Systems Programming with Zig

Build Real Tools with No Hidden Cost

Mihalis Tsoukalos

<packt>

Systems Programming with Zig

Portfolio Director: Kunal Chaudhari
Relationship Lead: Denim Pinto
Project Manager: Ankit Maroli
Content Engineer: Srishty Goyal
Technical Editor: Aditya Bharadwaj
Indexer: Tejal Soni
Proofreader: Srishty Goyal
Production Designer: Aparna Bhagat
Growth Lead: Rithika Shetty

First published: June 2026

Production reference: 1190626

Published by Packt Publishing Ltd.
Grosvenor House
11 St Paul's Square
Birmingham
B3 1RB, UK.

ISBN 978-1-80742-643-9
www.packtpub.com

I would like to dedicate the book to the Zig community.

– Mihalis Tsoukalos

Contributors

About the author

Mihalis Tsoukalos is a UNIX Systems Engineer and a Technical Writer. He is the author of Practical Systems Programming in Go, Time Series Indexing, and Mastering Go. He holds a B.Sc. in Mathematics from the University of Patras (Greece) and an M.Sc. in IT from University College London (UK). He has written more than 300 technical articles for magazines including Sys Admin, MacTech, Linux User and Developer, Usenix ;login:, Linux Format, and Linux Journal. His research interests include Time Series, Data Mining, Machine Learning, and Indexing.

I would like to thank Sushma Reddy, Ankit Maroli, Denim Pinto, and Srishty Goyal for helping me during the writing process – a book is a team process. I would also like to thank the Technical Reviewers of the book, Alex Rios and Jefferson Marchetti, who did an excellent job and corrected many of my errors, bugs, and inconsistencies.

Finally, I would like to thank you, the reader of the book, for choosing this book. I hope you find it helpful and that it will keep you good company in your Zig journey.

About the reviewers

Jefferson Marchetti is a Senior Software Engineer with more than 26 years of experience in software development. He specializes in Golang, Rust, distributed systems, data engineering, Apache Kafka, and cloud-native architectures. Throughout his career, he has worked on large-scale enterprise and financial platforms, focusing on high-performance systems, scalable APIs, and data-intensive applications. Jefferson is passionate about software craftsmanship and modern engineering practices.

Alex Rios is an established Brazilian software engineer with a 15-year track record of success in large-scale solution development. He specializes in Go and creates high-throughput systems that address diverse needs across fintech, telecom, and gaming industries. As a Staff Engineer at Stone Co., Alex applies his expertise using unconventional system designs, ensuring top-notch delivery. He also uses his expertise to evaluate books and publications as a technical reviewer. He is an enthusiastic community member, actively participating in its growth and development as Curitiba's Go meetup organizer. His dedication is evident in his regular presence as a speaker at major national tech events like GopherCon Brazil.

Table of Contents

Preface **xvii**

Free benefits with your book .... **xxv**

Part 1: Zig Foundations **1**

Chapter 1: Building Essential UNIX Tools **3**

Implementing ztee, a stream duplicator **4**

Understanding standard input, output, and error • 4

What does breaking changes mean for Zig? • 5

Writergate (Zig 0.15.1) • 5

Learning about the Zig 0.16 breaking changes • 5

Learning how to print on screen • 7

Using std.ArrayList • 9

Reading user input • 11

Reading and opening files for writing or appending • 13

Implementing ztee • 19

The I/O loop: buffering data efficiently • 23

Testing ztee • 25

Implementing zwhich, an executable locator **27**

Reading environment variables • 27

Splitting the PATH environment variable • 28

Connecting the dots • 29

Calling C code from Zig **31**

Creating secure passwords with zpass **33**

Two ways to generate random values • 33

Generating unpredictable passwords • 36

What did Zig get right **37**

Summary ... 38
Exercises ... 38
Additional resources ... 39

Chapter 2: Systems Infrastructure: Builds, Testing, and Distribution 41

Formatting strings with std.fmt ... 42
Understanding memory allocators ... 45
Verification strategy ... 50
Writing unit tests with std.testing • 50
Writing tests for zwhich • 50
Detecting memory leaks automatically during tests • 54
Generating documentation (-femit-docs) • 55
Fetching and using external libraries ... 60
The build system as infrastructure as code • 61
Managing dependencies with build.zig.zon • 61
Understanding build.zig • 62
Compiling a library to create an executable binary • 64
Developing zuuid, a UUID generator ... 66
Making a library from the zuuid code ... 70
Using GitHub • 70
Preparing the library for others to reuse • 71
Writing tests for the library • 72
Using our zuuid library • 73
Benchmarking zuuid against uuidgen • 77
Test filtering and coverage analysis • 78
Summary ... 79
Exercises ... 79
Additional resources ... 79

Chapter 3: Direct Memory Access and Binary Formats 81

Pointers ... 82

Pointer arithmetic • 83
Composing Null-Terminated C strings • 86
Putting structures on stack and heap • 88
Programming a custom memory allocator (wrapper) 90
Zunzip, a Zip file lister 98
Enforcing wire format correctness with comptime 106
Working with Endianness 113
Reading Little-Endian integers from raw bytes • 115
Casting raw byte slices to structured data types 117
Benchmarking memory allocators 120
Summary 127
Exercises 128
Additional resources 128

Chapter 4: Processing Streams, Buffers, and Data Encoding 129

Developing zcat 130
The cost of system calls • 132
Developing zwc, a wc(1) clone 135
Counting lines, words, and characters • 136
Achieving high-performance text counting with SIMD • 139
Comparing the two ZWC implementations • 144
Comparing zwc with wc • 145
Developing z64, a high-performance Base64 tool 146
Bitwise manipulation operations (<<, >>, &, |) • 146
Implementing the encoder logic • 147
Decoding streams • 150
Benchmarking reading and writing operations 153
Benchmarking reading speed for various buffer sizes • 154
How the buffer size affects writing speed • 157
Benchmarking file seeking with sequential reading • 159
Practical guidance for Zig programs • 163
Summary 164

Exercises 164

Additional resources 164

Part 2: Systems Programming in Practice 165

Chapter 5: Navigating Directories and Filesystem Events 167

The required theory 167

Understanding inodes, file permissions, and symlinks • 168

Resolve a relative path to its absolute counterpart • 169

Listing directory entries • 172

Finding the kind of file • 174

Finding file metadata • 175

Creating symbolic links • 178

Deleting a file • 179

Deleting a directory • 180

Moving a file • 182

Implementing ztree, a directory tree visualizer 183

Recursively walking directories • 183

Developing the utility • 187

Implementing zwatch, a filesystem watcher 190

Finding out the active operating system • 190

Understanding file events • 191

Using OS primitives: inotify (Linux) vs. kqueue (BSD/macOS) • 191

The event loop: polling for changes • 192

Implementing the chmod logic 198

Implementing the chown logic 200

Summary 203

Exercises 204

Additional resources 204

Chapter 6: Programming the Network Stack 205

Writing an Echo server using TCP 206

Testing the Echo server • 208

Writing a TCP Echo client 208

Performing low-level hostname resolution • 211

Improving the TCP Echo client • 214

Writing a UDP Echo server 216

Writing a UDP Echo client 220

Creating Docker images 223

Working with the HTTP protocol 226

Developing a minimal web server • 226

Creating a web service that generates random numbers • 229

Developing HTTP clients 232

Creating a system monitor service 240

Reading memory information • 240

The server process • 245

The service client • 246

Enforcing protocol correctness with comptime 250

Summary 254

Exercises 255

Additional resources 255

Subscribe to Deep Engineering 255

Chapter 7: Managing Threads, Processes, and Signals 257

UNIX signal handling 258

Using signals intentionally • 259

Processes and Threads 262

Forking processes • 263

Putting your CPU to work with threads 265

Running a variable number of threads • 266

Executing Shell Commands 268

Writing a concurrent TCP server 271

Writing a concurrent TCP client • 274

Creating zcron, a minimal cron variation 278

Explaining the design decisions • 278
Detaching from the terminal (fork, setsid) • 280
Using fork and exec to run periodic tasks • 282
Handling SIGTERM and SIGCHLD • 285
The zcron implementation details • 285
Summary **291**
Exercises **292**

Chapter 8: Orchestrating Concurrency and Synchronization 293

Avoiding race conditions **294**
Sharing memory safely: mutexes and RwLocks • 294
Using RwLock • 296
Avoiding race conditions by design • 299
Atomics: when to use them • 303
Changing a variable using atomic operations • 305
What would happen without atomics? • 307
Preventing data corruption in shared writing **308**
Writing without atomic operations • 308
Writing with atomic operations • 310
Improving the memory info server **312**
Using a separate memory allocator for each thread • 313
Thread pools: reusing threads for performance **316**
The Producer-Consumer pattern **318**
Implementing the Producer-Consumer pattern with atomics • 319
Implementing Producer-Consumer with condition variable • 322
The ring buffer data structure **325**
Logging information concurrently **330**
zlocate: A concurrent file indexer **331**
The Scatter-Gather pattern (parallelism) • 333
Implementation details • 333
Using the zlocate utility • 338
Summary **340**

Exercises 340

Chapter 9: Implementing Asynchronous I/O 341

Asynchrony is not Concurrency 341
Coroutines vs. OS Threads • 342
Event loops: how io_uring and kqueue work under the hood • 343
Writing nonblocking code • 343
Seeing async and await in action 343
Using async and await • 344
Using async and await for write operations • 348
Being interested in the first result only • 350
An asynchronous TCP proxy 351
Refactoring the TCP proxy using async and await 357
Comparing the performance of the two proxies 361
Low-Level I/O multiplexing: io_uring and kqueue 364
Summary 370
Exercises 370
Additional resources 371

Chapter 10: Building a High-Performance In-Memory Cache Server 373

The required theory 373
Developing zcache 374
Architecture: Event-driven vs. Thread-per-connection • 375
Wire protocol: designing a binary protocol (ZEMP) • 377
Defining the binary frame structure (header, length, payload) • 377
Implementing a state machine to parse streaming TCP data • 378
Handling partial reads and buffer fragmentation • 379
Why do we need both a hash map and a linked list • 379
Storage engine: implementing the LRU cache • 380
The doubly linked list • 381
The Hash Map wrapper • 382
Memory management • 383

Learning about server implementation details • 384

Developing a client 399

Explaining zemp_client.zig • 400

Explaining zcache_cli.zig • 401

Explaining bench.zig • 403

Summary 410

Exercises 410

Additional resources 413

Chapter 11: Persisting Structured Data with SQLite3 415

Working with JSON and nested structures 416

Converting date and time formats in JSON records • 419

Using SQLite3 426

Connecting to SQLite3 • 426

Inserting data into SQLite3 • 428

Querying data • 432

Deleting data • 435

Putting JSON data into a database 438

Advanced comptime • 438

Reflection: using @typeInfo to inspect struct fields • 438

Using anytype for generic database mapping • 439

Using comptime to map SQL rows to Zig structs • 439

Implementing the utility • 439

Using the utility • 443

Building a note-taking service 445

Specifying the functionality of the web service • 446

Implementing the web service • 446

Testing the web service with curl(1) • 456

Building a client for the note-taking service 458

Summary 462

Exercises 462

Additional resources 464

Chapter 12: Developing a Domain-Specific Language 467

The zcalc language 468

The EBNF grammar of zcalc • 468

Lexing: breaking strings into tokens • 472

Parsing: abstract syntax trees (ASTs) and recursion • 479

Evaluation: tree-walking execution • 485

REPL: building an interactive shell 490

Summary 496

Exercises 497

Additional resources 498

Chapter 13: Unlock Your Exclusive Benefits 499

Unlock this Book's Free Benefits in 3 Easy Steps 500

Other Books You May Enjoy 504

Subscribe to Deep Engineering 507

Index 509

Preface

Welcome to the *1st Edition* of *Systems Programming with Zig*! Systems programming has always been a discipline defined by honesty. Honest about what the hardware can do. Honest about where the memory came from and where it goes. Honest about the cost of every abstraction. For decades, C was the language that embodied that honesty — not because it was elegant but because it hid almost nothing. You saw the pointers. You managed the memory. You felt the machine beneath your fingers.

Zig carries that tradition forward but it does something C never quite managed: it makes the honest path also the convenient one. There is no hidden control flow. There is no global allocator quietly doing work on your behalf. There is no runtime making decisions you did not ask for. What you write is what runs, and the compiler will tell you — loudly, at build time — when what you wrote does not match what the machine requires. That quality, that refusal to let complexity hide in corners, is what makes Zig a genuinely interesting language for systems work rather than merely another contender.

This book is for programmers who want to understand systems, not just use them. We assume you can read Zig code and navigate a UNIX terminal. What we do not assume is that you already know why a TCP echo server blocks on `accept()`, what the kernel I/O scheduler is doing while your buffered writer accumulates bytes or why the wrong allocator choice in a hot loop can cost you an order of magnitude in throughput. Those are the questions this book is built around.

We build real tools throughout. A `tee(1)` clone, a Zip file lister, a file watcher backed by platform-specific kernel primitives, a concurrent job scheduler, a production-grade in-memory cache with a custom binary protocol, a note-taking service backed by SQLite3, and, finally, a working interpreter for a small programming language built from scratch. These are not toy examples dressed up as projects. They are the kind of programs that force you to make architectural decisions, feel the consequences of those decisions in the benchmark output, and understand why the systems community settled on the patterns it did.

In the tradition of foundational texts such as *The UNIX Programming Environment* and *The C Programming Language*, we frequently pause to examine the why. When we introduce a mutex, we explain what goes wrong without one. When we choose an arena allocator, we benchmark the alternative. When we design a binary protocol, we show what `comptime` can enforce that a runtime check cannot. The code is a vehicle for understanding engineering tradeoffs, and those tradeoffs are the real curriculum.

Zig 0.16.x arrived with significant changes — new I/O abstractions, a renamed allocator, a reworked networking API — and this book is written against that version throughout. Every code listing compiles and runs on Zig 0.16.0. Where the language made an interesting choice or broke with an older convention, we say so explicitly, because understanding why a language evolves is part of understanding the language.

Systems programming is not a finishing school for programmers who have mastered everything else. It is a way of thinking — about resources, about time, about the gap between what you asked the machine to do and what it actually did. Zig is an exceptionally clear lens for developing that way of thinking, because it refuses to blur the picture.

Thank you for choosing and reading *Systems Programming with Zig*. Let us dive in and unlock the full potential of Zig together! Happy coding!

Soli Deo gloria

Who this book is for

This book is for programmers who already understand Zig at a basic level and want to use it to do serious systems work, as well as intermediate and experienced systems programmers in Go, Python, Java, C, C++ or Rust who are curious about what Zig brings to the discipline. You do not need to be a Zig expert — a working familiarity with the syntax, the type system, and the basic standard library is enough to follow every chapter from the start.

If you have written application code in higher-level languages and are making your first serious contact with systems programming, some sections will challenge you. The chapters on memory allocators, data structures, and binary protocol parsing in particular assume a willingness to sit with unfamiliar ideas before they fully resolve. A second reading of a difficult section often reveals details that were invisible the first time through. That is not a failure of comprehension — it is how systems knowledge accumulates. Throughout the book, you will find working programs, benchmark results, and exercises grounded in real problems. The tools we build — a job scheduler, a file indexer, a cache server, an interpreter — are not simplified illustrations of the concepts. They are the concepts, expressed in code that compiles and runs. Read them, run them, modify them, break them, and observe what changes! Passive reading will take you only so far in systems programming.

Finally, be prepared for the compiler to argue with you, for benchmarks to produce surprising numbers, and for bugs to hide in places that seem unrelated to where you made the change. This is not a sign that you are doing something wrong. It is the nature of the discipline. Systems programming is an ongoing negotiation between your intentions and the machine's reality, and Zig is unusually honest about where the gaps are. That honesty is uncomfortable at first and invaluable thereafter.

What this book covers

Chapter 1, Building Essential UNIX Tools, introduces Zig as a modern systems language built on the premise of complete programmer control — no hidden control flow, no implicit allocations, and no surprise operator overloads. Rather than explaining Zig syntax from scratch, the chapter assumes working fluency and immediately puts the language to work building three real UNIX utilities: `ztee`, a `tee(1)` clone; `zwhich`, a `which(1)` clone; and `zpass`, which demonstrates calling C code directly from Zig via `@cImport()`.

Chapter 2, Systems Infrastructure: Builds, Testing, and Distribution, treats the build process as a first-class systems programming concern. Zig `build.zig` defines the project build graph using the same syntax as application code, enabling cross-compilation and dependency management without separate tooling. The chapter covers string formatting with `std.fmt`, memory allocators, unit testing with `std.testing`, the development of `zuuid`, and publishing packages using the Zig build system.

Chapter 3, Direct Memory Access and Binary Formats, bridges the gap between abstract variables and the physical machine by exploring Zig pointer mechanics and memory management strategies in depth. The chapter covers pointer arithmetic, custom allocator design, endianness handling, and binary file parsing, culminating in the construction of `zunzip`, a fully functional Zip file lister built from raw bytes. The chapter closes by benchmarking different memory allocation strategies to connect architectural choices to real-world performance.

Chapter 4, Processing Streams, Buffers, and Data Encoding, shifts focus to I/O efficiency and stream processing. Working through a suite of classic UNIX tools — `zcat`, `zwc`, and `z64` for Base64 encoding and decoding — the chapter examines buffering strategies, the cost of system calls, SIMD-accelerated data processing, and bitwise encoding logic, closing with benchmarks that quantify the tradeoffs between different reading and writing approaches.

Chapter 5, Navigating Directories and Filesystem Events, explores the mechanics of filesystem interaction at the level of OS primitives. The chapter builds `ztree`, a recursive directory tree visualizer that correctly handles symbolic links and edge cases, then constructs `zwatch`, a real-time file monitoring utility backed by Linux `inotify` or BSD `kqueue` depending on the platform. The chapter concludes by implementing the core functionality of `chmod(1)` and `chown(8)`.

Chapter 6, Programming the Network Stack, works up from raw TCP/IP sockets to a complete System Monitor API, building a TCP Echo server and client, a UDP Echo server and client, Docker images for network services, and a minimal HTTP server and client along the way. The chapter treats the network stack as a sequence of increasingly structured abstractions — bytes, frames, protocol, service — and closes by showing how `comptime` can enforce protocol correctness at compile time rather than runtime.

Chapter 7, Managing Threads, Processes, and Signals, gives direct access to the OS process model through the Zig C interoperability layer. The chapter covers UNIX signal handling with `signal(3)` and `sigaction(2)`, process creation with `fork(2)` and `exec(3)`, executing shell commands, and writing a concurrent TCP server and client. All of these concepts converge in `zcron`, a minimal `cron(8)`-style job scheduler that detaches from the terminal, manages child processes, and responds correctly to `SIGTERM`, `SIGHUP`, and `SIGCHLD`.

Chapter 8, Orchestrating Concurrency and Synchronization, examines the distinction between concurrency and parallelism and the practical consequences of getting it wrong. The chapter covers mutexes, atomic operations, and condition variables through progressively more demanding examples — race condition avoidance, data corruption prevention, thread pools, ring buffers, and the Producer-Consumer pattern — before applying these tools to `zlocate`, a concurrent file indexer that distributes filesystem traversal across a worker pool using the Scatter-Gather pattern.

Chapter 9, Implementing Asynchronous I/O, addresses the fundamental scalability problem of synchronous I/O under high concurrency. The chapter establishes the distinction between asynchrony and concurrency, introduces Zig 0.16 `async` and `await` model, builds an asynchronous TCP proxy, and refactors it using the `std.Io` event loop. It closes with a direct performance comparison between the synchronous and asynchronous implementations and includes platform-specific coverage of `io_uring` on Linux and `kqueue` on macOS for readers who want to see the kernel machinery directly.

Chapter 10, Building a High-Performance In-Memory Cache Server, constructs `zcache`, a production-grade in-memory cache built around three cleanly separated layers: an LRU storage engine combining a hash map with an intrusive doubly linked list, a custom binary wire protocol (ZEMP) with fixed-width frame parsing, and a thread-per-connection server. The chapter develops three client tools — a test client, a command-line client, and a benchmark — that together verify correctness, demonstrate usability, and put concrete throughput and latency numbers against the architectural claims.

Chapter 11, Persisting Structured Data with SQLite3, moves from in-memory to persistent storage. The chapter covers reading and writing JSON, parsing structured data into Zig types, and generating JSON from in-memory structures. It then connects to SQLite3 through the Zig C interoperability layer, building a complete note-taking service with an HTTP API and a dedicated client, demonstrating how battle-tested C libraries can be integrated into Zig programs without sacrificing compile-time safety.

Chapter 12, Developing a Domain-Specific Language, closes the book by building a small interpreted programming language called `zcalc` from scratch in Zig. The chapter implements all three pillars of an interpreter — a Lexer that transforms raw text into tokens, a Parser that structures those tokens into an Abstract Syntax Tree, and an Evaluator that executes the tree — and wraps them in an interactive REPL. Building a language from scratch in Zig demonstrates how `comptime`, explicit memory management, and the standard library combine to tackle one of the most intellectually demanding problems in software.

To get the most out of this book

This book requires a machine running macOS, Linux, or any UNIX-like operating system with Zig 0.16.0 or later installed. Most of the code examples rely on POSIX interfaces — `fork(2)`, `signal(3)`, `kqueue`, and similar — that are not available on Windows, so a UNIX environment is a genuine requirement rather than a recommendation. Familiarity with the command line, the filesystem, and basic `git(1)` usage is assumed throughout.

This book is written against Zig 0.16.0, and every code listing has been verified against that version. Install Zig 0.16.0 or later from the official Zig website at `https://ziglang.org/download/` or use a version manager such as `mise` or `zigup` to keep your installation current. Verify your installation with `zig version` before running any of the examples. If you are running a version newer than 0.16.0, the vast majority of the code will compile without changes, but be aware that Zig is a fast-moving language and any release may introduce breaking changes — particularly in the I/O and networking APIs that several chapters depend on heavily. The asynchronous I/O chapter in particular uses `std.Io` features introduced in 0.16, so anything earlier than that will not work regardless of how close the version number appears.

The source code for every example in this book is available on GitHub. Clone the repository and follow along — reading code is useful, but running it, modifying it, and breaking it deliberately is where the real understanding comes from. When a benchmark produces a number, change a parameter, and see what moves. When a `comptime` assertion fires, read the error carefully before fixing it. The compiler feedback is part of the learning experience, not an obstacle to it.

Systems programming rewards patience and curiosity in equal measure. Zig is a language that gives you the full picture of what the machine is doing, and that picture is worth spending time with.

Download the example code files

The code bundle for the book is hosted on GitHub at `https://github.com/mactsouk/zigSP`. We also have other code bundles from our rich catalog of books and videos available at `https://github.com/PacktPublishing/`. Check them out!

Download the color images

We also provide a PDF file that has color images of the screenshots/diagrams used in this book. You can download it here: `https://packt.link/gbp/9781807426439`.

Conventions used

There are a number of text conventions used throughout this book.

`CodeInText`: Indicates code words in text, database table names, folder names, filenames, file extensions, pathnames, dummy URLs, user input, and Twitter handles. For example: Mount the downloaded `WebStorm-10*.dmg` disk image file as another disk in your system.

A block of code is set as follows:

```
const std = @import("std");

pub fn main(_: std.process.Init.Minimal) !void {
    std.debug.print("Hello {s}!\n", .{"World"});
}
```

When we wish to draw your attention to a particular part of a code block, the relevant lines or items are set in bold:

```
    const pathEnv = init.environ_map.get("PATH") orelse {
        std.debug.print("Error: PATH variable not found\n", .{});
        return;
    };
```

Any command-line input or output is written as follows:

```
$ zig run ch01/stdArrayList.zig
Adding numbers 0, 10, 20, 30, 40...
Modified index 2 to 999.
List contents: 0 10 999 30 40
```

```
Popped last item: 40
Final count: 4
```

Bold: Indicates a new term, an important word, or important information. For instance, words in menus or dialog boxes appear in the text like this. For example: The `wordByWord()` function uses *regular expressions to separate the words* found in each line of the input file.

> **Note**
>
> Warnings or important notes appear like this.

Get in touch

Feedback from our readers is always welcome.

General feedback: Email `feedback@packtpub.com` and mention the book's title in the subject of your message. If you have questions about any aspect of this book, please email us at `questions@packtpub.com`.

Errata: Although we have taken every care to ensure the accuracy of our content, mistakes do happen. If you have found a mistake in this book, we would be grateful if you reported it to us. Please visit `http://www.packtpub.com/submit-errata`, click **Submit Errata**, and fill in the form.

Piracy: If you come across any illegal copies of our works in any form on the internet, we would be grateful if you would provide us with the location address or website name. Please contact us at `copyright@packtpub.com` with a link to the material.

If you are interested in becoming an author: If there is a topic that you have expertise in and you are interested in either writing or contributing to a book, please visit `http://authors.packtpub.com`.

Join us on Discord!

Read this book alongside other users, developers, experts, and the author himself.

Ask questions, provide solutions to other readers, chat with the authors via Ask Me Anything sessions, and much more. Scan the QR or visit the link to join the community.

`https://packt.link/deep-engineering-golang`

Free benefits with your book

This book comes with free benefits to support your learning. Activate them now for instant access (see the "*How to Unlock*" section for instructions).

Here's a quick overview of what you can instantly unlock with your purchase:

How to Unlock

Scan the QR code (or go to `packtpub.com/unlock`). Search for this book by name, confirm the edition, and then follow the steps on the page.

UNLOCK NOW

Note: Keep your invoice handy. Purchases made directly from Packt don't require one

Share your thoughts

Once you've read *Systems Programming with Zig*, we'd love to hear your thoughts! Scan the QR code below to go straight to the Amazon review page for this book and share your feedback.

`https://packt.link/r/1807426432`

Your review is important to us and the tech community and will help us make sure we're delivering excellent quality content.

Part 1

Zig Foundations

In this first part of the book, we establish the foundations that every subsequent chapter builds on. We begin by putting Zig to work immediately on real UNIX utilities, then examine the build system, testing infrastructure and distribution tooling that make Zig projects maintainable. From there, we go deeper into the language's most distinctive territory: explicit memory management, pointer arithmetic, custom allocator design, and the comptime machinery that enforces correctness at compile time rather than runtime. The part closes with stream processing, buffering strategies, and data encoding — the I/O primitives that underpin every networked and filesystem-facing program in the rest of the book.

This part of the book includes the following chapters:

- *Chapter 1, Building Essential UNIX Tools*
- *Chapter 2, Systems Infrastructure: Builds, Testing, and Distribution*
- *Chapter 3, Direct Memory Access and Binary Formats*
- *Chapter 4, Processing Streams, Buffers, and Data Encoding*

Part I

Introduction

1

Building Essential UNIX Tools

Zig emerges not merely as another contender in the crowded field of systems languages but as a *deliberate and focused effort to modernize the legacy of C without sacrificing its simplicity.* At its core, Zig is built on the radical premise that the programmer must be in complete control, eliminating the hidden control flow, implicit memory allocations, and surprise operator overloads that plague other ecosystems. It introduces a fresh paradigm where compile-time logic is executed with the same syntax as runtime code, allowing for powerful metaprogramming that remains readable and easy to debug. In this chapter, we are going to implement three UNIX command-line tools. As we construct these UNIX tools, you will discover how the lack of hidden control flow, the powerful compile-time logic execution, and the obsession with explicit allocation do not just make Zig code safer but make systems programming feel less like navigating a minefield and more like engineering. The I/O patterns, filesystem interactions, memory allocation strategies, and process environment access introduced through these three utilities are not isolated techniques but fundamental building blocks that reappear in every subsequent chapter, from the concurrent file indexer in *Chapter 8, Orchestrating Concurrency and Synchronization,* to the cache server in *Chapter 10, Building a High-Performance In-Memory Cache Server* and the language interpreter in *Chapter 12, Developing a Domain-Specific Language.* We proceed with the assumption that *you are already comfortable with the basics of Zig syntax and possess a working fluency in the UNIX environment.* We will not spend time explaining what a pipe is or how to declare a variable; instead, we will examine in more detail the specific mechanics that make Zig an exceptional tool for the modern systems architect.

> **Note**
>
> Have in mind that all code listings in this chapter assume `const std = @import("std");` at the top of the file; partial listings that focus on a specific function

> or block omit this import for brevity, but the complete source for every example is available in the accompanying GitHub repository.

This chapter covers:

- Developing `ztee`
- Developing `zwhich`
- Calling C code from Zig
- Developing `zpass`
- What did Zig get right

Let us begin our journey by implementing `ztee`, a `tee(1)` clone

> Note
>
> **Your purchase includes a free PDF copy + exclusive extras**
>
> Your purchase includes a DRM-free PDF copy of this book, 7-day trial to the Packt+ library (no credit card required), and additional exclusive extras. See the *Free benefits with your book* section in the *Preface* to unlock them instantly and maximize your learning.

Implementing ztee, a stream duplicator

The `tee(1)` command is a tool that allows a single data stream to exist in two places at once: captured on disk and flowing live to the terminal. Implementing `ztee` challenges us to coordinate multiple output targets without blocking the flow of data, a task that perfectly demonstrates the composability of `std.io` interfaces. But first, let us understand the three fundamental and standard streams.

Understanding standard input, output, and error

Every UNIX operating system has three files open all the time for its processes. UNIX uses file descriptors, which are non-negative integer values, as an internal representation for accessing open files, which is much prettier than using long paths. By default, all UNIX systems support three special and standard filenames: `/dev/stdin`, `/dev/stdout`, and `/dev/stderr`, which can also be accessed using file descriptors `0`, `1`, and `2`, respectively. These three file descriptors are also called **standard input**, **standard output** and **standard error**, respectively.

What does breaking changes mean for Zig?

The term **breaking changes** refers to modifications in a language, library, or tool that can cause existing code to stop working or require changes to keep working. For example, a function might change its signature, a feature might be removed, or behavior might be adjusted in a way that is not backward compatible. While this might sound negative at first, breaking changes are not always a bad thing. In fact, they often reflect improvements — such as cleaner design, better performance or more consistent behavior. Especially in a language like Zig, which is still evolving, breaking changes are part of refining the language and fixing earlier design decisions. Although they may require you to update your code from time to time, they ultimately lead to a more robust and well-designed ecosystem.

Writergate (Zig 0.15.1)

In the recent history of Zig development, few events have sparked as much debate, confusion, and eventual enlightenment as the overhaul of the standard library's I/O subsystem in version 0.15.1. This shift marked a departure from the comfortable, implicit unbuffered writes of the past to a stricter, performance-first model where *buffering is no longer an optional optimization but an architectural requirement.* While the transition broke countless builds and forced developers to rethink simple `print()` statements, it laid the groundwork for a zero-cost I/O abstraction that mirrors the hardware's reality: system calls are expensive, and batching is essential. In previous Zig versions, writing was performed as follows:

```
const std = @import("std");
pub fn main() !void {
    // The Naive Approach: Unbuffered
    // Every call to print() triggers a distinct 'write' syscall.
    const stdout = std.io.getStdOut().writer();

    try stdout.print("Processing item: {d}\n", .{1});
    try stdout.print("Processing item: {d}\n", .{2});
    // ... more code
}
```

However, starting with Zig 0.15.1, *the previous way generates an error and does not compile.* As if this was not enough, *Zig 0.16 introduced more breaking changes,* so code that used to work with Zig 0.15.1 does not work anymore.

Learning about the Zig 0.16 breaking changes

Zig 0.16 reorganizes several fundamental APIs in ways that touch almost every program in the book. The headline change is the removal of `std.time.milliTimestamp()`, `std.time.sleep()`, `std.Thread.sleep()`, `std.Thread.Mutex`, `std.crypto.random`, `std.net`, `std.time.Timer`, `std.time.nanoTimestamp()`, and `std.process.argsAlloc`, `argsWithAllocator`, among others. The `std.heap.GeneralPurposeAllocator` memory allocator is renamed `std.heap.DebugAllocator` and its initialization syntax changes from `var gpa = std.heap.DebugAllocator(.{}) = .init` to `var gpa: std.heap.DebugAllocator(.{}) = .init`. String helpers `std.mem.trimRight()` and `trimLeft()` are renamed `std.mem.trimStart()` and `trimEnd()`. File and directory operations move from `std.fs` into the new `std.Io.Dir` and `std.Io.File` namespaces, and virtually every call acquires an io parameter, making all I/O concurrency-aware by design. In Zig 0.14 and 0.15 the entry point was simply `pub fn main() !void`. Zig 0.16 changes this to `pub fn main(init: std.process.Init) !void`. The `std.process.Init` struct is the runtime gift to `main()`: it bundles everything a program typically needs at startup into one value. Its most important fields are `init.io`, a `std.Io` instance required by all async-aware APIs; `init.gpa`, a ready-to-use general-purpose allocator; `init.arena`, an arena allocator freed automatically on exit; `init.minimal.args`, which provides access to command-line arguments and `init.environ_map`, which exposes environment variables. In practice the first thing most programs do is extract `io` and set up buffered output. Note that `std.Io.File.stdout().writer()` now requires both the `io` instance and an explicit stack buffer — there is no global, zero-configuration writer anymore. If your program does not need the allocator or the `Io` instance, the runtime also accepts the lighter `std.process.Init.Minimal`, which exposes only `args` and environment. As for getting command-line arguments, `init.minimal.args.argsAlloc` and `argsWithAllocator` are both gone. Instead, you iterate directly through `init.minimal.args` by calling `init.minimal.args.iterate()` to obtain an iterator, skipping the first element, which is the program name, and then calling `iter.next()` in a loop to retrieve each subsequent argument as a `[]const u8` slice. Calling `iter.deinit()` is mandatory, since the iterator may allocate on some platforms. If you need a slice of all arguments at once, for example, to pass to a library, you can get one via the provided arena using `init.minimal.args.toSlice(init.arena.allocator())`. Environment variables follow the same pattern: `std.process.getEnvVarOwned` is removed and replaced by a direct map lookup through `init.environ_map.get("KEY")`, which requires no allocation and no explicit free, returning an optional `?[]const u8`. Taken together, these changes push programs toward a model where the runtime hands you everything you need up front, rather than having you construct allocators, fetch environment variables, and parse arguments independently.

But it is time to see all these changes in action. So, let us begin by presenting the famous Hello World program in Zig 0.16.

Learning how to print on screen

We are going to present three ways of printing information on screen, using the *Hello World!* program as an example. The first version (`ch01/hwv1.zig`) is the following:

```
const std = @import("std");
pub fn main(_: std.process.Init.Minimal) !void {
    std.debug.print("Hello {s}!\n", .{"World"});
}
```

In Zig 0.16, the entry point signature changed. So, programs that used to use `pub fnmain() !void` should use `pub fn main(_: std.process.Init.Minimal) !void`. Apart from this detail, the code uses `std.debug.print()` for generating output that is directed to standard error. The formatting syntax uses `{s}` as a placeholder for a string slice, which is filled by the arguments provided in the anonymous struct `.{ "World" }`.

The second version (`ch01/hwv2.zig`), which prints to standard output, is the following:

```
const std = @import("std");

pub fn main(init: std.process.Init) !void {
    try std.Io.File.stdout().writeStreamingAll(
        init.io,
        "Hello World!\n",
    );
}
```

In this case, we explicitly acquire a handle to the standard output file descriptor via `std.Io.File.stdout()`. We then invoke `writeStreamingAll()`, a raw method that attempts to write the exact slice of bytes provided to the file. The use of the `try` keyword ensures that if this system call fails, the error is propagated up the stack, allowing the runtime to handle the exit code appropriately. The distinction between this and the previous `std.debug.print()` example is fundamental to UNIX philosophy. While the previous example wrote to *Standard Error*, this program writes to *Standard Output*, which is the primary channel for data, allowing the text to be piped into other tools or redirected to files. Furthermore, `writeStreamingAll()` is a lower-level primitive than `print()` and does not support format specifiers like `{s}` or `{d}`.

So, what happens if you want *to print to standard output and want to use format specifiers and a buffer*? Here is an improved version of `ch01/hwv2.zig` called `ch01/hwv3.zig` that supports format specifiers and uses a buffer:

```
const std = @import("std");

pub fn main(init: std.process.Init) !void {
    var buffer: [4096]u8 = undefined;
    var stdout_impl = std.Io.File.stdout().writer(init.io,&buffer);
    const stdout=&stdout_impl.interface;
    try stdout.print("Hello {s}!\n", .{"Buffered World"});
    try stdout.print("Writing number: {d}\n", .{42});
    try stdout.flush();
}
```

This program illustrates the canonical pattern for high-performance input/output in Zig, striking the necessary balance between raw system efficiency and developer ergonomics. The implementation begins with the explicit allocation of a memory buffer on the stack: `var buffer: [4096]u8`. *Unlike higher-level languages that obscure this allocation behind the scenes, Zig requires us to declare exactly where our bytes will live before they are sent to the kernel, giving us complete control over memory usage and locality*. We then initialize the writer implementation by binding this buffer to the standard output file descriptor. The most distinct aspect of this pattern is the retrieval of the generic writer interface via `&stdout_impl.interface`. This step bridges the gap between our specific, concrete implementation (a buffered writer wrapping a file) and the general-purpose `std.io.Writer` interface. By accessing this interface, we gain access to high-level convenience methods like `.print()`, which allows us to use familiar formatting specifiers such as `{s}` and `{d}`. This abstraction layer means our code can remain expressive and readable without sacrificing the underlying performance benefits of buffering. However, this power comes with a responsibility: because `print()` operations merely *copy bytes into our stack buffer rather than triggering immediate system calls*, the data remains local to our process until the buffer fills up. Consequently, the explicit call to `.flush()` at the end of the program is mandatory; without it, any partial data remaining in the buffer when the program exits would be discarded, never reaching the terminal. In practice, this means that if you miss calling `stdout.flush()`, the program will print no output!

While fixed-size stack buffers provide excellent performance for streaming output, many system tasks, such as collecting lines from a file or accumulating search results, require us to handle data of indeterminate size, necessitating a shift to dynamic memory management via `std.ArrayList`.

Using std.ArrayList

`std.ArrayList` (**dynamic array implementation**) is a fundamental part of Zig and the most frequently used data structure in the Standard Library. The `ch01/stdArrayList.zig` program, which introduces `std.ArrayList`, begins with the following code:

```
const std = @import("std");

pub fn main(init: std.process.Init) !void {
    const allocator = init.gpa;

    // 1. Initialize ArrayList
    var numbers = std.ArrayList(i32).empty;
    defer numbers.deinit(allocator);

    const stdout = std.Io.File.stdout();
    try stdout.writeStreamingAll(init.io, "Adding numbers 0, 10, 20, 30,
40...\n");

    // 2. Append
    var i: i32 = 0;
    while (i < 5) : (i += 1) {
        try numbers.append(allocator, i * 10);
    }

    // 3. Modify
    if (numbers.items.len > 2) {
        numbers.items[2] = 999;
        try stdout.writeStreamingAll(init.io, "Modified index 2 to 999.\n");
    }
```

`std.ArrayList`, the default dynamic array in Zig, demonstrates the new "explicit allocation" philosophy for Zig data structures. The code begins by initializing the list with `var numbers = std.ArrayList(i32).empty;`. Unlike previous versions of Zig or other languages like C++, *this initialization does not allocate any memory or capture an allocator*; it simply creates a lightweight struct containing *a pointer* and *a length*, initialized to zero. The heavy lifting happens later in the loop: when we call `numbers.append(allocator, i * 10)`, we explicitly pass `init.gpa` to the method. If a function does not take an allocator parameter, you can be certain it will not grow the heap. Finally, `numbers.deinit(allocator)` completes this pattern, requiring the same allocator to free the underlying memory, ensuring that the lifecycle of the data is completely transparent and under your control.

The rest of the `main()` implementation, which demonstrates how to iterate, manipulate, and report on the data stored within the dynamic list, is as follows:

```
    // 4. Iterate and Print
    try stdout.writeStreamingAll(init.io, "List contents: ");
    for (numbers.items) |num| {
        const num_str = try std.fmt.allocPrint(allocator, "{d} ", .{num});
        defer allocator.free(num_str);
        try stdout.writeStreamingAll(init.io, num_str);
    }
    try stdout.writeStreamingAll(init.io, "\n");

    // 5. Pop (returns optional ?i32)
    const last = numbers.pop();
    const pop_msg = try std.fmt.allocPrint(allocator, "Popped last item: {?d}
\n", .{last});
    defer allocator.free(pop_msg);
    try stdout.writeStreamingAll(init.io, pop_msg);

    const len_msg = try std.fmt.allocPrint(allocator, "Final count: {d}\n", .
{numbers.items.len});
    defer allocator.free(len_msg);
    try stdout.writeStreamingAll(init.io, len_msg);
}
```

To display the contents, we loop through `numbers.items`, which provides a direct slice of the underlying memory. Inside the loop, we encounter `std.fmt.allocPrint()`, a function that formats data into a newly allocated string on the heap. This requires us to pass our allocator once again and to immediately schedule the memory for release using `defer allocator.free(num_str)`. This pattern (allocate, use, defer free) is the epicenter of safe memory management in Zig, ensuring we do not leak strings while iterating. After that, the program demonstrates the `.pop()` method, which efficiently removes and returns the last element of the list. Notice that `.pop()` returns the value directly (or `null` if the list were empty, though here we know it is not), allowing us to immediately print the modified state. Finally, we confirm that the list has shrunk by accessing `numbers.items.len`.

Run `ch01/stdArrayList.zig` on your machine to get the following output:

```
$ zig run ch01/stdArrayList.zig
Adding numbers 0, 10, 20, 30, 40...
Modified index 2 to 999.
List contents: 0 10 999 30 40
Popped last item: 40
Final count: 4
```

After understanding the use of `std.ArrayList`, let us find out how to read user input from a running program.

Reading user input

The `ch01/readUserInput.zig` program illustrates how to read user input while a program is running. First, we present the `main()` implementation:

```
pub fn main(init: std.process.Init) !void {
    const stdout = std.Io.File.stdout();
    try stdout.writeStreamingAll(init.io, "What is your name? ");
    const name = try readLine(init.io, init.gpa);

    if (name) |n| {
        defer init.gpa.free(n);
        const clean_name = std.mem.trimEnd(u8, n, "\r\n");

        const msg = try std.fmt.allocPrint(init.gpa, "Hello, {s}! Welcome to Zig.
\n", .{clean_name});
        defer init.gpa.free(msg);
        try stdout.writeStreamingAll(init.io, msg);
    } else {
        try stdout.writeStreamingAll(init.io, "\nNo input received.\n");
    }
}
```

The program uses `init.gpa` because user input is unpredictable — we cannot know the length of a name at compile time, so we must be ready to allocate memory dynamically on the heap. After prompting the user with a raw write to standard output (`stdout.writeStreamingAll()`), we call a helper function, `readLine()`, passing the allocator to it. This design choice is critical: the function that requests the memory (`main()`) provides the means to allocate it and, consequently, takes responsibility for freeing it. Upon receiving the result, we *unwrap the optional value* using `if` `(name)` `|n|`. Inside this block, our very first action is to `defer allocator.free(n)`, ensuring that the memory holding user input is returned to the system the moment we are done, regardless of how the block exits. We then encounter a common nuance of command-line tools: the *Enter* key. Since standard input captures the newline characters (`\r` or `\n`) generated by the user, we use `std.mem.trimEnd()` to strip them away, preventing our output from breaking onto a new line unexpectedly. Finally, we construct the greeting using `std.fmt.allocPrint()`. This generates a second allocated string — the formatted message — which we also must `defer` freeing, before writing the final clean result to the console. As we are using the *unbuffered* `writeStreamingAll()`, we do not need to `flush()`.

The program concludes with the implementation of the `readLine()` helper function, which offers a view into how dynamic buffers grow in response to unpredictable input:

```
fn readLine(io: std.Io, allocator: std.mem.Allocator) !?[]u8 {
    const stdin = std.Io.File.stdin();
    var list = std.ArrayList(u8).empty;
    errdefer list.deinit(allocator);

    while (true) {
        var byte: [1]u8 = undefined;
        const amt = stdin.readStreaming(io, &.{&byte}) catch |err|
            {
                if (err == error.EndOfStream) break;
                return err;
            };
        if (amt == 0) {
            if (list.items.len == 0) return null;
            break;
        }

        if (byte[0] == '\n') break;
        try list.append(allocator, byte[0]);
    }
    return try list.toOwnedSlice(allocator);
}
```

We obtain the standard input handle via `std.Io.File.stdin()`, which provides a high-level, io-aware handle to standard input. To manage the incoming data, we instantiate a `std.ArrayList(u8)`. Then, we place an `errdefer list.deinit(allocator)` immediately after initialization. This is a vital Zig pattern for robustness: *if memory allocation fails during the append step later in the loop, this statement ensures that any memory already claimed by the list is cleaned up before the error propagates, preventing leaks in failure states.* The reading loop reads one byte at a time into a stack-allocated array. While inefficient for high-throughput systems, it allows us to precisely inspect the stream for the newline (\n) character. When `error.EndOfStream` is signaled by the runtime, we break out of the loop. When valid data is found, we call `list.append(allocator, byte[0])`, forcing the list to dynamically resize its backing memory if it runs out of capacity. Finally, the function concludes with `list.toOwnedSlice(allocator)`. This method is the bridge between our dynamic builder and the caller; it shrinks the allocated memory to fit the data exactly, effectively dismantling the `ArrayList` structure and handing raw ownership of the byte slice to the caller. This explains why the `main()` function is responsible for freeing the memory: `readLine()` built it, but `main()` bought it.

Execute `ch01/readUserInput.zig` to get an output similar to the next:

```
$ zig run ch01/readUserInput.zig
What is your name? Mihalis
Hello, Mihalis! Welcome to Zig.
```

So far, we have treated data as bytes that flow from the keyboard to the screen and then vanish into the void of the terminal history. To build truly useful tools, however, we must master the art of persistence. In the next subsection, we step out of the transient world of standard streams and into the filesystem, where we will learn to open, create, and modify files on disk.

Reading and opening files for writing or appending

In this subsection, we will explore how `std.fs` abstracts the complexity of OS-level flags, allowing us to choose precisely whether to overwrite existing data or append to a growing log, giving our programs the memory they need to leave a lasting impact. The `ch01/empty.zig` source code shows how to create an empty file — *if the file already exists, it will be truncated*:

```
pub fn main(init: std.process.Init) !void {
    const file = try std.Io.Dir.cwd().createFile(
        init.io,
        "/tmp/empty.txt",
        .{
            .truncate = true,
        },
    );
    defer file.close(init.io);
```

```
    std.debug.print("Created empty file: /tmp/empty.txt\n", .{});
}
```

The execution begins by obtaining a reference to the current working directory via `std.Io.Dir.cwd()`, which acts as the anchor for file system operations. Using this directory handle, the program calls the `createFile()` method to initialize a new file located at the absolute path `/tmp/empty.txt`. The `try` keyword is utilized here to handle any potential errors during the creation process by immediately returning them, while the successful result is stored in the `file` constant. The specific behavior of the file creation is strictly controlled by *the anonymous struct passed as the second argument,* which sets the `std.fs.File.CreateFlags`. The `.truncate = true` option determines how the program handles a situation where `/tmp/empty.txt` already exists. By setting this to `true`, the system is instructed to wipe any existing content in the file, resetting its size to zero bytes, effectively ensuring that you start with a clean slate every time the program runs. Finally, the program employs `defer` to ensure resource safety. The line `defer file.close(io)` guarantees that the underlying file descriptor is freed when the `main()` scope exits, regardless of whether the function finishes normally or encounters an error. Once the file is successfully created, a confirmation message is printed to standard error, signaling the completion of the task.

The `ch01/emptyIfNotExists.zig` shows how to create an empty file if it does not already exist, which is the professional way to operate:

```
pub fn main(init: std.process.Init) !void {
    const file_result = std.Io.Dir.cwd().createFile(
        init.io,
        "/tmp/empty.txt",
        .{
            .exclusive = true,
            .truncate = false,
        },
    ) catch |err| {
        if (err == error.PathAlreadyExists) {
            std.debug.print("File already exists.\n", .{});
            return;
        } else {
            return err;
        }
    };

    defer file_result.close(init.io);
```

```
        std.debug.print("Created empty file.\n", .{});
    }
```

This program demonstrates a safer approach to file creation known as *exclusive creation*, which prevents accidental overwriting of existing data. Like the previous example, it starts by accessing the current working directory via `std.Io.Dir.cwd()`, but this time `createFile()` is configured with distinct flags to enforce strict creation rules. The critical option here is `.exclusive = true`. This flag instructs the operating system to create the file if and only if it does not already exist. If the file is present, the operation fails immediately with a specific error rather than opening the existing file. Consequently, the `.truncate = false` option is set because truncation is irrelevant when we are guaranteed to be creating a brand-new file; we never open an existing file to wipe it. The error handling logic is also more granular than a simple `try`. Instead of automatically propagating all errors, the program uses a `catch |err|` block to inspect the specific cause of failure. It explicitly checks if the error is `error.PathAlreadyExists`, which is the result of the `.exclusive` flag encountering an existing file. In this scenario, the program prints a user-friendly message and exits gracefully. Any other error — such as a permission denial or a read-only filesystem — is returned to the caller. Finally, if the file is successfully created, the `defer file_result.close()` statement ensures the handle is properly closed before the program terminates.

After creating a file, the code in `ch01/write.zig` shows how to write data to a file:

```
pub fn main(init: std.process.Init) !void {
    const args = try init.minimal.args.toSlice(init.arena.allocator());
    if (args.len < 2) {
        std.debug.print("Usage: {s} <file1>\n", .{args[0]});
        return;
    }
    const filePath = args[1];

    const file = std.Io.Dir.cwd().createFile(init.io, filePath, .{
        .exclusive = true,
        .truncate = false,
    }) catch |err| {
        if (err == error.PathAlreadyExists) {
            std.debug.print("File already exists.\n", .{});
            return;
        } else {
            return err;
        }
```

```
    };
    defer file.close(init.io);
    try file.writeStreamingAll(init.io, "Writing to the file.\n");
}
```

This program *stops using hardcoded paths by integrating command-line argument processing* with safe file creation and writing operations. Execution begins by initializing `init.arena.allocator()`, which is necessary for `init.minimal.args.toSlice()` to dynamically allocate memory for the command-line arguments. The program immediately enforces input validation; if the argument count is insufficient (less than 2), it prints a usage message and exits, protecting against invalid access. Once the target filename is extracted from `args[1]`, the program uses `createFile()` with the `.exclusive = true` option, which acts as a safety guard. This specific error, `error.PathAlreadyExists`, is caught and handled gracefully by notifying the user, while other errors propagate up. Finally, if the file is successfully created, the defer mechanism schedules the file to close and the argument memory to be freed, allowing the program to safely execute `file.writeStreamingAll()` to store the desired data in the new file before terminating. Running the program generates the following output:

```
$ zig run ch01/write.zig -- /tmp/newFile
$ cat /tmp/newFile
Writing to the file.
$ zig run ch01/write.zig -- /tmp/newFile
File already exists.
```

In the first execution, the program successfully creates `/tmp/newFile` because it does not exist yet; the subsequent `cat(1)` command confirms that the string `"Writing to the file."` was written correctly. However, when the exact same command is run a second time, the `.exclusive = true` flag triggers an `error.PathAlreadyExists`. Instead of crashing or overwriting the data, the program catches this specific error in the `catch` block and prints the user-friendly message `"File already exists."` before exiting, effectively preventing accidental data loss. The double dash `--` serves as a critical delimiter that separates arguments intended for the Zig compiler from arguments intended for your compiled program. When you run `zig run`, the CLI first parses flags meant to configure the build. The `--` signals the end of these compiler options, telling Zig that everything following it should be passed as a command-line argument. Without the `--`, the Zig compiler would try to interpret those flags as build instructions and likely fail.

Next, `ch01/append.zig` illustrates how to add data at the end of a file (*append*):

```
pub fn main(init: std.process.Init) !void {
    const args = try init.minimal.args.toSlice(init.arena.allocator());

    if (args.len < 2) {
        std.debug.print("Usage: {s} <file>\n", .{args[0]});
        return;
    }
    const filePath = args[1];

    // Open file for read+write (fails if file does not exist)
    const file = try std.Io.Dir.cwd().openFile(init.io, filePath, .
                                             { .mode = .read_write });
    defer file.close(init.io);

    // Get current file size, then write at the end (append)
    const stat = try file.stat(init.io);
    try file.writePositionalAll(init.io, "Appended line\n", stat.size);
}
```

The core logic of the program involves opening a file specifically for modification. Unlike `createFile()`, which makes a new file, `std.Io.Dir.cwd().openFile()` is used here with the `.mode = .read_write` option. *This function assumes the file already exists; if the user provides a path to a non-existent file, the program will return an error and terminate.* This distinction is critical for tools that are meant to update logs or add to existing datasets rather than overwrite them. To achieve the *append behavior*, the program must manually adjust the file cursor. When a file is first opened, the write cursor is positioned at the beginning (byte 0). If the program wrote data immediately, it would overwrite the existing content. Finally, `file.writePositionalAll(init.io, "Appended line\n", stat.size)` writes the new data starting from that end position. Trying `ch01/append.zig` produces the following kind of output:

```
$ zig run ch01/append.zig -- /tmp/newFile
$ cat /tmp/newFile
Writing to the file.
Appended line
```

Last, `ch01/readAll.zig` loads an entire file into memory in a single operation:

```
pub fn main(init: std.process.Init) !void {
    const allocator = init.gpa;
    const args = try init.minimal.args.toSlice(init.arena.allocator());

    if (args.len < 2) {
        std.debug.print("Usage: {s} <file>\n", .{args[0]});
        return;
    }
    const filePath = args[1];
    const file = try std.Io.Dir.cwd().openFile(init.io, filePath, .{});
    defer file.close(init.io);
    const stat = try file.stat(init.io);

    const buffer = try allocator.alloc(u8, stat.size);
    defer allocator.free(buffer);

    _ = try file.readPositionalAll(init.io, buffer, 0);
    std.debug.print("File contents:\n{s}\n", .{buffer});
}
```

The process begins by acquiring a memory allocator and parsing the command-line arguments to locate the target file path. Once the file is successfully opened using `std.Io.Dir.cwd().openFile()`, the code immediately calls `file.stat(io)` to inspect file metadata. This step retrieves the exact size of the file in bytes at that moment. Using this size, the program asks the allocator for a single contiguous block of memory (`buffer`) that fits the file perfectly. Finally, it invokes `file.readPositionalAll(init.io, buffer, 0)`, which attempts to fill that entire allocated slice with data from the disk before printing the result to the console.

This *check-measure-allocate pattern* works reliably only under specific conditions: when reading static, regular files that are smaller than available RAM and are not being actively modified. It is fragile in several critical scenarios. First, it suffers from a *Time-of-Check to Time-of-Use race condition*: if another process appends data to the file between the `stat()` call and the `readPositionalAll()` call, your buffer will be too small to hold the new content, and the extra data will be silently truncated. Conversely, if the file shrinks, your buffer will contain uninitialized garbage at the end. Second, this method completely fails for special UNIX files like those in `/proc` or named pipes; these files often report a size of `0` in their metadata even though they contain content, causing `allocator.alloc()` to create an empty buffer and `readPositionalAll()` to read nothing. Finally, because it attempts to allocate the entire file size at once, running this on a massive file will immediately crash the program with an *Out of Memory error*, unlike a streaming approach that processes data in small, fixed-size chunks. You will learn more about file I/O in *Chapter 4, Processing Streams, Buffers, and Data Encoding,* and about working with files and directories in *Chapter 5, Navigating Directories and Filesystem Events.*

With all that information in mind, which acts as a solid foundation to our Zig journey, let us present the Zig implementation of `tee(1)`.

Implementing ztee

The `tee(1)` utility represents a significant step up in complexity from our previous simplistic tools. While conceptually simple — reading from standard input and duplicating that data to both standard output and files — the implementation forces us to confront the realities of resource orchestration. We must manage multiple file descriptors simultaneously, ensuring that a write failure in one output target does not catastrophically interrupt the others. The `ztee` implementation (`ch01/ztee.zig`) is presented in multiple parts, starting with this:

```
const std = @import("std");

pub fn main(init: std.process.Init) !void {
    const allocator = init.arena.allocator();
    const args = try init.minimal.args.toSlice(allocator);
```

We begin the implementation of `ztee` by establishing a memory management strategy that is specifically optimized for the short, finite lifecycle of a command-line utility. Rather than tracking and freeing every individual allocation manually — a tedious process that often leads to leaks in complex control flows — we call `init.arena.allocator()` to get an allocator backed by the runtime-managed arena. This arena acts as a monotonic memory region: it allows us to allocate objects freely during setup, such as the slice of command-line arguments returned by `init.minimal.args.toSlice()`, with the guarantee that they will all be released as the arena is freed automatically when the process exits. This pattern drastically simplifies our initialization logic; we can parse flags, store filenames, and build configuration structs without worrying about individual `free()` calls, knowing that the `defer` statement guarding the arena will handle the cleanup of the entire memory pool the moment our tool finishes its work. Next, we have this:

```
    const stdout = std.Io.File.stdout();
    const stdin = std.Io.File.stdin();
    const stderr = std.Io.File.stderr();
```

This step establishes the structural foundation of our utility by *explicitly acquiring the three standard file descriptors that connect our process to the operating system.* By assigning `std.Io.File.stdin()`, `stdout`, and `stderr` to local constants, we define the primary conduits for data flow within `ztee`. We are preparing to connect the incoming data stream with its multiple destinations, ensuring we have direct control over standard input, output, and error from the very start. Before diving into the core logic of stream duplication, we address the user interface by implementing a standard help mechanism:

```
// Check for Help
if (args.len > 1) {
    const arg1 = args[1];
    if (std.mem.eql(u8, arg1, "-h") or std.mem.eql(u8, arg1,
                                                    "--help")) {
        const help_text =
            \\Usage: ztee [OPTION]... [FILE]...
            \\Copy standard input to each FILE, and also to standard
              output.
            \\
            \\  -a, --append          append to the given FILEs, do not
              overwrite
            \\  -h, --help            display this help and exit
            \\
        ;
        try stdout.writeStreamingAll(init.io, help_text);
        return;
    }
}
```

We perform a preliminary check on the command-line arguments; if any are present (`args.len > 1`), we inspect the first one to see if it matches the standard help flags, `-h` or `--help`. We utilize `std.mem.eql` for this comparison because Zig does not overload the == operator for string slices, requiring us to be explicit about checking byte-for-byte equality. If a match is found, we define the usage instructions using Zig's multiline string literal syntax. The \\ prefix allows us to embed formatted text directly into the source code without the visual noise of escape sequences or concatenation, keeping the help message readable and easy to maintain. Finally, we write this block to standard output and return immediately, ensuring the program exits cleanly without performing any unwanted operations. With the help text handled, we initialize the internal state that controls our tool's behavior:

```
// Default configuration
var append_mode = false;
var files_start_index: usize = 1;
```

```
    // Check for -a / --append flag
    if (args.len > 1) {
        const arg1 = args[1];
        if (std.mem.eql(u8, arg1, "-a") or std.mem.eql(u8, arg1,
                                                         "--append")) {

            append_mode = true;
            files_start_index = 2;
        }
    }
```

We define append_mode as a Boolean, defaulting to `false` (overwrite) and set `files_start_index` to `1` so that we begin looking for filenames immediately after the program name. We then perform a manual check for the `-a` or `--append` flag in the first argument position. If detected, we toggle the append mode to `true` and increment our start index to 2. This adjustment is important as it effectively *consumes the flag*, ensuring that when we later iterate through the arguments to open files, we do not mistakenly attempt to open a file named `-a` or `--append` on the disk. This approach represents a simple, positional parsing strategy — common in lightweight tools — where flags are expected to appear before the list of operands.

To manage the variable number of output destinations, we initialize a `std.ArrayList(std.Io.File)` to store our file handles:

```
    // Open Output Files
    var output_files = std.ArrayList(std.Io.File).empty;
    defer {
        for (output_files.items) |file| file.close(init.io);
        output_files.deinit(allocator);
    }
    var write_offsets = std.ArrayList(u64).empty;
    defer write_offsets.deinit(allocator);
```

Right after declaring the list, we establish a block-based `defer` statement that acts as a comprehensive safety net for the resources we are about to acquire. This block ensures that when the program exits — whether successfully or due to an error halfway through opening files — we will iterate through every file handle currently stored in the list and close it, followed by freeing the relevant memory. `ztee.zig` can write to multiple output files at the same time and in append mode each of those files may already contain a different amount of data. Because `writePositionalAll()` takes an explicit byte offset rather than using a hidden file cursor, the program needs to remember, for each file, where the next write should land. `write_offsets` serves exactly that purpose: it is a parallel array to `output_files` where each slot holds the current write position for the corresponding file. When a file is opened, its slot is seeded with `stat.size` if append mode is active (so writes start after the existing content) or with zero if the file was just truncated. By defining this cleanup logic *before a single file is even opened*, we ensure that our tool remains leak-free and robust, adhering to the principle that resource acquisition and destruction should be coupled as tightly as possible. With the configuration set, we proceed to iterate over the provided filenames, transforming string paths into active file descriptors:

```
var i = files_start_index;
while (i < args.len) : (i += 1) {
    const path = args[i];

    const file = std.Io.Dir.cwd().createFile(init.io, path, .{
        .truncate = !append_mode,
    }) catch |err| {
        const msg = try std.fmt.allocPrint(
            allocator,
            "ztee: {s}: {s}\n",
            .{ path, @errorName(err) },
        );
        try stderr.writeStreamingAll(init.io, msg);
        continue;
    };

    const initial_offset: u64 = if (append_mode) blk: {
        const stat = try file.stat(init.io);
        break :blk stat.size;
    } else 0;

    try output_files.append(allocator, file);
    try write_offsets.append(allocator, initial_offset);
}
```

The loop iterates over the command-line arguments starting from `files_start_index`, which is the index of the first filename argument after any flags have been parsed. For each path, `createFile()` is called with `.truncate = !append_mode` — when append mode is off, the file is truncated to zero on open, matching the default `tee(1)` behavior of overwriting existing content. When append mode is on, truncation is suppressed, and the existing content is preserved. If the file cannot be opened — because of a permissions error, an invalid path or any other OS-level failure — the error is caught, formatted into a human-readable message using `std.fmt.allocPrint()` and written to stderr before continue moves to the next filename. The `initial_offset` block determines where writes should begin. If append mode is active, `file.stat(init.io)` retrieves the file metadata and `stat.size` gives the byte offset of the end of the existing content — this is where new data should start. If append mode is off, the offset is simply zero since the file was just truncated. The labeled block `blk:` with `break :blk` is the Zig syntax for a block expression that returns a value, used here to conditionally compute the offset without a separate variable declaration for each branch. Finally, both the file handle and its corresponding write offset are appended to their respective `ArrayList` values — `output_files` and `write_offsets` — keeping the two arrays in sync so that later write calls can pair each file with the correct starting position.

With the output file handles securely stored in our list and the append mode logic applied, the initialization phase of `ztee` is complete. To transform this static configuration into a working utility, we must now implement a mechanism that actively pulls bytes from the source and pushes them to every waiting destination.

The I/O loop: buffering data efficiently

At the heart of every stream-processing tool lies the I/O loop, the mechanical engine that drives the utility. Because standard input is often an infinite stream or a file larger than available RAM, we cannot simply read the entire content into a massive array. Instead, we must process the data in manageable chunks, creating a cycle of *read*, *write*, and *repeat*. This approach not only keeps our memory footprint constant — regardless of whether we are processing a kilobyte or a terabyte — but also optimizes system throughput by aligning our operations with the underlying hardware's page sizes. In this section, we implement this cycle using a fixed-size buffer, establishing a pipeline that efficiently ferries bytes from the input to multiple destinations without blocking the flow.

```
while (true) {
const bytes_read = stdin.readStreaming(
    init.io,
    &.{&buf},
) catch |err| {
    if (err == error.EndOfStream) break;
    return err;
};
if (bytes_read == 0) break;

const chunk = buf[0..bytes_read];
```

```
        try stdout.writeStreamingAll(init.io, chunk);

        for (output_files.items, 0..) |file, idx| {
            if (append_mode) {
                file.writePositionalAll(
                    init.io,
                    chunk,
                    write_offsets.items[idx],
                ) catch |err| {
                    const msg = try std.fmt.allocPrint(
                        allocator,
                        "ztee: write error: {s}\n",
                        .{@errorName(err)},
                    );
                    try stderr.writeStreamingAll(init.io, msg);
                };
                write_offsets.items[idx] += chunk.len;
            } else {
                file.writeStreamingAll(init.io, chunk) catch |err| {
                    const msg = try std.fmt.allocPrint(
                        allocator,
                        "ztee: write error: {s}\n",
                        .{@errorName(err)},
                    );
                    try stderr.writeStreamingAll(init.io, msg);
                };
            }
        }
    }
```

The implementation begins by allocating a 4096-byte buffer on the stack using `var buf: [4096]u8 = undefined;`. We use `undefined` here for performance as initializing this memory is unnecessary; we will only ever access the bytes that the kernel explicitly fills. Inside the infinite `while (true)` loop, we call `stdin.readStreaming(init.io, &.{&buf})`, *a blocking operation that pauses execution until data is available.* `readStreaming()` signals EOF via `error.EndOfStream`, which is caught and breaks the loop. The `tee(1)` functionality is implemented by immediately writing this chunk to standard output via `stdout.writeStreamingAll()`. *We then iterate over our list of auxiliary files, writing the same chunk to each one.* The write path branches on `append_mode`. When append mode is off, `file.writeStreamingAll()` writes the chunk sequentially from wherever the file position currently sits. When append mode is on, `file.writePositionalAll()` is used instead, writing the chunk at the explicit byte offset stored in `write_offsets.items[idx]`. After each successful positional write, that offset is advanced by `chunk.len`, so the next iteration writes immediately after the bytes just written rather than overwriting them.

Testing ztee

We are going to need the following program named `ch01/stdOutErr.zig` for testing `ch01/ztee.zig`, which acts as a generator of mixed output streams designed to simulate a process that actively communicates on both Standard Output and Standard Error:

```
const std = @import("std");

pub fn main(init: std.process.Init) !void {
    // 1. Allocate buffers for the streams
    var out_buf: [4096]u8 = undefined;
    var err_buf: [4096]u8 = undefined;

    // 2. Initialize Buffered Writers
    var stdout_impl = std.Io.File.stdout().writer(init.io,&out_buf);
    var stderr_impl = std.Io.File.stderr().writer(init.io,&err_buf);

    // 3. Get the Generic Writer Interfaces
    const stdout=&stdout_impl.interface;
    conststderr=&stderr_impl.interface;

    var i: usize = 0;
    while (i < 5) : (i += 1) {
        try stdout.print("OUT: This is stdout message #{d}\n", .{i});
        try stderr.print("ERR: This is stderr warning #{d}\n", .{i});
    }

    // 4. Flush
    try stdout.flush();
    try stderr.flush();
}
```

The code begins by allocating two 4KB arrays, `out_buf` and `err_buf`, which serve as memory buffers. It then initializes buffered writers for `stdout` and `stderr` handles, linking them to these allocated arrays; this ensures that text written to these writers accumulates in memory rather than appearing on the console immediately. The core logic enters a loop that runs five times, formatting and printing a status message to the `stdout` buffer and a corresponding warning to the `stderr` buffer in each iteration. Finally, the program calls `.flush()` on both streams, which forces the accumulated data in the buffers to be discharged to the operating system and displayed on the screen or sent to the pipe.

This specific behavior is crucial for testing a utility like `ztee` because `ztee` is architecturally required to handle input streams selectively. The primary function of `ztee` is to read from Standard Input and duplicate that content to files and the console, while *completely ignoring Standard Error*. By piping this Zig program into `ztee`, we can verify stream isolation, as the output file must contain only the lines starting with `OUT`, while the lines starting with `ERR` should bypass `ztee` entirely and appear directly on your terminal. Let us try that and see what happens:

```
$ zig run ch01/stdOutErr.zig | zig run ch01/ztee.zig -- /tmp/output.txt
ERR: This is stderr warning #0
ERR: This is stderr warning #1
ERR: This is stderr warning #2
ERR: This is stderr warning #3
ERR: This is stderr warning #4
OUT: This is stdout message #0
OUT: This is stdout message #1
OUT: This is stdout message #2
OUT: This is stdout message #3
OUT: This is stdout message #4
```

Now, let us examine the contents of `/tmp/output.txt`:

```
$ cat /tmp/output.txt
OUT: This is stdout message #0
OUT: This is stdout message #1
OUT: This is stdout message #2
OUT: This is stdout message #3
OUT: This is stdout message #4
```

So, `/tmp/output.txt` got the output of standard output without containing any output that went to standard error (`ERR`). Having said that, `ztee` works as expected. Let us continue by implementing the famous `which(1)` utility in Zig.

Implementing zwhich, an executable locator

We begin the implementation of `zwhich` by presenting two utilities that illustrate how to read the value of `PATH` and how to split that value into individual directories.

Reading environment variables

This is how you read UNIX environment variables in Zig as found in `ch01/readEnv.zig`:

```
pub fn main(init: std.process.Init) !void {
    // Get the PATH environment variable from the environ map
    const pathEnv = init.environ_map.get("PATH") orelse {
        std.debug.print("Error: PATH variable not found\n", .{});
        return;
    };

    std.debug.print("PATH: {s}\n", .{pathEnv});
}
```

The centerpiece of this example is the `init.environ_map.get()` function, which is new in Zig 0.16. Unlike the old `std.process.getEnvVarOwned()`, which allocated a fresh heap buffer for every lookup and required an explicit `free()` when you were done, `init.environ_map` is a read-only map that the runtime populates once at startup, before `main()` is called. It holds slices that point directly into memory already owned by the process, meaning a lookup performs no allocation whatsoever. Calling `.get("PATH")` returns a `?[]const u8` — an optional slice. If the variable exists in the environment, you receive a non-owning view of its value; if it does not, you receive `null`. Because we do not own the memory, there is nothing to free, and the returned slice remains valid for the entire lifetime of the process. We handle the `null` case immediately with `orelse`, printing a user-friendly message and returning cleanly. If successful, we display the value of `PATH` to the console. Execute the program on your machine as follows:

```
$ zig run ch01/readEnv.zig
PATH: /opt/homebrew/bin:/usr/local/bin:/usr/bin:/bin:/usr/sbin:/sbin
```

Now, let us learn how to split the `PATH` environment variable into its parts.

Splitting the PATH environment variable

Instead of treating the `PATH` variable as a monolithic block of text, we recognize it as a colon-delimited list of directories and split it accordingly. This is the `main()` function from `ch01/splitPATH.zig`:

```
pub fn main(init: std.process.Init) !void {
    // Get the PATH environment variable
    const pathEnv = init.environ_map.get("PATH") orelse {
        std.debug.print("Error: PATH variable not found\n", .{});
        return;
    };

    // Split PATH into individual directories
    var dirs = std.mem.splitScalar(u8, pathEnv, ':');
    while (dirs.next()) |dir| {
        std.debug.print("Directory: {s}\n", .{dir});
    }
}
```

We split the retrieved `PATH` string using `std.mem.splitScalar()`. This function creates a lightweight iterator that scans the string for the specified separator (:) without allocating any additional memory for the substrings. As we cycle through this iterator with `dirs.next()` inside the `while` loop, it calculates the boundaries on the fly, yielding a temporary view of the original `pathEnv` string for each directory. This approach allows us to traverse and inspect every search path in `PATH` sequentially without any additional memory allocations. The generated output should look as follows:

```
$ zig run ch01/splitPATH.zig
Directory: /opt/homebrew/bin
Directory: /usr/local/bin
Directory: /usr/bin
Directory: /bin
Directory: /usr/sbin
Directory: /sbin
```

Now, let us complete the `zwhich` implementation by explaining how to get file permissions and check if we are dealing with a regular file or not. You will learn more about working with files and directories in *Chapter 5, Navigating Directories and Filesystem Events.*

Connecting the dots

With all these utilities in mind, we are ready to present the implementation of `zwhich` as found in `ch01/zwhich.zig`, beginning with the `canAccess()` helper function:

```
pub fn canAccess (io: std.Io, path: []const u8) bool {
    var found: bool = true;
    std.Io.Dir.cwd().access(io, path, .{}) catch |e| switch (e) {
        error.FileNotFound => found = false,
        else => found = false,
    };
    return found;
}
```

This function checks if the filesystem can access the specified path. The logic lies in the `catch` block, which intercepts any errors returned by the system call. We switch on the specific error e: if it matches `error.FileNotFound`, we know the path is invalid, so we set the value of `found` to `false`. The `else` branch handles all other failure scenarios (such as `AccessDenied`), which we also treat as *not found* for the purpose of this check.

The `isFile()` function checks whether a given path refers to a regular file or not:

```
pub fn isFile(io: std.Io, path: []const u8) bool {
    const stat = std.Io.Dir.cwd().statFile(io, path, .{}) catch return false;
    return stat.kind == .file;
}
```

The function takes a string slice path as input and uses the current working directory (`cwd`) to call `statFile()`, which attempts to retrieve the metadata of the file at that path. If this operation fails, the function catches the error and returns `false`. If metadata retrieval is successful, it inspects the kind field of the metadata, which indicates the type of the file system object. If kind is equal to `.file`, the function concludes that the path refers to a regular file and returns `true`; otherwise, it returns `false`.

The `isExecutable()` function determines whether a given file has executable permissions set for the user, group, or others on UNIX-like systems:

```
pub fn isExecutable(io: std.Io, path: []const u8) bool {
    const stat = std.Io.Dir.cwd().statFile(io, path, .{}) catch return false;
    const mode = stat.permissions.toMode();
```

```
    return (mode & 0o111) != 0;
}
```

The function accepts a file path as input and retrieves the file metadata using `statFile()`. If the metadata lookup fails because the file does not exist or cannot be accessed, the function returns `false`. It then checks the mode field of the file metadata, which encodes the file permission bits. By performing a bitwise AND with `0o111`, the function isolates the execute permission bits for the owner (`0o100`), group (`0o010`), and others (`0o001`). If any of these bits are set, it indicates that the file is marked as executable and the function returns `true`; otherwise, it returns `false`.

The interesting part of the `main()` function lies in the following `while` block:

```
    while (dirs.next()) |dir| {
        var pathBuf = std.ArrayList(u8).empty;
        defer pathBuf.deinit(init.gpa);
        try pathBuf.appendSlice(init.gpa, dir);
        try pathBuf.append(init.gpa, '/');
        try pathBuf.appendSlice(init.gpa, command);
        const fullPath = pathBuf.items;

        if (canAccess (init.io, fullPath) and
            isFile(init.io, fullPath) and
            isExecutable(init.io, fullPath))
        {

            try stdout.writeStreamingAll(init.io, fullPath);
            try stdout.writeStreamingAll(init.io, "\n");
            found = true;
            break;
        }
    }
```

This loop implements the core search logic of `zwhich`, systematically probing each directory in `PATH` for the requested command. Inside the iteration, we construct a candidate file path by concatenating the current directory (`dir`), a standard path separator (/), and the target command name. Once the full path string is constructed, we check if the path exists, verify it is a regular file (not a directory), and confirm it has the executable permission bit set. If all three conditions are met, we have found our match; the program prints the full path to standard output, flags the success, and immediately breaks the loop, adhering to the standard behavior of returning only the first valid executable found. It is worth noting that this implementation is

UNIX-specific. The path separator / and the PATH delimiter: are both hard-coded, which is correct on Linux and macOS but wrong on Windows, where paths use \ and PATH entries are separated by ;. For a UNIX systems programming book, the hard-coded approach is the clearest way to show the logic. Now, let us try `ch01/zwhich.zig`:

```
$ zig run ch01/zwhich.zig -- ls
/bin/ls
$ zig run ch01/zwhich.zig -- doesNotExist
error: Command 'doesNotExist' not found in PATH
error: FileNotFound
. . .
```

The first command finds `ls` at `/bin/ls`, confirming that `zwhich` correctly walks the PATH directories and returns the first match it finds — exactly as `which(1)` does.

The second command searches for `doesNotExist`, finds nothing, and produces two lines of output. The first is the explicit diagnostic message the program writes before returning. The second, `error: FileNotFound`, is Zig's standard error propagation output showing the underlying error value that traveled up the call stack. The `...` indicates a stack trace that has been truncated for brevity. In a production tool, you would suppress the raw Zig error and show only the user-facing message, but here both lines together illustrate how application-level error reporting and Zig's error system work in tandem.

In a production build, the trace is suppressed, and only the application-level message appears. If you always want clean output regardless of build mode, the alternative is to catch the error explicitly at the top level, print the diagnostic, and call `std.process.exit(1)` rather than returning an error from `main()`. Either approach is valid — the current implementation prioritizes simplicity and transparency during development, which suits a learning example.

So, the `zwhich` utility works as expected. While implementing standard utilities in pure Zig is an excellent way to master a programming language, a big part of the versatility of Zig lies in the ability to leverage the vast ecosystem of existing C libraries.

Calling C code from Zig

Zig lets you call C code. In fact, sometimes you need C functionality to access certain low-level or platform-specific features. So, this is not just a matter of style or preference but a real need. Here is a Zig program (`ch01/isExecutableC.zig`) that checks whether a given file is executable or not by using the `access(2)` call while demonstrating how Zig treats C functions as native citizens that simply need a forward declaration:

```
const std = @import("std");
const c = @cImport(@cInclude("unistd.h"));

// Import the `access()` function from C
extern fn access(path: [*:0]const u8, mode: c_int) c_int;

pub fn main(init: std.process.Init) !void {
    const args = try init.minimal.args.toSlice(init.arena.allocator());

    if (args.len < 2) {
        std.debug.print("Usage: isExecutableC <file>", .{});
        return;
    }

    const filePath = args[1];

    // Call C function `access()` to check executability
    if (access(filePath, c.X_OK) == 0) {
        std.debug.print("{s} is executable", .{filePath});
    } else {
        std.debug.print("{s} is NOT executable or does not exist",
                    .{filePath});
    }
}
```

The core mechanism here is the extern block: by writing `extern fn access(...)`, we manually define the function signature of the POSIX `access(2)` syscall found in the C library of the active system. Notice the precise type usage: `c_int` is used instead of `i32` to guarantee compatibility regardless of the target architecture's C integer definition, and `[*:0]const u8` is used to represent a C-string, which is *a pointer to an array of bytes terminated by a sentinel zero value.* The actual invocation of the function inside `main()` highlights one of Zig's most powerful convenience features: automatic type coercion for sentinel-terminated slices. Although `args[1]` is a Zig slice (containing a length and a pointer), `init.minimal.args.toSlice()` guarantees these strings are null-terminated (`[:0]u8`). When we pass `filePath` to the C `access(2)` function, *Zig automatically unwraps the slice, discarding the length, and passing just the pointer to the raw, null-*

terminated data. This allows us to write Zig code that verifies the executable permission (X_OK) directly without the need for glue code or marshaling layers.

Let us try ch01/isExecutableC.zig on a macOS Tahoe machine:

```
$ zig run ch01/isExecutableC.zig -- /bin/ls
/bin/ls is executable
$ zig run ch01/isExecutableC.zig -- /bin
/bin is executable
$ zig run ch01/isExecutableC.zig -- /etc/hosts
/etc/hosts is NOT executable or does not exist
```

Running the previous command on an Omarchy Linux system creates an error message due to issues with not linking against the *libc library*. The way to correct that is by adding -lc at the end of the command before the -- part. This applies to all Zig programs that include C code under my Omarchy machine. Your Linux machine may behave differently or the same. Just keep in mind that there is nothing wrong with the Zig code.

Have in mind that currently the program cannot differentiate between a regular file and a directory. With all the wisdom in mind, let us learn how to create secure passwords.

Creating secure passwords with zpass

Difficult to guess passwords can be very handy when creating new user or database accounts. In this section, we are going to learn how to create random passwords in Zig. But first, we are going to learn how to generate random values in Zig.

Two ways to generate random values

Zig distinguishes between two primary categories of randomness: cryptographically secure random bytes and pseudo-random numbers, each serving distinct use cases. For security-critical applications — such as generating passwords, session keys, nonces, or salts — you should use init.io.randomSecure(&buf). This call always goes directly to the operating system's entropy source (/dev/urandom on UNIX, BCryptGenRandom on Windows) with no fallback, guaranteeing that the output is unpredictable and safe for sensitive operations. init.io.random(&buf) is a related but weaker alternative: it uses a PRNG seeded by randomSecure() where possible but may fall back to a less secure mechanism on failure, making it unsuitable for cryptographic purposes. When performance is paramount and cryptographic strength is unnecessary — such as in simulations, games or shuffling logic — std.Random.DefaultPrng is the right choice. This generator is deterministic once seeded and is fast, but it is not a CSPRNG regardless of how its seed is obtained. zpass.zig uses randomSecure() directly since it is generating passwords. Both approaches are illustrated in the following utility. Both ways are illustrated in the following utility:

```
const std = @import("std");
const builtin = @import("builtin");
const print = std.debug.print;

pub fn main(init: std.process.Init) !void {
    // --- Securely seeded PRNG ---
    // io.random() seeds from the OS entropy source where possible,
    // but falls back to a less secure mechanism on failure.
    // This makes the initial state unpredictable but the algorithm
    // (Xoshiro256++) remains deterministic and is NOT a CSPRNG.
    var seed_bytes: [8]u8 = undefined;
    init.io.random(&seed_bytes);
    var seeded_prng = std.Random.DefaultPrng.init(
        @bitCast(seed_bytes),
    );
    const rand_seeded = seeded_prng.random();

    print("Seeded PRNG u8:         {}\n", .{rand_seeded.int(u8)});
    print(
        "Seeded PRNG u8 < 10:   {}\n",
        .{rand_seeded.uintLessThan(u8, 10)},
    );
    print("Seeded PRNG u16:        {}\n", .{rand_seeded.int(u16)});
    print("Seeded PRNG u32:        {}\n", .{rand_seeded.int(u32)});
    print("Seeded PRNG i32:        {}\n", .{rand_seeded.int(i32)});
    print("Seeded PRNG float:      {d}\n", .{rand_seeded.float(f64)});

    var data = [_]u8{ 1, 2, 3, 4, 5, 6, 7, 8, 9, 10, 20, 30, 40, 50 };
    rand_seeded.shuffle(u8,&data);
    print("Shuffled data:          {any}\n", .{data});

    // --- Fixed-seed PRNG (reproducible) ---
    // Seeding with a constant produces the same sequence every run.
    // Use this for debugging, simulations or procedural generation
    // where reproducibility matters.
    var fixed_prng = std.Random.DefaultPrng.init(0);
    const rand_fixed = fixed_prng.random();
```

```
    print("Fixed-seed float:      {d}\n", .{rand_fixed.float(f32)});
    print("Fixed-seed boolean:    {}\n", .{rand_fixed.boolean()});
    print("Fixed-seed u8:         {}\n", .{rand_fixed.int(u8)});
    print(
        "Fixed-seed u8 [0,255]: {}\n",
        .{rand_fixed.intRangeAtMost(u8, 0, 255)},
    );
}
```

This program acts as a comprehensive tour of the `std.Random` interface, demonstrating how the same set of methods can be driven by two fundamentally different engines. It begins by calling `init.io.random(&seed_bytes)`, which fills an 8-byte stack buffer from the OS entropy source where possible, though it may fall back to a less secure mechanism on failure. Those bytes are then bit-cast into a 64-bit integer and used to seed a `DefaultPrng`. It is important to understand what this buys and what it does not: seeding from OS entropy makes the initial state unpredictable, so the sequence will differ on every run. However, the underlying algorithm — Xoshiro256++ — is deterministic and is not a CSPRNG. This means the seeded PRNG is suitable for unpredictable shuffles, simulations, and games, but not for cryptographic purposes such as key generation. For those use cases, `init.io.randomSecure()` is the correct call. Through `rand_seeded`, the code generates a variety of types — integers of different widths, signed and unsigned, floating-point numbers — and performs a shuffle on a byte array via `std.Random.shuffle()`.

The second half of the program shifts focus to reproducibility by initializing a `DefaultPrng` with the fixed seed `0`. This means the sequence of numbers it produces will be identical every time the program runs — behavior that is essential for debugging simulations, writing deterministic tests, or implementing procedural generation where the same seed should always produce the same world. Calling `.random()` on either generator returns the same generic `std.Random` interface, which is the point: the code that consumes random numbers does not need to know or care which engine is behind it. You can swap a fixed-seed PRNG for an OS-seeded one — or vice versa — by changing a single line. Now, let us use `ch01/randomValues.zig`:

```
$ zig run ch01/randomValues.zig
Random u8: 72
Random u8 < 10: 4
Random u16: 25163
Random u32: 1077443060
Random i32: 354857164
Random float: 0.960382148832826
```

```
Shuffled data: { 4, 9, 30, 8, 3, 10, 5, 50, 7, 6, 40, 20, 2, 1 }
Random float: 0.27175805
Random boolean: true
Random u8: 252
Random u8: 26
```

The first block – everything up to `Shuffled data` – displays values generated by `io.random(&buf)`, whereas the remaining output is from the seeded `DefaultPrng`.

With all the information in mind, let us generate unpredictable passwords!

Generating unpredictable passwords

The following program (`ch01/zpass.zig`) creates a simple random password generator, introducing an OS entropy-based seeding strategy to ensure different outputs across runs:

```
const std = @import("std");

pub fn main(init: std.process.Init) !void {
    // Customize this set to match your target password policy.
    const set = "abcdefghijklmnopqrstuvwxyzABCDEFGHIJKLMNOPQRSTUVWXYZ0123456789!
@#$%^&*-_";
    const charsetLen = set.len;

    var stringLength: u32 = 16;
    var iter = init.minimal.args.iterate();
    defer iter.deinit();
    _ = iter.next();
    if (iter.next()) |arg| {
        stringLength = try std.fmt.parseInt(u32, arg, 10);
    }

    const result = try init.gpa.alloc(u8, stringLength);
    defer init.gpa.free(result);

    // Rejection sampling avoids modulo bias when mapping
    // a uniform byte to the charset.
    const threshold = 256 - (256 % charsetLen);
    for (result) |*ch| {
        var byte: [1]u8 = undefined;
        while (true) {
            try init.io.randomSecure(&byte);
```

```
            if (byte[0] < threshold) {
                ch.* = set[byte[0] % charsetLen];
                break;
            }
        }
    }

    std.debug.print("Random string: {s}\n", .{result});
}
```

We begin by processing command-line arguments using the `init.minimal.args.iterate` iterator pattern, which processes arguments sequentially, allowing us to define a default length of 16 and override it only if the user provides a number. We define a string literal `set` containing our allowed characters — lowercase, uppercase, digits, and common special characters — giving 72 possibilities per position. The character set is a plain string constant and can be customized to match any password policy. We allocate a destination buffer of the desired length on the heap and then fill it one byte at a time using `init.io.randomSecure`, which reads directly from the OS cryptographic entropy source without going through a PRNG. To avoid modulo bias when mapping a uniform random byte to the 72-character set, we use rejection sampling: bytes at or above the largest multiple of 72 that fits in a byte are discarded and redrawn. Accepted bytes are mapped to a charset index with `%`. Finally, we print the constructed string to the console. Let us see that:

```
$ zig run ch01/zpass.zig
Random string: X^JWTMpxna012r8#
$ zig run ch01/zpass.zig -- 8
Random string: t5UGAXss
```

This is how simple it is to generate secure paths in Zig – it turns out that Zig designers got many things right!

What did Zig get right

Zig designers and developers got many things right about Zig, including:

- Zig is fine-tuned for performance and safety and is being marketed as an alternative to C. Therefore, it can be used for writing software such as TCP/IP servers and Web services.
- Zig offers manual memory management, which is the price that we must pay for its speed. If you want a garbage-collected programming language, then maybe you should

look at Go or even Python. However, if you need to process lots of data fast, then Zig is a rational choice.

- Error handling is an essential part of modern programming languages, and Zig does a great job! So, you can easily write secure and bug-free tools in Zig.
- Zig offers compatibility with C code! This means that existing C libraries can be used immediately in Zig without using any magic tricks. However, this is a feature that should be used with care, as existing C code might contain bugs and invalid memory accesses that might crash your Zig program. So, if you have existing C code that you want to use, Zig can help a lot!
- Zig is relatively easy to learn, especially when compared to programming languages such as Rust and C++. As a result, it can be used by both amateur and experienced engineers either for developing applications in production or for learning programming and studying Computer Science at a University.

Nevertheless, Zig is not perfect, which is true for all programming languages! Zig is still in the development phase. Additionally, it takes time to learn its idiosyncrasies and use it effectively and productively. Lastly, Zig documentation is still maturing and can be sparse in some advanced areas. We hope this book helps fill that gap.

Summary

In this chapter, we have moved from the simplicity of printing text to the console to the architectural reality of building robust, UNIX-compliant utilities like `ztee` and `zwhich`.

In the next chapter, we will explore the build system of Zig (`build.zig`) and learn about Memory Allocators. Alongside this, we will deepen our understanding of software verification by writing tests for `zwhich`, manage external dependencies and develop `zuuid`, a utility for generating unique identifiers.

Exercises

- Change the code in `ch01/append.zig` to create a file if it does not exist.
- Modify the output of `ch01/zwhich.zig` when running a command such as `zig run ch01/zwhich.zig - doesNotExist`.
- Make the necessary changes to `ch01/zwhich.zig` so that it finds all the paths where the given binary executable can be found.

- Make the necessary changes to `ch01/zwhich.zig` so that it can process multiple command-line arguments.
- Rewrite `ch01/zpass.zig` so that it uses the secure random generator.

Additional resources

- Zig: `https://ziglang.org/`

Get this book's PDF version and more

2

Systems Infrastructure: Builds, Testing, and Distribution

Discussing build systems is usually the driest part of systems programming. This usually includes talking about *Makefiles* and *shell scripts* that feel entirely detached from the code we write. Zig changes this dynamic entirely by treating the build process as a Zig program. In this chapter, we explore `build.zig`, where you define your project's build graph using the same syntax and standard library available to your main application, as well as the less crucial `build.zig.zon`. We see how this approach allows you to handle complex cross-compilation targets and manage dependencies. This way, Zig empowers you to create reproducible builds that work seamlessly across different operating systems. We also bridge the gap between writing code and shipping it by developing a complete Zig library and enforcing reliability through `std.testing`.

This chapter covers:

- Formatting strings with `std.fmt`
- Understanding Memory Allocators
- Writing unit tests with `std.testing`
- Generating documentation with `-femit-docs`
- Developing `zuuid`
- Using GitHub to host a Zig library
- Publishing packages and the Zig Build System

We start this chapter by discussing `std.fmt` and memory allocators.

Formatting strings with std.fmt

In Zig, string formatting is centralized in the `std.fmt` namespace, which powers everything from simple console debugging to the serialization of complex data structures. Zig leverages compile-time logic to verify that your data types match your format specifiers, preventing a whole class of runtime errors. In this section, we explore how to use specifiers to control the presentation of numbers and text and how to direct that formatted output to different destinations — whether it be directly to standard output, into a fixed-size stack buffer, or into a dynamically allocated string on the heap. We use `ch02/stdFmt.zig` to showcase formatting and present it in multiple snippets, starting with the following:

```
const std = @import("std");
const User = struct {
    name: []const u8,
    id: u32,
};
```

The `User` struct acts as a simple blueprint for grouping related data, containing two fields: `name`, which is typed as `[]const u8`, and `id`, a 32-bit unsigned integer. We continue with the beginning of the `main()` function:

```
pub fn main(init: std.process.Init) !void {
    const io = init.io;
    // page_allocator is used here for brevity before the full
    // allocator discussion in the next section. In production
    // code and in the rest of this book, prefer init.gpa.
    const allocator = std.heap.page_allocator;
    const stdout = std.Io.File.stdout();
    std.debug.print("Debug: Program started.\n", .{});
```

We begin by preparing the necessary resources that we will need in the process, and we continue with code that shows dynamic string construction:

```
    const number = 255;
    const msg_nums = try std.fmt.allocPrint(
        allocator,
        "Decimal: {d}, Hex: {x}, Binary: {b}, Octal: {o}\n",
        .{ number, number, number, number },
    );
```

```
defer allocator.free(msg_nums);
try stdout.writeStreamingAll(io, msg_nums);
```

We define a constant 255 and use `std.fmt.allocPrint()` to format it. Unlike simple printing functions, `allocPrint()` calculates the exact required size for the output string and *allocates memory on the heap to store it*. Within the format string, we apply four distinct filters to the same number: `{d}` for standard decimal, `{x}` for hexadecimal, `{b}` for binary, and `{o}` for octal. Because this operation creates new memory, the pattern is completed with a `defer allocator.free(msg_nums)` statement, ensuring that the allocated string is freed once we have written it to standard output. Next, we move from numerical bases to formatting floating-point numbers for cleaner presentation:

```
const pi = 3.14159;
const msg_float = try std.fmt.allocPrint(
    allocator,
    "Pi (2 decimals): {d:.2} | Padded: {d: >10.2}\n",
    .{ pi, pi },
);
defer allocator.free(msg_float);
try stdout.writeStreamingAll(io, msg_float);
```

We apply two distinct formatting rules within a single string using an approximation of Pi. The first specifier, `{d:.2}`, instructs the formatter to present the value in standard decimal notation but truncates the output to exactly two decimal places, rounding the value to `3.14`. The second specifier, `{d: >10.2}`, combines this precision control with layout management: the `>10` syntax forces the output to be *right-aligned* within a field of ten characters, padding the left side with spaces. This alignment capability is essential for generating readable plain text tables or financial reports where columns of numbers must line up perfectly. As before, we handle the memory responsibly by allocating the string and deferring its destruction.

The next code snippet shows how to format complex data types automatically:

```
const user = User{ .name = "Alice", .id = 101 };
const numbers = [_]u8{ 1, 2, 3 };
const msg_struct = try std.fmt.allocPrint(
    allocator,
    "User: {any}, Array: {any}\n",
    .{ user, numbers },
);
```

```
    defer allocator.free(msg_struct);
    try stdout.writeStreamingAll(io, msg_struct);
```

We instantiate a `User` struct and a simple array of bytes and pass them to `std.fmt.allocPrint()` using the `{any}` specifier. This is a *generic placeholder* that instructs the compiler to generate a default text representation for the data, regardless of its type. For the struct, `{any}` recursively walks through the fields, printing the type name followed by the field names and values. For the array, it lists the elements enclosed in braces. Finally, we demonstrate the high-performance alternative to heap allocation: formatting directly into a fixed-size stack buffer:

```
    var buffer: [64]u8 = undefined;
    const slice = try std.fmt.bufPrint(
        &buffer,
        "Stack buffer: {s}-{d}",
        .{ "Data", 42 },
    );
    try stdout.writeStreamingAll(io, slice);
    try stdout.writeStreamingAll(io, "\n");
}
```

Instead of requesting dynamic memory from the system, we manually declare a local array `buffer` of 64 bytes using `undefined`, reserving a small scratchpad directly on the function's stack frame. We then utilize `std.fmt.bufPrint()`, passing a pointer to this buffer alongside our format string. This function writes the text `Data-42` directly into our reserved memory and returns a slice representing only the bytes that were used. This mechanism allows us to obtain a valid string view without touching the heap, eliminating the need for `free()` calls or leak checking. The trade-off for this speed is the size limit; if the formatted output were to exceed our 64-byte capacity, `bufPrint()` would fail with `error.NoSpaceLeft`, forcing us to handle the truncation or choose a larger buffer. We can now execute `ch02/stdFmt.zig` to get the following output:

```
$ zig run ch02/stdFmt.zig
Debug: Program started.
Decimal: 255, Hex: ff, Binary: 11111111, Octal: 377
Pi (2 decimals): 3.14 | Padded:       3.14
User: .{ .name = { 65, 108, 105, 99, 101 }, .id = 101 }, Array: { 1, 2, 3 }
Stack buffer: Data-42
```

The `.name` field prints as `{ 65, 108, 105, 99, 101 }` rather than `Alice` because `{any}` is a generic formatter that inspects the underlying type and, for a `[]const u8` slice, prints each byte as a decimal integer. This is technically correct — those are the ASCII values of `A`, `l`, `i`, `c`, `e` — but it is rarely what you want when printing a string. To get a human-readable string, use `{s}` instead of `{any}`. The distinction matters whenever you are working with byte slices: `{s}` treats the bytes as a UTF-8 string and prints them as text, while `{any}` treats them as a sequence of raw values and prints each one numerically. As a rule of thumb, use `{s}` for strings and `{any}` for everything else when you want to see the contents rather than the byte representation.

With string formatting established as a foundation, we now turn to one of the most consequential decisions in any Zig program: how memory is allocated. This is not a theoretical concern — it is infrastructure. The networking server in *Chapter 6, Programming the Network Stack*, uses an arena allocator to manage per-connection memory and discard it instantly when the connection closes. The concurrent file indexer in *Chapter 8, Orchestrating Concurrency and Synchronization*, gives each worker thread its own allocator to eliminate contention. The cache server in *Chapter 10, Building a High-Performance In-Memory Cache Server*, passes a single allocator through every layer of the system so the memory strategy can be swapped without touching the logic. Every one of those designs depends on understanding what allocators are, how they differ, and why the choice matters. That understanding starts here.

Understanding memory allocators

The allocator model in Zig is not just a design preference; it reflects a fundamental philosophy about where complexity should live in a systems program. In most languages, the allocator is a global, invisible service that the runtime manages on your behalf. This convenience comes at a cost: you cannot easily change allocation strategy per subsystem, you cannot trivially detect leaks in a specific code path, and you cannot run the same logic against a stack buffer in one context and the system heap in another without rewriting it. Zig eliminates the global allocator entirely. Every function that needs dynamic memory declares that need explicitly by accepting a `std.mem.Allocator` parameter. The function does not know or care whether the bytes it receives came from the OS heap, a pre-allocated arena, or a fixed array on the stack. That decision belongs to the caller, who is the only party with enough context to make it correctly. The `std.mem.Allocator` type is an interface in the Zig sense: a struct containing a pointer to an implementation and a pointer to a vtable of function pointers covering `alloc()`, `resize()`, and `free()`. Every concrete allocator — `DebugAllocator`, `ArenaAllocator`, `FixedBufferAllocator`, and any custom allocator you write — satisfies this interface by providing those three operations. When you call `allocator.alloc(u32, 4)`, you are calling through that vtable, and the compiler has no obligation to inline or specialize the call. This is a tradeoff by design: the polymorphism costs one indirect call per allocation, but it buys complete decoupling between the code that uses memory and the code that manages it.

Understanding when each allocator is the right tool requires understanding what each one optimizes for. The `DebugAllocator` — known as `GeneralPurposeAllocator` in earlier Zig versions — prioritizes correctness over raw speed. It tracks every live allocation in an internal metadata structure and, when you call `deinit()`, reports any that were never freed. It also detects double-frees and use-after-free accesses in debug builds by poisoning freed memory with a sentinel pattern. This overhead is exactly what you want during development and exactly what you want to remove in production. The allocator is designed to be swapped out, not optimized around. The `ArenaAllocator` makes the opposite tradeoff: it prioritizes throughput and simplicity of cleanup at the cost of the ability to free individual allocations. Internally, it maintains a linked list of large memory blocks obtained from its child allocator. Each call to `alloc()` simply advances a pointer within the current block — an operation that takes a handful of CPU instructions with no locking, no metadata update, and no fragmentation concern. Individual frees are accepted but do nothing; the only deallocation that matters is `arena.deinit()`, which walks the block list and returns every block to the child allocator in a single sweep. This model maps perfectly onto any workload that has a natural batch lifetime: parse a configuration file into a tree, use it, discard the whole tree at once. Build a request response object, send it, and destroy everything. In these patterns, the arena eliminates an entire category of memory management error — the forgotten free — because the question of "did I free every node in this tree?" simply does not arise. The `FixedBufferAllocator` takes the arena concept to its logical extreme by removing the child allocator entirely. You hand it a slice of memory that you already own — typically a stack-allocated array — and it manages that slice as a bump allocator. The implementation is a single pointer and a length; `alloc()` checks that the requested bytes fit, advances the pointer, and returns the slice. There is no `free` implementation worth mentioning and no `deinit()`. When the function that owns the backing array returns, the memory disappears automatically as the stack frame is popped. The `FixedBufferAllocator` is the right choice whenever you know an upper bound on the memory you need, that bound is small enough to live on the stack, and you want the absolute minimum allocation overhead. Embedded systems, hot paths inside tight loops, and temporary scratch buffers during serialization are all natural fits.

Beyond these three, the allocator interface is open to extension. A `MemoryPoolAllocator` can serve fixed-size objects from a pre-allocated array with *O(1)* allocation and deallocation, eliminating fragmentation entirely for homogeneous workloads. A logging allocator can wrap any existing allocator and record every allocation and free to a file, giving you a complete trace of memory activity without modifying the code under test. A failing allocator can be configured to return `OutOfMemory` on the Nth call, enabling systematic testing of every allocation failure path in your program. All of these are possible because the interface is just a struct with three function pointers — there is no runtime or compiler magic involved. The practical consequence of this design is that the allocator strategy becomes an architectural decision rather than an implementation detail. When you write a parser, you decide at the call site whether it should use an arena (fast, bulk-free), a debug allocator (safe, leak-detecting), or a fixed buffer (zero-overhead, stack-local). That decision is visible in the code, reviewable in a pull request, and changeable without touching the parser itself. This is what Zig means when it says there is no hidden control flow and no hidden memory management — the costs are explicit, and the person who bears them is the person best positioned to reason about them.

As discussed, *there is no default global allocator*, and functions and data structures that need dynamic memory must accept a `std.mem.Allocator` as a parameter. *This approach forces you to think about the lifecycle and cost of your data.* It also grants you immense power: you can seamlessly swap memory strategies without rewriting your application logic. You might use a `DebugAllocator` during development to catch memory leaks, switch to an `ArenaAllocator` in production to group allocations for instant cleanup, or rely on a `FixedBufferAllocator` to run on the stack in constrained embedded environments. The `std.mem.Allocator` interface unifies these distinct strategies, allowing the same code to adapt to vastly different system constraints. `ch02/memAllocators.zig` demonstrates how the exact same function (`createNumbers()`) can behave differently depending on the `std.mem.Allocator` passed to it:

```
const std = @import("std");
fn createNumbers(allocator: std.mem.Allocator) ![]u32 {
    const slice = try allocator.alloc(u32, 4);
    for (slice, 0..) |*item, i| {
        item.* = @intCast(i * 10);
    }
    return slice;
}
```

This helper function is *agnostic to how memory is managed*. By accepting a `std.mem.Allocator` interface as an argument, it allows the caller to dictate the memory source — whether it be the system heap, a temporary arena, or a stack buffer. Inside, we use `allocator.alloc(u32, 4)` to request a slice of four 32-bit integers; the `try` keyword ensures that if the allocation fails, the error is propagated immediately. The subsequent loop populates the data using the syntax `for (slice, 0..) |*item, i|`. Two details are critical here: first, the `0..` syntax allows us to capture the index `i` alongside the element. Second, we capture `*item` as a *pointer* rather than a value. If we had captured `item` directly, we would be holding a read-only copy; by capturing the pointer, we can dereference it (`item.*`) to modify the actual data in the slice. Finally, we use `@intCast()` to safely convert the index (a machine-sized `usize`) into a `u32` before returning the populated slice, transferring ownership as well as the responsibility to free it, back to the caller. Next, we do a little bit of setup before we put any memory allocator to work:

```
pub fn main(init: std.process.Init) !void {
    const io = init.io;
    const stdout_file = std.Io.File.stdout();
    var buf: [4096]u8 = undefined;
    var stdout_impl = stdout_file.writer(io,&buf);
    conststdout=&stdout_impl.interface;
    // ignoring flush error in demo context
    defer stdout.flush() catch {};
```

We begin by acquiring the raw file handle for standard output via `std.Io.File.stdout()`. However, writing to this handle directly for every small string would be inefficient due to frequent system calls. To solve this, we manually allocate a `4096` byte buffer on the stack (`var buf`) and pass it to `stdout_file.writer(io, &buf)`. This call constructs a specialized writer implementation that fills our buffer first, only triggering a costly write to the OS when the buffer is full. We then capture the address of its `.interface` field, which gives us a polymorphic `Writer` pointer (`stdout`). This standardized interface allows us to use high-level methods like `print()` and `writeAll()` seamlessly. Finally, because the buffer is managed in user space, we must ensure that any remaining data is pushed to the terminal before the program ends; the line `defer stdout.flush() catch {}` guarantees this cleanup happens automatically, preventing truncated output. We begin with the **General Purpose Allocator** (GPA), which is now called **Debug Allocator** in Zig 0.16, implemented as `std.heap.DebugAllocator`:

```
    var gpa: std.heap.DebugAllocator(.{}) = .init;
    defer _ = gpa.deinit();
    const gpa_allocator = gpa.allocator();
    const numbers = try createNumbers(gpa_allocator);
    try stdout.print("GPA Numbers: {any}\n", .{numbers});
    gpa_allocator.free(numbers);
```

The Debug Allocator is designed to balance performance with safety. *Its defining characteristic is safety checking.* When `gpa.deinit()` is called, the `DebugAllocator` does two things simultaneously. First, it writes any leak information directly to stderr as a side effect — this happens unconditionally regardless of what you do with the return value. Second, it returns a `Check` enum value that indicates whether any leaks were detected, allowing you to act on the result programmatically. The pattern `defer _ = gpa.deinit()` discards that return value with _ =, which silences the compiler warning about an unused result but does not suppress the stderr output. Leak reports will still appear on the terminal. If you want to assert that no leaks occurred — for instance, in a test — you would write `defer std.debug.assert(gpa.deinit() == .ok)` instead, which turns a leak into a panic rather than a silent log message. For development and learning purposes, `defer _ = gpa.deinit()` is sufficient: you will see the leak report on stderr and the program will exit cleanly regardless. In this section, we follow the traditional manual memory management pattern: we allocate the `numbers` slice, print it, and then explicitly call `gpa_allocator.free(numbers)`. If we had forgotten that line, the GPA would have printed a leak warning to the console upon program exit, making it invaluable for debugging. Next, we introduce the **Arena Allocator**, which wraps the GPA to fundamentally change how memory is reclaimed:

```
    var arena = std.heap.ArenaAllocator.init(gpa_allocator);
    defer arena.deinit();
    const arena_allocator = arena.allocator();
    const n1 = try createNumbers(arena_allocator);
    const n2 = try createNumbers(arena_allocator);
    try stdout.print("Arena Numbers: {any}, {any}\n", .{ n1, n2 });
```

The `std.heap.ArenaAllocator` takes a child allocator and acts as a monolithic memory pool. Notice that we call `createNumbers()` twice here to generate `n1` and `n2`, yet we never free them individually. This is the superpower of arena: instead of tracking thousands of tiny objects, we simply defer `arena.deinit()`. When that line runs, the arena frees every single allocation it ever made in one efficient sweep. This pattern is ideal for request-based systems (like web servers) where you want to construct a complex graph of objects and destroy them all instantly when the request finishes, eliminating the risk of dangling pointers or forgotten frees within that scope. Finally, we demonstrate the **Fixed Buffer Allocator** (FBA), which completely bypasses the heap for raw speed:

```
    var stack_buffer: [1024]u8 = undefined;
    var fba = std.heap.FixedBufferAllocator.init(&stack_buffer);
    const fba_allocator = fba.allocator();
    const n3 = try createNumbers(fba_allocator);
    try stdout.print("Stack Numbers: {any}\n", .{n3});
}
```

We initialize `std.heap.FixedBufferAllocator` using a slice of memory residing directly on the stack (`stack_buffer`). Because this allocator simply bumps a pointer forward within that fixed array, *it is the fastest possible way to allocate memory* — essentially zero overhead. However, it is also the most constrained; if we requested more than 1024 bytes, the allocator would return an

`OutOfMemory` error. Crucially, there is no `free` or `deinit` logic required here at all. Since the memory lives on the stack, it is automatically reclaimed by the CPU the moment the `main()` function returns, *making the FBA perfect for temporary, high-performance buffers where the upper size limit is known in advance.* Now, we can execute `ch02/memAllocators.zig`:

```
$ zig run ch02/memAllocators.zig
GPA Numbers: { 0, 10, 20, 30 }
Arena Numbers: { 0, 10, 20, 30 }, { 0, 10, 20, 30 }
Stack Numbers: { 0, 10, 20, 30 }
```

The output confirms that our `createNumbers()` function acts identically regardless of the memory strategy backing it. This uniformity is the ultimate proof of the pattern's success: we swapped the underlying memory engine three times — from the general heap to a monolithic pool to the stack — without changing a single line of the data generation code. In the next chapter, we are going to benchmark the performance of memory allocators.

Next, we are going to learn how to create tests for Zig code, taking `zwhich` as an example.

Verification strategy

We are going to create tests for the `zwhich` command-line tool we created in the previous chapter. But first, we are going to explain the way testing works in Zig.

Writing unit tests with std.testing

In Zig, testing is not a secondary concern delegated to external frameworks but is directly integrated into the core of the language. The `std.testing` namespace provides the essential primitives for verification, allowing you to assert conditions and compare values using functions like `expect()`, `expectEqual()`, and `expectError()`. Instead of maintaining separate directory trees for tests that can easily drift out of sync, Zig encourages you to *write test blocks within the same source files as your implementation code.* These blocks are strictly compile-time constructs; they are only compiled and run when you explicitly issue the `zig test` command, ensuring that your production binaries are lean and optimized. We showcase testing by writing tests for `zwhich`.

Writing tests for zwhich

Now that we understand the logic of `std.testing`, we can apply these principles to verify the correctness of the `ch01/zwhich.zig` utility. Unlike simple mathematical functions, testing a command-line tool like `zwhich` requires interacting with the external environment. In this subsection, we will write tests that validate the `zwhich` helper functions. The testing code can be found in `ch02/test_zwhich.zig` and starts as follows:

```
test "filesystem helpers" {
    const testing = std.testing;
    var t: std.Io.Threaded = .init_single_threaded;
    const io = t.io();
    var tmp = testing.tmpDir(.{});
    defer tmp.cleanup();
```

Have in mind that, unlike `main()`, which receives a `std.process.Init` parameter from the runtime containing a ready-to-use `init.io` handle, test blocks receive no such parameter — they are standalone functions called directly by the test runner with no event loop attached. `std.Io.Threaded` provides a way to construct a minimal `std.Io` instance manually for exactly this situation. Declaring `var t: std.Io.Threaded = .init_single_threaded` and calling `t.io()` gives you a valid `std.Io` value that you can pass to any function that requires one, making it the standard pattern for writing tests that exercise code depending on the `std.Io` interface.

We begin by defining a *test block* titled `"filesystem helpers"` using the `test` keyword. This block serves as a specialized container for our assertions, ensuring that this logic runs only during the `zig test` phase and *is stripped entirely from the final production binary*. For convenience, we create a local alias `const testing = std.testing`, a common Zig idiom that keeps our subsequent assertions and helper calls concise and readable. The core of this snippet is the establishment of the testing environment, as the testing of filesystem operations directly on the hard drive is dangerous. To prevent this, `var tmp = testing.tmpDir(.{})` generates a *strictly isolated temporary directory*. This sandbox provides a safe, throwaway playground where we can create, modify, and delete files freely without any side effects on the host operating system. Finally, we clean up the environment with `defer tmp.cleanup()`. This line registers a deferred action that executes strictly when the scope exits — whether the test passes, fails, or crashes with an error. By calling `cleanup()`, Zig recursively deletes the temporary directory and all its contents, guaranteeing that our test suite is going to leave no trace, keeping the development machine clean without requiring any manual intervention. Next, we populate the sandbox with a dummy file to act as our target executable:

```
    const filename = "test_bin";
    const file = try tmp.dir.createFile(io, filename, .{});
    defer file.close(io);
```

We define the name `test_bin` and then utilize `tmp.dir.createFile()`, which creates the file relative to our isolated temporary directory rather than the current working directory of the project. This function returns an open `File` handle. While we might typically close a file immediately if we only needed it to exist, we keep this handle open (stored in `file`) because we will soon need to manipulate its metadata — specifically its executable permissions — without race conditions. After that, we issue `defer file.close(io)` to guarantee that the file descriptor is released back to the OS the moment the test finishes, regardless of the outcome.

Next, we create a subdirectory named `test_subdir` using `tmp.dir.createDir()`:

```
const dirname = "test_subdir";
try tmp.dir.createDir(io, dirname, .default_dir);

var path_buffer: [std.fs.max_path_bytes]u8 = undefined;
const abs_file_len = try tmp.dir.realPathFile(
    io,
    filename,
    &path_buffer,
);
const abs_file_path = path_buffer[0..abs_file_len];

var dir_buffer: [std.fs.max_path_bytes]u8 = undefined;
const abs_dir_len = try tmp.dir.realPathFile(
    io,
    dirname,
    &dir_buffer,
);
const abs_dir_path = dir_buffer[0..abs_dir_len];
```

This is a critical test because a robust system tool must be able to distinguish between a file and a directory; by having both present, we can later verify that the `isFile()` function correctly accepts the binary while rejecting the folder. To perform these verifications, we need to convert our relative names into fully qualified absolute paths that the operating system can recognize. In Zig, fetching a path requires a destination for the resulting string, so we manually declare a stack buffer (`path_buffer`) sized to `std.fs.max_path_bytes` — a constant ensuring we have enough space for the longest possible path the OS supports. We then call `tmp.dir.realPathFile()`, which resolves the location of `test_bin` relative to our temporary directory and writes the full path into our buffer. We repeat this process for the directory, resulting in two valid, absolute path slices (`abs_file_path` and `abs_dir_path`) ready to be passed into our helper functions. The final segment of our test suite moves from setup to verification, asserting that our helper functions behave exactly as expected:

```
        // --- TEST: doesItExist ---
        try testing.expect(doesItExist(io, abs_file_path));
        try testing.expect(!doesItExist(io, "non_existent_junk_file_123"));

        // --- TEST: isFile ---
        try testing.expect(isFile(io, abs_file_path));
        try testing.expect(!isFile(io, abs_dir_path));

        // --- TEST: isExecutable ---
        if (@import("builtin").os.tag != .windows) {
            // Case A: Make it executable (755)
            _ = std.c.fchmod(file.handle, 0o755);
            try testing.expect(isExecutable(io, abs_file_path));

            // Case B: Make it non-executable (644)
            _ = std.c.fchmod(file.handle, 0o644);
            try testing.expect(!isExecutable(io, abs_file_path));
        }
    }
```

We start with the fundamental check, `doesItExist()`, confirming both the positive case — that our physically created file is detected — and the negative case, ensuring that a nonsense string correctly returns `false` without crashing the program. Immediately following this, we verify type strictness with `isFile()`. By asserting that `abs_file_path` is accepted while `abs_dir_path` is rejected, we ensure our search logic will filter out false positives effectively. The most complex logic is reserved for `isExecutable()`, which requires interacting with the operating system's permission bits. Because Windows uses Access Control Lists rather than simple permission bits, we wrap this block in a conditional check (`if ... != .windows`) to run strictly on POSIX systems like Linux and macOS. Inside, we leverage the open file handle we saved earlier to call `std.c.fchmod()`. We first set the permissions to `0o755` (making the file executable by everyone) and assert that our function returns `true`. We then flip the bits to `0o644` and assert that the function returns `false`. As `std.c.fchmod()` is a direct binding to the POSIX C library function, it requires libc to be linked explicitly. When running tests that use it, pass `-lc` to the test command. For readers who prefer to avoid the libc dependency entirely, `std.Io.File.setPermissions()` is the idiomatic Zig 0.16 alternative. It takes a `Permissions` struct describing the desired access rights and requires no `-lc` flag.

We are now ready to execute our tests:

```
$ zig test ch02/test_zwhich.zig -lc
All 1 tests passed.
```

Verifying that our functions return the correct values is only the first step in ensuring robust software. In a systems language, logical correctness is insufficient if the program mishandles resources, as a tool that works perfectly for five minutes but crashes after an hour due to memory exhaustion is effectively useless. While logic errors are often obvious in output, *resource leaks* are silent killers that typically go unnoticed until the system is under heavy load.

Detecting memory leaks automatically during tests

With the use of `std.testing.allocator`, which is a *specialized memory manager that tracks every allocation made during testing*, you have automatic memory leak detection. When the test block concludes, this allocator performs a mandatory audit: if any memory remains unfree, it fails the test completely. This mechanism provides a built-in safety net that matches external tools like Valgrind, pinpointing the exact source of leaks within your code and ensuring that your application remains as efficient as it is correct. Here is the relevant testing code as found in `ch02/memoryLeak.zig`:

```
test "leak from helper function" {
    const testing = std.testing;
    const fib_sequence = try computeFibonacci(testing.allocator, 10);
    // BUG: We intentionally forget to free 'fib_sequence' here!
    // defer testing.allocator.free(fib_sequence);
    try testing.expectEqual(@as(u32, 34), fib_sequence[9]);
}
```

The `computeFibonacci()` function accepts an allocator and a count `n`, allocates a slice of `n u32` values on the heap using `allocator.alloc()`, and fills it with the Fibonacci sequence before returning the slice to the caller. Ownership of the slice — and the responsibility to free it — transfers to the caller at the point of return. This is the standard Zig ownership pattern: the function that allocates does not free, and the caller decides when the memory is no longer needed. That transfer of responsibility is exactly what the leak detector is designed to catch when the matching `allocator.free()` call is deliberately omitted in the examples that follow. The full source is available in `ch02/memoryLeak.zig` in the accompanying repository.

So, by intentionally omitting `defer testing.allocator.free(fib_sequence)`, we *retain ownership of the heap memory without ever releasing it*. The code then proceeds to the assertion `try` `testing.expectEqual(...)`, which verifies that the 10th Fibonacci number is indeed 34. While this logical check succeeds, the test framework will ultimately flag a failure the moment the block exits, reporting that the memory allocated for `fib_sequence` was *leaked*. Let us now try `zig test` on `ch02/memoryLeak.zig`:

```
$ zig test ch02/memoryLeak.zig
. . .
All 1 tests passed.
1 errors were logged.
1 tests leaked memory.
error: the following test command failed with exit code 1:
~/.cache/zig/o/156c5c21576044f9d/test --seed=0xad8759b5
```

The line `All 1 tests passed` indicates that our code executed successfully without crashing and that every assertion evaluated to `true`. Mathematically, the Fibonacci function calculated the correct number. However, the subsequent line `1 tests leaked memory` signals that the post-execution audit failed. The `std.testing.allocator` detected that memory was allocated during the test but never released. Because Zig treats resource leaks as critical defects comparable to logic bugs, the test runner overrides the "passed" status of the assertions and forces the overall command to fail (`exit code 1`). So, the compiler is telling you: *Your math is correct, but your housekeeping is flawed.*

This distinction matters more than it might appear in a simple test. A Fibonacci function that leaks a few bytes is harmless in isolation, but the same pattern in a long-running server is a slow-motion failure. A TCP proxy that allocates a buffer per connection and never frees it will exhaust available memory over hours or days under real load — not crashing immediately but degrading gradually until the OS kills the process. Zig's test-time leak detection exists precisely to catch these patterns before they reach production, where the consequence is a 3 a.m. incident rather than a failed test run.

Now that we have verified the correctness of our logic through testing, we must address the human side of software infrastructure. A tool that works perfectly is of little value if its interface is opaque or its usage undocumented. In the next subsection, we will see how Zig allows us to generate professional documentation directly from our source code.

Generating documentation (-femit-docs)

Documentation is often the first casualty of rapid development, usually because the tools to generate it are cumbersome or disconnected from the build process. Zig solves this by integrating documentation generation directly into the compiler itself. By using the `-femit-docs` flag, the Zig compiler parses your source code — looking for triple-slash `///` *documentation comments* — and automatically synthesizes a complete, searchable static HTML website. This generated site reflects the exact state of your code, including public functions, types, and their relationships, ensuring that your documentation never drifts out of sync with your implementation. To illustrate all these, we are going to generate documentation for `zwhich`, which can be found in `ch02/zwhich.zig`. We are not going to present the actual code, just the triple-slash comments, starting with `canAccess()`:

````
/// Checks if a file system entry exists at the given path.
///
/// This function attempts to access the specified path and returns:
/// - `true` if the path exists (file, directory, symlink, etc.)
/// - `false` for any error (including non-existence)
///
/// # Parameters
/// - `io`: Io instance for async filesystem access
/// - `path`: File system path to check
///
/// # Example
/// ```zig
/// const exists = canAccess(io, "myfile.txt");
/// std.debug.print("File exists: {}\n", .{exists});
/// ```
pub fn canAccess(io: std.Io, path: []const u8) bool {}
````

This code snippet illustrates *doc comments,* which use a triple-slash prefix to distinguish them from standard source code comments. Unlike the double-slash syntax, which is ignored by the compiler, these comments are strictly associated with the declaration that follows them. When the documentation generator runs, it parses this text as Markdown; *the first paragraph serves as a high-level summary for list views,* while the subsequent sections provide the deep-dive details. The inclusion of the fenced code block (` ```zig `) allows the documentation to feature syntax-highlighted usage examples, turning the source code into a living user manual that is both machine-readable and human-friendly.

Next, we present the documentation of `isFile()`:

```
/// Determines if a path points to a regular file.
///
/// Returns `false` for directories, symlinks, or any access errors.
///
/// # Parameters
```

```
/// - `io`: Io instance for async filesystem access
/// - `path`: Path to check
///
/// # See Also
/// - `canAccess`: For generic existence check
/// - `isExecutable`: For executable verification
pub fn isFile(io: std.Io, path: []const u8) bool { }
```

Here, the documentation expands beyond a simple definition to offer context and navigation through the `# See Also` section. While the initial lines define the strict boundaries of `isFile()`, clarifying that it rejects directories and symbolic links, the `See Also` block connects this specific tool to the broader utility belt of the library. By explicitly referencing `canAccess()` and `isExecutable()`, we create associations.

After that, we show the example documentation of `isExecutable()`:

```
/// Checks if a file is executable by any user (UNIX permissions).
///
/// Examines the file mode's executable bits (owner/group/others).
/// Returns `false` for non-files or inaccessible paths.
///
/// # Parameters
/// - `io`: Io instance for async filesystem access
/// - `path`: File path to check
///
pub fn isExecutable(io: std.Io, path: []const u8) bool { }
```

The documentation for `isExecutable()` illustrates how to effectively communicate *platform-specific* nuances in a codebase. The summary and parameter sections describe the standard UNIX behavior — checking the owner, group, and others' permission bits. Last, the documentation of `main()`, which provides information for using the utility:

```
/// UNIX `which` command implementation in Zig.
///
/// Finds the first executable instance of a command in PATH.
///
/// # Usage
/// ```sh
/// $ zig run zwhich.zig -- ls
/// /usr/bin/ls
```

```
/// ```
///
/// # Behavior
/// 1. Parses command-line argument
/// 2. Splits PATH environment variable
/// 3. Checks each directory for executable file matching command
/// 4. Prints first valid executable path found
/// 5. Exits with error if not found
///
/// # Error Handling
/// - Returns `error.FileNotFound` when command is missing
/// - Prints usage error for incorrect arguments
/// - Handles PATH lookup failures
pub fn main(init: std.process.Init) !void { }
```

The documentation for `main()` shifts the focus from internal API details to the user-facing behavior of the application itself. Because `main()` is the entry point, the `# Usage` section abandons Zig syntax in favor of a shell command example, showing exactly how to invoke the tool from the command line. The `# Behavior` block serves as a high-level specification, breaking down the application logic into a clear, step-by-step algorithm, from parsing arguments to iterating through the `PATH`. This is complemented by the `# Error Handling` section, which establishes a contract with the user, clearly defining how the tool communicates failure when a target cannot be found.

To transform these comments into a navigable website, we rely on the Zig *built-in documentation generator*. By running the command `zig build-exe -femit-docs zwhich.zig` in your terminal, you instruct the compiler to perform a standard build while simultaneously extracting all triple-slash comments and function signatures. This process creates a new subdirectory named `docs/` within your current folder. Inside, you will find an `index.html` file. In this case, we are also going to rename the generated `docs/` directory into `zwhich.docs`, but feel free to use your own directory name. Viewing the documentation locally requires running a local HTTP server. This happens because browsers do not allow JavaScript `fetch()` from `file://` URLs due to security reasons; therefore, browsers restrict cross-origin HTTP requests initiated from scripts. Python offers such a capability by default, so it is Python that we are going to use. Run `python3 -m http.server 8000` inside the documentation directory (`zwhich.docs`) and then open your browser to `http://localhost:8000/` and you are done. The steps are the following:

```
$ cd ch02
$ zig build-exe -femit-docs zwhich.zig
```

```
$ mv docs zwhich.docs
$ cd zwhich.docs
$ python3 -m http.server 8000
Serving HTTP on :: port 8000 (http://[::]:8000/) ...
```

After that, you should visit `http://localhost:8000/`. The root documentation page can be seen in the image that follows:

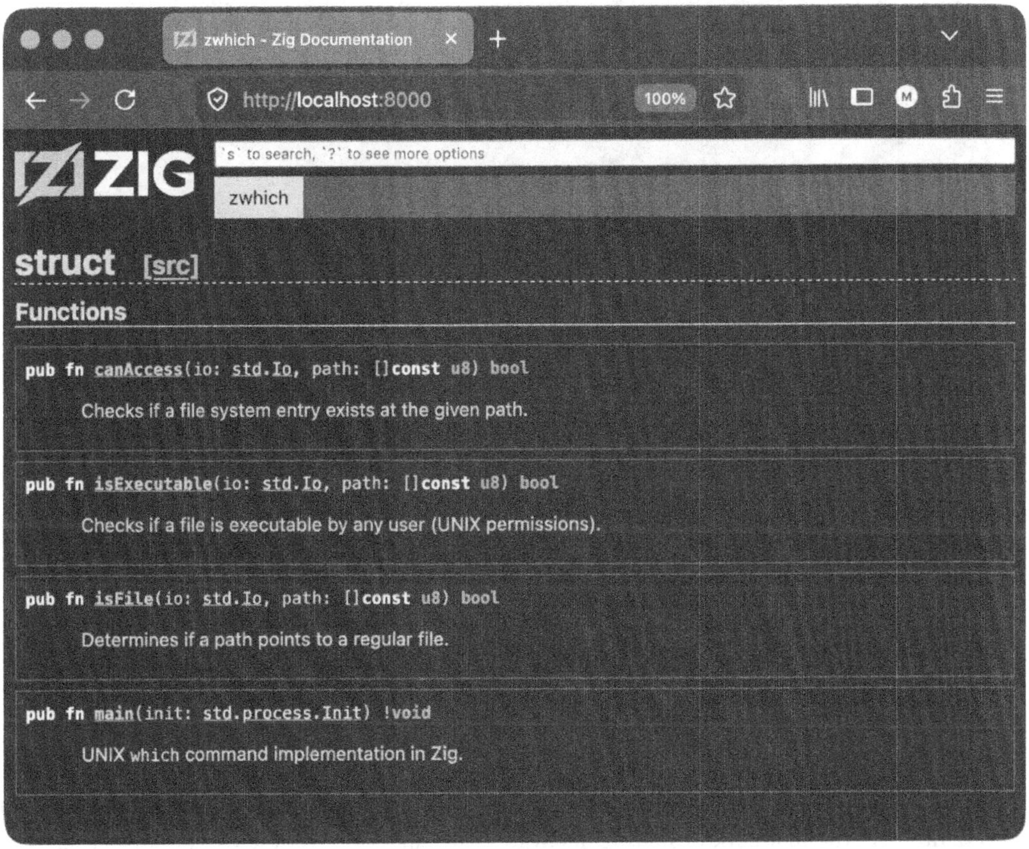

Figure 2.1 – The root documentation page of zwhich.zig

Press on the documentation of the `main()` function to get the following image – at the bottom of the image, you can see a small part of the `main()` implementation, which is true for all presented functions:

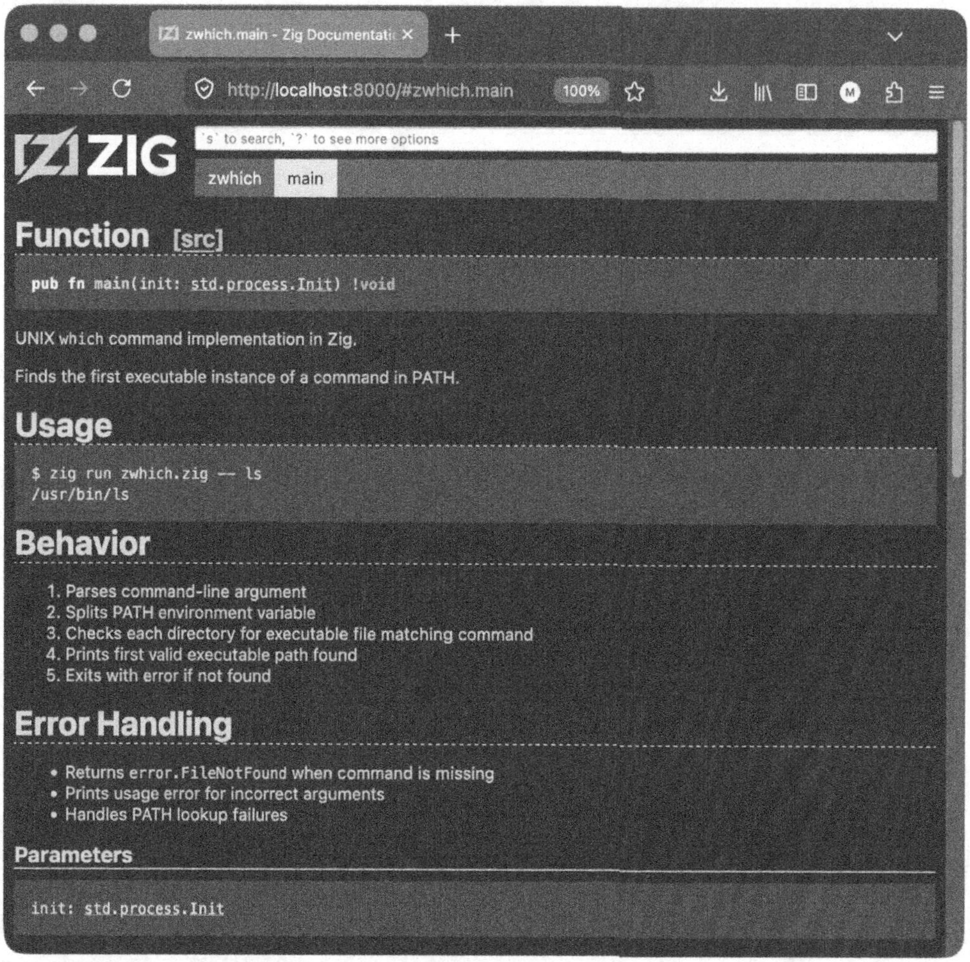

Figure 2.2 – The documentation page of main()

With our code now verified by tests and explained by documentation, we have a solid internal foundation. Yet the hallmark of mature software is not just how well it works in isolation, but how effectively it leverages the work of others. Instead of wasting time re-implementing algorithms that have already been solved and optimized by the community, we can dramatically accelerate our development by integrating existing packages.

Fetching and using external libraries

For the purposes of this section, we are going to use an external library found at `https://github.com/mactsouk/tsdist-zig` and host all relevant files inside `ch02/ts`. To manage these integrations, Zig employs a decentralized package manager powered by a file named `build.zig.zon` (*Zig Object Notation*). This manifest defines the project dependencies not by vague names or registry tags but by *precise URLs and cryptographic hashes.* This design guarantees reproducible builds: because every dependency is pinned to a specific hash, you can be certain that if your project compiles today, it will compile the same way in the future, even if the upstream source changes.

The build system as infrastructure as code

Zig reimagines the build process by discarding static configuration files in favor of a full-fledged imperative programming model. Instead of dealing with Makefiles or CMake lists, you define your build pipeline using standard Zig code within a `build.zig` file. This means the entire build graph — defining executables, libraries, tests, and their dependencies — is constructed programmatically at runtime. You can use Standard Library features to detect system properties, write loops to generate multiple targets, and share logic between your application and its build scripts.

Managing dependencies with build.zig.zon

While `build.zig` is the imperative Zig program that defines *how* to compile your code — setting up targets, optimization levels, and linking steps — `build.zig.zon` is strictly declarative, defining *what* your project needs. This separation ensures that the compiler can resolve, download, and verify external code before your build logic even begins execution. For our project, we are going to use the following `build.zig.zon` file:

```
.{
    .name = .my_project,
    .version = "0.1.0",
    .fingerprint = 0xa54a7cc201649d8a,

    .dependencies = .{
        .tsdist = .{
            .url = "git+https://github.com/mactsouk/tsdist-zig?
ref=main#467e99ba95d29657de06920f38b419dabccad7a9",
            .hash = "zig_distances-0.1.0-EOpI-
h4jAAAI7mMBGf4gMtGVm0GN47oLfcNDcMfzKTOj",
            .branch = "main",
        },
    },
    .paths = .{"."},
}
```

This configuration file represents the declarative root manifest for a Zig project, serialized in **Zig Object Notation** (ZON), a format structurally identical to the Zig anonymous struct literals. At the top level, the `.name` and `.version` fields establish the package identity within the dependency graph, allowing it to be referenced and resolved by downstream consumers. The `.fingerprint` field serves as a 64-bit unique identifier used by the global Zig cache system; unlike a content hash, which verifies data integrity, the `fingerprint` aids the build system in quickly recognizing the project across different contexts and builds without needing to re-scan the entire directory tree initially. The core of this manifest lies within the `.dependencies` struct, which maps the local import name `.tsdist` to a specific remote resource. The `.url` field utilizes the `git+https` scheme, explicitly pinning the dependency to a precise Git commit hash (the alphanumeric string following the #). This guarantees that the build system will always fetch that exact snapshot of history, preventing the build from breaking if the remote `main` branch changes. On top of that, the `.hash` field acts as a cryptographic integrity check of the downloaded content itself. Even if the Git server is compromised or returns different data for the same commit ID, Zig will reject the dependency if the computed hash of the files does not match this expected string. Finally, the `.paths` field set to `.{"."}` instructs the package manager to include the entire root directory when this project is bundled, exposing all files to the build process. Let us now explain `build.zig` in more detail.

Understanding build.zig

With the metadata and dependencies strictly defined in `build.zig.zon`, we now turn our attention to `build.zig`. In this subsection, we analyze the anatomy of a `build.zig` file, exploring how to define executable targets, configure optimization modes, and map the dependencies we declared in our manifest into the actual compilation units. We are going to be using the following `build.zig` file for our project:

```
const std = @import("std");

pub fn build(b: *std.Build) void {
    const target = b.standardTargetOptions(.{});
    const optimize = b.standardOptimizeOption(.{});

    // Fetch the tsdist package
    const tsdist_dep = b.dependency("tsdist", .{
        .target = target,
        .optimize = optimize,
    });
```

```
    // Create root module for your executable
    const exe_mod = b.createModule(.{
        .root_source_file = b.path("src/main.zig"),
        .target = target,
        .optimize = optimize,
    });

    // Add tsdist as import (matches root module name
    // in tsdist-zig: "distances")
    exe_mod.addImport("distances", tsdist_dep.module("distances"));

    // Build the executable
    const exe = b.addExecutable(.{
        .name = "ts",
        .root_module = exe_mod,
    });
    b.installArtifact(exe);

    // Run command
    const run_cmd = b.addRunArtifact(exe);
    run_cmd.step.dependOn(b.getInstallStep());
    if (b.args) |args| {
        run_cmd.addArgs(args);
    }

    const run_step = b.step("run", "Run the app");
    run_step.dependOn(&run_cmd.step);
}
```

This `build.zig` script is utilizing the `std.Build` API to construct a Directed Acyclic Graph of build steps. The entry point, `pub fn build()`, accepts a `std.Build` pointer, which acts as the centralized coordinator for all artifacts and commands. `build()` begins by invoking `standardTargetOptions()` and `standardOptimizeOption()`. These calls do not immediately set values; rather, they register command-line flags (like `-Dtarget=...` and `-Doptimize=ReleaseFast`) and resolve them into concrete configuration objects (`target` and `optimize`). These objects encapsulate the cross-compilation constraints and optimization levels (`Debug`, `ReleaseSafe`, etc.) that will be propagated throughout the compilation process. The next phase involves dependency resolution and module composition. The line `b.dependency("tsdist", ...)` queries the package manifest (`build.zig.zon`) to locate the `tsdist` package. We pass the resolved `target` and `optimize` options into this dependency, ensuring that the external library is compiled with the exact same architecture and optimization settings as our main application, preventing any mismatches. We then define a compilation unit for our local code using `b.createModule()`, specifying `src/main.zig` as the root source file. The connection between the local code and the remote library is established via `exe_mod.addImport`. This function explicitly maps the string literal `"distances"` — which will be used in the source code as `@import("distances")` — to the specific module object exposed by the `tsdist` dependency. This decoupling allows the internal module name of the dependency to differ from the `import` name used in the source code. Last, the script defines the build artifacts and execution logic. The `b.addExecutable()` function consumes the previously created module to define a binary artifact named `"ts"`. The `b.installArtifact(exe)` call registers a "side effect" step in the graph that copies the compiled binary to the standard installation directory (`zig-out/bin`). The concluding block sets up a `"Run"` step using `b.addRunArtifact()`. This creates a virtual command that executes the resulting binary. It includes logic to forward command-line arguments (checking `b.args`) from the build tool to the application and strictly defines step dependencies (`dependOn`), ensuring that the application is only executed after it has been successfully compiled and installed. We all have that in mind, we are ready to present `src/main.zig` and execute our project.

Compiling a library to create an executable binary

In this subsection, we are going to use the library, compile it, and create a binary executable. The source file with the `main()` function can be found at `ch02/ts/src/main.zig` and comes with the following Zig code:

```
const std = @import("std");
const distances = @import("distances");

pub fn main(_: std.process.Init.Minimal) !void {
    const allocator = std.heap.page_allocator;
    var a = [_]f64{ 1.0, 2.0, 3.0 };
    var b = [_]f64{ 2.0, 3.0, 4.0 };

    const ed = try distances.euclideanDistance(&a,&b);
    std.debug.print("Euclidean distance: {d:.5}\n", .{ed});
    const man = try distances.manhattanDistance(&a,&b);
    std.debug.print("Manhattan distance: {}\n", .{man});
    const che = try distances.chebyshevDistance(&a,&b);
    std.debug.print("Chebyshev distance: {}\n", .{che});
```

```
    const lcss = try distances.lcssDistance(allocator,&a,&b,0.001);
    std.debug.print("LCSS distance: {d:.5}\n", .{lcss});
    const edr = try distances.edrDistance(allocator,&a,&b,0.001);
    std.debug.print("EDR distance: {}\n", .{edr});
}
```

This code uses the external Zig library we just configured. It begins by importing the dependency using the name we mapped in `build.zig` (`@import("distances")`), proving that the build system is correctly resolving the package. Inside `main()`, the code sets up two test vectors and initializes a memory allocator, which is required for the more complex algorithms like LCSS and EDR that need dynamic memory. The logic then systematically calls each metric function — passing pointers for simple calculations and the allocator for the complex ones — and prints the results. *This serves as the final integration test, confirming that our application can successfully link against, invoke, and utilize the logic from the third-party dependency.* Now, you can compile the project and execute it as follows:

```
$ zig build run
Euclidean distance: 1.73205
Manhattan distance: 3
Chebyshev distance: 1
LCSS distance: 0.33333
EDR distance: 2
```

The generated output serves as the definitive confirmation that our Zig project has transitioned from a collection of source and configuration files into a functioning, compiled executable. The command `zig build run` successfully invoked the Zig compiler, resolved all dependencies, built the binary, and immediately executed it, printing the results of your distance algorithms to the standard output! With `zig build run`, all your build configuration — such as include paths, library paths, linked libraries, optimization modes, and target settings — is stored in the `build.zig` file rather than typed out every time you run the program. This means you avoid retyping or remembering long flag sequences like `-I/opt/homebrew/include`, `-L/opt/homebrew/lib`, and `-lsqlite3`, reducing errors and making your project easier to share and build on other machines. It also simplifies running your program with arguments: you just write `zig build run -- [program args]`, and Zig takes care of compiling and linking with the correct settings before executing the binary. This approach improves reproducibility, encourages cleaner project organization, and makes it easier for collaborators to run your program without knowing all the low-level compilation details.

After that, the contents of the project directory are as follows:

```
$ tree
.
|— build.zig
|— build.zig.zon
|— src
|   └— main.zig
└— zig-out
    └— bin
        └— ts

4 directories, 4 files
```

We have successfully integrated third-party code into our project. However, a healthy ecosystem relies not just on consumption but on contribution. Now, we will shift our perspective from consumer to producer by creating our own standalone library: `zuuid`, a simple yet robust UUID generator. This exercise will take us through the full lifecycle of library authorship, teaching us how to structure a project for distribution, design a clean public API, and package it effectively so that other developers can import it into their `build.zig.zon` files just as easily as we imported our dependencies. But first, we are going to begin by presenting an autonomous utility that generates UUID values.

Developing zuuid, a UUID generator

A **Universally Unique Identifier** (*UUID*) is a 128-bit number used to uniquely identify information in computer systems, designed to be generated across distributed systems without any need for central coordination. In the context of our tools, a UUID serves as a digital fingerprint — a sequence so statistically improbable to duplicate that we can safely assume it is unique across all space and time. Standardized by RFC 4122, these identifiers are typically represented as 32 hexadecimal characters (displayed in five groups separated by hyphens, such as `550e8400-e29b-41d4-a716-446655440000`) and come in several "versions" based on how they are constructed. While some versions rely on time and hardware MAC addresses (Version 1) or namespace hashing (Versions 3 and 5), the most common for general programming tasks is Version 4. This version is constructed almost entirely from random numbers, providing a robust collision resistance that makes it ideal for database keys, transaction IDs, and any scenario where you need to label an object uniquely without checking a central registry first. We present `ch02/zuuid.zig` in multiple snippets, beginning with the following:

```
const std = @import("std");

pub fn main(init: std.process.Init) !void {
    const io = init.io;

    var buffer: [4096]u8 = undefined;
    var stdout_impl = std.Io.File.stdout().writer(io,&buffer);
    conststdout=&stdout_impl.interface;
    defer stdout.flush() catch {};
    var count: usize = 1;
    var use_uppercase: bool = false;
    var iter = init.minimal.args.iterate();
    defer iter.deinit();

    // Skip the first argument (the program name itself)
    _ = iter.next();
```

This code establishes the foundational infrastructure required for a command-line utility. The code optimizes terminal output by setting up a *buffered writer*. The program allocates a 4KB buffer on the stack and wraps standard output to write data in efficient chunks. The `defer stdout.flush()` line acts as a safety mechanism, ensuring that any data remaining in the buffer is physically written to the console before the program terminates. Finally, the argument iterator skips its first entry, leaving the iterator positioned at the start of the user-provided flags, ready for the parsing loop, which is the following:

```
    while (iter.next()) |arg| {
        if (std.mem.eql(u8, arg, "-u")) {
            use_uppercase = true;
        } else if (std.mem.eql(u8, arg, "-n")) {
            // If -n is found, the *next* argument must be the number.
            if (iter.next()) |num_str| {
                count = try std.fmt.parseInt(usize, num_str, 10);
            } else {
                std.debug.print(
                    "Error: -n requires a number argument.\n",
                    .{},
                );
```

```
                return error.InvalidArgs;
            }
        }
    }
```

This code snippet defines the core logic for interpreting user input from the command line, utilizing a linear iterator pattern. The `while` loop advances through the argument list one token at a time; for every iteration, `iter.next()` captures the current string slice into `arg`. The code then uses `std.mem.eql()` to check if this token matches known flags. While the `-u` flag acts as a simple Boolean toggle, the handling of `-n` demonstrates special treatment. When the program encounters `-n`, it immediately calls `iter.next()` a second time within the same loop cycle. This action *steals* the subsequent token from the list, treating it as the numeric value associated with the flag rather than a standalone argument. This value is then parsed into a machine-native integer using `std.fmt.parseInt()`. If the user provides `-n` as the final argument with no value following it, the inner `iter.next()` returns `null`, triggering a descriptive error message and causing the function to return `error.InvalidArgs` rather than crashing. The rest of the program is the following:

```
    var i: usize = 0;
    while (i < count) : (i += 1) {
        var uuid: [16]u8 = undefined;

        // io.random() uses a PRNG seeded from a secure source —
        // fast but not guaranteed to make a syscall per invocation.
        // For UUIDs used as database IDs, session tokens, or any
        // security-sensitive context, use io.randomSecure(), which
        // always calls the OS entropy source
        // and returns error.EntropyUnavailable on failure.
        try io.randomSecure(&uuid);
        uuid[6] = (uuid[6] & 0x0f) | 0x40;
        uuid[8] = (uuid[8] & 0x3f) | 0x80;

        if (use_uppercase) {
            try stdout.print(
                "{X:0>2}{X:0>2}{X:0>2}{X:0>2}-{X:0>2}{X:0>2}-" ++
                    "{X:0>2}{X:0>2}-{X:0>2}{X:0>2}-" ++
                    "{X:0>2}{X:0>2}{X:0>2}{X:0>2}{X:0>2}{X:0>2}\n",
                .{
                    uuid[0], uuid[1], uuid[2], uuid[3],
```

```
                uuid[4],  uuid[5],  uuid[6],  uuid[7],
                uuid[8],  uuid[9],  uuid[10], uuid[11],
                uuid[12], uuid[13], uuid[14], uuid[15],
            },
        );
    } else {
        try stdout.print(
            "{x:0>2}{x:0>2}{x:0>2}{x:0>2}-{x:0>2}{x:0>2}-" ++
                "{x:0>2}{x:0>2}-{x:0>2}{x:0>2}-" ++
                "{x:0>2}{x:0>2}{x:0>2}{x:0>2}{x:0>2}{x:0>2}\n",
            .{
                uuid[0],  uuid[1],  uuid[2],  uuid[3],
                uuid[4],  uuid[5],  uuid[6],  uuid[7],
                uuid[8],  uuid[9],  uuid[10], uuid[11],
                uuid[12], uuid[13], uuid[14], uuid[15],
            },
        );
    }
}

try stdout.flush();
}
```

The execution loop iterates count times to satisfy the user request. Inside each iteration, the code allocates a 16-byte array and immediately populates it using `io.randomSecure()`, which always calls the OS entropy source (such as `getrandom` or `arc4random`) and can return `error.EntropyUnavailable` on failure — hence the `try`. This differs from `io.random()`, which uses a PRNG seeded from a secure source: faster but not guaranteed to make a syscall on every invocation and therefore unsuitable for UUIDs used as database IDs, session tokens, or other security-sensitive values. To transform these raw random bytes into a valid Version 4 UUID compliant with RFC 4122, the code performs two precise bitwise operations: it masks the high nibble of the 7th byte (index 6) to set the version to 4 (`0100`), and it adjusts the high nibble of the 9th byte (index 8) to ensure the variant bits match the standard (`10xx`). The subsequent printing logic handles the textual representation of these bytes. Depending on the `use_uppercase` flag, the code selects a format string using either `{X}` for uppercase or `{x}` for lowercase hexadecimal output. The format specifiers, such as `{x:0>2}`, instruct the writer to pad single-digit hex values with a leading zero, ensuring that every byte occupies exactly two characters. Notably, the code utilizes Zig's compile-time string concatenation operator (++) to break the long UUID format pattern into multiple lines for readability without incurring any runtime performance penalty.

Finally, after the loop concludes, the critical `try stdout.flush()` call ensures that any remaining data sitting in the memory buffer is pushed to the terminal. Now, you can execute `ch02/zuuid.zig`:

```
$ zig run ch02/zuuid.zig
44cb2754-b58d-428c-8c95-d6d299fb650c
$ zig run ch02/zuuid.zig -- -u
57F81D65-B887-4024-B2DC-875E3F56531B
```

Before diving into the mechanics of the refactor, it is worth naming the architectural principle at work. The original `zuuid` implementation bundles two distinct concerns into a single file: the logic that generates UUIDs and the command-line interface that presents them to the user. These are not the same thing and keeping them separate is one of the most important habits in systems programming. The UUID generation logic — the algorithm, the random byte sourcing, the formatting — is a reusable, testable unit that has no inherent dependency on `stdin`, `stdout`, or command-line arguments. The CLI is just one consumer of that logic. By extracting the core logic into a library, we make it independently testable with `zig build test`, independently benchmarkable, and independently importable by any other program in this book or beyond.

Making a library from the zuuid code

In this section, we will extract the generation algorithms into a standalone library named `zuuid`, transforming a specific tool into a *reusable component that can be easily shared, versioned, and integrated into any future Zig project.* Having fully examined the monolithic implementation, we have identified exactly which parts of the code belong to the domain of the application (like the handling of the `-n` flag) and which belong to the domain of the data type itself. We are now ready to perform the refactoring. But first, we are going to discuss the use of GitHub for hosting our Zig library.

Using GitHub

We are going to use the `https://github.com/mactsouk/zuuid` repository for hosting our Zig library. You do not need to download it if you only intend to use the library, but you need to have it locally during development. So, we start the development process by cloning and initializing the empty GitHub repository as follows:

```
$ git clone git@github.com:mactsouk/zuuid.git
$ cd zuuid
$ zig init
$ tree
```

```
.
├── build.zig
├── build.zig.zon
├── README.md
└── src
    ├── main.zig
    └── root.zig

2 directories, 5 files
```

The good thing is that the default `build.zig` file works fine for simple projects and offers support for both `zig build test` and `zig build run` commands, which is what we are going to need here. However, as by default `build.zig` comes with many comments; you might need to clean it up a little. At this point, we are going to populate the `src/root.zig` file with Zig code based on `ch02/zuuid.zig`, which is a trivial task. But we are not done!

Preparing the library for others to reuse

Before publishing the library, we need to make sure that everything works as expected. In practice, we need to make sure that both `zig build test` and `zig build run` commands work the way we want. The first time you try to test the library, you are going to see a message like the following:

```
$ zig build test
/Users/mtsouk/zuuid/build.zig.zon:1:2: error: missing top-level 'fingerprint'
field; suggested value: 0x857b80c93a33b403
.{
 ^
```

In this case, you should get the suggested value and put it in the `build.zig.zon` file, which is going to look as follows:

```
.{
    .name = .zuuid,
    .version = "0.1.0",
    .minimum_zig_version = "0.16.0",
    .dependencies = .{},

    // If Zig suggests a different fingerprint when you run `zig build`,
    // replace this value with the suggested one.
    .fingerprint = 0x857b80c93a33b403,
```

```
        .paths = .{
            "build.zig",
            "build.zig.zon",
            "src",
        },
}
```

After fixing that, we should write the actual tests, which depend on the library itself.

Writing tests for the library

Having a property defined in the `build.zig.zon` file means we should write and place the testing code at the end of `src/root.zig`, which in our case is the following:

```
test "basic v4 generation" {
    var t: std.Io.Threaded = .init_single_threaded;
    const io = t.io();
    const uuid = Uuid.v4(io);
    try std.testing.expectEqual(@as(u8, 4), uuid.bytes[6] >> 4);
    try std.testing.expectEqual(@as(u8, 2), uuid.bytes[8] >> 6);
}
```

After that, running `zig build test` is going to create no output, which means that the tests ran successfully. However, there is another critical test that we need to generate, which is the actual use of the library in an external program so that `zig build run` does something. For that kind of unofficial testing, we should populate `src/main.zig`:

```
const std = @import("std");
const zuuid = @import("root.zig");

pub fn main(init: std.process.Init) !void {
    var count: usize = 1;
    var use_uppercase: bool = false;

    var iter = init.minimal.args.iterate();
    defer iter.deinit();
    _ = iter.next(); // skip program name
    while (iter.next()) |arg| {
        if (std.mem.eql(u8, arg, "-u")) {
            use_uppercase = true;
```

```
        } else if (std.mem.eql(u8, arg, "-n")) {
            if (iter.next()) |num_str| {
                count = try std.fmt.parseInt(usize, num_str, 10);
            }
        }
    }

    var buf: [37]u8 = undefined; // 36 for UUID + 1 for \n
    var i: usize = 0;
    while (i < count) : (i += 1) {
        const id = zuuid.Uuid.v4(init.io);
        const s = if (use_uppercase)
            std.fmt.bufPrint(&buf, "{f}\n", .{id.fmtUpper()}) catch
                unreachable
        else
            std.fmt.bufPrint(&buf, "{f}\n", .{id}) catch unreachable;
        try std.Io.File.stdout().writeStreamingAll(init.io, s);
    }
}
```

What is important in the previous program is the use of `const zuuid = @import("root.zig");` for *accessing the local copy* of the `zuuid` library. Apart from that, the rest of the code is straightforward. Using the project produces the next kind of output:

```
$ zig build run
d708e5ef-32c8-4d77-b5c1-f2df2cdba86e
```

So, `build.zig` defines how your module is built and `build.zig.zon` describes package metadata and dependencies using ZON syntax.

Using our zuuid library

So, we found our `zuuid` Zig library on GitHub, and we want to use it in one of our projects. Previously, we presented some ready to use `build.zig.zon` and `build.zig` files, but now we are going to learn how to construct them. So, in this subsection, you will learn how to manually configure your `build.zig.zon` and `build.zig` files. We start a new Zig project:

```
$ mkdir ch02/zuuid-cli
$ cd ch02/zuuid-cli
$ zig init
$ rm src/root.zig
```

Before presenting the listing, a word of warning: the `build.zig.zon` file shown below is intentionally incomplete. The commit hash in the URL and the `.hash` field are omitted to demonstrate Zig's error-driven workflow — the compiler will inspect the remote archive and tell you the correct values, which you then paste in. Do not copy this listing as your final configuration. Treat it as the starting point for a two-step process: write the incomplete file, run `zig build`, and let the compiler fill in what is missing. The corrected version with all fields populated is shown immediately after. So, we begin with the following bare bones version of `build.zig.zon`; you just have to make sure that the `.url` value is correct:

```
.{
    .name = .my_zuuid,
    .version = "0.1.0",
    .minimum_zig_version = "0.16.0",
    .dependencies = .{
        .zuuidcli = .{
            .url = "git+https://github.com/mactsouk/zuuid",
            .branch = "main",
        },
    },
    .paths = .{"."},
}
```

Now, execute `zig build` on your machine:

```
$ zig build
/Users/mtsouk/Desktop/zuuid-cli/build.zig.zon:1:2: error: missing top-level
'fingerprint' field; suggested value: 0x857b80c93a33b403
.{
 ^
```

The previous output suggests a value for `fingerprint`. Let us now add that. Do not forget to put a dot, making it `.fingerprint`. Now, execute `zig build` again (the output is edited):

```
$ zig build
/Users/mtsouk/Desktop/zuuid-cli/build.zig.zon:8:20: error: url field is missing an
explicit ref
            .url = "git+https://github.com/mactsouk/zuuid",
                   ^~~~~~~~~~~~~~~~~~~~~~~~~~~~~~~~~~~~~~~~
```

```
note: try .url = "git+https://github.com/mactsouk/
zuuid#50b710eaf7500153b17ea4d7aa283cf212efacbb",
```

Now, update the value of `.url` to the suggested one and run `zig build` again:

```
$ zig build
/Users/mtsouk/Desktop/zuuid-cli/build.zig.zon:8:20: error: dependency is missing
hash field
            .url = "git+https://github.com/mactsouk/
zuuid#50b710eaf7500153b17ea4d7aa283cf212efacbb",

^~~~~~~~~~~~~~~~~~~~~~~~~~~~~~~~~~~~~~~~~~~~~~~~~~~~~~~~~~~~~~~~~~~~~~~~~~~~~~~~
note: expected .hash = "zuuid-0.1.0-A7QzOlETAADHugCVKL5y2AelR2xjz2GdmynY4yKawL7L",
```

Now add the `.hash` key and value as suggested, and we are done. However, we still need to modify `build.zig` and write `src/main.zig`. The final version of `build.zig` is the following:

```
const std = @import("std");

pub fn build(b: *std.Build) void {
    const target = b.standardTargetOptions(.{});
    const optimize = b.standardOptimizeOption(.{});
    const zuuid_dep = b.dependency("zuuidcli", .{
        .target = target,
        .optimize = optimize,
    });

    const exe_mod = b.createModule(.{
        .root_source_file = b.path("src/main.zig"),
        .target = target,
        .optimize = optimize,
    });

    exe_mod.addImport("zuuid", zuuid_dep.module("zuuid"));
    const exe = b.addExecutable(.{
        .name = "zuuid-cli",
        .root_module = exe_mod,
    });
    b.installArtifact(exe);

    const run_cmd = b.addRunArtifact(exe);
```

```
        run_cmd.step.dependOn(b.getInstallStep());
        if (b.args) |args| {
            run_cmd.addArgs(args);
        }
        const run_step = b.step("run", "Run the app");
        run_step.dependOn(&run_cmd.step);
}
```

As before, the script begins by importing the standard library and defining the public `build()` function, which accepts a `*std.Build` object. The dependency resolution phase is handled by the `b.dependency()` function call. This method queries the project's package manifest (`build.zig.zon`) to locate the package named `"zuuidcli"`. So, the script passes the `target` and `optimize` parameters into this dependency. The result, `zuuid_dep`, is a handle to the external package build logic, allowing us to access its exposed artifacts and modules. After that, we create the main module via `b.createModule()`. This script first defines an abstract compilation unit rooted at `src/main.zig`. This module object, exe_mod, acts as a container for source code and its relationships. The subsequent call to `exe_mod.addImport("zuuid", ...)` forms the logical link between the application and the library; it maps the string `"zuuid"`, which will be used inside the source code file as `@import("zuuid")`, to the actual module object exposed by the dependency. This separation of module definition from artifact creation allows for more granular control over dependencies and compilation units.

Finally, the script defines the build artifacts and execution logic. The `b.addExecutable()` function consumes the fully configured `exe_mod` to create a compilation step for the binary named `zuuid-cli`. The `b.installArtifact(exe)` call registers this binary as a primary output, ensuring it is copied to the standard installation directory (typically `zig-out/bin`) upon a successful build. To facilitate rapid development, a `run` step is defined using `b.addRunArtifact()`. This executes the binary immediately after compilation and forwards any arguments provided by the user (`zig build run -- [args]`) to the application using `run_cmd.addArgs()`. This entire chain is bound to the command `zig build run`, allowing developers to compile, link, and test the application in a single command. The `src/main.zig` source code file is the one that contains the `main()` function. The external library is used as follows:

```
const std = @import("std");
const zuuid = @import("zuuid");
```

We are now ready to use the project! Execute the following commands on your machine:

```
$ zig build run
b84d6cfe-495a-4fd4-bc15-557c3f31d729
$ zig build run -- -u
367190D9-D19C-42A5-AC7A-A3E44FEE326A
```

Great! Let us now compare the performance of our `zuuid` against the system `uuidgen(1)`.

Benchmarking zuuid against uuidgen

For the purposes of this subsection, we are going to need the `hyperfine` utility. Please install it on your machine if it is not already there. We are going to use a bash shell script to conduct our benchmarking – the path of the script is `ch02/zuuid-cli/benchmark.sh` and its output looks like the following:

```
$ /benchmark.sh
Compiling zuuid-cli in ReleaseFast mode...
Starting Benchmark...
--------------------------------------------------
Benchmark 1: System uuidgen
  Time (mean ± σ):   1.4 ms ±   0.1 ms    [User: 0.7 ms, System: 0.3 ms]
  Range (min … max):      1.3 ms …    1.9 ms    2015 runs

Benchmark 2: Zig zuuid (ReleaseFast)
  Time (mean ± σ): 856.1 µs ± 39.9 µs [User: 343.7 µs, System: 284.7 µs]
  Range (min … max):    788.2 µs … 1371.0 µs    3358 runs

Summary
  Zig zuuid (ReleaseFast) ran
    1.64 ± 0.10 times faster than System uuidgen
--------------------------------------------------
Results saved to benchmark_results.md
```

The results indicate that `zuuid-cli` is significantly faster than the pre-installed system tool (`uuidgen(1)`), specifically outperforming it by a factor of `1.64`x for single executions.

With our performance benchmarks confirming that the `zuuid` library is not only functional but highly efficient, we must now shift our focus from speed to stability and comprehensive verification. Raw throughput is of little value if the underlying logic harbors unverified edge cases or dead code paths.

Test filtering and coverage analysis

In this subsection, we examine methods for *filtering tests* to isolate and debug specific behaviors without running the entire suite, and we conduct *coverage analysis* to visualize exactly which lines of code are being exercised, ensuring that our bitwise manipulations and formatting logic are rigorously proven correct. For the purposes of this subsection, we are going to use a simplistic Zig source code file named `ch02/filterCoverage.zig`. In our code example, the test suite is divided into distinct semantic groups: mathematical operations and utility checks. During the development of the `add()` or `maybeDouble()` functions, running unrelated tests generates unnecessary noise and latency. By invoking the test runner with `zig test filterCoverage.zig --test-filter "math"`, we instruct the compiler to pattern-match against test descriptions, executing only those labeled with `"math"`. This targeted approach significantly accelerates the inner development loop, allowing for rapid iteration on specific features while temporarily ignoring the broader system:

```
$ cd ch02
$ zig test filterCoverage.zig --test-filter "math"
All 2 tests passed.
$ zig test filterCoverage.zig
All 3 tests passed.
```

While filtering confirms that selected tests pass, *coverage analysis reveals which parts of the codebase were actually exercised by those tests,* effectively highlighting *dead zones* in the logic. To perform this analysis on `ch02/filterCoverage.zig`, we first compile a dedicated test binary using `-femit-bin`, separating the compilation step from execution. Running this binary through a coverage tool like `kcov` (you might need to install it on your machine) generates a visual report that maps executed instructions back to source lines. In our example, such a report would immediately flag the `else` branch of the `maybeDouble()` function in red. This visual cue informs the developer that while the "doubling" logic is verified, the "identity" behavior (where `should_double` is `false`) remains purely theoretical and untested, necessitating the addition of a new test case to ensure comprehensive reliability. Before running the coverage commands, note that `kcov` must be installed separately. On Linux, install it via your package manager. On macOS, install it via Homebrew with `brew install kcov`.

```
$ cd ch02
$ zig test filterCoverage.zig -femit-bin=/tmp/testing
$ kcov /tmp/report /tmp/testing
```

After that, the coverage report can be found in `/tmp/report`. Feel free to look into it. Discussing more about code coverage is beyond the scope of this book.

Summary

The Zig build system is a flexible, programmatic approach to compiling, testing, and managing projects, driven by a `build.zig` file written in Zig itself. Instead of relying on static configuration files, you define the build steps using Zig code, which gives you full control over compilation options, dependencies, testing, and installation. This system uses the `std.Build` API, where you typically create a build object, add executable or library targets with `addExecutable()`, `addStaticLibrary()`, or `addSharedLibrary()`, set target and optimization options, and declare default build steps like `install`.

But the chapter covered more than building tooling. Reproducible builds, dependency isolation, test discipline, memory leak verification, documentation generation, benchmarking, and package publishing are not incidental features — they are the operational foundations of maintainable infrastructure software. A cache server that cannot be tested in isolation is a liability. A concurrent indexer with no memory verification is a time bomb. A networking library with no documented API is a maintenance burden. The practices introduced in this chapter are what separate a program that works today from a system that can be understood, extended, and deployed with confidence tomorrow. Every subsequent chapter in this book depends on them.

We are now ready to examine how the language interacts directly with the machine resources. While our previous examples focused primarily on logic and flow, real-world systems programming requires a precise understanding of where data lives and how it is accessed to prevent bottlenecks and ensure safety. In the next chapter, we will transition from writing code that simply runs to writing code that efficiently manages memory, exploring the critical role of pointers, the implementation of custom allocators, and the techniques required to parse complex binary formats directly from raw bytes.

Exercises

- Change `ch02/ts/src/main.zig` so that it generates a random time series.
- Change `ch02/ts/src/main.zig` so that it generates a random time series whose length is given as a command-line argument.

Additional resources

- RFC 4122: `https://www.rfc-editor.org/rfc/rfc4122`
- Zig documentation: `https://ziglang.org/documentation/master/`

3

Direct Memory Access and Binary Formats

What distinguishes a high-level script from a performant, hardware-aware application is the ability to directly manipulate memory. This chapter bridges the gap between abstract variables and the physical machine by diving deep into the pointer mechanics and memory management strategies of Zig. We will move beyond simple variable declarations to explore how data is really structured in memory, building a custom allocator and a fully functional Zip file lister (`zunzip`) from scratch. Along the way, we will tackle the practical realities of binary file formats, including handling *endianness*, performing pointer arithmetic to navigate raw bytes, and benchmarking different allocation strategies to ensure our architectural choices result in real-world performance gains. By the end of this chapter, you will think about memory differently — not as an invisible resource that appears on demand but as a finite, structured medium that you lay out with purpose, navigate with precision, and reclaim on your own terms. You will be able to look at a binary file format and see a struct. You will be able to look at an allocation and ask who owns it, when it will be freed, and what happens if it is not. That shift in perspective is what separates systems programming from application programming.

This chapter covers:

- Pointers and pointer arithmetic
- Programming a custom memory allocator (wrapper)
- Developing `zunzip`, a Zip file lister
- Working with Endianness
- Benchmarking memory allocators

Pointers

A **Pointer** in Zig is a variable that holds the memory address of another value, allowing you to reference, modify, or pass data without creating copies. Pointers are strongly typed, meaning that they are associated with a specific type of data, which helps maintain safety and clarity in code. Here is a simple code example that illustrates pointers in Zig:

```
const std = @import("std");

pub fn main(_: std.process.Init.Minimal) void {
    var x: i32 = 42;
    constptr:*i32=&x
    std.debug.print("Memory address of x: {}\n", .{ptr});
    std.debug.print("Value of x via pointer: {}\n", .{ptr.*});
    ptr.* = 100;
    std.debug.print("Modified value of x via pointer: {}\n", .{x});
}
```

The code begins by declaring a mutable integer variable `x` on the stack, followed by the creation of `ptr`, which captures the memory address of `x` using the `&` (*address-of*) operator. Zig requires you to explicitly append `.*` to dereference the pointer, signaling clearly that you are accessing the value stored at that address rather than the address itself. When the code executes `ptr.* = 100`, it modifies the memory location that `x` occupies; consequently, when `x` is printed afterward, it reflects the updated value. Running `ch03/ptr.zig` produces the following output:

```
$ zig run ch03/ptr.zig
Memory address of x: i32@16dbe2c44
Value of x via pointer: 42
Modified value of x via pointer: 100
```

Now, let us understand a subtle but important detail. The placement of the `const` keyword relative to the pointer declaration changes the permission rules for that memory. The declaration `const ptr: *i32` creates a *constant pointer to a mutable value*. This means the pointer variable itself is immutable (you cannot make `ptr` point to a different address later), but the data it points to is fully mutable (you are allowed to write `ptr.* = 100`). In contrast, if you declare `const ptr: *const i32`, you create *a pointer to a constant value*. Any attempt to write `ptr.* = 100` would result in a compile-time error because the *type system enforces read-only access through that specific pointer*.

Pointer arithmetic

Pointer arithmetic is the process of calculating new memory addresses by adding or subtracting offsets from an existing pointer. Unlike C, where any pointer can be treated as a number, Zig enforces a strict type distinction to prevent accidental bounds violations. Standard single-item pointers (`*T`) strictly forbid arithmetic; to perform these operations, you must explicitly coerce your pointer into a many-item pointer (`[*]T`). Here is the code in `ch03/ptrArithmetic.zig` that illustrates pointer arithmetic:

```
const std = @import("std");

pub fn main(_: std.process.Init.Minimal) void {
    var arr = [_]i32{ 1, 2, 3, 4 };
varptrArr:[*]i32=&arr
    constfirst:[*]i32=&arr

    ptrArr[0] = -9;
    std.debug.print(
        "ptrArr[0]: {} , arr[0]: {}\n",
        .{ ptrArr[0], arr[0] },
    );
    std.debug.print("array: {any}\n", .{ arr });
```

The code declares a fixed-size array of four integers allocated on the stack (`arr`). In here, we have an explicit type coercion from a safe, bounds-checked pointer (`&arr`) to a *many-item pointer* (`[*]i32`). By explicitly annotating `ptrArr` and `first` with `[*]i32`, we instruct the compiler to treat these variables not as references to a single object but as starting points for a contiguous block of memory of unknown size. Next, we demonstrate *aliasing*, where multiple variables refer to the same physical memory location. Even though `ptrArr` is a pointer, Zig allows us to use the familiar array indexing syntax `ptrArr[0]` to access the first element. When the code assigns `-9` to this index, it is not modifying a copy; it is writing directly to the memory address where `arr` starts.

Next, we present a loop that illustrates the concept of a **sliding pointer**, a technique often used in parsing algorithms where a cursor consumes data sequentially:

```
    for (0..arr.len) |i| {
        std.debug.print(
            "ptrArr[0]: {} , arr[i]: {}\n",
            .{ ptrArr[0], arr[i] },
```

```
        );
        // Points to the next array element
        ptrArr += 1;
    }
```

Unlike a standard iteration, where the base address remains static and an array index updates (`arr[i]`), here the pointer variable `ptrArr` is mutated in every iteration. The operation `ptrArr += 1` does not add a single byte to the address but advances the pointer forward by the *byte size of the type* — in this case, the size of an `i32` (4 bytes). Therefore, the expression `ptrArr[0]` always reads the value at the pointer's current location. As the loop progresses, `ptrArr` walks down the stack, abandoning the previous elements and treating the current position as the new start of the memory block.

The next code snippet introduces **offset addressing**, which is a *non-destructive form* of pointer arithmetic:

```
    var tmp: [*]i32 = undefined;
    for (0..arr.len) |i| {
        tmp = first + i;
        std.debug.print(
            "tmp[0]: {} , arr[i]: {}\n",
            .{ tmp[0], arr[i] },
        );
    }
```

In this case, the `first` pointer remains anchored at the beginning of the array as it was declared as `const` – it cannot be moved. Instead, we generate a new, temporary address in each iteration by adding the index `i` to the base address. The expression `first + i` calculates the memory location of the i-th element (offset by `i * @sizeOf(i32)` bytes) and assigns it to `tmp`. *This pattern can be used when you need random access to different parts of a buffer without losing your reference to the start of the memory block.*

The next segment serves as a crucial counterpoint to the previous manual arithmetic, demonstrating the safe, idiomatic way to handle memory and nullability in Zig:

```
    constmyPtr=&arr
    for (myPtr, 0..) |*item, i| {
        std.debug.print("Element {}: {} {}\n", .{i, item, item.*});
    }
    const nullPtr: ?*i32 = null;
```

```
        if (nullPtr == null) {
            std.debug.print("The pointer is null.\n", .{});
        }
    }
```

The loop `for (myPtr, 0..) |*item, i|` showcases an idiomatic mechanism for iterating over buffers. Unlike the manual `ptr += 1` approach, which relies on the programmer to track boundaries, this construct safely abstracts the pointer arithmetic. By capturing `*item`, we receive a pointer to the current element (rather than a copy of its value), allowing us to efficiently access or modify the data in place using `item.*`. So, we retain the performance benefits of pointers — avoiding unnecessary data copying — while eliminating the risk of straying past the memory end of the buffer, being protected by the compiler and runtime. The final block introduces the **Optional Pointer**, denoted by the `?*i32` syntax. A standard pointer (`*T`) is guaranteed to never be `null`, a feature that eliminates an entire category of runtime crashes. To express the possibility of a "missing" value, you must explicitly opt in using the ? prefix. This forces you to handle the `null` case (as shown in the `if` check) before you can unwrap and use the underlying pointer. Execute `ch03/ptrArithmetic.zig` on your machine:

```
$ zig run ch03/ptrArithmetic.zig
ptrArr[0]: -9 , arr[0]: -9
array: { -9, 2, 3, 4 }
ptrArr[0]: -9 , arr[i]: -9
ptrArr[0]: 2 , arr[i]: 2
ptrArr[0]: 3 , arr[i]: 3
ptrArr[0]: 4 , arr[i]: 4
tmp[0]: -9 , arr[i]: -9
tmp[0]: 2 , arr[i]: 2
tmp[0]: 3 , arr[i]: 3
tmp[0]: 4 , arr[i]: 4
Element 0: i32@16d676c00 -9
Element 1: i32@16d676c04 2
Element 2: i32@16d676c08 3
Element 3: i32@16d676c0c 4
The pointer is null.
```

The output confirms that `ptrArr` acts as a direct alias to `arr` since the modification of `ptrArr[0]` to `-9` is reflected in the original array. The subsequent lines verify that our pointer arithmetic strategies navigate the memory to retrieve the sequence `-9`, 2, 3, 4. The `Element` lines expose the physical memory layout, where the hexadecimal addresses increase by exactly 4 bytes for each iteration. Finally, the output confirms that the optional pointer `nullPtr` was correctly initialized to `null` and trapped by the safety check.

The following subsection explores how to construct compliant C-strings from dynamic Zig data without sacrificing safety or performance. This can be handy in cases where we are combining the elements of a slice or a `std.ArrayList` into a single string to create a log entry, formatted output, or a proper error message.

Composing Null-Terminated C strings

String literals in Zig are null-terminated, which means that they can be passed into a C function without any issues. However, *Zig strings are generally not compatible with C strings when generated dynamically*. As the reality of Systems Programming is that we often need to communicate with the outside world — specifically, C libraries and the operating system kernel – we show how to create a null-terminated Zig string that can be passed into a C function as a pointer using the items of a `std.ArrayList` as an example. The technique is illustrated in `ch03/convertPtr.zig`, which starts with the following code:

```
const std = @import("std");
const c = @cImport({
    @cInclude("stdio.h");
});

pub fn printC(s: [*:0]const u8) c_int {
    return c.printf("%s\n", s);
}
```

The `printC()` function explicitly defines the type required for C string interoperability. The argument `s` accepts a `[*:0]const u8`, which denotes a *sentinel-terminated many-item pointer*. Unlike a standard Zig slice (`[]const u8`), which stores a pointer and a length, this type is a raw pointer (`*`) to an array of unknown size (`[*]`) that ends with a specific sentinel value (`:0`), which indicates that the terminator is a null byte, which matches the C definition of a string (`const char*`). This type safety ensures that the compiler treats the data as a null-terminated string, preventing common errors associated with missing terminators. The function returns a `c_int`, which maps directly to the `int` return type used by `printf(3)` to indicate the number of characters written. Inside the function body, `c.printf()` performs the actual output. Because the argument `s` is already typed as `[*:0]const u8`, it is compatible with the C function expectation of a `const char*` and can be passed directly without casting.

Next is the implementation of the `main()` function:

```
pub fn main(_: std.process.Init.Minimal) !void {
    const allocator = std.heap.page_allocator;
    const dir = "/usr";
    const util = "ls";
    _ = printC(dir);

    var pathBuf = std.ArrayList(u8).empty;
    defer pathBuf.deinit(allocator);
    try pathBuf.appendSlice(allocator, dir);
    try pathBuf.append(allocator, '/');
    try pathBuf.appendSlice(allocator, util);

    const fullPath = pathBuf.items;
    std.debug.print("Zig Slice: {s}\n", .{fullPath});
    // Manual C-String conversion
    const buffer = try allocator.alloc(u8, fullPath.len + 1);
    defer allocator.free(buffer);
    std.mem.copyForwards(u8, buffer[0..fullPath.len], fullPath);
    buffer[fullPath.len] = 0;
    _ = printC(@as([*:0]const u8, @ptrCast(buffer.ptr)));
}
```

The `main()` function immediately highlights the difference between compile-time string literals and runtime string slices. The variable `dir` is initialized with the literal `"/usr"`. In Zig, string literals are stored as null-terminated arrays, with the type `*const [4:0]u8` (a pointer to a null-terminated array of 4 bytes). Because the null terminator is guaranteed at compile time, this literal implicitly coerces to the `[*:0]const u8` type required by `printC()`. This explains why `printC(dir)` works without manual conversion; the compiler knows the memory is already safe for C consumption. As the code constructs `pathBuf` using an `ArrayList`, the resulting `fullPath` variable (accessed via `.items`) is a standard Zig slice (`[]u8`). A slice is technically a struct containing a pointer and a length field (`usize`). As it does not rely on a sentinel value to determine its end, there is no guarantee that the byte immediately following the slice in memory is a null terminator (it could be garbage data or unmapped memory). Therefore, you cannot pass `fullPath` directly to `printC()`; doing so would cause the C function to read past the end of the buffer until it hits a random zero, likely resulting in a segmentation fault. Since the standard slice lacks the terminator, we must allocate a new block of memory sized `fullPath.len + 1`. This extra byte is strictly reserved for the null character. The function then uses std.mem.copyForwards() to duplicate the content of the Zig slice into this new buffer. Last, the code explicitly sets the terminator with buffer[fullPath.len] = 0. At this point, the memory layout matches C expectations, but the type system still views buffer as a standard Zig slice. To satisfy the printC() signature, the code performs a pointer cast: @as([*:0]const u8, @ptrCast(buffer.ptr)). This extracts the raw multi-item pointer (.ptr) from the slice and casts it to a sentinel-terminated pointer ([*:0]). This cast is an assertion by the programmer to the compiler that the memory at that address is indeed null-terminated. Execute the program on your machine:

```
$ zig run ch03/convertPtr.zig
/usr
Zig Slice: /usr/ls
/usr/ls
```

The output verifies our program logic by first printing the compatible string literal, then confirming the intermediate dynamic slice construction, and finally proving that our manual conversion successfully produced a valid C string.

Next, we see how Zig handles custom data structures in memory. Whether you need the speed of the *stack* for temporary data or the flexibility of the *heap* for long-lived objects, Zig puts the decision directly in your hands.

Putting structures on stack and heap

The decision of where to store data — on the efficient, automatic *stack* or the flexible, manual *heap* — is a fundamental architectural choice that directly impacts performance and memory safety. This section explores the mechanics of instantiating structures in both memory regions. Look at the first part of ch03/stackHeapStruct.zig:

```
const std = @import("std");

const Person = struct {
    name: []const u8,
    age: u8,
};

pub fn main(init: std.process.Init) !void {
    const allocator = init.gpa;

    const stack = Person{
        .name = "Mihalis",
```

```
        .age = 10,
    };
    std.debug.print(
        "Stack: N = {s}, A = {}\n",
        .{ stack.name, stack.age },
    );
```

The program begins by establishing the shape of our data with a simple `Person` struct. Inside `main()`, we immediately get the allocator provided by `init.gpa`. The core of this snippet is the creation of the `stack` constant. *By simply declaring the variable and filling in the struct fields, we are instructing Zig to place this data structure directly on the stack.* This is the default mode of operation in Zig and represents the "fast path" for memory usage. *There are no calls to allocate memory and no matching calls to free it*; the `Person` instance exists solely within the scope of the `main()` function and is automatically cleaned up the moment the function exits. Let us continue with the remaining code:

```
    const heap_ptr = try allocator.create(Person);
    defer allocator.destroy(heap_ptr);
    heap_ptr.* = Person{
        .name = "Epifanios",
        .age = 18,
    };

    std.debug.print(
        "Heap: N = {s}, A = {}\n",
        .{ heap_ptr.name, heap_ptr.age },
    );
}
```

When we want heap allocation, the syntax changes to reflect the manual control we are taking over memory. Instead of declaring a variable, we use `allocator.create(Person)`. This function asks the allocator to find a free spot in memory large enough to hold a `Person` struct and returns a pointer to that location, which we store in `heap_ptr`. *As we asked for this memory explicitly, we are also responsible for giving it back.* That is why the `defer allocator.destroy(heap_ptr)` line appears immediately after; it ensures that no matter how the function ends, the memory is properly freed, preventing leaks. The way we access and modify the data also shifts. Since `heap_ptr` is a pointer, not the struct itself, we use the dereference syntax `heap_ptr.*` to assign the actual `Person` data into that allocated slot. However, Zig offers a convenient syntactic sugar here: when we want to read the fields later in the `debug.print()` statement, we can just write heap_ptr.name. The compiler understands we want to access the fields inside the structure that the pointer is pointing to. This keeps the code readable even when managing the complexities of heap memory. Running ch03/stackHeapStruct.zig produces the following output:

```
$ zig run ch03/stackHeapStruct.zig
Stack: N = Mihalis, A = 10
Heap: N = Epifanios, A = 18
```

The output validates that both methods of creating a Person worked perfectly. The first line confirms our stack variable ("Mihalis") was stored and read correctly, while the second proves we successfully managed the manual lifecycle of the heap-allocated instance ("Epifanios"), properly accessing its fields through the pointer. Now that we have mastered using the standard tools, it is time to implement our own custom memory allocator to understand exactly how Zig manages memory under the hood.

Programming a custom memory allocator (wrapper)

The three standard allocators covered in the previous chapter handle the vast majority of real-world workloads. But understanding what an allocator actually is — not just how to use one — requires building one from scratch. Zig makes this unusually accessible because std.mem.Allocator is not a special compiler construct or a privileged runtime object. It is an ordinary *interface*: a struct containing a pointer to an implementation and a vtable of three function pointers covering alloc(), resize(), and free(). Any struct that satisfies those three operations and exposes an .allocator() method to produce a vtable-bound value is a fully interchangeable std.mem.Allocator — passable to std.ArrayList, standard library containers, and any function that accepts the interface. The TrackingAllocator we built in this section takes a slightly different approach: it exposes allocation methods directly rather than wiring into the vtable, which keeps the implementation visible and easy to follow. We note where it diverges from full interchangeability and what would be needed to close that gap. Writing a custom allocator is therefore less about memory management wizardry and more about implementing a well-defined interface — which is exactly the kind of systems programming task Zig is designed to make explicit and approachable. The implementation that follows is organized in four stages: first, we define the wrapper struct and its internal state, then we implement the allocation and deallocation methods, then we add the reporting helpers that make the tracking visible, and finally, we exercise the whole thing in main() against a mix of types and allocation styles. By the end, you will have seen every moving part of an allocator from the inside.

While the standard library provides excellent general-purpose tools, there are times when "good enough" simply is not enough. You might be working on a game engine that needs to free millions of objects instantly, an embedded system with hard memory limits, or a real-time application where every microsecond of allocation latency counts. *Writing a custom allocator allows you to bypass the overhead of generic logic, tailoring the memory management strategy to fit the exact shape and lifecycle of your data.* Beyond performance, this is an insightful learning experience; implementing the `Allocator` interface reveals the mechanical heart of Zig, transforming memory from a mysterious resource into a predictable, controllable asset. The implementation begins with a struct that establishes the internal state for our allocator:

```
const std = @import("std");
const bitsInByte = 8;

pub const TrackingAllocator = struct {
    allocator: std.mem.Allocator,
    allocBytes: usize,
```

As we are not building a raw memory manager that speaks directly to the operating system kernel, we are creating a "wrapper" or "middleware" allocator. The `allocator` field stores a pointer to a parent allocator, to which we will delegate the actual heavy lifting of finding free memory. The `allocBytes` field is our custom addition: it serves as a running counter, tracking how much memory has been requested through this wrapper. This setup allows us to inject our own logic — in this case, simple accounting — into the allocation pipeline.

Next, we have the `init()` function that serves as the constructor:

```
    // Initialize the Tracking Allocator
    pub fn init(allocator: std.mem.Allocator) TrackingAllocator {
        return TrackingAllocator{
            .allocator = allocator,
            .allocBytes = 0,
        };
    }
```

The function accepts a `std.mem.Allocator` value, which establishes the "parent-child" relationship of our design. By storing this parent allocator and setting our `allocBytes` counter to zero, we prepare the struct to intercept memory requests.

After that, we have `alloc()`, which is the heart of our interception logic:

```
    pub fn alloc(
        self: *TrackingAllocator,
        comptime T: type,
```

```
        n: usize,
    ) ![]T {
        const initialValue: usize = self.allocBytes;
        const slice: []T = try self.allocator.alloc(T, n);
        self.allocBytes += @sizeOf(T) * n;
        const AFTER = self.allocBytes - initialValue;
        std.debug.print(
            "Allocated {}. Current: {}\n",
            .{ AFTER, self.allocBytes },
        );
        return slice;
    }
```

Instead of managing raw memory pages itself, `alloc()` acts as a middleman. When you call `alloc()`, it immediately delegates the hard work to the parent allocator we stored earlier (`self.allocator.alloc`). This ensures that the memory is allocated safely and correctly, whether that is the page allocator or a fixed buffer. Once the parent allocator successfully returns the memory, our custom logic kicks in. We calculate exactly how many bytes were just reserved using `@sizeOf(T) * n` and add this to our running total, `allocBytes`. Before handing the memory back to the user, we print a status update to the console. This gives us real-time visibility into memory consumption.

Just as we track memory going out, we must account for it coming back in. The `free()` function mirrors the logic of `alloc()`, completing the lifecycle of our tracked memory:

```
    pub fn free(
        self: *TrackingAllocator,
        comptime T: type,
        slice: []T,
    ) void {
        if (slice.len > 0) {
            const initialValue: usize = self.allocBytes;
            self.allocBytes -= @sizeOf(T) * slice.len;
            self.allocator.free(slice);
            const FREED: usize = initialValue - self.allocBytes;
            std.debug.print(
                "{} freed. Current: {}\n",
                .{ FREED, self.allocBytes },
            );
```

```
        }
    }
```

When you pass a slice to be freed, the function first calculates the size of that memory block and subtracts it from our running total, ensuring `allocBytes` reflects the reduction in usage. Once this is done, the function delegates the actual cleanup work to the parent allocator using `self.allocator.free(slice)`. This order of operations — update the stats, then release the resource — ensures that our internal state is always consistent before the memory is returned to the system. Finally, it prints a confirmation message, giving you immediate feedback that the memory has been successfully reclaimed and showing the new current total. While `alloc()` is designed for creating arrays (slices) of multiple items, `create()` is the specialized tool for allocating a single object, such as a struct instance, directly on the heap:

```
    pub fn create(self: *TrackingAllocator, comptime T: type) !*T {
        const initialValue: usize = self.allocBytes;
        const memory: *T = try self.allocator.create(T);
        self.allocBytes += @sizeOf(T);
        const AFTER = self.allocBytes - initialValue;
        std.debug.print(
            "Allocated {}. Current {}\n",
            .{ AFTER, self.allocBytes },
        );
        return memory;
    }
```

The logic here is simpler because there is no element count to manage; we are reserving exactly enough space for one instance of type `T`. Just like the previous methods, this function acts as a wrapper. It delegates the actual memory request to the parent allocator using `self.allocator.create(T)`. Once the pointer is returned, we add the size of that specific type (`@sizeOf(T)`) to our counter and log the action.

Finally, we need a way to clean up those single objects we made with `create()`. The `destroy()` function is the closing bracket to `create()`'s opening one:

```
    pub fn destroy(
        self: *TrackingAllocator,
        comptime T: type,
        memory: *T,
    ) void {
        const initialValue: usize = self.allocBytes;
```

```
            self.allocBytes -= @sizeOf(T);
            self.allocator.destroy(memory);
            const FREED: usize = initialValue - self.allocBytes;
            std.debug.print(
                "{} freed. Now: {}\n",
                .{ FREED, self.allocBytes },
            );
        }
```

While `free()` handles slices (lists of things), `destroy()` is focused on deleting just one specific instance pointed to by memory. The logic follows the same disciplined pattern we established earlier: first, we subtract the size of the object from `allocBytes`. Once the accounting is done, we hand the pointer over to the parent allocator to perform the actual memory reclamation. The function ends with a log message, confirming that the object is gone and showing the updated memory usage.

The final piece of our `TrackingAllocator` is a set of helper functions designed to expose the data we have been carefully collecting:

```
        pub fn bytesAllocated(self: *TrackingAllocator) usize {
            return self.allocBytes;
        }
        pub fn printBits(self: TrackingAllocator) void {
            std.debug.print(
                "Memory: {} bits\n",
                .{self.allocBytes * bitsInByte},
            );
        }
        pub fn printBytes(self: TrackingAllocator) void {
            std.debug.print("Memory: {} bytes\n", .{self.allocBytes});
        }
    };
```

`bytesAllocated()` is a simple *getter* method that allows external code to query exactly how much memory is currently held by the allocator without giving direct access to modify the `allocBytes` field. `printBits()` and `printBytes()` are used for reporting. `printBytes()` outputs the raw counter value while `printBits()` performs a simple calculation (multiplying by `bitsInByte`, which we defined as 8 earlier) to display the usage in a finer granularity. While debugging, having these quick-access print functions prevents you from having to write `std.debug.print()`

statements repeatedly throughout your codebase. The `main()` function is where we put our custom memory allocator to work:

```
pub fn main(_: std.process.Init.Minimal) !void {
    const allocator = std.heap.page_allocator;
    var trackingAllocator = TrackingAllocator.init(allocator);
    trackingAllocator.printBytes();

    const n = 250;
    const slice = try trackingAllocator.alloc(i16, n);
    for (slice, 0..) |*item, index| {
        item.* = @as(i16, @intCast(index)) * 2;
    }
```

We start by initializing the standard `page_allocator`, but instead of using it directly, we pass its address (`&allocator`) into our `TrackingAllocator.init()` function. This wraps the standard allocator, ensuring that any request we make goes through our tracking logic first before reaching the system. When we call `trackingAllocator.alloc(i16, n)`, we are invoking the custom method we wrote earlier. This single line does two things: it successfully reserves space for 250 integers using the underlying page allocator and updates our internal byte counter. Once we have the slice, however, the difference disappears. We treat it exactly like any other Zig slice, iterating through it, and filling it with data (using `@intCast()` to satisfy the strict type requirements of Zig). The code consuming the memory is unaware that it is being audited by our custom allocator.

The final block of code is a stress test for our accounting logic as it deliberately mixes types (`i16`, `i32`, `i64`) and allocation styles (slices vs. single objects) to ensure our `TrackingAllocator` can handle real-world usage patterns:

```
    _ = try trackingAllocator.alloc(i32, n);
    trackingAllocator.free(i16, slice);
    trackingAllocator.printBytes();

    const anInt = try trackingAllocator.create(i64);
    anInt.* = 42;
    _ = try trackingAllocator.create(i64);

    trackingAllocator.destroy(i64, anInt);
    trackingAllocator.printBytes();
```

```
    trackingAllocator.printBits();
}
```

First, we allocate a second slice of i32 integers. Notice that we do not store the pointer (using _ =), which would be a memory leak in a real program, but here it serves to bump up the allocBytes counter so we can see it rise. Then, we call free() on the original i16 slice. After that, our custom free() function should subtract exactly 250 * 2 bytes (500 bytes) from the total, proving that the subtraction logic works as well as the addition. Finally, we test the single-item logic with create. We allocate an i64, assign it the value 42, and then immediately allocate another one that we ignore. This verifies that our allocator correctly handles small, singular requests just as well as large arrays. By calling destroy() on the first integer and printing the final stats, we get a snapshot of the net memory usage. The final calls to printBytes() and printBits() give us the summary, confirming that our wrapper has successfully tracked every byte in and out of the system.

Running ch03/customMemoryAllocator.zig produces the following output:

```
$ zig run ch03/customMemoryAllocator.zig
Memory: 0 bytes
Allocated 500. Current: 500
Allocated 1000. Current: 1500
500 freed. Current: 1000
Memory: 1000 bytes
Allocated 8. Current 1008
Allocated 8. Current 1016
8 freed. Current: 1008
Memory: 1008 bytes
Memory: 8064 bits
```

The logs verify the array logic first: allocating 250 i16 values adds exactly 500 bytes and a subsequent slice of 250 i32 values adds 1000 more, while freeing the initial slice drops the total back to 1000, proving the subtraction logic matches the addition. The single-item tracking is validated next: two i64 values of 8 bytes each are allocated, bringing the total to 1016, and then one is destroyed, dropping it back to 1008. The final Memory: 1008 bytes and Memory: 8064 bits lines reflect the net outstanding allocation at exit — 500 bytes from the unreleased i32 slice, 8 bytes from the second unreleased i64, and the 500 bytes of the original i16 slice that was freed, leaving exactly 1008 bytes unaccounted for. The counter got the arithmetic right throughout.

The `TrackingAllocator` presented here is a **wrapper allocator** rather than a raw allocator — it delegates actual memory management to a parent allocator and intercepts the calls to inject accounting logic. This is one of the two fundamental patterns in custom allocator design. The other is a **backing allocator**, which manages raw memory directly without a parent: a slab allocator that carves fixed-size objects from a pre-allocated pool, a bump allocator that advances a pointer through a contiguous block, or a stack allocator that supports LIFO deallocation with zero overhead. Wrapper allocators are generally easier to write and compose well — you can stack a tracking allocator on top of an arena on top of a debug allocator, and each layer sees only the interface below it.

It is worth noting what this implementation omits. There is no thread safety: `allocBytes` is a plain `usize` with no atomic protection, so concurrent allocations from multiple threads would produce a data race. A production tracking allocator would use `std.atomic.Value(usize)` for the counter or protect it with a mutex. There is also no `resize()` implementation, which means this allocator cannot participate in in-place slice growth — any call to `allocator.resize()` through the standard interface would fail. Adding `resize()` support requires tracking not just total bytes but the size of each individual allocation, which typically means maintaining a hash map of pointer-to-size entries. These are not oversights in the example — they are deliberate omissions that keep the code focused on the core concept. They are also exactly the kind of tradeoff you reason about explicitly in Zig, because the language never makes them for you silently.

The deeper lesson here is about what the Zig allocator design enables at the architectural level. Because every allocation is explicit and every allocator is swappable, you can instrument any subsystem of a running program without modifying the subsystem itself. Pass a `TrackingAllocator` to your parser, run it against a representative workload, and you have an exact measurement of its allocation behavior. Pass a `FixedBufferAllocator` to the same parser, and you know immediately whether it fits within your memory budget. Pass a failing allocator that returns `OutOfMemory` on the third call, and you can verify that every allocation failure path in the parser is handled correctly. None of this requires mocking, monkey-patching, or runtime instrumentation frameworks. It requires only that the code accept an allocator parameter in the first place, which, in Zig, it always does.

With the mechanics of memory management and custom allocators now firmly in our grasp, we are ready to put them to work on a problem that cannot be solved without them. `zunzip` is not a standalone topic — it is where everything covered so far converges. Parsing a binary file format requires understanding how data is laid out in memory at the byte level, exactly what pointer arithmetic and struct layout taught us. Handling variable-length records without knowing their size in advance requires deliberate allocation and ownership decisions, exactly what the allocator sections prepared us for. The `comptime` layout validation we introduced earlier becomes not just a technique but a necessity when the cost of a misaligned struct is a silently corrupted filename rather than a compiler error. By building `zunzip` from raw bytes up to a working command-line utility, we close the loop on everything this chapter has introduced and demonstrate that these are not isolated mechanics but a coherent toolkit for systems-level problem solving.

Zunzip, a Zip file lister

Building a ZIP lister is an excellent exercise for systems programmers because it forces you to see the reality of how data is stored on disk. Unlike text files, which are typically processed line-by-line from the beginning, a ZIP archive is effectively constructed backward, with its master index (*Central Directory*) located at the very end of the file. In this section, we implement `zunzip`, a utility that navigates this non-linear structure by seeking to the end of the file and scanning backward for specific binary signatures.

Unlike simple text files, where data is read linearly from the first byte to the last, a ZIP archive is engineered to be read backward. This design choice, dating back to the era of floppy disks, places the "master index" — known as the **Central Directory** — at the very end of the file. This presents a unique challenge for our parser: we cannot simply open the file stream and start reading. Instead, we must jump to the end of the file and hunt for a specific **End of Central Directory** (EOCD) record, which contains the map coordinates for every other file in the archive. If we were to read from the beginning, we would be flying blind, unaware of where the compressed data streams begin or end.

To interpret the raw bytes of the EOCD record, we move away from error-prone manual offsets and instead define a rigid memory template using an `extern struct`. By declaring a struct like EOCD with fields that match the ZIP specification — such as `signature` (4 bytes), `disk_num` (2 bytes), and `cd_offset` (4 bytes) — we create a direct mapping between our code and the binary data on disk. This approach allows us to *cast a slice of raw bytes directly into a usable object.* However, because the ZIP format strictly uses Little Endian byte order, we must remain vigilant: while the structure layout organizes the bytes correctly, the integer values themselves may still need to be swapped if our host machine uses Big Endian architecture—we will talk about Little and Big Endian in a while.

Locating the EOCD record requires a precise mix of file seeking and pointer arithmetic. Since the EOCD record ends with a variable-length comment field (up to 65,535 bytes), its signature is not at a fixed location; it is "floating" somewhere in the last 66 kilobytes of the file. To find it, we calculate the starting position of the search window — the file size minus the maximum possible tail length — and pass that offset directly to `file.readPositionalAll()`, which reads that entire tail chunk into a buffer in a single operation without moving any file cursor. We then perform a backward linear scan looking for the 4-byte signature `0x06054b50`. The scan begins at `buffer.len - EOCD_SIZE` — the last byte offset where a full 22-byte record could fit — and steps backward toward the start of the buffer, mirroring the physical layout of the file: in the common case, where an archive carries no comment or a short one, the signature sits at or very near that starting position and is found on the first or second check. A fully defensive implementation would also validate each candidate by confirming that the parsed `comment_len` field equals the number of bytes remaining between the end of the fixed header and the end of the file; for real-world archives, the four-byte signature pattern is rare enough in comment data that a simple first-match scan is sufficient. Once the EOCD struct is cast and parsed, the program extracts the memory offset for the Central Directory. The next phase passes that *offset* directly to `file.readPositionalAll()` and enters a loop: it reads the fixed-size header for a file, extracts the filename, and then uses pointer arithmetic to jump over variable-length extra fields, landing precisely at the start of the next entry without reading unnecessary data. With all that in mind, let us see the implementation of `ch03/listZipContents.zig`:

```
const std = @import("std");

// ZIP file constants
const EOCD_SIGNATURE = 0x06054b50;
const CD_SIGNATURE = 0x02014b50;
const EOCD_SIZE = 22;
const CD_HEADER_SIZE = 46;

const EOCD = struct {
    signature: u32,
    disk_num: u16,
    disk_start: u16,
    num_entries_disk: u16,
    num_entries_total: u16,
    cd_size: u32,
    cd_offset: u32,
    comment_len: u16,
};

const CentralDirectoryHeader = struct {
    signature: u32,
    version_made: u16,
    version_needed: u16,
    flags: u16,
    method: u16,
```

```
    mod_time: u16,
    mod_date: u16,
    crc32: u32,
    compressed_size: u32,
    uncompressed_size: u32,
    filename_len: u16,
    extra_len: u16,
    comment_len: u16,
    disk_start: u16,
    internal_attrs: u16,
    external_attrs: u32,
    local_header_offset: u32,
};

comptime {
    var eocd_wire: usize = 0;
    for (std.meta.fields(EOCD)) |f| eocd_wire += @sizeOf(f.type);
    if (eocd_wire != EOCD_SIZE)
        @compileError("EOCD field sizes do not sum to EOCD_SIZE");

    var cd_wire: usize = 0;
    for (std.meta.fields(CentralDirectoryHeader)) |f| cd_wire += @sizeOf(f.type);
    if (cd_wire != CD_HEADER_SIZE)
        @compileError("CentralDirectoryHeader field sizes do not sum to
CD_HEADER_SIZE");
}
```

This section establishes the vocabulary our program uses to interpret the raw binary stream of a ZIP file. In systems programming, we cannot read files as vague chunks of text — we must treat them as strict data structures with fields at exact byte offsets. The constants `EOCD_SIGNATURE` (`0x06054b50`) and `CD_SIGNATURE` (`0x02014b50`) act as navigational signals within the byte stream. Since a binary file offers no inherent structural markers like newlines, the program relies on these unique hexadecimal patterns to identify the starting points of critical records. When the parser encounters the byte sequence corresponding to `0x06054b50`, it knows it has located the End of Central Directory record and can anchor the rest of the parsing logic from that position. The `EOCD` and `CentralDirectoryHeader` structs are plain Zig structs — not `extern` or `packed` — used purely as named containers for the values we parse. This is fundamentally different from the "overlay" approach, where a struct is cast directly onto raw memory. The overlay approach is tempting because it appears zero-copy and elegant, but it is fragile: the Zig compiler is free to insert padding between fields for alignment, and that padding does not exist in the file. A struct that looks correct on screen may silently read the wrong bytes at runtime. Instead, each field is populated explicitly by `eocdFromBytes()` and `cdHeaderFromBytes()`, which call `std.mem.readInt()` with precise byte ranges matching the ZIP specification. The struct becomes a named value holder; the parsing functions are where the wire format is actually enforced. The size constants `EOCD_SIZE = 22` and `CD_HEADER_SIZE = 46` represent the exact number of bytes each record occupies on disk, as defined by the PKZIP specification. They are not derived from `@sizeOf()` — which would include any compiler-inserted padding — but from the specification itself. These constants drive the pointer arithmetic that advances through the file, ensuring the parser stays synchronized with the packed data stream.

Before moving on to the parsing logic, we take a moment to apply compile-time layout validation — a technique we will examine in much more depth in the next section. Consider this a practical preview: seeing the pattern applied to a real problem first will make the deeper discussion that follows land with greater force. An assertion is a statement that something must be true — if it is not, the program refuses to proceed. In most languages, assertions fire at runtime, after the program is already running and potentially after corrupt data has already been processed. Zig's `comptime` assertions fire at build time, before a single byte of the binary exists. For a binary format parser like `zunzip`, this distinction is critical. The ZIP specification defines exact byte offsets for every field in both the End of Central Directory record and the Central Directory Header. If a field type is accidentally widened or a field is reordered, the parsing functions will read the wrong bytes from the wrong positions in the file. The bug will not appear immediately — it will surface as a corrupted filename, a wrong file size, or a misreported entry count, far from the point where the struct was defined. The `comptime` block takes a different approach from a simple `@sizeOf` check. Rather than asserting the total struct size, it iterates over `std.meta.fields()` and sums the individual field sizes, verifying that they add up to the expected wire size. This is more precise: it catches the case where a field type is accidentally widened — for example, changing `filename_len` from `u16` to `u32` — without being fooled by a compensating change elsewhere that happens to preserve the total. If either assertion fails, `@compileError` halts the build with a message that names the problem directly. The size constants stop being magic numbers — they become the wire-format specification, and the compiler enforces that the field types match them on every build, unconditionally.

The entry point of our program (`main()`) handles the essential setup before executing the optimized search strategy:

```
pub fn main(init: std.process.Init) !void {
    const allocator = init.gpa;
    const args = try init.minimal.args.toSlice(init.arena.allocator());
    if (args.len != 2) {
```

```
        std.debug.print("Usage: {s} <archive.zip>\n", .{args[0]});
        return;
    }
    const file = try std.Io.Dir.cwd().openFile(init.io, args[1], .{});
    defer file.close(init.io);
    const file_size = (try file.stat(init.io)).size;

    // 1. Smart Seek - read the last part of the file
    const search_len = @min(file_size, 65535 + EOCD_SIZE);
    const search_start_pos = file_size - search_len;
    const buffer = try allocator.alloc(u8, search_len);
    defer allocator.free(buffer);
    _ = try file.readPositionalAll(init.io, buffer, search_start_pos);
```

We begin by acquiring a memory allocator and parsing the command-line arguments to obtain the target ZIP filename. Once the file is opened, we immediately query its total size using `file.stat()`. Rather than reading the file from start to finish — which would be drastically inefficient for large archives — we implement a *Smart Seek* to isolate the specific region where our target data must hide. The core of this logic lies in the `search_len` calculation. According to the ZIP specification, the EOCD record is always the last structural element, but it can be followed by a variable-length comment field of up to `65,535` bytes. This means the crucial EOCD signature could be floating anywhere within the last 65,557 bytes of the file (the maximum comment size plus the 22-byte header itself). By strictly defining this window and using `file.readPositionalAll()`, we jump directly to the end of the file and load only this tiny tail into a buffer. This optimization makes the performance independent of the file size, allowing it to open a 10 GB archive just as instantly as a 10 KB one.

This remaining part of `main()` implements the critical *backward scan* algorithm required to correctly identify the ZIP file's structural anchor:

```
    // 2. Backward Scan for EOCD Signature
    var found_eocd: ?EOCD = null;
    if (buffer.len >= EOCD_SIZE) {
        var i: usize = buffer.len - EOCD_SIZE;
        while (true) {
            if (std.mem.readInt(
                u32,
                buffer[i..][0..4],
                .little,
            ) == EOCD_SIGNATURE) {
```

```
                found_eocd = eocdFromBytes(buffer[i..][0..EOCD_SIZE]);
                break;
            }
            if (i == 0) break;
            i -= 1;
        }
    }

    if (found_eocd) |record| {
        try listEntries(init.io, file, record);
    } else {
        std.debug.print(
            "Error: valid EOCD signature not found.\n",
            .{},
        );
    }
}
```

The backward scan starts at `buffer.len - EOCD_SIZE` — the last position where a complete 22-byte EOCD record could begin — and works toward the start of the buffer one byte at a time. At each position, `std.mem.readInt(u32, buffer[i..][0..4], .little)` reads four bytes and interprets them as a little-endian `u32`, checking whether they match `EOCD_SIGNATURE`. Scanning backward guarantees that the first match found is the last signature in the file, which is the legitimate EOCD record even if a ZIP comment earlier in the file happens to contain the same byte sequence. Once the signature is found, `eocdFromBytes()` is called with a fixed-size slice of exactly `EOCD_SIZE` bytes, populating the `EOCD` struct field by field using `std.mem.readInt()` with explicit byte ranges. This gives us immediate access to critical fields like `cd_offset`, which tells us where the central directory begins, and `num_entries_total`, which tells us how many entries to expect.

The `listEntries()` function executes the final phase of extraction: traversing the master index itself:

```
fn listEntries(io: std.Io, file: std.Io.File, eocd: EOCD) !void {
    std.debug.print(" ZIP file listing:\n-------------------\n", .{});

    var i: usize = 0;
    var offset: u64 = eocd.cd_offset;
    while (i < eocd.num_entries_total) : (i += 1) {
        var raw_header: [CD_HEADER_SIZE]u8 = undefined;
        _ = try file.readPositionalAll(io,&raw_header,offset);
```

```
        offset += CD_HEADER_SIZE;

        const header = cdHeaderFromBytes(&raw_header);
        if (header.signature != CD_SIGNATURE) break;

        var filename_buf: [256]u8 = undefined;
        const read_len = @min(header.filename_len, filename_buf.len);
        _ = try file.readPositionalAll(
            io,
            filename_buf[0..read_len],
            offset,
        );
        offset += header.filename_len +
            header.extra_len +
            header.comment_len;

        std.debug.print("{d:>9} bytes (c)  -> {s}\n", .{
            header.compressed_size,
            filename_buf[0..read_len],
        });
    }

    std.debug.print(
        "--------------------\nTotal files: {d}\n",
        .{eocd.num_entries_total},
    );
}
```

Before we can list the files, we must accurately decipher the "map coordinates" hidden within the EOCD record. The first few lines of the function tackle a subtle but critical systems programming challenge: *endianness*. The ZIP format, created in the MS-DOS era, strictly stores integers in Little Endian format (least significant byte first). However, if your program runs on a Big Endian machine (like some mainframes or older networking hardware), reading these raw bytes directly would yield gibberish values. In this implementation, endianness is handled inside `eocdFromBytes()` and `cdHeaderFromBytes()` via `std.mem.readInt(..., .little)`, which converts each field to native byte order at parse time. By the time `listEntries()` receives the `EOCD` struct, all fields are already in the correct order for the host machine — the function can use them directly without any further byte-swapping. Each iteration reads exactly `CD_HEADER_SIZE` bytes from the current `offset` into a fixed-size stack buffer `raw_header` using `file.readPositionalAll()`, which reads at an explicit file position without moving any file cursor. `offset` is then immediately advanced by `CD_HEADER_SIZE`. `cdHeaderFromBytes()` deserializes those bytes into a `CentralDirectoryHeader` struct, populating every field with the correct little-endian values. The signature check `header.signature != CD_SIGNATURE` guards against reading past the end of the central directory or into malformed data — if the expected signature is absent, the loop exits immediately. Once the fixed-size header is parsed, the filename is read into a 256-byte stack buffer. The length is capped with `@min(header.filename_len, filename_buf.len)`, which silently truncates filenames longer than 256 bytes — a known limitation of this implementation that a production tool would handle with an error or a heap-allocated buffer. After the filename is read, `offset` is advanced by `header.filename_len + header.extra_len + header.comment_len`, skipping over the full filename, any extra data field, and the per-entry comment in a single arithmetic step with no I/O. This moves `offset` to the start of the next central directory entry. The compressed size and filename are then printed, and the loop continues until all entries have been listed.

It is worth noting that this implementation supports standard ZIP files only — archives up to 4 GiB in size with no more than 65,535 entries. ZIP64, the extension that lifts those limits for larger archives, uses a different EOCD record format with 64-bit offset and entry count fields. A production tool would need to detect and handle ZIP64, but for the purposes of this chapter, the standard format is sufficient to demonstrate the core parsing techniques. Try `ch03/listZipContents.zig` on your machine to get an analogous output:

```
$ zig run ch03/listZipContents.zig -- tsouk.zip
ZIP file listing:
-------------------
 21032530 bytes (c)  -> DSW00286.png
       92 bytes (c)  -> __MACOSX/._DSW00286.png
 17837053 bytes (c)  -> DSW00063.png
       92 bytes (c)  -> __MACOSX/._DSW00063.png
 23268707 bytes (c)  -> DSC09853.png
       92 bytes (c)  -> __MACOSX/._DSC09853.png
 16903849 bytes (c)  -> DSW09850.png
       92 bytes (c)  -> __MACOSX/._DSW09850.png
 17047752 bytes (c)  -> DSW09304.png
       92 bytes (c)  -> __MACOSX/._DSW09304.png
 19984224 bytes (c)  -> DSW09416.png
       92 bytes (c)  -> __MACOSX/._DSW09416.png
-------------------
Total files: 12
```

The output confirms that our utility is successfully parsing the Central Directory of the `tsouk.zip` archive. Each line represents a single file header extracted from the binary data. The output reveals the presence of hidden `__MACOSX` directories and `._`-prefixed files, which are metadata resource forks created by macOS that are often invisible to users but physically present in the file structure.

Every binary parser we have written so far carries a silent assumption: that the struct we are reading into matches the byte layout of the data on disk or on the wire. So far, that assumption has held because we wrote both sides. But in a real system, structs evolve — a field grows from `u16` to `u32`, a new field gets inserted, a developer reorders members to satisfy alignment requirements — and the parser silently starts producing garbage. The bug does not appear at the point of change. It appears later, in production, when a malformed record arrives and the values coming out of the parser make no sense. Zig gives us a way to make that class of bug impossible. By moving the layout verification into a `comptime` block, we turn a runtime mystery into a build error that fires at the exact moment the struct diverges from the wire specification, on every build, unconditionally. The following example shows exactly how that works.

Enforcing wire format correctness with comptime

Before diving into the code, it helps to see `comptime` through a few concrete scenarios that capture why it matters in systems programming. Consider a network protocol that reserves exactly 4 bytes for a sequence number. A developer later decides a `u64` would be safer and widens the field — a perfectly reasonable change in isolation. Without `comptime` validation, the struct silently grows from the expected size, and every peer that parses the old format now reads garbage, with no error until a production message arrives and the values make no sense. With a `comptime` size assertion in place, the build fails the moment the field is widened, before a single binary is produced. The fix happens at the keyboard, not in a debugger at 2 am. A second scenario involves field reordering. A developer notices that grouping the two `u32` fields together would improve readability and swaps them. The struct still compiles, the size is unchanged, but the `crc32` field is now where length used to be, and every parser that reads the old layout silently interprets the checksum as a payload size. A `comptime` offset assertion catches this immediately — `@offsetOf(Record, "crc32")` no longer equals 8, the build halts, and the message tells the developer exactly which field is at the wrong position. A third scenario is less obvious but equally dangerous: adding a field without checking alignment. Inserting a `u32` after a `u8` in a non-`extern` struct can cause the compiler to insert 3 bytes of padding to satisfy alignment requirements. The struct grows by 7 bytes instead of 4, every field after the insertion point shifts, and nothing in the language warns you unless you are actively checking. The `@sizeOf` assertion fires on the next build and points directly at the discrepancy. These three scenarios share a common pattern: the bug is introduced by a local, apparently safe change, and manifests remotely, under load, in a way that is hard to reproduce and harder to diagnose. `comptime` turns all three into build errors. That is the value proposition — not just catching bugs earlier but making an entire category of bugs structurally impossible to ship.

The program with the long filename (`ch03/comptimeBinaryValidation.zig`) demonstrates one of the most practical applications of Zig `comptime` machinery: *guaranteeing that a struct's in-memory layout matches a binary wire format* before a single byte is ever sent or received. The protocol defined here is ZMP (*Zig Message Protocol*), a 12-byte record header with fields at fixed offsets — `magic` at byte 0, `version` at byte 2, `kind` at byte 3, `length` at byte 4, and `crc32` at byte 8. The first design decision is the use of `extern struct` rather than a plain Zig struct. A regular Zig struct gives the compiler freedom to insert padding between fields and reorder them for performance. `extern struct` removes that freedom, enforcing C-compatible layout rules: fields appear in declaration order with no padding inserted. On a wire protocol, this distinction matters enormously — a padding byte silently inserted between `version` and `kind` would shift every subsequent field by one byte, corrupting every message without producing a single compiler warning. Here is the relevant code:

```
const RecordKind = enum(u8) {
    data = 0,
    ack = 1,
    err = 2,
    fin = 3,
};

const Record = extern struct {
    magic: u16,
    version: u8,
    kind: RecordKind,
    length: u32,
    crc32: u32,
};
```

The `comptime` block that follows is where the real safety guarantee lives. It runs before `main()` and before any binary is produced. It checks that `@sizeOf(Record)` is exactly 12, and that `@offsetOf(Record, "magic")` is 0, `@offsetOf(Record, "version")` is 2, and so on through every field. If any assertion fails, `@compileError` halts the build with a message that names the exact problem. The consequence is significant: any future change to a field type, any accidental reordering, or any struct modification that introduces unexpected padding immediately becomes a build error rather than a runtime data-corruption bug that only manifests when a malformed message arrives at a remote host.

```
comptime {
    if (@sizeOf(Record) != 12)
        @compileError(
            "Record must be exactly 12 bytes; check for unexpected
             padding",
        );

    if (@offsetOf(Record, "magic") != 0) @compileError(
        "magic must be at wire offset 0",
    );
    if (@offsetOf(Record, "version") != 2) @compileError(
        "version must be at wire offset 2",
    );
    if (@offsetOf(Record, "kind") != 3) @compileError(
        "kind must be at wire offset 3",
    );
    if (@offsetOf(Record, "length") != 4) @compileError(
        "length must be at wire offset 4",
    );
    if (@offsetOf(Record, "crc32") != 8) @compileError(
        "crc32 must be at wire offset 8",
    );
}
```

Next, the `assertLayout()` function generalizes this pattern. It accepts any type `T` and the expected size and alignment as `comptime_int` parameters, then produces a compiler error that names both the type and the conflicting values. This makes the validator reusable across any protocol struct in the codebase — you define your wire spec once in the assertion call, and the compiler enforces it permanently.

```
fn assertLayout(
    comptime T: type,
    comptime expected_size: comptime_int,
    comptime expected_align: comptime_int,
) void {
    if (@sizeOf(T) != expected_size) @compileError(
        @typeName(T) ++ " size mismatch: got " ++
```

```
            std.fmt.comptimePrint("{d}", .{@sizeOf(T)}) ++
            ", expected " ++
            std.fmt.comptimePrint("{d}", .{expected_size}),
    );
    if (@alignOf(T) != expected_align) @compileError(
        @typeName(T) ++ " alignment mismatch: got " ++
            std.fmt.comptimePrint("{d}", .{@alignOf(T)}) ++
            ", expected " ++
            std.fmt.comptimePrint("{d}", .{expected_align}),
    );
}

comptime {
    assertLayout(Record, 12, 4);
}
```

The argument type of `parseRecord()` is itself a form of `comptime` safety. By declaring the parameter as `*const [@sizeOf(Record)]u8`, the function requires the caller to supply exactly the right number of bytes. The type system enforces this at compile time, eliminating the need for runtime bounds checks on the input slice:

```
const MAGIC: u16 = 0xBEEF;
const VERSION: u8 = 1;

fn parseRecord(bytes: *const [@sizeOf(Record)]u8) Record {
    return std.mem.bytesToValue(Record, bytes);
}
```

The `validateRecord()` function handles runtime checks that `comptime` cannot: verifying that the magic bytes match the expected constant `0xBEEF`, that the version field carries a supported value, and that the declared payload length does not exceed a safe threshold. These checks belong at runtime because their inputs are not known until a message actually arrives.

```
fn validateRecord(r: Record) !void {
    if (std.mem.littleToNative(
        u16,
        r.magic,
    ) != MAGIC) return error.BadMagic;
    if (r.version != VERSION) return error.UnsupportedVersion;
    if (std.mem.littleToNative(
```

```
            u32,
            r.length,
        ) > 0xFFFF) return error.PayloadTooLarge;
}
```

The CRC-32 implementation uses the IEEE 802.3 polynomial `0xEDB88320`, the same one used by zlib and gzip, computed with a standard bit-by-bit loop. The `inline for` directive unrolls the eight-iteration inner loop at compile time, producing straight-line code rather than a branch per bit:

```
fn crc32(data: []const u8) u32 {
    var crc: u32 = 0xFFFFFFFF;
    for (data) |byte| {
        crc ^= byte;
        inline for (0..8) |_| {
            const mask: u32 = @as(u32, 0)-%(crc&1);
            crc = (crc >> 1) ^ (0xEDB88320&mask);
        }
    }
    return ~crc;
}
```

In `main()`, the program constructs a synthetic ZMP frame by serializing a `Record` header into a byte array using `std.mem.asBytes()` — a zero-copy operation that produces a typed view of the struct's memory — and appending a literal payload string. It then parses the header back using `parseRecord()`, validates the fields, extracts the payload slice using the parsed length, and verifies the CRC. Finally, it prints both the decoded field values and the `comptime`-verified layout with each field's offset and size, giving the reader a concrete picture of exactly what the wire format looks like in memory.

```
pub fn main(_: std.process.Init.Minimal) !void {
    const payload = "hello from ZMP";
    const checksum = crc32(payload);
    const hdr = Record{
        .magic = MAGIC,
        .version = VERSION,
        .kind = .data,
        .length = @intCast(payload.len),
        .crc32 = checksum,
    };
```

```
var frame: [@sizeOf(Record) + payload.len]u8 = undefined;
@memcpy(frame[0..@sizeOf(Record)], std.mem.asBytes(&hdr));
@memcpy(frame[@sizeOf(Record)..], payload);
const r = parseRecord(frame[0..@sizeOf(Record)]);
try validateRecord(r);

const body = frame[@sizeOf(Record)..][0..r.length];
if (r.crc32 != crc32(body)) return error.CrcMismatch;
std.debug.print("Record parsed and validated:\n", .{});
std.debug.print("  magic   = 0x{X:0>4}\n", .{r.magic});
std.debug.print("  version = {d}\n", .{r.version});
std.debug.print("  kind    = {s}\n", .{@tagName(r.kind)});
std.debug.print("  length  = {d}\n", .{r.length});
std.debug.print("  crc32   = 0x{X:0>8}\n", .{r.crc32});
std.debug.print("  payload = \"{s}\"\n", .{body});

std.debug.print(
    "\nComptime-verified layout ({d} bytes):\n",
    .{@sizeOf(Record)},
);
std.debug.print(
    "  [+{d}] magic   ({d}B)\n",
    .{ @offsetOf(Record, "magic"), @sizeOf(u16) },
);
std.debug.print(
    "  [+{d}] version ({d}B)\n",
    .{ @offsetOf(Record, "version"), @sizeOf(u8) },
);
std.debug.print(
    "  [+{d}] kind    ({d}B)\n",
    .{ @offsetOf(Record, "kind"), @sizeOf(u8) },
);
std.debug.print(
    "  [+{d}] length  ({d}B)\n",
    .{ @offsetOf(Record, "length"), @sizeOf(u32) },
);
std.debug.print(
    "  [+{d}] crc32   ({d}B)\n",
    .{ @offsetOf(Record, "crc32"), @sizeOf(u32) },
```

```
    );
}
```

Let us now see `ch03/comptimeBinaryValidation.zig` in action:

```
$ zig run ch03/comptimeBinaryValidation.zig
Record parsed and validated:
  magic   = 0xBEEF
  version = 1
  kind    = data
  length  = 14
  crc32   = 0xB2BE7B14
  payload = "hello from ZMP"

Comptime-verified layout (12 bytes):
  [+0] magic   (2B)
  [+2] version (1B)
  [+3] kind    (1B)
  [+4] length  (4B)
  [+8] crc32   (4B)
```

The first block confirms that the round-trip worked correctly. The magic value `0xBEEF` matches the protocol constant, confirming that the parser read the first two bytes correctly and that no misalignment shifted the field. The version field reads as `1`, matching the `VERSION` constant defined in the source. The `kind` field prints as `data` rather than `0` because Zig resolves the `RecordKind` enum tag name at runtime, making the output human-readable without any extra formatting code. The `length` field shows `14`, which is the exact byte count of the string `"hello from ZMP"`. The `crc32` value `0xB2BE7B14` is the IEEE 802.3 checksum computed over that payload, and the fact that validation passed confirms that the checksum computed during parsing matched the one embedded in the header — the payload arrived intact. The `payload` line then prints the raw bytes extracted from the frame using the parsed length as the slice boundary, confirming that the data region of the frame is correctly separated from the header region. The second block is the `comptime`-verified layout report. It shows the offset and size of every field in the `Record` struct as the compiler sees them. `magic` sits at offset 0 and occupies 2 bytes, `version` at offset 2 occupies 1 byte, `kind` at offset 3 occupies 1 byte, `length` at offset 4 occupies 4 bytes, and `crc32` at offset 8 occupies 4 bytes, for a total of 12 bytes. The fact that this output matches the wire specification exactly — with no gaps, no padding, and no field overlap — is precisely what the `comptime` assertions verified before the program was allowed to compile. If any of these numbers were different, the binary would not exist.

The takeaway is that `comptime` does not just move checks earlier — it changes their nature. A runtime check can be skipped, can fail only under certain inputs, or can be forgotten entirely during a refactor. A `comptime` assertion runs on every build, unconditionally, and cannot be bypassed. For binary protocols where a one-byte misalignment silently corrupts data across process or machine boundaries, that unconditional guarantee is precisely what correctness requires.

The ZIP parser we just built depends on an assumption we have not yet made explicit: that every multi-byte integer in the file is stored in a specific byte order that matches what our parsing functions expect. When `std.mem.readInt(u32, b[0..4], .little)` reads the EOCD signature; the `.little` argument is not a stylistic choice — it is a correctness requirement. Get it wrong, and the signature check fails, the EOCD record is never found, and the entire parser produces nothing. This dependency on byte ordering is not specific to ZIP files; it is a fundamental property of every binary format, every network protocol, and every hardware interface you will encounter in systems programming. We must now formalize our understanding of how bytes are translated into numerical values. This leads us directly to the concept of endianness — a fundamental property of computer architecture that dictates the specific order in which multi-byte data types are stored in memory, and one that the ZIP parser has already been quietly relying on throughout this chapter.

Working with Endianness

Endianness refers to the sequential order in which bytes are arranged into larger numerical values, distinguishing between systems that place the most significant byte first (*Big Endian*) and those that place it last (*Little Endian*). While this distinction is often invisible in high-level application code, it becomes the defining factor when reading binary file formats, communicating over networks, or porting software between architectures like x86 and ARM. In this section, we explore how Zig provides explicit tools to handle these conversions with the help of `ch03/endianness.zig`, which begins by importing the usual `std` library for general functionality and the `builtin` package that provides compile-time information about the target architecture:

```
const std = @import("std");
const builtin = @import("builtin");

pub fn main(_: std.process.Init.Minimal) void {
    const value: u32 = 0x12345678;
    const native_bytes = std.mem.asBytes(&value);
    std.debug.print(
        "Native ({s}):   {x}\n",
```

```
        .{ @tagName(builtin.cpu.arch.endian()), native_bytes.* },
    );
```

Inside `main()`, we define a 32-bit integer value with the hexadecimal pattern `0x12345678`. The core operation uses `std.mem.asBytes(&value)` to create a slice of bytes (`[]u8`) that directly aliases the memory address of that integer. This allows the program to inspect exactly how the multi-byte integer is physically stored in memory without modifying it. Finally, `std.debug.print()` outputs the architecture's endianness by reading `builtin.cpu.arch.endian()`, followed by the raw byte sequence. On a typical Little Endian system (like x86 or ARM64), the bytes will appear in reverse order (`78 56 34 12`), revealing the underlying storage layout.

The second half of the program shows how to decouple data representation from the underlying architecture, ensuring consistency for file formats and network protocols:

```
    const big_val = std.mem.nativeToBig(u32, value);
    const big_bytes = std.mem.asBytes(&big_val);
    std.debug.print("Big Endian:      {x}\n", .{big_bytes.*});

    const little_val = std.mem.nativeToLittle(u32, value);
    const little_bytes = std.mem.asBytes(&little_val);
    std.debug.print("Little Endian:   {x}\n", .{little_bytes.*});
}
```

By calling `std.mem.nativeToBig()`, the code forces the integer into Big Endian order (`0x12`, `0x34`, `0x56`, `0x78`), aligning the bytes to match the human-readable hexadecimal sequence; this is the standard "network byte order" used in Internet communication. Conversely, `std.mem.nativeToLittle()` translates the integer into Little Endian format (`0x78`, `0x56`, `0x34`, `0x12`), placing the least significant byte first.

Execute `ch03/endianness.zig` on your machine to learn about its endianness:

```
$ zig run ch03/endianness.zig
Native (little):   78563412
Big Endian:        12345678
Little Endian:     78563412
```

As I ran this on a standard x86 or ARM laptop, you can see the "Native" bytes match the "Little Endian" bytes (`78 56 34 12`). However, the "Big Endian" output will always be `12 34 56 78`, preserving the logical order of the hex digits.

With the theoretical foundation of endianness established, we can now turn our attention to the practical task of *extracting meaningful numbers from a raw file buffer*. Since we cannot simply cast a pointer to a byte array and hope for the best, we need a robust method to assemble these values.

Reading Little-Endian integers from raw bytes

The `ch03/bigLittle.zig` program provides a practical demonstration of how high-level Zig structures can be serialized into raw byte streams and reconstructed, bridging the gap between type-safe programming and binary file formats:

```
const std = @import("std");
const Io = std.Io;

const Person = packed struct(u16) {
    age: u8,
    value: u8,
};
```

The program begins by defining `Person`, a *packed struct* backed by a 16-bit integer (`u16`). This `packed` modifier is crucial for Systems Programming because it instructs the compiler to compress the fields — age (8 bits) and `value` (8 bits) — tightly into the adjacent bits of a generic integer, eliminating the padding bytes that would normally be inserted for memory alignment. *This guarantees that the struct occupies exactly 2 bytes in memory, matching the layout of the hardware registers or binary protocols it might represent.*

After that, the `main()` function orchestrates the serialization process using a custom I/O wrapper (`Io.Writer` and `Io.Reader`):

```
pub fn main(_: std.process.Init.Minimal) !void {
    const gpa = std.heap.smp_allocator;
    const p: Person = .{ .age = 20, .value = 100 };

    var writer_state: Io.Writer.Allocating = .init(gpa);
    constw=&writer_state.writer;
    try w.writeInt(u16, @bitCast(p), .little);
    std.debug.print("Written: {any}\n", .{writer_state.written()});

    var reader: Io.Reader = .fixed(writer_state.written());
    const readP: Person = @bitCast(try reader.takeInt(u16, .little));
    std.debug.print("Read: {any}\n", .{readP});
}
```

`std.heap.smp_allocator` is a lock-free, thread-safe allocator introduced in Zig 0.16, optimized for symmetric multi-processing (SMP) workloads where multiple threads allocate and free memory concurrently. It is used here because `Io.Writer.Allocating` requires an allocator to grow its internal buffer dynamically. For a single-threaded program like this one, `std.heap.page_allocator` would also work, but `smp_allocator` is a convenient global allocator that requires no setup or teardown. Before explaining the code, four Zig 0.16 I/O types appear here that have not been introduced elsewhere in the chapter and deserve a brief explanation. `Io.Writer.Allocating` is a writer that accumulates bytes into a dynamically growing heap buffer rather than a fixed-size stack array — it is the right choice when the total output size is not known in advance. Once writing is complete, `writer_state.written()` returns a slice of exactly the bytes written so far, giving you a clean view of the accumulated output without copying. On the reading side, `Io.Reader.fixed()` creates a reader over an existing byte slice, treating it as a stream — each read advances an internal cursor through the slice exactly as it would through a file or socket. Finally, `reader.takeInt(u16, .little)` reads exactly two bytes from the current cursor position and interprets them as a little-endian `u16`, advancing the cursor by two bytes in the process. Together, these four primitives give the example a complete write-then-read round-trip: bytes are encoded into the allocating writer, the written slice is handed to a fixed reader, and the reader reserializes the values back out, confirming that the encoding was correct.

So, the core operation happens when the program writes the struct to the buffer: `w.writeInt(u16, @bitCast(p), .little)`. Here, `@bitCast()` acts as a zero-cost reinterpretation, tricking the compiler into treating the `Person` struct as a raw `u16` integer. By specifying `.little` (Little-Endian), the code explicitly controls the byte order — writing the least significant byte first — which is essential for cross-platform compatibility. Finally, the program verifies this process by creating a reader, pulling the integer back from the raw bytes using the same endianness and bitcasting it back into a `Person` struct, proving that the original data has been perfectly preserved through the round-trip conversion. This can be verified by running `ch03/bigLittle.zig`:

```
$ zig run ch03/bigLittle.zig
Written: { 20, 100 }
Read: .{ .age = 20, .value = 100 }
```

The output validates the mechanism of Little-Endian serialization. The first line reveals the raw byte layout in memory. Because `Person` is a *packed struct*, the compiler placed age (20) into the lower 8 bits and `value` (100) into the upper 8 bits of the backing `u16`. When `writeInt()` serialized this integer using Little-Endian mode (`.little`), it wrote the Least Significant Byte (the lower bits containing age) first, followed by the Most Significant Byte (`value`). This is why you see 20 followed by 100 in the byte stream. The second line confirms the successful reversal of this process: the reader consumed those bytes in the exact same Little-Endian order, reconstructing the original 16-bit integer and bitcasting it back into a Person struct with the fields intact.

While reading integers byte-by-byte gives us granular control, it quickly becomes tedious and error-prone when dealing with complex file headers containing dozens of fields. Instead of manually stitching together every u16 or u32 from raw indices, Zig offers a far more powerful and expressive approach: mapping the binary layout directly to our code. In the next section, we will explore how to define extern structs.

Casting raw byte slices to structured data types

One of the most frequent tasks in Systems Programming is interpreting a raw stream of bytes as a structured data type. Whether you are parsing a binary network protocol, reading a file header, or decoding a hardware register, you often start with a generic []u8 slice and need to treat it as a specific struct to access fields like header.version or packet.id. Zig provides powerful tools to bridge this gap, allowing you to either "view" the raw memory directly as a struct or safely deserialize it into a new variable. However, this capability comes with strict responsibilities regarding memory alignment and safety, which the language enforces explicitly to prevent the subtle, architecture-dependent bugs that frequently plague C and C++ codebases. Unlike normal structs, where the compiler is free to rearrange fields to optimize for CPU cache lines, an extern struct guarantees that the fields remain in the exact order they are defined. This rigid layout allows us to define a Zig type like EOCD that perfectly mirrors the byte sequence of the ZIP End of Central Directory record, turning a stream of hex codes into meaningful fields like disk_num and cd_offset.

Look at the code of ch03/castRawBytes.zig, which begins as follows – this illustrates the preparation required to interpret raw memory as a structured type in Zig:

```
const std = @import("std");

const Header = extern struct {
    magic: u16,
    version: u8,
    command: u8,
};

pub fn main(_: std.process.Init.Minimal) !void {
    const err = std.debug;
```

```
const raw_bytes align(@alignOf(Header)) = [_]u8{
    0x34,
    0x12,
    0x01,
    0x05,
};
const slice: []constu8=&raw_bytes;
```

We begin by defining an `extern` structure named `Header`. The `extern` keyword is crucial here as it guarantees a specific, C-compatible memory layout, ensuring the fields `magic` (2 bytes), `version` (1 byte), and `command` (1 byte) appear in that exact order. The most significant detail in `main()` is the alignment directive attached to the `raw_bytes` array: `align(@alignOf(Header))`. By default, an array of `u8` can be placed at any memory address (1-byte alignment). However, our `Header` struct contains a `u16`, which typically requires an even memory address (2-byte alignment) for efficient CPU access. By strictly enforcing this alignment on the source array, we satisfy the safety requirements needed to cast these raw bytes into a `Header` pointer later, preventing potential runtime crashes or undefined behavior associated with misaligned memory access.

The next snippet demonstrates the *unsafe* but *highly efficient* way to parse binary data: *pointer casting*. Instead of reading bytes one by one and copying them into a new variable, we simply tell the compiler to treat the existing memory address of the byte array as if it were already a `Header` struct:

```
const header_ptr: *const Header = @ptrCast(@alignCast(slice.ptr));
err.print("Method 1 (Pointer Cast):\n", .{});
err.print(
    "  Magic: 0x{X}, Cmd: {}\n",
    .{ header_ptr.magic, header_ptr.command },
);
```

The transformation happens in two specific steps. First, `@alignCast()` acts as a runtime assertion, verifying that the memory address of `slice.ptr` satisfies the alignment requirements of the `Header` struct. This is why the `align` directive in the previous snippet was mandatory; without it, this cast could trigger a panic or undefined behavior. Second, `@ptrCast()` performs the actual type reinterpretation, converting the pointer from "*many bytes*" to "*single struct*". When we print `header_ptr.magic`, the CPU reads bytes `0x34` and `0x12` directly from the array. Because most modern CPUs are Little Endian, this sequence is interpreted as the integer `0x1234`, demonstrating that this method implicitly relies on the native endianness matching the data format.

The second method solves the alignment dangers of the pointer-casting approach:

```
    const big_buffer = [_]u8{ 0xFF, 0x34, 0x12, 0x01, 0x05 };
    const unaligned_slice = big_buffer[1..5];
    const safe_header = std.mem.bytesToValue(Header, unaligned_slice);

    err.print("\nMethod 2 (bytesToValue):\n", .{});
    err.print(
        "  Magic: 0x{X}, Cmd: {}\n",
        .{ safe_header.magic, safe_header.command },
    );
}
```

First, we create a *misalignment scenario*: `big_buffer` creates an array and `unaligned_slice` starts reading from index `1` – the extra byte (`0xFF`) at the beginning is a deliberate trick to force a misaligned memory address. Because the CPU often expects multi-byte integers (like the `u16` in our `Header`) to sit at even memory addresses, pointing a `Header` pointer directly at index 1 (an odd address) would be illegal and could cause a crash on many architectures. `std.mem.bytesToValue()` sidesteps this problem entirely. Instead of trying to "overlay" a struct definition onto the existing raw memory, it reads the bytes from the slice and copies them into a completely new `Header` instance created safely on the stack. This operation effectively works like a `memcpy(3)`. While it involves a small performance cost due to the copying, it is robust: it works perfectly even if the source data is at an odd memory address, making it ideal for parsing packed file formats where data fields are crunched together without padding. Note, however, that like the previous method, this still performs a raw copy, so it interprets the bytes (`0x34`, `0x12`) using the native endianness (resulting in `0x1234` on Little Endian systems).

Now, execute `ch03/castRawBytes.zig` to see its magic in action:

```
$ zig run ch03/castRawBytes.zig
Method 1 (Pointer Cast):
  Magic: 0x1234, Cmd: 5

Method 2 (bytesToValue):
  Magic: 0x1234, Cmd: 5
```

You can see here that the mapping of specific bytes to specific fields is determined entirely by the `extern struct` definition. Whether you use Method 1 (which looks at the bytes directly in their original location) or Method 2 (which copies the bytes into a new location first), the rule remains the same: the first 2 bytes always fill the `magic` field, the 3rd byte fills `version`, and the 4th byte fills `command`. *The only difference between the methods is safety — Method 1 requires the original data to be perfectly aligned in memory, while Method 2 safely handles messy, unaligned data by copying it first.*

On architectures such as ARM or SPARC memory alignment is a strict hardware requirement. Accessing a multi-byte type like a `u16` or `u64` from a memory address that is not a multiple of its size can trigger a CPU fault, causing the application to crash instantly. Zig prevents this class of errors by encoding alignment directly into the pointer type, refusing to implicitly cast a generic, 1-byte aligned `[*]u8` into a strictly aligned struct pointer. This forces a deliberate architectural choice: you must either guarantee the buffer's physical alignment and assert it via `@alignCast()` for high-performance zero-copy access or accept the minor overhead of `std.mem.bytesToValue()` to safely deserialize unaligned data into a fresh variable.

With a solid grasp of how to cast raw bytes into structured data, we have learned the mechanics of low-level memory management. However, in systems programming, the true differentiator is efficiency. It is not enough to simply allocate memory; we must *understand the latency and throughput implications* of those allocations under load.

Benchmarking memory allocators

Knowing which allocator to reach for is one skill. Knowing by how much it matters in your specific workload is another. Intuition about allocator performance is notoriously unreliable — developers frequently over-engineer allocation strategies for code that is not allocation-bound and equally frequently leave genuine bottlenecks untouched because the cost was never measured. The only way to reason confidently about allocator choice is to benchmark it under conditions that resemble your actual workload: the same data sizes, the same iteration patterns, the same hardware. That is what this section does. The four allocators measured here — `DebugAllocator`, `PageAllocator`, `FixedBufferAllocator`, and `ArenaAllocator` — all satisfy the same `std.mem.Allocator` interface and all produce correct results. The benchmark exists to quantify how differently they produce those results, turning the abstract tradeoffs discussed in the previous section into concrete microsecond numbers. So, in this section, we transition from implementation to measurement. By quantifying the performance delta between different memory allocators, we demonstrate that memory management is not just a safety concern but a critical optimization lever. The program of this section establishes a benchmarking framework designed to compare its memory allocators against each other under identical conditions.

The first code snippet of `ch03/benchMemoryAllocators.zig` is the following:

```
const std = @import("std");
```

```
const KiB = 1024;
const MiB = 1024 * 1024;

fn benchmarkStandard(
    io: std.Io,
    allocator: std.mem.Allocator,
    name: []const u8,
    count: usize,
    repeat: usize,
) !void {
    var total_alloc_ns: u64 = 0;

    for (0..repeat) |_| {
        const t_start = std.Io.Timestamp.now(io, .awake);
        const arr = try allocator.alloc(i32, count);
        const elapsed: u64 =
@intCast(t_start.durationTo(std.Io.Timestamp.now(io, .awake)).nanoseconds);

        total_alloc_ns += elapsed;
        allocator.free(arr);
    }

    printStats(name, count, repeat, total_alloc_ns);
}
```

The core of our testing suite is the `benchmarkStandard()` function. It is designed to be generic, accepting any `std.mem.Allocator` interface, which allows us to pass in different allocator implementations without changing the test logic. The benchmarking code uses `std.Io.Timestamp`, Zig 0.16's replacement for the older `std.time.nanoTimestamp()`. Four elements work together to measure elapsed time. `std.Io.Timestamp.now(io, .awake)` captures the current timestamp using the wall-clock source — the `.awake` argument selects real elapsed time excluding any time the process spent sleeping or suspended, which is exactly what you want for a performance measurement. Taking two timestamps, one before the operation and one after, then calling `.durationTo()` on the first computes the interval between them as a `Duration` value. Finally, `.nanoseconds` converts that duration to a plain integer nanosecond count that can be accumulated across iterations and divided to produce a mean. This four-step pattern — now, now, `durationTo`, `.nanoseconds` — is the standard timing idiom in Zig 0.16 and replaces the subtract-two-integers approach that `std.time.nanoTimestamp()` required.

The function runs a loop determined by the repeat parameter to average out system noise. Inside each iteration, the critical performance metric is captured by recording a `std.Io.Timestamp` immediately before the `allocator.alloc()` call and another immediately after, then computing the elapsed nanoseconds via `.durationTo()`, isolating the measurement strictly to the allocation cost. The `allocator.free(arr)` call is placed after the timer reading. This separation ensures that we are benchmarking only the "cost of asking" for memory, not the "cost of cleaning up," which might vary independently.

The next function tests the Arena Allocator only. We require a separate function for the Arena Allocator because it follows a unique memory lifecycle that is incompatible with the symmetrical `alloc/free` pattern of the standard benchmark. While `benchmarkStandard()` relies on calling `free()` to reclaim memory after every iteration, the Arena is designed to ignore individual free requests, meaning the standard loop would simply accumulate memory indefinitely until the program crashed from exhaustion. Furthermore, the ability of Arena to instantly recycle pre-allocated memory for the next cycle relies on the specific `arena.reset(.retain_capacity)` method. Since this reset functionality is not part of the generic `std.mem.Allocator` interface, we need a dedicated function to access the Arena struct directly and simulate the high-speed "frame reuse" pattern that makes this allocator so efficient:

```
fn benchmarkArena(
    io: std.Io,
    parent_allocator: std.mem.Allocator,
    name: []const u8,
    count: usize,
    repeat: usize,
) !void {
    var total_alloc_ns: u64 = 0;
    var arena = std.heap.ArenaAllocator.init(parent_allocator);
    defer arena.deinit();
    const allocator = arena.allocator();

    for (0..repeat) |_| {
        const t_start = std.Io.Timestamp.now(io, .awake);
        _ = try allocator.alloc(i32, count);

        const elapsed: u64 =
@intCast(t_start.durationTo(std.Io.Timestamp.now(io, .awake)).nanoseconds);
        total_alloc_ns += elapsed;
        _ = arena.reset(.retain_capacity);
    }
```

```
        printStats(name, count, repeat, total_alloc_ns);
    }
```

Here we initialize the `ArenaAllocator` once outside the loop. Inside the timing block, the allocation (`allocator.alloc()`) is incredibly fast because the arena simply advances an internal pointer rather than searching for a free block or making expensive system calls. The crucial difference lies in how memory is reclaimed. As discussed, instead of freeing the array individually, we call `arena.reset(.retain_capacity)` at the end of each iteration. This method rewinds the arena's internal pointer to the beginning without returning the memory to the operating system. This means that for every loop iteration after the first one, the allocator is reusing the exact same block of pre-allocated memory. This simulates a high-performance "frame allocator" pattern often used in game loops or request handlers, where memory is used temporarily and then wiped clean for the next cycle. Next, a helper function serves as the reporting engine for our benchmark suite:

```
fn printStats(
    name: []const u8,
    count: usize,
    repeat: usize,
    total_ns: u64,
) void {
    const totalBytes = count * @sizeOf(i32);
    const totalMib = @as(f64, @floatFromInt(totalBytes))/@as(f64, MiB);
    const mean_alloc_us = (total_ns / repeat) / 1_000;

    std.debug.print(
        "{s:24}: {d:6.2} MiB x {d:2} -> alloc: {d:5} µs\n",
        .{ name, totalMib, repeat, mean_alloc_us },
    );
}
```

First, the code converts count into a MiB value, giving us a clear sense of the memory volume involved. Then, it calculates the mean latency by averaging the total accumulated nanoseconds over the number of repetitions and scaling the result down to microseconds (µs), which is a more readable unit for system operations. The final `std.debug.print()` aligns the output into columns, ensuring that when the different benchmarks run sequentially, their results stack perfectly for easy visual analysis.

Next, we present the first part of `main()`, which allows us to tweak test parameters directly from the command line:

```
pub fn main(init: std.process.Init) !void {
    const allocator = std.heap.page_allocator;
    const args = try init.minimal.args.toSlice(init.arena.allocator());
    const default_count: usize = 10_000_000;
    const default_repeat: usize = 10;

    var count: usize = default_count;
    var repeat: usize = default_repeat;
    if (args.len >= 2) count = try std.fmt.parseInt(usize, args[1], 10);
    if (args.len >= 3) repeat = try std.fmt.parseInt(usize, args[2], 10);
```

We begin by fetching and parsing the command-line arguments via `init.minimal.args.toSlice()`. The program defines robust defaults but includes logic to override these values. By checking `args.len` and parsing the subsequent strings into `usize` integers, the script allows us to scale the test down for quick checks or up for heavy stress testing.

The program concludes by arranging a direct head-to-head comparison of four distinct memory management strategies:

```
    std.debug.print(
        "  - Benchmarking allocators: {d} i32s x {d} runs -   \n",
        .{ count, repeat },
    );
    // 1. Debug Allocator (formerly GeneralPurposeAllocator)
    var gpa_state: std.heap.DebugAllocator(.{}) = .init;
    defer _ = gpa_state.deinit();
    try benchmarkStandard(
        init.io,
        gpa_state.allocator(),
        "DebugAllocator",
        count,
        repeat,
    );

    // 2. Page Allocator
    try benchmarkStandard(
        init.io,
        std.heap.page_allocator,
```

```
            "PageAllocator",
            count,
            repeat,
        );

        // 3. Fixed Buffer Allocator (Stack based for speed)
        const fba_size = 64 * MiB;
        const backing_buffer = try std.heap.page_allocator.alloc(u8, fba_size);
        defer std.heap.page_allocator.free(backing_buffer);
        var fba = std.heap.FixedBufferAllocator.init(backing_buffer);
        try benchmarkStandard(
            init.io,
            fba.allocator(),
            "FixedBufferAllocator",
            count,
            repeat,
        );

        // 4. Arena Allocator (uses specialized function)
        try benchmarkArena(
            init.io,
            allocator,
            "ArenaAllocator",
            count,
            repeat,
        );
    }
```

After printing the test parameters, it first benchmarks the Debug Allocator (formerly `GeneralPurposeAllocator`), which balances performance with safety features like leak detection. It then tests the `PageAllocator`, which interacts directly with the operating system kernel, often serving as a slower baseline due to the overhead of system calls. To test the `FixedBufferAllocator`, the code must first manually allocate a large 64 MiB backing buffer; this upfront cost allows the FBA to subsequently issue memory with blazing speed by simply subdividing that pre-existing block. Finally, the suite calls our specialized `benchmarkArena()` function.

It is time to see our benchmark in action by running `ch03/benchMemoryAllocators.zig`:

```
$ zig run ch03/benchMemoryAllocators.zig
  - Benchmarking allocators: 10000000 i32s x 10 runs -
         DebugAllocator:  38.15 MiB x 10 -> alloc:  2711 µs
          PageAllocator:  38.15 MiB x 10 -> alloc:  1888 µs
   FixedBufferAllocator:  38.15 MiB x 10 -> alloc:   343 µs
         ArenaAllocator:  38.15 MiB x 10 -> alloc:   476 µs
```

The Debug Allocator (2711 µs) is the slowest, which is expected; it is doing the most work behind the scenes, managing bucket sizes and tracking allocations to provide safety features like leak detection. Interestingly, the `PageAllocator` (1888 µs) is faster here because our allocation size is very large; requesting one massive block directly from the OS is relatively efficient compared to the `DebugAllocator` internal bookkeeping for smaller objects. However, the real story is the order-of-magnitude leap in performance with the `FixedBufferAllocator` (343 µs) and `ArenaAllocator` (476 µs). Both are nearly 5x to 8x faster than the standard allocators. This speed comes from their simplicity: they do not search for free space; they merely increment a pointer. The FBA is the absolute fastest because it has zero overhead, as it just slices a pre-existing array. The Arena is a close second, with only a tiny overhead for managing its list of memory nodes. This confirms that for high-performance loops (like game frames or request handlers), pre-allocated strategies are vastly superior to general-purpose malloc-style calls.

The numbers deserve a closer reading than *faster is better*. The `DebugAllocator` 2711 µs is not a waste — it is the cost of the safety guarantees it provides. Every allocation it makes is tracked in an internal metadata structure so that `deinit()` can report any that were never freed. In a development build, that cost is worth paying unconditionally. The question is never "should I use `DebugAllocator` in production?" — you should not — but rather "what is the actual penalty of leaving it in during development?" The answer, here, is roughly 800 µs over ten rounds compared to `PageAllocator`, which is a rounding error on human perception and well worth the leak detection it buys.

The `PageAllocator` result is the most instructive in terms of what it reveals about OS interaction. At 1888 µs it is faster than `DebugAllocator` despite doing something more expensive at the kernel level — it issues a system call to request memory pages from the OS directly. The reason it wins is that our benchmark allocation is large: 10 million `i32` values is roughly 38 MiB, and requesting one contiguous 38 MiB block from the kernel is cheaper than asking `DebugAllocator` to bookkeep it across its internal bucket structure. This result would invert for small, frequent allocations. If the benchmark allocated 10 bytes at a time across a million iterations,

`PageAllocator` would lose badly because the syscall overhead per allocation would dominate. Allocator performance is not absolute — it is load-shaped.

The gap between `FixedBufferAllocator` at 343 µs and `ArenaAllocator` at 476 µs is also worth examining. Both use bump-pointer allocation — advancing an internal offset rather than searching for free space — and both avoid syscalls after their initial setup. The `FixedBufferAllocator` advantage comes from having zero bookkeeping: it is a pointer, a length, and nothing else. The `ArenaAllocator` maintains a linked list of backing blocks so it can grow beyond a fixed size, and that list management introduces a small but measurable overhead. If you know your upper memory bound in advance and it fits on the stack or in a pre-allocated buffer, `FixedBufferAllocator` is the right choice. If you need the arena's ability to grow dynamically, the 133 µs premium is a reasonable price.

One thing the benchmark does not measure is *fragmentation*. Over a long-running process with many small allocations and frees of varying sizes, the `DebugAllocator` and `PageAllocator` can develop fragmented heaps where large contiguous allocations fail even though sufficient total free memory exists. The `ArenaAllocator` and `FixedBufferAllocator` are structurally immune to fragmentation because they never reuse freed space within a session — they only move forward. For long-running servers and background services, this immunity can matter more than raw allocation speed.

Summary

By mastering pointers and memory allocators, you have unlocked the core capability of systems programming: *total control over memory*. We have navigated the architectural trade-offs between the stack and the heap, built a custom allocator to demystify how memory is managed under the hood, and applied these concepts to decode the raw binary structure of a Zip file. Additionally, our benchmarks demonstrated that the choice of allocator is a critical performance decision. With these tools in hand, you are no longer limited to the memory management strategies dictated by the standard library; you can now architect solutions that are precisely tuned to the lifecycle and performance requirements of your specific application. Keep in mind that *pointers can create nasty bugs and program crashes*. If you are lucky and your program cannot compile, you are going to find the cause of your bug(s) early. However, if you are not lucky and you are using pointers carelessly, then you are in real trouble! Be particularly careful with pointer arithmetic and do not use pointers without knowing exactly what you are doing. Ask any C software engineer about pointers!

In the next chapter, we are going to learn how to build high-performance data pipelines by mastering the stream and buffer capabilities of Zig. We will start by building `zcat`, a tool that teaches us to efficiently pipe raw data between file descriptors. From there, we will tackle `zwc` to explore high-speed text counting and finally z64, where we will use bitwise operations to implement a custom Base64 encoder and decoder. Finally, we are going to benchmark reading and writing operations!

Exercises

- Modify `ch03/bigLittle.zig` to use big-endian.
- Write `sumArray()` that accepts a many-item pointer (`[*]const i32`) and a length, then calculates the total sum of the elements. The strict constraint here is that you are forbidden from using the square bracket index operator; instead, you must construct a loop that either physically increments the pointer variable itself (`ptr += 1`) in each iteration or calculates the explicit address offset manually to dereference the value. Test your code with an array containing the values `10`, `20`, `30`, `40`, `50`, ensuring the result is `150`.
- Imagine you are processing a raw buffer defined as `const raw = [_]u8{ 0xFF, 0x01, 0x00, 0x05, 0x00 }`, where the first byte `0xFF` is irrelevant padding and the valid payload begins at index 1. Define a packed struct named `Packet` containing two `u16` fields (an ID and a set of flags). Your goal is to create a slice starting at the second byte (`raw[1..]`) and decode it into a `Packet` instance. Because this slice begins at an odd memory address, a direct pointer cast would be unsafe on many architectures; therefore, you must utilize `std.mem.bytesToValue()` to safely deserialize the unaligned bytes into a fresh struct, printing the fields to verify that the ID is `1` and the flags are `5`.

Additional resources

- Endianness: `https://en.wikipedia.org/wiki/Endianness`

4

Processing Streams, Buffers, and Data Encoding

Data flows in from various sources through command-line utilities and transforms on the fly before ever touching permanent storage. In this chapter, we shift our focus to **stream processing** with a single unifying question behind every tool we build: how fast can we make it, and why? This is performance-oriented systems programming — the discipline of understanding not just whether code is correct, but whether it is working with the hardware or against it. We will build a suite of classic UNIX tools to explore how Zig handles I/O efficiency, moving beyond simple file reading to master the art of buffering, understand the high cost of system calls, harness the power of SIMD instructions for data-parallel processing, and implement high-performance encoding logic using bitwise operations. By the end of the chapter, every benchmark result will have an explanation rooted in hardware behavior, and every design decision will have a measurable consequence.

So, this chapter covers:

- Implementing `zcat`
- Implementing `zwc`
- Implementing `z64` for Base64 encoding and decoding
- Benchmarking reading and writing operations

Developing zcat

We begin this chapter by creating a `cat(1)` clone. In the first part of `ch04/zcat.zig`, the `main()` function establishes the memory strategy and routes data streams before any actual processing begins:

```
const std = @import("std");

pub fn main(init: std.process.Init) !void {
    var arena = std.heap.ArenaAllocator.init(std.heap.page_allocator);
    defer arena.deinit();
    const allocator = arena.allocator();
    const stdout = std.Io.File.stdout();
    const stderr = std.Io.File.stderr();
    const args = try init.minimal.args.toSlice(allocator);

    if (args.len == 1) {
        try catStream(init.io, std.Io.File.stdin(), stdout);
    } else {
        var i: usize = 1;
        while (i < args.len) : (i += 1) {
            const path = args[i];
            const file = std.Io.Dir.cwd().openFile(
                init.io,
                path,
                .{},
            ) catch |err| {
                const msg = try std.fmt.allocPrint(
                    allocator,
                    "cat: {s}: {s}\n",
                    .{ path, @errorName(err) },
                );
                try stderr.writeStreamingAll(init.io, msg);
                continue;
            };
            defer file.close(init.io);
            try catStream(init.io, file, stdout);
        }
    }
}
```

The code begins by setting up an `ArenaAllocator`, which provides a simple way to manage memory without tracking individual allocations; when the function returns, the `defer` statement ensures that all memory used for arguments or error messages is reclaimed at once. This approach avoids the complexity of manual memory management for short-lived tasks. After that, the program retrieves command-line arguments and checks their count to decide between reading from standard input or processing a list of paths. When paths are provided, a loop iterates through each one, skipping the program name at the first index. For each path, the utility attempts to open the file relative to the current working directory. If a file cannot be opened, an error message is printed to standard error, and the loop continues, allowing the program to process any remaining files. The `defer file.close()` statement inside the loop ensures that each file descriptor is closed as soon as its contents are processed, preventing resource exhaustion during long runs. Finally, valid files are passed to the `catStream()` function, which serves as the core data transfer engine, designed to be generic enough to handle any input or output source:

```
fn catStream(
    io: std.Io,
    reader: std.Io.File,
    writer: std.Io.File,
) !void {
    var buf: [128]u8 = undefined;
    while (true) {
        const n = reader.readStreaming(io, &.{&buf}) catch |err| {
            if (err == error.EndOfStream) break;
            return err;
        };
        try writer.writeStreamingAll(io, buf[0..n]);
    }
}
```

The `catStream()` function defines a small, fixed-size buffer on the stack, which serves as temporary storage and avoids the need for heap allocation. Within a continuous loop, the function calls `readStreaming()` to pull data into this buffer. In Zig 0.16, `readStreaming()` signals end-of-file by returning `error.EndOfStream` rather than a zero byte count, so the call is wrapped in a `catch` block that breaks the loop cleanly on that specific error while propagating any other unexpected error to the caller. If bytes are successfully read, the function then calls `writeStreamingAll()` to push that specific subset of the buffer to the output. By using the `buf[0..n]` slice, the code ensures that only the valid portion of the buffer is transmitted, preventing the output of stale data from previous iterations. This iterative approach allows the utility to process files of any size while maintaining a constant, minimal memory footprint.

Try `ch04/zcat.zig` on your machine by giving it input from standard input:

```
$ zig run ch04/zcat.zig
Test
Test
Bye!
Bye!
```

Everything works as expected. Although `ch04/zcat.zig` is correct, we can make it more efficient by utilizing a larger buffer and a different approach.

The cost of system calls

In this subsection, we see why buffered writing matters even on simple programs like `zcat.zig`. The updated version of `zcat.zig` is called `ch04/zcatBuffer.zig` and uses optimized buffering to speed up its operation. Put simply, it adapts its behavior to the environment, solving the tension between seeing data immediately and moving data fast. When you pipe data, the standard output is not a terminal, so the program detects this via `isTty()` and disables line scanning, filling the 4KB buffer completely before issuing a single `write()` system call. When the output is to a terminal, the program enables line scanning, which results in higher system call overhead (most likely one per line) but guarantees immediate responsiveness, ensuring you see log entries the moment they are processed rather than waiting for 4KB of data to accumulate.

Here is the first part of `ch04/zcatBuffer.zig`, which is the preparation stage:

```
const std = @import("std");

pub fn main(init: std.process.Init) !void {
    var arena = std.heap.ArenaAllocator.init(std.heap.page_allocator);
    defer arena.deinit();
    const allocator = arena.allocator();
    const stdout_file = std.Io.File.stdout();
    const stderr_file = std.Io.File.stderr();
    var stdout_buf: [4096]u8 = undefined;
    var stdout_impl = stdout_file.writer(init.io,&stdout_buf);
    const stdout=&stdout_impl.interface;
    var stderr_impl = stderr_file.writer(init.io, &.{});
    conststderr=&stderr_impl.interface;
    const is_terminal = try stdout_file.isTty(init.io);
```

The core of the optimization lies in how the writers are constructed. We allocate a 4096-byte array (`stdout_buf`) directly on the stack to serve as our intermediate storage. The variable `stdout_impl` is a writer structure that uses this stack array for buffering. Then we define `stdout` by taking the address of the interface field (`&stdout_impl.interface`). We repeat a similar process for standard error, but we pass an empty slice (`&.{}`) to create an unbuffered writer, ensuring error messages are displayed immediately without waiting for a buffer to fill. Finally, the code determines the execution context by calling `stdout_file.isTty()`, which queries the operating system to see if the standard output is connected to an interactive terminal or a file/pipe. Note that `isTty()` returns `Cancelable!bool` and requires `try`. The result is stored in the `is_terminal` flag, which controls our smart buffering strategy: when `true`, the program enables line scanning to flush output immediately after each newline, giving interactive users instant feedback; when `false`, it skips that check entirely and lets the buffer fill completely before writing, maximizing throughput for piped or redirected output. As before, the program continues by looking at the given command-line arguments.

Two things worth noticing here. First, stderr is created with an empty buffer slice (`&.{}`), which is the idiomatic way to opt out of buffering entirely. When the internal buffer has zero capacity, the writer has nowhere to accumulate data, so every `writeAll` call goes directly to the OS as its own `write(2)` syscall. This is the right choice for `stderr`: error messages must appear immediately, regardless of whether a flush has been issued. Second, `stdout`, by contrast, gets a 4 096-byte buffer. That buffer lets the writer coalesce many small writes into fewer, larger syscalls, which matters for throughput when printing file contents. The trade-off is that a manual `flush()` is required at the end of `main()` to drain any bytes still held in the buffer before the program exits. If stderr were buffered the same way as `stdout`, a fatal error message could sit unprinted in the buffer and never reach the terminal — for example, if the program crashes or exits before the buffer is flushed. Unbuffered `stderr` is a long-standing UNIX convention for exactly this reason.

The listing above shows the argument parsing and setup portion of `main()`. Two details in the remainder of the function are worth calling out explicitly, even though the full listing is available in the repository. First, the `is_terminal` flag computed here is passed to `catStream()` to control whether ANSI color codes are emitted — piping to a file should never produce escape sequences, but printing to a terminal can. Second, `main()` calls try `stdout.flush()` after all `catStream()` calls complete. This is not optional. The buffered writer accumulates bytes in a 4096-byte stack buffer and only writes to the OS when that buffer is full or when `flush()` is called explicitly. Without the final `flush()`, any bytes remaining in the buffer when `main()` returns are silently dropped — the program exits cleanly, the output appears truncated, and there is no error message to explain why. Forgetting `flush()` is the most common bug with buffered I/O, and it is particularly insidious because it only manifests when the total output is not an exact multiple of the buffer size.

Next, here is the updated `catStream()` implementation:

```
fn catStream(
    io: std.Io,
    reader: std.Io.File,
    writer: anytype,
    line_buffer: bool,
) !void {
    var buf: [4096]u8 = undefined;
    while (true) {
        const n = reader.readStreaming(io, &.{&buf}) catch |err| {
            if (err == error.EndOfStream) break;
            return err;
        };
        if (n == 0) break;

        const chunk = buf[0..n];
        try writer.writeAll(chunk);
        if (line_buffer) {
            if (std.mem.indexOfScalar(u8, chunk, '\n') != null) {
                try writer.flush();
            }
        }
    }
}
```

The code repeatedly calls `reader.readStreaming(io, &.{&buf})`, which fills the buffer with available data and returns the number of bytes read. In Zig 0.16, end-of-file is signaled by `error.EndOfStream` rather than a zero byte count, so the call is wrapped in a `catch` block that breaks the loop cleanly on that specific error while propagating any other unexpected error to the caller. The valid data is extracted via `const chunk = buf[0..n]` and passed to `writer.writeAll(chunk)` to ensure only the bytes actually read in this iteration are transmitted, not stale data from a previous loop. If `line_buffer` is set (indicating an *interactive terminal output*), the function scans this chunk for a newline character using `std.mem.indexOfScalar()`; if found, it triggers `writer.flush()`, forcing the buffered data to appear on screen without delay, while non-interactive destinations skip this check to maximize throughput. Efficiency at its best!

We suspect that `ch04/zcatBuffer.zig` is more efficient than `ch04/zcat.zig` but we cannot prove that this is true without comparing them – the first command creates a big file that we are going to be using, whereas the next two commands create executable binaries for each program. The last command does the actual testing using `hyperfine`:

```
$ dd if=/dev/urandom of=/tmp/bigfile.dat bs=1M count=1000
$ zig build-exe ch04/zcat.zig -O ReleaseFast -femit-bin=zcat
$ zig build-exe ch04/zcatBuffer.zig -O ReleaseFast -femit-bin=zcatBuffer
$ hyperfine --warmup 3 \
  "./zcat /tmp/bigfile.dat > /dev/null" \
  "./zcatBuffer /tmp/bigfile.dat > /dev/null"
Benchmark 1: ./zcat /tmp/bigfile.dat > /dev/null
  Time (mean ± σ):   5.247 s ±  0.052 s [User: 1.100 s, System: 4.145 s]
  Range (min … max):    5.169 s …  5.320 s    10 runs

Benchmark 2: ./zcatBuffer /tmp/bigfile.dat > /dev/null
  Time (mean ± σ): 206.1 ms ±  1.2 ms [User: 44.1 ms, System: 159.8 ms]
  Range (min … max):   203.6 ms … 208.0 ms    13 runs

Summary
  ./zcatBuffer /tmp/bigfile.dat > /dev/null ran
   25.46 ± 0.29 times faster than ./zcat /tmp/bigfile.dat > /dev/null
```

The results show a massive `25.46x` speedup when using larger buffering. The `zcat` binary took `5.25` seconds to process the file, but the most revealing metric is the "System" time of `4.145` seconds. This indicates that the program spent nearly `80%` of its total execution time waiting for the operating system kernel to handle individual read and write requests.

The moral of the story is that efficiency is not about how fast you work but how rarely you are interrupted. By loading 4KB or more into memory, you reduce the number of interruptions by thousands. So, always batch your I/O operations to keep the CPU doing actual work instead of waiting on the kernel. With the foundations of efficient, buffered file reading now in place, we can shift our focus from merely moving data to analyzing it by building zwc, a high-performance clone of the standard `wc(1)` utility.

Developing zwc, a wc(1) clone

Implementing `wc(1)` is a great exercise in file reading and processing. However, in this section, we are going to take it to the next level, as we are going to present a version that uses SIMD commands, which makes it extremely fast! But first, let us show the rational implementation, starting with a function that counts lines, words, and characters.

Counting lines, words, and characters

The `Counts` struct is a simple data container designed to hold the statistical results of the text analysis. It comprises three public fields of type `usize`: `lines`, `words`, and `bytes`, which serve as accumulators for the number of newline characters, whitespace-delimited words, and total bytes processed, respectively. The design choice worth noting before entering the implementation is that all three counters are updated in a single pass over the input. A naive implementation might count lines first, then rewind and count words, then rewind again for bytes — three passes, three times the I/O cost. By accumulating all three metrics simultaneously as bytes arrive from the stream, `zwc` touches each byte exactly once regardless of input size. For small files, this is a minor concern, but for a tool designed to process large log files or piped output from other commands, single-pass processing is the difference between a tool that keeps up with the data and one that becomes the bottleneck. The struct is the architectural expression of that commitment: one pass, one set of accumulators, one result.

So, we use a single function for counting lines, words, and characters on a per-file basis. This is important because we access the input only once. Here is `processStream()` from `ch04/zwc.zig` used for processing the input, which is read from a file or standard input:

```
fn processStream(io: std.Io, file: std.Io.File) !Counts {
    var buffer: [16 * 1024]u8 = undefined;
    var lines: usize = 0;
    var words: usize = 0;
    var bytes: usize = 0;
    var in_word = false;

    while (true) {
        const n = file.readStreaming(io, &.{&buffer}) catch |err| {
            if (err == error.EndOfStream) break;
            return err;
        };
        if (n == 0) break;
        bytes += n;
        for (buffer[0..n]) |c| {
            if (c == '\n') {
                lines += 1;
            }
            if (std.ascii.isWhitespace(c)) {
```

```
                in_word = false;
            } else if (!in_word) {
                in_word = true;
                words += 1;
            }
        }
    }
    return Counts{ .lines = lines, .words = words, .bytes = bytes };
}
```

The `processStream()` computes line, word, and byte counts from an input source using a 16KB buffer. It begins by initializing counters and a flag, `in_word`, which tracks whether the parser is currently inside a word or not. The function then enters a loop that continuously reads from the provided `reader` into a stack-allocated buffer until the end of the stream is reached. A line is counted whenever a newline character (`\n`) is encountered, whereas for word counting, the logic detects transitions: if the current character is whitespace, the state is reset to *not in a word*; if it is a non-whitespace character and the previous state was *not in a word*, it registers the start of a new word and increments the counter. This ensures that multiple spaces between words do not trigger false counts. The function finally returns the aggregated statistics in a `Counts` struct. Next, we present the remaining code, starting with the `printCounts()` function that is responsible for printing totals:

```
fn printCounts(
    writer: anytype,
    counts: Counts,
    filename: []const u8,
    showLines: bool,
    showWords: bool,
    showBytes: bool,
) !void {
    if (showLines) {
        try writer.print("{d: >12}", .{counts.lines});
    }
    if (showWords) {
        try writer.print("{d: >12}", .{counts.words});
    }
    if (showBytes) {
        try writer.print("{d: >12}", .{counts.bytes});
    }
    if (filename.len != 0) {
```

```
        try writer.print(" {s}", .{filename});
    }
    try writer.writeByte('\n');
}
```

The function accepts a `Counts` struct containing the tallied values and three Boolean flags (`showLines`, `showWords`, and `showBytes`), which determine which metrics are displayed. For each enabled metric, the function prints the corresponding count right-aligned within a field width of 12 spaces, ensuring neat columnar alignment even for large numbers. Finally, if a filename is provided, it is appended to the line, and the output is terminated with a newline character, mimicking the standard format of the `wc(1)` utility.

The `main()` function serves as the entry point for the utility, orchestrating initialization, argument parsing, and file processing. The function inspects command-line arguments to determine which metrics to display; if a flag string is detected, it selectively enables counting for lines, words, or bytes, otherwise defaulting to showing all three. Depending on the remaining arguments, the program either processes data from standard input or iterates through a list of provided file paths. For each file, it calculates statistics using `processStream()`, prints the individual results, and accumulates them into a global total. If multiple files are processed, the function concludes by printing an aggregated `total` line, providing a summary across all inputs. Feel free to look at `ch04/zwc.zig` for more.

Let us now use `ch04/zwc.zig` and see it in action:

```
$ echo 'Hi there\n\n\n' | zig run ch04/zwc.zig
          4           2          12
$ zig run ch04/zwc.zig -- ch12/*.zig
        457        2015       16665 ch12/evaluator.zig
        210         689        6037 ch12/lexer.zig
        351        1467       13341 ch12/parser.zig
        629        2199       19649 ch12/repl.zig
       1647        6370       55692 total
$ zig run ch04/zwc.zig -- -l ch12/*.zig
        457 ch12/evaluator.zig
        210 ch12/lexer.zig
        351 ch12/parser.zig
        629 ch12/repl.zig
       1647 total
```

In the first command, data is piped via standard input, confirming that the tool correctly defaults to reading from stdin when no file arguments are present. The second command illustrates the tool's ability to handle multiple file arguments (expanded from the wildcard), providing individual statistics for each file and automatically calculating a total row at the bottom, mirroring the behavior of `wc(1)`. Finally, the third command verifies the argument parsing logic; by passing the `-l` flag, the output is correctly filtered to display only the line counts.

While our current byte-by-byte approach works, it leaves significant performance on the table. So, next, we exploit modern processor parallelism by implementing high-performance text counting with SIMD.

Achieving high-performance text counting with SIMD

Modern processors are capable of incredible parallelism, not just by using multiple cores, but by using special instructions within a single core. Traditional code is *scalar*, meaning it processes one piece of data per instruction. This approach leaves a significant portion of the CPU's sophisticated circuitry idle as it waits for individual data points to move through the pipeline. **SIMD (Single Instruction, Multiple Data)** breaks this bottleneck by allowing the processor to execute the same operation on multiple data points simultaneously. By utilizing wide vector registers, we can load chunks of 16, 32, or even 64 bytes at once and compare them all against a target character in a single clock cycle. For our word counter, this effectively means we can process text 16 to 32 times faster than a standard loop, transforming a sequential crawl through memory into a high-speed sprint.

The name of the new implementation is `ch04/zwcOptimized.zig`. For this version, we are only going to update the `processStream()` function – the rest of the program does not need to change. The first code snippet of `processStream()` is the following:

```
fn processStream(io: std.Io, file: std.Io.File) !Counts {
    // 64KB buffer for high throughput
    var buffer: [64 * 1024]u8 = undefined;
    var lines: usize = 0;
    var words: usize = 0;
    var bytes: usize = 0;
    // SIMD Configuration
    const VSize = 32; // Processes 32 bytes at a time
    const Vector = @Vector(VSize, u8);
    const U1Vec = @Vector(VSize, u1);
```

The improved `processStream()` begins by aggressively optimizing for throughput. We quadruple the buffer size from 16KB to 64KB, a change that significantly reduces the frequency of system calls and ensures the CPU vector units are kept fed with data without waiting on memory controller overhead. The true power of this implementation lies in the type definitions. We define `VSize` as 32, meaning we will process 32 bytes (256 bits) *simultaneously* per cycle. The `Vector` type acts as a direct mapping to CPU SIMD registers, capable of holding 32 characters at once. The `U1Vec` type represents the result of a SIMD comparison, storing 32 Boolean results as single bits. This setup moves us away from checking one character at a time to performing logic on entire blocks of text in parallel.

Have in mind that `@Vector(32, u8)` requests 32-byte vectorization from the compiler; on x86-64 with AVX2, this maps to a single 256-bit instruction, while on arm64 (such as Apple Silicon) it lowers to two 128-bit NEON operations. Compiling with `-mcpu=native` ensures the backend uses the widest SIMD registers available on the target CPU.

To facilitate parallel comparison, we initialize several constant vectors using `@splat`, which broadcasts a single scalar value across all 32 lanes of a SIMD register:

```
const ones_u1: U1Vec = @splat(1);
const zeros_u1: U1Vec = @splat(0);
const space_char: Vector = @splat(' ');
const tab_char: Vector = @splat('\t');
const cr_char: Vector = @splat('\r');
const nl_char: Vector = @splat('\n');
var prev_was_space: u32 = 1;
```

For instance, `space_char` becomes a vector filled entirely with ASCII spaces. This allows the processor to later compare a 32-byte chunk of input data against this constant in a single clock cycle, instantly identifying every space character in the block. We similarly create mask vectors for tabs, carriage returns, and newlines. We also prepare helper vectors like `ones_u1` (filled with 1s) to perform parallel arithmetic for counting matches. Finally, the `prev_was_space` variable handles the critical boundary condition between chunks. Because word counting depends on detecting transitions (changing from whitespace to non-whitespace), we must remember the state of the last character of the previous 32-byte block. This ensures that if a word is split precisely between two buffer reads, the algorithm correctly identifies it as a single word rather than two.

The core processing loop begins by filling our large 64KB buffer with data from the `reader`:

```
while (true) {
    const n = file.readStreaming(io, &.{&buffer}) catch |err| {
        if (err == error.EndOfStream) break;
        return err;
```

```
        };
        if (n == 0) break;
        bytes += n;
        var i: usize = 0;
```

The `while (true)` construct ensures we continue processing chunks until the file is exhausted. Immediately upon reading, we add the number of bytes read, `n`, to our total byte count. Inside the loop, we initialize an index variable that will track our position within the current buffer as we iterate through it. Instead of processing byte-by-byte from index `0` to `n`, we are preparing to jump through the buffer in strides of 32 bytes (our vector size), allowing the SIMD instructions to consume large swaths of data at once.

The next section represents the heart of the high-performance engine, where the code processes data in 32-byte strides (using 256-bit vectors):

```
        while (i + VSize <= n) : (i += VSize) {
            const v: Vector = buffer[i..][0..VSize].*;
            const is_nl = v == nl_char;
            const nl_bits: u32 = @bitCast(
                @select(u1, is_nl, ones_u1, zeros_u1),
            );
            lines += @popCount(nl_bits);

            const is_white = (v == space_char) |
                ((v >= tab_char) & (v <= cr_char));
            const curr_bits: u32 = @bitCast(
                @select(u1, is_white, ones_u1, zeros_u1),
            );
            const prev_bits = (curr_bits << 1) | prev_was_space;
            const word_starts = (~curr_bits)&prev_bits;
            words += @popCount(word_starts);
            prev_was_space = curr_bits >> 31;
        }
```

Inside the loop, the code loads a vector `v` containing 32 characters from the buffer and immediately performs two parallel tasks. First, to count lines, it compares the entire vector against the newline character `\n`. The resulting Boolean vector is compressed into a single 32-bit integer (`nl_bits`), where each set bit represents a newline. The `@popCount()` function (which maps to a specialized hardware instruction) then instantly tallies these bits, allowing us to count up to 32 lines in a handful of CPU cycles.

The word counting logic is even more ingenious, relying on bitwise transitions rather than `if` statements. We first create a whitespace mask (`curr_bits`) where a `1` indicates a space, tab or carriage return. To detect the start of a word, we look for the specific pattern: Whitespace followed by Non-Whitespace. By shifting the current mask left (`curr_bits << 1`) and combining it with the stored state from the previous iteration (`prev_was_space`), we align the *previous* character state with every *current* character. The expression `(~curr_bits) & prev_bits` asks *Where is the current character not a space AND the previous character was a space?* The result is a bitmask of word starts, which is again instantly summed up using `@popCount()`. Finally, the loop saves the last bit of the current chunk to `prev_was_space` to maintain continuity across the next 32-byte iteration.

This final section of the code handles the remaining bytes that did not fit into the 32-byte chunks processed by the SIMD loop:

```
        while (i < n) : (i += 1) {
            const c = buffer[i];
            if (c == '\n') lines += 1;
            const is_space = std.ascii.isWhitespace(c);
            const is_space_int: u32 = if (is_space) 1 else 0;
            if (!is_space and prev_was_space == 1) {
                words += 1;
            }
            prev_was_space = is_space_int;
        }
    }
    return Counts{
        .lines = lines,
        .words = words,
        .bytes = bytes,
    };
}
```

Because files rarely have a length that is a perfect multiple of 32, there are almost always a few bytes (between 1 and 31) left at the end of the buffer. This `while` loop picks up exactly where the SIMD loop left off index `i`, and iterates one byte at a time until it reaches the end of the valid data `n`. Inside the loop, the logic mirrors the SIMD approach but uses standard conditional statements. It checks each character `c` to see if it is a newline, incrementing the line count if so. For word counting, it determines if the current character is whitespace and compares this state against `prev_was_space`. Just like the bitwise logic in the vectorized loop, a word is counted only when a transition occurs from whitespace (previous) to non-whitespace (current). The `prev_was_space` variable preserves the state across the boundary between the fast SIMD loop and this scalar loop, as well as between different buffer loads, ensuring that a word split across a 32-byte chunk or a 64KB buffer boundary is correctly identified as a single word. Finally, the accumulated statistics are packaged into the `Counts` struct and returned.

To understand what `word_starts = (~curr_bits) & prev_bits` is computing, it helps to work through a short example. Take the five-byte sequence `"  Hi "` — two spaces, the letters H, and i, then a space. We want to count one word start, at the position of `H`. The first step builds `curr_bits`, a bitmask where a `1` at position `i` means `buffer[i]` is whitespace:

```
position:   0   1   2   3   4
character: ' ' ' ' 'H' 'i' ' '
curr_bits:  1   1   0   0   1
```

The second step builds `prev_bits`, which answers the question "was the byte immediately before position `i` whitespace?" In other words, `prev_bits[i] = curr_bits[i-1]`. Position `0` has no predecessor within this chunk, so it is filled with `prev_was_space` — the whitespace state of the last byte from the previous chunk. Assuming that byte was not whitespace, `prev_was_space = 0`:

```
position:   0   1   2   3   4
prev_bits:  0   1   1   0   0
```

With both masks ready, the expression selects every position where the current byte is not whitespace and the previous byte was whitespace — the precise definition of a word start:

```
~curr_bits: 0   0   1   1   0   ← 1 where current byte is NOT whitespace
prev_bits:  0   1   1   0   0   ← 1 where previous byte WAS whitespace
word_starts: 0  0   1   0   0   ← AND: only position 2 matches
```

Position 2 is `H` — the only word start in this sequence, which is correct. `std.math.popcount(word_starts)` counts the `1` bits in the final mask in a single instruction, giving the word count for the entire 32-byte chunk without a single branch or loop iteration.

Now that we have both a simple scalar implementation and a highly optimized SIMD version, it is time to put them head-to-head to quantify exactly how much performance our vectorization efforts have unlocked.

Comparing the two ZWC implementations

We created `ch04/benchWC.zig` for comparing the two `wc(1)` implementations – feel free to look at its code before executing it as follows:

```
$ zig run ch04/benchWC.zig -O ReleaseFast -mcpu=native
Allocating 100MB of test data...
Benchmarking Scalar implementation...
Benchmarking SIMD implementation...

Results (100MB input):
-------------------------------------------
Scalar: 0.2142 s  |  0.4560 GB/s
SIMD:   0.0065 s  |  14.9564 GB/s
-------------------------------------------
Speedup: 32.80x
```

The massive 33x speedup observed on my macOS machine comes from a fundamental difference in how the CPU processes data. In the *Scalar* implementation, the processor is scanning items one by one. For every single byte of the 100MB file, the CPU must load the byte, check if it is a newline, check if it is a space, update the counters and then loop back. This means that to process 100 million bytes, the CPU must execute hundreds of millions of individual instructions. Furthermore, because the text data is random, the `if (!is_space)` check becomes unpredictable. Modern CPUs try to guess the outcome of an `if` statement to run faster, a process that is called **branch prediction**, but when the data is random, they guess wrong about 50% of the time. Every wrong guess forces the CPU to flush its "pipeline" of upcoming work and start over, wasting valuable cycles. SIMD fundamentally changes this dynamic by widening the road. It is effectively doing the work of 32 loop iterations in a single clock cycle. Additionally, the SIMD version eliminates the `if` statements that troubled the scalar version. Instead of branching, it uses *bitwise mathematics* — AND, OR, and NOT operations — to calculate the word counts. Because math is deterministic and flows linearly without branching, the CPU pipeline never stalls or flushes. The combination of processing 32 times more data per cycle and removing the costly branch mispredictions results in the order-of-magnitude performance leap you just witnessed. Internal benchmarks are useful, but the ultimate validation for any core utility is how it stands up against the tool it aims to replace. For decades, `wc(1)` has served as the gold standard for text counting, benefitting from years of optimization in C.

Comparing zwc with wc

In this section, we step out of our own development environment and pit our high-performance zwc directly against the system's native `wc(1)` to see if our modern Zig implementation has what it takes to outperform a UNIX classic. Prepare the experiments with the following commands:

```
$ zig build-exe ch04/zwc.zig -O ReleaseFast -mcpu=native
$ zig build-exe ch04/zwcOptimized.zig -O ReleaseFast -mcpu=native
$  dd if=/dev/urandom of=/tmp/bigfile.dat bs=1M count=1000
1000+0 records in
1000+0 records out
1048576000 bytes transferred in 2.033589 secs (515628281 bytes/sec)
```

After preparing the stage for the benchmarks, we are ready to execute them:

```
$ hyperfine --warmup 3 "wc /tmp/bigfile.dat" "./zwc /tmp/bigfile.dat" "./
zwcOptimized /tmp/bigfile.dat"
Benchmark 1: wc /tmp/bigfile.dat
  Time (mean ± σ):   3.914 s ±  0.028 s [User: 3.857 s, System: 0.056 s]
  Range (min … max):    3.876 s …  3.957 s    10 runs

Benchmark 2: ./zwc /tmp/bigfile.dat
  Time (mean ± σ):   624.4 ms ± 2.8 ms [User: 561.0 ms, System: 62.9 ms]
  Range (min … max):   620.9 ms … 629.8 ms    10 runs

Benchmark 3: ./zwcOptimized /tmp/bigfile.dat
  Time (mean ± σ):   111.0 ms ±  1.0 ms [User: 68.1 ms, System: 42.4 ms]
  Range (min … max):   109.7 ms … 114.2 ms    26 runs

Summary
  ./zwcOptimized /tmp/bigfile.dat ran
    5.63 ± 0.06 times faster than ./zwc /tmp/bigfile.dat
   35.27 ± 0.41 times faster than wc /tmp/bigfile.dat
```

The standard macOS `wc(1)` utility is taking `3.91` seconds to process the 1GB file. This relatively slow performance suggests that the default `wc(1)` implementation is not optimized for modern hardware. zwc is finishing in `624` milliseconds, which is roughly `6.3x` faster than the system utility. Even without explicit SIMD instructions, the CPU branch predictor worked reasonably well, and the compiler likely auto-vectorized small parts of the code. Last, the `zwcOptimized` version is completing the task in just `111` milliseconds. This represents a 35x speedup over the system `wc(1)` and is `5.6x` faster than `zwc`. By processing 32 bytes per cycle and eliminating branch mispredictions via bitwise logic, the CPU is no longer bounded by program logic but by memory bandwidth!

Having pushed the limits of read-only analysis with word counting, we now face a more complex challenge: data transformation. While counting bytes is largely a matter of observation, encoding and decoding require efficiently mapping, bit-shifting, and rewriting every byte of input into a new format.

Developing z64, a high-performance Base64 tool

Before examining the encoding and decoding mechanics in detail, it is worth understanding what system problem Base64 solves and why the implementation approach matters. Binary data — the kind produced by image compression, cryptographic operations, or serialized structs — contains byte values that many text-oriented protocols cannot handle safely. A single null byte or control character in a binary payload can truncate a string, corrupt a parser, or break a protocol that was never designed to handle arbitrary bytes. Base64 was designed to eliminate that risk entirely. The implementation approach matters because Base64 appears in hot paths: encoding a large file upload, decoding a JWT token on every authenticated request, or processing a stream of binary sensor data in real time. A naive character-by-character implementation that allocates on every call will become the bottleneck in exactly these scenarios. The implementation that follows uses bitwise operations on fixed-size stack buffers to keep allocations out of the hot path entirely — the systems programming answer to a problem that higher-level languages typically solve with a library call and a heap allocation.

Base64 is a binary-to-text encoding scheme designed to ensure data integrity when transferring binary content over channels that only reliably support text. Systems like email or JSON are built to handle ASCII characters and raw binary bytes — which might look like control characters or whitespace — can be corrupted or misinterpreted during transmission. Base64 solves that by taking the input stream of 8-bit bytes and regrouping them into 6-bit chunks. Each chunk represents a value from 0 to 63, which is then mapped to a printable character from a standardized 64-character alphabet (`A-Z`, `a-z`, `0-9`, `+` and `/`). If the data length is not divisible by three, padding characters (=) are added to the end. The trade-off for this safety is size: *because 3 bytes of input become 4 bytes of output, the encoded data is approximately 33% larger than the original.* In this section, we develop a Base64 clone called `z64` (`ch04/z64.zig`).

Bitwise manipulation operations (<<, >>, &, |)

Base64 encoding is fundamentally an exercise in bitwise operations. We take a stream of 8-bit bytes and repackage them into 6-bit chunks because 2^6=64 characters in the standard alphabet. To achieve this, `z64` treats a group of three input bytes (24 bits) as a single unit. It combines them into a temporary 32-bit integer using left shifts (<<) and logical ORs (|) to place them side-by-side. Once combined, the code extracts four 6-bit indices by shifting right (>>) and masking with `& 0x3F` (which is binary `00111111`). For example, to get the first index, we shift the 24-bit block right by 18 positions; to get the second, we shift by 12, and so on. This transforms the input `[b0, b1, b2]` into four distinct indices that map directly to our defined `BASE64_ALPHABET` array, enabling the textual representation of binary data.

As an example, to encode the string `Zig!` We must process the input in 24-bit chunks. The first complete chunk is the substring `"Zig"`. In ASCII, these characters correspond to the byte values `90`, `105`, and `103`. When their binary representations (`01011010`, `01101001`, `01100111`) are concatenated, they form a continuous 24-bit stream. We then split this stream into four 6-bit groups: `010110`, `100110`, `100101`, and `100111`. Mapping these decimal values (22, 38, 37, 39) to the standard Base64 alphabet yields the characters `W`, `m`, `l`, and `n`. The remaining input is the single character `"!"`, which presents a misalignment because Base64 requires groups of three bytes. To resolve this, we take the byte value of `"!"` (33 or `00100001`) and conceptually pad the missing 16 bits with zeros to complete the 24-bit block. The first 6 bits (`001000`) map to `I` (index 8) and the next 6 bits (`010000`) map to `Q` (index 16). Since the remaining 12 bits of the block are entirely padding, they are converted into two `=` symbols to indicate that those bytes did not exist in the original source. Combining these parts, the final encoded string is `WmlnIQ==`. We can now integrate this logic into a complete encoder function that efficiently handles data streams of any size.

Implementing the encoder logic

The encoder function, `encode()`, orchestrates the transformation process by iterating through the input in 3-byte strides. Unlike a naive implementation that might process one byte at a time, z64 calculates the maximum processable length for the current buffer—the largest multiple of 3 that fits within the data read. This allows the main loop to run without conditional checks for end-of-buffer scenarios, maximizing throughput. Inside the loop, the code loads three bytes, performs the bitwise extraction described above, and writes four characters to the output buffer. The efficiency in the z64 implementation comes from minimizing system calls and memory copying. Here is the first part of the `encode()` implementation:

```
fn encode(io: std.Io, infile: std.Io.File, outfile: std.Io.File) !void {
    var in_buf: [4096]u8 = undefined;
    var out_buf: [6000]u8 = undefined;
    var leftover_len: usize = 0;

    while (true) {
```

```
        const bytes_read = infile.readStreaming(
            io,
            &.{in_buf[leftover_len..]},
        ) catch |err| blk: {
            if (err == error.EndOfStream) break :blk @as(usize, 0);
            return err;
        };
        const total_bytes = leftover_len + bytes_read;
        if (total_bytes == 0) break; // End of File

        const chunks = total_bytes / 3;
        const processable_len = chunks * 3;
        var i: usize = 0;
        var out_idx: usize = 0;

        while (i < processable_len) : (i += 3) {
            const b0 = in_buf[i];
            const b1 = in_buf[i + 1];
            const b2 = in_buf[i + 2];
            const temp: u32 = (@as(u32, b0) << 16) |
                (@as(u32, b1) << 8) |
                @as(u32, b2);

            out_buf[out_idx] = BASE64_ALPHABET[@as(usize, (temp >> 18)&0x3F)];
            out_buf[out_idx + 1] = BASE64_ALPHABET[@as(usize, (temp >> 12)&0x3F)];
            out_buf[out_idx + 2] = BASE64_ALPHABET[@as(usize, (temp >> 6)&0x3F)];
            out_buf[out_idx + 3] = BASE64_ALPHABET[@as(usize,temp&0x3F)];
            out_idx += 4;
        }
```

The `encode()` function uses two static buffers: a 4KB input buffer to minimize system call overhead and a proportionally larger (6KB) output buffer. The buffer size is not arbitrary: Base64 encodes every 3 bytes of input as 4 bytes of output, so a 4096-byte input chunk produces at most `ceil(4096/3)*4 = 5464` encoded bytes. The additional headroom to 6000 accounts for the `=` padding characters appended when the final input group is not a complete 3-byte triple. Any code that adapts this implementation for a different chunk size should recalculate the output buffer using the same formula rather than copying the constant blindly.

To handle arbitrary read sizes without complex state machines, the code employs a *leftover tracking strategy*. Each read operation appends new data immediately after any bytes remaining from the previous cycle, ensuring a contiguous stream of valid data. Once the buffer is filled, the function calculates the processable length — the largest subset of the data that is perfectly divisible by three. This calculation allows the inner encoding loop to operate in a *fast path mode*, iterating with a fixed stride of 3 bytes without needing to check for buffer boundaries or partial chunks on every iteration. As explained, inside this loop, three 8-bit bytes are fused into a 24-bit temporary integer, which is then sliced into four 6-bit indices to look up the corresponding characters in the `BASE64_ALPHABET`. This design concentrates the heavy computational work into a tight, branch-free loop for maximum efficiency.

The rest of the function implementation is as follows:

```
        if (out_idx > 0) {
            try outfile.writeStreamingAll(io, out_buf[0..out_idx]);
        }
        const new_leftover = total_bytes - processable_len;
        if (bytes_read == 0) {
            if (new_leftover > 0) {
                try encodeLastChunk(
                    io,
                    in_buf[processable_len..total_bytes],
                    outfile,
                );
            }
            break;
        }

        if (new_leftover > 0) {
            std.mem.copyForwards(
                u8,
               ∈_buf,
                in_buf[processable_len..total_bytes],
            );
        }
        leftover_len = new_leftover;
    }
}
```

After the main loop has processed the aligned data, the function flushes the generated characters to the output "file". The critical challenge here is managing the "seam" between buffer reads: `total_bytes` rarely divides perfectly by three, leaving one or two bytes (`new_leftover`) at the end of the buffer. If the stream has ended (`bytes_read == 0`), these remaining bytes are treated as the final partial block. The code calls encodeLastChunk() to apply the necessary padding (adding = characters) and then terminates the loop. However, if the stream is still active, these leftover bytes must be preserved to maintain alignment. The function uses std.mem.copyForwards() to shift them to the very beginning of in_buf. This effectively re-queues them, ensuring that the next read() operation appends new data directly after them, seamlessly reuniting the split 3-byte group in the next iteration. A critical edge case arises at the end of the file: if the input length is not divisible by 3, there will be one or two leftover bytes. The encodeLastChunk() function handles this by manually padding the remaining bits with zeros and appending the appropriate number of = padding characters (one or two) to the final output, ensuring the generated Base64 string is valid and compliant with the standard. Here is the implementation of encodeLastChunk():

```
fn encodeLastChunk(io: std.Io, bytes: []const u8, outfile: std.Io.File) !void {
    var out_buf: [4]u8 = undefined;
    var temp: u32 = @as(u32, bytes[0]) << 16;
    if (bytes.len > 1) {
        temp |= @as(u32, bytes[1]) << 8;
    }
    out_buf[0] = BASE64_ALPHABET[@as(usize, (temp >> 18)&0x3F)];
    out_buf[1] = BASE64_ALPHABET[@as(usize, (temp >> 12)&0x3F)];

    if (bytes.len > 1) {
        out_buf[2] = BASE64_ALPHABET[@as(usize, (temp >> 6)&0x3F)];
    } else {
        out_buf[2] = '=';
    }
    out_buf[3] = '=';
    try outfile.writeStreamingAll(io,&out_buf);
}
```

While processing chunks in isolation is straightforward, high-performance file I/O requires a more sophisticated approach to ensure we do not drop data between buffer reads. Now that we have a robust encoder, we must implement its inverse: a decoder capable of reconstructing binary files from Base64 text, even when that text is interrupted by newlines or formatting characters.

Decoding streams

The decode() function reconstructs the original binary data from a Base64 stream by processing input in efficient 4KB buffered chunks while maintaining a stateful accumulator for incomplete data. Because Base64 streams often contain ignorable characters like newlines, the function iterates through the input byte-by-byte, using the pre-computed `DECODE_TABLE` to instantly filter out invalid characters and map valid ones to their 6-bit integer values. The core logic revolves around a small "quad" buffer that collects these valid 6-bit values. Once four characters are accumulated, the function combines them into a single 24-bit integer using bitwise shifts and logical ORs, which is then split into three standard 8-bit bytes and appended to the output buffer. The function handles stream termination by detecting the padding character (=); upon encountering it, the code immediately processes any remaining partial chunk via `flushQuad()`, flushes the output buffer to disk, and exits. This ensures that even if the input stream is interrupted or contains irregular formatting, the binary output remains accurate and complete. Here is the `decode()` function implementation:

```
fn decode(io: std.Io, infile: std.Io.File, outfile: std.Io.File) !void {
    var in_buf: [4096]u8 = undefined;
    var out_buf: [4096]u8 = undefined;
    var out_len: usize = 0;
    var quad: [4]u8 = undefined;
    var quad_count: usize = 0;

    while (true) {
        const bytes_read = infile.readStreaming(
            io,
            &.{∈_buf},
        ) catch |err| {
            if (err == error.EndOfStream) break;
            return err;
        };
        if (bytes_read == 0) break;
        for (in_buf[0..bytes_read]) |char| {
            // 1. Handle Padding (End of Data)
            if (char == '=') {
                if (quad_count > 1) {
                    flushQuad(quad[0..quad_count], &out_buf,&out_len);
                }
                // Flush whatever is in the main output buffer and exit
                if (out_len > 0) try outfile.writeStreamingAll(
                    io,
                    out_buf[0..out_len],
                );
                return;
            }
```

The code begins by allocating 4KB buffers for both reading and writing to minimize system call overhead and defining a `quad` accumulator to preserve state across buffer boundaries. The reading loop iterates through the input stream byte by byte. The first critical check inside this loop is for the padding character (=), which acts as the explicit end-of-stream marker in Base64. Upon detecting it, the code stops processing new input, flushes any partially accumulated characters in `quad` (using `flushQuad()` to handle the final 1 or 2 bytes), writes the remaining output buffer to disk, and immediately returns. This effectively ignores any subsequent data (like newlines or garbage) that might follow the padding, ensuring a clean exit.

If the character is not padding, the function consults the `DECODE_TABLE` to determine its 6-bit integer value. This lookup table design allows for immediate filtering: if the value is `0xFF` (representing invalid characters like newlines or whitespace), the loop continues to the next byte, essentially stripping non-data characters without complex logic:

```
// 2. Lookup Value (Filter out newlines/whitespace)
const val = DECODE_TABLE[char];
if (val == 0xFF) continue;
// 3. Accumulate valid 6-bit chunk
quad[quad_count] = val;
quad_count += 1;
// 4. Process Full Quad (4 * 6 bits = 24 bits -> 3 bytes)
if (quad_count == 4) {
    const temp: u32 = (@as(u32, quad[0]) << 18) |
        (@as(u32, quad[1]) << 12) |
        (@as(u32, quad[2]) << 6) |
        @as(u32, quad[3]);

    out_buf[out_len] = @as(u8, @truncate(temp >> 16));
    out_buf[out_len + 1] = @as(u8, @truncate(temp >> 8));
    out_buf[out_len + 2] = @as(u8, @truncate(temp));
    out_len += 3;
    quad_count = 0;

    // Flush output buffer if full
    if (out_len >= out_buf.len - 3) {
        try outfile.writeStreamingAll(
            io,
            out_buf[0..out_len],
        );
        out_len = 0;
```

```
                }
            }
        }
    }
    // Final flush if we hit EOF without padding
    if (quad_count > 1) {
        flushQuad(quad[0..quad_count], &out_buf,&out_len);
    }
    if (out_len > 0) try outfile.writeStreamingAll(
        io,
        out_buf[0..out_len],
    );
}
```

Valid values are pushed into the `quad` accumulator. Once this small buffer holds four 6-bit integers, the function combines them into a single 24-bit temporary value using left shifts (`<< 18`, `<< 12`, etc.) and logical ORs. This 24-bit block is then sliced into three standard 8-bit bytes, which are appended to `out_buf`. To ensure efficient I/O, the function checks if `out_buf` is nearing capacity; if full, it writes the entire chunk in one operation and resets the index, repeating this cycle until the input stream is exhausted. With all the information in mind, let us try to use `ch04/z64.zig`:

```
$ echo -n "Zig Lang" | zig run ch04/z64.zig
WmlnIExhbmc=
$ echo -n "Zig" | zig run ch04/z64.zig | zig run ch04/z64.zig -- -d
Zig
```

The second output demonstrates a successful round-trip verification of the `z64` utility, proving that the encoder and decoder are correctly implemented as inverse operations. After code correctness, we usually want speed. The next section introduces tools and methodologies for effectively benchmarking file reading and writing operations.

Benchmarking reading and writing operations

Benchmarking Zig code is a critical step in evaluating the performance characteristics of our code, allowing developers to measure execution speed, memory usage, and resource efficiency against other languages or implementations. We start by measuring how buffer size affects the speed of reading operations.

Benchmarking reading speed for various buffer sizes

The Zig program implements a flexible and configurable file reading benchmark that allows the user to specify different buffer sizes via command-line arguments. It is organized for clarity and reuse, combining practical benchmarking with robust error handling and clear output formatting. The user must supply at least three parameters: the file size in megabytes, the number of trials, and one or more buffer sizes. If the user provides fewer arguments, the program displays a helpful usage message and exits early. The core logic of `ch04/benchmarkReading.zig` is found in `benchmarkBufferSize()`:

```
fn benchmarkBufferSize(
    io: std.Io,
    allocator: std.mem.Allocator,
    file_path: []const u8,
    buffer_size: usize,
    trials: usize,
) !void {
    const file_check = try std.Io.Dir.cwd().openFile(
        io,
        file_path,
        .{},
    );
    const file_size = (try file_check.stat(io)).size;
    file_check.close(io);

    const file_size_mb_float = @as(
        f64,
        @floatFromInt(file_size),
    ) / (1024.0 * 1024.0);
    const buffer = try allocator.alloc(u8, buffer_size);
    defer allocator.free(buffer);
    var durations: std.ArrayListUnmanaged(f64) = .empty;
    try durations.ensureTotalCapacity(allocator, trials);
    defer durations.deinit(allocator);
```

The `benchmarkBufferSize()` function initiates the performance test by first establishing the baseline metrics and resources. It opens the target file briefly to retrieve its size via `stat()` — calculating the megabyte count upfront for later throughput math — and then immediately closes it. The function also performs the necessary memory allocations before the benchmarking loop begins. It allocates the read buffer of the requested `buffer_size` and pre-initializes an

`ArrayListUnmanaged` with exact capacity for the trial results. This pre-allocation strategy isolates the I/O performance being measured, ensuring that the timing results reflect raw disk speed rather than the overhead of memory management or dynamic array resizing.

The core benchmark loop executes the specified number of trials, treating each as an isolated event. For every iteration, the file is opened fresh, ensuring that the measurement captures the full lifecycle of the file handle interaction. A `while` loop then consumes the file content, repeatedly filling the test buffer until the end of the file is reached:

```
var total_time_ms: f64 = 0;
for (0..trials) |_| {
    const file = try std.Io.Dir.cwd().openFile(io, file_path, .{});
    defer file.close(io);

    const t_start = std.Io.Timestamp.now(io, .awake);
    var total_read: usize = 0;
    while (true) {
        const bytes_read = file.readStreaming(
            io,
            &.{buffer},
        ) catch |err| {
            if (err == error.EndOfStream) break;
            return err;
        };
        if (bytes_read == 0) break;
        total_read += bytes_read;
    }

    // durationTo returns i96 nanoseconds; safe to @intCast to
    // u64 because the .awake (monotonic) clock never goes backwards.
    const elapsed_ns: u64 = @intCast(t_start.durationTo(
        std.Io.Timestamp.now(io, .awake),
    ).nanoseconds);
    const elapsed_ms = @as(
        f64,
        @floatFromInt(elapsed_ns),
    ) / 1_000_000.0;
    try durations.append(allocator, elapsed_ms);
    total_time_ms += elapsed_ms;
}
```

Please have in mind that `Io.Duration.nanoseconds` is typed as `i96` — a signed 96-bit integer — because durations in Zig's I/O abstraction are designed to represent time differences that could theoretically be negative (for example, when comparing timestamps from a wall clock that can be adjusted backward by NTP). However, when both timestamps are taken from the `.awake` monotonic clock, as is the case here, the elapsed time is guaranteed to be non-negative: the monotonic clock only ever moves forward. The `@intCast` to `u64` is therefore safe in practice, but Zig's type system cannot prove this statically, so the cast will still panic in debug builds if the value is ever negative — a useful safety net should the clock source be changed in the future.

A high-resolution timer brackets this entire operation, capturing the elapsed nanoseconds, which are then converted to milliseconds. By storing each individual result in the `durations` list rather than keeping a running average, the function preserves the granular data needed to calculate variance and standard deviation later, offering a more complete picture of I/O stability. After the loop concludes, the function synthesizes the raw timing data into actionable metrics. It first computes the arithmetic mean of the execution times to establish a baseline performance figure. From this average, it derives the throughput by dividing the known file size in megabytes by the average duration in seconds:

```
    const avg_time_ms = total_time_ms / @as(f64, @floatFromInt(trials));
    const avg_throughput = file_size_mb_float / (avg_time_ms / 1000.0);
    const std_dev_ms = calculateStdDev(durations.items, avg_time_ms);
    print("{d:<5} bytes    {d:>8.3} ms    {d:>10.2} MB/s    {d:>8.3} ms\n", .{
        buffer_size,
        avg_time_ms,
        avg_throughput,
        std_dev_ms,
    });
}
```

However, the code does not stop at averages as it calculates the standard deviation using the stored trial data. This metric quantifies the instability of the disk operations, revealing whether the performance is consistent or fluctuating due to system noise. Finally, the function prints these statistics using precise format specifiers, aligning the output into neat columns to facilitate easy visual comparison between different buffer sizes.

Now, let us try `ch04/benchmarkReading.zig` on an M4 Pro macOS machine:

```
$ zig run ch04/benchmarkReading.zig -- 100 10 128 512 1024 4096 16384

File Reading Benchmark - 100 MB File - 10 Trials
```

```
===================================================================
Buffer Size     Avg Time (ms)   Avg Throughput       Std Dev
-------------------------------------------------------------------
128   bytes     245.689 ms        407.02 MB/s        0.889 ms
512   bytes      64.156 ms       1558.71 MB/s        0.611 ms
1024  bytes      33.742 ms       2963.64 MB/s        0.303 ms
4096  bytes      10.854 ms       9212.90 MB/s        0.118 ms
16384 bytes       5.579 ms      17924.72 MB/s        0.124 ms
```

This benchmark output shows the results of reading a 100 MB file, repeated over 10 trials for various buffer sizes. Smaller buffer sizes result in slower and less efficient performance. For instance, reading with a tiny 128-byte buffer takes an average of `245.689 ms` and delivers a modest throughput of `407.02 MB/s`. This is because the system must repeatedly request small chunks of data from disk, which adds significant overhead. As the buffer size increases, performance improves dramatically. With a 512-byte buffer, the time drops to `64.156 ms` and throughput nearly quadruples to `1558.71 MB/s`. At 4096 bytes (4 KiB), throughput jumps to over `9212 MB/s`, and with 16384 bytes (16 KiB), it reaches a peak of `17924.72 MB/s`. With all this information in mind, let us see how the buffer size is related to file writing.

How the buffer size affects writing speed

We will not present the code for `ch04/benchmarkWriting.zig` here, as it largely mirrors the structure of the reading benchmark. The implementation iterates through the same set of buffer sizes, writing random data to a temporary file and measuring the throughput by recording a `std.Io.Timestamp` before and after each write operation, then computing the elapsed nanoseconds via `.durationTo()`. We encourage you to examine the source code in `ch04/benchmarkWriting.zig` independently. However, there is one helper function that deserves our attention:

```
fn generateTestData(
    io: std.Io,
    allocator: std.mem.Allocator,
    size_mb: usize,
) ![]u8 {
    const size_bytes = size_mb * 1024 * 1024;
    const buffer = try allocator.alloc(u8, size_bytes);
    var seed_bytes: [8]u8 = undefined;
    io.random(&seed_bytes);
    var prng = std.Random.DefaultPrng.init(@bitCast(seed_bytes));
    const rand = prng.random();
```

```
    for (buffer) |*byte| {
        byte.* = rand.intRangeAtMost(u8, 32, 126);
    }
    return buffer;
}
```

The `generateTestData()` function creates a heap-allocated buffer of a specified size to serve as the workload for the benchmark. Instead of filling this memory with zeroes or purely random binary noise, the function generates a stream of printable ASCII characters to simulate realistic text data. By constraining the random values to the range `[32, 126]` — which spans from the space character to the tilde (~) — it ensures the output mimics legitimate text content that is safe for terminal display and text-processing tools. Now, execute the benchmark on your machine – expect to get the following kind of output:

```
$ zig run ./ch04/benchmarkWriting.zig -- 50 10 256 512 2048 8192 16384
Generating 50MB of random test data...

File Writing Benchmark - 50 MB File - 10 Trials
======================================================================
Buffer Size     Avg Time (ms)   Avg Throughput       Std Dev
----------------------------------------------------------------------
256   bytes     213.547 ms         234.14 MB/s       0.975 ms
512   bytes     118.837 ms         420.74 MB/s       0.783 ms
2048  bytes      47.297 ms        1057.15 MB/s       2.372 ms
8192  bytes      21.568 ms        2318.25 MB/s       3.877 ms
16384 bytes      10.803 ms        4628.43 MB/s       0.386 ms
```

The test writes a `50 MB` file ten times for each buffer size provided on the command line and then reports the average time taken, throughput in megabytes per second, and the standard deviation in milliseconds. As the buffer size increases, the average time to write the file consistently decreases. For example, using a small buffer of `256 bytes` results in a relatively slow write time of `213.547 ms` and a low throughput of `234.14 MB/s`. However, with a larger buffer size, such as `16384 bytes`, the write time drops significantly to just `10.803 ms`, and the throughput increases dramatically to `4628.43 MB/s`. This is because larger buffers reduce the number of system calls and allow more data to be written per operation. The standard deviation values indicate how consistent each measurement was over the ten trials. In this case, the smallest standard deviation (`0.386 ms`) occurs with the largest buffer, confirming that larger buffer sizes not only improve speed but also yield more stable performance.

With the performance characteristics of buffered writing now established, we turn our attention to the input side of the equation, where we compare the efficiency of sequential scanning against direct file seeking.

Benchmarking file seeking with sequential reading

When working with file I/O operations, the choice between file seeking and sequential access can significantly impact performance and efficiency. File seeking involves moving the file pointer to specific positions within a file to read or write data, while sequential access processes data in a linear, consecutive manner. So, this is something that needs to be benchmarked. Before presenting the benchmarking code and results, let us recall how seeking works in Zig using the code of `ch04/lseek.zig`, which is the following:

```
const std = @import("std");

pub fn main(init: std.process.Init) !void {
    const args = try init.minimal.args.toSlice(
        init.arena.allocator(),
    );

    if (args.len < 2) {
        std.debug.print("Usage: {s} <file>\n", .{args[0]});
        return;
    }
    const filePath = args[1];
    const file = try std.Io.Dir.cwd().openFile(init.io, filePath, .{});
    defer file.close(init.io);

    var byte_buf: [1]u8 = undefined;
    const n = try file.readPositionalAll(init.io, &byte_buf, 5);
    if (n > 0) {
        std.debug.print("Byte at offset 5: 0x{x}\n", .{byte_buf[0]});
    } else {
        std.debug.print("File is shorter than 5 bytes.\n", .{});
    }
    const stat = try file.stat(init.io);
    std.debug.print("File size: {d} bytes\n", .{stat.size});
}
```

The core operation happens with `try file.readPositionalAll()`. In Zig 0.16, file I/O uses *positional reads* instead of the traditional seek-then-read two-step. Rather than moving a shared file cursor with `seekTo()` and then issuing a separate `read()`, `readPositionalAll()` accepts the target byte offset as a direct argument, reading from that exact position in a single call without modifying any internal cursor state. This design is safer for concurrent use — multiple coroutines can read from different offsets of the same file simultaneously without interfering with each other — and it maps directly to the `pread(2)` system call on POSIX systems, which the kernel can satisfy more efficiently than a seek followed by a read.

We do not show the full source for `ch04/benchSeekingSequential.zig` here. As with the writing benchmark, the code is a straightforward exercise in setting up a controlled experiment: it generates a test file and then times three distinct functions — `benchmarkSequentialBuffered()`, `benchmarkPositionalDirect()`, and `benchmarkPositional()` — to measure their performance. We recommend reviewing the implementation yourself. Let us now try `ch04/benchSeekingSequential.zig` to get useful and practical insights:

```
$ zig run ch04/benchSeekingSequential.zig -- 100M 4K
Generating 100MB test file...

- Results -
Sequential (full read) speed:        0.69 MiB/s
Sequential (buffered)  speed:        0.71 MiB/s
Positional             speed:     1143.18 MiB/s
```

The benchmark results show a dramatic contrast between the three file reading strategies. Both the full-read approach, which allocates a buffer the size of the entire file and loads it in one call, and the sequential buffered approach, which reads through the file in chunks until the target range is covered, report speeds around `0.7 MiB/s`, while the positional read reaches an astonishing `1143.18 MiB/s`. This difference arises from the volume of data each method must traverse to reach the target. The sequential approaches are forced to read through the entire `100 MB` prefix just to access the requested slice, wasting distinct processing time on irrelevant data. While the buffered version (`0.71 MiB/s`) is marginally faster than the unbuffered version (`0.69 MiB/s`) due to fewer system calls, it remains bound by the linear scan. The seek-based version, however, jumps directly to the `100 MB` offset and reads only the requested `4 KiB`, completing almost instantly. Since the benchmark calculates throughput based on the useful data retrieved over a tiny duration, the resulting speed appears massive, proving that the fastest way to read data is to skip what you do not need.

So far in this chapter, we have treated the buffer as a purely application-level concern — a slice of memory that we fill before flushing, chosen for its effect on the number of `write(2)` calls we make. But a write that leaves our process does not go directly to storage. It enters the Linux block layer, where the kernel I/O scheduler decides when and in what order it will actually reach the device. Understanding that layer changes how you think about buffer sizing, flush frequency, and the tradeoff between latency and throughput. A program that flushes every 512 bytes is making a very different bargain with the scheduler than one that accumulates 64 KiB before writing, and the right choice depends not just on your workload but on which scheduler is sitting between your code and the disk.

The discussion that follows covers Linux-specific kernel internals, but the concepts are broadly applicable: every operating system has an I/O scheduling layer, and every system programmer benefits from understanding how the kernel arbitrates between competing I/O requests. However, the specific commands, `sysfs` paths, and scheduler names (`BFQ`, `mq-deadline`, `Kyber`) are Linux-only and will not work on macOS or Windows. Readers on those platforms can follow the conceptual discussion and apply the mental model to their own kernel's I/O subsystem — macOS uses its own I/O Kit framework, and Windows uses the I/O Manager — but the hands-on commands in this section require a Linux machine or a Linux virtual machine.

The Linux I/O scheduler occupies the block layer, the thin translation stratum between a filesystem and a storage driver. When a process issues a `read(2)` or `write(2)` call on a buffered file, the virtual filesystem resolves the request into one or more 512-byte (or 4 KB) sector-aligned block I/O requests and hands them to the scheduler. The scheduler's job is to decide the *order* in which those requests reach the device. On a spinning disk, reordering adjacent-sector requests into a single sweep of the read head — the classic elevator algorithm — can turn dozens of random seeks into one sequential pass, multiplying throughput by an order of magnitude. On an NVMe solid-state drive, the same reordering provides no benefit: the device's internal parallelism and near-zero seek time make the scheduler optimizations irrelevant or even counterproductive, so the kernel bypasses it entirely on fast devices.

Linux 5.x exposes several schedulers through `sysfs`, and you can inspect and change the active scheduler per device using `cat /sys/block/sda/queue/scheduler` to read the current setting and `echo mq-deadline | sudo tee /sys/block/sda/queue/scheduler` to change it. The active scheduler is reported in brackets in the output, for example `[mq-deadline] kyber bfq none`. The **none scheduler**, also called **noop** on older kernels, passes requests straight through with a simple FIFO queue. It is the default on NVMe drives and virtual block devices where reordering yields nothing and latency is paramount. **mq-deadline** is the standard choice for HDDs and SATA SSDs. It partitions requests into read and write queues with per-request deadlines, servicing whichever queue has the nearest deadline to prevent any single request from starving indefinitely. The read deadline defaults to 500 ms and the write deadline to 5 seconds, both tunable via `/sys/block/<dev>/queue/iosched/`. `Kyber` uses a token-bucket mechanism to give independent latency targets for read and synchronous-write traffic, making it particularly effective on fast multi-queue SSDs where the bottleneck is not *seek time* but fair access to device queues across processes. **BFQ (Budget Fair Queuing)** tracks per-process I/O budgets and provides bandwidth guarantees that survive large bursty neighbors. It is the default on desktop distributions such as Fedora and Ubuntu because it keeps interactive applications — video players, browsers — responsive even while a background build or backup is hammering the disk.

The I/O scheduler and the page cache readahead mechanism are distinct, though they interact. When the kernel detects a sequential read pattern — successive `read(2)` calls advancing through a file — the readahead algorithm issues speculative reads several pages ahead of the current position before the application asks for them. The default readahead window is 128 KB (`/sys/block/<dev>/queue/read_ahead_kb`), though the kernel adjusts it dynamically: a sustained sequential workload pushes the window up; random access collapses it to zero. Your buffer size choice intersects with readahead in a subtle way. If your application reads in 512-byte chunks, the kernel must issue many small requests, each potentially stalling until the scheduler acknowledges a CQE, and the readahead algorithm has few opportunities to observe a sequential pattern before you switch position. If you read in 64 KB chunks, each request covers 16 pages, the scheduler sees fewer but larger block requests that it can merge trivially, and the readahead window tracks comfortably ahead. The Zig benchmarks in this chapter (`ch04/benchmarkReading.zig`) consistently show an inflection around 4–16 KB: below that, syscall overhead and scheduler round-trips dominate; above 64 KB, the gains diminish because the readahead is already doing the prefetching for you.

The default `open(2)` call uses *buffered I/O*: every read populates the page cache, and subsequent reads of the same data return from memory without touching the disk. Every write goes to the page cache and is eventually written back to disk by the kernel dirty page writeback threads. Buffered I/O is almost always the right choice for programs that access files in a typical pattern: the cache absorbs both temporal locality (re-reading the same region) and write coalescing (multiple small writes to the same page are flushed in one disk I/O). *Direct I/O* (opened with `O_DIRECT`) bypasses the page cache entirely. The kernel transfers data straight between the user buffer and the device DMA engine. This is appropriate in two situations: when a process manages its own, larger cache — PostgreSQL and MySQL both do this — and when the workload is single-pass sequential (log ingestion, disk imaging), so cached pages would never be reused, only consuming memory. Direct I/O imposes a strict constraint: the user buffer, the file offset, and the transfer length must all be aligned to the logical block size, typically 512 bytes or 4 KB. How you satisfy this constraint depends on where your buffer lives. For stack-allocated buffers, `extern struct` and `@alignOf()` let you verify the alignment at compile time. For heap-allocated buffers — the common case for large I/O workloads — standard allocators in Zig align to 8 or 16 bytes by default, which is insufficient for `O_DIRECT`. A standard `allocator.alloc()` call will produce a buffer whose address does not meet the block-size alignment requirement, and the failure will be silent until the `write(2)` or `read(2)` call returns `EINVAL` at runtime. The correct approach is `allocator.alignedAlloc()` with the block size as the alignment argument:

```
// Allocate a buffer correctly aligned for O_DIRECT I/O.
// Both the address and the transfer length must be multiples
// of the device logical block size (512 B or 4 KiB).
const block_size = 4096;
const buf = try allocator.alignedAlloc(u8, block_size, transfer_len);
defer allocator.free(buf);
```

On POSIX systems, `posix_memalign()` is the C equivalent and is callable via `@cImport()` when working with C libraries that manage their own buffers. The alignment requirement applies equally to the file offset and the transfer length — all three must be multiples of the logical block size, or the kernel will reject the operation. Checking `@alignOf()` on a type tells you the compiler's alignment for that type in isolation, but it does not arrange correct alignment for heap allocations automatically. Always use `alignedAlloc()` when combining heap-allocated buffers with `O_DIRECT`.

Practical guidance for Zig programs

For sequential file processing — the common case in this chapter — a buffer of 4–64 KB gives near-optimal performance on both HDDs and SSDs. The exact sweet spot depends on the scheduler in use (BFQ penalizes very small requests more than none does), the page size (4 KB on x86-64 and aarch64), and the I/O depth: on an NVMe device, you may benefit from submitting multiple requests in flight simultaneously, which the Zig `Io` abstraction handles transparently via `io_uring` on Linux. The `ch04/benchmarkReading.zig` and `ch04/benchmarkWriting.zig` programs in this chapter are designed to find your system sweet spot empirically — run them with a range of buffer sizes and let the numbers guide your production defaults rather than relying on rules of thumb. For write-heavy workloads, the kernel writeback is controlled by `vm.dirty_ratio` (the ceiling at which writes start blocking) and `vm.dirty_background_ratio` (the softer threshold at which background flush begins). If your program writes at a sustained rate that keeps dirty memory above the background threshold, lowering `dirty_background_ratio` or increasing writeback frequency (`vm.dirty_writeback_centisecs`) can reduce latency spikes. These are system-wide tunables; for a production service, consider whether `O_SYNC` or `fdatasync()` after each logical transaction is a better tradeoff than relying on automatic writeback — it makes durability explicit in the code rather than depending on administrator configuration.

Summary

This chapter focused on high-performance I/O and data transformation. We implemented `zcat`, and we refined `zwc` from a scalar implementation to a vectorized one, using SIMD instructions to process 32-byte chunks in parallel. We then developed `z64`, a Base64 utility that manages bitwise realignment and buffer boundaries to handle arbitrary-sized streams. Benchmarks demonstrated that system call overhead dominates with small buffers; increasing buffer size to 4KB or 16KB saturates I/O bandwidth. Finally, we showed that the most efficient way to process data is to skip it entirely using seek operations rather than sequential scanning.

The deeper lesson connecting all these techniques is a single principle: performance in systems programming comes from reducing unnecessary work between your program and the hardware. Buffering reduces the number of times you cross the kernel boundary. SIMD reduces the number of iterations your CPU executes. Seeking reduces the number of bytes you read from storage. Each technique operates at a different layer of the stack, but all three are expressions of the same discipline — understanding exactly what the hardware costs and finding the shortest path through it. That discipline is what separates a tool that works from a tool that scales. The next chapter is about the persistent structures of the operating system and the exploration of the filesystem. You will examine the Zig way for traversing directories and reading file metadata, as well as the construction of practical tools like a recursive tree visualizer and a cross-platform filesystem watcher.

Exercises

- Implement a simplified version of `tail(1)` called `ztail` that prints the last `N` bytes of a file. First, determine the file size, then use `file.readPositionalAll(init.io, buffer, offset)` with a calculated `offset`, avoiding a full sequential read of the file.

Additional resources

- The `hyperfine` tool: `https://github.com/sharkdp/hyperfine`
- The SIMD (Single instruction, multiple data) Wikipedia article: `https://en.wikipedia.org/wiki/Single_instruction,_multiple_data`
- Base64: `https://en.wikipedia.org/wiki/Base64`

Part 2

Systems Programming in Practice

In the second part of the book, we apply the foundations from Part 1 to the full range of systems programming challenges: navigating filesystems, programming the network stack, managing processes and signals, orchestrating concurrent workloads, implementing asynchronous I/O and building production-grade services. Each chapter introduces a systems concept first and then builds a complete, working tool that makes the concept tangible and measurable. The part closes by persisting structured data with SQLite3 and building a domain-specific language interpreter from scratch — two projects that draw on every technique introduced across the book.

This part of the book includes the following chapters:

- *Chapter 5, Navigating Directories and Filesystem Events*
- *Chapter 6, Programming the Network Stack*
- *Chapter 7, Managing Threads, Processes, and Signals*
- *Chapter 8, Orchestrating Concurrency and Synchronization*
- *Chapter 9, Implementing Asynchronous I/O*
- *Chapter 10, Building a High-Performance In-Memory Cache Server*
- *Chapter 11, Persisting Structured Data with SQLite3*
- *Chapter 12, Developing a Domain-Specific Language*

5

Navigating Directories and Filesystem Events

Modern Systems Programming demands a delicate balance between high-level abstraction and granular control over hardware resources, a philosophy that lies at the heart of the Zig programming language. Zig provides the primitives necessary to interact directly with the underlying data structures and event notifications of the operating system. This chapter explores the mechanics of *navigating* directories and managing files, moving beyond basic I/O to address the technical realities of modern filesystems. We will begin by implementing basic tasks before constructing a directory tree visualizer, `ztree`, which requires an understanding of recursive traversal and the handling of edge cases like cyclic symbolic links. From there, the focus shifts to real-time interaction through `zwatch`, a file-monitoring utility that leverages platform-specific primitives such as Linux `inotify` or BSD `kqueue`. Finally, the chapter concludes with the implementation of core system utilities equivalent to `chmod(1)` and `chown(8)`.

This chapter covers:

- Interacting with the filesystem
- Implementing `ztree`
- Implementing `zwatch`, a file watcher
- Implementing the functionality of `chmod(1)` and `chown(8)`

The required theory

Interacting with the filesystem in Zig 0.16 centers on the `std.Io.Dir` and `std.Io.File` namespaces, which emphasize explicit resource management and platform-specific efficiency. At the core of this system is the `std.Io.Dir` struct, representing an open directory handle. Unlike older Zig versions, where iteration required a separate `IterableDir` type, in Zig 0.16, you enable iteration simply by passing `.iterate = true` when opening a directory handle and then calling `.iterate()` on it to obtain an iterator. This design ensures that the overhead of maintaining an iterator is only incurred when explicitly requested. Zig provides a robust abstraction for relative and absolute paths through `std.Io.Dir.cwd()`, which returns the current working directory as a starting point for operations, and `std.Io.Dir.openDirAbsolute()`, which allows you to work with absolute paths. When navigating these structures, the developer must be mindful of the `std.Io.File` and `std.Io.Dir` lifetimes; failing to close these handles can lead to resource leaks, which is why the `defer` keyword is ubiquitous in the implementation of `ztree`. Understanding the underlying `Stat` structure is also vital, as it provides the metadata — such as permissions, timestamps, and inode numbers — required to implement tools like `chmod(1)` and `chown(8)`. As you progress, keep in mind that the standard library prioritizes safety, often requiring explicit flags to handle symbolic links or to ensure that recursive operations do not fall into infinite loops caused by cyclic references. Before manipulating files through code, it is essential to understand the underlying data structures that the kernel uses to represent them on the disk. This requires a shift in perspective: from seeing a file as a mere name to seeing it as an inode — a unique index node that stores metadata such as size, timestamps, and ownership, independent of the filename itself. This distinction is the logical foundation for understanding how permissions are enforced through bitmasks and how symbolic links function as specialized files that point to other paths.

Understanding inodes, file permissions, and symlinks

To program the filesystem effectively, one must look past the convenience of filenames and interact with the UNIX kernel internal system. At the heart of every UNIX filesystem is the **inode** (*index node*), a data structure that serves as the identity of a file. While a filename is a human-readable entry in a directory table, the inode contains the essential metadata: the file size, its physical location on the disk blocks, and its **file permissions**. These permissions are stored as a bitmask, determining which users can read, write, or execute the content. When you change a file mode or owner, you are not modifying the file data but rather updating the fields within this inode. However, as operating systems evolved to support multiple types of filesystems simultaneously, the kernel required an even higher level of abstraction: the **vnode** (*virtual node*). While the inode is a static record tied to a specific physical disk, the vnode is a dynamic, in-memory object managed by the **Virtual File System** (VFS) layer. When a process opens a file, the kernel creates a vnode that acts as a universal interface, translating generic system calls like `read(2)` or `write()` into the specific operations required by the underlying filesystem. On systems like macOS and the BSDs, the vnode is the primary point of contact for the kernel event-monitoring subsystems. Because the vnode exists in the kernel's active memory, it can track real-time changes across various storage technologies through a single, consistent structure.

The logic of UNIX filesystem security is governed by three distinct categories: the *Owner*, the *Group*, and *Others*. These are not abstract concepts — they are the exact three axes that `chmod` manipulates when it sets permission bits and that `chown` reassigns when it transfers file ownership. Understanding the relationship between these categories and the permission bits they control is what makes the implementations of `iChmod` and `zchown` later in this chapter readable at a glance rather than opaque bit manipulation. The theory here is the direct specification for the code that follows.

Each category is assigned a 3-bit value representing read (4), write (2) and execute (1) capabilities. These are often expressed in octal notation; for instance, a mode of `755` (binary `111 101 101`) grants the owner full control while restricting the group and others to reading and executing. Zig interacts with these permissions through the `std.posix.mode_t` type, allowing you to programmatically enforce security boundaries that the kernel will respect during every subsequent I/O operation. Building upon the concept that inodes are **symbolic links** or **symlinks**, unlike a **hard link**, which is simply another name pointing to the same inode, a symlink is a unique file type that contains a text string representing a path to another file or directory. When the kernel encounters a symlink during path resolution, it diverts the operation to the target path. This distinction is vital for systems programmers because certain operations, such as `lstat(2)` or `fchownat(2)` with specific flags, allow you to manipulate the link itself rather than the target it points to, preventing accidental modifications in complex directory structures.

We begin the code examples of this chapter by showing how to resolve a relative path to its absolute path, a critical functionality that can create secure and reliable code.

Resolve a relative path to its absolute counterpart

A relative path is sometimes insufficient for operations requiring unambiguous file identification, such as security auditing or managing configuration across different working directories. Resolving a relative path to its absolute counterpart — known as **canonicalization** — involves expanding the path from the root directory and resolving all symbolic links and redundant segments like `.` or `..`. Zig provides two primary native methods for this: `std.Io.Dir.cwd().realPathFile()`, which populates a caller-provided fixed buffer, and `std.Io.Dir.realPathFileAlloc()`, which dynamically allocates the necessary memory. This section explores these functions, contrasting them with the legacy C `realpath(1)` function. The example code can be found in `ch05/rel2abs.zig`:

```
const std = @import("std");

const c = @cImport({
```

```
    @cInclude("stdlib.h");
});


pub fn main(init: std.process.Init) !void {
    const io = init.io;
    const allocator = init.arena.allocator();
    const args = try init.minimal.args.toSlice(init.arena.allocator());

    if (args.len != 2) {
        std.debug.print("Usage: {s} <relative-path>\n", .{args[0]});
        return error.InvalidArgs;
    }

    const inputPath = args[1];
    var c_buffer: [std.fs.max_path_bytes]u8 = undefined;
    const resolvedPath = c.realpath(inputPath,&c_buffer);
    if (resolvedPath == null) {
        const err = std.c._errno().*;
        std.debug.print("C realpath() failed with errno {}\n", .{err});
    } else {
        const absPath = std.mem.span(resolvedPath);
        std.debug.print("C:    {s}\n", .{absPath});
    }

    var zig_buffer: [std.fs.max_path_bytes]u8 = undefined;
    const zig_path_len = std.Io.Dir.cwd().realPathFile(
        io,
        inputPath,
        &zig_buffer,
    ) catch |err| {
        std.debug.print(
            "Zig realpath failed: {s}\n",
            .{@errorName(err)},
        );
        return;
    };
    std.debug.print("Zig:  {s}\n", .{zig_buffer[0..zig_path_len]});

    const absolutePath = std.Io.Dir.realPathFileAlloc(
        std.Io.Dir.cwd(),
```

```
            io,
            inputPath,
            allocator,
        ) catch |err| {
            std.debug.print(
                "Zig realpathAlloc failed: {s}\n",
                .{@errorName(err)},
            );
            return;
        };
        defer allocator.free(absolutePath);
        std.debug.print("Alloc: {s}\n", .{absolutePath});
    }
```

While `std.Io.Dir.cwd().realPathFile()` provides a safe, slice-returning wrapper around the system canonicalization logic, it requires the developer to handle the maximum path length constraint. In contrast, `std.Io.Dir.realPathFileAlloc()` abstracts this away at the cost of a dynamic allocation, providing a more convenient interface for general-purpose application code where path lengths are unpredictable. Choosing between the three canonicalization methods depends primarily on your performance requirements, memory constraints, and the expected complexity of the environment. The native Zig methods are almost always preferred over C to maintain safety and reduce external dependencies. The choice between `std.Io.Dir.cwd().realPathFile()` and `std.Io.Dir.realPathFileAlloc()` is a trade-off between deterministic performance and architectural flexibility. You should prefer the fixed-buffer approach of `std.Io.Dir.cwd().realPathFile()` in performance-critical sections, such as tight loops or resource-constrained embedded systems, because it operates entirely on the stack without the overhead of heap management. This method is technically superior when you can guarantee that the path will not exceed `std.fs.max_path_bytes`, allowing the logic of your program to remain allocation-free. Conversely, `std.Io.Dir.realPathFileAlloc()` is the better choice for general-purpose applications where path lengths are unpredictable or where you wish to avoid the memory footprint of a large, pre-allocated stack buffer. The decision mainly depends on whether your utility values the zero-cost execution of stack-based buffers or the robust, no-fail capacity of dynamic memory.

The `ch05/rel2abs.zig` utility produces the following kind of output:

```
$ zig run ch05/rel2abs.zig -- .
C:    /Users/username/zigSP/code
```

```
Zig:   /Users/username/zigSP/code
Alloc: /Users/username/zigSP/code
```

This output also serves as a practical form of *testing* and *cross-validation* within the development cycle. You are verifying that three distinct methods of path resolution all converge on the same absolute path.

Path resolution is not a standalone utility concern — it is a foundational operation that underlies almost every filesystem interaction a system's program performs. Before a file can be opened, its path must be resolved. Before a directory can be traversed, its absolute position in the filesystem hierarchy must be known. Before a symlink can be followed safely, its target must be resolved against a known base. The `rel2abs.zig` logic introduced here reappears implicitly in `ztree.zig`, where every directory entry must be resolved relative to the traversal root, and in `zwatch`, where the paths passed to `inotify`, or `kqueue`, must be absolute to guarantee that the kernel watches the intended location regardless of how the process's working directory changes at runtime. Building path resolution correctly once, and understanding what it is doing, pays dividends across every filesystem-facing tool in the chapter. So, after mastering the ability to resolve individual paths, the focus shifts to navigating a filesystem effectively, which requires listing its contents.

Listing directory entries

Navigating the filesystem requires a clear understanding of the distinction between process-relative paths and absolute locations within the global hierarchy. Zig facilitates this through the `std.Io` namespace, where `std.Io.Dir.cwd()` serves as the primary entry point for relative operations by returning a `Dir` handle to the current working directory. Conversely, accessing an absolute path involves using `std.Io.Dir.openDirAbsolute()`, which bypasses the current process context to target a specific root-anchored address. Both ways are illustrated in `ch05/ls.zig`, which comes with the following example code:

```
const std = @import("std");

pub fn main(init: std.process.Init) !void {
    const io = init.io;
    var cwdDir: std.Io.Dir = try std.Io.Dir.cwd().openDir(
        io,
        ".",
        .{ .iterate = true },
    );
    defer cwdDir.close(io);
```

```
    var cwdIterator = cwdDir.iterate();
    while (try cwdIterator.next(io)) |dirContent| {
        std.debug.print("{s}\n", .{dirContent.name});
    }

    std.debug.print("\n", .{});
    var rootDir: std.Io.Dir = try std.Io.Dir.openDirAbsolute(io, "/", .{ .iterate
= true });
    defer rootDir.close(io);

    var rootIterator = rootDir.iterate();
    while (try rootIterator.next(io)) |dirContent| {
        std.debug.print("{s}\n", .{dirContent.name});
    }
}
```

The logic of this program revolves around the acquisition and consumption of *directory iterators* to reveal the contents of specific filesystem locations. It begins by obtaining a handle to the current working directory via `std.Io.Dir.cwd().openDir()`, where the inclusion of the `.iterate = true` flag is a critical prerequisite that instructs the kernel to *prepare the directory for streaming entries rather than simple access*. Once the handle is secured, the program initializes a `dirIterator` through the `iterate()` method, entering a `while` loop that calls `next()` to retrieve entries one by one. This non-allocating iterator yields a `dirContent` struct for each item, allowing the program to print the name field until the kernel signals that no more entries remain. Next, the program reassigns the `dir` variable by invoking `std.Io.Dir.openDirAbsolute()` to target the root directory and applies the same iterative logic.

Let us try `ch05/ls.zig`, which should generate the following kind of output:

```
$ zig run ch05/ls.zig
ch07
. . .
ch10

home
. . .
cores
```

Once you have successfully acquired a handle to a directory and can iterate through its entries, the next logical step is to move beyond mere names and investigate the specific nature of each item discovered. Identifying whether a directory entry refers to a regular file, a subdirectory, or a symbolic link is essential for deciding how the program should handle that entry — whether to open it for reading, descend into it recursively, or simply report its presence.

Finding the kind of file

The presented example code functions as a basic file identification utility that determines the nature of a filesystem entry by querying its metadata. Here is the `ch05/fileType.zig` implementation:

```
const std = @import("std");

pub fn main(init: std.process.Init) !void {
    const io = init.io;
    const args = try init.minimal.args.toSlice(init.arena.allocator());

    if (args.len < 2) {
        std.debug.print("Usage: {s} <path>\n", .{args[0]});
        return;
    }
    const path = args[1];


    // follow_symlinks = false uses lstat(2) semantics so .sym_link
    // is reachable. openFile() + stat() would follow the link and
    // report the target type instead.
    const meta = try std.Io.Dir.cwd().statFile(
        io,
        path,
        .{ .follow_symlinks = false },
    );

    defer file.close(io);
    const meta = try file.stat(io);

    switch (meta.kind) {
        .file => std.debug.print("{s} is a regular file.\n", .{path}),
        .directory => std.debug.print("{s} is a directory.\n", .{path}),
        .sym_link => std.debug.print(
            "{s} is a symbolic link.\n",
            .{path},
        ),
```

```
        else => std.debug.print(
            "{s} is some other kind of file.\n",
            .{path},
        ),
    }
}
```

Once the program confirms a target path is provided, it invokes the openFile() method on the current working directory handle — acquired through std.Io.Dir.cwd() — which performs the underlying open system call with read-only access. To retrieve the specific characteristics of the entry, the program executes file.stat(), a core statement that triggers a fstat(2) system call to populate a metadata structure. Finally, the program evaluates the kind field of this metadata within a switch block, allowing it to distinguish between regular files, directories, and symbolic links based on the information returned by the kernel. The follow_symlinks = false option is important here. Without it, the underlying call would follow the symbolic link before inspecting it — reporting the type of the target rather than the link itself — making the .sym_link branch unreachable. This mirrors the difference between open(2) and lstat(2) in POSIX: open always resolves symlinks, while lstat stops at the link and reports its own type. Any filesystem tool that needs to distinguish a symlink from its target must take the lstat path.

Let us now try ch05/fileType.zig to see how it works:

```
$ zig run ch05/fileType.zig -- .
. is a directory.
$ zig run ch05/fileType.zig -- ch05/fileType.zig
ch05/fileType.zig is a regular file.
```

While identifying the general category of a file allows for basic filtering, many systems programming tasks require a deeper investigation into the specific attributes stored within the inode. Transitioning from the simple classification of a file type to retrieving its metadata — such as size or modification timestamps — provides the comprehensive state necessary for auditing, backup, or synchronization logic.

Finding file metadata

The ability to inspect file metadata programmatically is the foundation of an entire class of systems tools. Every administrative utility that reports disk usage, audits permissions, detects stale files, or monitors directory growth is built on exactly the metadata fields examined in this section. du(1) walks the filesystem summing block counts. find(1) filters entries by modification time, size, or permission bits. Security auditing tools flag files with unexpected ownership or world-writable permissions. Backup systems use `mtime` and `ctime` to decide which files have changed since the last snapshot. The data is always the same, and the tool is defined by how it interprets and acts on that data. What this section has given you is direct access to that layer, which means any of those tools is now within reach.

This subsection explores the `std.Io.File.stat()` method and the resulting `Stat` structure, demonstrating how to extract and interpret the bitmasks and timestamps provided by the operating system. The example code retrieves and displays metadata about a specified file, similar to the UNIX `stat(1)` command:

```
const std = @import("std");

pub fn main(init: std.process.Init) !void {
    const io = init.io;
    const args = try init.minimal.args.toSlice(init.arena.allocator());
    if (args.len < 2) {
        std.debug.print("Usage: {s} <path>\n", .{args[0]});
        return;
    }
    const path = args[1];
    const file = try std.Io.Dir.cwd().openFile(
        io,
        path,
        .{ .mode = .read_only },
    );
    defer file.close(io);
    const meta = try file.stat(io);

    std.debug.print("File: {s}\n", .{path});
    std.debug.print("Size: {} bytes\n", .{meta.size});
    std.debug.print(
        "Permissions: 0o{o}\n",
        .{meta.permissions.toMode()},
    );
    std.debug.print("Last accessed: {?}\n", .{meta.atime});
    std.debug.print("Last modified: {}\n", .{meta.mtime});
    std.debug.print("Created: {}\n", .{meta.ctime});
    std.debug.print("Kind: {}\n", .{meta.kind});
}
```

The code prints a usage message showing the expected command format and returns early without raising an error if insufficient arguments are provided. The core file access operation uses `std.Io.Dir.cwd().openFile()` to open the specified file in read-only mode from the current working directory. The `.mode = .read_only` option ensures the program only needs read permissions, making it safer, and preventing accidental modifications. Once the file is open, the program calls `file.stat()` to retrieve the file metadata, which returns a structure containing comprehensive information about the file. This single system call efficiently gathers all the file statistics rather than making multiple separate queries. The metadata structure contains fields like size, permissions, timestamps, and file type, all of which are standard components of UNIX-like file systems. The program then prints this metadata in a human-readable format using `std.debug.print()`. The file size is displayed in bytes using the default decimal format. The permissions are particularly interesting: they are printed using the `0o{o}` format specifier, where `0o` is the Zig octal literal prefix and `{o}` tells the formatter to output the value in octal notation, which is the conventional way to represent UNIX file permissions (like `0755` or `0644`). The three timestamp fields show when the file was last accessed (`atime`), last modified (`mtime`), and when its metadata was last changed (`ctime`). Finally, the program displays the entry kind. The generated output is similar to the following:

```
$ zig run ch05/metadata.zig -- .
File: .
Size: 640 bytes
Permissions: 0o40755
Last accessed: 1770911423089384708
Last modified: 1770911423039374554
Created: 1770911423039374554
Kind: .directory
```

The `Size` reflects the bytes allocated for the directory entry table, while `Permissions` has a value of `0o40755`, which breaks into two parts: the prefix `40`, which encodes the file type (`S_IFDIR = 0o040000`, occupying bits 12–15 of the mode word), and the permission bits `755` — read, write, and execute for the owner; read and execute for group and others. This distinction matters when reading or writing mode values programmatically, since `0o40755` and `0o755` are not interchangeable. The timestamps are rendered as raw nanoseconds since the UNIX Epoch, representing the high-precision temporal data stored in the inode. Finally, the `Kind` field confirms the kernel classification of the path as a `.directory`.

Once the program can successfully retrieve file metadata, it becomes possible to manipulate the filesystem by creating references that point to existing data. Moving from passive inspection to the creation of *symbolic links* introduces a layer of abstraction where a single path on the disk acts as a pointer to another, allowing for flexible organization without duplicating the underlying storage blocks.

Creating symbolic links

Creating a symbolic link involves the `symlink(2)` system call, which tells the filesystem to treat the new entry as a shortcut. In this section, we explore the `std.Io.Dir.symLink()` method using the following example code (`ch05/symbolicLink.zig`):

```
const std = @import("std");
const Allocator = std.mem.Allocator;

pub fn main(init: std.process.Init) !void {
    const io = init.io;
    const args = try init.minimal.args.toSlice(init.arena.allocator());

    if (args.len < 3) {
        std.debug.print(
            \\Usage: {s} [--dir] <target> <link_name>
            \\  --dir    : Create directory symlink (Windows)
            \\Example:
            \\  {s} source.txt link.txt
            \\  {s} --dir my_dir dir_link
            \\
        , .{ args[0], args[0], args[0] });
        return;
    }

    var is_dir_flag = false;
    var arg_index: usize = 1;
    if (std.mem.eql(u8, args[1], "--dir")) {
        is_dir_flag = true;
        arg_index = 2;

        if (args.len < 4) {
            std.debug.print("Missing arguments for --dir flag\n", .{});
            return error.InvalidArguments;
        }
    }
```

```
    const target = args[arg_index];
    const link_name = args[arg_index + 1];
    try std.Io.Dir.cwd().symLink(
        io,
        target,
        link_name,
        .{ .is_directory = is_dir_flag },
    );

    std.debug.print(
        "Created symlink: '{s}' -> '{s}'\n",
        .{ link_name, target },
    );
}
```

The code uses `init.arena.allocator()` to manage the lifecycle of command-line arguments. The program then implements a simple state machine to check for a `--dir` flag; this is a critical detail for Windows compatibility, where the underlying system must be explicitly told whether a link points to a file or a directory at the moment of creation. Once the `target` and `link_name` are extracted from the remaining arguments, the program invokes the `symLink()` method on a handle to the current working directory. This core statement executes the `symlink(2)` system call on POSIX systems or the `CreateSymbolicLink()` API on Windows, utilizing the `.is_directory` option to pass the previously determined flag.

Execute `ch05/symbolicLink.zig` on your own machine:

```
$ zig run ch05/symbolicLink.zig -- ch01/hwv1.zig /tmp/myLink.zig
Created symlink: '/tmp/myLink.zig' -> 'ch01/hwv1.zig'
$ ls -l /tmp/myLink.zig
lrwxr-xr-x  1 mtsouk  wheel  13 Feb 26 21:08 /tmp/myLink.zig -> ch01/hwv1.zig
```

After establishing how to create pointers to data through symbolic links, the logical progression leads to the final stage of a file lifecycle: removal. Moving from the creation of filesystem entries to the act of deleting a file requires a shift in focus toward how the kernel manages resource cleanup and reference counting.

Deleting a file

In Zig, the delete operation is handled via the `deleteFile()` method, which serves as a safeguard against accidentally targeting directories — which require a different set of system calls for removal. The following program (`ch05/deleteFile.zig`) functions as a minimal implementation of the `rm(1)` utility, designed to remove a single file from the filesystem:

```
const std = @import("std");

pub fn main(init: std.process.Init) !void {
    const io = init.io;
    const args = try init.minimal.args.toSlice(init.arena.allocator());
    if (args.len < 2) {
        std.debug.print("Usage: {s} <file>\n", .{args[0]});
        return;
    }
    const file = args[1];
    try std.Io.Dir.cwd().deleteFile(io, file);
}
```

By invoking the `deleteFile()` method, the program triggers the underlying `unlink(2)` system call. This system call is technically significant because it does not *necessarily erase* data; rather, it removes the directory entry associated with the filename and decrements the inode link count. If the link count reaches zero and no processes have the file open, the kernel marks the storage blocks as available for reuse. Try `ch05/deleteFile.zig` on your machine, but make sure that you do not delete any valuable data.

While the removal of a single file is a straightforward matter of unlinking an entry, the logic required for deleting a directory is more restrictive to ensure the structural integrity of the filesystem. Transitioning from file deletion to directory removal introduces the `rmdir(2)` system call, which imposes a strict prerequisite: the target directory must be entirely empty.

Deleting a directory

In this section, we show how to delete a directory. The example code (`ch05/rmdir.zig`) removes a directory while demonstrating a logic flow that prioritizes explicit path validation before attempting a destructive operation:

```
const std = @import("std");

pub fn doesItExist(io: std.Io, path: []const u8) bool {
    std.Io.Dir.cwd().access(io, path, .{}) catch |e| switch (e) {
        error.FileNotFound => return false,
        else => return false,
    };
```

```
    return true;
}

pub fn main(init: std.process.Init) !void {
    const io = init.io;
    const args = try init.minimal.args.toSlice(init.arena.allocator());
    if (args.len < 2) {
        std.debug.print("Usage: {s} <directory>\n", .{args[0]});
        return;
    }
    const directory = args[1];

    if (!doesItExist(io, directory)) {
        std.debug.print("Path {s} does not exist!\n", .{directory});
        return error.PathDoesNotExist;
    }
    try std.Io.Dir.cwd().deleteDir(io, directory);
}
```

The `doesItExist()` function utilizes the `std.Io.Dir.cwd().access()` method, triggering the `access(2)` system call with an empty set of flags to verify the existence of the path without requiring specific read or write permissions. Within this helper, the logic relies on Zig error handling to catch a `FileNotFound` error, returning a Boolean that determines the subsequent execution path. If the directory is confirmed to exist, the program proceeds to call `deleteDir()` on the current working directory handle, which executes the `rmdir(2)` system call. It is technically significant to note that this specific system call will only succeed if the target directory is empty; if the directory contains any files or subdirectories, the kernel will return an error, which the program then propagates through the `try` keyword. Try `ch05/rmdir.zig` on your machine:

```
$ mkdir /tmp/testFolder
$ zig run ch05/rmdir.zig -- /tmp/testFolder
$ zig run ch05/rmdir.zig -- ~/IdeaProjects
error: DirNotEmpty
/opt/homebrew/Cellar/zig/0.16.0/lib/zig/std/posix.zig:2592:22: 0x1005d085f in
unlinkatZ (rmdir)
            .NOTEMPTY => return error.DirNotEmpty,
```

The stack trace in the output is not a bug — it is expected behavior in Debug mode. When an error is propagated with `try` and reaches `main()` without getting handled, the Zig runtime prints a backtrace to help with debugging. A production tool would catch `error.DirNotEmpty` explicitly and print a user-friendly message instead, which is exactly what a real `rm(1)` implementation would do.

Once the program can successfully create and destroy filesystem entries, the focus shifts to the logic of relocation. Moving from the simple deletion of a file to moving a file introduces the `rename(2)` system call, an operation that is technically more sophisticated than it appears. This transition moves us away from the two-step *copy and delete* process toward an atomic transaction that updates the directory structure without necessarily touching the actual data blocks on the disk.

Moving a file

The logic of a move operation depends heavily on the relationship between the source and the destination. If both paths reside on the *same physical partition*, the kernel simply unlinks the old name and creates a new directory entry pointing to the existing inode. This is an *O(1)* operation — instantaneous regardless of file size. However, if the destination is on a different filesystem, the operation fails at the system call level with an `EXDEV` error (*Invalid cross-device link*), requiring the application to manually copy the data and delete the original. The following code functions as a minimal implementation of the `mv(1)` command, designed to move or rename filesystem entries *within the same volume*:

```
const std = @import("std");

pub fn main(init: std.process.Init) !void {
    const io = init.io;
    const args = try init.minimal.args.toSlice(init.arena.allocator());

    if (args.len != 3) {
        std.debug.print("Usage: {s} <source> <dest>\n", .{args[0]});
        return error.InvalidArgs;
    }

    const src = args[1];
    const dst = args[2];
    const cwd = std.Io.Dir.cwd();
    if (std.Io.Dir.rename(cwd, src, cwd, dst, io)) |_| {
        return;
    } else |err| {
        std.debug.print("Error: {}\n", .{err});
```

```
    }
}
```

The core operation is performed by the `rename()` method on the `std.Io.Dir()` handle, which executes the `rename(2)` system call. As already discussed, this system call is an *atomic operation* within the same filesystem, meaning it updates the directory entry to point to the new name of the existing inode without moving the underlying data blocks. If the destination already exists, the kernel replaces it with the source entry in a single transaction, ensuring that no other process sees a partially moved state. The program prints a diagnostic message if the operation fails due to issues like missing source files or cross-device movement restrictions, while simply exiting on successful completion. Try `ch05/mv.zig` with care to avoid any surprises:

```
$ zig run ch05/mv.zig -- README.md pleaseREADME.md
$ ls -l pleaseREADME.md
-rw-r--r--  1 mtsouk  staff  37 Jan  2 10:45 pleaseREADME.md
```

Building a directory tree visualizer requires more than just visiting a list of files; it demands a logical framework for representing the hierarchical relationship between containers and their contents. This involves a transition from inspecting individual metadata entries to visualizing a collective structure. While our previous examples dealt with solitary files and directories, `ztree` must maintain a persistent state as it descends through nested folders, using the recursion depth to decide which visual connectors correctly illustrate the branching of the filesystem.

Implementing ztree, a directory tree visualizer

The `ztree` utility we implement in this section serves as a practical application of the concepts of recursion and directory iteration, transforming the flat results into a human-readable tree. By implementing this tool, we move from simple path resolution to managing deep directory traversals, learning how to track nesting levels and handle the technical challenges of modern filesystems, such as cyclic symbolic links or restricted access permissions. We begin our journey by showing how to recursively walk directories.

Recursively walking directories

The core of the program logic rests on the ability to distinguish between leaf nodes (regular files) and branch nodes (directories) and then decide whether to terminate the path or descend further. This exercise provides an ideal introduction to the `std.Io.Dir` pattern, which allows us to stream entries from the kernel without the overhead of loading an entire directory listing into memory at once. Based on that, the implementation of `ztree` relies on a recursive function, `printTree()`, to navigate the filesystem hierarchical structure:

```
const DirEntry = struct {
    name: []const u8,
    is_dir: bool,
    symlink_target: ?[]const u8 = null,
};

fn printTree(
    allocator: std.mem.Allocator,
    io: std.Io,
    dir: std.Io.Dir,
    depth: usize,
    prefix: []const u8,
    show_all: bool,
    max_depth: ?usize,
    stdout: *std.Io.Writer,
) !void {
    if (max_depth) |limit| {
        if (depth >= limit) return;
    }

    var entries: std.ArrayListUnmanaged(DirEntry) = .empty;
    var it = dir.iterate();
    while (try it.next(io)) |entry| {
        if (!show_all and entry.name.len > 0 and entry.name[0] == '.')
            continue;

        const name_copy = try allocator.dupe(u8, entry.name);

        if (entry.kind == .sym_link) {
            // Resolve the link target for display only; ztree
            //  does not recurse into symlinked directories to avoid
            // infinite loops on cyclic links.
            var link_buf: [4096]u8 = undefined;
            const target = dir.readLink(io, entry.name, &link_buf) catch
                null;
            const target_copy = if (target) |len|
                try allocator.dupe(u8, link_buf[0..len])
            else
```

```
                null;
            try entries.append(allocator, .{
                .name = name_copy,
                .is_dir = false,
                .symlink_target = target_copy,
            });
        } else {
            try entries.append(
                allocator,
                .{
                    .name = name_copy,
                    .is_dir = (entry.kind == .directory),
                },
            );
        }
    }

    std.mem.sort(DirEntry, entries.items, {}, struct {
        fn lessThan(_: void, a: DirEntry, b: DirEntry) bool {
            return std.mem.lessThan(u8, a.name, b.name);
        }
    }.lessThan);

    const count = entries.items.len;
    for (entries.items, 0..) |item, index| {
        const is_last = (index == count - 1);
        const connector = if (is_last) "└── " else "├── ";
        if (item.symlink_target) |target| {
            try stdout.print(
                "{s}{s}{s} -> {s}\n",
                .{ prefix, connector, item.name, target },
            );
        } else {
            try stdout.print(
                "{s}{s}{s}\n",
                .{ prefix, connector, item.name },
            );
        }

        if (item.is_dir) {
            const extension = if (is_last) "    " else "│   ";
```

```
                const new_prefix = try std.fmt.allocPrint(
                    allocator,
                    "{s}{s}",
                    .{ prefix, extension },
                );
                if (dir.openDir(
                    io,
                    item.name,
                    .{ .iterate = true },
                )) |sub_dir| {
                    var sub_dir_mut = sub_dir;
                    defer sub_dir_mut.close(io);
                    try printTree(
                        allocator,
                        io,
                        sub_dir_mut,
                        depth + 1,
                        new_prefix,
                        show_all,
                        max_depth,
                        stdout,
                    );
                } else |_| {}
            }
        }
    }
```

The logic begins by obtaining an iterator from the current directory handle using `dir.iterate()`. However, to produce a sorted tree like the standard UNIX utility, we must collect these entries into a temporary `ArrayListUnmanaged` and sort them by name before beginning the print cycle. This ensures that the visual output remains deterministic regardless of how the underlying filesystem returns directory entries. Once the entries are sorted, the function iterates through the list, calculating the appropriate visual connector — either a branch (├──) or a corner (└──) — based on whether the current item is the last in the list. When a folder is encountered, the function prepares for a deeper descent. It calculates a new `prefix` by appending either a vertical bar or empty spaces to the current `prefix`, ensuring that the tree members are drawn correctly for nested levels. The function then calls itself with the new subdirectory handle, incrementing the `depth` counter to respect any user-defined limits passed via the `-L` flag.

`ztree.zig` displays symbolic links with an arrow annotation showing their target — for example, `lib -> ../lib64` — using `dir.readLink()` to resolve the link path at display time. It does not recurse into symlinked directories, even when a symlink points to a directory. This is a deliberate safety decision: on systems where symlinks form cycles (for example, a directory that contains a symlink back to one of its own ancestors), blindly following them would send `ztree.zig` into an infinite loop. The well-known `tree(1)` utility applies the same policy by default. If you need to traverse symlinked subtrees, a production tool would track visited inodes and stop recursion when an already-seen inode is encountered, but that complexity is left as an exercise for the reader.

Developing the utility

The main detail that is currently missing from `ztree` is the `main()` implementation:

```
pub fn main(init: std.process.Init) !void {
    const io = init.io;
    const allocator = init.arena.allocator();
    const args = try init.minimal.args.toSlice(init.arena.allocator());

    var show_all = false;
    var max_depth: ?usize = null;
    var start_path: []const u8 = ".";

    var i: usize = 1;
    while (i < args.len) : (i += 1) {
        const arg = args[i];
        if (std.mem.eql(u8, arg, "--all") or std.mem.eql(u8, arg, "-a")) {
            show_all = true;
        } else if (std.mem.eql(u8, arg, "-L")) {
            i += 1;
            if (i >= args.len) {
                std.debug.print("Error: missing depth value after -L\n", .{});
                return error.MissingDepthValue;
            }
            max_depth = try std.fmt.parseInt(usize, args[i], 10);
        } else if (arg.len > 0 and arg[0] == '-') {
            std.debug.print("Usage: tree [--all] [-L <depth>] [path]\n", .{});
            return error.InvalidArgument;
        } else {
            start_path = arg;
```

```
        }
    }
```

Once the memory allocator is initialized, the program retrieves the command-line arguments into a slice using `init.minimal.args.toSlice()`. Next, we enter a manual `while` loop to parse these arguments, starting from index `1`. The state of the program is tracked through three primary variables: `show_all` (a Boolean for hidden files), `max_depth` (an optional integer), and `start_path` (the root of our search, defaulting to the current directory). When the loop encounters `-L`, it manually increments the index `i` to consume the subsequent value. We include a safety check here to ensure a value exists before attempting to parse it with `std.fmt.parseInt()`. Any other argument beginning with a hyphen that we do not recognize triggers a usage message and an error. If an argument does not start with a hyphen, we treat it as the target path for the directory traversal. This manual approach to argument parsing mirrors the style found in classical UNIX utilities, providing full control over the program initial configuration. The remaining code of the `main()` function implementation is the following:

```
    var buf: [4096]u8 = undefined;
    var w_impl = std.Io.File.stdout().writer(io,&buf);
    const stdout=&w_impl.interface;

    var root_dir = try std.Io.Dir.cwd().openDir(
        io,
        start_path,
        .{ .iterate = true },
    );
    defer root_dir.close(io);

    try stdout.print("{s}\n", .{start_path});
    try printTree(
        allocator,
        io,
        root_dir,
        0,
        "",
        show_all,
        max_depth,
        stdout,
    );
```

```
    try stdout.flush();
}
```

To optimize output performance, we wrap `stdout` in a buffered writer. This prevents the system from performing a costly `write(2)` system call for every individual branch or filename; instead, small strings are aggregated into a 4096-byte buffer and flushed in bulk. The logic then shifts to the filesystem. We obtain a handle to the starting path using `std.Io.Dir.cwd().openDir()`. As you already know, it is critical to set `.iterate = true` in the options; without this flag, the kernel will not allow us to call `iterate()` on the directory handle later. We use `defer root_dir.close(io)` to ensure the file descriptor is released regardless of whether the subsequent recursion succeeds or fails. The core of the utility is the recursive call to `printTree()`. We pass the `allocator` for prefix strings and entry sorting, the initial `root_dir` handle, a starting `depth` of `0`, and an empty `prefix` string. Once the recursive traversal completes, we perform a final `bw.flush()` to ensure any remaining data in the buffer is pushed to the terminal before the program exits. This manual flush is a critical final step in the program execution; without a final call to `flush()` in the `main()` function, any data remaining in the buffer that did not reach the 4,096-byte threshold would be lost when the process terminates, resulting in a truncated directory tree.

It is time to try `ztree` and see it in action:

```
$ zig run ch05/ztree.zig -- -L 1
.
├── LICENSE
├── README.md
├── ch01
. . .
├── ch11
└── ch12
```

By passing the `-L 1` argument, the program logic limits the recursive traversal to the first level of the filesystem hierarchy, effectively flattening the view to show only immediate children.

While `ztree` provides a static snapshot of a filesystem hierarchy at a single point in time, modern system utilities often require the ability to react to changes as they happen. Transitioning from a one-time directory traversal to implementing `zwatch`, a Filesystem Watcher, shifts our focus from structural visualization to event-driven monitoring.

Implementing zwatch, a filesystem watcher

Building a practical filesystem monitor requires moving beyond static metadata inspection toward a dynamic engagement with kernel-level event systems. The `zwatch` utility serves as a bridge between the filesystem concepts explored earlier and the asynchronous nature of modern operating systems, providing real-time notifications whenever files are created, modified, or deleted within a directory. In this section, we implement a cross-platform watcher that utilizes Linux `inotify` and macOS/BSD `kqueue` APIs. The first task we need to perform is determining the current UNIX variant in order to utilize the appropriate system call.

Finding out the active operating system

Before creating the filesystem watcher, we need to be able to differentiate between macOS and Linux because these two operating systems use different ways of understanding file events. The following example code (`ch05/linuxMac.zig`) allows you to determine the current operating system:

```
const std = @import("std");
const builtin = @import("builtin");

pub fn main(_: std.process.Init.Minimal) !void {
    if (builtin.os.tag == .linux) {
        std.debug.print("This is a Linux machine!\n", .{});
    } else if (builtin.os.tag == .macos or builtin.os.tag.isBSD()) {
        std.debug.print("This is a macOS machine!\n", .{});
    } else {
        @compileError("Unsupported operating system");
    }
}
```

This code demonstrates Zig's powerful *compile-time introspection* capabilities, which allow a single codebase to support multiple operating systems without the overhead of runtime checks. By importing the `builtin` module, the program gains access to information about the target architecture and operating system known at the moment the code is compiled.

The logic relies on `builtin.os.tag`, an enumeration that identifies the target platform. Because the value of `builtin.os.tag` is a compile-time constant (known as `comptime` in Zig), the compiler evaluates the `if` and `else if` branches during the compilation phase itself. It identifies which branch matches the current target and includes only that specific code in the final binary, pruning the branches that do not apply. This ensures that the resulting executable is as slim as possible and contains no unnecessary logic for platforms it is not running on. The final `else` branch introduces the `@compileError()` builtin function, which is a directive that instructs the compiler to stop and issue a fatal error if execution reaches this point during compilation. By placing this in the final branch, we create a *compile-time guard* that prevents the program from even being built on unsupported systems like Windows. This pattern is fundamental to systems programming in Zig, as it forces the developer to handle platform differences explicitly and safely before the code reaches a user's machine.

Running `ch05/linuxMac.zig` on a macOS machine generates the following output:

```
$ zig run ch05/linuxMac.zig
This is a macOS machine!
```

Now that we know how to distinguish between different UNIX variants, it is time to talk about file events, which implement the core logic of `zwatch`.

Understanding file events

Understanding file events requires shifting from a model where the application polls the filesystem for changes to one where the *kernel proactively notifies the application of specific occurrences*. A file event is essentially a signal generated by the operating system kernel when a transition occurs in the lifecycle of a filesystem object, such as a write operation, a name change, or a deletion.

Technically, these events are delivered through a specialized file descriptor that acts as a queue. When the kernel detects an action that matches a "mask" or "filter" previously registered by the program, it pushes an event structure into this queue. The application then reads this queue, often using a blocking read that sleeps until data is available, ensuring high efficiency by consuming zero CPU cycles while the filesystem is idle. For a tool like `zwatch`, the logic must account for the variable-size nature of these notifications — particularly in `inotify`, where the filename is appended directly to the event header — requiring careful pointer arithmetic and alignment to extract the data safely.

Using OS primitives: inotify (Linux) vs. kqueue (BSD/ macOS)

Different kernels categorize these file events with varying degrees of granularity: Linux `inotify` system provides a detailed stream of individual file actions, including the specific name of the affected file, whereas BSD-derived systems like macOS use `kqueue` to monitor file descriptors for broad changes like *vnode* modifications. Grasping this logic is fundamental because it determines how an application must parse incoming data; it must distinguish between the event itself and the context — such as the file path or the process ID — that triggered it.

With that in mind, let us proceed with the event loop, which handles the logic of the utility.

The event loop: polling for changes

Once the monitoring system is initialized and the kernels are instructed to watch specific paths, the program must transition into a persistent state of readiness. The **event loop** is the heart of `zwatch`; it is where the logic shifts from configuration to execution. So, the program enters an infinite `while (true)` loop that blocks execution until the kernel broadcasts a notification. This approach is significantly more efficient than manual polling — where a program might check a file timestamp every second — because the process remains dormant and consumes nearly zero CPU cycles until the OS signals that an I/O event has occurred. In the Linux implementation, the logic revolves around the `std.posix.read()` system call. The program provides a buffer, and the kernel fills it with one or more `inotify_event` structures. Because these structures are *variable-length* (due to the file name field), the loop must manually increment a pointer through the buffer, carefully aligning, and casting memory to extract each event. In contrast, the kqueue logic on macOS and BSD uses the `kevent` system call to retrieve a *fixed-size* array of `struct_kevent`. While `inotify` provides the specific name of the file that changed, `kqueue` notifies us that a change happened on a specific file descriptor. This distinction is vital: it highlights the difference between an event-centric API and a descriptor-centric API. Handling these events requires a robust parsing strategy to ensure the program does not misinterpret the stream of data. By using `@ptrCast()` and `@alignCast()`, we safely navigate the raw bytes returned by the kernel, transforming them back into meaningful structures that our program can act upon. This event loop represents the bridge between the static filesystem and the dynamic reality of a running operating system, allowing `zwatch` to provide immediate feedback the moment a file is created, modified, or deleted.

With all the information in mind, let us see the Linux-related implementation:

```
fn runInotify(
    io: std.Io,
    stdout: std.Io.File,
    dirs: []const [:0]const u8,
) !void {
    const linux = std.os.linux;
    const rc_init = linux.inotify_init1(linux.IN.CLOEXEC);
    const init_errno = std.posix.errno(rc_init);
    if (init_errno != .SUCCESS)
        return std.posix.unexpectedErrno(init_errno);
    const fd: std.posix.fd_t = @intCast(rc_init);
    defer _ = linux.close(fd);
```

```
    var msg_buf: [512]u8 = undefined;
    const msg = try std.fmt.bufPrint(
        &msg_buf,
        "zwatch: Monitoring via inotify (Linux) - {d} director{s}...\n",
        .{ dirs.len, if (dirs.len == 1) "y" else "ies" },
    );
    try stdout.writeStreamingAll(io, msg);

    for (dirs) |dir| {
        const rc_watch = linux.inotify_add_watch(
            fd,
            dir.ptr,
            linux.IN.MODIFY | linux.IN.CREATE | linux.IN.DELETE,
        );
        const watch_errno = std.posix.errno(rc_watch);
        if (watch_errno != .SUCCESS)
            return std.posix.unexpectedErrno(watch_errno);
        const dir_msg = try std.fmt.bufPrint(
            &msg_buf,
            "  Watching: {s}\n",
            .{dir},
        );
        try stdout.writeStreamingAll(io, dir_msg);
    }
```

The `runInotify()` function establishes the monitoring infrastructure by first creating an `inotify` instance through `inotify_init1()`. This returns a file descriptor that acts as a single centralized queue for all filesystem events. The logic then utilizes a loop to register each directory provided in the arguments. For every directory, we call `inotify_add_watch()` and provide a bitmask consisting of `IN.MODIFY`, `IN.CREATE` and `IN.DELETE`. This bitmask explicitly tells the Linux kernel which specific state changes in the inode should trigger a notification to our program. By using a single file descriptor (`fd`) to watch multiple paths, the function sets up a highly efficient multiplexing system where the kernel does the heavy lifting of tracking changes across various points in the filesystem hierarchy. The use of `std.fmt.bufPrint()` with a fixed-size `msg_buf` demonstrates a memory-conscious approach to logging. Instead of allocating new strings on the heap for every directory we monitor, we reuse a stack-allocated buffer to format our status messages. This reflects the "low-overhead" philosophy of the tool, ensuring that even the setup phase of the monitoring loop is as lightweight as possible. Once the loop completes, the kernel is fully primed with our list of targets, and the file descriptor is ready to be used in the subsequent blocking read loop to capture events:

```
    var buf: [4096]u8 align(@alignOf(linux.inotify_event)) = undefined;while
(true) {
        const bytes_read = try std.posix.read(fd,&buf);
        var i: usize = 0;
        while (i < bytes_read) {
            const event = @as(
                *const linux.inotify_event,
                @ptrCast(@alignCast(&buf[i])),
            );
            if (event.len > 0) {
                const name_ptr = @as(
                    [*:0]const u8,
                    @ptrCast(&buf[i + @sizeOf(linux.inotify_event)]),
                );
                const name = std.mem.span(name_ptr);
                const event_msg = try std.fmt.bufPrint(
                    &msg_buf,
                    "Event detected on: {s}\n",
                    .{name},
                );
                try stdout.writeStreamingAll(io, event_msg);
            }
            i += @sizeOf(linux.inotify_event) + event.len;
        }
    }
}
```

This event loop processes raw byte streams from the Linux kernel. The `buf` array is explicitly aligned to `linux.inotify_event` to ensure that the initial cast is hardware safe. Inside the loop, `std.posix.read()` blocks until the kernel populates the buffer with one or more events. Because inotify events are variable-length — consisting of a fixed-size header followed by a null-terminated filename — the logic uses pointer arithmetic to navigate the buffer. For each event, `@ptrCast()` and `@alignCast()` convert the current buffer offset into a struct pointer. If `event.len` is greater than zero, the filename is extracted by offsetting the pointer by `@sizeOf(linux.inotify_event)`. The `std.mem.span()` function converts the resulting null-terminated C-pointer into a safe Zig slice. Finally, the loop increments the index `i` by the total size of the header and the padded name field, ensuring the next iteration begins exactly at the start of the subsequent event header.

The `runKqueue()` function demonstrates the BSD-style approach to event monitoring, which is strictly descriptor-oriented:

```
fn runKqueue(
    io: std.Io,
    stdout: std.Io.File,
    dirs: []const [:0]const u8,
    allocator: std.mem.Allocator,
) !void {
    const kq = std.c.kqueue();
    if (kq == -1) return error.KqueueFailed;
    defer _ = std.c.close(kq);

    var msg_buf: [512]u8 = undefined;
    const msg = try std.fmt.bufPrint(
        &msg_buf,
        "zwatch: Monitoring via kqueue - {d} director{s}...\n",
        .{ dirs.len, if (dirs.len == 1) "y" else "ies" },
    );
    try stdout.writeStreamingAll(io, msg);

    var events: std.ArrayListUnmanaged(c.struct_kevent) = .empty;
    defer events.deinit(allocator);

    for (dirs) |dir| {
        const dir_fd = try std.posix.openat(
            std.posix.AT.FDCWD,
            dir,
            .{ .ACCMODE = .RDONLY },
            0,
        );
        // dir_fd must stay open for the lifetime of the monitoring
        // session; kqueue holds a reference to it. A production tool
        // would collect these fds and close them on SIGTERM/SIGINT
        // before exiting.

        const event = c.struct_kevent{
            .ident = @intCast(dir_fd),
```

```
            .filter = c.EVFILT_VNODE,
            .flags = c.EV_ADD | c.EV_ENABLE | c.EV_CLEAR,
            .fflags = c.NOTE_WRITE | c.NOTE_DELETE | c.NOTE_RENAME,
            .data = 0,
            .udata = null,
        };
        try events.append(allocator, event);

        const dir_msg = try std.fmt.bufPrint(
            &msg_buf,
            "  Watching: {s}\n",
            .{dir},
        );
        try stdout.writeStreamingAll(io, dir_msg);
    }
```

The code begins by creating a kernel event queue via `kqueue()`, which returns a file descriptor used to manage a list of active monitors. As kqueue monitors specific open file descriptors, it requires the program to manually `open()` each directory it intends to watch. Note that we do not close these directory descriptors immediately; they must remain open for the duration of the watch as the kernel uses the descriptor lifecycle to track the *vnode* (the kernel internal representation of the file) being monitored. For each directory, the function constructs a `struct_kevent` to define the monitoring parameters. The `ident` field holds the folder file descriptor, while the `filter` is set to `EVFILT_VNODE`, indicating we are watching for filesystem-level changes. The `flags` specify that we want to add and enable the event (`EV_ADD | EV_ENABLE`) and that the event should be cleared automatically after it is triggered (`EV_CLEAR`). The `fflags` field is the most critical part of the logic as it tells the kernel exactly which operations to report — specifically writes, deletions, and renames occurring within that directory. These event structures are collected into a `std.ArrayList`, allowing the program to register multiple watches in a single batch. This setup phase highlights the trade-off inherent in kqueue: while it provides a powerful, unified interface for monitoring everything from sockets to files, it imposes an administrative burden on the programmer to manage an open file descriptor for every watched entry. By the time the loop finishes, the kernel is primed with a collection of *vnode* filters, and the program is ready to transition into the event-processing loop:

```
    _ = c.kevent(
        kq,
        events.items.ptr,
        @intCast(events.items.len),
```

```
            null,
            0,
            null,
        );

        while (true) {
            var event_list: [10]c.struct_kevent = undefined;
            const n = c.kevent(
                kq,
                null,
                0,
                &event_list,
                event_list.len,
                null,
            );
            if (n > 0) {
                for (0..@intCast(n)) |idx| {
                    const evt = event_list[idx];
                    const change_msg = try std.fmt.bufPrint(
                        &msg_buf,
                        "Changes detected in directory (fd: {d})\n",
                        .{evt.ident},
                    );
                    try stdout.writeStreamingAll(io, change_msg);
                }
            }
        }
    }
```

The code utilizes the `kevent()` system call for two distinct purposes: registration and event polling. The first call passes the `events` array to the kernel, which registers the monitoring filters for all directories in a single atomic operation. By setting the `eventlist` parameters to `null` and `0`, this call returns immediately after updating the kernel interest set. The program then enters an infinite loop, calling `kevent()` again, but this time with the `changelist` parameters set to `null`. This transition shifts the system call into *waiting mode*, where it blocks the thread until at least one of the registered vnode changes occurs. When the kernel wakes the process, it populates the `event_list` buffer with fixed-size `struct_kevent` entries. Unlike the inotify implementation, which requires *parsing* a variable-length byte stream, the kqueue logic simply iterates through the returned array. The `evt.ident` field provides the file descriptor of the modified directory, allowing the program to report activity relative to the specific handle. Using a fixed-size array for event_list ensures deterministic memory usage within the loop, reflecting the descriptor-centric, high-efficiency design of BSD-style event notification.

Running the program on macOS produces the following kind of output:

```
$ zig run ch05/zwatch.zig -- /tmp
zwatch: Monitoring via kqueue - 1 directory...
  Watching: /tmp
Changes detected in directory (fd: 4)
Changes detected in directory (fd: 4)
```

In the kqueue architecture, the ident field of the returned kevent structure contains the file descriptor of the object that triggered the filter. In this case, fd: 4 is the descriptor the program received when it opened /tmp. Each time a file is created, deleted or renamed within that directory, the kernel triggers a NOTE_WRITE event.

Running the program on Linux produces the following kind of output:

```
$ zig run ch05/zwatch.zig -- /tmp
zwatch: Monitoring via inotify (Linux) - 1 directory...
  Watching: /tmp
Event detected on: newFile
```

The final line, Event detected on: newFile, reveals the primary advantage of the inotify API: the kernel provides the specific name of the file that triggered the event.

Moving from the structural relocation of files to the administrative control of their access rights requires a shift from managing paths to managing security metadata. The permission bits and ownership fields that chmod(1) and chown(8) manipulate are stored in the same inode that ztree and zwatch read when traversing the filesystem — changing them is a direct write to that metadata, not to the file contents.

Implementing the chmod logic

In UNIX variants, the *mode* of a file is a fundamental component of the kernel permission model, and changing it allows a program to lock down sensitive data or mark a newly created script as an executable. The example code can be found in ch05/iChmod.zig:

```
const std = @import("std");

pub fn main(init: std.process.Init) !void {
```

```
    const io = init.io;
    const args = try init.minimal.args.toSlice(init.arena.allocator());

    if (args.len != 3) {
        std.debug.print("Usage: {s} <mode> <file>\n", .{args[0]});
        return error.InvalidArgs;
    }
    const modeStr = args[1];
    const filePath = args[2];

    const mode = std.fmt.parseInt(u16, modeStr, 8) catch {
        std.debug.print("Invalid mode: {s}\n", .{modeStr});
        return error.InvalidMode;
    };

    const file = std.Io.Dir.cwd().openFile(io, filePath, .{}) catch {
        std.debug.print("chmod failed for file: {s}\n", .{filePath});
        return error.ChmodFailed;
    };
    defer file.close(io);

    if (std.c.fchmod(file.handle, @as(std.posix.mode_t, mode)) != 0) {
        std.debug.print("chmod failed for file: {s}\n", .{filePath});
        return error.ChmodFailed;
    }

    std.debug.print(
        "Set permissions {s} for {s}\n",
        .{ modeStr, filePath },
    );
}
```

In `main()`, the program validates that exactly three arguments are provided: the program name itself, the permission mode, and the target file path. If the argument count is incorrect, it prints a usage message showing the expected format and returns an error. The program extracts the mode string and file path from the arguments array, where `args[1]` contains the permission mode (like `"755"` or `"644"`) and `args[2]` contains the file path. The mode string is then parsed as an octal number (base 8) into a 16-bit unsigned integer using `std.fmt.parseInt()`. *The use of base 8 is crucial here because UNIX file permissions are conventionally expressed in octal notation.* If the string is not a valid octal value, the program returns `error.InvalidMode`. The target file is then opened via `std.Io.Dir.cwd().openFile()` and the underlying file descriptor is passed directly to `std.c.fchmod()`, which is the C `fchmod(2)` system call. This avoids the need to `@cImport` any C headers — Zig exposes `fchmod()` through `std.c` directly. If the call fails, the program reports the error and returns `error.ChmodFailed`.

Try `ch05/iChmod.zig`, but be careful and reset any changes you made afterward:

```
$ zig run ch05/iChmod.zig -- 644 README.md
Set permissions 644 for README.md
```

After establishing the methods for modifying file access modes, the logical next step is to address the identity of the file manager. Implementing the `chown(8)` logic shifts our focus from what can be done with a file to who owns it.

Implementing the chown logic

Implementing the `chown(8)` logic requires moving beyond the contents of a file to modify its relationship with the system users and groups. This program (`ch05/zchown.zig`) is an implementation of the `chown(8)` functionality in Zig, which changes file ownership by setting the user ID (UID) and group ID (GID) for a specified file:

```
const std = @import("std");
const builtin = @import("builtin");

const c = @cImport({
    @cInclude("unistd.h");
    @cInclude("fcntl.h");
});

pub fn main(init: std.process.Init) !void {
    const io = init.io;
    const stdout = std.Io.File.stdout();
    const stderr = std.Io.File.stderr();
    const args = try init.minimal.args.toSlice(init.arena.allocator());

    if (args.len != 4) {
        try stderr.writeStreamingAll(
            io,
            "Usage: zchown <uid> <gid> <file>\n",
        );
```

```
        std.process.exit(1);
    }

    const uid = std.fmt.parseInt(c.uid_t, args[1], 10) catch {
        try stderr.writeStreamingAll(io, "Error: Invalid UID\n");
        return;
    };

    const gid = std.fmt.parseInt(c.gid_t, args[2], 10) catch {
        try stderr.writeStreamingAll(io, "Error: Invalid GID\n");
        return;
    };
```

The implementation begins by importing the standard Zig library and the `builtin` module, then uses `@cImport` to include two critical C header files: `unistd.h` and `fcntl.h`, which provide the `fchownat(2)` function and related constants needed for file ownership operations. The main function begins by getting the file handles for stdout and stderr. After memory allocation and retrieving command-line arguments, the program validates that exactly four arguments are provided: the program name, the target UID, the target GID, and the file path. If this condition is not met, an error message is written to stderr, and the program exits with status code 1. The use of `stderr.writeStreamingAll()` directly instead of `std.debug.print()` is notable because it provides more control over where output goes and is appropriate for command-line use.

The program then parses the UID and GID arguments as decimal integers (base 10) into their respective C types (`c.uid_t` and `c.gid_t`). Each parsing operation includes error handling that catches parse failures and writes descriptive error messages to stderr before returning early. The core operation uses the `fchownat(2)` function, which is a modern POSIX primitive that is more flexible than the traditional `chown(2)`:

```
    const path = args[3];
    // Produce a null-terminated copy; fchownat expects a C string.
    var path_buf: [std.fs.max_path_bytes:0]u8 = undefined;
    const path_z = std.fmt.bufPrintZ(&path_buf, "{s}", .{path}) catch {
        try stderr.writeStreamingAll(io, "Error: path too long\n");
        return;
    };

    const result = c.fchownat(c.AT_FDCWD, path_z.ptr, uid, gid, 0);
    if (result != 0) {
        const err: std.posix.E = @enumFromInt(std.c._errno().*);
```

```
        var msg_buf: [256]u8 = undefined;
        const msg = try std.fmt.bufPrint(
            &msg_buf,
            "zchown: error: {s}\n",
            .{@tagName(err)},
        );
        try stderr.writeStreamingAll(io, msg);
        std.process.exit(1);
    }

    var success_buf: [256]u8 = undefined;
    const success_msg = try std.fmt.bufPrint(
        &success_buf,
        "Changed {s} to {d}:{d}\n",
        .{ path, uid, gid },
    );
    try stdout.writeStreamingAll(io, success_msg);
}
```

The `fchownat(2)` function is called with five arguments: `c.AT_FDCWD` (a special constant meaning *current working directory*), `path.ptr` (the pointer to the null-terminated file path string), the parsed UID and GID values, and a flags value of `0`. The `AT_FDCWD` constant tells the kernel to resolve the path relative to the current directory, mimicking the behavior of standard `chown(8)`, while the zero flag value indicates that the function should follow symbolic links (as opposed to changing the ownership of the link itself). The error handling for the `fchownat(8)` call is more sophisticated than a simple success check. If the result is non-zero (indicating failure), the program uses `std.posix.errno()` to convert the raw result into a *Zig error enum*, then formats this error into a human-readable message using `std.fmt.bufPrint()` and a stack-allocated buffer. Finally, upon successful execution, the program formats and writes a confirmation message to standard output showing the file path and the new `UID:GID` ownership values, giving clear feedback that the operation completed as expected. Try `ch05/zchown.zig` on your machine – use your own user ID and group ID values or reset any changes afterwards:

```
$ zig run ch05/zchown.zig -- 501 20 /tmp/testFile
Changed /tmp/testFile to 501:20
$ ls -l /tmp/testFile
-rw-r--r--  1 mtsouk  staff  0 Feb 26 21:26 /tmp/testFile
```

While the program used numeric IDs (`501` and `20`), `ls(1)` performs a reverse lookup in the system user and group databases (typically `/etc/passwd` and `/etc/group`). On my machine, UID 501 is associated with my username (`mtsouk`) and GID `20` with the group `staff`. With this utility, we have reached the end of this chapter, having moved from the basic opening of files to the administrative control of the entire filesystem hierarchy.

Summary

In the tradition of classical systems programming, we created many *self-contained programs. By ensuring that the logic, the data structures, and the system calls are all contained within a single, readable source file, we provide a complete map of the program's intent and execution.* This is an invaluable way to learn because there are no hidden configuration files, opaque third-party dependencies, or external frameworks to distract from the core mission: communicating with the operating system. Furthermore, self-contained code ensures reproducibility and longevity. A program that relies only on its own source and the standard library is far more likely to compile and run correctly years from now, even if the Zig programming language introduces breaking changes, than one tethered to a shifting ecosystem of external packages.

So, in this chapter, we have explored how Zig interacts with the filesystem. By constructing the `ztree` utility, we navigated the complexities of recursive directory traversal and learned to handle the nuanced logic of symbolic links and metadata inspection via `std.Io.Dir`. The implementation of `zwatch` demonstrated the power of interfacing directly with platform-specific event subsystems. Finally, by building native versions of `chmod(1)` and `chown(8)`, we grounded these high-level concepts in the granular reality of UNIX permissions and ownership. This foundation in filesystem mechanics is not just about building clones of classic utilities but about gaining the technical confidence to build the next generation of systems software that is both efficient and platform-aware.

In the next chapter, we transition from the isolated environment of the local filesystem to the interconnected world of the network stack. Programming at the socket level provides a unique perspective on how modern software communicates, stripping away the convenience of high-level frameworks to reveal the fundamental mechanics of data exchange. We will construct basic TCP and UDP servers and show how a single server can manage multiple client interactions simultaneously. Finally, we will implement a custom HTTP-based System Monitor API, bridging the gap between raw binary streams and the structured JSON responses that power the modern web.

Exercises

- Modify `ch05/ls.zig` to accept the paths as command-line arguments.
- The current `zwatch` implementation highlights a fundamental architectural difference between Linux and BSD-derived systems like macOS. While `inotify` provides the name of the changed file directly in the event stream, `kqueue` only signals that a change occurred on a specific directory file descriptor. Modify the `runKqueue()` function to identify the specific file that was created or deleted within a watched directory. To achieve this, the program logic must transition from a reactive model to a stateful one. When a directory is first registered for monitoring, the program should store a *snapshot* of its current contents. Upon receiving a `NOTE_WRITE` event from `kqueue`, the program must rescan the directory and compare the new state against the stored snapshot to find the discrepancy. This exercise will require you to use a `std.StringHashMap` to store the filenames for each directory file descriptor and implement a *comparison function* that identifies whether a file was added or removed by checking the results of a new `std.Io.Dir.iterate()` call against the map.

Additional resources

- Zig 2026: `https://www.youtube.com/watch?v=iqddnwKF8HQ`
- UNIX inode: `https://en.wikipedia.org/wiki/Inode`

6

Programming the Network Stack

Networks are the connective tissue of modern software — understanding how to program them at the socket level gives us insight that no amount of high-level abstraction can replace. First, you need to understand *TCP/IP* – the foundational protocol suite that powers the Internet and most local networks. TCP/IP stands for **Transmission Control Protocol/Internet Protocol**, a layered set of rules that govern how data is packaged, addressed, transmitted, and received between computers. At a high level, IP handles addressing and routing, ensuring that data reaches the correct destination, while TCP ensures that data is delivered reliably and in order. Together, they enable computers to exchange information transparently across diverse hardware and networks. **Port numbers** help identify specific services or applications running on a device. While an IP address identifies a host on the network, a port number specifies which process on that host should handle incoming or outgoing data. Think of it like sending a letter to an apartment building (the IP address) and including an apartment number (the port) to reach the right person. Port numbers are 16-bit unsigned integers, ranging from 0 to 65535. Ports *0–1023* are well-known ports used by standard services like HTTP (port 80) or SSH (port 22). Ports *1024–49151* are registered ports used by third-party services, while ports *49152–65535* are dynamic or private ports, used for temporary connections.

We start with the humble Echo server and progressively work toward more sophisticated services. Along the way, you will see how TCP and UDP differ and how the HTTP protocol you interact with every day is just structured text flowing over a TCP connection. Our approach remains consistent with the previous chapters: we try to avoid the convenience of external libraries in favor of the Standard Library and raw system calls. This ensures that every program we write is self-contained, transparent, and easy to modify and adapt to your needs. This chapter covers:

- Writing a TCP Echo server and client
- Writing a UDP Echo server and client

- Creating Docker images
- Working with the HTTP protocol
- Creating a System Monitor API
- Enforcing Protocol Correctness with `comptime`

Writing an Echo server using TCP

Now that we understand the basics of TCP/IP and how port numbers work, let us put that knowledge into practice by writing a simple **Echo server** in Zig. Echo servers have been a foundational learning tool in network programming since the earliest days of UNIX — RFC 862 standardized the protocol in 1983 — because they isolate the mechanics of connection handling, data framing, and error propagation from application logic, making every assumption about the underlying transport visible and testable. A TCP Echo server listens for incoming TCP connections, reads data sent by clients, and immediately sends the same data back – just like an echo. It is a classic example of learning socket programming because it involves key networking tasks: creating sockets, binding to a port, accepting connections, reading data, and writing data. Consider the following example code (`ch06/echoServer.zig`) for the implementation of a sample TCP Echo server – you can use that as a template when developing TCP servers in Zig and change the logic of the server according to your needs:

```
const std = @import("std");

pub fn main(init: std.process.Init) !void {
    const io = init.io;
    const args = try init.minimal.args.toSlice(init.arena.allocator());

    if (args.len < 2) {
        std.debug.print("Usage: echo_server <port>\n", .{});
        return error.MissingPort;
    }
    const port = try std.fmt.parseInt(u16, args[1], 10);
    const address = try std.Io.net.IpAddress.parseIp4("0.0.0.0", port);
    var server = try address.listen(io, .{});
    defer server.deinit(io);
    std.debug.print("Listening on 0.0.0.0:{d}\n", .{port});

    while (true) {
        const stream = server.accept(io) catch |err| {
            std.log.err("accept: {}", .{err});
```

```
                continue;
            };
            defer stream.close(io);
            std.debug.print("Accepted connection\n", .{});

            var rbuf: [1024]u8 = undefined;
            var wbuf: [1024]u8 = undefined;
            var reader_impl = stream.reader(io,&rbuf);
            var writer_impl = stream.writer(io,&wbuf);
            constreader=&reader_impl.interface;
            constwriter=&writer_impl.interface;

            while (true) {
                var buf: [1024]u8 = undefined;
                const n = reader.readSliceShort(&buf) catch break;
                if (n == 0) break;
                writer.writeAll(buf[0..n]) catch break;
                writer.flush() catch break;
            }
        }
    }
```

This program implements a basic *synchronous TCP echo server*. The logic begins by transforming a port number into a network-ready format using `std.Io.net.IpAddress.parseIp4()`, which binds the service to the `0.0.0.0` interface, allowing it to *accept traffic from any network adapter available to the host.* Once the address is defined, the core command `address.listen()` initializes a socket, sets it to a listening state. The execution then enters an infinite `while(true)` loop, acting as the primary event loop where the server blocks on `server.accept()`. This statement pauses execution until a client initiates a TCP handshake; once successful, it returns a `std.Io.net.Stream`. To manage resources correctly, the program uses a nested block containing `defer stream.close()`. This ensures that as soon as the inner echo logic finishes, the file descriptor for that specific connection is released, preventing the server from hitting the operating system limit on open files. Inside this connection block, the program enters a secondary `while` loop to facilitate the actual Echo behavior. It utilizes `reader.readSliceShort()` to pull data into a local 1024-byte buffer. The logic here relies on the return value `n`: if `n` is zero, it signals that the client has closed the connection (EOF), triggering a `break` to exit the loop. If data is present, the server sends it back to the client using `writer.writeAll()`, making sure that every byte received is accurately transmitted back to the source before the next read operation begins. In a *synchronous* or *single-threaded* approach like the one shown, *the server handles exactly one client at a time*. The logic is straightforward because the program flow is linear: the CPU waits at `server.accept()` for a client, and once connected, it remains entirely occupied by the inner `readSliceShort()` and `writeAll()` loop until that specific client disconnects. While this is simple to debug and mirrors the style of early UNIX network utilities, its primary limitation is that any other clients attempting to connect will be held in the listen queue and appear to *hang* until the current session is terminated. In *Chapter 7, Managing Threads, Processes, and Signals*, we see how to develop concurrent TCP servers. However, it will be in *Chapter 8, Orchestrating Concurrency and Synchronization,* that we are going to have full control over what is happening in our TCP servers.

For now, let us see how to test the TCP server using an existing UNIX tool to make sure that it works as expected. After that, we are going to develop a client in Zig.

Testing the Echo server

Until we test a server or a service, we cannot be sure whether it works or not. As we do not have an Echo client written in Zig yet, we are going to use UNIX utilities to do so. In this case, `socat(1)`. First, execute `zig runch06/echoServer.zig-- 1234` to start the server at port `1234` before using the following `socat(1)` commands:

```
$ echo "ping" | socat - TCP:localhost:1234
ping
$ echo "Hi again." | socat - TCP:localhost:1234
Hi again.
```

Now that we have a TCP Echo server up, running, and tested, it is time to build in Zig a client that can talk to it.

Writing a TCP Echo client

In this section, we write a TCP Echo client. This client will connect to the server, send a message, and wait for the server to echo it back. This is a small but important step in understanding how client-server communication works; you learn how to establish TCP connections, send data, and read responses. The goal here is to get a feel for the basics because whether you are writing chat apps, file transfer tools or game servers, the core mechanics are the same. Here is the example code as found in `ch06/echoClient.zig`:

```
const std = @import("std");

pub fn main(init: std.process.Init) !void {
    const io = init.io;
```

```
    var iter = init.minimal.args.iterate();
    defer iter.deinit();
    _ = iter.next();
    const host = iter.next() orelse {
        std.debug.print("Usage: echoClient <host> <port>\n", .{});
        return error.MissingHost;
    };
    const port_str = iter.next() orelse {
        std.debug.print("Usage: echoClient <host> <port>\n", .{});
        return error.MissingPort;
    };
    const port = try std.fmt.parseInt(u16, port_str, 10);
    const address = try std.Io.net.IpAddress.parseIp4(host, port);
    const stream = try address.connect(io, .{ .mode = .stream });
    defer stream.close(io);

    const message = "Hello from Zig client!\n";
    var rbuf: [1024]u8 = undefined;
    var wbuf: [1024]u8 = undefined;
    var reader_impl = stream.reader(io,&rbuf);
    var writer_impl = stream.writer(io,&wbuf);
    constreader=&reader_impl.interface;
    constwriter=&writer_impl.interface;

    try writer.writeAll(message);
    try writer.flush();
    try stream.shutdown(io, .send);
    const n = reader.readSliceShort(&rbuf) catch 0;
    if (n == 0) {
        std.debug.print("Server closed connection.\n", .{});
        return;
    }

    const response = rbuf[0..n];
    var out_buf: [1024]u8 = undefined;
    var stdout_impl = std.Io.File.stdout().writer(io,&out_buf);
    conststdout=&stdout_impl.interface;
    try stdout.print("Received: {s}", .{response});
    try stdout.flush();
}
```

The program begins by iterating over command-line arguments using `init.minimal.args.iterate()`. The iterator's first value is always the program name, so it is discarded with `_ = iter.next()`. The next two calls retrieve the host and port strings; if either is absent, the program prints a usage message and returns an error immediately, before any network activity has begun. The port string is then parsed into a `u16` with `std.fmt.parseInt()`, catching malformed input at the earliest possible point. With a valid host and port in hand, the client calls `std.Io.net.IpAddress.parseIp4(host, port)` to construct a binary network address. This function is strictly a parser — it accepts only dotted-decimal IPv4 literals such as `127.0.0.1` and will return `error.ParseFailed` on anything else, including hostnames like `localhost`. There is no DNS lookup involved. This limitation is intentional at this stage of the chapter and is addressed in `echoClientResolve.zig`, which introduces proper hostname resolution. Once an address is available, `address.connect(io, .{ .mode = .stream })` performs the TCP three-way handshake and returns an `Io.net.Stream` representing the live connection. The `.{ .mode = .stream }` option explicitly selects TCP as opposed to `.dgram` for UDP. A `defer stream.close(io)` is registered immediately, so the connection is torn down cleanly regardless of how the function exits. The I/O setup follows the idiomatic Zig 0.16 pattern. `stream.reader(io,&rbuf)` and `stream.writer(io,&wbuf)` each return a concrete implementation struct that owns its stack-allocated buffer; the actual `*std.Io.Reader` and `*std.Io.Writer` interfaces, live at `.interface` on those structs. The two-step var `reader_impl=...; const reader = &reader_impl.interface;` a pattern is necessary because the interface pointer must remain stable in memory, which requires taking the address of a named local rather than a temporary. The message is staged into the write buffer with `writer.writeAll(message)` and pushed over the socket with `writer.flush()`. The client then calls `stream.shutdown(io, .send)`, which performs a TCP half-close — equivalent to POSIX `shutdown(SHUT_WR)`. This signals to the server that no further data will arrive from the client side, causing the server to see EOF on its next read. In an echo protocol, this is important: without the shutdown, the server has no way to know the client has finished sending and may block indefinitely waiting for more data before it echoes anything back. With the *write side* closed, the client calls `reader.readSliceShort(&rbuf)`, which reads however many bytes are currently available and returns the count. The `catch 0` converts any read error into a zero, treating a dropped connection the same as an empty response. If the count is zero, the server has closed the connection, and the program exits with a message; otherwise, `rbuf[0..n]` is a correctly bounded slice of only the received bytes. Finally, the response is printed to stdout through its own buffered writer — `std.Io.File.stdout().writer(io, &out_buf)` with the same .interface indirection

— and `stdout.flush()` ensures the output reaches the terminal before the program exits. Let us now try the TCP client:

```
$ zig run ch06/echoClient.zig -- 127.0.0.1 1234
Received: Hello from Zig client!
```

Let us give it another try now, this time giving the hostname of the server instead of its IP address. As we are going to connect to the same machine, the server will be `localhost`:

```
$ zig run ch06/echoClient.zig -- localhost 1234
error: ParseFailed
. . .
else => return error.ParseFailed,
. . .
```

The root of the problem is found in `error.ParseFailed`. Put simply, our Echo client cannot work with hostnames such as `localhost`. So, we need to learn how to find the IP address of a hostname, which can be more than one. This is illustrated next.

Performing low-level hostname resolution

The presented Zig program resolves a hostname to its corresponding IP addresses, supporting both IPv4 and IPv6. Strictly speaking, we are going to learn how to convert a hostname to one or more IP addresses. Here (`ch06/resolveHostname.zig`) is the example code that demonstrates the technique — prepare yourselves for some low-level C code:

```
const std = @import("std");
const c = @cImport({
    @cInclude("netdb.h");
    @cInclude("sys/socket.h");
    @cInclude("arpa/inet.h");
    @cInclude("netinet/in.h");
});

pub fn main(init: std.process.Init) !void {
    var iter = init.minimal.args.iterate();
    defer iter.deinit();
    _ = iter.next();

    const hostname = iter.next() orelse {
        std.debug.print("Usage: resolveHostname <hostname>\n", .{});
```

```
        return;
    };

    var hints: c.addrinfo = .{};
    hints.ai_family = c.AF_UNSPEC; // Accept both IPv4 and IPv6
    hints.ai_socktype = c.SOCK_STREAM; // TCP stream sockets
    hints.ai_flags = 0;

    var res: ?*c.addrinfo = null;

    const err = c.getaddrinfo(hostname,null,&hints,&res);
    if (err != 0) {
        const errStr = c.gai_strerror(err);
        std.debug.print("getaddrinfo error: {s}\n", .{errStr});
        return;
    }
    defer c.freeaddrinfo(res);

    var ai = res;
    while (ai != null) : (ai = ai.?.ai_next) {
        const family = ai.?.ai_family;

        if (family == c.AF_INET) {
            const sockaddr4: *const c.sockaddr_in =
                @ptrCast(@alignCast(ai.?.ai_addr));
            var ipBuf: [16]u8 = undefined;

            const ip_ptr: *const u8 = @ptrCast(&sockaddr4.sin_addr);
            const ip_cstr = c.inet_ntop(
                family,
                ip_ptr,
                &ipBuf,
                ipBuf.len,
            );

            if (ip_cstr == null) {
                std.debug.print(
                    "inet_ntop failed for IPv4 address.\n",
                    .{},
                );
                continue;
```

```
                }

                const ipStr = std.mem.sliceTo(ipBuf[0..], 0);
                std.debug.print("IPv4: {s}\n", .{ipStr});
            } else if (family == c.AF_INET6) {
                const sockaddr6: *const c.sockaddr_in6 =
                    @ptrCast(@alignCast(ai.?.ai_addr));
                var ipBuf: [46]u8 = undefined;

                const ip_ptr: *const u8 = @ptrCast(&sockaddr6.sin6_addr);
                const ip_cstr = c.inet_ntop(
                    family,
                    ip_ptr,
                    &ipBuf,
                    ipBuf.len,
                );
                if (ip_cstr == null) {
                    std.debug.print(
                        "inet_ntop failed for IPv6 address.\n",
                        .{},
                    );
                    continue;
                }

                const ipStr = std.mem.sliceTo(ipBuf[0..], 0);
                std.debug.print("IPv6: {s}\n", .{ipStr});
            }
        }
    }
```

At the top, the program imports several C headers with `@cImport()`. Specifically, `netdb.h`, `sys/socket.h`, `arpa/inet.h` and `netinet/in.h`. These provide access to structures and functions like `addrinfo`, `getaddrinfo(3)`, and `inet_ntop`. The program prepares a `hints` struct of type `c.addrinfo` to configure the behavior of `getaddrinfo()`. It sets the address family to `c.AF_UNSPEC` to support both IPv4 and IPv6, the socket type to `c.SOCK_STREAM` for TCP and leaves `flags` unset. It then calls `c.getaddrinfo()` to resolve the hostname. If the call fails, it uses `c.gai_strerror` to print the human-readable error string. On success, the result is a linked list of `addrinfo` structs; the program iterates through them using a `while` loop. For each result, it checks whether the address is IPv4 (`c.AF_INET`) or IPv6 (`c.AF_INET6`). It uses `@ptrCast()` and

@alignCast() to convert the generic socket address pointer into either c.sockaddr_in or c.sockaddr_in6. It then extracts the address and converts it into a human-readable string using c.inet_ntop. Finally, the code uses std.mem.sliceTo() to trim the null-terminated C string and prints the resulting IP address with std.debug.print(). After finishing, we call c.freeaddrinfo() to release the resources. Let us see ch06/resolveHostname.zig in action:

```
$ zig run ch06/resolveHostname.zig -lc -- www.mtsoukalos.eu
IPv4: 65.21.59.44
$ zig run ch06/resolveHostname.zig -lc -- www.google.com
IPv6: 2a00:1450:4001:807::2004
IPv4: 142.251.141.100
```

When you examine www.mtsoukalos.eu, the program resolves the hostname to its corresponding IP address and prints IPv4: 65.21.59.44, indicating that the domain has an IPv4 address but no IPv6 address was returned. When you run the same program with a more globally distributed domain like www.google.com, the output shows both IPv6: 2a00:1450:4001:807::2004 and IPv4: 142.251.141.100, proving that Google supports both IP versions. With all that information in mind, an updated version of the Echo client is in order and will be presented next.

Improving the TCP Echo client

Having learned how to resolve a hostname manually, we can now enhance the Echo client by incorporating this functionality. However, we are not going to need C code as we are going to use the native std.Io.net.HostName.init() function. Here is the implementation of ch06/echoClientResolve.zig:

```
const std = @import("std");

pub fn main(init: std.process.Init) !void {
    const io = init.io;
    var iter = init.minimal.args.iterate();
    defer iter.deinit();
    _ = iter.next();

    const host = iter.next() orelse {
        std.debug.print("Usage: <program> <host> <port>\n", .{});
        return error.MissingHost;
    };
    const port_str = iter.next() orelse {
        std.debug.print("Usage: <program> <host> <port>\n", .{});
```

```
        return error.MissingPort;
    };

    const port = try std.fmt.parseInt(u16, port_str, 10);
    const hn = try std.Io.net.HostName.init(host);
    const stream = try hn.connect(io, port, .{ .mode = .stream });
    defer stream.close(io);

    const message = "Hello from Zig client!\n";
    var rbuf: [1024]u8 = undefined;
    var wbuf: [1024]u8 = undefined;
    var reader_impl = stream.reader(io,&rbuf);
    var writer_impl = stream.writer(io,&wbuf);
    constreader=&reader_impl.interface;
    constwriter=&writer_impl.interface;

    try writer.writeAll(message);
    try writer.flush();
    try stream.shutdown(io, .send);

    const n = reader.readSliceShort(&rbuf) catch 0;
    if (n == 0) {
        std.debug.print("Server closed connection.\n", .{});
        return;
    }

    const response = rbuf[0..n];
    var out_buf: [1024]u8 = undefined;
    var stdout_impl = std.Io.File.stdout().writer(io,&out_buf);
    conststdout=&stdout_impl.interface;
    try stdout.print("Got: {s}", .{response});
    try stdout.flush();
}
```

The most interesting part is `std.Io.net.HostName.init(host)`. This creates a lightweight struct that stores and validates the hostname string, but does no network activity yet. The actual DNS resolution happens when you call `.connect(io, port, .{ .mode = .stream })` on it. That single call resolves the hostname to an IP address and opens a TCP connection to that address on the given port, returning an `Io.net.Stream`. The `.{ .mode = .stream }` option selects TCP (as opposed to `.dgram` for UDP). This is the high-level 0.16 replacement for the old `std.net.tcpConnectToHost` — it handles hostnames rather than requiring you to first parse a literal IP string yourself. Once connected, the program sets up buffered I/O over the socket. In Zig 0.16, readers and writers require an explicit user-supplied buffer rather than doing internal heap allocation. `stream.reader(io, &rbuf)` and `stream.writer(io, &wbuf)` each return a concrete implementation struct, and the actual `*std.Io.Reader` or `*std.Io.Writer` interface — with methods like `writeAll()`, `print()`, `flush()` and `readSliceShort()` — lives at `.interface` on that struct. The two-step `varreader_impl=...; const reader = &reader_impl.interface;` pattern is the idiomatic 0.16 way to get a usable reader or writer pointer. The communication itself is straightforward. The client buffers the message with `writer.writeAll(message)`, flushes it to actually send the bytes over the socket, then calls `stream.shutdown(io, .send)`. That last call is a TCP half-close (equivalent to POSIX `shutdown(SHUT_WR)`): it tells the server that no more data is coming from the client side, so the server sees EOF on its read — a common technique in echo-style protocols where the server echoes everything back until it sees the client is done writing. The client then calls `reader.readSliceShort(&rbuf)`, which reads up to 1024 bytes and returns the count actually received. If zero bytes come back, the connection was closed by the server; otherwise, the response slice is printed to stdout using the same buffered writer pattern (`std.Io.File.stdout().writer(io, &out_buf)`), which is the 0.16 replacement for the old `std.io.getStdOut().writer()`. A final `flush()` ensures the output actually reaches the terminal before the program exits. Let us try our more powerful version:

```
$ zig run ch06/echoClientResolve.zig -- 127.0.0.1 1234
Got: Hello from Zig client!
$ zig run ch06/echoClientResolve.zig -- localhost 1234
Got: Hello from Zig client!
```

While the TCP echo server we just built provides a reliable, connection-oriented stream, many network applications prioritize low latency over perfect reliability, dictating a shift to the **User Datagram Protocol (UDP)**. The choice between TCP and UDP is not a matter of one being better than the other — it is a tradeoff driven by application requirements. When delivery guarantees and ordering matter, TCP is the right tool. When low latency, simplicity, or broadcast semantics matter more than reliability, UDP is the better fit. DNS, video streaming, and game state updates are classic examples of protocols that choose UDP for these reasons.

Writing a UDP Echo server

A UDP echo server functions as a *stateless listener*, treating every incoming packet as an *independent event* rather than part of a continuous stream. This lack of session state makes UDP significantly faster and more resource-efficient for tasks like real-time gaming or streaming, but it shifts the burden of reliability and packet ordering onto the application layer. Zig 0.16's `std.Io.net` API does not yet expose UDP socket creation directly, so the UDP server and client use raw C socket bindings via `@cImport`. This is a practical reminder that systems programming occasionally requires dropping below the standard library — Zig makes this straightforward through its C interoperability layer. Here is the example code as found in `ch06/udpServer.zig`:

```
const std = @import("std");
const c = @cImport({
    @cInclude("sys/socket.h");
    @cInclude("netinet/in.h");
    @cInclude("arpa/inet.h");
    @cInclude("unistd.h");
});

pub fn main(init: std.process.Init) !void {
    const args = try init.minimal.args.toSlice(init.arena.allocator());
    if (args.len != 2) {
        std.debug.print("Usage: {s} <port>\n", .{args[0]});
        return error.InvalidUsage;
    }

    const port = try std.fmt.parseInt(u16, args[1], 10);
    const sock = c.socket(c.AF_INET, c.SOCK_DGRAM, 0);
    if (sock < 0) return error.SocketCreateFailed;
    defer _ = c.close(sock);

    var addr: c.struct_sockaddr_in = std.mem.zeroInit(c.struct_sockaddr_in, .{
        .sin_family = @as(c.sa_family_t, @intCast(c.AF_INET)),
        .sin_port = std.mem.nativeToBig(u16, port),
        .sin_addr = .{ .s_addr = c.INADDR_ANY },
    });

        if (c.bind(
        sock,
        @ptrCast(&addr),
        @sizeOf(c.struct_sockaddr_in),
    ) < 0)
        return error.BindFailed;

    std.debug.print("Listening on 0.0.0.0:{}...\n", .{port});
```

```
    var buf: [1024]u8 = undefined;
    var other_addr: c.struct_sockaddr_in = undefined;
    var other_addrlen: c.socklen_t = @sizeOf(c.struct_sockaddr_in);
```

This program initializes a UDP networking socket using C bindings imported via `@cImport`. The execution begins by ensuring the user has provided exactly one parameter: the target port. Once the port is validated and converted into a numeric `u16` type, the program calls `c.socket()` to request a communication handle from the kernel. By passing `c.AF_INET`, the code specifies the IPv4 address family, while `c.SOCK_DGRAM` configures the socket for connectionless UDP datagrams. The address structure `c.struct_sockaddr_in` is initialized with `std.mem.zeroInit()` to zero all fields before setting the address family – we cast to `c.sa_family_t` directly rather than a fixed-width integer, since `sa_family_t` is `u8` on macOS but `u16` on Linux, making the concrete C type the portable choice – the port (converted to big-endian byte order via `std.mem.nativeToBig()`) and the bind address `c.INADDR_ANY`, which tells the kernel to accept packets on all available network interfaces. The `c.bind()` call then registers this address with the socket, after which the program is ready to receive incoming datagrams. The `defer _ = c.close(sock)` statement ensures the file descriptor is returned to the OS regardless of how the function exits. Next, we have the rest of the implementation:

```
        while (true) {
        const n_recv = c.recvfrom(
            sock,
            &buf,
            buf.len,
            0,
            @ptrCast(&other_addr),
            &other_addrlen,
        );
        if (n_recv < 0) {
            std.debug.print("recvfrom failed\n", .{});
            continue;
        }
        std.debug.print("Received {d} byte(s)\n", .{n_recv});
        const n_sent = c.sendto(
            sock,
            &buf,
            @intCast(n_recv),
            0,
            @ptrCast(&other_addr),
```

```
            other_addrlen,
        );
        if (n_sent < 0) {
            std.debug.print("sendto failed\n", .{});
            continue;
        }
        std.debug.print("Sent {d} byte(s)\n", .{n_sent});
    }
}
```

The core of the server is an infinite loop driven by `c.recvfrom()`, which blocks the thread until a datagram arrives. This call is distinct from a standard stream read because it simultaneously populates the `other_addr` structure with the sender IP address and port, providing the return address necessary for the echo functionality. The received byte count is returned as `n_recv`; a negative value indicates a failure, in which case the loop logs the error and continues rather than crashing. Once data has been captured into the 1024-byte buffer, the program immediately invokes `c.sendto()` to transmit exactly `n_recv` bytes back to the source. Because UDP is connectionless, each call to `c.sendto()` must explicitly reference the `other_addr` captured during the preceding receive, addressing the response packet to the specific client that initiated the contact. The `other_addrlen` variable is passed to both calls, so the kernel knows the size of the address structure it is reading from or writing into. Let us now try the UDP server with `socat(1)` – first execute it as `zig run ch06/udpServer.zig -- 1234`. Then, run the following:

```
$ echo "ping" | socat - UDP:localhost:1234
ping
$ echo "ping" | socat - UDP:127.0.0.1:1234
ping
```

First, `socat(1)` sends the message to `localhost:1234`, and second, to `127.0.0.1:1234`. Both addresses refer to the local machine, so they are functionally equivalent. The fact that `ping` is printed back to the terminal in both cases confirms that the UDP server received the datagram and responded correctly, echoing the message back. This behavior is expected from a properly functioning Echo server and demonstrates that it can handle UDP packets sent to it using both hostname and IP address.

With our UDP Echo server successfully tested for handling incoming datagrams and bouncing messages back to clients, we have completed our work for the server side. But there is still something missing, which is the development of a UDP client in Zig.

Writing a UDP Echo client

In this section, we write a UDP Echo client that sends a message to the server and prints out the echoed response. Consider the following example code (`ch06/udpClient.zig`) when creating UDP clients:

```
const std = @import("std");

pub fn main(init: std.process.Init) !void {
    const io = init.io;
    const args = try init.minimal.args.toSlice(init.arena.allocator());

    var err_buf: [1024]u8 = undefined;
    var stderr_impl = std.Io.File.stderr().writer(io,&err_buf);
    conststderr=&stderr_impl.interface;
    var out_buf: [1024]u8 = undefined;
    var stdout_impl = std.Io.File.stdout().writer(io,&out_buf);
    conststdout=&stdout_impl.interface;

    if (args.len != 4) {
        try stderr.print(
            "Usage: {s} <hostname> <port> <message>\n",
            .{args[0]},
        );
        try stderr.flush();
        std.process.exit(1);
    }
    const hostname = args[1];
    const port_str = args[2];
    const message = args[3];
    const port = try std.fmt.parseInt(u16, port_str, 10);

    const hn = try std.Io.net.HostName.init(hostname);
    var lookup_buf: [16]std.Io.net.HostName.LookupResult = undefined;
    var lookup_queue: std.Io.Queue(
        std.Io.net.HostName.LookupResult,
    ) = .init(&lookup_buf);
    try hn.lookup(io,&lookup_queue,.{.port=port});

    var dest_addr: ?std.Io.net.IpAddress = null;
```

```
while (lookup_queue.getOne(io)) |result| {
    switch (result) {
        .address => |addr| if (dest_addr == null) {
            dest_addr = addr;
        },
        .canonical_name => {},
    }
} else |err| switch (err) {
    error.Canceled => return error.Canceled,
    error.Closed => {},
}
const dest = dest_addr orelse return error.UnknownHostName;

const local = try std.Io.net.IpAddress.parseIp4("0.0.0.0", 0);
const sock = try local.bind(io, .{ .mode = .dgram });
defer sock.close(io);
```

The program begins by setting up buffered writers for both stdout and stderr, then validates that exactly three arguments are provided: a hostname, a port, and a message. The port string is parsed into a `u16` immediately, so any invalid input is caught before any system calls are made. Hostname resolution is handled entirely through the `std.Io.net` API. `HostName.init(hostname)` creates a lightweight wrapper around the hostname, then `hn.lookup(io, &lookup_queue, .{ .port = port })` initiates an asynchronous DNS lookup that streams results into a fixed-capacity queue backed by a stack-allocated buffer of 16 `LookupResult` slots. Each result pulled from the queue with `getOne(io)` is either an `.address` — an `IpAddress` ready to use — or a `.canonical_name`, which is ignored here. The loop ends when the queue signals `error.Closed`, meaning all results have been delivered; `error.Canceled` is the only other terminal case and is propagated immediately. If no `.address` result was received, the program returns `error.UnknownHostName`. Once a valid destination address is in hand, `IpAddress.parseIp4("0.0.0.0", 0)` constructs a local bind address where port 0 instructs the OS to assign an ephemeral port automatically. Calling `.bind(io, .{ .mode = .dgram })` on that address creates and binds a UDP socket, with a `defer sock.close(io)`, ensuring the socket is released when the function exits.

Data transmission in this program is handled by the following code:

```
try sock.send(io,&dest,message);
try stdout.print(
    "Sent {d} bytes to {s}:{d}: {s}\n",
```

```
        .{ message.len, hostname, port, message },
    );
    try stdout.flush();
```

With the socket created and the destination address resolved, the program calls `sock.send(io, &dest, message)` to transmit the message. Unlike a TCP connection, where the destination is established once during a handshake, send requires the target address to be passed explicitly as `&dest` on every call — reflecting the stateless nature of UDP, where each datagram is an independent packet with no persistent association to a remote endpoint. Any failure is surfaced as a Zig error and propagated immediately via `try`. On success, the program prints a confirmation showing the byte count, destination hostname, port, and the original message, then flushes the buffered writer to ensure the output reaches the terminal before the process continues.

With the datagram sent, the program calls `sock.receive(io, &buffer)` to block until the server's echo response arrives:

```
    var buffer: [1024]u8 = undefined;
    // Receive the response.
    // Note: sock.receive() blocks indefinitely if the server
    // does not reply. In a real application you would set a receive
    // timeout (e.g. SO_RCVTIMEO) to handle packet loss or an
    // unresponsive server gracefully.
    const incoming = try sock.receive(io,&buffer);
    try stdout.print(
        "Received {d} bytes: {s}\n",
        .{ incoming.data.len, incoming.data },
    );
    try stdout.flush();
}
```

Unlike the raw C `recvfrom()`, which required separate address and length arguments to capture the sender's identity, `sock.receive()` returns a structured result — here bound to `incoming` — that bundles the received data together with the source address, making the API self-contained and eliminating the need to manually track how many bytes were written into the buffer. The `incoming.data` slice already has the correct length, so there is no risk of reading uninitialized bytes beyond the received content. Once the response is printed and the buffered writer is flushed, the function returns, and the deferred `sock.close(io)` releases the socket back to the OS. Let us now try to use the UDP client:

```
$ zig run ch06/udpClient.zig -- localhost 1234 "Hi there\!"
Sent 9 bytes to localhost:1234: Hi there!
Received 9 bytes: Hi there!
$ zig run ch06/udpClient.zig -- 127.0.0.1 1234 "Hi there\!"
Sent 9 bytes to 127.0.0.1:1234: Hi there!
Received 9 bytes: Hi there!
```

The output confirms that the Zig UDP client successfully sent a message to a local server using an IP address or a hostname and received a response, which demonstrates that the basic UDP communication path is working as expected.

Manually setting up dependencies and configurations can be error-prone and tedious, especially when deploying to servers or sharing your application with others. This is where Docker comes in. By packaging our Zig servers into a lightweight, portable Docker image, we can ensure they run consistently — whether on your local machine, the laptop of a colleague, or a cloud-hosted container platform. Let us now explore how to create a Docker image for our TCP/IP servers.

Creating Docker images

Docker is a platform that makes it easier to build, run, and manage applications in *isolated environments called* **containers**. A container is like a lightweight, standalone box that packages your application code, dependencies, and configuration — everything it needs to run — into a single unit. Internally, Docker uses Linux distributions and commands, but it can run on many operating systems. In this section, we are going to create a Docker image for running two Zig programs, which are going to be a TCP and a UDP Echo server. All necessary files are located inside the `ch06/dock` directory.

```
$ tree ch06/dock
ch06/dock
├── docker-compose.yaml
├── Dockerfile
├── tcp.zig
└── udp.zig
1 directory, 4 files
```

We are not going to deal with `tcp.zig` and `udp.zig` as the code in these two files is covered in previous sections. So, first, let us see and understand the contents of `Dockerfile`, which is used for generating the Docker image:

```
FROM alpine:latest AS builder
RUN apk add --no-cache zig build-base

WORKDIR /app
COPY tcp.zig .
COPY udp.zig .

RUN zig build-exe tcp.zig -O ReleaseSafe -target native-native-musl -static -lc
RUN zig build-exe udp.zig -O ReleaseSafe -target native-native-musl -static -lc

# Final image
FROM alpine:latest
WORKDIR /app
COPY --from=builder /app/tcp .
COPY --from=builder /app/udp .
EXPOSE 1234 1235
CMD ["/bin/sh", "-c", "./tcp 1234 & ./udp 1235"]
```

This `Dockerfile` defines a two-stage build process to compile and package two Zig networking programs into a minimal Docker image. In the first stage, named `builder`, the image is based on `alpine:latest`, a lightweight Linux distribution. It installs Zig and basic build tools and sets the working directory to `/app`. After that, it copies both Zig source files inside the container and compiles them using `zig build-exe` with options `-O ReleaseSafe` (for safe optimizations), `-target native-native-musl` (for native CPU and musl libc), `-static`, and `-lc`, which ensures statically linked binaries suitable for minimal containers. The second stage also uses `alpine:latest` as its base image to keep things small. It sets the working directory to `/app`, then copies the compiled `tcp` and `udp` binaries from the `builder` stage. The `EXPOSE` directive opens ports `1234` and `1235`, making them available for network communication. Finally, the container starts both servers, where the TCP server runs in the background, and the UDP server runs in the foreground. You usually run a single server per Docker image.

Next, we need a proper `docker-compose.yaml` for giving instructions to the Docker image on how it is going to get executed, which ports are going to be exposed to the outer word and the mapping of the internal ports to the external ports; this is very important in network services because a wrongly defined mapping of internal and external ports might make the Docker image unavailable to the outer word. So, consider the following `docker-compose.yaml` file for running simple TCP/IP services:

```
services:
  zig-echo-server:
    build: .
    ports:
      - "1234:1234"       # TCP
      - "1235:1235/udp"   # UDP
    restart: unless-stopped
```

This `docker-compose.yaml` file defines a single service named `zig-echo-server`, which is intended to run the TCP and UDP servers we included in the `Docker` image. The `build: .` directive tells Docker Compose to build the service image using the `Dockerfile` found in the current directory. Under `ports`, two mappings are specified: `1234:1234` maps TCP port 1234 on the host to port 1234 in the container, and `1235:1235/udp` does the same for UDP port 1235. This ensures that clients can connect to both protocols externally. The `restart: unless-stopped` policy ensures that the container will automatically restart if it crashes or the system reboots — unless it has been manually stopped.

Having Docker installed on your Linux machine, build the new Docker image named `echo` as specified by the value of the `-t` option:

```
$ docker build --no-cache -f Dockerfile -t echo .
. . . lots of output
```

The `--no-cache` option in Docker is used during the build process to force Docker to ignore all previously cached layers and rebuild the image entirely from scratch. This ensures that every instruction in the `Dockerfile` is re-executed, which is particularly useful when dependencies may have changed or when cached results lead to inconsistent behavior. It also helps avoid subtle bugs caused by stale or outdated build layers, ensuring a clean, fresh build every time. Use it when you want absolute certainty that your image reflects the current state of your source code and dependencies.

Now, verify the existence of the `echo` Docker image with the following command:

```
$ docker images # You might get lots of output
IMAGE                 ID             DISK USAGE   CONTENT SIZE   EXTRA
echo:latest       9c0e5c8bcb4f       13.2MB             0B
```

You are now ready to use that image with the help of the `docker-compose up` command:

```
$ docker-compose up
. . .lots of output
```

Now, try to connect to the TCP and UDP Echo servers in that order. We are going to use the handy `socat(1)` utility for that:

```
$ echo "ping" | socat - TCP:localhost:1234
ping
$ echo "pong" | socat - UDP:localhost:1235
pong
```

Both commands generate log entries in the output of `docker-compose up`. Once your TCP/IP server is running inside a Docker container and its ports are properly published, it becomes indistinguishable from a natively running service as far as the client is concerned. Whether the server is bound directly to the network or routed through Docker virtual interfaces, the underlying TCP/IP behavior remains the same. Docker abstracts away the internals so effectively that clients do not need to know — or care — whether the service is running on bare metal or in a container.

Now that we have wrapped up containerizing our networking tools using Docker, it is time to shift gears from how we run our applications to what they communicate. While TCP and UDP give us the building blocks for raw data exchange, most real-world applications use higher-level protocols built on top of them. One of the most important of these is HTTP. Let us explore how to work with HTTP directly in Zig and see how to build both clients and servers that speak the language of the web.

Working with the HTTP protocol

So far, we have explored low-level networking by working directly with TCP and UDP sockets. Now it is time to move up the stack and tackle one of the most widely used protocols on the Internet: HTTP. Whether you are building web clients, lightweight servers, or tools that interact with APIs, understanding how to speak HTTP is essential. In this section, we dive into the structure of HTTP requests and responses, learn how to send and receive them using Zig, and build some practical tools that leverage the protocol to fetch and serve data over the web.

Developing a minimal web server

First, let us build something concrete: a web server. So, we are going to develop a minimal HTTP server that listens for incoming requests and responds with simple content. The goal is not to create a full-featured HTTP service but to show you how HTTP works and how you can handle it directly using Zig networking and I/O facilities. Here is the example code of `ch06/minimalHTTP.zig`:

```
const std = @import("std");

pub fn main(init: std.process.Init) !void {
    const io = init.io;
    const address = try std.Io.net.IpAddress.parseIp4(
        "127.0.0.1",
        8080,
    );
    var server = try address.listen(io, .{});
    defer server.deinit(io);
    while (true) {
        const stream = try server.accept(io);
        handleConnection(io, stream) catch |err| {
            std.log.err("connection error: {}", .{err});
        };
    }
}
```

The core command of the code snippet is `address.listen()`, which initializes the socket and sets it to a listening state. The program execution then enters an infinite while loop where `server.accept()` blocks until a client completes the TCP handshake, returning a `std.Io.net.Stream` that is immediately passed to `handleConnection()`. Because this model is synchronous, the server process remains occupied by the current connection and cannot accept new clients until `handleConnection()` completes its execution:

```
fn handleConnection(io: std.Io, stream: std.Io.net.Stream) !void {
    defer stream.close(io);
    var reader_buf: [1024]u8 = undefined;
    var writer_buf: [1024]u8 = undefined;
    var reader_impl = stream.reader(io,&reader_buf);
    var writer_impl = stream.writer(io,&writer_buf);
    var http_server = std.http.Server.init(
        &reader_impl.interface,
        &writer_impl.interface,
    );
    var req = try http_server.receiveHead();
```

```
    try req.respond("Hello world\n", .{});
}
```

This function processes an *individual TCP connection* as a specialized HTTP transaction. A 1KB buffer is allocated on the stack for reading the request and `std.http.Server` is initialized to parse the HTTP headers. Once a request is received using `receiveHead()`, the server immediately sends back a plain response with the message `Hello world\n`.

Execute `minimalHTTP.zig` on your machine and interact with it in any way you want. I used to interact with services like SMTP and HTTP using `telnet(1)`, which is rarely used nowadays. An alternative to this archaic approach is to use `curl(1)`. The `-v` option creates *verbose output* showing what happens behind the scenes:

```
$ curl localhost:8080 -v
* Host localhost:8080 was resolved.
* IPv6: ::1
* IPv4: 127.0.0.1
*   Trying [::1]:8080...
* connect to ::1 port 8080 from ::1 port 58224 failed: Connection refused
*   Trying 127.0.0.1:8080...
* Connected to localhost (127.0.0.1) port 8080
> GET / HTTP/1.1
> Host: localhost:8080
> User-Agent: curl/8.7.1
> Accept: */*
>
* Request completely sent off
< HTTP/1.1 200 OK
< content-length: 12
<
Hello world
* Connection #0 to host localhost left intact
```

The `curl(1)` command tries to connect to a server running on your local machine at port `8080` and prints a detailed breakdown of the HTTP transaction. The tool first resolves localhost to both an IPv6 address (`::1`) and an IPv4 address (`127.0.0.1`) and attempts to connect via IPv6 first, but the connection is refused because the server is not listening on that interface. It then falls back to IPv4 and successfully connects to `127.0.0.1:8080`. According to the HTTP protocol, the client sends an HTTP `GET` request to the root path, including headers like `Host`, `User-Agent`, and `Accept`. The server responds with an HTTP `200 OK` status, a `content-length` of 12 bytes, and the body `Hello world`. This confirms that the server is correctly receiving and responding to HTTP requests over IPv4. The connection is left open, following HTTP/1.1 default behavior unless the server sends a `Connection: close` header.

> **Note**
>
> Creating an IPv6-capable HTTP server in Zig is essentially identical to the IPv4 process, as the standard library abstracts the protocol family through the `std.Io.net.IpAddress` union type. The core logic shifts only during the address initialization phase, where you replace `parseIp4()` with `std.Io.net.IpAddress.parseIp6("::1", 8080)` to target the IPv6 loopback or `std.Io.net.IpAddress.parseIp6("::", 8080)` to bind to the IPv6 unspecified address. Note that `"::"` is not merely "all IPv6 interfaces" — on most operating systems, binding to it enables a dual-stack socket that also accepts incoming IPv4 connections, which arrive mapped as IPv6 addresses in the `::ffff:x.x.x.x` form. For static addresses, you can skip string parsing and use the dedicated constructors `std.Io.net.Ip6Address.loopback(port)` and `std.Io.net.Ip6Address.unspecified(port)`, which are the cleaner choice when no runtime address string is involved. Once an `IpAddress` value is in hand, all downstream calls — listen, connect, and stream handling — are identical for both protocol families.

Now that we have built a minimal web server and explored how to handle basic HTTP requests, it is time to turn our focus outward. In the next subsection, we will write a web service that generates random numbers. This will give us hands-on experience with making HTTP services with support for multiple endpoints.

Creating a web service that generates random numbers

In this subsection, we will flip the script once again by creating our own web service that generates random numbers. The server responds to HTTP requests with pseudo-random values. This is a practical way to combine everything we have covered so far: handling HTTP requests, generating data on the fly, and serving it to a client — perfect for testing, demos, or just having a bit of fun.

The most interesting part of the web service is the function that handles connections:

```
fn handleConnection(
    io: std.Io,
    stream: std.Io.net.Stream,
    allocator: std.mem.Allocator,
```

```
) !void {
    defer stream.close(io);

    var reader_buf: [1024]u8 = undefined;
    var writer_buf: [1024]u8 = undefined;
    var reader_impl = stream.reader(io,&reader_buf);
    var writer_impl = stream.writer(io,&writer_buf);

    var http_server = std.http.Server.init(
        &reader_impl.interface,
        &writer_impl.interface,
    );
    var req = try http_server.receiveHead();

    const path = req.head.target;
```

This function wraps the TCP stream in buffered interfaces, extracting `.interface` pointers to initialize the `std.http.Server` state machine. `http_server.receiveHead()` parses the incoming byte stream into a structured request, specifically capturing `req.head.target` to identify the *requested URL path*. Capturing the `path` provides the necessary metadata for routing logic, allowing the server to branch its execution based on the client's destination. This concluding logic of the `handleConnection()` function implements a basic routing engine that dispatches responses based on the HTTP request destination path:

```
    if (std.mem.eql(u8, path, "/")) {
        try req.respond(
            "Welcome to the Zig Web Server!\n",
            .{
                .status = .ok,
                .extra_headers = &.{
                    .{ .name = "Content-Type", .value = "text/plain" },
                },
            },
        );
    } else if (std.mem.eql(u8, path, "/rand")) {
        var rand_bytes: [4]u8 = undefined;
        io.random(&rand_bytes);
        const random_num = std.mem.readInt(u32,&rand_bytes,.little)%1_000_001;
        const body = try std.fmt.allocPrint(
            allocator,
```

```
            "Random number: {}\n",
            .{random_num},
        );
        defer allocator.free(body);
        try req.respond(body, .{
            .status = .ok,
            .extra_headers = &.{
                .{ .name = "Content-Type", .value = "text/plain" },
            },
        });
    } else {
        try req.respond("404 Not Found\n", .{
            .status = .not_found,
            .extra_headers = &.{
                .{ .name = "Content-Type", .value = "text/plain" },
            },
        });
    }
}
```

The flow begins with a conditional check comparing the path string against the root route `/`. If a match occurs, the server calls `req.respond()` to transmit a static greeting, explicitly setting the HTTP status to `.ok` and defining the `Content-Type` as plain text through the `.extra_headers` field. This ensures the client interprets the raw byte stream correctly as human-readable text rather than a binary download. For the second route `/rand`, the server generates dynamic content. Rather than using a pseudo-random number generator, the code calls `io.random(&rand_bytes)` to fill a 4-byte array with cryptographically random bytes sourced from the operating system. These bytes are then reinterpreted as a `u32` integer via `std.mem.readInt()` and reduced to the range 0–1,000,000 with a modulo operation. Note that reducing a u32 to a range of 1,000,001 values via `% 1_000_001` introduces a negligible statistical bias of roughly 0.023%, since 2^32 is not evenly divisible by 1,000,001 — values in the lower part of the range appear fractionally more often. For a demonstration endpoint, this is entirely acceptable; a cryptographic use case would require rejection sampling to eliminate the bias entirely. The resulting number is formatted into a response body string using `std.fmt.allocPrint()`, which requires a heap allocation; the matching `defer allocator.free(body)` ensures this memory is reclaimed immediately after the response is sent. The final `else` block serves as the *catch-all handler* for any undefined routes, implementing a standard 404 Not Found response. By setting the status to `.not_found`, the server communicates a specific protocol-level error to the client, indicating that while the server is active, the requested resource does not exist. This structured approach to routing — branching between static strings, dynamically allocated content, and error states — demonstrates the fundamental logic of a simple web API, where the server behavior is entirely dictated by the path captured during the initial request parsing phase. The full source of `ch06/webServer.zig` contains one addition beyond what is described above. At the top of the file, the program imports `signal.h` via `@cImport` and registers a C-callable handler with `c.signal(c.SIGINT, handle_sigint)` at the start of `main()`. The handler itself calls `std.process.exit(0)` when the process receives `SIGINT` — the signal delivered by Ctrl+C — so the server shuts down cleanly rather than printing a raw termination message to the terminal. This is a practical necessity for any long-running server you will interact with repeatedly during development: without it, pressing Ctrl+C leaves no visible confirmation that the process stopped. Signal handling in Zig is covered in depth in *Chapter 7, Managing Threads, Processes, and Signals*; for now, treat this as boilerplate that keeps the development experience tidy. Let us now try `ch06/webServer.zig` with the help of `curl(1)`:

```
$ curl localhost:8080
Welcome to the Zig Web Server!
$ curl localhost:8080/rand
Random number: 91767
$ curl localhost:8080/doesNotExist
404 Not Found
```

When you run `curl localhost:8080`, the request targets the root path (/), and the server replies with a plain-text welcome message, indicating that the server is up and running. When the request targets `/rand`, the server generates a random number and sends it back in the response body. This confirms that the server can return dynamic content. Finally, accessing an unknown path such as `/doesNotExist` triggers a `404 Not Found` response, showing that the server handles invalid or unrecognized routes gracefully.

Let us now create an HTTP client. Although Zig offers a high-level HTTP client, it also provides the essential building blocks you need to construct reliable and efficient clients on your own. In this chapter, we are going to create our own HTTP client using relatively low-level commands. However, in *Chapter 11, Persisting Structured Data with SQLite3*, we are going to use the HTTP client offered by Zig to interact with a note-taking web service.

Developing HTTP clients

In this section, we dive into the practical world of building HTTP clients with Zig. You learn how to send requests, receive server responses, and handle data coming from web servers. The client is structured around a clear separation of concerns: argument parsing, connection setup, request construction, and response handling are each handled by a dedicated function. This decomposition is worth internalizing — as networked applications grow in complexity, keeping these responsibilities separate is what makes them testable, maintainable, and extensible.

We present the most important parts of `ch06/webClient.zig`, starting with `fetch()`:

```
pub fn fetch(
    io: std.Io,
    allocator: mem.Allocator,
    server: []const u8,
    url: []const u8,
) ![]const u8 {
    const address = try parseAddress(allocator, server);
    defer if (!address.is_ip) allocator.free(address.host);
    const stream = try connectToAddress(io, address);
    defer stream.close(io);
    try sendRequest(
        io,
        allocator,
        stream,
        address.host,
        url,
        address.port,
    );
    return try readResponse(io, allocator, stream);
}
```

The `fetch()` function arranges a synchronous network transaction through a sequential pipeline of operations. The process begins with `parseAddress()`, which validates and resolves the target server information into a compatible network structure. This is followed by the core command `connectToAddress()`, which initiates the TCP handshake to create a functional communication stream. Once connected, `sendRequest()` pushes the HTTP protocol commands to the remote host. The transaction concludes with `readResponse()`, which reads the resulting data stream from the socket into a buffer, ensuring the connection is closed via `defer` immediately after the data is retrieved.

Next, we have the parseAddress() function, which implements a parser that transforms a raw string into a structured Address object by isolating the hostname and port number:

```
fn parseAddress(allocator: mem.Allocator, server: []const u8) !Address {
    const colon_index = mem.indexOf(u8, server, ":") orelse {
        if (std.Io.net.IpAddress.parseIp4(server, 80)) |ip| {
            return Address{
                .host = try allocator.dupe(u8, server),
                .port = 80,
                .is_ip = true,
                .ip = ip,
            };
        } else |_| {
            const host = try allocator.dupe(u8, server);
            return Address{
                .host = host,
                .port = 80,
                .is_ip = false,
                .ip = undefined,
            };
        }
    };

    const host_part = server[0..colon_index];
    const port_part = server[colon_index + 1 ..];
    const port = fmt.parseUnsigned(u16, port_part, 10) catch {
        return WebClientError.InvalidPort;
    };

    if (std.Io.net.IpAddress.parseIp4(host_part, port)) |ip| {
        return Address{
            .host = try allocator.dupe(u8, host_part),
            .port = port,
            .is_ip = true,
            .ip = ip,
        };
    } else |_| {
        const host = try allocator.dupe(u8, host_part);
        return Address{
            .host = host,
            .port = port,
```

```
                .is_ip = false,
                .ip = undefined,
            };
        }
    }
```

The function begins by searching for a colon character to determine whether an explicit port is provided. If no colon is found, the program defaults to port `80` and attempts to parse the entire input as an IPv4 address using `std.Io.net.IpAddress.parseIp4()`. If that succeeds, the function stores the pre-parsed binary address directly in the `Address` struct so that DNS resolution can be skipped later. If parsing fails, the input is assumed to be a plain hostname. In both cases, `allocator.dupe()` creates a heap-owned copy of the string, ensuring the resulting `Address` object owns its data and remains valid independent of the lifetime of the original input slice. When a colon is present, the logic splits the string into a host part and a port part using slice indexing, converting the port portion into a u16 integer via `fmt.parseUnsigned()`. If that conversion fails, for example, because the port string contains non-numeric characters — the function returns `WebClientError.InvalidPort`. The host part is then subjected to the same `std.Io.net.IpAddress.parseIp4()` check as the no-colon path, producing either a resolved IP address or a hostname for later DNS lookup. This dual-path design ensures the client handles both bare hostnames and explicit `host:port` formats such as `localhost` or `127.0.0.1:8080`, consistently. The `connectToAddress()` function serves as the bridge between a logical network address and a live communication stream:

```
fn connectToAddress(io: std.Io, address: Address) !std.Io.net.Stream {
    if (address.is_ip) {
        return address.ip.connect(io,.{.mode = .stream}) catch |err| {
            std.log.err("Failed to connect to IP: {}", .{err});
            return err;
        };
    } else {
        const resolved = std.Io.net.IpAddress.resolve(
            io,
            address.host,
            address.port,
        ) catch {
            return WebClientError.ResolutionFailed;
        };
        return resolved.connect(io, .{ .mode = .stream }) catch |err| {
            std.log.err("Failed to connect to host: {}", .{err});
```

```
                return err;
            };
        }
    }
```

The function branches on whether the input address was already identified as a numeric IP or remains a symbolic hostname. If `address.is_ip` is true, the function calls `address.ip.connect()` directly with `.mode = .stream` to initiate a TCP connection, bypassing name resolution entirely since the binary address is already available. If the address is a hostname, the function first calls `std.Io.net.IpAddress.resolve()`, which queries the operating system's DNS resolver to translate the hostname and port into a usable `IpAddress`. If resolution fails for any reason, the function returns `WebClientError.ResolutionFailed` rather than propagating a low-level OS error, keeping the error surface clean for the caller. Once a resolved address is obtained, the function calls `.connect()` on it with the same `.mode = .stream` option to establish the TCP connection. In both paths, any connection failure is logged via `std.log.err()` before the error is returned, giving the caller visibility into what went wrong without swallowing the error. The return value in the success case is a `std.Io.net.Stream`, which the caller can use immediately for reading and writing data over the established connection.

> **Note**
>
> `std.Io.net.IpAddress.resolve()` returns a single `IpAddress` and is the straightforward choice when you just need something to connect to. `hn.lookup()` — where `hn` is a `std.Io.net.HostName`, a validated hostname wrapper — performs DNS resolution and delivers results into a caller-supplied queue rather than returning a single address. The queue receives `LookupResult` items, each of which is either an `.address` (a resolved `IpAddress`) or a `.canonical_name`; you drain the queue in a loop until it signals it is closed. This gives you the full DNS response — multiple A/AAAA records and the canonical name — and lets you act on the first address that arrives before the rest have been delivered. Both functions take an std.Io handle, so neither is inherently more or less blocking than the other; the runtime backend decides that. Choose `resolve()` for simplicity; choose `lookup()` when you need the complete picture or want to try multiple addresses.

The `sendRequest()` function translates the abstract web request into a formatted byte stream that complies with the HTTP/1.1 protocol:

```
fn sendRequest(
    io: std.Io,
    allocator: mem.Allocator,
    stream: std.Io.net.Stream,
    host: []const u8,
    url: []const u8,
    port: u16,
) !void {
    const request = if (port == 80)
        try fmt.allocPrint(
            allocator,
            "GET {s} HTTP/1.1\r\nHost: {s}\r\nConnection: close\r\n\r\n",
            .{ url, host },
        )
    else
        try fmt.allocPrint(
            allocator,
            "GET {s} HTTP/1.1\r\nHost: {s}:{d}\r\nConnection: close\r\n\r\n",
            .{ url, host, port },
        );
    defer allocator.free(request);

    var wbuf: [4096]u8 = undefined;
    var writer_impl = stream.writer(io,&wbuf);
    constwriter=&writer_impl.interface;
    try writer.writeAll(request);
    try writer.flush();
}
```

The function constructs a minimal HTTP/1.1 GET request string by branching on the port number. If the port is the standard 80, it is omitted from the `Host` header to follow convention; any non-standard port is appended explicitly so the remote server can identify the correct virtual host. The string is built dynamically using `fmt.allocPrint()`, which formats the method, path, host, and the mandatory `\r\n` line terminators required by the HTTP specification into a single heap-allocated buffer. The `Connection: close` header instructs the server to terminate the connection after sending its response, keeping the interaction as a single clean transaction rather than an idle persistent connection. A `defer allocator.free(request)` ensures the temporary request buffer is released once the function exits. To actually transmit the request, the function wraps the stream in a buffered writer using `stream.writer(io, &wbuf)`, where `wbuf` is a 4096-byte stack buffer. The request bytes are passed to `writer.writeAll()` to stage them in the buffer, and then `writer.flush()` pushes the buffered data across the network socket in a single operation, minimizing the number of underlying system calls.

Last, we have `readResponse()`, which implements the final stage of the client transaction by progressively harvesting the raw byte stream from the network socket:

```
fn readResponse(
    io: std.Io,
    allocator: mem.Allocator,
    stream: std.Io.net.Stream,
) ![]const u8 {
    var buffer: std.ArrayListUnmanaged(u8) = .empty;
    defer buffer.deinit(allocator);

    var rbuf: [4096]u8 = undefined;
    var reader_impl = stream.reader(io,&rbuf);
    constreader=&reader_impl.interface;

    while (true) {
        const n = reader.readSliceShort(&rbuf) catch |err| {
            std.log.err("Failed to read response: {}", .{err});
            return WebClientError.ReadFailed;
        };
        if (n == 0) break;
        try buffer.appendSlice(allocator, rbuf[0..n]);
    }

    return buffer.toOwnedSlice(allocator);
}
```

The function wraps the stream in a buffered reader using `stream.reader(io, &rbuf)`, where `rbuf` is a 4096-byte stack buffer that serves as the intermediate staging area for incoming data. The continuous loop invokes `reader.readSliceShort()`, which reads however many bytes are currently available without waiting for the buffer to fill completely — making it well suited for network responses where data may arrive in irregular chunks. A return value of zero signals that the remote server has closed the connection after finishing its transmission, at which point the loop breaks. If the read fails for any other reason, the error is logged via `std.log.err()` and the function returns `WebClientError.ReadFailed`. During each successful iteration, `buffer.appendSlice()` copies the newly arrived bytes from the fixed stack buffer into a growing `ArrayListUnmanaged`, accumulating the full response in heap memory. Once the stream is exhausted, `buffer.toOwnedSlice()` transfers ownership of the internal allocation to the caller, returning the complete HTTP response as a single contiguous slice. The `defer buffer.deinit(allocator)` is safe here because `toOwnedSlice()` relinquishes the list internal pointer before the `defer` runs, so no double-free occurs.

The code includes a suite of unit tests designed to ensure that `parseAddress()` handles the nuances of network strings with precision. The logic behind these tests focuses on three primary scenarios: the successful separation of a hostname from an explicit port, the identification of a literal IP address as a numeric type, and the correct application of the default HTTP port when no port is specified. By exercising these different paths, the tests confirm that the parser reliably differentiates between symbolic domain names and binary-ready IP addresses, a distinction that is vital for determining whether the client needs to perform a DNS lookup or can proceed directly to a connection.

Now, go and execute the tests to make sure that `parseAddress()` works as expected:

```
$ zig test ch06/webClient.zig
All 3 tests passed.
```

Great! It is now time to start using this generic web client and put the code into action:

```
$ zig run ch06/webClient.zig -- localhost:8080 /rand
HTTP/1.1 200 OK
connection: close
content-length: 22
Content-Type: text/plain

Random number: 516022
```

This output shows the successful execution of `webClient.zig` that connects to a local server at `localhost:8080` and sends a request to the `/rand` endpoint. The server responds with an *HTTP 1.1 message*, starting with the status line `HTTP/1.12000K`, indicating a successful request. The headers `connection: close`, `content-length: 22`, and `Content-Type:text/plain` describe how the connection will be managed and the nature of the response body. The final line, `Random number: 516022`, is the actual content returned by the server, generated dynamically by its random number logic.

Now that we have both sides of an HTTP conversation working — a server that can respond to requests and a client that can parse those responses — we can put them together in something more practical: a service for getting system memory (RAM) in use.

Creating a system monitor service

In this section, we build a small HTTP service that reads memory in use from the operating system, serializes it as JSON, and serves it over HTTP to its clients. We begin by presenting an autonomous program that can read active memory – this is just a utility.

Reading memory information

The program (`ch06/memInfo.zig`) is a memory monitor that prints RAM usage every two seconds in an infinite loop. The `main()` function obtains an allocator from `init.gpa` and an `io` handle from `init.io`, then enters a `while (true)` loop that repeatedly calls `printUsedMemory()`. Any error returned by that function is caught and printed via `std.debug.print()` without terminating the process, ensuring the monitor keeps running even if a single read fails. After each call, the loop suspends for two seconds using `std.Io.sleep(io, std.Io.Duration.fromSeconds(2), .awake)`, which is the Zig 0.16 way to perform a timed sleep through the Io interface rather than the older `std.Thread.sleep()`:

```
pub fn main(init: std.process.Init) !void {
    const io = init.io;
    const allocator = init.gpa;

    while (true) {
        printUsedMemory(io, allocator) catch |err| {
            std.debug.print("Error: {}\n", .{err});
        };
        try std.Io.sleep(io, std.Io.Duration.fromSeconds(2), .awake);
    }
}
```

`printUsedMemory()` does the real work and its behavior branches at compile time based on the operating system using `switch (builtin.os.tag)`:

```
fn printUsedMemory(io: std.Io, allocator: std.mem.Allocator) !void {

    const ts = std.Io.Timestamp.now(io, .real);
    const now: i64 = ts.toSeconds();
```

On Linux, it reads `/proc/meminfo` into a stack buffer using `file.readPositionalAll()`, then tokenizes the content line by line, looking for the `MemTotal:` and `MemAvailable:` fields. Both values are in kilobytes, so subtracting available from total gives used memory, which is then converted to megabytes for display:

```
switch (builtin.os.tag) {
    .linux => {
        const file = try std.Io.Dir.cwd().openFile(
            io,
            "/proc/meminfo",
            .{},
        );
        defer file.close(io);
        var buf: [4096]u8 = undefined;
        const n = try file.readPositionalAll(io,&buf,0);
        if (n >= buf.len)
            std.debug.print(
                "warning: /proc/meminfo may be truncated\n",
                .{},
            );
        const content = buf[0..n];
        var total: u64 = 0;
        var available: u64 = 0;

        var lines = std.mem.tokenizeScalar(u8, content, '\n');
        while (lines.next()) |line| {
            if (std.mem.startsWith(u8, line, "MemTotal:")) {
                total = parseLine(line);
            } else if (std.mem.startsWith(
                u8,
                line,
                "MemAvailable:",
            )) {
                available = parseLine(line);
            }
        }

        const used_mb = (total - available) / 1024;
        const total_mb = total / 1024;
        std.debug.print(
            "[{d}] Linux Used RAM: {d} MB / {d} MB\n",
```

```
            .{ now, used_mb, total_mb },
        );
    },
```

On macOS the same information requires two separate sources:

```
    .macos => {
        const total_bytes = try getSysctl(
            io,
            allocator,
            "hw.memsize",
        );
        const page_size = try getSysctl(
            io,
            allocator,
            "hw.pagesize",
        );
        const vm_stat_cmd = try std.process.run(allocator, io, .{
            .argv = &[_][]const u8{"vm_stat"},
        });
        defer {
            allocator.free(vm_stat_cmd.stdout);
            allocator.free(vm_stat_cmd.stderr);
        }

        var active_pages: u64 = 0;
        var wired_pages: u64 = 0;
        var compressed_pages: u64 = 0;

        var lines = std.mem.tokenizeScalar(u8, vm_stat_cmd.stdout, '\n');
        while (lines.next()) |line| {
            if (std.mem.containsAtLeast(u8, line, 1, "Pages active:")) {
                active_pages = parseLine(line);
            } else if (std.mem.containsAtLeast(
                u8,
                line,
                1,
                "Pages wired down:",
            )) {
                wired_pages = parseLine(line);
            } else if (std.mem.containsAtLeast(
```

```
                    u8,
                    line,
                    1,
                    "Pages occupied by compressor:",
                )) {
                    compressed_pages = parseLine(line);
                }
            }

            const used_bytes = (active_pages + wired_pages + compressed_pages) *
page_size;
            const used_mb = used_bytes / 1024 / 1024;
            const total_mb = total_bytes / 1024 / 1024;
            std.debug.print(
                "[{d}] macOS Used RAM: {d} MB / {d} MB\n",
                .{ now, used_mb, total_mb },
            );
        },
        else => @compileError("Unsupported OS"),
    }
}
```

The macOS branch retrieves total memory and page size by calling `getSysctl()` twice with the `hw.memsize` and `hw.pagesize` keys, respectively. Because macOS does not expose a simple memory usage file like Linux `/proc/meminfo`, the code instead runs the `vm_stat` command as a child process using `std.process.run()`, capturing its standard output into an allocated string that is freed via `defer` once parsing is complete. The output is tokenized line by line using `std.mem.tokenizeScalar()`, and three specific counters are extracted — active pages, wired pages, and pages occupied by the compressor — by matching each line with `std.mem.containsAtLeast()` and passing it to the shared `parseLine()` helper. Used memory is then calculated by summing those three page counts and multiplying by the page size.

Both platforms finish by printing a timestamped line showing used RAM versus total RAM, where now is a timestamp value passed into the function. The helper `parseLine ()` is shared across both platforms and works by tokenizing a line on spaces, dots, and colons, then attempting to parse each token as a `u64`, returning the first one that succeeds and zero if none do.

The `getSysctl()` function is a thin wrapper around the macOS `sysctl(8)` command-line tool that retrieves a single named kernel parameter and returns it as a `u64`:

```
fn getSysctl(
    io: std.Io,
    allocator: std.mem.Allocator,
    name: []const u8,
) !u64 {
    const result = try std.process.run(allocator, io, .{
        .argv = &[_][]const u8{ "sysctl", "-n", name },
    });
    defer {
        allocator.free(result.stdout);
        allocator.free(result.stderr);
    }
    return try std.fmt.parseInt(
        u64,
        std.mem.trim(u8, result.stdout, " \n\r\t"),
        10,
    );
}
```

The function takes an allocator and a parameter name such as `"hw.memsize"` or `"hw.pagesize"` as input. The allocator is needed because `std.process.run()` allocates the subprocess stdout and stderr as heap strings that must be freed by the caller. The code spawns `sysctl -n <name>` as a child process. The `-n` flag tells `sysctl(8)` to print only the value with no label, so for `hw.memsize` you get back something like `"17179869184\n"` rather than `"hw.memsize: 17179869184"`. Both `result.stdout` and `result.stderr` are freed immediately via `defer` regardless of whether parsing succeeds, since the raw strings are no longer needed once the value is extracted. Before parsing, `std.mem.trim()` strips any surrounding whitespace and newline characters from stdout because `parseInt()` will fail if the string contains a trailing newline. The function propagates both the subprocess error and the parse error to the caller with `try`, so if `sysctl(8)` fails to run or returns something that is not a valid integer, the error bubbles up naturally. Using `ch06/memInfo.zig` produces the following kind of output on macOS:

```
$ zig run ch06/memInfo.zig
[1772818492] macOS Used RAM: 19188 MB / 65536 MB
[1772818494] macOS Used RAM: 19156 MB / 65536 MB
```

With all the information in mind, let us proceed with the server part of the service.

The server process

The server (`ch06/memServer.zig`) is a raw TCP service that listens on `127.0.0.1:8080` and responds to every incoming connection with a JSON snapshot of current memory usage. It binds by calling `std.Io.net.IpAddress.parseIp4()` followed by `address.listen()`, then enters an infinite loop that blocks on `server.accept()` until a client connects. Any accept error is logged, and the loop continues rather than crashing. The accept loop is the following:

```
while (true) {
    const stream = server.accept(io) catch |err| {
        std.debug.print("Accept error: {}\n", .{err});
        continue;
    };
    defer stream.close(io);

    const stats = try getMemoryStats(io, allocator);
    const json_str = try std.fmt.allocPrint(
        allocator,
        "{f}\n",
        .{std.json.fmt(stats, .{})},
    );
    defer allocator.free(json_str);

    var wbuf: [4096]u8 = undefined;
    var writer_impl = stream.writer(io,&wbuf);
    constwriter=&writer_impl.interface;
    try writer.writeAll(json_str);
    try writer.flush();
}
```

The loop calls `server.accept()` on each iteration, blocking until a client connects. Accept errors are caught and logged without terminating the server — the continue statement returns control to the top of the loop immediately, leaving the server running. Once a connection is accepted, `getMemoryStats()` reads the current memory figures and `std.json.fmt()` serializes them into a heap-allocated JSON string. A stack-allocated 4096-byte buffer backs the stream writer, which sends the response and flushes it before the `defer` statements at the top of the loop body run — closing the stream and freeing the JSON string — and the next `accept()` call begins. This is a single-client-at-a-time design: each connection is fully served before the next one is accepted.

JSON serialization is handled by the `MemStats` struct and `std.json.fmt()`. The `MemStats` struct defines the shape of the response with four fields: os, a string identifying the operating system; `used_mb` and `total_mb`, both `u64` values representing memory in megabytes; and `timestamp`, an `i64` UNIX timestamp. Once `getMemoryStats()` populates and returns a `MemStats` value, the server serializes it using `std.fmt.allocPrint()` with the `{f}` format specifier and `std.json.fmt(stats, .{})`. A newline is appended, and the result is staged into a buffered writer wrapping the connection stream, then flushed in a single operation. The program combines everything discussed in this section and in `memInfo.zig` — the `MemStats` struct, `getMemoryStats()`, `getSysctl()` and `parseNumber()` — into a single file. All the logic has been explained in detail above, so rather than walking through it line by line again, we encourage you to read through the full listing. With the server written and running, we can now turn to the other side of the conversation. The server sits and waits, collecting memory statistics and serializing them as JSON on demand — but on its own, it produces no visible output. We need a client that connects to it, reads the response, and presents the data in a meaningful way.

The service client

With the server in place, we need a client that can connect to it, deserialize the JSON response, and display the results in a human-readable format. Unlike the general-purpose HTTP client built earlier in this chapter, *this client is purpose-built for the memory monitoring service* — it knows exactly what the server sends and polls it on a fixed interval, printing a timestamped summary of memory usage each time. The core of the client is the `pollServer()` function. The `main()` function is responsible for reading the host and port from the command line, then calling `pollServer()` in a loop with a configurable sleep between each call. `pollServer()` opens a TCP connection to the memory server, reads one response, parses it as JSON, and prints a formatted summary. It is intentionally narrow — one connection, one read, one response — because it is designed to be called in a loop by the caller rather than looping internally:

```
fn pollServer(
    io: std.Io,
    allocator: std.mem.Allocator,
    host: []const u8,
    port: u16,
) !void {
    const ip = try resolveHostname(allocator, host);
    defer allocator.free(ip);
    const address = try std.Io.net.IpAddress.parseIp4(ip, port);
    const stream = try address.connect(io, .{ .mode = .stream });
    defer stream.close(io);
```

```
    var rbuf: [64]u8 = undefined;
    var data: [1024]u8 = undefined;
    var reader_impl = stream.reader(io,&rbuf);
    constreader=&reader_impl.interface;

    const bytes_read = try reader.readSliceShort(&data);
    if (bytes_read == 0) return error.EmptyResponse;
```

The connection is established by first calling the local `resolveHostname()` helper, which translates the hostname string into a raw IPv4 address string that is heap-allocated and freed via `defer`. That resolved IP string is then passed to `std.Io.net.IpAddress.parseIp4()` alongside the port to produce a binary address, after which `address.connect()` with `.mode = .stream` opens the TCP connection. The reading setup uses two distinct buffers deliberately: `rbuf` is a small 64-byte stack buffer that serves as the reader's internal staging area, while `data` is the 1024-byte destination buffer passed to `readSliceShort()` — the actual slice that receives the incoming bytes. This separation keeps the reader's internal bookkeeping independent from the application buffer. The `readSliceShort()` call reads however many bytes are currently available in one operation, which is safe here because the JSON payload from the server is always small and arrives in one chunk over loopback. If the read returns zero bytes, the server has closed the connection without sending anything, so `error.EmptyResponse` is returned rather than attempting to parse an empty buffer. The most deliberate decision in the function is the use of an anonymous struct directly inside the `std.json.parseFromSlice()` call rather than importing or redefining the `MemStats` type from the server. This is a common Zig pattern for JSON parsing at the boundary of a program — you declare exactly the shape you care about inline, and the compiler wires up the field mapping at compile time. The `.ignore_unknown_fields = true` option means the parser will not fail if the server later adds new fields to its response, making the client forward compatible by default. `parsed.deinit()` is deferred to ensure the parsed memory is freed even if subsequent lines fail:

```
    const parsed = try std.json.parseFromSlice(
        struct {
            os: []const u8,
            used_mb: u64,
            total_mb: u64,
            timestamp: i64,
        },
        allocator,
        data[0..bytes_read],
        .{ .ignore_unknown_fields = true },
```

```
    );
    defer parsed.deinit();

    const stats = parsed.value;
    std.debug.print("[{d}] {s} Memory: {d}/{d} MB ({d}%)\n", .{
        stats.timestamp,
        stats.os,
        stats.used_mb,
        stats.total_mb,
        (stats.used_mb * 100) / stats.total_mb,
    });
}
```

Finally, for the percentage calculation, the multiplication happens first to preserve precision before the division discards the remainder, giving a whole-number percentage without needing floating-point.

Here is the `resolveHostname()` helper function implementation:

```
fn resolveHostname(allocator: std.mem.Allocator, host: []const u8) ![]const u8 {
    // If it already looks like an IPv4 literal, return a copy.
    if (std.Io.net.IpAddress.parseIp4(host, 0)) |_| {
        return allocator.dupe(u8, host);
    } else |_| {}

    // Use getaddrinfo to resolve the hostname.
    const host_z = try allocator.dupeZ(u8, host);
    defer allocator.free(host_z);

    var hints = std.mem.zeroes(c.struct_addrinfo);
    hints.ai_family = c.AF_INET; // IPv4 only
    hints.ai_socktype = c.SOCK_STREAM;

    var res: ?*c.struct_addrinfo = null;
    const rc = c.getaddrinfo(host_z.ptr,null,&hints,&res);
    if (rc != 0) return error.HostNotFound;
    defer c.freeaddrinfo(res);

    const sa = @as(*c.struct_sockaddr_in, @ptrCast(@alignCast(res.?.ai_addr)));
    var buf: [16]u8 = undefined;
    const ip = c.inet_ntop(c.AF_INET,&sa.sin_addr,&buf,buf.len);
```

```
    if (ip == null) return error.HostNotFound;

    const ip_str = std.mem.sliceTo(ip, 0);
    return allocator.dupe(u8, ip_str);
}
```

`resolveHostname()` takes a hostname string and always returns a dotted-decimal IPv4 address string, allocating the result on the caller-supplied allocator. It first checks whether the input is already an IPv4 literal using `std.Io.net.IpAddress.parseIp4()` — if the parse succeeds, a copy of the input is returned immediately, avoiding an unnecessary DNS lookup. If the input is a hostname, the function creates a null-terminated copy using `allocator.dupeZ()` since `c.getaddrinfo()` requires a C string. A zeroed `struct_addrinfo` hints structure constrains the lookup to IPv4 (`AF_INET`) stream sockets, and `getaddrinfo()` is called to perform the resolution. On failure, the function returns an `error.HostNotFound`; on success, `defer c.freeaddrinfo(res)` ensures the result list is released regardless of what follows. The first result's address is cast from the generic `struct_sockaddr` to `struct_sockaddr_in`, and `inet_ntop()` converts the binary address into a human-readable dotted-decimal string written into a 16-byte stack buffer — large enough for any IPv4 address. The resulting string is duplicated onto the allocator and returned to the caller.

Let us see both server and client in action – begin the server process before trying to use the client. The output from the client should be analogous to the following:

```
$ zig run ch06/memClient.zig -lc -- localhost 8080 3
Polling localhost:8080 for 3 samples...
[1772818962] macos Memory: 18771/65536 MB (28%)
[1772818963] macos Memory: 18842/65536 MB (28%)
[1772818964] macos Memory: 18842/65536 MB (28%)
```

In this section, we built a complete client-server system for monitoring memory usage in real time. Starting from the OS-level primitives — `/proc/meminfo` on Linux and `sysctl(8)` plus `vm_stat(1)` on macOS — we collected live memory statistics, packaged them into a typed struct, and serialized them as JSON over a raw TCP connection. On the client side, we deserialized that JSON using an anonymous struct and presented the results as a human-readable, timestamped summary. Not bad!

The `memServer.zig` and `memClient.zig` pair we just built serializes data as JSON text, which is readable and flexible but leaves an entire class of bugs undetected until runtime. Rename a field, widen a `u32` to a `u64`, or insert a new field in the middle of a struct, and the parser will silently produce wrong values — or simply stop working — only when a live message arrives. Zig `comptime` gives us a way to make that impossible. The following section implements a comptime-driven encoder and decoder for ZEMP that is parameterized by the message struct type itself. The parser is generated at compile time from the struct's field declarations, so it is always in sync with the data it encodes. Adding a field requires no parser changes, removing a field removes it from the wire format automatically, and using an unsupported field type, such as `f64` or a pointer, is a `@compileError` at the point of definition rather than a runtime panic discovered in testing.

Enforcing protocol correctness with comptime

Before examining the code, it is worth grounding the `comptime` parser in concrete terms. Consider what happens with a hand-written parser when the `MemQueryResp` struct gains a new field — say, a `swap_mb` value to report swap usage. With a hand-written approach, you must remember to update the encoder, update the decoder, update any size constants, and update any documentation that describes the wire format. Miss any one of those, and the parser silently reads the wrong value into the wrong field with no error until a live message produces nonsense output. With the `comptime` parser, adding the field to the struct is the only change required. The encoder and decoder are regenerated automatically on the next build because they are derived from `@typeInfo(MemQueryResp)` at compile time. There is no separate parser file to synchronize. A second scenario involves field types. Suppose a developer tries to add a `f64` field to store a CPU utilization percentage, reasoning that a floating-point percentage is more natural than a scaled integer. The `comptime` parser rejects this immediately with a `@compileError` naming the unsupported type and the field that introduced it. The build fails before any binary is produced, before any test is run, and before any message is sent over the network. The developer is forced to make a conscious decision — use a `u32` scaled by 100 or keep floating-point values out of the wire format entirely — rather than shipping a parser that silently produces platform-dependent byte representations of `f64` values. A third scenario is buffer sizing. A hand-written approach typically declares a buffer with a hardcoded size — `var buf: [256]u8 = undefined` — chosen by the developer at the time of writing and silently wrong the moment the struct grows beyond that estimate. With `frameSize(MemQueryResp)` returning a `comptime_int`, the buffer declaration `var buf: [frameSize(MemQueryResp)]u8 = undefined` is always exactly right. It cannot be stale, cannot be too small, and requires no heap allocation. The compiler enforces it. These three scenarios share the same pattern seen in *Chapter 3, Direct Memory Access and Binary Formats*: a local, apparently safe change produces a remote, hard-to-diagnose failure. The comptime parser closes all three gaps simultaneously. Adding a field updates the parser. Adding an unsupported type stops the build. Changing field sizes adjusts the buffer. The struct definition becomes the single source of truth for the entire wire format, and comptime makes that truth impossible to contradict at compile time.

The program defines **ZEMP (Zig Exchange Memory Protocol)** as a binary framing where every message consists of a fixed 8-byte `FrameHeader` followed by a variable-length payload whose size is determined entirely at compile time by the payload struct type. The header carries an opcode, flags, and a sequence number, all stored as little-endian integers. A `comptime` assertion verifies that `FrameHeader` is exactly 8 bytes before any binary is produced.

Three payload structs are defined. `MemQueryReq` is a client request carrying a flags field and a maximum response size. `MemQueryResp` is the server response carrying total, used, and available memory in megabytes and a UNIX timestamp. `PingPayload` carries a single nonce for connectivity checks. All three use extern struct to guarantee C-compatible layout with no compiler-inserted padding.

```
const MemQueryReq = extern struct {
    flags: u32, // reserved, must be 0
    limit: u32, // max response bytes the client can accept
};

const MemQueryResp = extern struct {
    total_mb: u64,
    used_mb: u64,
    available_mb: u64,
    timestamp: i64, // Unix seconds
};

const PingPayload = extern struct {
    nonce: u64,
};
```

The `frameSize()` function computes the total byte count of a frame — header plus payload — as a `comptime_int`. Because this value is known at compile time, callers can write `var buf: [frameSize(MemQueryResp)]u8 = undefined` and the compiler allocates exactly the right stack buffer with no runtime calculation and no heap involvement.

```
fn frameSize(comptime Payload: type) comptime_int {
    return HEADER_SIZE + @sizeOf(Payload);
}
```

The `encode()` function accepts a `FrameHeader` and a payload value and writes them into a buffer whose size is enforced by the type system to be exactly `frameSize(Payload)` — passing the wrong size buffer is a compile error, not a runtime bounds violation. It writes the header using `std.mem.asBytes()` for a zero-copy cast, then iterates over the payload struct fields using `@typeInfo(Payload).@"struct".fields` inside an `inline for` loop. Because `inline for` is unrolled at compile time, the resulting machine code contains straight-line serialization instructions with no runtime type dispatch, no virtual calls, and no allocations.

```
fn encode(
    comptime Payload: type,
    hdr: FrameHeader,
    payload: Payload,
    buf: *[frameSize(Payload)]u8,
) void {
    // Write header (extern struct - safe direct cast)
    @memcpy(buf[0..HEADER_SIZE], std.mem.asBytes(&hdr));

    // Write each payload field in declaration order
    var offset: usize = HEADER_SIZE;
    inline for (@typeInfo(Payload).@"struct".fields) |field| {
        const FieldT = field.type;
        const value = @field(payload, field.name);
        const wire_value = wireInt(FieldT, value);
        const bytes = std.mem.asBytes(&wire_value);
        @memcpy(buf[offset..][0..@sizeOf(FieldT)], bytes);
        offset += @sizeOf(FieldT);
    }
}
```

The `wireInt()` helper handles endianness conversion for each field. It switches over `@typeInfo(T)` at compile time: integer types are passed through `std.mem.nativeToLittle()` and enum types have their tag integer extracted, converted, and re-wrapped. Any other type — `f64`, a pointer, a slice — hits the `else` branch, which calls `@compileError`, producing a build failure that names the unsupported type and the field that introduced it. This means the error appears at the moment you add the problematic field, not when a test happens to exercise that code path.

```
fn wireInt(comptime T: type, value: T) T {
    return switch (@typeInfo(T)) {
        .int => std.mem.nativeToLittle(T, value),
        .@"enum" => |ei| {
            const I = ei.tag_type;
            const v = std.mem.nativeToLittle(I, @intFromEnum(value));
```

```
                return @enumFromInt(v);
            },
            else => @compileError(
                "ZEMP field type '" ++ @typeName(T) ++
                    "' not supported; use integers or integer-backed enums",
            ),
        };
    }
```

The `decode()` function mirrors `encode()` exactly, reading fields back from the buffer in declaration order using `std.mem.bytesToValue()` and applying `fromWireInt()` for the reverse endianness conversion. It checks the buffer length before reading and returns an `error.BufferTooShort` if the input is insufficient. Feel free to look at its implementation.

Last, in `main()`, the program constructs a `MemQueryResp` value with realistic memory statistics, encodes it into a stack-allocated buffer, prints the raw hex bytes of the resulting frame, decodes it back, and verifies that every field survived the round-trip exactly. It then prints the `comptime` frame sizes for all three payload types. This is `MemQueryResp`:

```
const resp = MemQueryResp{
        .total_mb = 16384,
        .used_mb = 4200,
        .available_mb = 12184,
        .timestamp = 1_700_000_000,
    };
```

Let us see `ch06/comptimeParser.zig` in action:

```
$ zig run ch06/comptimeParser.zig
Encoded 40-byte ZEMP frame:
02 00 00 00 2A 00 00 00
00 40 00 00 00 00 00 00
68 10 00 00 00 00 00 00
98 2F 00 00 00 00 00 00
00 F1 53 65 00 00 00 00

Decoded frame:
  opcode        = 0x0002
  seq           = 42
  total_mb      = 16384
```

```
    used_mb      = 4200
    available_mb = 12184
    timestamp    = 1700000000
  Round-trip OK.

  Comptime frame sizes:
    MemQueryReq  = 16 bytes
    MemQueryResp = 40 bytes
    PingPayload  = 16 bytes
```

The first block shows the raw 40-byte frame as hex pairs, eight bytes per line. The first line `02 00 00 00 2A 00 00 00` is the 8-byte header. The first two bytes `02 00` are the opcode `0x0002` (`MEM_QUERY_RESP`) in little-endian order. The next two bytes `00 00` are the flags field set to zero. The final four bytes `2A 00 00 00` are the sequence number 42 in little-endian — `0x2A` is decimal 42. The remaining four lines are the 32-byte payload. Each line is one field: `00 40 00 00 00 00 00 00` is `total_mb = 16384` (`0x4000` in little-endian u64), `68 10 00 00 00 00 00 00` is `used_mb = 4200` (`0x1068`), `98 2F 00 00 00 00 00 00` is `available_mb = 12184` (`0x2F98`) and `00 F1 53 65 00 00 00 00` is the timestamp `1700000000` (`0x6553F100`) in little-endian `i64`. The decoded block confirms that every field survived the round-trip intact. The opcode prints as `0x0002`, matching `Opcode.MEM_QUERY_RESP`. The sequence number is 42. All four payload fields match the values that were encoded. The `Round-trip OK` line confirms that all four `std.debug.assert()` calls passed. The final block shows the `comptime` frame sizes. `MemQueryReq` is 16 bytes (8-byte header plus two u32 fields). `MemQueryResp` is 40 bytes (8-byte header plus four 8-byte fields). `PingPayload` is 16 bytes (8-byte header plus one `u64` nonce). These values are `comptime_int` constants — they exist entirely at compile time and impose zero runtime cost.

Summary

In this chapter, you learned how to program TCP/IP applications in Zig. You realized how TCP and UDP differ in code and how the HTTP protocol can be programmed. We concluded the chapter by applying these concepts to a real-world scenario: building a system monitoring API, serializing live system data into JSON responses, and serving them over a minimal web server. These patterns — *listen, accept, read, write, close* — repeat themselves endlessly across networked software, and having implemented them by hand means you now understand what every higher-level library is doing underneath.

In the next chapter, we turn our attention to threads, processes, commands, and signals — the building blocks of concurrent and parallel systems programming in Zig. You will see how to use `std.Thread()`, how to fork child processes using the C interoperability layer, and how to handle

UNIX signals for graceful shutdown and inter-process communication. We will put all these ideas together in a practical project: `zcron`, a minimal `cron(8)`-like service that schedules and runs periodic tasks, detaches from the terminal, and responds correctly to signals like `SIGTERM` and `SIGCHLD`.

Exercises

- Modify `echoClientResolve.zig` to accept the message as an argument.
- Modify `memServer.zig` to listen on the provided port.

Additional resources

- Docker: `https://www.docker.com/`
- The `docker-compose` utility: `https://github.com/docker/compose`
- The HTTP protocol: `https://www.w3.org/Protocols/`

7

Managing Threads, Processes, and Signals

Zig gives you low-level control over system programming tasks, including process management and concurrency. At the same time, the Zig Standard Library provides native support for *threads* via `std.Thread()`, it does not yet offer high-level abstractions for direct process control. However, the C interoperability of Zig lets you call functions like `fork(2)` and `exec(3)` directly from the underlying operating system, empowering you to create child processes and execute shell commands. **Signals** are a fundamental part of inter-process communication in UNIX systems, enabling processes to respond to *asynchronous events* like `SIGINT` (interrupt), `SIGTERM` (terminate), or `SIGHUP` (hangup). Even though the Standard Library does not yet include built-in abstractions for signal handling, you can also use C functions such as `signal(3)`, `sigaction(2)` and `kill(2)` via `@cImport()` to register signal handlers, block or mask signals, and send signals between processes. Each of these capabilities — signal handling, process creation, thread management, and command execution — is introduced individually before converging in `zcron`, a minimal `cron(8)`-style job scheduler that ties them all together into a single production-oriented tool.

This chapter covers:

- UNIX signal handling
- Processes and Threads
- Executing Shell Commands
- Writing a concurrent TCP server and client
- Creating `zcron`, a minimal Cron variation

UNIX signal handling

With UNIX signals, we can achieve asynchronous communication with a running process, which can be very handy at times. The single most useful case for UNIX signals is finding out what an application is doing or its current status without taking any extreme measures (we are going to see such a case in a while), provided that such functionality has been implemented. For now, we will start with a small Zig program (`ch07/sigInt.zig`) that showcases the handling of the `SIGINT` signal:

```
const std = @import("std");

const c = @cImport({
    @cInclude("signal.h");
    @cInclude("unistd.h");
});

var running: std.atomic.Value(bool) = std.atomic.Value(bool).init(true);

fn handle_sigint(_: c_int) callconv(.c) void {
    running.store(false, .seq_cst);
}
```

By importing the C header `signal.h`, the program gains access to the low-level signal handling infrastructure of the OS. The `handle_sigint()` function is marked with `callconv(.c)` to ensure it is compatible with the C calling convention required by the kernel's signal delivery mechanism. When the user presses Ctrl+C, the OS sends SIGINT to the process, interrupting the main execution flow to invoke this handler. Because POSIX strictly limits which functions may be safely called inside a signal handler — prohibiting anything that acquires locks, allocates memory, or flushes buffers — the handler does nothing more than set an atomic flag. The main loop detects the flag on its next iteration and handles printing and exit in a safe context.

In the `main()` function, the program registers the handler by calling `c.signal()`, which informs the kernel that instead of performing the default action — immediate termination — it should invoke our custom handler when `SIGINT` arrives:

```
pub fn main(init: std.process.Init) !void {
    const io = init.io;
    _ = c.signal(c.SIGINT, handle_sigint);
    std.debug.print("Running... Ctrl+C to trigger SIGINT.\n", .{});
```

```
        while (running.load(.seq_cst)) {
            try std.Io.sleep(io, std.Io.Duration.fromSeconds(1), .awake);
        }
        std.debug.print("Caught SIGINT, exiting.\n", .{});
        std.process.exit(0);
    }
```

The loop runs until the atomic flag is cleared by the handler, sleeping for one second on each iteration to prevent the CPU from spinning at 100% capacity. Once the flag is set, the loop exits, and `main()` prints a diagnostic message and calls `std.process.exit(0)` in a safe context — outside the signal handler, where standard library functions may be called freely.

Now, let us use `ch07/sigInt.zig` by pressing `Ctrl+C`:

```
$ zig run ch07/sigInt.zig
Running... Ctrl+C to trigger SIGINT.
^CCaught SIGINT! Cleaning up before exit...
```

When we press `Ctrl+C`, the terminal sends a `SIGINT` to the foreground process, which handles it on its own instead of letting the OS handle it itself.

Now that we have learned how to handle signals in Zig, let us use that knowledge to do something more rewarding. In the next section, we will create something meaningful, like getting information from a running program.

Using signals intentionally

In the presented example code, we use signals for two reasons: first, to get back a random value and second, to learn the uptime of the program. This use of signals offers a technique for understanding what is going on behind the scenes without terminating the application or having to look at logs. This pattern is also useful for debugging, monitoring, and managing long-running services in a UNIX environment — a process that can report its internal state on demand, without being restarted or recompiled, is far easier to operate in production than one that requires external tooling or log scraping to understand what it is doing.

Here is the code of `ch07/getInformation.zig`:

```
const std = @import("std");
const c = @cImport({
    @cInclude("signal.h");
    @cInclude("unistd.h");
```

```
});

var randomValue = std.atomic.Value(i32).init(0);
var sRunning = std.atomic.Value(usize).init(0);
var newValueRequested = std.atomic.Value(bool).init(false);
var uptimeRequested = std.atomic.Value(bool).init(false);

fn handle_sigusr1(_: c_int) callconv(.c) void {
    newValueRequested.store(true, .monotonic);
}

fn handle_sigusr2(_: c_int) callconv(.c) void {
    uptimeRequested.store(true, .monotonic);
}
```

The program defines two custom signal handlers that interact with a shared atomic state. When the process receives `SIGUSR1`, the handler sets the `newValueRequested` flag; the main loop checks it on its next iteration, generates a new random value using `io.random()`, and stores it atomically in `randomValue`. When the process receives `SIGUSR2`, the handler sets the `uptimeRequested` flag; the main loop checks it and prints the current value of `sRunning`, which is incremented by 2 on every two-second iteration to track uptime in seconds. Because signal handlers can execute at any point between instructions, all shared variables are declared as `std.atomic.Value` and accessed with appropriate memory ordering — `.monotonic` in the handlers, where only the atomic write itself matters, and `.seq_cst` in the main loop, where a consistent view of all shared state is required. This pattern is common in system utilities that need to report internal metrics or respond to external signals without stopping the primary execution loop.

`main()` serves as the entry point that wires the signal handlers to the OS event system:

```
pub fn main(init: std.process.Init) !void {
    const io = init.io;
    _ = c.signal(c.SIGUSR1, handle_sigusr1);
    _ = c.signal(c.SIGUSR2, handle_sigusr2);

    std.debug.print(
        "Use -USR1 <pid> and -USR2 <pid> to send signals.\n",
        .{},
    );
    std.debug.print("PID: {}\n", .{c.getpid()});
```

```
        while (true) {
            try std.Io.sleep(io, std.Io.Duration.fromSeconds(2), .awake);
            _ = sRunning.fetchAdd(2, .seq_cst);
            if (newValueRequested.load(.seq_cst)) {
                newValueRequested.store(false, .seq_cst);
                var buf: [4]u8 = undefined;
                io.random(&buf);
                randomValue.store(
                    std.mem.readInt(i32, &buf, .little),
                    .seq_cst,
                );
                std.debug.print(
                    "randomValue: {d}\n",
                    .{randomValue.load(.seq_cst)},
                );
            }
            if (uptimeRequested.load(.seq_cst)) {
                uptimeRequested.store(false, .seq_cst);
                std.debug.print(
                    "Uptime: {d} seconds\n",
                    .{sRunning.load(.seq_cst)},
                );
            }
        }
    }
```

The program overrides the default signal behaviors by calling `c.signal()` for both `SIGUSR1` and `SIGUSR2`, then prints its own process ID via `c.getpid()` so the user knows which target to pass to `kill(1)`. On each iteration, the loop sleeps for two seconds and increments `sRunning` by 2 to track uptime in seconds. It then checks the `newValueRequested` flag — if `SIGUSR1` was received since the last iteration, the loop clears the flag and generates a new random value using `io.random()`, which draws from the platform's cryptographically secure random source (`getrandom(2)` on Linux, `arc4random` on macOS), storing the result atomically in `randomValue`. For a signal-handling demonstration, a simple PRNG would be sufficient; `io.random()` is used here because it is the standard way to obtain random bytes in Zig 0.16 and requires no additional setup. If `SIGUSR2` was received, the loop clears the `uptimeRequested` flag and prints the current uptime. All shared state is accessed through atomic operations, ensuring that concurrent signal delivery never produces a torn read or write. Now, let us use `ch07/getInformation.zig`:

```
$ zig run ch07/getInformation.zig
Use -USR1 <pid> and -USR2 <pid> to send signals.
PID: 7206
```

Given that in this case the process ID is `7206` (yours is going to vary), send `SIGUSR1` to the process with `kill(1)` by executing `kill -USR17206` from another terminal window. Next, send the `SIGUSR2` signal to the process. These two signals produce the following output:

```
[SIGUSR1] Current random value: -1820054701
[SIGUSR2] Seconds running: 96
```

While signals provide a powerful mechanism for inter-process communication and event handling, another fundamental way to manage and create new execution flows in UNIX systems is through processes and threads.

Processes and Threads

In UNIX systems, **threads** and **processes** are fundamental building blocks for parallelism and multitasking. A **process** is an independent execution environment with its own memory space, while **threads** are lightweight units of execution within a process that share memory and resources. The `fork(2)` system call is a classic UNIX mechanism used to create a new child process by duplicating the current process. After a `fork(2)`, both parent and child continue executing from the same point but with different process IDs. The child can perform a different task or replace its code using `execve(3)` to run another program entirely. Unlike threads, which communicate via shared memory, processes typically communicate via **inter-process communication** (IPC) mechanisms like pipes, signals, or sockets. Let us first learn about creating new processes. The choice between processes and threads is one of the most consequential decisions in systems programming. Threads share the same address space, making communication cheap but requiring careful synchronization to avoid data races. Processes are isolated — each has its own address space, file descriptor table, and signal mask — making them more robust in the face of failure but more expensive to create and slower to communicate across. As a rule of thumb: use threads when tasks need to share data tightly, and performance is the primary concern; use processes when isolation, fault tolerance, or the ability to run different executables matters more. A process has its own isolated address space — the kernel duplicates the page tables and file descriptor table on `fork(2)`, which makes creation more expensive but guarantees that a crash in one process cannot corrupt another. A thread, by contrast, shares the address space of its parent process: creation is cheap, requiring only a new stack and thread control block, but a null pointer dereference, or stack overflow in any thread, brings down the entire process. Communication reflects the same tradeoff — threads can share variables directly, protected by mutexes or atomics, while processes must use IPC mechanisms such as pipes, sockets, or signals. In practice, many production systems combine both models — a process-per-core model with threads inside each process. `zcron` forks a child process per job precisely because a crashing job must not corrupt the scheduler's state or terminate the entire program — isolation is worth the overhead. A web server handling thousands of short-lived requests per second would make the opposite choice, using a thread pool to avoid the repeated cost of `fork(2)`.

Forking processes

Process forking, which only works on operating systems that support the `fork(2)` call, is the mechanism by which a running process creates a new process by *duplicating itself*. This new process is called the *child* process, while the original is called the *parent*. The two processes run concurrently and initially share the same code and memory contents, although they operate independently after the fork. So, a process calls `fork(2)` and creates a copy of itself. The call *returns twice*: once in the parent process (returning the PID of the child process) and once in the child process (returning `0`). Here is the example code of `ch07/forkMe.zig`, which demonstrates process creation using `fork(2)`:

```
const std = @import("std");
const c = @cImport({
    @cInclude("unistd.h");
    @cInclude("sys/wait.h");
});

pub fn main(init: std.process.Init) !void {
    _ = init;
    const myPID = c.getpid();
    const pid = c.fork();
    if (pid < 0) {
        std.debug.print("Fork failed.\n", .{});
        return error.ForkFailed;
    } else if (pid == 0) {
        std.debug.print("Hello from the child process!\n", .{});
    } else {
        std.debug.print("Hello from the parent process!\n", .{});
        std.debug.print(
            "Parent PID: {} - Child PID: {}\n",
```

```
            .{ myPID, pid },
        );
        const wait_result = c.waitpid(pid, null, 0);
        if (wait_result < 0) {
            std.debug.print("waitpid failed.\n", .{});
        }
    }
}
```

The result of `c.fork()` is two nearly identical processes running the same code. The logic depends entirely on the return value of `fork(2)`, which allows the two processes to distinguish themselves — in the parent, `fork(2)` returns the PID of the newly created child, while in the child, the return value is always 0. If the return value is negative, the system was unable to allocate resources for a new process, and the program handles this as an error. By using an `if/else` structure, the program directs the two execution flows into different logical paths. The child process identifies itself and prints a greeting, while the parent prints its own identity along with the PID of its child. Once the child has finished, the parent calls `waitpid(2)` to collect the child's exit status. This is not optional — without it, the kernel retains the child's entry in the process table after it exits, producing a zombie process that remains visible in `ps(1)` output as `<defunct>` until the parent itself exits. In a long-running service that forks repeatedly, uncollected zombies will eventually exhaust the process table. The `zcron` scheduler avoids this problem entirely by installing a `SIGCHLD` handler that calls `waitpid(2)` with `WNOHANG`, reaping finished children automatically without blocking the main loop — a pattern worth adopting in any production code that spawns child processes.

Now try `ch07/forkMe.zig` on your machine:

```
$ zig run ch07/forkMe.zig
Hello from the parent process!
Parent PID: 7300 - Child PID: 7303
Hello from the child process!
```

The parent process (`7300`) successfully receives the PID of the new child (`7303`) as the return value, while the child process receives `0`, and the program is executed as planned.

Forking provides robust process isolation, but creating a new process can be resource-intensive. For scenarios where concurrent execution is needed without the overhead of full process duplication, threads offer a lighter alternative *within the same process*.

Putting your CPU to work with threads

Although concurrent programming is the subject of the next chapter, in this section, we are going to learn how to create threads in order to unlock the full potential of modern hardware and build software that can effectively manage multiple tasks simultaneously. Unlike forking, which creates entirely separate processes, spawning a thread creates a new execution path that shares the same memory space as the parent process.

The following example code (`ch07/threads.zig`) demonstrates the use of native concurrency in Zig via the `std.Thread` module:

```
const std = @import("std");

fn threadFunc(arg: usize) void {
    std.debug.print("Hello from thread! Arg = {}\n", .{arg});
}

pub fn main(init: std.process.Init) !void {
    _ = init;
    const thr1 = try std.Thread.spawn(.{}, threadFunc, .{1234});
    std.debug.print("Hello from main thread!\n", .{});
    const thr2 = try std.Thread.spawn(.{}, threadFunc, .{4321});
    thr1.join();
    thr2.join();
    std.debug.print("All threads have finished.\n", .{});
}
```

The code begins with the definition of the `threadFunc()` function. In the `main()` function, `std.Thread.spawn()` is called twice to initialize these new execution paths. The first argument to `spawn()` is a configuration struct (left as default here), followed by the function to execute and a tuple containing the arguments for that function. Because thread creation can fail due to system resource limits, the `try` keyword is used to handle potential errors. The program uses the `join()` method on the thread handles `thr1` and `thr2`. This is a *synchronization point* that tells the main thread to *wait* until the specific background threads have finished their execution. Without these calls, the `main()` function might reach its end and terminate the entire process before the background threads have a chance to print their messages. This pattern ensures that all concurrent tasks are completed in an orderly fashion before the program exits. Let us try `ch07/threads.zig` on our machines – you should get a similar output:

```
$ zig run ch07/threads.zig
Hello from main thread!
Hello from thread! Arg = 1234
Hello from thread! Arg = 4321
All threads have finished.
```

The logic behind the first line, `Hello from main thread!`, appearing before the spawned threads is a matter of timing. Spawning a thread involves a system call and some overhead to set up a new stack and execution context. Because the main thread is already running, it often hits its own print statement before the OS has fully initialized and switched context to the first worker thread. However, *this is not guaranteed*; on a heavily loaded system or a different architecture, you might see the worker threads interleave their output differently. The sequence of the arguments, `1234` then `4321`, suggests a sequential startup, but again, this is purely at the discretion of the scheduler. The most critical observation is the position of the final line. Because of the `join()` calls, this message is guaranteed to appear last. The next section picks up where this leaves off, demonstrating how to spawn and coordinate several threads simultaneously.

Running a variable number of threads

Now we are going to create a program that produces N threads, where N is a user-provided parameter. We are creating the threads using a `for` loop, and each thread gets a parameter from 0 to N - 1, which is printed on screen. The following example code (`ch07/nThreads.zig`) illustrates how to execute a variable number of threads at runtime:

```
const std = @import("std");

fn threadFunc(arg: usize) void {
    std.debug.print("{} ", .{arg});
}

pub fn main(init: std.process.Init) !void {
    const allocator = init.gpa;
    const argv = try init.minimal.args.toSlice(init.arena.allocator());
    if (argv.len < 2) {
        std.debug.print("Usage: {s} <N>\n", .{argv[0]});
        return;
    }
```

```
    const nStr = argv[1];
    const value = std.fmt.parseInt(usize, nStr, 10) catch {
        std.debug.print("Invalid number: {s}\n", .{nStr});
        return;
    };

    const threads = try allocator.alloc(std.Thread, value);
    defer allocator.free(threads);
    for (0..value) |i| {
        const thread = try std.Thread.spawn(.{}, threadFunc, .{i});
        threads[i] = thread;
    }

    for (0..value) |i| {
        threads[i].join();
    }
    std.debug.print("\nAll threads have finished.\n", .{});
}
```

This program expands the previous threading concept by introducing *dynamic concurrency*, where the number of execution paths is determined at runtime via command-line input. It utilizes the Debug Allocator to request a block of memory from the OS, allowing the program to store an arbitrary number of thread handles based on user input. The logic follows a three-stage lifecycle: **parsing**, **spawning**, and **synchronizing**. First, the program converts the command-line string into a `usize` integer using `std.fmt.parseInt()`. Once the count is known, `allocator.alloc()` creates a slice of `std.Thread` objects. This is a critical step because the compiler cannot know how much stack or heap space to reserve for these handles until the program is actually running. In the second stage, a `for` loop iterates, calling `std.Thread.spawn()` for each `i` index. Each thread receives its unique index `i` as an argument, but because they run concurrently, the order in which they print their numbers to the terminal is non-deterministic and managed by the OS scheduler. Finally, a second loop iterates through the slice to call `join()` on every handle. Let us now try `ch07/nThreads.zig` with just 4 threads:

```
$ zig run ch07/nThreads.zig -- 4
0 1 3 2
All threads have finished.
$ zig run ch07/nThreads.zig -- 4
0 3 1 2
All threads have finished.
```

These two execution traces provide a perfect laboratory demonstration of thread non-determinism. Although we passed the same argument (4) to both runs, the sequence of the thread IDs changed. This happens because while we may spawn threads in a specific order in your code, *we have no control over the order in which the OS scheduler actually places them on a CPU core to execute.*

While threads provide powerful tools for managing concurrent tasks, applications need to interact with the broader system environment. This leads us to executing external shell commands, a crucial method for leveraging existing system utilities and other programs.

Executing Shell Commands

To extend their reach beyond internal program logic, Zig applications often need to execute external shell commands, a fundamental way to leverage existing system utilities. The presented example illustrates how to launch external programs as child processes using `std.process.run()`, which handles spawning, waiting, and output capture in a single call. The program demonstrates two invocations: the first runs a command that is expected to fail, exercising the error path of the termination switch, while the second runs a command that succeeds and captures its standard output and standard error into heap-allocated strings. Both examples showcase how to interpret the result using a switch over the termination union, giving us fine-grained control over process execution, output handling, and error management. Consider the following example code (`ch07/executeCommand.zig`):

```
const std = @import("std");

pub fn main(init: std.process.Init) !void {
    const allocator = init.gpa;
    const io = init.io;

    // First command: Execute a process and ignore stdout and stderr
    const argv1 = [_][]const u8{ "ls", "./doesNotExist" };
    const proc1 = try std.process.run(
        allocator,
```

```
        io,
        .{ .argv = &argv1 },
    );
    defer allocator.free(proc1.stdout);
    defer allocator.free(proc1.stderr);
    switch (proc1.term) {
        .exited => |eCode| {
            if (eCode != 0) {
                std.debug.print(
                    "P1 did not exit cleanly with code {}\n",
                    .{eCode},
                );
            } else {
                std.debug.print("P1 completed successfully.\n", .{});
            }
        },
        .signal => {
            std.debug.print("P1 was killed by a signal.\n", .{});
        },
        .stopped => {
            std.debug.print("P1 was stopped.\n", .{});
        },
        .unknown => {
            std.debug.print("P1 terminated: unknown status.\n", .{});
        },
    }
```

The program defines the command-line arguments for the first child process as `{ "ls", "./doesNotExist" }`, setting it up to list the contents of a non-existent directory — a choice that guarantees a non-zero exit code. `std.process.run()` is called with the allocator and `io` handle, which spawns the child, waits for it to complete, and returns a result containing the termination status along with heap-allocated `stdout` and `stderr` strings. The `defer` statements ensure those strings are freed regardless of how the switch resolves. The code then switches over `proc1.term` to handle different outcomes: a clean exit with code zero, a non-zero exit indicating failure, termination by a signal, a stopped process, or an unknown status. Each branch prints a diagnostic message, giving a transparent view of exactly how the child process ended. For the second child process, its command-line arguments are defined in the code that follows. In this instance, it is set to run the `uptime(1)` command, which does not require any additional arguments:

```
const argv2 = [_][]const u8{"uptime"};
const proc2 = try std.process.run(
    allocator,
    io,
    .{ .argv = &argv2 },
);
defer allocator.free(proc2.stdout);
defer allocator.free(proc2.stderr);
```

This child process starts with `std.process.run()`, configured to capture its standard output and standard error using the provided allocator. The memory allocated for standard output is marked for automatic deallocation when it goes out of scope. Similarly, the code ensures the same cleanup for standard error, preventing any memory leaks. The program then switches over the termination status (`proc2.term`) of this second child process to manage its outcome:

```
switch (proc2.term) {
    .exited => |eCode| {
        if (eCode != 0) {
            std.debug.print(
                "P2 did not exit cleanly with code {}\n",
                .{eCode},
            );
            return;
        }
        std.debug.print("P2 completed successfully.\n", .{});
    },
    .signal => {
        std.debug.print("P2 was killed by a signal.\n", .{});
        return;
    },
    .stopped => {
        std.debug.print("P2 was stopped.\n", .{});
        return;
    },
    .unknown => {
        std.debug.print("P2 terminated: unknown status.\n", .{});
        return;
```

```
        },
    }

    std.debug.print("P2 stdout:\n{s}\n", .{proc2.stdout});
    std.debug.print("P2 stderr:\n{s}\n", .{proc2.stderr});
}
```

The program prints the standard output collected from the second child process as well as the collected output from standard error, if any.

It is now time to execute `ch07/executeCommand.zig` on our machines:

```
$ zig run ch07/executeCommand.zig
P1 did not exit cleanly with code 1
P2 completed successfully.
P2 stdout:
21:29  up  1:41, 9 users, load averages: 1.38 1.49 1.72

P2 stderr:
```

The first line, `P1 did not exit cleanly with code 1`, indicates that the first process (`P1`) failed to complete its task successfully. In UNIX systems, an exit code of `0` typically signifies success, whereas any non-zero value denotes an error. The second half of the output describes the success of the second process (`P2`). The message `P2 completed successfully.` confirms that this process returned an exit code of `0`. Because `P2` was configured to capture its output, the program then prints the contents of its standard output buffer. Finally, the empty `P2 stderr:` line shows that the `uptime(1)` command did not produce any error messages. Since the command executed exactly as expected, its error stream remained empty. By capturing both `stdout` and `stderr`, the parent program can provide a transparent view of what happened inside the child process.

After seeing how to manage isolated tasks, it is time to revisit the TCP server we built in the previous chapter and make it concurrent.

Writing a concurrent TCP server

While a simple server might process one request at a time, a concurrent TCP server can manage many clients at once. This transition from local task management to network-based concurrency is essential for building scalable system utilities, as it allows your program to remain responsive to new incoming connections while existing ones are still being processed autonomously. Consider the example code in `ch07/concTCP.zig` when implementing a concurrent TCP server –

the `handleConnection()` function that handles each connection is omitted from the listing below for brevity, as its implementation does not depend on whether we are dealing with a concurrent TCP server or not:

```
const std = @import("std");
const Io = std.Io;
const Thread = std.Thread;
const AtomicUsize = std.atomic.Value(usize);

var thread_counter = AtomicUsize.init(0);

pub fn main(init: std.process.Init) !void {
    var gpa: std.heap.DebugAllocator(.{}) = .init;
    defer _ = gpa.deinit();
    const allocator = gpa.allocator();
    const io = init.io;

    const argv = try init.minimal.args.toSlice(init.arena.allocator());
    if (argv.len < 2) {
        std.debug.print("Usage: echo_server <port>\n", .{});
        return error.MissingPort;
    }

    const port = try std.fmt.parseInt(u16, argv[1], 10);
    const address = try Io.net.IpAddress.parseIp4("0.0.0.0", port);
    var server = try address.listen(io, .{});
    defer server.deinit(io);

    std.debug.print("Listening on 0.0.0.0:{d}\n", .{port});
```

This code establishes the foundation of a concurrent server by initializing the networking stack and preparing for thread-safe state management. The program begins by defining a global `AtomicUsize` counter, which provides a thread-safe way to track active connections without the performance overhead or complexity of a mutex. The server binds to `0.0.0.0` with `Io.net.IpAddress.parseIp4()`; this means that it accepts connections on any available network interface at the specified port. *Atomics* and *mutexes* are explained in *Chapter 8, Orchestrating Concurrency and Synchronization.*

The block that follows implements the accept loop, the engine of a concurrent network service, which represents the transition from a passive listener to an active responder:

```
    while (true) {
        const stream = server.accept(io) catch |err| {
            std.debug.print("Accept failed: {}\n", .{err});
            continue;
        };

        const thread_num = thread_counter.fetchAdd(1, .seq_cst);
        const thread = Thread.spawn(.{
            .allocator = allocator,
        }, handleConnection, .{
            io,
            stream,
            thread_num,
        }) catch |err| {
            std.debug.print("Failed to spawn thread: {}\n", .{err});
            stream.close(io);
            continue;
        };

        thread.detach();
    }
}
```

By placing the `server.accept()` call inside an infinite `while` loop, the program enters a state of constant readiness, *blocking until a client initiates a connection*. The concurrency logic is handled through the combination of atomic incrementing and thread detachment. When a connection is accepted, `thread_counter.fetchAdd()` generates a unique, thread-safe identifier for that specific session. The program then attempts to spawn a new worker thread to execute `handleConnection()`. We call `thread.detach()` after spawning, which in a server context tells the OS that the *thread will manage its own lifecycle* and that the main thread does not need to (and cannot) wait for it to finish. This **fire and forget** pattern prevents the main loop from becoming blocked by the work of a single client, allowing it to remain responsive to hundreds of simultaneous connections. The error handling here is also intentionally robust. If a thread fails to spawn, the program catches the error, manually closes the specific client stream to avoid a file descriptor leak and continues with the loop. This ensures that a localized failure with one client does not crash the entire server, maintaining high availability for other users. Once we have a server that handles multiple connections, the focus shifts to the other side of the socket: the concurrent client. While a standard client typically performs a single request-response cycle, a concurrent version is designed to initiate multiple simultaneous connections or perform background data processing while maintaining an active network stream.

Writing a concurrent TCP client

The necessity for concurrent TCP clients arises from the shift from simple, sequential tasks to complex, high-performance systems. A client that can handle one request at a time might become a bottleneck, failing to utilize the full bandwidth and processing power of the host machine. By spawning multiple threads or using asynchronous I/O – the subject of *Chapter 9, Implementing Asynchronous I/O* – to manage several connections at once, a client can initiate a new request without waiting for the previous one to complete. This is critical in web browsers, which must download dozens of images, scripts, and stylesheets simultaneously to render a single page quickly. Without concurrency, each file would have to wait in a queue, leading to an unacceptable user experience. Here is the important code of `ch07/concClient.zig` – the `connectAndEcho()` function handles the actual connection:

```
fn connectAndEcho(io: Io, address_str: []const u8, port: u16, index: u32) void {
    const addr = Io.net.IpAddress.resolve(
        io,
        address_str,
        port,
    ) catch |err| {
        std.debug.print(
            "Client {d} resolve error: {}\n",
            .{ index, err },
        );
        return;
    };
    const stream = addr.connect(io, .{ .mode = .stream }) catch |err| {
        std.debug.print(
            "Client {d} connect error: {}\n",
            .{ index, err },
        );
        return;
    };
    defer stream.close(io);

    var msg_buf: [64]u8 = undefined;
    const msg = std.fmt.bufPrint(
        &msg_buf,
```

```
        "ping from client #{}\n",
        .{index},
    ) catch return;

    var wbuf: [256]u8 = undefined;
    var w = stream.writer(io,&wbuf);
    w.interface.writeAll(msg) catch return;
    w.interface.flush() catch return;

    stream.shutdown(io, .send) catch return;

    var reader_buf: [1]u8 = undefined;
    var r = stream.reader(io,&reader_buf);
    var reply_buf: [64]u8 = undefined;
    const n = r.interface.readSliceShort(reply_buf[0..msg.len]) catch
        return;

    std.debug.print(
        "Client {d} received: {s}",
        .{ index, reply_buf[0..n] },
    );
}
```

`connectAndEcho()` begins by resolving the server hostname or IP address and port into a usable network address using `Io.net.IpAddress.resolve()`. If that fails, it prints an error and returns early. It then calls `addr.connect` to open a TCP stream to the server, with `defer stream.close(io)`, ensuring the connection is always cleaned up when the function exits. Next, it formats a short identifying message — `ping from client #N` — into a stack buffer using `std.fmt.bufPrint()`, creates a buffered writer over the stream, writes the message, and flushes it so the bytes are actually sent. Once the message is on the wire, it calls `stream.shutdown()` with `.send` to send a TCP FIN, signaling to the server that no more data is coming from this client; without this, the server's read loop would block indefinitely waiting for more input. Finally, `connectAndEcho()` sets up a buffered reader over the same stream and calls `r.interface.readSliceShort()` to receive the server's echo, then prints whatever came back to standard error with `std.debug.print()`.

The `main()` function serves as the orchestrator for a high-concurrency stress test, responsible for parsing environment inputs and rapidly deploying worker threads:

```
pub fn main(init: std.process.Init) !void {
    var gpa: std.heap.DebugAllocator(.{}) = .init;
    defer _ = gpa.deinit();
    const allocator = gpa.allocator();
    const io = init.io;

    const argv = try init.minimal.args.toSlice(
        init.arena.allocator(),
    );

    if (argv.len != 4) {
        std.debug.print(
            "Usage: {s} <address> <port> <numConn>\n",
            .{argv[0]},
        );
        return;
    }

    const server_addr = argv[1];
    const server_port = try std.fmt.parseInt(u16, argv[2], 10);
    const num_connections = try std.fmt.parseInt(u32, argv[3], 10);

    const threads = try allocator.alloc(Thread, num_connections);
    defer allocator.free(threads);

    for (threads, 0..) |*t, i| {
        t.* = try Thread.spawn(
            .{ .allocator = allocator },
            connectAndEcho,
            .{ io, server_addr, server_port, @as(u32, @intCast(i)) },
        );
    }

    for (threads) |t| t.join();
}
```

`main()` begins by initializing a `DebugAllocator` for heap allocation and parsing four command-line arguments: the server address, port, and the number of concurrent connections to spawn. If the argument count is incorrect, a usage message is printed, and the program exits. The port and connection count are parsed from strings into their respective numeric types — `u16` for the port and `u32` for the connection count. The function then allocates a slice of `Thread` handles sized to the requested connection count. A `for` loop spawns one thread per connection, each running `connectAndEcho()` with the server address, port, and a unique zero-based connection index passed as arguments. The `io` handle is also forwarded to each thread so it can perform network I/O using the standard library's I/O API. A second `for` loop calls `join()` on every thread, blocking `main()` until all connections have completed. This ensures the allocator is not torn down while threads are still running, and that the program exits cleanly only after all concurrent work is finished.

Let us now use `ch07/concClient.zig`. But before that, start the server process. I used `zig run ch07/concTCP.zig -- 1234` for mine. Now, run 10 concurrent connections:

```
$ zig run ch07/concClient.zig -- 127.0.0.1 1234 10
Client 3 received: ping from client #3
Client 0 received: ping from client #0
Client 4 received: ping from client #4
Client 7 received: ping from client #7
Client 9 received: ping from client #9
Client 8 received: ping from client #8
Client 5 received: ping from client #5
Client 1 received: ping from client #1
Client 2 received: ping from client #2
Client 6 received: ping from client #6
```

This trace confirms that the TCP server managed 10 simultaneous connections by spawning independent threads. Each line shows that the server correctly associated the unique `ping` message with the specific thread that sent it, proving that the atomic counter and thread-local data remained distinct across the concurrent sessions.

With the foundational mechanics of signal handling, process detachment, and concurrent networking now established, we have moved beyond the abstract study of system primitives. To demonstrate how these disparate pieces converge into a single utility, we will now synthesize them into a practical project. In the following section, we implement `zcron`, a minimal yet robust job scheduler.

Creating zcron, a minimal cron variation

Building a minimal `cron(1)` service in Zig provides a practical way to combine threads, processes, and signal handling into a single utility. We call this tool `zcron`. Let us first present the files that compose the `zcron` project as found in `ch07/zcron`:

```
$ tree
.
├── build.zig
└── src
    ├── config.zig
    ├── main.zig
    ├── repl.zig
    ├── schedule.zig
    ├── scheduler.zig
    └── signals.zig
2 directories, 7 files
```

`schedule.zig` defines the data the rest of the program works with: what a job is and what a collection of jobs looks like. It has no knowledge of files, terminals or processes. `config.zig` reads the configuration file and turns it into a populated schedule. It owns the config file format and nothing else. The code in `signals.zig` handles the three UNIX signals the program cares about: `SIGTERM` for shutdown, `SIGHUP` for reload and `SIGCHLD` for reaping finished child processes. It translates asynchronous signal deliveries into simple Boolean flags that the rest of the program can check safely. `repl.zig` provides the interactive interface. It reads commands from the terminal, acts on them, and prints results back to the user. It knows about the schedule and can trigger reloads and job spawning, but it has no knowledge of the event loop that drives it. `scheduler.zig` is the engine. It runs the main event loop, waits for either user input or a one-second tick, fires any jobs that are due, and checks whether a reload or shutdown has been requested. It is the only file that forks and execs child processes. Last, `main.zig` connects everything together. It installs signal handlers, finds and loads the config file, and then hands control to the scheduler. It contains no logic of its own. Clearly explaining the design decisions of a program is a very important task for understanding its limitations, its philosophy, and its strengths. This is coming next!

Explaining the design decisions

Each major design choice addresses a specific challenge in managing concurrent events and system resources. Therefore, the architecture of `zcron` favors simplicity and clarity, prioritizing patterns that demonstrate robust systems programming over performance. We want to build a utility that would not demand you change your system status, as this can lead to system instabilities. These are the design characteristics of `zcron`:

The Single-Threaded Event Loop: Choosing to stay in the foreground while using `poll()` as the heartbeat of the application is a fundamental structural decision. A common but naive alternative involves two threads: one sleeping in a loop to fire jobs and another blocking on `stdin.readLine()`. This multithreaded approach immediately introduces shared mutable state, requiring a mutex to protect the schedule during every tick, list operation, and reload. By using `poll(stdin_fd, 1000ms)`, the process remains completely idle until either a character arrives on standard input or one second elapses. The program handles both events sequentially in a single thread, eliminating synchronization problems. This pattern is a cornerstone of systems programming. It mirrors the event-loop architecture found in high-performance tools like Redis and Nginx.

Leveraging the Shell for Command Execution: Routing commands through `/bin/sh -c` keeps the configuration logic simple and grants the user full shell expressiveness. The scheduler treats the first whitespace-delimited token as the interval and passes everything following it verbatim to the shell. This design removes the need for complex argument splitting, quoting rules, or escape sequences within the Zig code. Users can write redirections, pipelines, and shell builtins directly in their schedule. While every job pays the overhead of forking a shell process rather than executing a binary directly, this cost is negligible for intervals measured in minutes or hours.

Stack-Based Memory Management: Using fixed-size stack arrays for the schedule removes heap allocation from the execution path. A limit of `MAX_JOBS = 128` provides ample space for a personal service while allowing the entire schedule to fit into a `[128]Job` array. This approach eliminates the need to thread an allocator through the scheduler, avoids memory fragmentation, and removes the risk of allocation failures during a critical timing tick. While a dynamic `ArrayList` offers more flexibility, the fixed-stack array provides a more predictable and resilient design for this specific problem.

Atomic Signal Handling: Using atomic Boolean flags for communication between the signal handler and the main loop is the most direct and correct approach. POSIX strictly limits the functions one can safely call inside a signal handler; it forbids `malloc`, `printf` and most locking mechanisms. An atomic store in the handler combined with an atomic load in the main loop satisfies these safety requirements without the complexity of extra file descriptors. While techniques like the *self-pipe trick* are valid, they add management overhead that atomic flags avoid in this context. The **self-pipe trick** is a classic UNIX programming pattern designed to solve a fundamental concurrency problem: the race condition that occurs when a program needs to wait for both signals and I/O events (like data arriving on a socket) at the same time. In a standard event loop using `select(2)` or `poll(2)`, the process blocks until a file descriptor is ready. However, if a signal arrives while the process is blocked, the signal handler runs, but it cannot easily wake up the event loop to tell it to check a new state. The logic of the trick is to turn an asynchronous signal into a synchronous I/O event. You create a pipe using `posix.pipe()` and add the read end of that pipe to your event loop watched file descriptors. Inside your signal handler, you simply write a single byte into the write end of that pipe. Because the read end is being monitored by your `poll(2)` or `select(2)` call, the arrival of that byte immediately wakes up the main loop. The program then reads the byte, recognizes it as a signal notification, and proceeds to handle the event safely within the main execution flow rather than inside the restricted context of a signal handler. See how complicated this sounds?

Following UNIX Conventions: Assigning `SIGHUP` as the reload signal follows deep-rooted UNIX conventions. Historically used to signal that a modem line had dropped, `SIGHUP` has evolved into the standard trigger for a service to reread its configuration. Operators accustomed to tools like Nginx or SSH instinctively use `kill -HUP` to refresh the service. By exposing this same action through the REPL, the program remains equally accessible to interactive users and external scripts.

While these architectural choices ensure that the core logic remains robust and synchronous, they represent only half of what defines a true system utility. Even a perfectly designed event loop is of limited use if it remains tethered to a specific terminal session. To transform this code into a persistent background process, we must move beyond the foreground and implement the classic detach sequence. By utilizing `fork(2)` and `setsid(2)`, we can orphan our process and break its link to the controlling terminal, allowing it to live independently as a managed background entity that persists after the initial shell has closed.

Detaching from the terminal (fork, setsid)

The program demonstrates how to transform a foreground process into a background service that detaches from the terminal and communicates through a monitored file — a technique directly applicable to running `zcron` as a system service. In `main()`, the program begins by registering a `SIGTERM` handler using `posix.sigaction()`. The handler performs an atomic store on the global g_`running` flag with `.release` ordering, while the main loop reads it with `.acquire` ordering. This pairing guarantees that a shutdown signal is immediately and safely visible across memory boundaries, preventing the service from spinning in its polling loop after termination has been requested. Before entering the monitoring loop, `main()` creates the target file with an initial entry and then calls `detach()`, which transforms the process into a proper background service. Once detached, the loop polls the target file's modification time every second using `file.stat()`. When the modification time increases, the program reads the file content and appends a timestamped entry to a separate log file. Timestamps are obtained via `std.c.clock_gettime()`, and the log entry is formatted into a fixed 8192-byte stack buffer, keeping the memory footprint predictable and allocation-free in the hot path. The `detach()` function itself, as found in `ch07/detachMe.zig`, implements the full daemonization sequence and is worth examining in detail:

```
fn detach() !void {
    const pid = std.c.fork();
    if (pid < 0) return error.ForkFailed;
    if (pid > 0) std.c.exit(0);

    // Become a new session leader with no controlling terminal.
    if (std.c.setsid() < 0) return error.SetsidFailed;

    const pid2 = std.c.fork();
    if (pid2 < 0) return error.ForkFailed;
    if (pid2 > 0) std.c.exit(0);

    if (std.c.chdir("/") < 0) return error.ChdirFailed;

    const dev_null = std.c.openat(
        std.c.AT.FDCWD,
        "/dev/null",
        .{ .ACCMODE = .RDWR },
    );
    if (dev_null < 0) return error.OpenDevNullFailed;

    if (std.c.dup2(dev_null, std.c.STDIN_FILENO) < 0)
        return error.Dup2Failed;
    if (std.c.dup2(dev_null, std.c.STDOUT_FILENO) < 0)
        return error.Dup2Failed;
    if (std.c.dup2(dev_null, std.c.STDERR_FILENO) < 0)
        return error.Dup2Failed;

    if (dev_null > std.c.STDERR_FILENO) {
        _ = std.c.close(dev_null);
    }
}
```

The `detach()` function is responsible for severing the process's connection to the interactive terminal environment. It begins with a first `fork(2)` call, which creates a duplicate child process.

The parent exits immediately, returning control to the shell and leaving the child to continue as an orphan. The orphan then calls `setsid(2)` to become the leader of a new session and process group, permanently shedding the controlling terminal. A second `fork(2)` follows immediately after `setsid(2)`. This is the step that distinguishes a production-grade daemon from a naive implementation: a session leader can inadvertently reacquire a controlling terminal on System V-derived systems simply by opening a terminal device without `O_NOCTTY`. By forking again and having the session leader exit, the surviving grandchild is guaranteed never to be a session leader and can therefore never acquire a controlling terminal, regardless of which terminal devices it opens later. The function then calls `chdir("/")` to ensure the service does not prevent administrators from unmounting the filesystem where the program was originally launched. Finally, `dup2(2)` redirects standard input, output, and error to `/dev/null`, ensuring that residual print statements or library errors do not attempt to write to a terminal that no longer exists. By the time `detach()` returns, the process has no terminal, is immune to session-based signals like `SIGHUP`, and its lifecycle is entirely independent of the user who started it. Two hardening steps present in production daemon code are omitted here for clarity: calling `umask(0)` to reset the file creation mask, and writing the daemon's PID to a file under `/var/run` so that init systems and administrators can identify and signal the process by name. Both are worth adding before deploying this pattern in a real service. Running `ch07/detachMe.zig` produces the following kind of output:

```
$ zig run ch07/detachMe.zig
$ ps ax | grep detach
10727   ??  Ss     0:00.00 /Users/mtsouk/.cache/zig/o/xyz/detachMe
```

A proper way to terminate that process is by running `kill -SIGTERM 10727`. Experiment with `watch_me.txt` and see how `background_process.log` logs the activities.

The core mission of a scheduler like `zcron` is not merely to track time but to bridge the gap between a persistent background process and the ephemeral tasks it must launch. To achieve this without interrupting the service, we rely on `fork(2)` and `exec(3)`.

Using fork and exec to run periodic tasks

By creating a nearly identical child process with `fork(2)`, a service can effectively make the parent continue monitoring the schedule for the next duties while the child undergoes a transformation via `execve(3)`. The replacement of the child memory space with a new executable allows the system to run any arbitrary command or script in total isolation, ensuring that a failing task or a long-running process never stalls the primary dispatching loop.

The main loop in `ch07/forkExec.zig` acts as the clock, waking up every second to invoke tick, which iterates through a static array of Task objects. Each task maintains its own state — specifically its command string and the timestamp of its last execution — using the `isDue()` method to determine if the required interval has elapsed. When a task is ready, the scheduler calls `spawn()`, then updates the task metadata and continues its loop without waiting for the task to finish. This non-blocking architecture is essential for a scheduler as it ensures that a long-running command (like a backup script) does not cause the entire system to lose track of time. The `spawn()` function is the critical juncture where the program transitions from internal logic to external system execution. It utilizes the classic UNIX **fork-and-exec pattern**, which is a two-stage process. Consider the following example code of `spawn()` as found in `ch07/forkExec.zig` when running isolated tasks:

```
fn spawn(command: [:0]const u8) void {
    const pid = std.c.fork();
    if (pid < 0) {
        std.log.err("fork failed", .{});
        return;
    }

    if (pid != 0) {
        std.log.info("spawned pid {d}: {s}", .{ pid, command });
        return;
    }

    const argv = [_:null]?[*:0]const u8{
        "/bin/sh",
        "-c",
        command.ptr,
    };
    const envp = [_:null]?[*:0]const u8{
        "PATH=/usr/local/bin:/usr/bin:/bin",
    };
    _ = std.c.execve("/bin/sh",&argv,&envp);
    std.c._exit(127);
}
```

The logic begins with `c.fork()`. Inside the child process, the environment is transformed using `c.execve()`. This call does not start a new program in the traditional sense; rather, it replaces the entire memory image of the current child process with a new executable, which in this case is /

`bin/sh`. By passing the `-c` flag along with the user command, the child hands off execution to the system shell. To ensure the new process has a sane environment, the code explicitly defines an `argv` array (the command-line arguments) and an `envp` array (the environment variables, such as `PATH`). A subtle but vital detail in this implementation is the use of `c._exit(127)` as a fallback. Because a successful `execve()` never returns — the original program code is literally gone — any code following that call is only reached if the execution failed (for example, if `/bin/sh` could not be found). By using the raw `c._exit()` instead of a higher-level library function, the child ensures it *terminates immediately* without flushing standard I/O buffers that were inherited from the parent, preventing duplicate log entries or corrupted output. Let us now see `ch07/forkExec.zig` in action – it runs for 30 seconds and exits automatically:

```
$ zig run ch07/forkExec.zig
info: fork_exec starting - 3 task(s)
info: spawned pid 21764: date
info: spawned pid 21765: echo 'hello from forkExec child'
info: spawned pid 21766: ls /tmp
hello from forkExec child
MozillaUpdateLock-2656FF1E876E9973      zeb_def_ipc_18159
. . .
```

In the first four lines of output, we see the parent process rapidly dispatching its duties; it identifies that all three tasks are due at startup and spawns them in quick succession. The parent logs the specific PID assigned by the kernel for each — `21764`, `21765` and `21766` — before immediately returning to its own timing loop. Notice that `hello from forkExec child` appears after the parent has already announced the spawning of the third process. This occurs because the child process must go through the overhead of the `execve()` system call, loading `/bin/sh`, and parsing the command string before it can finally write to the console. The parent, meanwhile, has moved on to its next tick without being delayed by the work of its children. Finally, the appearance of file names like `MozillaUpdateLock` and `zeb_def_ipc` confirms that the third child executed `ls /tmp`.

Running background tasks is good, but it should be performed with care. The signal handling strategy in `zcron` ensures the service remains responsive to system events while adhering to the strict safety requirements of asynchronous execution. Moreover, as the scheduler begins to populate the system with child processes, we encounter the necessity of rigorous process accounting. In UNIX, a parent process remains responsible for its children even after they have finished execution; if we fail to acknowledge their termination, they persist as *zombies*, cluttering the process table with defunct entries.

Handling SIGTERM and SIGCHLD

By using `std.posix.sigaction()`, the program replaces default behaviors for `SIGTERM`, `SIGHUP`, and `SIGCHLD` with custom handlers. To communicate safely with the main execution loop, the handlers use *atomic Boolean flags*; this avoids the hazards of heap allocation or locking within an interrupt, which POSIX explicitly forbids. `SIGTERM` initiates a graceful shutdown by clearing the running flag, while `SIGHUP` triggers a configuration reload, mirroring standard UNIX service conventions. A critical component of this implementation is the `SIGCHLD` handler, which prevents the accumulation of zombie processes. When a child process completes its task, the kernel keeps its exit status in the process table until the parent acknowledges it. The `onSigchld()` handler uses a `while` loop with the `WNOHANG` flag to reap all terminated children immediately. This loop is necessary because POSIX does not queue signals; if multiple children exit at the same time, the system may only deliver a single `SIGCHLD` notification. By installing this handler with the `SA_RESTART` flag, we ensure that these background reaping actions do not interrupt the `poll()` heartbeat of the main loop, maintaining a steady one-second tick for the scheduler.

With the architectural blueprints for process management and signal handling established, we can turn our attention to the logic and code that bring `zcron` to life.

The zcron implementation details

First, let us revisit the files that compose the `zcron` project in more detail. `schedule.zig` sits at the bottom of the dependency graph and is the only file with no imports beyond the Standard Library. It defines two types: `Job`, which holds a single scheduled task, and `Schedule`, a fixed-capacity array of jobs. `Job` stores its command in a `[MAX_CMD + 1]u8` buffer with an explicit null terminator, so the command slice can be handed directly to `std.c.execve()` without any copying or conversion. The `isDue()` method encapsulates the scheduling logic in the entire program: It compares the current time against `last_run + interval_sec` and returns a Boolean. Because this file has no I/O, no syscalls, and no side effects, all six of its unit tests run with `zig build test` in complete isolation. Everything else in the project depends on `schedule.zig`; it depends on nothing.

The code in `config.zig` is responsible for turning a text file into a populated `Schedule`. It opens the config file through `std.Io.Dir.cwd().openFile(io, path, .{})`, which accepts both absolute and relative paths, reads it entirely into a 64 KiB stack buffer, and then splits on newlines. Each non-blank, non-comment line is expected to have an interval in seconds as its first whitespace-delimited token, followed by a shell command that occupies the rest of the line. Malformed lines emit a warning via `std.log()` and are skipped; the function only returns an error if the file cannot be opened at all. The `reload()` function wraps `load()` with a warning on failure, giving the REPL and the SIGHUP handler a safe call site that never propagates an error into the event loop.

The functionality in `signals.zig` manages the three signals the program cares about: `SIGTERM`, `SIGHUP`, and `SIGCHLD`. It owns two module-level atomic Booleans — `g_running` and `g_reload` — and exposes them through accessor functions that use acquire/release memory ordering. The signal handlers themselves are deliberately minimal: `onSigterm()` writes `false` to `g_running`, `onSighup()` writes `true` to `g_reload`, and `onSigchld()` loops calling `std.c.waitpid()` with `WNOHANG` until no more terminated children remain. That last point is important: because POSIX does not queue signals, two children exiting simultaneously may produce only one `SIGCHLD` delivery, so the loop is not optional. We call `std.c.waitpid()` directly rather than `posix.waitpid()` because the Zig 0.16 wrapper treats `ECHILD` — the normal stop condition — as unreachable. When using the high-level `std.posix.waitpid()` wrapper, the library assumes that if you are calling it, you must certainly have child processes to wait for. According to the library view, attempting to wait on a non-existent child is a logic error, so it marks the `ECHILD` error code as `unreachable`. The raw C function returns `-1` on `ECHILD`, which we check for cleanly.

The `repl.zig` file implements the interactive command interface. It exposes two public functions: `printPrompt()`, which writes the `zcron>` prompt to stdout and `dispatch()`, which reads one line from stdin and acts on it. Reading from stdin uses `posix.read()` directly on `STDIN_FILENO`, bypassing the standard file API. Writing to stdout goes through `std.Io.File.stdout().writeStreamingAll()`, keeping output consistent with the rest of the codebase. This makes the read path immune to buffering API changes while the write path benefits from the 0.16 streaming interface. The six supported commands — `list`, `run`, `reload`, `status`, `help`, and `quit` — are each implemented as a small private function. `list` formats relative timestamps using a stack-allocated `SmallBuf` helper so there is no heap allocation at any point during command handling. The `quit` command calls `signals.requestStop()`, which sets `g_running` to `false` through the same atomic path as a real `SIGTERM`, ensuring a clean and consistent shutdown regardless of how the user chooses to stop the program.

The code in `scheduler.zig` is the heart of the program. Its `run()` function enters a loop that calls `poll()` on stdin with a one-second timeout, then branches on the result: if stdin is readable, it calls `repl.dispatch`; if the timeout fires, it calls `tick()`, which walks the schedule and spawns any jobs whose interval has elapsed. After every iteration it checks the `g_reload` and `g_running` flags from `signals.zig`. This single-threaded design means the schedule, the REPL, and the signal flags are all accessed sequentially with no synchronization required. Job execution follows the classic UNIX pattern: `spawnJob()` forks, the parent returns immediately and the child calls `execCommand()`, which overlays itself with `/bin/sh -c <command>` via `std.c.execve()`. Routing commands through the shell means users can write redirections, pipes, and shell builtins in their config file without `zcron` needing to understand any of it. This file has many interesting functions, including `tick()`, `spawnJob()`, and `execCommand()`, which are fully presented, starting with `tick()`, which acts as the repetitive heartbeat of `zcron`, operating as the bridge between the passage of time and the execution of tasks:

```
fn tick(schedule: *Schedule) void {
    const now = unixNow();
    for (schedule.slice()) |*job| {
        if (!job.isDue(now)) continue;
        log.info("spawning: {s}", .{job.command()});
        spawnJob(job);
        job.last_run = now;
    }
}
```

The code logic is straightforward: every time it is called — typically once per second — it captures the current system time via `unixNow()` and performs a linear scan through the active schedule. By iterating over a slice of jobs, it evaluates each one against its specific timing requirements. If a job's internal `isDue()` logic determines that the necessary interval has not yet elapsed, the function simply skips it and moves to the next entry, ensuring that the scheduler remains efficient even as the list of jobs grows.

To illustrate this logic in a live scenario, imagine `zcron` wakes up and captures the current UNIX timestamp as `1741812000`. The function begins iterating through its schedule, first encountering a backup task configured with a sixty-second interval and a recorded `last_run` of `1741811940`. By performing the subtraction `1741812000-1741811940`, the code determines that precisely sixty seconds have elapsed since the job last executed. Because this value meets the required threshold, the scheduler emits an informational log, triggers `spawnJob()` to launch the script in the background, and immediately updates the `last_run` field to `1741812000`. Continuing its scan, the loop evaluates a temporary file cleanup script designed to run every five minutes or three hundred seconds. This job currently holds a `last_run` value of `1741811800`, meaning only two hundred seconds have passed since its prior activation. When the `isDue()` check compares the current time against the scheduled interval, the calculation `1741812000-1741811800=200` results in a value that is strictly less than the required three hundred seconds. Therefore, the function executes a `continue` statement, bypassing the spawning logic for this specific task and moving on to the next entry in the schedule without performing any external system calls.

Next, we have the `spawnJob()` implementation:

```
pub fn spawnJob(job: *const Job) void {
    const pid = std.c.fork();
    if (pid < 0) {
        log.err("fork failed for '{s}'", .{job.command()});
        return;
    }

    if (pid != 0) return;

    execCommand(job.command());
    std.c._exit(127);
}
```

By accepting a `Job` object, the function encapsulates the command logic within the job's own context, calling `job.command()` to resolve the executable string at the moment of execution. This separation of concerns means that `spawnJob()` does not need to know how the command is stored or formatted; it simply acts as the mechanism that bridges the job-defined intent with the OS process manager.

Last, we present the `execCommand()` implementation:

```
fn execCommand(cmd: [:0]const u8) void {
    const argv = [_:null]?[*:0]const u8{ SHELL, "-c", cmd.ptr };
    _ = std.c.execve(SHELL,&argv,&CHILD_ENV);
}
```

The `execCommand()` function serves as the transition from the Zig runtime to the system shell, preparing the necessary data structures for the `execve(2)` system call. The function passes `CHILD_ENV` to establish a sanitized environment, ensuring the task has a predictable `PATH` for locating utilities. The return value of `std.c.execve()` is discarded with `=`, which reflects the unique nature of the exec family of calls: a successful invocation never returns because the child's memory image is completely replaced by the new executable. A return to the Zig code only occurs if the system call fails — such as if the shell executable is missing or permissions are denied — at which point the function simply finishes, allowing the child to reach the `std.c._exit(127)` fallback in `spawnJob()`.

`main.zig` is minimal by design: It installs signal handlers, resolves the config file path — checking the command-line argument first, then falling back to `~/.config/zcron/zcron.conf`, then to `./zcron.conf` in the current directory — loads the schedule and calls `scheduler.run()`. The only non-trivial logic is in `defaultConfigPath()`, which reads `$HOME` at runtime to construct the XDG path. Everything else is a delegation. Keeping `main.zig` as an orchestrator with no business logic of its own means every meaningful piece of the program is in a file that clearly owns it, and the startup sequence reads as a straightforward list of steps rather than a complication of concerns.

XDG stands for the Cross-Desktop Group, a freedesktop.org standard that defines where applications should store their files on Linux and UNIX-like systems. Rather than scattering configuration files across arbitrary locations, the XDG Base Directory Specification says that user configuration belongs in `~/.config/<appname>/`. So, first, let us create a valid `zcron` configuration file (`~/.config/zcron/zcron.conf`) with the following contents:

```
$ cat ~/.config/zcron/zcron.conf
5   echo "job 0 fired" >> /tmp/zcron_test.log
10  date >> /tmp/zcron_test.log
20  uptime >> /tmp/zcron_test.log
```

Job 0 (`echo`) runs every 5 seconds and writes a fixed string. It is the heartbeat — the most frequent job and the one that confirms the scheduler is alive and ticking even when nothing interesting is happening. Job 1 (`date`) runs every 10 seconds and appends the current date and time. It lets you verify that the intervals are accurate: every second entry in the log should be a timestamp, and the gap between consecutive timestamps should be close to 10 seconds. Job 2 (`uptime`) runs every 20 seconds and appends the system uptime and load averages. It is the least frequent job and the one most likely to interleave with the others in the log. It is now time to try `zcron` – I used the following example commands:

```
$ cd ch07/zcron
$ zig build run 2>/tmp/zcron.log # redirect stderr to a file
```

If we do not redirect standard error messages to a file, messages that start with `info(scheduler):` would appear on the terminal and interleave with the REPL prompt. The `info(scheduler):` prefix comes from `std.log.scoped(.scheduler)` in `scheduler.zig`, which writes to stderr. It is one of the concrete reasons UNIX services redirect stderr to a log file rather than leaving it attached to a terminal.

We continue by giving commands to the zcron REPL:

```
zcron> list
  #  interval   last run        next run        command
  -  ---------  ------------    ------------    -----------------------
  0  5s       2s ago      in 3s          echo "job 0 fired" >> /tmp/zcron_test
  1  10s    7s ago     in 3s        date >> /tmp/zcron_test.log
  2  20s    17s ago    in 3s        uptime >> /tmp/zcron_test.log
zcron> status
  uptime : 0h 2m 5s
  jobs   : 3
  config : /Users/mtsouk/.config/zcron/zcron.conf
zcron> run 1
spawning job #1: date >> /tmp/zcron_test.log
zcron> help
Commands:
  list          show all scheduled jobs and their timing
  run <n>       force-run job #n right now
  reload        reload the config file from disk
  status        show uptime and job count
  help          show this message
  quit / exit   stop zcron gracefully

Signals:
  SIGHUP        same as 'reload'
  SIGTERM       same as 'quit'
```

The `list` command shows the live state of the schedule at the moment you typed it. Each row shows one job: its index number, how often it runs, when it last ran, expressed as seconds ago, when it will next run, expressed as seconds from now, and the command itself. All three jobs show `in 3s` for the next run, which means we happened to type `list` at a moment when the entire schedule was about to tick simultaneously — the 5-second, 10-second, and 20-second intervals all aligned at that instant. The `status` command confirms the service has been running for 2 minutes and 5 seconds, is managing 3 jobs, and loaded its configuration from the expected XDG path under your home directory. The `run 1` command forces job 1 to be fired immediately, outside of its normal schedule. `zcron` spawned the `date` command on the spot and updated `last_run` for that job, so its next scheduled run will be 10 seconds from that moment rather than from whenever it would have fired naturally. This is useful for testing a new job without waiting for its interval to elapse. The `help` command lists everything the REPL accepts, including the two signals. The signal entries are there as a reminder that `zcron` can also be controlled from another terminal without touching the REPL — `SIGHUP` and `SIGTERM` are the scriptable equivalent of `reload` and `quit`. The first 10 lines of `/tmp/zcron_test.log`:

```
$ head /tmp/zcron_test.log
job 0 fired
Thu Mar 12 21:06:11 EET 2026
21:06  up 1 day,  5:20, 9 users, load averages: 17.96 19.41 19.31
job 0 fired
job 0 fired
Thu Mar 12 21:06:21 EET 2026
job 0 fired
job 0 fired
Thu Mar 12 21:06:31 EET 2026
21:06  up 1 day,  5:20, 9 users, load averages: 19.03 19.58 19.38
```

`zcron` touches every major concept in foreground UNIX Systems Programming: the process model, the fork and exec pattern, signal safety, zombie prevention, and the poll-based event loop that ties them together without threads. Who would have imagined at the start of this journey that you would be building something as robust as `zcron` with a few hundred lines across six files?

The distance from `sigInt.zig` to `zcron` is worth pausing to appreciate. The chapter opened with a single signal handler setting an atomic flag — the smallest meaningful unit of OS interaction. From there, each concept built on the last: process creation with `fork(2)`, session management with `setsid(2)`, thread coordination with `std.Thread`, command execution with `execve(2)`, and signal-driven child reaping with `SIGCHLD`. `zcron` is not a new idea introduced at the end of the chapter — it is the same ideas, composed. Every design decision in the scheduler has a direct counterpart in an earlier example, and that is precisely the point: *Systems Programming is not a collection of unrelated primitives but a set of composable tools that combine predictably when you understand what each one does.*

Summary

In this chapter, we explored how Zig empowers systems programming through support for threads, processes, forking, and signal handling. Threads allow concurrent execution within a program, making it easier to perform multiple tasks simultaneously and put multiple CPU cores to work. Forking, through the `fork(2)` system call, enables a process to create child processes that run independently, forming the foundation of UNIX-style multitasking. By learning to handle signals like `SIGINT` and `SIGTERM`, we provided our programs with the mechanisms necessary to clean up resources and exit gracefully, ensuring our background services remain robust and responsive. We synthesized these concepts by building `zcron`, which demonstrates how to make a process run in the background and maybe become a service, manage periodic task execution through `execve(2)`, and respond to asynchronous events.

In the next chapter, we are going to create professional concurrent applications that take advantage of multiple CPU cores by spawning threads, coordinating their execution, and using synchronization techniques to manage shared data safely and avoid resource locking and race conditions.

Exercises

- Change the code in `ch07/detachMe.zig` so that the file that is being watched can be given as a command-line argument.
- Change the code in `ch07/detachMe.zig` so that it can watch multiple files.

8

Orchestrating Concurrency and Synchronization

We briefly talked about threads in the previous chapter. However, in this chapter, we are going to discuss concurrency in more detail, which in practice means working and synchronizing multiple threads, avoiding race conditions and deadlocks, collecting results from multiple threads, and implementing concurrent patterns such as Consumer-Producer, Thread Pool, and Ring Buffer with the help of mutexes, atomic operations, and condition variables. Although threads can, in theory, take advantage of multiple processors or cores, it is not always that simple or straightforward. It is a common misconception that *concurrency* and *parallelism* are the same thing, which is far from the truth! Concurrency is a way of structuring components so that they can be independently executed without issues, when possible, whereas parallelism is the simultaneous execution of multiple things. Having lots of threads waiting for a shared resource and doing nothing while waiting does not make your application faster. Similarly, having multiple threads torturing a shared variable does not result in a proper use of multiple CPU cores. It is only when you build things concurrently that you can safely execute them in parallel, when and if your OS and hardware permit it. The Erlang programming language did this a long time ago, long before CPUs had multiple cores and computers had lots of RAM. In a valid concurrent design, adding concurrent entities makes the whole system run faster because more things can run in parallel. So, the desired parallelism comes from a better concurrent expression and implementation of the problem. We are responsible for taking concurrency into account during the design phase of a system and benefiting from the potential parallel execution of the components of the system. So, we should not think about parallelism but about breaking things into independent components that solve the initial problem when combined.

This chapter covers:

- Avoiding race conditions
- Improving the memory info server
- Preventing data corruption
- Thread Pools and Ring Buffers
- Producers and Consumers
- Logging information concurrently
- `zlocate`: a concurrent file indexer

Avoiding race conditions

The single most important issue that exists in concurrent programming is *shared* variables and *shared* memory. When multiple threads or processes attempt to read from and write to the same memory location concurrently without proper coordination, it can lead to a lot of subtle and often obscure bugs. These issues, collectively known as race conditions, manifest when the final outcome of a program becomes dependent on the unpredictable interleaving of operations from different threads. This non-determinism makes debugging incredibly challenging as the erroneous behavior may only appear intermittently and under specific, hard-to-reproduce timing conditions. Consequently, ensuring data consistency and preventing corruption in shared memory environments is paramount to developing robust and reliable concurrent applications. This is precisely where a mutex becomes indispensable.

Sharing memory safely: mutexes and RwLocks

A **mutex** (short for mutual exclusion) is a synchronization primitive used in concurrent programming to ensure that only one thread at a time can access a particular section of code or data. It acts like a lock: when a thread acquires the mutex, other threads attempting to acquire it are blocked until the first thread releases it. This prevents data races and ensures consistency when multiple threads need to read from or write to shared resources such as variables, files, or memory buffers. Put simply, a mutex ensures that only one thread can access a *designated critical section of code* — the part that interacts with shared variables — at any given moment. When a thread locks a mutex, it gains exclusive access to the shared resource, preventing other threads from entering that critical section until the mutex is unlocked. This enforced serialization of access eliminates race conditions, guaranteeing that operations on shared data are performed atomically and in a predictable order, thus preserving data integrity in a concurrent system. In Zig, the `std.Io.Mutex` type provides this functionality, allowing you to explicitly lock and unlock around critical sections to guard shared data in multithreaded programs. Here is the example code (`ch08/mutex.zig`) that illustrates how to use a mutex to safely update a shared variable (`counter`) from multiple threads (just two in this case):

```
const std = @import("std");

var mutex: std.Io.Mutex = .init;
var counter: u32 = 0;
const ThreadArgs = struct { io: std.Io, id: usize };

fn incrementThread(args: ThreadArgs) void {
    var i: u32 = 0;
    while (i < 1000) : (i += 1) {
        mutex.lock(args.io) catch return; // Begin critical section
        counter += 1;
        mutex.unlock(args.io); // End critical section
    }

    std.debug.print("Thread {d} done.\n", .{args.id});
}

pub fn main(init: std.process.Init) !void {
    const io = init.io;
    const t1 = try std.Thread.spawn(
        .{},
        incrementThread,
        .{ThreadArgs{ .io = io, .id = 1 }},
    );
    const t2 = try std.Thread.spawn(
        .{},
        incrementThread,
        .{ThreadArgs{ .io = io, .id = 2 }},
    );

    t1.join();
    t2.join();
    std.debug.print("Final counter value: {d}\n", .{counter});
}
```

We define a global variable (`counter`) and a `Mutex` from the Standard Library to protect that shared variable. Two threads are spawned, each executing the `incrementThread()` function, which increments the counter 1000 times. Inside that function, the `mutex` is locked before updating the `counter` and unlocked immediately afterward to ensure that only one thread can access the counter at any given time, preventing data races. After completing their increments, the threads print a message indicating they are done. The main thread waits for both threads to finish using `join()` and then prints the final value of `counter`. Thanks to the mutex, the output is reliably 2000, confirming that all increments were safely performed across the threads. Without the mutex, simultaneous access to `counter += 1` would cause data races, potentially leading to an incorrect final value. The mutex prevents concurrent modification, preserving correctness. It goes without saying that the more threads we have, the higher the chance of a data race.

While a mutex is highly effective for ensuring exclusive access, its all-or-nothing approach can sometimes be overly restrictive, particularly in scenarios where data is read far more frequently than it is written. If a shared resource is primarily used for reading, and writes are rare, a mutex would still force all reading threads to wait for each other, even though their operations do not conflict. This can unnecessarily limit concurrency and introduce performance bottlenecks. To address this common pattern, a more specialized synchronization primitive known as a Read-Write Lock comes into play.

Using RwLock

An `RwLock` offers a more nuanced locking mechanism, distinguishing between read operations and write operations. It allows multiple threads to acquire a read lock simultaneously, enabling concurrent reads of the shared data, as long as no thread holds a write lock. However, for write operations, an `RwLock` behaves like a mutex; only one thread can acquire a write lock at a time, and no other reads or writes are permitted until the write lock is released. This intelligent differentiation between read and write access patterns can significantly improve the throughput of read-heavy concurrent applications by maximizing parallelism for non-modifying operations. If your program is not that busy, you are not going to see any real difference in execution time.

`std.Io.RwLock` provides `lock()` for exclusive write access and `lockShared()` for shared read access; these are released using `unlock()` and `unlockShared()`, respectively. Look at the following code example (`ch08/rwmutex.zig`) that showcases the use of `std.Io.RwLock`:

```
const std = @import("std");

var rwlock: std.Io.RwLock = .init;
var counter: u32 = 0;
const WriterArgs = struct { io: std.Io, id: usize };
const ReaderArgs = struct { io: std.Io, id: usize };

fn writerThread(args: WriterArgs) void {
```

```
    var i: u32 = 0;
    while (i < 1000) : (i += 1) {
        rwlock.lock(args.io) catch return;
        counter += 1;
        rwlock.unlock(args.io);
    }
    std.debug.print("Writer {d} done.\n", .{args.id});
}

fn readerThread(args: ReaderArgs) void {
    var i: u32 = 0;
    while (i < 5) : (i += 1) {
        rwlock.lockShared(args.io) catch return;
        const value = counter;
        rwlock.unlockShared(args.io);
        std.debug.print(
            "Reader {d} sees counter = {d}\n",
            .{ args.id, value },
        );
        std.Io.sleep(
            args.io,
            std.Io.Duration.fromMilliseconds(200),
            .awake,
        ) catch {};
    }
}

pub fn main(init: std.process.Init) !void {
    const io = init.io;
    const writer = try std.Thread.spawn(
        .{},
        writerThread,
        .{WriterArgs{ .io = io, .id = 1 }},
    );
    const reader1 = try std.Thread.spawn(
        .{},
        readerThread,
        .{ReaderArgs{ .io = io, .id = 1 }},
    );
    const reader2 = try std.Thread.spawn(
        .{},
```

```
            readerThread,
            .{ReaderArgs{ .io = io, .id = 2 }},
        );

        writer.join();
        reader1.join();
        reader2.join();
        std.debug.print("Final counter value: {d}\n", .{counter});
    }
```

The code uses a read-write lock (`rwlock`) to protect access to the shared counter variable, allowing concurrent reads and exclusive writes. It spawns one writer thread and two reader threads, each performing its tasks in parallel. The observations of the counter shared variable in the reader threads depend on timing — how far the writer had progressed at the moment the reader was allowed to read.

Running `ch08/rwmutex.zig` produces the following kind of output:

```
$ zig run ch08/rwmutex.zig
Reader 1 sees counter = 610
Writer 1 done.
Reader 2 sees counter = 820
Reader 1 sees counter = 1000
Reader 2 sees counter = 1000
Reader 1 sees counter = 1000
Reader 2 sees counter = 1000
Reader 1 sees counter = 1000
Reader 2 sees counter = 1000
Reader 1 sees counter = 1000
Reader 2 sees counter = 1000
Final counter value: 1000
```

The output reflects the contention dynamics of a read-write lock in action. The first two lines — `Reader 1 sees counter = 610`, and `Reader 2 sees counter = 820` — occur because the writer briefly releases the exclusive lock between iterations, giving the readers a narrow window to acquire a read lock and take a snapshot of the in-progress value. While the writer holds the exclusive lock, both readers block entirely — they cannot proceed until the writer releases, which is why the early values are sparse rather than continuous. Once the writer finishes and releases the lock for the last time, the behavior changes entirely. The long sequence of `= 1000` entries reflects the core advantage of an `RwLock` over a plain `Mutex`: with no writer competing for the exclusive lock, multiple readers can hold the read lock simultaneously and interleave freely with each other. A plain `Mutex` would serialize every read, forcing `Reader 1` and `Reader 2` to take turns even when no write is in progress. The `RwLock` eliminates that unnecessary serialization — and that is precisely the tradeoff that justifies its added complexity over a plain `Mutex`.

While a mutex and RwLock provide robust mechanisms for managing shared resources by controlling access, they inherently introduce blocking. This means that when a thread tries to acquire a locked resource, it is forced to pause and wait, potentially leading to performance bottlenecks and even deadlocks if not handled carefully. Because of that, we should try to avoid using mutexes when possible. The next section shows a design that allows you to do that.

Avoiding race conditions by design

The presented approach focuses on structuring data and algorithms in ways that minimize or eliminate shared mutable state to ensure correctness without ever forcing threads to wait for each other. Although this might not work in every case, it is still a good technique to consider. Consider the `main()` implementation of `ch08/avoidLock.zig` that calculates a Fibonacci sequence using multiple threads, demonstrating a concurrent approach without explicit locks like mutexes:

```
const AtomicU64 = std.atomic.Value(u64);
// sentinel stored in every slot before the computing thread writes it
const unset: u64 = std.math.maxInt(u64);

const FibArgs = struct {
    io: std.Io,
    index: usize,
    fibs: []AtomicU64,
};

pub fn main(init: std.process.Init) !void {
    const io = init.io;
    var gpa: std.heap.DebugAllocator(.{}) = .init;
    const allocator = gpa.allocator();
    const argv = try init.minimal.args.toSlice(init.arena.allocator());

    if (argv.len != 2) {
        std.debug.print("Usage: {s} <n>\n", .{argv[0]});
        return error.InvalidArguments;
    }
```

```
    const n = try std.fmt.parseInt(usize, argv[1], 10);
    if (n == 0) return error.InvalidArguments;

    const fibs = try allocator.alloc(AtomicU64, n);
    defer allocator.free(fibs);
    for (fibs) |*f| f.* = AtomicU64.init(unset);

    var threads = try allocator.alloc(std.Thread, n);
    defer allocator.free(threads);

    var nArgs = try allocator.alloc(FibArgs, n);
    defer allocator.free(nArgs);
    var i: usize = 0;
    while (i < n) : (i += 1) {
        nArgs[i] = FibArgs{ .io = io, .index = i, .fibs = fibs };
        threads[i] = try std.Thread.spawn(
            .{},
            fib_worker,
            .{&nArgs[i]},
        );
    }

    for (threads) |t| t.join();

    std.debug.print("Fibonacci sequence:\n", .{});
    var j: usize = 0;
    while (j < fibs.len) : (j += 1) {
        std.debug.print(
            "  fib[{d}] = {d}\n",
            .{ j, fibs[j].load(.acquire) },
        );
    }
}
```

The program begins by defining a `FibArgs` struct, which serves as a container for the arguments passed to each worker thread — specifically, the `io` handle needed for sleeping during the busy-wait, the index of the Fibonacci number to be calculated, and a slice `fibs` where all results will be stored. Every element of `fibs` is initialized to `unset` — the maximum value of `u64` — to signal that no Fibonacci number has been computed yet. The sentinel value is the coordination mechanism: a worker reading `unset` in a predecessor slot knows the result is not yet ready and must wait. `main()` then allocates arrays for `std.Thread` objects and `FibArgs` instances, both of size `n`. A loop iterates from `0` to `n-1`, preparing a `FibArgs` instance for each index and spawning a thread that executes `fib_worker()` with a pointer to its respective arguments. After all threads have been spawned, a second loop calls `join()` on each one, blocking `main()` until every worker has finished. Once all threads have completed, `main()` iterates through the fibs slice and prints the computed Fibonacci sequence to the console. The core logic resides in the `fib_worker()` function, which is executed by each thread:

```
fn fib_worker(arg: *FibArgs) void {
    const i = arg.index;
    const fibs = arg.fibs;

    if (i == 0) {
        fibs[0].store(0, .release);
        return;
    }
    if (i == 1) {
        fibs[1].store(1, .release);
        return;
    }

    while (fibs[i - 1].load(.acquire) == unset or
        fibs[i - 2].load(.acquire) == unset)
    {
        std.Io.sleep(
            arg.io,
            std.Io.Duration.fromMicroseconds(1),
            .awake,
        ) catch {};
    }

    fibs[i].store(
        fibs[i - 1].load(.acquire) + fibs[i - 2].load(.acquire),
        .release,
    );
}
```

`fib_worker()` takes a pointer to a `FibArgs` instance and begins by extracting the index and the `fibs` slice. For the base cases, index 0 and index 1, the worker stores the known values directly into `fibs[0]` and `fibs[1]` using `.release` ordering and returns immediately. For all other indices, the worker enters a busy-wait loop, repeatedly loading `fibs[i-1]` and `fibs[i-2]` with `.acquire` ordering until neither holds the sentinel value `unset`. During each iteration, the thread sleeps for one microsecond to avoid consuming an entire CPU core while waiting. Once both predecessors are available, the worker computes their sum and stores the result into `fibs[i]` with `.release` ordering.

Why does this work? Each thread writes exclusively to its own index in the `fibs` slice — no two threads ever write to the same memory location, which eliminates write-write data races. Reads of already-computed values are safe for the same reason: by the time a thread reads `fibs[i-1]` or `fibs[i-2]`, the thread responsible for that slot has already finished writing to it. The `.release`/`.acquire` pairing is what makes this guarantee formal and portable: the `.release` store in the writing thread and the `.acquire` load in the reading thread establish a happens-before relationship, ensuring the reader sees the fully written value rather than a stale one from the CPU store buffer or cache. On architectures with weak memory models, such as ARM, omitting this pairing would allow the processor to reorder operations and produce incorrect results even when the code appears logically correct. The broader lesson is that lock-free design is not about removing synchronization — it is about replacing coarse-grained locking with precise, targeted memory ordering that makes only the guarantees the program actually needs. Let us try `ch08/avoidLock.zig` – expect to get the following output:

```
$ zig run ch08/avoidLock.zig -- 5
Fibonacci sequence:
  fib[0] = 0
  fib[1] = 1
  fib[2] = 1
  fib[3] = 2
  fib[4] = 3
```

Lock avoidance by partitioning writes works well when each thread owns a distinct memory location and dependencies between threads are known in advance. But many concurrent problems do not fit that shape — multiple threads need to update a shared counter, append to a shared list, or coordinate access to a resource whose ownership cannot be statically partitioned. A mutex solves this by serializing access entirely, which is correct but introduces contention: every thread that wants the lock must wait, even when the critical section is a single integer increment. **Atomic operations** occupy the space between these two approaches. They operate on a single memory location without a lock, using hardware primitives that guarantee the read-modify-write sequence is indivisible. The tradeoff is scope — atomics work on one value at a time, while a mutex can protect an arbitrarily complex invariant. Choosing between them is a matter of matching the synchronization primitive to the shape of the problem.

Atomics: when to use them

Atomics are a way to perform thread-safe operations on shared memory without explicit locks, ensuring that reads, writes, and modifications are indivisible (one thread cannot interrupt another mid-operation) even on complex data types or across multiple memory accesses. The best example of atomics is when you get money from your bank account; this is an atomic operation that cannot be interrupted in the middle of it, and it can either succeed or fail as an entity. We are going to see atomics in action in many examples in this chapter, starting with the following (`ch08/atomic.zig`) example code:

```
const std = @import("std");
const Val = std.atomic.Value(u32);
const Order = std.builtin.AtomicOrder;

fn toRunInThread(v: *Val) void {
    const value = v.load(Order.acquire);
    v.store(value + 1, Order.release);
}

pub fn main(init: std.process.Init) !void {
    const allocator = init.gpa;
    var value = Val.init(42);
    const thread = try std.Thread.spawn(.{
        .allocator = allocator,
        .stack_size = 1024,
},toRunInThread,.{&value});

    thread.join();
    std.debug.print(
        "Expected value 43: {}\n",
        .{value.load(Order.acquire)},
    );
}
```

This program utilizes `std.atomic.Value()`, a generic wrapper that guarantees indivisible access to its underlying data. We alias this type as `Val` for a 32-bit unsigned integer and import `std.builtin.AtomicOrder` to dictate how the processor and compiler are allowed to reorder memory operations around our atomic accesses. In concurrent programming, simply making a variable atomic is not enough; we must also explicitly define the memory visibility rules to prevent the CPU from aggressively optimizing reads and writes in ways that break thread coordination. The core logic resides in the `toRunInThread()` function, which accepts a pointer to our atomic value. It retrieves the current integer using `v.load(Order.acquire)`. The `acquire` is a directive to the hardware and compiler, ensuring that no subsequent memory accesses in the current thread are moved before this atomic load. Next, the function calculates the incremented value and writes it back using `v.store(value + 1, Order.release)`. The `release` acts as the counterpart, guaranteeing that all memory operations written before this point become visible to any other thread that subsequently performs an acquire load on the same atomic variable.

The `main()` function orchestrates the execution by initializing the atomic value to `42` and spawning a single worker thread. This implementation takes advantage of the `std.Thread.spawn()` configuration struct to explicitly set a custom stack size of 1024 bytes and provide a memory allocator. This demonstrates how to finely control the resources allocated to a thread, which is vital in systems programming where default stack sizes might be wasteful for simple tasks. Finally, the main thread calls `join()` to wait for the worker to finish its execution before verifying and printing the expected outcome.

acquire and **release** are memory ordering modes used with atomic operations to control how memory visibility and instruction reordering behave across threads. These orderings are essential for writing safe concurrent programs without relying on heavier synchronization primitives like mutexes. Acquire ordering is typically used with atomic loads. When a thread performs a load with acquire, it prevents any following memory operations (reads or writes) from being reordered before that load. This ensures that once the load completes, the thread sees not only the loaded value but also all writes that occurred in another thread before a corresponding release store. In simpler terms, acquire guarantees that any data published by another thread using a release store becomes visible. Release ordering is used with atomic stores. When a thread performs a store with release, it ensures that all preceding memory operations cannot be reordered after that store. This means any writes to shared data that happen before the release store become visible to other threads that later load the same atomic variable using acquire. Effectively, release publishes data so it can be safely read by others. Together, release and acquire establish a happens-before relationship: a write with release guarantees that all preceding operations in the writing thread are visible to a reading thread that performs a corresponding load with acquire. This creates a reliable synchronization point between threads without requiring locks.

Think of it this way: imagine a teammate writing a report and then emailing you when it is ready. The **release ordering** is like them making sure the document is fully saved and uploaded to the cloud before hitting send — this guarantees that all their work is complete and visible before the notification goes out. The **acquire ordering** is like your email client, ensuring that when you see that "report ready" message, it also waits for any pending file downloads to finish before letting you open the attachment. So, when you receive the email and see it is true, you can safely open the document knowing you are getting the complete, up-to-date version rather than a partial or stale copy. This is exactly how *acquire* and *release* work together in multithreaded programming: one thread publishes data with a release store, another consumes it with an acquire load, and together they create a reliable happens-before relationship that ensures safe communication without locks.

The previous program has an issue. Although it uses atomics for the individual load and store operations, it performs these as two separate steps rather than a single atomic read-modify-write. This creates a window where another thread could modify the value between the load and the store, leading to lost updates — a classic race condition. The correct approach is to use an atomic operation like `fetchAdd()`, which combines the entire increment into one indivisible step that is truly thread safe. Therefore, a better `toRunInThread()` implementation would be the following (`ch08/atomicFetchAdd.zig`):

```
fn toRunInThread(v: *Val) void {
    _ = v.fetchAdd(1, Order.monotonic);
}
```

This pattern is widely used in lock-free algorithms to safely share data between threads with minimal synchronization overhead. Let us now present more representative code.

Changing a variable using atomic operations

The program illustrates the safe, concurrent mutation of shared memory using hardware-level atomic operations. Here is the example code of `ch08/atomicIncrease.zig`:

```
const std = @import("std");
const Thread = std.Thread;

pub fn main(init: std.process.Init) !void {
    _ = init;
    var counter: usize = 0;
    const thread_count = 4;
    const increments = 100_000;
    const threads = try std.heap.page_allocator.alloc(
        Thread,
        thread_count,
    );
    defer std.heap.page_allocator.free(threads);
```

```
    for (threads) |*t| {
        t.* = try Thread.spawn(
            .{},
            threadMain,
            .{ &counter, increments },
        );
    }

    for (threads) |t| {
        t.join();
    }

    const final = @atomicLoad(usize,&counter,.seq_cst);
    std.debug.print("Final counter value: {d}\n", .{final});
}

fn threadMain(counter_ptr: *usize, increments: usize) void {
    var i: usize = 0;
    while (i < increments) : (i += 1) {
        _ = @atomicRmw(usize, counter_ptr, .Add, 1, .seq_cst);
    }
}
```

In the main routine, a single integer `counter` is initialized on the stack alongside constants dictating the creation of four separate worker threads, each tasked with incrementing the counter *one hundred thousand times*. As each thread is spawned, it receives a direct memory address to this shared `counter`. The logic behind passing a pointer rather than a value is fundamental: all threads must operate on the exact same location in memory to consolidate their work. The main thread then blocks, systematically joining each worker to ensure all concurrent execution halts before the final tally is read. The critical synchronization mechanism resides within the thread worker function. Rather than employing a mutex to lock the counter during updates, the routine leverages the `@atomicRmw()` built-in function to perform a *read-modify-write cycle*. This translates directly to a locked CPU instruction, ensuring that the act of reading the current value, adding one, and writing it back occurs as a single, indivisible event. The logic behind specifying `.seq_cst`, or *sequentially consistent memory ordering*, is to enforce a strict, global synchronization barrier. This prevents both the compiler and the processor from reordering memory accesses in ways that might obscure the true sequence of operations from other threads. Consequently, race conditions are entirely avoided, and the final atomic load in the main thread is guaranteed to observe exactly four hundred thousand increments. Execute `ch08/atomicIncrease.zig` to make sure that it works as expected:

```
$ zig run ch08/atomicIncrease.zig
Final counter value: 400000
```

By running four separate threads that each perform one hundred thousand increments, the final tally reaches exactly 400,000. Let us now see what happens if we do not use atomics, using a slightly different example.

What would happen without atomics?

Here is a simple program named `ch08/noAtomic.zig` where multiple threads are modifying a variable without any safety mechanism:

```
const std = @import("std");

var counter: u32 = 0;
fn incrementCounter() void {
    counter += 1;
}

pub fn main(init: std.process.Init) !void {
    _ = init;
    var threads: [200]std.Thread = undefined;
    for (&threads) |*t| {
        t.* = try std.Thread.spawn(.{}, incrementCounter, .{});
    }

    for (threads) |t| {
        t.join();
    }
    std.debug.print("Counter: {} (Expected: 200)\n", .{counter});
}
```

In this case, 200 threads read `counter`, increment it locally, and write back, causing lost updates. The reason for using 200 threads instead of just two is that it makes the race condition far more obvious because it dramatically increases the chances of threads interfering with each other. However, the issue might still appear with fewer threads. It is just more difficult to replicate.

Running ch08/noAtomic.zig multiple times produces the following kind of output:

```
$ zig run ch08/noAtomic.zig
Counter: 199 (Expected: 200)
$ zig run ch08/noAtomic.zig
Counter: 200 (Expected: 200)
```

The output illustrates race conditions in action. Due to the unpredictable execution order of threads, the output is not the same all the time, and it might be incorrect.

The next section shows how to use atomic operations when writing data, as well as what would have happened without the use of atomic operations.

Preventing data corruption in shared writing

In multithreaded programs, *writing to a shared file* can easily lead to data corruption if not handled properly. When multiple threads attempt to write simultaneously, their output can become interleaved, incomplete, or lost entirely. However, this is just a part of the story. The other part is that you should also take good care of the variables that you want to write to that file. This section explores how to prevent such issues. But first, let us begin with learning what would happen if we attempted to write a variable to a file without using atomic operations or any synchronization mechanisms to protect the variable.

Writing without atomic operations

It is highly instructive to examine a flawed approach to fully appreciate the necessity of proper concurrent design. By analyzing a program that attempts to update shared memory without the strict guarantees of atomic hardware instructions, we can observe firsthand how data races silently corrupt the state of an application. Here is the function implementation as found in ch08/noAtomicWrite.zig:

```
fn threadMain(args: ThreadArgs) void {
    var buf: [32]u8 = undefined;
    var i: usize = 0;
    while (i < args.increments) : (i += 1) {
        // This is *NOT* thread-safe!
        const new_val = args.counter_ptr.* + 1;
        args.counter_ptr.* = new_val;

        const line = std.fmt.bufPrint(&buf, "{}\n", .{new_val}) catch
            continue;
        args.file_mutex_ptr.lock(args.io) catch return;
```

```
        args.logFile_ptr.writeStreamingAll(args.io, line) catch {};
        args.file_mutex_ptr.unlock(args.io);
    }
}
```

The threadMain() function attempts to combine shared memory manipulation with synchronized file logging, but its underlying logic contains a severe concurrency flaw. The routine accepts pointers to a shared counter, a mutex, and a log file, intending to increment the counter a specified number of times and record each new value to the disk. Inside the loop, the thread reads the current value of the counter, adds one to it, and writes the new value back into memory. This is a classic *read-modify-write operation*. However, because this specific operation is neither performed using atomic hardware instructions nor protected by a mutex, it introduces a blatant data race. When multiple threads execute this exact sequence simultaneously, they will inevitably read the same initial value, perform the addition in their local registers, and blindly overwrite each other's results. The logic assumes that each thread executes its instructions in perfect, uninterrupted isolation, completely ignoring the preemptive nature of the OS scheduler.

After calculating what it incorrectly believes to be the definitive new value, the thread formats the number into a local string buffer. Only after this formatting step does it acquire the lock to safely append the text to the log file. While the file writing itself is correctly synchronized to ensure that lines of text do not become garbled or interleaved, the data being written is fundamentally unreliable due to the earlier race condition. Furthermore, separating the state change from the synchronization mechanism creates a chronological disconnect. Even if the counter increment were made atomic, formatting the string outside the critical section means a thread might increment the counter, get suspended by the OS, and allow other threads to increment and log a higher number first.

Let us try ch08/noAtomicWrite.zig and see the issue in practice:

```
$ zig run ./ch08/noAtomicWrite.zig -- /tmp/logs.log 25
Done: attempted to log 25 * 100000 increments to /tmp/logs.log
Final counter value (expected 2500000): 2499996
$ wc /tmp/logs.log
 2500000 2500000 18888894 /tmp/logs.log
$ sort /tmp/logs.log | uniq -d
1382807
1425957
1676509
65756
```

In this run, 25 threads were incrementing the global counter `100,000` times, which should result in a final value of `2,500,000`. However, the final reported counter value is `2,499,996`, indicating that 4 increments were lost due to interleaved, non-atomic reads and writes. Despite this, `/tmp/logs.log` contains 2,500,000 lines, which suggests that some values were written multiple times. This is confirmed by the `sort | uniq -d` output, which lists duplicate values that were logged more than once. These duplicates occurred because two or more threads read the same counter value simultaneously and each logged it after incrementing, overwriting each other's intended unique values.

As a rule of thumb, the more threads you are using, the more likely a data race might occur. Now, let us present a concurrent-safe version of the function.

Writing with atomic operations

Now, let us go back to the original problem, which is modifying a variable atomically to prevent corruption. In this case, we use two mechanisms: a mutex for the writing operations and atomic operations when dealing with the changes to the counter variable.

The technique is presented using the example code found in `ch08/atomicWrite.zig`, which you might want to consider in similar scenarios:

```
fn threadMain(args: ThreadArgs) void {
    var buf: [32]u8 = undefined;
    var i: usize = 0;

    while (i < args.increments) : (i += 1) {
        const previous = @atomicRmw(
            usize,
            args.counter,
            .Add,
            1,
            .seq_cst,
        );
        const new_val = previous + 1;
        const line = std.fmt.bufPrint(&buf, "{}\n", .{new_val}) catch
            continue;

        // Lines may appear out of order: the lock is
        // acquired after the increment, so another thread can
        // win the lock and write a higher value first. Ordering would
        // require holding the lock across both
        // the increment and the write.
```

```
            args.file_mutex.lock(args.io) catch return;
            defer args.file_mutex.unlock(args.io);
            args.logFile.writeStreamingAll(args.io, line) catch {};
        }
    }
```

The improved version of the Zig program introduces thread-safe counter manipulation using atomics, which eliminates the data race present in the earlier version. Although the original program used a Mutex to serialize access to the log file, it failed to protect the `counter`, which is just as critical. In contrast, the improved version replaces the unsafe increment logic with an atomic read-modify-write operation using `@atomicRmw()` with the `.Add` operation and a sequential consistency memory ordering (`.seq_cst`). **Sequential consistency memory ordering** is the strongest and most intuitive form of memory ordering, ensuring that all threads observe atomic operations in a single, global order. By treating these operations as if they were executed sequentially, it prevents the compiler or CPU from reordering instructions and ensures a consistent view of shared memory across the entire system. In practice, this provides a straightforward mental model that matches what most of us would expect: When one thread writes a value, another thread reading that value will see the change in a predictable way. In Zig, you can specify this ordering with operations like `@atomicLoad`, `@atomicStore`, or `@atomicRmw`, using `.seq_cst` as the ordering argument. Keep in mind that while sequential consistency simplifies reasoning about concurrency, it can incur a performance cost due to the strict ordering guarantees it imposes. Therefore, it is often chosen when correctness and clarity are more important than maximum performance. So, `.seq_cst` ensures that updates to `counter` are performed *atomically* and observed in a consistent global order across threads. Additionally, the final value of the counter is read with `@atomicLoad` to guarantee a synchronized and accurate result. These changes ensure that the number of increments exactly matches the total expected, regardless of thread interleaving or CPU scheduling. We can verify our code by running `ch08/atomicWrite.zig`:

```
$ zig run ch08/atomicWrite.zig -- /tmp/logs.log 25
Done: attempted to log 25 * 100000 increments to /tmp/logs.log
Final counter value (expected 2500000): 2500000
$ sort /tmp/logs.log | uniq -d
```

In this case, the final value is indeed `2,500,000`, and the log file `/tmp/logs.log` contains no duplicate values, resulting in a correct execution of the program!

The Memory Info server from *Chapter 6, Programming the Network Stack*, bound to a single address using `0.0.0.0`, which is sufficient for most use cases. The next section improves on that design by applying the thread-per-listener pattern introduced earlier in this chapter.

Improving the memory info server

While binding to `0.0.0.0` is the pragmatic solution for most cases, there are situations where you want explicit control over which addresses your server listens on — for example, exposing a service on an internal network interface while keeping it off a public-facing one. In those cases, you need one listener per address, since each `listen()` call binds to exactly one IP. The approach is to store your target addresses in a fixed array, then iterate over them: for each address, you call `address.listen()` to get a server, print a confirmation, and spawn a dedicated `std.Thread` to run the accept loop. The thread handles are stored in a parallel array so the main function can call `join()` on each one at the end, blocking until all listeners shut down. The *accept loop* itself is factored out into a `serveLoop()` function that takes ownership of the server and an allocator, runs `accept()` in a `while(true)` loop, and handles each connection — catching errors at each step with `catch` so that a single bad connection or failed stats read does not bring down the whole listener. Because multiple threads share the same `DebugAllocator`, it is worth noting that this might not be very efficient; *in production, you would give each thread its own allocator* – we are going to see this implementation in a while, but first, let us begin with the simplistic implementation (`ch08/multiTCP.zig`) – the program logic can be found in `main()`:

```
pub fn main(init: std.process.Init) !void {
    var gpa: std.heap.DebugAllocator(.{}) = .init;
    defer _ = gpa.deinit();
    const allocator = gpa.allocator();
    const io = init.io;
    const addresses = [_][]const u8{
        "127.0.0.1",
        "192.168.1.168", // replace with your actual IP
    };

    var threads: [addresses.len]std.Thread = undefined;

    for (addresses, 0..) |addr_str, i| {
        const address = try Io.net.IpAddress.parseIp4(addr_str, 8080);
        const server = try address.listen(io, .{});
        std.debug.print(
            "Memory Service listening on {s}:8080...\n",
```

```
            .{addr_str},
        );
        threads[i] = try std.Thread.spawn(
            .{},
            serveLoop,
            .{ io, server, allocator },
        );
    }

    for(&threads)|*t|t.join();
}
```

The function defines an array of IP addresses and prepares a corresponding array of `std.Thread` handles. By iterating through each address, the code parses the IPv4 string and configures a listening socket on port `8080`. The concurrency model is established as each iteration spawns a new OS thread. The logic here is to pass both the unique server socket and the shared allocator into `serveLoop()`, allowing each network interface to operate in parallel without blocking the others.

Rather than attempting to multiplex multiple listening sockets within a complex, single-threaded event loop, the next server parses the command-line arguments and spawns a dedicated background thread for every provided IP address. The logic behind this decision prioritizes architectural simplicity and isolation. Each network interface operates entirely independently, blocking on its own accept call without interfering with the others.

Using a separate memory allocator for each thread

The improved version (`ch08/tcpMemoryAllocator.zig`) makes two changes visible right in `main()`. First, the addresses are no longer hardcoded — they are read from the command-line arguments, making the program reusable without recompilation. Second, and more importantly, the `std.Thread.spawn` call passes only `.{ io, server }` instead of `.{ io, server, allocator }`:

```
pub fn main(init: std.process.Init) !void {
    var gpa: std.heap.DebugAllocator(.{}) = .init;
    defer _ = gpa.deinit();
    const allocator = gpa.allocator();
    const io = init.io;

    const argv = try init.minimal.args.toSlice(
        init.arena.allocator(),
```

```
    );

    if (argv.len < 2) {
        std.debug.print(
            "Usage: {s} <ip1> [ip2] [ip3] ...\n",
            .{argv[0]},
        );
        std.debug.print(
            "Example: {s} 127.0.0.1 192.168.1.100\n",
            .{argv[0]},
        );
        return error.NoAddressProvided;
    }

    const addr_args = argv[1..];
    const threads = try allocator.alloc(std.Thread, addr_args.len);
    defer allocator.free(threads);

    for (addr_args, 0..) |addr_str, i| {
        const address = try Io.net.IpAddress.parseIp4(addr_str, 8080);
        const server = try address.listen(io, .{});
        std.debug.print(
            "Memory Service listening on {s}:8080...\n",
            .{addr_str},
        );
        threads[i] = try std.Thread.spawn(
            .{},
            serveLoop,
            .{ io, server },
        );
    }

    for (threads) |*t| t.join();
}
```

The gpa here is used only to allocate the `threads` slice — it is no longer shared with the worker threads. Each thread is responsible for its own memory, so the allocator does not need to cross thread boundaries at all. The `serveLoop()` signature drops the allocator parameter entirely, and the thread creates its own allocator internally, as we will see next. This is the implementation of `serveLoop()` as found in `ch08/tcpMemoryAllocator.zig`:

```
fn serveLoop(io: Io, server: Io.net.Server) void {
    var gpa: std.heap.DebugAllocator(
        .{ .thread_safe = false },
    ) = .init;
    defer _ = gpa.deinit();
    const allocator = gpa.allocator();

    var srv = server;
    defer srv.deinit(io);

    while (true) {
        const stream = srv.accept(io) catch |err| {
            std.debug.print("Accept error: {}\n", .{err});
            continue;
        };
        defer stream.close(io);
        var arena = std.heap.ArenaAllocator.init(allocator);
        defer arena.deinit();
        const arena_alloc = arena.allocator();
        const stats = getMemoryStats(io, arena_alloc) catch |err| {
            std.debug.print("Stats error: {}\n", .{err});
            continue;
        };

        const json_str = std.fmt.allocPrint(
            arena_alloc,
            "{f}\n",
            .{std.json.fmt(stats, .{})},
        ) catch continue;

        var wbuf: [4096]u8 = undefined;
        var w = stream.writer(io,&wbuf);
        w.interface.writeAll(json_str) catch |err| {
            std.debug.print("Write error: {}\n", .{err});
            continue;
        };
        w.interface.flush() catch {};
```

```
    }
}
```

The code begins by initializing a memory allocator scoped to the lifetime of `serveLoop()`. By declaring the `DebugAllocator` with `.thread_safe = false` before the `while` loop starts, we ensure that the same instance is reused across every connection handled by this thread. The logic behind this local, unsynchronized allocator is to eliminate the need for internal mutexes. Since each thread possesses its own heap, the hardware avoids the cache-coherency traffic and atomic overhead usually required to keep a global allocator consistent. This implementation utilizes a *two-layered allocation strategy* to protect the long-term stability of the server. While the GPA provides the backing memory for the thread, an `ArenaAllocator` is initialized inside the loop to handle the specific requirements of a single connection. This shifts the paradigm from microscopic tracking of individual variables to bulk management of client sessions. In a global heap, processing millions of ephemeral requests often leads to memory fragmentation as blocks are freed out of order. Here, the logic of the arena allocator ensures that the entire memory footprint for a client interaction is managed in isolation. When the connection terminates, a single call to `arena.deinit()` reclaims all associated memory instantly, preventing slow-burning leaks and keeping the underlying GPA heap compact.

It is now time to consider a more structured and scalable approach to managing concurrency: thread pools. In the next section, we will learn how to use `std.Thread.Pool` to streamline task execution and manage workloads more effectively.

Thread pools: reusing threads for performance

While manually spawning and joining threads gives you fine-grained control, it can become cumbersome and inefficient as the number of tasks grows. A **thread pool** is a programming pattern that manages a set of pre-created threads to perform work concurrently without the overhead of constantly creating and destroying threads.

`std.Thread.Pool` was removed in Zig 0.16 as part of the broader shift toward the event-driven `std.Io` concurrency model. Where the old pool required an allocator, a job count, and an explicit `init/deinit` lifecycle, `std.Io.Group` needs none of that: it is declared as a zero-initialized value, tasks are added with `group.async(io, func, .{args})`, and a single `group.await(io)` call blocks until every task finishes — with `defer group.cancel(io)` provides the cleanup guarantee on early exit. Because `Io.Group` tasks are coroutines scheduled by the event loop rather than OS threads. The mechanism also changes: a task that never suspends on I/O simply runs to completion without yielding, which means purely CPU-bound functions like work plug in directly without needing an `io` parameter of their own. The practical consequence is that code which previously needed to size a thread pool and manage its lifetime now reduces to three lines — declare the group, fire the tasks, await them — while the runtime handles the rest.

Consider the example code of `ch08/threadPool.zig` when developing a thread pool:

```
const std = @import("std");

// Io.Group is an abstraction over async execution. Behavior depends
// on the Io vtable in use. Under the default Threaded Io, it dispatches
// to a worker thread pool; effectively the same model std.Thread.Pool
// provides. Under an evented Io (io_uring-based), CPU-bound functions
// that never suspend would block the event loop.
pub fn main(init: std.process.Init) !void {
    const io = init.io;
    var group: std.Io.Group = .init;
    defer group.cancel(io);

    group.async(io, work, .{@as(u32, 3)});
    group.async(io, work, .{@as(u32, 5)});
    group.async(io, work, .{@as(u32, 7)});
    try group.await(io);
}

fn work(inc: u32) void {
    std.debug.print("Start Inc = {d}\n", .{inc});
    var total: u32 = 0;
    var i: u32 = 0;
    while (i < 100000) : (i += 1) {
        total += inc;
    }
    std.debug.print("Total = {d}, Inc = {d}\n", .{ total, inc });
}
```

In `main()`, an `Io.Group` is declared as a zero-initialized value, and three tasks are enqueued with `group.async()`, each invoking `work()` with a different increment value (3, 5, and 7). The `work()` function performs a simple computation: it iterates 100,000 times, adding the given increment to the total on each iteration and prints the increment and the resulting total before and after the computation. A `defer group.cancel(io)` at the top of `main()` ensures cleanup on any early exit and `group.await(io)` at the end waits for all three tasks to complete before the program returns. Run `ch08/threadPool.zig` on your machines:

```
$ zig run ch08/threadPool.zig
Start Inc = 5
Start Inc = 3
Start Inc = 7
Total = 300000, Inc = 3
Total = 700000, Inc = 7
Total = 500000, Inc = 5
```

Each of the three threads spawned by the pool begins by printing its unique increment value, as seen in messages like `Start Inc = 5`, `Start Inc = 3`, and `Start Inc = 7`. These start messages may appear in any order due to the non-deterministic nature of thread scheduling. Each thread then performs a computation loop, adding its increment value to a local total variable `100000` times. Once completed, it prints the result, such as `Total = 300000, Inc = 3`, indicating that it added 3 a hundred thousand times. Similarly, threads with increments of 5 and 7 produce totals of 500000 and 700000, respectively.

Next to the Thread Pool, another very popular concurrency pattern is the *Producer-Consumer* pattern, which is presented in the section that follows.

The Producer-Consumer pattern

The **Producer-Consumer pattern** is a fundamental concurrency design model used to manage the interaction between threads that generate data and those that process it. In this pattern, one or more producer threads create or generate data and place it into a shared buffer, while one or more consumer threads retrieve and process that data. This separation allows the production and consumption of data to occur at independent rates, improving system responsiveness and throughput. Since both producers and consumers access the same buffer, synchronization mechanisms such as mutexes, condition variables, semaphores, or atomic operations are required to prevent race conditions and ensure thread-safe operations. For instance, a producer might need to wait if the buffer is full, while a consumer might wait if the buffer is empty, and both can be woken up appropriately using signaling. This pattern is widely used in real-world systems like logging services, job queues, and streaming data pipelines, and helps build reliable and scalable multithreaded applications.

We are going to create two implementations of the Producer-Consumer pattern: the first, using Atomics, and the second using *Condition Variables*. When implementing the Producer-Consumer pattern in Zig, the choice between using Atomics and a Condition Variable significantly impacts the design, complexity, and performance of your concurrency model. Atomics provide low-level, lock-free access to shared data, making them ideal for high-performance, low-latency systems where efficiency is critical. They allow safe concurrent modification of shared variables, such as read/write indices in a ring buffer, but require careful handling of memory ordering and race conditions. On the other hand, condition variables offer a higher-level abstraction for thread coordination. With a `std.Io.Condition`, consumers can block and wait for a signal from producers, which is much more CPU-efficient than busy-waiting, as it allows threads to sleep when idle. While atomic-based implementations are often more performant, they tend to be complex and error-prone, especially in managing wraparound and synchronization correctness. In contrast, condition variables simplify the coordination logic and are generally easier to implement and reason about, making them suitable for most general-purpose applications. Ultimately, the decision depends on your goals — use atomics for maximum speed and control and condition variables for clearer, more maintainable synchronization. In more advanced systems, it is common to combine both approaches to strike a balance between performance and clarity.

Implementing the Producer-Consumer pattern with atomics

Here is a Producer Consumer pattern implementation using atomics as found in `ch08/producerConsumer.zig`. The goal is to transfer five integer values from a producer to a consumer through a single-slot buffer while avoiding data races or lost updates.

```
const std = @import("std");

// Atomic producer-consumer with a single-slot buffer.
// Both threads busy-wait with 10us sleep loops, so this is NOT faster
// than a condvar design - a condvar suspends the thread until signaled,
// with zero polling. Atomics give fine-grained control; misapplied
// (busy-wait on a single slot), they trade simplicity for higher CPU
// usage and lower throughput than std.Thread.Mutex + std.Thread.Condition
const AtomicU32 = std.atomic.Value(u32);
const AtomicBool = std.atomic.Value(bool);
const Order = std.builtin.AtomicOrder;
var buffer: AtomicU32 = AtomicU32.init(0);
var full: AtomicBool = AtomicBool.init(false);
var done: AtomicBool = AtomicBool.init(false);
```

At the core of the implementation are three global variables. First, `buffer`, an `AtomicU32` value, which represents a single shared memory slot for passing integer values. Then, we have `full`, an `AtomicBool` value, which signals whether the buffer is currently holding a value (`true` if full).

Last, there is `done`, another `AtomicBool`, which indicates when the producer has finished producing all values. This program uses atomic memory operations (`load()` and `store()` with `Order.acquire` and `Order.release`) to enforce correct visibility and ordering across threads, ensuring safe communication without requiring mutexes or condition variables. Next, we have the producer and consumer implementations:

```
fn producer(args: WorkerArgs) void {
    var value: u32 = 1;
    while (value <= 5) {
        while (full.load(Order.acquire)) {
            std.Io.sleep(
                args.io,
                std.Io.Duration.fromMicroseconds(10),
                .awake,
            ) catch {}; // wait until buffer is free
        }

        buffer.store(value, Order.release);
        full.store(true, Order.release);
        std.debug.print("Produced: {d}\n", .{value});
        value += 1;
    }

    done.store(true, Order.release);
}

fn consumer(args: WorkerArgs) void {
    while (true) {
        if (done.load(Order.acquire) and !full.load(
            Order.acquire,
        )) break;

        if (full.load(Order.acquire)) {
            const val = buffer.load(Order.acquire);
            std.debug.print("Consumed: {d}\n", .{val});
            full.store(false, Order.release);
        } else {
            std.Io.sleep(
                args.io,
                std.Io.Duration.fromMicroseconds(10),
```

```
                .awake,
            ) catch {}; // wait for producer
        }
    }
}
```

The `producer()` function increments a local value from 1 to 5. Before placing a new value into the buffer, it checks whether `full` is set; if so, it sleeps briefly and retries. Once the buffer is free, it stores the new value in the buffer using `Order.release`, which ensures that all prior writes are visible to other threads, and sets `full` to `true`, signaling to the consumer that data is available. After all values are produced, it sets done to `true`. The `consumer()` runs in a loop, checking whether the producer is done and whether the buffer is empty. If `full` is `true`, the consumer reads the value from the buffer, prints it, and sets `full` back to `false`, indicating it has consumed the value. If there is no data available, it sleeps briefly to avoid busy waiting.

In the `main()` function, the program creates two threads, one for the producer and one for the consumer. It then waits for both to finish using `join()`:

```
pub fn main(init: std.process.Init) !void {
    _ = init;
    const t1 = try std.Thread.spawn(.{}, producer, .{});
    const t2 = try std.Thread.spawn(.{}, consumer, .{});
    t1.join();
    t2.join();
}
```

Now, let us execute `ch08/producerConsumer.zig` – expect the following kind of output:

```
$ zig run ch08/producerConsumer.zig
Produced: 1
Consumed: 1
Produced: 2
Consumed: 2
Produced: 3
Consumed: 3
Produced: 4
Consumed: 4
Produced: 5
Consumed: 5
```

The output reflects the correct and synchronized execution of the `producer()` and `consumer()` threads. For each value from 1 to 5, the producer successfully writes the number into the *atomic buffer*, sets the full flag to indicate data availability, and then prints a message indicating the value produced. Almost immediately after, the consumer detects that the buffer is full, reads the value, prints a message showing it was consumed, and resets the full flag so the producer can continue. The fact that each `Produced` line is followed directly by the corresponding `Consumed` line shows that the single-slot buffer is being used cooperatively and safely by both threads, thanks to the proper use of atomic `load()` and `store()` operations with `Order.acquire` and `Order.release`.

Next, we present the producer-consumer pattern using condition variables.

Implementing Producer-Consumer with condition variable

A **Cond** (*condition variable*) in Zig is a synchronization primitive used in conjunction with a mutex to coordinate threads based on a shared condition. It allows threads to wait (block) until another thread signals that some condition has been met. This is especially useful in Producer-Consumer patterns or other scenarios where threads need to wait for a resource or state change. As before, the main idea is that one thread (the producer) generates values and places them into a shared buffer, while another thread (the consumer) takes those values out for processing. To avoid race conditions and ensure proper coordination, the program uses a `std.Io.Mutex` to guard access to the buffer and a `std.Io.Condition` to allow threads to wait and be notified when the buffer state changes. Here is the example code of the producer (`ch08/condProdCons.zig`):

```
fn producerThread(args: ProducerArgs) void {
    var i: u32 = 1;
    while (i <= args.n) : (i += 1) {
        mutex.lock(args.io) catch return;
        while (count == max_buffer_size) {
            std.debug.print("Producer waiting: Buffer full\n", .{});
            cond.wait(args.io, &mutex) catch {
                mutex.unlock(args.io);
                return;
            };
        }

        buffer[tail] = i;
        tail = (tail + 1) % max_buffer_size;
        count += 1;
        std.debug.print("Produced: {}\n", .{i});

        cond.signal(args.io);
```

```
            mutex.unlock(args.io);
            std.Io.sleep(
                args.io,
                std.Io.Duration.fromMilliseconds(100),
                .awake,
            ) catch {};
        }
        std.debug.print("Producer finished.\n", .{});
    }
```

The `producerThread()` function attempts to insert values from `1` to `n` into a shared buffer. If the buffer is full (`count == max_buffer_size`), it waits on the condition variable until the consumer removes at least one item. After adding a value to the buffer, the producer signals the condition variable to wake up a potentially waiting consumer and unlocks the mutex. Similarly, the `consumerThread()` function tries to consume `n` values from the buffer. If the buffer is empty (`count == 0`), it waits on the condition variable until there is something to consume. When an item is available, it removes the oldest value in the buffer (making the buffer operate as a FIFO queue), prints it, signals the producer that there is now space available, and unlocks the mutex.

```
fn consumerThread(args: ConsumerArgs) void {
    var i: usize = 0;
    while (i < args.n) : (i += 1) {
        mutex.lock(args.io) catch return;
        while (count == 0) {
            std.debug.print("Consumer waiting: Buffer empty\n", .{});
            cond.wait(args.io, &mutex) catch {
                mutex.unlock(args.io);
                return;
            };
        }

        const item = buffer[head];
        head = (head + 1) % max_buffer_size;
        count -= 1;
        std.debug.print("Consumed: {}\n", .{item});
        cond.signal(args.io);
        mutex.unlock(args.io);
        std.Io.sleep(
            args.io,
            std.Io.Duration.fromMilliseconds(200),
```

```
                .awake,
            ) catch {};
        }
        std.debug.print("Consumer finished.\n", .{});
}
```

Let us now try `ch08/condProdCons.zig` – expect the following output:

```
$ zig run ch08/condProdCons.zig -- 5 3
Produced: 1
Consumed: 1
Produced: 2
Consumed: 2
Produced: 3
Produced: 4
Consumed: 4
Produced: 5
Producer finished.
Consumer finished.
```

The producer is set to generate 5 items, and the consumer is to consume 3. Initially, the producer creates item 1, and the consumer immediately consumes it. The same happens with item 2 — demonstrating that the buffer had space and both threads were running concurrently with well-synchronized access. When item 3 is produced, it is not immediately consumed; instead, the producer proceeds to create item 4, showing that the consumer was either waiting or simply slower due to the longer sleep time in its loop (*200 ms* vs. the producer's *100 ms*). Item 4 is then consumed, and the producer continues to produce item 5. The final two lines, `Producer finished.` and `Consumer finished.`, confirm that both threads have completed their tasks — producing 5 values and consuming 3. What is notable is that items 3 and 5 were not consumed (only items 1, 2, and 4 were), which aligns with the arguments of the program. Since the consumer was only instructed to consume 3 items, the remaining values are left in the buffer unprocessed. This demonstrates the bounded and symmetric nature of this implementation: producers and consumers do exactly as much work as they are told, and the buffer enforces correct access throughout.

While the classic Producer-Consumer pattern effectively manages synchronization between threads, it often relies on traditional queue structures that can introduce overhead and complexity in certain high-throughput or real-time scenarios. To address these challenges, the **Ring Buffer pattern** offers a streamlined, fixed-size circular queue approach that enables efficient, lock-free data exchange between producers and consumers. Using a ring buffer, systems can achieve lower latency and better cache performance, making it an attractive alternative for scenarios requiring fast and continuous data streaming.

The ring buffer data structure

A **Ring Buffer** (also known as a **circular buffer**) is a fixed-size data structure that efficiently manages a continuous flow of data in a first-in-first-out (FIFO) manner. When the buffer fills up, new data overwrites the oldest data, making it ideal for streaming and real-time applications. It consists of a preallocated array with two key pointers: a front (read pointer) for removing the oldest data and a rear (write pointer) for inserting new data. When the buffer is full, new data overwrites the oldest entries, allowing seamless handling of streaming data without dynamic resizing. The circular nature of the buffer comes from its use of modulo arithmetic, which causes the pointers to wrap around to the start once they reach the end of the array. This design ensures *O(1)* time complexity for both insertions and removals, making it ideal for real-time systems like audio processing or embedded applications where memory efficiency and speed are critical. However, edge cases like buffer *underflow* (reading when empty) or *overflow* (writing when full) must be handled explicitly, often with checks or thread-safe mechanisms in concurrent environments.

Ring buffers appear throughout Systems Programming precisely because they solve a problem that comes up constantly: two components running at different speeds need to exchange data without either blocking the other or allocating memory dynamically. A fixed-size circular buffer gives the producer a place to deposit work and the consumer a place to retrieve it, with the buffer absorbing the difference in their rates. You will find this pattern in kernel I/O queues, network packet buffers, audio pipelines, and inter-thread communication layers — anywhere bounded, allocation-free, concurrent data transfer is needed.

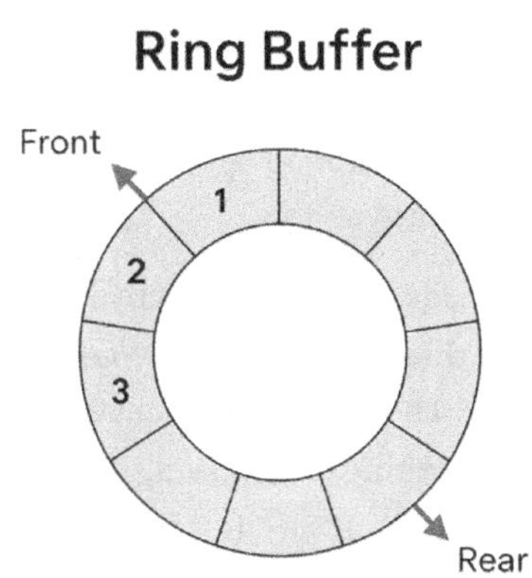

Figure 8.1 – A sample Ring Buffer data structure

Consider the following implementation of a ring buffer as found in `ch08/ringBuffer.zig`, which *implements a lock-free ring buffer for inter-thread communication between a producer and a consumer using atomics* and provides a more scalable alternative to a simple single-slot buffer by allowing multiple items to be in-flight at once while avoiding traditional locks or condition variables. At its core, the program uses a fixed-size buffer of `AtomicU32` elements (`buffer`) along with a corresponding array of `AtomicBool` flags (`fullFlags`) to indicate which slots are occupied:

```
const std = @import("std");

const Order = std.builtin.AtomicOrder;
const AtomicU32 = std.atomic.Value(u32);
const AtomicBool = std.atomic.Value(bool);
const size = 4;

// Ring buffer with atomic slots
var buffer: [size]AtomicU32 = [_]AtomicU32{
    AtomicU32.init(0),
} ** size;
var fullFlags: [size]AtomicBool = [_]AtomicBool{
    AtomicBool.init(false),
} ** size;
```

Let us discuss the statement that defines the `buffer` variable and declares a mutable variable as a fixed-size array of `AtomicU32` elements with length `size`. It initializes the array so that every element is an atomic 32-bit unsigned integer set to zero by using the slice literal `[_]AtomicU32{AtomicU32.init(0)}`, which creates a single-element slice containing an `AtomicU32` initialized to zero, and then the ** size operator repeats this element size times to fill the array. This creates a size-length array where each entry is an `AtomicU32` initialized to `0`, making the buffer ready for thread-safe atomic operations. The same thing takes place on the next line, where we define the `fullFlags` variable.

The `producerIndex` and `consumerIndex` track the respective positions in the ring buffer, and they are updated independently by each thread. Each thread wraps its index using modulo arithmetic (`% size`) to cycle around the buffer. The `producer()` function loops from 1 to 10, attempting to store a value into the buffer. Before writing, it checks if the corresponding `fullFlags[index]` is `false`, meaning the slot is empty. If it is, the producer stores the value using buffer[index].store, sets the flag to true, and advances its index and value counters. If the slot is full, it sleeps briefly, and tries again:

```
var producerIndex = std.atomic.Value(usize).init(0);
var consumerIndex = std.atomic.Value(usize).init(0);
var done = AtomicBool.init(false);

fn producer(args: WorkerArgs) void {
    var value: u32 = 1;
    while (value <= 10) {
        const pi = producerIndex.load(Order.acquire);
        const index = pi % size;
        if (!fullFlags[index].load(Order.acquire)) {
            buffer[index].store(value, Order.release);
            fullFlags[index].store(true, Order.release);
            std.debug.print(
                "Produced: {d} at {d}\n",
                .{ value, index },
            );
            producerIndex.store(pi + 1, Order.release);
            value += 1;
        } else {
            std.Io.sleep(
                args.io,
                std.Io.Duration.fromMicroseconds(10),
                .awake,
            ) catch {}; // buffer slot is full
        }
    }
    done.store(true, Order.release);
}
```

The consumer() function continually checks if there is a value available at its current index. If fullFlags[index] is true, it loads the value, prints it, clears the full flag by setting it to false and moves to the next slot. It continues this process until the producer signals it is done and there are no more filled slots to consume, at which point the consumer exits.

```
fn consumer(args: WorkerArgs) void {
    while (true) {
        const ci = consumerIndex.load(Order.acquire);
```

```
        const index = ci % size;

        if (done.load(Order.acquire) and !fullFlags[index].load(
            Order.acquire,
        )) {
            break;
        }

        if (fullFlags[index].load(Order.acquire)) {
            const val = buffer[index].load(Order.acquire);
            std.debug.print("Consumed: {d} from {d}\n", .{ val, index });
            fullFlags[index].store(false, Order.release);
            consumerIndex.store(ci + 1, Order.release);
        } else {
            std.Io.sleep(
                args.io,
                std.Io.Duration.fromMicroseconds(10),
                .awake,
            ) catch {}; // wait for data
        }
    }
}
```

Last, the `main()` function orchestrates the process by starting the relevant threads:

```
pub fn main(init: std.process.Init) !void {
    const io = init.io;
    const prod = try std.Thread.spawn(
        .{},
        producer,
        .{WorkerArgs{ .io = io }},
    );
    const cons = try std.Thread.spawn(
        .{},
        consumer,
        .{WorkerArgs{ .io = io }},
    );
    prod.join();
    cons.join();
}
```

Overall, this program showcases how atomic variables and careful buffer management can be used to implement efficient, lock-free communication between threads, making it suitable for high-performance concurrent applications.

Execute the program on your machine – the output should look similar to the following:

```
$ zig run ch08/ringBuffer.zig
Produced: 1 at 0
Produced: 2 at 1
Produced: 3 at 2
Produced: 4 at 3
Consumed: 1 from 0
Consumed: 2 from 1
Consumed: 3 from 2
Consumed: 4 from 3
Produced: 5 at 0
Produced: 6 at 1
Produced: 7 at 2
Produced: 8 at 3
Consumed: 5 from 0
Consumed: 6 from 1
Consumed: 7 from 2
Consumed: 8 from 3
Produced: 9 at 0
Produced: 10 at 1
Consumed: 9 from 0
Consumed: 10 from 1
```

The program begins with the producer thread rapidly filling up the buffer with values 1 through 4 at indices 0 through 3, cycling through the ring buffer. Since the consumer has not yet consumed anything at this point, these entries are simply marked as full. Shortly afterward, the consumer thread begins processing these entries in order, consuming values 1 to 4 from the same indices, freeing up the slots. This cycle continues with the producer writing values 5 through 8 at the same indices (0 through 3), followed again by the consumer reading and clearing them. Finally, the producer writes values 9 and 10 at indices 0 and 1, and the consumer completes by consuming those. This output reflects how both threads are correctly synchronizing using atomics: the producer waits for free slots, and the consumer waits for full ones, all without needing locks. The ring buffer wraps around as expected, showcasing a stable and efficient concurrency pattern. The next section presents a solution for logging information concurrently.

Logging information concurrently

Logging information concurrently is a real-world case where multiple threads write to the same log file. What we want is to prevent mixing information from the threads. The solution to that problem is the use of a mutex to ensure thread-safe access to the shared log file. The following example code (`ch08/sharedLog.zig`) illustrates the technique – feel free to see the implementation of `main()` at the book GitHub repository:

```
const std = @import("std");

const Thread = std.Thread;

const LogContext = struct {
    io: std.Io,
    file: std.Io.File,
    mutex: *std.Io.Mutex,
    tID: usize,
};
```

The `LogContext` structure passes both shared and thread-specific state into our concurrent workers. By bundling a copy of the `std.Io.File` handle, a pointer to a shared `Mutex`, and a unique thread identifier, we provide each thread with the exact environment it needs to operate. The logic behind passing the file by value rather than by pointer is rooted in how Zig manages file descriptors; the struct itself is essentially a lightweight handle to the underlying operating system resource. Conversely, the mutex must be passed by pointer to ensure all threads synchronize against the exact same lock in memory, preventing them from independently locking their own isolated copies.

`threadLog()` demonstrates a vital principle of concurrent systems design: minimizing the critical section. Rather than acquiring the lock immediately, the thread first allocates a 128-byte array on its local stack and formats the log message using `std.fmt.bufPrint()`. The logic behind this decision is to maximize throughput, as string formatting is a relatively CPU-intensive operation. By performing this work using local memory before requesting the lock, we allow multiple threads to prepare their messages simultaneously, thereby maintaining high concurrency and keeping the processor cores busy:

```
fn threadLog(ctx: *LogContext) void {
    var buf: [128]u8 = undefined;
    const text = std.fmt.bufPrint(
```

```
            &buf,
            "[Thread {}]: value = {}\n",
            .{ ctx.tID, ctx.tID * 10 },
        ) catch return;

        ctx.mutex.lock(ctx.io) catch return;
        defer ctx.mutex.unlock(ctx.io);
        ctx.file.writeStreamingAll(ctx.io, text) catch {};
    }
```

Once the text is fully prepared, the thread enters the critical section by calling `ctx.mutex.lock()`. The `defer ctx.mutex.unlock()` statement guarantees that the lock will be released securely when the function exits. With exclusive access granted, the thread executes `writeStreamingAll(ctx.io, text)`. This function is chosen over higher-level buffered writers because it translates into a direct system call, writing the exact slice of formatted bytes to the file descriptor. By restricting the locked portion of the code solely to the actual I/O operation, we ensure that threads only block each other for the absolute minimum time required to safely append their data to the shared log.

Building a concurrent logger is only part of the story. However, building a practical tool is what often provides the best environment for understanding abstract programming concepts. To see how concurrency operates outside of isolated, synthetic examples, we will construct `zlocate`, a high-performance concurrent file indexer.

zlocate: A concurrent file indexer

Building a utility like a **Concurrent File Indexer** requires a shift from simple sequential logic to an architecture designed for maximum throughput. A modern file indexer faces the challenge of crawling through millions of files across diverse storage media, where the bottleneck shifts rapidly between disk I/O and CPU-bound metadata processing. To address this, we must move beyond the basic threading models and implement a system that efficiently distributes the heavy lifting of file traversal and indexing across all available processor cores. Using `zlocate`, we explore how the theoretical concepts of concurrency — mutual exclusion, atomic state management, and the efficient reuse of *threads in a pool* — come together to solve the real-world problem of building a responsive, scalable, and robust systems tool.

The tool provides a comprehensive suite of commands to manage indexed data directly from the command line. Users can maintain a persistent list of search targets using the `add`, `remove`, and `roots` commands, which store configured paths in a local cache directory. The core indexing logic is triggered via `zlocateupdate`, which supports configuration options such as thread count adjustments, directory exclusions, recursion depth limits, and the ability to follow symbolic links. Once an index is built, the `search` command enables fast, memory-efficient pattern matching across the database using either simple substring filters or glob wildcards like * and ?. Additionally, the `stats` command provides metadata about the current index, including its age, total entry count, and physical file size on disk. The files that compose the project are the following:

```
$ tree
.
├── build.zig
├── build.zig.zon
└── src
    ├── database.zig
    ├── indexer.zig
    ├── main.zig
    └── search.zig
2 directories, 6 files
```

`main.zig` serves as the central orchestrator for the application, defining the command-line configuration structure and the command dispatch logic. To keep call sites readable, the module defines two small helpers, `stdoutWrite()` and `stdoutPrint()`, that wrap `std.Io.File.stdout().writeStreamingAll()` — a choice that avoids repeating the full call at every output point, not an abstraction over API stability. It also manages the persistent storage of *roots* (the directories targeted for indexing) by reading and writing to a flat-text configuration file located in the user's cache directory. The performance core of the tool resides in `indexer.zig`. It implements a parallel **Breadth-First Search** (BFS) using a thread-safe `WorkQueue` that manages directory paths awaiting processing. The queue uses a `std.Io.Mutex` to protect the underlying `ArrayList` and a `std.Io.Condition` to handle worker synchronization and termination detection. Worker threads pull items from this queue, traverse directories using the `std.Io.Dir.iterate()` interface, and update global counters — such as total files and bytes — using lock-free `std.atomic.Value` primitives. `database.zig` defines a custom, little-endian binary format optimized for high-speed serialization and deserialization. The database schema includes a 24-byte header containing magic bytes, a version number, a UNIX timestamp, and a 64-bit entry count. Rather than using streaming writers, the save function pre-calculates the required buffer size, serializes the entire index into memory, and performs an atomic write using a temporary file and a rename operation. The load function mirrors this by reading the entire file into a single memory block for rapid parsing. `search.zig` implements the pattern-matching engine through a lazy `Iterator` that yields matching paths without additional heap allocations.

It supports two primary matching strategies: a recursive `globMatch` for patterns containing * or ? wildcards and a standard `substringMatch` for plain text. By default, the module handles case-insensitive comparisons by normalizing characters to lowercase using `std.ascii.toLower()` during the matching phase.

The logic of `zlocate` is governed by the Scatter-Gather pattern, which serves as the architectural foundation, enabling the system to distribute a massive filesystem traversal task across a pool of concurrent worker threads and later coalesce their individual discoveries into a unified result. This is presented next.

The Scatter-Gather pattern (parallelism)

In the context of `zlocate`, the **Scatter-Gather pattern** is a fundamental parallel programming strategy used to distribute a large workload across multiple execution units and then consolidate the results. The pattern operates in two distinct phases: the **scatter phase**, where a single coordinator breaks a large problem into smaller, independent tasks and distributes them to a pool of workers, and the **gather phase**, where the results from those workers are collected and combined into a final output. In the scatter phase, the logic focuses on decomposition and distribution. For a file indexer, this means a primary thread traverses the directory tree and "scatters" file paths into a work queue. This phase is critical for performance because it determines how well the workload is balanced; if tasks are too small, the overhead of distribution outweighs the benefits, but if they are too large, some CPU cores may sit idle while others are still working. By decoupling the discovery of files from the actual processing, the system can begin indexing the first few files found while the discovery thread is still searching deeper into the filesystem. The gather phase occurs as workers complete their individual tasks and report back to a shared structure or a central coordinator. This requires careful synchronization to ensure that as metadata flows back from various threads, it is merged correctly without data loss or corruption. In a lock-free design, this might involve updating atomic counters or writing to independent memory locations that are joined at the very end. In a more traditional design, it might involve a mutex-protected hash map where each worker "gathers" its findings. The Scatter-Gather pattern turns a linear, time-consuming process into a parallel operation that scales with the number of available processor cores.

Let us now present key functions and methods from the `zlocate` utility.

Implementation details

The most vital component of the project is the concurrent worker architecture as found in `indexer.zig` starting with `WorkQueue.pop()`, which is the heart of the concurrency model as it demonstrates the **classic parallel-BFS invariant**, where threads use a Condition variable to wait while the queue is empty but active workers are processing directories:

```
fn pop(self: *WorkQueue, io: std.Io) ?WorkItem {
    self.mutex.lock(io) catch return null;
    defer self.mutex.unlock(io);
    while (true) {
        if (self.items.items.len > 0) {
            self.active += 1;
            return self.items.pop();
        }
        if (self.active == 0) {
            self.cond.broadcast(io);
            return null;
        }
        self.cond.wait(io, &self.mutex) catch return null;
    }
}
```

The `pop()` function is the core synchronization engine of `zlocate`, responsible for distributing work items while determining exactly when the entire indexing process has concluded. By using a combination of a mutual exclusion lock and a condition variable, the function ensures that threads coordinate their activity without wasting CPU cycles on busy waiting. The operation begins by acquiring the `WorkQueue` mutex, ensuring that only one thread can inspect or modify the queue state at a time. Once the lock is held, the function enters an infinite loop to handle various thread states. If the internal `ArrayList` contains work items, the thread increments the active counter and returns the next directory to be processed. This transition from the queue to the active state prevents the system from shutting down prematurely if the queue momentarily hits zero while a worker is still discovering new subdirectories. If the queue is empty, the function evaluates whether any other threads are still active. If the active count is zero, it confirms that all branches of the file system have been fully explored; the function then broadcasts a signal to wake any remaining waiting threads and returns null to indicate completion. However, if other workers are still active, the current thread calls `self.cond.wait(&self.mutex)`, which atomically releases the lock and suspends the thread, allowing it to remain dormant until a fellow worker either pushes new work into the queue or signals that the entire process is finished.

workerThread() closes the termination loop; its body is a simple while that calls queue.pop() for each item and, in a defer block, calls queue.finish() before moving to the next iteration:

```
fn workerThread(shared: *Shared) void {
    const io = shared.io;
    while (shared.queue.pop(io)) |item| {
        defer {
            shared.allocator.free(item.path);
            shared.queue.finish(io);
        }
        crawlDirectory(shared, item.path, item.depth) catch |err| {
            std.log.debug(
                "skipping '{s}': {s}",
                .{ item.path, @errorName(err) },
            );
            _ = shared.n_errors.fetchAdd(1, .monotonic);
        };
    }
}
```

finish() acquires the mutex, decrements active, and — if active has reached zero and the queue is empty — broadcasts on the condition variable. That broadcast is what wakes every worker that is blocked inside pop() waiting for more work; they each re-check the termination condition (active == 0 and queue empty), find it true, and return null, ending their loop. The defer placement is deliberate: finish() is called after crawlDirectory() returns, meaning the slot stays "active" for the entire duration of directory processing — including any push() calls that add sub-directories. This prevents a false termination signal mid-crawl, which would occur if active were decremented before the worker had finished enqueuing its children.

Next, we have the crawlDirectory() function, which is the primary engine of the file-system traversal logic, responsible for recursively exploring the directory hierarchy and populating the results list. It operates by first attempting to obtain an absolute directory handle using std.Io.Dir.openDirAbsolute() with iteration enabled. The logic is designed to be resilient; it explicitly catches and ignores common environmental errors, such as AccessDenied or FileNotFound, to ensure that a single restricted folder does not terminate the entire indexing process. Once the directory is opened, the function increments the global directory counter using an atomic fetch-and-add operation to maintain accurate statistics across threads. The function then initializes a directory iterator and enters a loop to process each entry discovered within the current path. For every entry, it first checks against the user-defined exclusion list — such as .git or `node_modules` — to skip irrelevant branches of the file system. If an entry is valid, the function constructs its full absolute path by joining the current directory path with the entry name. This newly formed path is then appended to the shared results list under the protection of a dedicated results mutex, ensuring thread-safe updates to the final index. The final stage of the operation involves dispatching sub-tasks based on the entry file type. If the entry is a directory and the current depth has not reached the configured maximum limit, the function pushes the new path back into the global `WorkQueue`, allowing other worker threads to pick up the task and explore that sub-branch. The logic also includes specialized handling for symbolic links; if configured to follow them, the function resolves the link to its real path and, if it points to a directory, re-queues it for processing. Feel free to examine the implementation details in the source to see how these recursive dispatches and atomic counter updates are precisely synchronized. Next, `buildIndex()` acts as the primary entry point for concurrent operations, coordinating the transition from a single-threaded configuration to a multi-threaded execution environment. The logic begins by initializing a high-resolution timer to capture the total duration of the crawl. It then determines the optimal degree of parallelism by checking the user configuration; if no specific thread count is provided, the function queries the system to detect the number of available CPU cores, ensuring the workload scales naturally with the hardware. Once the concurrency level is established, the function initializes a `Shared` state structure, which acts as the central repository for the thread-safe work queue, the results list, and the atomic performance counters. The operation moves into its initial seeding phase by pushing each user-provided root directory into the queue, priming the system for the worker threads. The logic then proceeds to allocate an array of thread handles and spawns the worker pool, passing a pointer to the shared state to each thread. This creates a parallel execution block where the main thread suspends its own progress to wait for the workers to join, signaling that the entire filesystem tree has been exhausted and all directory branches have been processed. In the final phase of the operation, the function performs a clean teardown of the concurrent infrastructure, transforms the gathered results into a stable slice, and populates a `Result` structure with the accumulated filesystem paths and the finalized statistics gathered from the atomic counters. By capturing the final timer reading, the function provides the caller with a complete profile of the indexing run, including entry counts and precise duration. While this overview explains the high-level orchestration, feel free to look at the implementation details and the exact sequence of thread spawning and resource cleanup.

As this project avoids the evolving `std.io` reader/writer abstractions, it uses manual byte-level serialization in `database.zig`. The `database.save()` function implements a robust, single-shot serialization strategy designed to maintain data integrity and performance without relying on complex streaming abstractions. The operation begins by performing a complete pre-calculation of the required file size, iterating through the list of paths to account for both the fixed-size header and the variable-length string entries. Once the total memory footprint is determined, the logic allocates a single contiguous buffer and populates it with little-endian representations of the magic bytes, version number, and file metadata using manual byte-slice offsets. To ensure that the database is never left in a corrupted state during a crash or power failure, the function employs an atomic write pattern. It first writes the entire serialized buffer to a temporary file with a `.tmp` extension and then uses a filesystem-level rename operation to replace the existing database file in a single, uninterruptible step. While this overview covers the high-level persistence strategy, feel free to look at the implementation details to see how the code handles paths that exceed the 16-bit length limit. In contrast, the `database.load()` function is architected for maximum retrieval speed by minimizing individual I/O calls. The code opens the target file and reads its entire contents into a heap-allocated memory block in one shot, bypassing the overhead of traditional line-by-line or buffered reading. To navigate this block, the function utilizes a specialized internal helper that validates the remaining data length before advancing a position pointer, effectively creating a safe, localized parsing environment. The parsing phase strictly validates the *ZLOC* magic bytes and the format version before proceeding to allocate the final path array. Each path entry is reconstructed by reading its 16-bit length prefix and duplicating the subsequent bytes into the result set. This approach ensures that the database is loaded into a structured format ready for immediate use. You are encouraged to look at the implementation details and observe the `errdefer` logic, which carefully manages memory cleanup if a file is truncated or contains invalid data.

Next, let us discuss the `matches()` function and the `Iterator.next()` method from `search.zig`. The `matches()` function serves as the central dispatch hub for the project's search engine, determining the most efficient strategy for comparing a search pattern against a file path. The logic begins by identifying the subject of the search; depending on the user configuration, it may evaluate the full absolute path or isolate only the final component using `std.fs.path.basename()`. Once the subject is defined, the function inspects the pattern for the presence of glob wildcards, specifically * or ?. If these characters are detected, the operation branches to a recursive glob-matching algorithm; otherwise, it defaults to a faster, iterative substring scan. The `Iterator.next()` method implements a **lazy search pattern**, which is essential for maintaining a low memory footprint when filtering through a database potentially containing millions of entries. Instead of pre-calculating and allocating a new list of all matching results, the code maintains an internal index to track its progress through the existing array of paths. During each invocation, the method enters a loop that advances through the path list, applying the match logic to each entry sequentially. As soon as a match is identified, the function immediately yields that specific path to the caller and pauses its execution. If the end of the list is reached without further success, it returns null to signal that the search is exhausted. Having explored the underlying architecture and the precise logic of the core modules and functions, let us now use `zlocate`.

Using the zlocate utility

After creating the `zlocate` binary, execute the following commands on your machines:

```
$ cd ch08/zlocate
$ zig build
$ ./zig-out/bin/zlocate add /var/log
Added '/private/var/log' to index roots.
$ ./zig-out/bin/zlocate add ~/Desktop
Added '/Users/mtsouk/Desktop' to index roots.
```

So, the first step is defining which areas of the filesystem should be indexed. In this case, we have added two directories as verified by the next command:

```
$ ./zig-out/bin/zlocate roots
/private/var/log
/Users/mtsouk/Desktop
```

A notable technical detail here is the automatic path normalization: the shell-expanded `~/Desktop` is resolved to its absolute representation, `/Users/mtsouk/Desktop`, and `/var/log` is resolved to `/private/var/log`. This resolution (`std.Io.Dir.realPathFile()`) ensures that the path stored in the configuration file matches the actual physical location on the filesystem, preventing duplicate entries or broken references. But we are not done yet; we need to build the index by running the `update` command:

```
$ ./zig-out/bin/zlocate update
Indexing 2 root(s) with 14 thread(s) …
  /private/var/log
  /Users/mtsouk/Desktop
Crawled 13324 dirs, found 25908 entries in 0.26s
Saved 25908 entries → /Users/mtsouk/.cache/zlocate/files.db
```

And now, we are ready to search by looking for `build.zig` files:

```
$ ./zig-out/bin/zlocate search --basename --case-sensitive "build.zig"
. . .
22 match(es)
```

`zlocate` found 22 paths matching `build.zig`. Next, let us see some statistics:

```
$ ./zig-out/bin/zlocate stats
Database path : /Users/mtsouk/.cache/zlocate/files.db
Entries       : 25908
File size     : 2019538 bytes
Index age     : 0h 2m
Indexed at    : 1773765172 (Unix)
Roots         :
  /private/var/log
  /Users/mtsouk/Desktop
```

Last, let us remove both existing root directories:

```
$ ./zig-out/bin/zlocate remove ~/Desktop
Removed '/Users/mtsouk/Desktop' from index roots.
$ ./zig-out/bin/zlocate remove /var/log
Removed '/private/var/log' from index roots.
$ ./zig-out/bin/zlocate update
No roots configured — saved empty index to /Users/mtsouk/.cache/zlocate/files.db
$ ./zig-out/bin/zlocate stats
Database path : /Users/mtsouk/.cache/zlocate/files.db
Entries       : 0
File size     : 24 bytes
Index age     : 0h 0m
Indexed at    : 1773765406 (Unix)
Roots         : (none configured)
```

In the first two commands, the utility removed the specified directories from its tracking list. When `zlocate update` is executed after these removals, the orchestrator in `main.zig` finds that the root configuration file is empty. Because there are no starting points for the `WorkQueue` in `indexer.zig`, the crawler terminates immediately without spawning worker threads. However, the program still proceeds to finalize the state by calling `database.save()`. This ensures that any previous index is overwritten with a clean state. The message indicates that an empty index has been saved to the default cache path, preserving the integrity of the database file even if it contains no file entries. The `zlocate stats` output confirms the internal structure of the resulting binary file. The report of a 24-byte file size is a direct consequence of the database schema defined in `database.zig`. Even with zero entries, the file must contain the mandatory header, which consists of 4 bytes for the Magic number (*ZLOC*), 4 bytes for Format version, 8 bytes for the UNIX timestamp (the "Indexed at" value), and 8 bytes for a 64-bit integer representing the entry count, stored in the `Header` struct that serves as the immutable preamble of the `zlocate` database file. This consistency allows the `load()` function to verify the file integrity by inspecting the first few bytes before committing to a larger memory allocation.

Building a high-performance tool like `zlocate` demonstrates how the principles of systems programming — concurrency, memory safety, and efficient binary I/O — converge into a single, solid application. By prioritizing a thread-safe architectural design through the `WorkQueue`, the project leverages modern hardware to minimize the latency inherent in deep filesystem traversals. The shift away from evolving library abstractions toward manual, single-shot binary serialization in `database.zig` ensures long-term stability and maximum throughput for data persistence. The project serves as a practical model for how Zig empowers developers to build tools that are not only performant but also predictable in their resource consumption. Through the combination of parallel execution and lazy evaluation, `zlocate` provides a robust foundation for anyone looking to master the complexities of modern systems development.

Summary

As we conclude this exploration of concurrency, it becomes clear that the move from sequential to parallel execution is as much about *architectural discipline* as it is about raw speed. We have moved from the basic mechanics of thread creation to the sophisticated management of shared state, learning that the true power of a multi-core system is only unlocked when we design for independence. By mastering the coordination of producers and consumers through thread pools and ring buffers and by protecting our data with the surgical application of mutexes and atomic operations, we have built a toolkit capable of handling the most demanding system tasks. The implementation of `zlocate` serves as a testament to these principles, proving that a well-structured concurrent design naturally paves the way for efficient parallelism. As you move forward, remember that the complexities of race conditions and deadlocks are not just obstacles to be avoided, but signals that the components of a system are too tightly coupled. By thinking in terms of independent, communicating entities, you can build software that scales gracefully with the hardware of tomorrow.

The natural evolution of systems programming leads toward even more efficient ways of handling massive throughput. This transition brings us to the next chapter, where we shift our focus from the parallel execution of threads to the event-driven world of *non-blocking operations*. In the coming pages, we will demystify the core theory behind *asynchrony*, explore the mechanics of high-performance event loops, and build a practical, non-blocking TCP proxy.

Exercises

- Modify `ch08/multiTCP.zig` to accept the port number as a command-line argument.

9

Implementing Asynchronous I/O

The shift toward asynchronous I/O is primarily driven by the need to handle a high volume of concurrent operations without the overhead of traditional threading. In a synchronous model, each I/O request — such as reading from a disk or waiting for a network packet — blocks the execution of the calling thread. This blocking behavior forces the OS to perform a context switch to another thread to keep the CPU busy, a process that involves saving and restoring registers and kernel-level bookkeeping. As the number of concurrent connections grows into the thousands, the memory consumed by individual thread stacks and the CPU cycles lost to context switching become a major bottleneck. *Asynchronous programming* addresses this by allowing a single thread to initiate multiple I/O operations and continue executing other logic while the hardware or kernel processes those requests.

This chapter covers:

- Asynchrony is not Concurrency
- Seeing async and await in action
- An Asynchronous TCP Proxy
- Refactoring the TCP proxy using async and await
- Comparing the performance of the two proxies

Asynchrony is not Concurrency

A common point of confusion in systems programming is the conflation of asynchrony with concurrency. While they often appear together, they address different architectural concerns. *Concurrency* is about structure — it is the ability of a program to handle multiple tasks at once by breaking them into independent units of execution. In contrast, asynchrony is about *latency* and the elimination of blocking. A concurrent system might use multiple CPU cores to run tasks in parallel, but an asynchronous system focuses on ensuring that the CPU does not sit idle while waiting for a slow I/O device. You can have a single-threaded asynchronous program that manages thousands of network connections efficiently without ever running two pieces of code at the same physical moment. Understanding this distinction is vital for Zig developers, as the language provides the primitives to build concurrent structures, but leaves the choice of asynchronous execution strategy entirely in the hands of the programmer. This separation of concerns runs through every example in the chapter. The foundational examples establish how `std.Io` abstracts the underlying event mechanism, the `fanOut.zig` example shows how asynchrony handles multiple concurrent operations without threads, and the TCP proxy brings both ideas together in a system where the distinction between concurrency and asynchrony directly shapes the architecture. By the end of the chapter, the difference between the two will not be just a definition but a design instinct.

Before looking at `std.Io` and the event mechanisms it abstracts, it is worth examining the two fundamental execution models that underpin all asynchronous programming: coroutines and OS threads. The choice between them is not just an implementation detail, as it determines the scheduling model, the memory cost per concurrent task, and the synchronization primitives your code will need. Understanding the tradeoffs here will make every design decision in the async examples that follow immediately legible.

Coroutines vs. OS Threads

The choice between **coroutines** and **OS threads** is a choice between user-space management and kernel-space management. OS threads are *preemptive*, meaning the OS scheduler can interrupt a thread at any time to give another thread CPU time. This requires each thread to have its own dedicated stack memory, often several megabytes, which limits how many you can spawn before exhausting system resources. *Coroutines* or *green threads* are *cooperative*. They yield control back to a scheduler only when they hit a natural waiting point, such as an I/O request. Because coroutines can share a single OS thread and utilize much smaller, dynamically sized stacks, a system built on coroutines can handle orders of magnitude more simultaneous tasks than one relying on raw OS threads. In Zig 0.16.x, we utilize these lightweight execution units to maintain high throughput without the heavy memory footprint of traditional threading.

It is important to note that these coroutine benefits apply only when you explicitly opt into an event-driven `std.Io` backend. The default backend, `std.Io.Threaded`, uses real OS threads: a bounded pool defaulting to one less than the logical CPU count, each with a standard 16 MiB stack on Linux, with tasks beyond the pool size running inline. A reader who runs `basic.zig` or `fanOut.zig` without explicitly selecting a backend gets this threaded model — not the lightweight coroutine model described above. The claim that coroutines support orders of magnitude more simultaneous tasks than OS threads does not hold under the default. If your program needs the scheduling and memory advantages of coroutines, you must select an evented backend explicitly and understand that the behavior of your program will differ meaningfully between backends.

Event loops: how io_uring and kqueue work under the hood

To achieve true high-performance I/O, we must move beyond the overhead of the `read()` and `write()` system calls, which require a transition from user space to kernel space for every operation. Modern kernels provide specialized interfaces like Linux `io_uring` and BSD `kqueue` to facilitate "event-driven" programming. At the heart of these systems is the event loop: a continuous cycle that polls the kernel for completed I/O events. With `io_uring`, for instance, the application places I/O requests into a shared submission queue and later harvests the results from a completion queue. This design minimizes the number of expensive system calls and allows the kernel to process I/O asynchronously in the background. By using these primitives, a Zig application can submit a batch of disk and network operations and continue processing data, only reacting when the kernel signals that the data is ready.

Writing nonblocking code

Writing non-blocking code requires a shift in mindset from a linear, imperative flow to a state-driven approach. In a standard synchronous function, you might call `file.read()` and wait for the data to arrive before moving to the next line. In a non-blocking context, you must handle the possibility that the data is not yet available. If a read operation would block, the system returns a specific error — often `WouldBlock` — signaling the developer to register interest in the file descriptor and yield control. The logic is then resumed only when the event loop notifies the program that the descriptor is ready for progress. In Zig, this is typically handled by wrapping I/O operations in functions that return a "future" or a task handle. This ensures that the CPU is always performing meaningful work, never stalled by the inherent slowness of external hardware or network latency.

With the theory of asynchronous I/O established, it is time to see it expressed directly in Zig 0.16 code.

Seeing async and await in action

The `async` and `await` keywords are not magic — they are syntactic handles on the coroutine machinery provided by the `std.Io` interface. When a function is launched with `io.async()`, it becomes a *coroutine*: a unit of work that can suspend itself at any I/O boundary and yield the thread to other coroutines rather than blocking it. When the I/O completes, the runtime resumes the coroutine from exactly the point it left off. The `await` call on the returned handle is simply the caller saying *I need this result before I can continue*. What makes this model powerful is that the calling code reads almost identically to synchronous code — there are no callbacks, no explicit state machines, and no manually managed continuation objects — yet the runtime is free to interleave dozens of concurrent operations on a single thread whenever any one of them is waiting for the OS.

Using async and await

In Zig 0.16, `async` and `await` are not language keywords but methods on the `io` instance. Calling `io.async(function, .{arguments})` schedules a function asynchronously and immediately returns a `Future` handle — the caller does not block. When the result is needed, `task.await(io)` suspends the caller until the task completes and delivers its return value. The following program (`ch09/basic.zig`) demonstrates the complete lifecycle of a single async task:

```
const std = @import("std");
const Io = std.Io;

fn longComputation(io: Io, input: u64) !u64 {
    // Simulate some work (in a real program this could be CPU work or I/O)
    try io.sleep(Io.Duration.fromSeconds(1), .awake);
    return input * input;
}

pub fn main(init: std.process.Init) !void {
    const io = init.io;

    // Launch two independent computations concurrently
    var task1 = io.async(longComputation, .{ io, 42 });
    defer _ = task1.cancel(io) catch {};
    var task2 = io.async(longComputation, .{ io, 7 });
    defer _ = task2.cancel(io) catch {};

    // Do unrelated work while both tasks run in the background
    var buf: [128]u8 = undefined;
    const working = std.fmt.bufPrint(
        &buf,
        "Tasks launched; doing other work...\n",
        .{},
    ) catch unreachable;
    try std.Io.File.stdout().writeStreamingAll(io, working);

    // Simulate additional CPU work the main thread can do concurrently
    var sum: u64 = 0;
```

```
    for (0..1_000_000) |i| sum +%= i;

    // Now collect both results
    const result1 = try task1.await(io);
    const result2 = try task2.await(io);

    const s = std.fmt.bufPrint(
        &buf,
        "42^2={d}, 7^2={d}, side-sum={d}\n",
        .{ result1, result2, sum },
    ) catch unreachable;
    try std.Io.File.stdout().writeStreamingAll(io, s);
}
```

The function `longComputation` accepts an `io` instance and an integer. The `io.sleep` call suspends the coroutine for one second, simulating slow I/O without blocking an OS thread. In `main()`, `io.async` is called twice, launching both computations concurrently and storing the returned futures in `task1` and `task2`. The `defer _ = taskN.cancel(io) catch {}` lines are safety nets: if `main()` exits early, any in-flight task is canceled and its resources freed. While both tasks sleep in the background, `main()` prints a status message and performs an independent CPU-bound loop — work that runs concurrently with the sleeping coroutines. Only after that does the main call `task1.await(io)` and `task2.await(io)` to collect both results. Because the two one-second sleeps overlap with each other and with the main-thread work, the total wall time stays near one second rather than two — this overlap between async launch and deferred await is the foundation of the asynchronous programming model.

You can see that in action by running `ch09/basic.zig`:

```
$ zig run ch09/basic.zig
Tasks launched; doing other work...
42^2=1764, 7^2=49, side-sum=499999500000
```

When multiple independent tasks must all be completed before proceeding, Zig provides `io.concurrent`, which is similar to `io.async` but may return a `ConcurrentError` if scheduling resources are exhausted — hence the `try`. The `ch09/fanOut.zig` program launches three parallel data-fetch operations, each simulating a different network latency, and waits for all three:

```
const std = @import("std");
const Io = std.Io;
```

```
fn fetchData(io: Io, id: u32, out: *u64) !void {
    try io.sleep(
        Io.Duration.fromMilliseconds(300 + @as(i64, id) * 100),
        .awake,
    );
    out.* = 1000 * id;
}

pub fn main(init: std.process.Init) !void {
    const io = init.io;
    var results: [3]u64 = undefined;

    // Start three tasks concurrently
    var t1 = try io.concurrent(
        fetchData,
        .{ io, @as(u32, 1), &results[0] },
    );
    defer _ = t1.cancel(io) catch {};

    var t2 = try io.concurrent(
        fetchData,
        .{ io, @as(u32, 2), &results[1] },
    );
    defer _ = t2.cancel(io) catch {};

    var t3 = try io.concurrent(
        fetchData,
        .{ io, @as(u32, 3), &results[2] },
    );
    defer _ = t3.cancel(io) catch {};

    // Wait for all tasks
    try t1.await(io);
    try t2.await(io);
    try t3.await(io);

    var buf: [128]u8 = undefined;
    const s = std.fmt.bufPrint(
        &buf,
        "Results: {d} {d} {d}\n",
        .{ results[0], results[1], results[2] },
```

```
    ) catch unreachable;
    try std.Io.File.stdout().writeStreamingAll(io, s);
}
```

Each call to `try io.concurrent(fetchData, ...)` launches an independent task that writes its result directly to a pre-allocated slot in the `results` array. Because all three tasks start before any is awaited, their simulated I/O overlaps in time. The sequential `await` calls then collect each result. The total wall-clock time approaches the duration of the slowest individual task rather than the sum of all three.

The fan-out pattern gets its name from the shape of execution: one path fans out into N parallel paths, then fans back in to collect results. This pattern appears constantly in distributed systems and network services — any time a program needs to query multiple backends, fetch multiple resources, or run multiple independent computations before combining their results, fan-out is the natural shape of the solution. In `ch09/fanOut.zig`, three calls to `io.concurrent(fetchData, ...)` launch three independent tasks before any of them is awaited. The concurrent call is important here — unlike `io.async`, which lets the Io implementation choose how to execute the task — inline, on a worker thread, or as a coroutine — `io.concurrent` forces actual concurrent execution and returns `ConcurrencyUnavailable` if the `Io` implementation cannot provide it. Because all three are launched before any `await`, their simulated sleeps genuinely overlap in time. Each task receives a pointer to a distinct slot in the pre-allocated results array and writes its output there directly. There is no heap allocation, no mutex, and no channel. This is safe precisely because each task touches a different slot — concurrent writes to the same slot would be a data race. The `defer _ = tX.cancel(io) catch {}` statements (where `X` takes the values of `1`, `2`, and `3`) are a safety net. If `main()` exits early — say, an `await` returns an error — the `defers` cancel any tasks still running. Without this, a task could continue writing into the stack memory that no longer belongs to it. The `await` calls, similar to `try t1.await(io)`, are sequential in source order, but that does not serialize the work. By the time `t1.await` is called, tasks 2 and 3 are already running on their own threads. Each `await` simply blocks until that one task finishes and re-raises any error the task produced. The total wall-clock time is therefore driven by the slowest task — roughly `600 ms` for task 3 — rather than the `1500 ms` sum of all three delays.

Let us try `ch09/fanOut.zig` – expect to get the following output:

```
$ zig run ch09/fanOut.zig
Results: 1000 2000 3000
```

The output shows three results collected from three concurrent tasks. Each task received a different ID — 1, 2, and 3 — and computed `1000 * id`, so the values 1000, 2000, and 3000 appear in the order the tasks were launched rather than the order they finished. All three tasks ran concurrently, meaning the total waiting time was determined by the slowest task alone, not by the sum of all three delays.

The fan-out pattern shown above focuses on reading or fetching data from multiple sources at once, but concurrent I/O does not stop at reads. The next section extends the model to write operations.

Using async and await for write operations

Reading data asynchronously is only half of the picture. Write operations carry their own set of challenges: a slow or back-pressured client can cause a naive server to block while trying to flush bytes into a socket, stalling every other coroutine on the same thread. The `std.Io` model handles this symmetrically — a write that cannot complete immediately suspends the coroutine and yields the thread, exactly as a read does, so the event loop remains free to service other connections while the OS drains the send buffer. The practical consequence is that the same `io.async()` and `await` pattern used for reads applies equally to writes, and a coroutine that interleaves reading from one stream with writing to another does so without any explicit coordination between the two operations.

In `ch09/multipleWrites.zig`, two independent file writes are launched concurrently using `io.async`. Because neither write depends on the result of the other, they can overlap in execution:

```
const std = @import("std");
const Io = std.Io;

fn saveFile(io: Io, data: []const u8, name: []const u8) !void {
    const file = try Io.Dir.cwd().createFile(io, name, .{});
    defer file.close(io);

    try file.writeStreamingAll(io, data);
}

pub fn main(init: std.process.Init) !void {
    const io = init.io;
    const data = "Hello from Zig 0.16 async I/O!\n";

    var task_a = io.async(saveFile, .{ io, data, "/tmp/output_a.txt" });
    defer _ = task_a.cancel(io) catch {};
    var task_b = io.async(saveFile, .{ io, data, "/tmp/output_b.txt" });
```

```
    defer _ = task_b.cancel(io) catch {};

    try task_a.await(io);
    try task_b.await(io);

    try std.Io.File.stdout().writeStreamingAll(io, "Both files written
successfully!\n");
}
```

The `saveFile()` helper opens a file, writes the payload with `writeStreamingAll` and closes the handle. Both `io.async(saveFile, ...)` calls return immediately, launching the writes in the background. The subsequent `await` calls collect completion. Both `createFile()` and `writeStreamingAll()` operations are submitted to the event loop and can be serviced in whichever order the I/O subsystem satisfies them.

`main()` begins by extracting the `io` handle from `init` – a popular pattern – and defining a short string literal that will be written to both files. It then launches two tasks with `io.async()` — one targeting `output_a.txt` and one targeting `output_b.txt` — before waiting on either. Using `async` rather than concurrent means the scheduler is free to run the tasks inline if it determines that is efficient, but because both are started before either is awaited, the two file writes can overlap. Each task handle gets a `defer` cancel guard so that if an error causes main to exit early, any still-running task is cleaned up rather than left writing into stale memory. The two `await()` calls then collect the results in order. If either `saveFile()` failed — for instance, because the file could not be created — the error propagates out of main here. Once both await return without error, a final `writeStreamingAll()` confirms success to `stdout`. Let us run `ch09/multipleWrites.zig`:

```
$ zig run ch09/multipleWrites.zig
Both files written successfully!
```

There are times when only the first result matters — the rest can be discarded, which is what is illustrated next.

Being interested in the first result only

`Io.Select` waits for whichever of several concurrent tasks finishes first and automatically cancels the losers. The `ch09/sleepSelect.zig` program races two timers and acts only on the winner:

```
const std = @import("std");
const Io = std.Io;

fn sleepFor(io: Io, seconds: i64) void {
    io.sleep(Io.Duration.fromSeconds(seconds), .awake) catch {};
}

pub fn main(init: std.process.Init) !void {
    const io = init.io;
    const Result = union(enum) { t1: void, t2: void };

    var buf: [2]Result = undefined;
    var sel = Io.Select(Result).init(io,&buf);
    defer sel.cancelDiscard();

    sel.async(.t1, sleepFor, .{ io, @as(i64, 1) });
    sel.async(.t2, sleepFor, .{ io, @as(i64, 2) });

    // Wait for the first one to complete
    const winner = try sel.await();

    switch (winner) {
        .t1 => try std.Io.File.stdout().writeStreamingAll(
            io,
            "Task 1 finished first\n",
        ),
        .t2 => try std.Io.File.stdout().writeStreamingAll(
            io,
            "Task 2 finished first\n",
        ),
    }
}
```

The `Result` union defines one variant per competing task. `Io.Select(Result).init(io, &buf)` allocates the selector with a backing buffer sized for all tasks. `sel.async(.t1, sleepFor, ...)` and `sel.async(.t2, sleepFor, ...)` launch both timers. `sel.await()` blocks until one completes and returns the winning tagged union value, which the `switch` statement then dispatches on — each arm maps directly to the corresponding `Result` variant and prints the appropriate message. `defer sel.cancelDiscard()` ensures the losing task is canceled and its result discarded. Note that `sleepFor()` returns `void` and swallows sleep errors with `catch {}`, which keeps the example focused on the select mechanics; in production code, the function would return `!void` and propagate the error instead. `Io.Select` is the natural building block for timeouts, backend races, and any pattern where only the fastest response matters. Let us see `ch09/sleepSelect.zig` in action:

```
$ zig run ch09/sleepSelect.zig
Task 1 finished first
```

The examples so far have demonstrated the core building blocks of the Zig async I/O model in isolation — launching concurrent tasks, writing to files in parallel, and racing tasks to pick the fastest result. The next step is combining these primitives into something more realistic. An asynchronous TCP proxy puts them all together: it accepts incoming connections, forwards data in both directions between client and remote, and uses `Io.Select` to tear down the session as soon as either direction closes — all without blocking on network I/O while data is in flight.

An asynchronous TCP proxy

Building a TCP proxy is a classic systems programming exercise that serves as an excellent litmus test for any language's I/O capabilities. In this section, we develop a utility that sits between a client and a destination server, forwarding raw byte streams in both directions. While a synchronous proxy would require two dedicated OS threads per connection — one for each direction of the data flow — our asynchronous implementation leverages the power of the `std.Io` interface to multiplex thousands of these proxy pairs onto a single execution thread. This project transitions from the abstract concepts of event loops into a concrete tool, demonstrating how to manage multiple file descriptors and maintain state across non-blocking boundaries.

The primary advantage of an **asynchronous TCP proxy** is its *horizontal scalability*. Because we are not allocating a 2MB or 8MB stack for every concurrent connection, the memory footprint of the proxy remains exceptionally lean, limited primarily by the size of the application-level buffers we define. Furthermore, by utilizing `io_uring` or `kqueue` through Zig's standard library, we minimize the *system call tax*. Instead of constantly switching between user mode and kernel mode to check if a socket has data, we batch our requests, allowing the kernel to notify us only when actionable data is available. This results in significantly higher throughput and lower jitter, especially under high-concurrency workloads where a thread-per-connection model would struggle with scheduler latency.

However, asynchrony introduces a higher degree of *architectural complexity*. In a synchronous program, the call stack implicitly tracks the state of a connection; in an asynchronous system, the developer must explicitly manage state machines to track what has been read and what is pending a write. This "state bookkeeping" can make the code harder to debug and reason about, as the execution flow is no longer linear. Additionally, while we avoid the overhead of OS threads, we introduce the risk of event loop starvation. If a single request involves a heavy computational task — such as complex packet inspection or encryption — it can block the entire event loop, delaying all other active connections. In Zig, where there is no hidden runtime to save you from these pitfalls, the responsibility for keeping the loop "spinning" rests entirely on the design of your functions.

We begin with `ch09/tcpProxy.zig`, a synchronous proxy that handles one TCP connection at a time. It accepts a local port, a remote host, and a remote port as command line arguments, then forwards all traffic between the two endpoints. This sequential baseline makes the architecture easy to reason about before introducing concurrency. The code presentation opens with `transferOneWay()`, the function that moves data in one direction between two streams — the building block that both the synchronous and asynchronous proxies share:

```
const std = @import("std");
const Io = std.Io;

fn transferOneWay(io: Io, src: Io.net.Stream, dst: Io.net.Stream) void {
    var data: [4096]u8 = undefined;
    var wbuf: [4096]u8 = undefined;
    // Zero-length internal buffer: readVec reads directly into
    // `data` without spilling overflow bytes into a secondary
    // buffer, giving true short reads.
    var r = src.reader(io, &[0]u8{});
    var w = dst.writer(io,&wbuf);
    var bufs: [1][]u8 = .{&data};
    while (true) {
        const n = r.interface.readVec(&bufs) catch break;
        if (n == 0) break;
        w.interface.writeAll(data[0..n]) catch break;
        w.interface.flush() catch break;
    }
    // Half-close so the peer knows the request is complete.
```

```
    // Production code should log errors via @errorName(err).
    dst.shutdown(io, .send) catch {};
}
```

`transferOneWay()` is the low-level workhorse. It takes two streams — a source and a destination — and pumps data from one to the other until the source is exhausted or the connection drops. A 4096-byte stack buffer `data` for each incoming chunk, and a second 4096-byte buffer `wbuf` backs the buffered writer. The reader is created with a zero-length internal buffer (`src.reader(io, &[0]u8{})`), which is an intentional and very important decision. When the Reader has a non-zero internal buffer, `readVec` adds it to the iovec array alongside `data`, which can cause overflow bytes to spill into the internal buffer and then block on a subsequent call trying to fill the remaining space — a deadlock when the sender has nothing more to write. With a zero-length internal buffer, `readVec` reads directly into `data` and returns as soon as the OS delivers any bytes, giving a true short read. Each chunk is immediately written to the destination and flushed, so data reaches the peer without delay. When the source closes (`n == 0`) or an error occurs, the loop exits, and `dst.shutdown(io, .send)` performs a TCP half-close, signaling the peer that no more data is coming. Errors inside the loop are silently discarded because a dropped connection is a normal condition here; production code should at minimum log `@errorName(err)`. Next, `handleSession()` orchestrates a full proxy session for one client:

```
fn handleSession(
    io: Io,
    client: Io.net.Stream,
    remote_addr: Io.net.IpAddress,
) !void {
    defer client.close(io);

    const remote = try remote_addr.connect(io, .{ .mode = .stream });
    defer remote.close(io);

    // Run both directions concurrently and wait for both to finish.
    var task_c2r = io.async(transferOneWay, .{ io, client, remote });
    defer task_c2r.cancel(io);
    var task_r2c = io.async(transferOneWay, .{ io, remote, client });
    defer task_r2c.cancel(io);

    task_c2r.await(io);
    task_r2c.await(io);
}
```

The code opens a connection to the remote address immediately on entry and registers deferred closes for both the client and remote streams, so they are always cleaned up when the function returns. The interesting part is the bidirectional forwarding: a TCP session carries data in both directions simultaneously, so a single `transferOneWay` call is not enough. Instead, `handleSession()` launches two independent async tasks — `task_c2r` for client-to-remote and `task_r2c` for remote-to-client — and then awaits both in sequence. When c2r reaches EOF, it half-closes the write side of the remote connection via `shutdown`, which signals the backend to send its response and close. That unblocks r2c, which forwards the remaining data back to the client and then also finishes. Only once both tasks have completed does `handleSession()` return, and the deferred stream closes. This means the session stays open long enough for a full request-response exchange, regardless of which side sends first. The tradeoff is that this proxy serves only one client at a time; `proxyAsync.zig` removes that limitation.

> **Note**
>
> The error handling in `handleClient()` is simplified for clarity. Failed backend connections, write errors, and broken client connections all result in silent session termination via `catch return` and `catch {}`. A production proxy would distinguish between these cases — logging each error type separately, implementing retry logic for transient backend failures and reporting connection statistics to a monitoring system. The simplification here if for keeping the focus on the async coordination pattern rather than the operational concerns of a production service.

Now, let us see `main()`:

```
pub fn main(init: std.process.Init) !void {
    const io = init.io;
    var iter = init.minimal.args.iterate();
    defer iter.deinit();
    _ = iter.next(); // skip program name

    var local_port: u16 = 8080;
    var remote_host: []const u8 = "127.0.0.1";
    var remote_port: u16 = 9000;
    const arg1 = iter.next();
    const arg2 = iter.next();
    const arg3 = iter.next();

    if (arg1) |arg| {
```

```
        local_port = std.fmt.parseInt(u16, arg, 10) catch |err| {
            std.debug.print("Invalid local port: {s}\n", .{arg});
            return err;
        };
    }

    if (arg2) |arg| {
        remote_host = arg;
    }

    if (arg3) |arg| {
        remote_port = std.fmt.parseInt(u16, arg, 10) catch |err| {
            std.debug.print("Invalid remote port: {s}\n", .{arg});
            return err;
        };
    }

    if (arg1 == null) {
        std.debug.print("Using default ports.\n", .{});
        std.debug.print(
            "To change: zproxy <local_port> <remote_host> <remote_port>\n",
            .{},
        );
        std.debug.print("Example: zproxy 3000 127.0.0.1 5000\n\n", .{});
    }

    std.debug.print(
        "zproxy: Listening on 0.0.0.0:{d} -> {s}:{d}\n",
        .{ local_port, remote_host, remote_port },
    );

    const local_addr = try Io.net.IpAddress.parseIp4("0.0.0.0", local_port);
    const remote_addr = try Io.net.IpAddress.resolve(io, remote_host,
remote_port);

    var server = try local_addr.listen(io, .{});
    defer server.deinit(io);

    while (true) {
        const client = try server.accept(io);
        std.debug.print("[New Connection]\n", .{});
```

```
            handleSession(io, client, remote_addr) catch |err| {
                std.debug.print("[Error] {s}\n", .{@errorName(err)});
            };
            std.debug.print("[Session closed]\n", .{});
        }
    }
```

`main()` begins by parsing its three optional command-line arguments — local port, remote host, and remote port — falling back to defaults of `8080`, `127.0.0.1`, and `9000` if none are provided. If no arguments are given at all, it prints a usage hint, so the user knows how to configure the proxy. Once the arguments are resolved, it prints a summary line showing the forwarding path that is about to be set up. The resolution of addresses happens in two steps. The local address is parsed directly from the literal string `0.0.0.0` combined with the local port, binding the server to all available network interfaces. The remote address goes through `Io.net.IpAddress.resolve()`. With both addresses in hand, main calls `local_addr.listen()` to open the server socket and then enters an infinite loop. Each iteration calls `server.accept(io)`, which blocks until a new client connects and returns its stream. That stream is passed directly to `handleSession()`, which takes over and blocks until the session ends. Any session-level error is caught and printed without crashing the server, and the loop immediately cycles back to accept for the next connection. Only one client is served at a time because the `accept()` loop cannot proceed while a session is active, which is the limitation that the async refactor in the next section addresses.

To see `tcpProxy.zig` in action, you need three things running concurrently: a backend service for the proxy to forward traffic to, the proxy itself, and a client that connects through it. The simplest backend is a TCP echo server. On most systems, `socat` can stand one up in a single command: `socat TCP-LISTEN:9000,fork EXEC:/bin/cat`.

With the backend listening on port 9000, we should start the proxy in a second terminal:

```
$ zig run ch09/tcpProxy.zig
Using default ports.
To change: zproxy <local_port> <remote_host> <remote_port>
Example:   zproxy 3000 127.0.0.1 5000

zproxy: Listening on 0.0.0.0:8080 -> 127.0.0.1:9000
```

Last, run the following command:

```
$ echo "hello from the proxy" | nc 127.0.0.1 8080
hello from the proxy
```

The feedback — the initial message returned — shows that the entire network loop works as expected.

The proxy, as written, handles one connection at a time — while a session is active, the accept loop sits idle waiting for it to finish before it can serve the next client. For a low-traffic tool, this is acceptable, but it leaves a clear opening for improvement. The natural next step is to refactor the proxy so that each incoming connection is handed off to its own concurrent task, freeing the accept loop to keep accepting. This is where `async` and `await` primitives move from demonstration examples into practical use.

Refactoring the TCP proxy using async and await

The synchronous proxy is fundamentally limited by its sequential accept loop. To serve many simultaneous clients on a single thread, `ch09/proxyAsync.zig` uses `Io.Group` to fire-and-forget each session handler. The group acts as a concurrent task pool: each accepted client is handed off to a `handleClient()` coroutine, and the accept loop immediately returns to wait for the next connection.

`transferOneWay()` is identical to the version in `ch09/tcpProxy.zig` and serves the same purpose: it copies data from one stream to another using two fixed 4096-byte stack buffers, looping until the source is exhausted or the connection drops. Errors are silently swallowed with `catch {}` because a closed connection is expected, not exceptional.

`handleClient()` is the async refactor of `handleSession()` from `ch09/tcpProxy.zig`:

```
// handleClient must return void because Io.Group.async requires
// it. All errors are therefore handled locally and logged
// rather than propagated.
fn handleClient(
    io: Io,
    client: Io.net.Stream,
    remote_addr: Io.net.IpAddress,
) void {
    defer client.close(io);

    const remote = remote_addr.connect(
        io,
        .{ .mode = .stream },
    ) catch |err| {
        std.debug.print(
            "[error] backend connect failed: {s}\n",
```

```
            .{@errorName(err)},
        );
        return;
    };
    defer remote.close(io);

    // Run both directions concurrently and wait for both to finish.
    var task_c2r = io.async(transferOneWay, .{ io, client, remote });
    defer task_c2r.cancel(io);
    var task_r2c = io.async(transferOneWay, .{ io, remote, client });
    defer task_r2c.cancel(io);

    task_c2r.await(io);
    task_r2c.await(io);

    std.debug.print("[session] closed\n", .{});
}
```

`handleClient()` comes with two differences. First, it returns `void` instead of `!void` — because it will be launched as a fire-and-forget task via `Io.Group`, there is no caller waiting to receive an error, so errors are handled locally with `catch return` or `catch {}` rather than propagated. Second, a failed connection to the backend prints a diagnostic and returns early instead of unwinding through an error union. The bidirectional forwarding logic is otherwise identical to `handleSession()`: two independent async tasks are launched for the two transfer directions, and both are awaited in sequence, making sure the full request-response exchange completes before the session is torn down.

`acceptLoop()` is the piece that was missing from `ch09/tcpProxy.zig`:

```
fn acceptLoop(io: Io, local_addr: Io.net.IpAddress, remote_addr:
Io.net.IpAddress) !void {
    var server = try local_addr.listen(io, .{});
    defer server.deinit(io);
    var group: Io.Group = .init;
    defer group.cancel(io);

    while (true) {
        const client = server.accept(io) catch |err| {
            std.debug.print(
                "[accept error] {s}\n",
                .{@errorName(err)},
```

```
            );
            continue;
        };
        // Fire-and-forget the session handler
        group.async(
            io,
            handleClient,
            .{ io, client, remote_addr },
        );
    }
}
```

The code opens the listening socket, initializes an `Io.Group`, and then enters an infinite loop accepting connections. Each accepted client stream is handed off immediately to `handleClient()` via `group.async()`, which launches it as a fire-and-forget concurrent task and returns instantly — the accept loop does not wait for the session to finish before accepting the next connection. The `Io.Group` tracks all the in-flight session tasks and `defer group.cancel(io)` ensures they are all canceled if `acceptLoop()` ever exits. This is the key structural difference from `ch09/tcpProxy.zig`: Many sessions can be active simultaneously.

Last, we have `main()`, which is noticeably shorter than its counterpart in `tcpProxy.zig`:

```
pub fn main(init: std.process.Init) !void {
    const io = init.io;

    var iter = init.minimal.args.iterate();
    defer iter.deinit();
    _ = iter.next(); // skip program name

    var local_port: u16 = 8080;
    var remote_host: []const u8 = "127.0.0.1";
    var remote_port: u16 = 9000;

    if (iter.next()) |arg| local_port = std.fmt.parseInt(
        u16,
        arg,
        10,
    ) catch
        local_port;
    if (iter.next()) |arg| remote_host = arg;
```

```
    if (iter.next()) |arg| remote_port = std.fmt.parseInt(
        u16,
        arg,
        10,
    ) catch
        remote_port;

    std.debug.print(
        "zproxy: Listening on 0.0.0.0:{d} -> {s}:{d}\n",
        .{ local_port, remote_host, remote_port },
    );

    const local_addr = try Io.net.IpAddress.parseIp4(
        "0.0.0.0",
        local_port,
    );
    const remote_addr = try Io.net.IpAddress.resolve(
        io,
        remote_host,
        remote_port,
    );

    var acceptor = io.async(
        acceptLoop,
        .{ io, local_addr, remote_addr },
    );
    defer _ = acceptor.cancel(io) catch {};

    try acceptor.await(io);
}
```

Argument parsing is condensed to three `if` statements that silently fall back to the default on a parse error rather than returning it. After resolving addresses, `main()` does something the synchronous version never needed to do; it wraps `acceptLoop()` itself in an `io.async` call. This is because `acceptLoop()` runs forever, and wrapping it in a future gives main a handle to cancel it cleanly on exit via the deferred `acceptor.cancel()`. The subsequent `acceptor.await()` then blocks `main()` for the lifetime of the server, keeping the process alive until an external signal or error brings it down.

With both proxies implemented, the natural question is which one performs better and by how much. The synchronous proxy in `tcpProxy.zig` handles one connection at a time, so its throughput under concurrent load is limited by session duration — a slow or long-lived client blocks every other client waiting to connect. The async proxy in `proxyAsync.zig` removes that bottleneck by dispatching each session to its own concurrent task, so the accept loop stays free regardless of how many sessions are active. Measuring the two under identical conditions makes the cost of that serialization concrete and gives a feel for how much async primitives buy you in a real network workload.

Comparing the performance of the two proxies

To measure the real-world impact of the architectural difference between the two proxies, we need a purpose-built load generator rather than a manual client. Manually opening connections one at a time would never expose the serialization bottleneck in `tcpProxy.zig`, because a human simply cannot issue fifty simultaneous TCP connections from a terminal. The `ch09/proxyBench.zig` utility fills this role. It operates in two independent modes: as a TCP echo server that acts as the proxy backend, and as a benchmark client that fires a configurable number of concurrent connections through whichever proxy is under test, measuring wall-clock time, total throughput, and average per-connection latency. The benchmark uses a simple length-prefix protocol to avoid requiring a TCP half-close. Each client connection sends a four-byte big-endian integer declaring the payload size, immediately followed by that many bytes of data. The echo server reads the length header, reads exactly that many bytes, and writes them back. The client then reads back the same number of bytes and records the elapsed time. Because both sides agree on the exact transfer size, neither needs to signal end-of-stream; the exchange completes deterministically after a fixed number of bytes in each direction.

Before comparing the two proxies, we need a controlled way to generate load and measure results and `ch09/proxyBench.zig` provides exactly that: it doubles as both a backend echo server and a benchmark client, so the entire test environment runs within a single codebase with no external dependencies. The echo server speaks a simple length-prefixed protocol — each connection sends a 4-byte big-endian payload length followed by that many bytes, and the server reads and writes them back, which keeps the backend trivial and ensures it is never the bottleneck. The benchmark client fires a configurable number of concurrent connections through whichever proxy is running, measures how long each one takes end-to-end, and reports wall-clock time, total throughput in MB/s, and average per-connection latency.

We begin by running the following in a terminal, which is the backend echo server with a latency of `50 ms`. This will help us understand the different techniques better:

```
$ zig run ch09/proxyBench.zig -- --server 9000 --latency 50
Echo server ready on 127.0.0.1:9000 (latency 50ms)
```

Then we run the proxy under test. First this:

```
$ zig run ch09/tcpProxy.zig -- 8080 127.0.0.1 9000
zproxy: Listening on 0.0.0.0:8080 -> 127.0.0.1:9000
```

And last, we have the benchmark client:

```
$ zig run ch09/proxyBench.zig -- --bench 127.0.0.1 8080 --conns 4 --bytes 4096
Benchmarking 127.0.0.1:8080 — 4 concurrent connections × 4096 bytes

=== Benchmark Results ===
Connections:      4 ok  /  0 failed
Total bytes:      16384
Wall-clock time:  220 ms
Throughput:       0.07 MB/s
Avg conn latency: 136.74 ms

NOTE: wall-clock time scales with --conns on tcpProxy (serial),
      but stays roughly constant on proxyAsync (concurrent).
```

Then, after benchmarking, we will stop `ch09/tcpProxy.zig` and run `ch09/proxyAsync.zig` as follows:

```
$ zig run ch09/proxyAsync.zig -- 8080 127.0.0.1 9000
zproxy: Listening on 0.0.0.0:8080 -> 127.0.0.1:9000
```

After that, we run the benchmark client:

```
$ zig run ch09/proxyBench.zig -- --bench 127.0.0.1 8080 --conns 4 --bytes 4096
Benchmarking 127.0.0.1:8080 — 4 concurrent connections × 4096 bytes

=== Benchmark Results ===
Connections:      4 ok  /  0 failed
Total bytes:      16384
Wall-clock time:  56 ms
```

```
Throughput:          0.28 MB/s
Avg conn latency: 55.71 ms

NOTE: wall-clock time scales with --conns on tcpProxy (serial),
      but stays roughly constant on proxyAsync (concurrent).
```

Both proxies completed all 4 connections without a single failure, confirming that correctness was not sacrificed in either implementation. The difference shows up in the performance numbers. `tcpProxy.zig` processed 16,384 bytes in `220 ms` at 0.07 MB/s with an average per-connection latency of `136.74 ms`. `proxyAsync.zig` processed the same workload in `56 ms` at 0.28 MB/s with an average latency of `55.71 ms` — roughly 75% faster in wall-clock time and about 59% lower in per-connection latency. The reason is architectural. `tcpProxy.zig` serializes connections: the accept loop blocks for the duration of each session, so the 4 connections are processed one after another, and the total time accumulates — `136 ms` per connection multiplied across all four produces the `220 ms` wall-clock total. `proxyAsync.zig` dispatches each session to its own concurrent task via `Io.Group`, so all 4 connections are in flight simultaneously, and the wall-clock time approaches that of a single connection rather than the sum of all four. It is worth keeping the numbers in perspective. The test runs entirely on `localhost`, which means network latency is essentially zero and the loopback interface is doing no real work compared to a production environment. The payload is small — 4096 bytes per connection — and the echo server is trivially fast. In a real deployment with genuine network latency, larger payloads, and a slower backend, the gap between the two proxies would be considerably wider, because each connection in `tcpProxy.zig` would hold the accept loop idle for much longer while waiting for the remote end to respond. The benchmark here captures the shape of the difference rather than its full magnitude.

Throughout this chapter, we have worked with the functionality of `std.Io`, which abstracts platform-specific I/O execution behind a common interface. The default backend, `std.Io.Threaded`, uses a real OS thread pool — one less than the logical CPU count by default. To opt into event-driven I/O, you must explicitly construct and initialize an evented backend: `std.Io.Uring` on Linux, `std.Io.Dispatch` on macOS (which uses Grand Central Dispatch), or `std.Io.Kqueue` on BSD systems. On Linux, `io_uring` and on BSD, `kqueue` exist precisely because the older `select(2)` and `poll(2)` interfaces require the kernel to scan every watched file descriptor on every call — an `O(n)` operation that becomes painful when a server is tracking thousands of connections simultaneously. The two programs that follow implement the same TCP echo server directly against each kernel interface, bypassing Zig's abstraction entirely, so the machinery is fully visible. Reading them side by side gives you a concrete picture of what the evented backends are doing on your behalf and why the abstraction is worth having.

> **Note**
>
> Although macOS supports `kqueue` as a system call, `std.Io` on macOS uses Grand Central Dispatch (`std.Io.Dispatch`) internally — not `kqueue` directly. The program that follows is a standalone low-level example that calls the `kqueue` API directly via C bindings. It runs on both macOS and BSD systems but it is not a reflection of what `std.Io` does on macOS. Think of it as a window into the kernel interface rather than a guide to what Zig's standard library uses under the hood on that platform.

However, keep in mind that the measurements that follow are independent — `kqueue` was benchmarked on an Apple M4 Pro and `io_uring` on on an Intel i7; therefore, the numbers reflect what each interface delivers on its respective platform, not a head-to-head comparison between the two.

Low-Level I/O multiplexing: io_uring and kqueue

Every server we have built in this chapter ultimately asks the same question: which of my connections has data ready right now? The answer to that question is what an I/O multiplexing mechanism provides, and the mechanism you choose has direct consequences for how many connections your server can handle, how many syscalls it makes per second, and how much work the kernel does on your behalf. Linux and macOS/BSD answer that question differently — Linux with **io_uring**, a *shared-memory ring* that lets the kernel and user space exchange batches of I/O operations without a syscall per operation, and macOS and BSD with **kqueue**, an *event notification queue* that delivers only the file descriptors that are actually ready, rather than requiring the application to scan the full set. Both are single-threaded solutions to the concurrency problem: one thread, no locks, no context switching between connection handlers, yet the server remains fully responsive to every client simultaneously. The two programs in this section implement exactly the same TCP echo server against each interface directly, without `std.Io` in the way, so you can see the kernel machinery in its raw form before `ch09/echoBench.zig` puts a number against it.

In both cases, the TCP echo server accepts multiple concurrent connections on a single thread and echoes every byte back to the client that sent it. The two implementations share the same structural skeleton: create and bind a listening socket using C Interoperability via `@cImport`, set the socket to non-blocking mode with `fcntl(2)`, enter an infinite event loop, and dispatch on the type of event that fires. Both use a heap-allocated array of per-connection buffers indexed by file descriptor value, capped at `MAX_FD = 1024`. Both set `SO_REUSEADDR` on the listening socket so the server can restart immediately without waiting for the OS to release the port. Both use `comptime` guards — `@compileError` — to produce a clear build failure if compiled on the wrong platform. Both print connection and disconnection events to stdout using `std.Io.File.stdout().writeStreamingAll()` and accept an optional port argument from the command line, defaulting to 9000.

The fundamental difference is how each program tells the kernel what to watch and how it learns what is ready. `ch09/kqueue.zig` creates a single kqueue file descriptor with `std.c.kqueue()` and registers interest in sockets using `kevent(2)` with `EV_ADD`. The event loop calls `kevent(2)` a second time with a null changelist to block until events arrive, receiving up to `MAX_EVENTS = 64` notifications per call. Each event carries the file descriptor that fired in its `ident` field. The loop checks whether `ident` matches the listening socket — in which case it calls `accept(2)` and registers the new client fd with `EV_ADD` — or whether it is a client socket, in which case it reads available bytes with `c.read()` and immediately writes them back with `c.write()`. Peer disconnection is detected via the `EV_EOF` flag on the event. The read and write operations are direct and synchronous within the event callback: data arrives, gets echoed, and the loop returns to waiting. `ch09/ioUring.zig` uses `io_uring` interface through the `std.os.linux.IoUring` Zig wrapper. Rather than making one syscall per I/O operation, `io_uring` uses a pair of shared memory rings between userspace and the kernel: the application writes **Submission Queue Entries** (SQEs) into the submission ring describing operations to perform, and the kernel writes **Completion Queue Entries** (CQEs) back into the completion ring when those operations finish. The program encodes the operation type (`accept`, `recv`, `send`) and the file descriptor into each SQE's 64-bit `user_data` field using bit-packing — the high 32 bits carry the operation type, the low 32 bits carry the file descriptor. The completion handler decodes this field to know what just finished and what to queue next. This means the control flow is asynchronous and continuation-based rather than the direct read/write style of `kqueue.zig`: after a `recv` completes, the handler queues a `send`; after a `send` completes, the handler queues the next `recv`; after an `accept` completes, the handler queues a `recv` on the new client and immediately re-queues another `accept` so the next connection does not require an extra syscall round-trip. The practical consequence of this difference is that `io_uring` can batch multiple operations into a single `io_uring_enter(2)` syscall, reducing kernel-crossing overhead significantly at high connection counts. `kqueue` makes one `kevent(2)` call per batch of events and then individual `read()`/`write()` calls per connection. For a simple echo server, the difference is modest, but under load with many concurrent connections, it becomes measurable, which is exactly what `ch09/echoBench.zig` quantifies.

`echoBench.zig` is a concurrent load generator designed to measure the throughput and latency of both echo servers under controlled conditions. It accepts a host, port, and three optional parameters: `--conns` for the number of concurrent connections per round (default 50), `--bytes` for the payload size per connection (default 4096 bytes), and `--rounds` for the number of measurement iterations (default 3). The benchmark allocates a payload buffer of the requested size and fills it with the byte `'X'`. For each round, it creates an `Io.Group` and fires one `group.async()` task per connection, each executing `benchConn()`. This means all connections are established and exercised concurrently as coroutines on the event loop rather than sequentially, which is essential for exercising the server's multiplexing behavior — a sequential benchmark would never saturate a single-threaded event-driven server. Each `benchConn()` task records a `std.Io.Timestamp` before connecting, establishes a TCP connection using `addr.connect(io, .{ .mode = .stream })`, sends the full payload using a buffered writer, reads back exactly the same number of bytes using `readSliceAll()` to ensure the complete echo is received, then records a second timestamp. It updates four shared atomic counters: `done` for successful completions, `failed` for any error, `bytes` for total bytes transferred, and `latency_ns` for the cumulative nanosecond latency across all connections. The use of atomic operations ensures these counters are updated safely across concurrent coroutines without a mutex. After `group.await(io)` returns, `runRound()` reads the counters and computes three metrics: throughput in MB/s (total bytes divided by wall-clock elapsed time), average per-connection latency in milliseconds (cumulative nanoseconds divided by successful connection count), and total wall-clock time in milliseconds. These are printed in a single line per round, making it straightforward to compare results across the two servers or across different `--conns` and `--bytes` values.

`benchConn()` is the unit of measurement for the benchmark: one call equals one complete round-trip to the echo server. It connects to the server, sends the full payload as raw bytes (no length prefix — the raw-echo servers just mirror whatever arrives), reads the same number of bytes back, and records three counters atomically: successful completions (`done`), payload bytes transferred (`bytes`), and end-to-end wall-clock latency in nanoseconds (`latency_ns`). Any failure — connection refused, a short write, or a short read — increments `failed` and returns immediately without touching the other counters, so the reported averages reflect only successful connections. The timestamp wraps the entire operation from `connect` to last byte received, making the reported average latency the client-observable round-trip time rather than server-side processing time alone.

```
fn benchConn(
    io:         Io,
    addr:       Io.net.IpAddress,
    payload:    []const u8,
    results:    *Results,
```

```
) void {
    const t0 = std.Io.Timestamp.now(io, .awake);

    const conn = addr.connect(io, .{ .mode = .stream }) catch {
        _ = results.failed.fetchAdd(1, .monotonic);
        return;
    };
    defer conn.close(io);

    var wbuf: [4096]u8 = undefined;
    var rbuf: [4096]u8 = undefined;
    var w = conn.writer(io,&wbuf);
    var r = conn.reader(io,&rbuf);

    // Send the whole payload.
    w.interface.writeAll(payload) catch {
        _ = results.failed.fetchAdd(1, .monotonic);
        return;
    };
    w.interface.flush() catch {
        _ = results.failed.fetchAdd(1, .monotonic);
        return;
    };

    // Read back the same number of bytes.
    const readback = std.heap.page_allocator.alloc(u8, payload.len) catch {
        _ = results.failed.fetchAdd(1, .monotonic);
        return;
    };
    defer std.heap.page_allocator.free(readback);

    r.interface.readSliceAll(readback) catch {
        _ = results.failed.fetchAdd(1, .monotonic);
        return;
    };

    const t1 = std.Io.Timestamp.now(io, .awake);
    _ = results.done.fetchAdd(1, .monotonic);
    _ = results.bytes.fetchAdd(payload.len, .monotonic);
    _ = results.latency_ns.fetchAdd(
        @as(u64, @intCast(t1.nanoseconds - t0.nanoseconds)),
```

```
        .monotonic,
    );
}
```

Note

The numbers that will be presented in a while are not a fair or direct comparison. The kqueue benchmark was run on an Apple M4 Pro, and the `io_uring` benchmark was run on an Intel i7 — two machines with significantly different memory bandwidth, loopback stack performance, and CPU characteristics. A reader who takes away *kqueue is six times faster than io_uring* from these numbers, has drawn a conclusion that the data cannot support. What the numbers really show is the ceiling each interface reaches on its native platform: this is what kqueue delivers on Apple silicon, and this is what `io_uring` delivers on that generation of Intel hardware. A meaningful comparison of the two kernel interfaces would require running both on the same hardware, which is not straightforward since kqueue is a macOS and BSD primitive and `io_uring` is Linux-specific.

Let us do the testing on macOS first. We begin by running `zig run ch09/kqueue.zig -- 9000`. Then, we execute the benchmarking utility in a different terminal as follows:

```
$ zig run ch09/echoBench.zig -- 127.0.0.1 9000 --conns 200 --bytes 8192 --rounds 5

echo-bench → 127.0.0.1:9000   conns=200  bytes=8192  rounds=5

Round 1:  200 ok  0 failed  |  89.87 MB/s  |  avg latency 0.73 ms  |  wall 17 ms
Round 2:  200 ok  0 failed  |  106.78 MB/s  |  avg latency 0.46 ms  |  wall 14 ms
Round 3:  200 ok  0 failed  |  126.32 MB/s  |  avg latency 0.09 ms  |  wall 12 ms
Round 4:  200 ok  0 failed  |  123.77 MB/s  |  avg latency 0.08 ms  |  wall 12 ms
Round 5:  200 ok  0 failed  |  120.16 MB/s  |  avg latency 0.09 ms  |  wall 13 ms

Done.
```

After that, we go on a Linux machine and run `zig run ch09/ioUring.zig -- 9000`. Then, we execute the benchmarking utility on a different terminal as follows:

```
$ zig run ch09/echoBench.zig -- 127.0.0.1 9000 --conns 200 --bytes 8192 --rounds 5

echo-bench → 127.0.0.1:9000   conns=200  bytes=8192  rounds=5
```

```
Round 1:  200 ok  0 failed  |  12.15 MB/s  |  avg latency 1.96 ms  |  wall 128 ms
Round 2:  200 ok  0 failed  |  18.99 MB/s  |  avg latency 1.85 ms  |  wall 82 ms
Round 3:  200 ok  0 failed  |  19.93 MB/s  |  avg latency 1.62 ms  |  wall 78 ms
Round 4:  200 ok  0 failed  |  19.45 MB/s  |  avg latency 1.36 ms  |  wall 80 ms
Round 5:  200 ok  0 failed  |  20.21 MB/s  |  avg latency 1.53 ms  |  wall 77 ms

Done.
```

Both runs completed all 200 connections across all 5 rounds with zero failures, which confirms that both servers handle concurrent load correctly. The numbers themselves, however, tell a more nuanced story than a simple `kqueue` versus `io_uring` comparison. The macOS run shows a clear warm-up pattern across the first three rounds. Round 1 delivers 89.87 MB/s with a `0.73 ms` average latency, round 2 jumps to 106.78 MB/s, and round 3 reaches 126.32 MB/s, where it stabilizes. Rounds 4 and 5 hold steady at around 120 – 126 MB/s with average latency dropping to just `0.08 - 0.09 ms` and wall-clock time settling at `12 - 13 ms` per round. The warm-up effect is characteristic of the OS page cache, CPU branch predictor, and connection-handling code all reaching a hot state after the first round. Once warm, the numbers are impressively consistent. The Linux run also shows warm-up behavior — Round 1 at 12.15 MB/s, climbing to around 20 MB/s by Round 3 and stabilizing there. The latency figures are higher, averaging around `1.4 - 1.9 ms`, and wall-clock time settles at roughly `77 - 82 ms` per round, significantly slower than the macOS numbers. The honest answer is that this benchmark is primarily measuring hardware, not the kernel interface. The Apple M4 Pro is an exceptionally fast chip with high memory bandwidth, low-latency caches, and an extremely efficient loopback network stack. The Intel i7 Linux machine, while capable, is an older architecture that cannot match the M4 Pro's raw throughput on loopback I/O. A fair comparison between `kqueue` and `io_uring` would require both servers running on identical hardware. On the same hardware, `io_uring` would be expected to pull ahead of `kqueue` at higher connection counts precisely because it reduces the number of syscalls through batching — an advantage that does not show up clearly here because the benchmark is dominated by memory bandwidth and CPU speed rather than syscall overhead. The results should therefore be read as *this is what each server achieves on its respective hardware,* rather than `kqueue` is faster than `io_uring`.

As you reach the end of this chapter, it is important to treat the provided examples as architectural blueprints rather than static boilerplate. In a language that evolves as rapidly as Zig, the specific syntax of a standard library function may shift, but the underlying systems principles remain constant. Your goal should be to understand how an event loop multiplexes I/O, how a task suspends to prevent blocking, and how an interface like `std.Io` decouples your business logic from the hardware. If you focus on the "why" behind the allocation of a session or the manual cleanup of a poll list, you will be able to adapt your code to any future version of the compiler or any new kernel primitive that arrives. Mastery in systems programming is not found in the ability to compile a specific snippet but in the ability to reason about how data flows through the kernel and into your application memory. If you come up with efficient logic, everything will be easier.

Summary

In this chapter, we have examined the fundamental transition from synchronous, blocking operations to the high-performance asynchronous model provided by Zig 0.16.x. We began by dismantling the common misconception that asynchrony and concurrency are identical, establishing instead how event loops like `io_uring` and `kqueue` allow a single thread to manage thousands of concurrent I/O events without the memory overhead of OS-level context switching. By implementing a TCP proxy, we moved from the theoretical mechanics of non-blocking code to a practical system capable of scaling under significant network load.

The next chapter puts these concurrency and networking primitives to work in a complete system: a production-ready in-memory cache server called `zcache`. It covers the internal data structures — a doubly linked list threaded through a hash map — that make *O(1)* eviction possible, a state machine for parsing a custom binary protocol arriving over a streaming TCP connection, and the development of three clients that exercise the server: a functional test client, an interactive CLI, and a load benchmark.

Exercises

- Run `proxyBench.zig` against both proxies with `--conns` set to `10`, `50`, `100`, and `200`, keeping `--bytes` fixed at `4096`. Record the wall-clock time for each combination and arrange the results in a table. Describe the shape of each proxy scaling curve and explain why they differ using the vocabulary introduced in the *Asynchrony is not Concurrency* section.
- Add a per-session timeout to `tcpProxy.zig`. Use `Io.Select` with three variants instead of two: the existing `c2r` and `r2c` directions, plus a new timeout variant that fires a coroutine sleeping for a configurable number of seconds. When `sel.await()` returns `.timeout`, print a message and close the session. Verify the timeout fires correctly by connecting with `nc` and staying idle.
- Add an active-connection counter to `proxyAsync.zig` using `std.atomic.Value(u32)`. Increment it when `handleClient()` starts and decrement it in the `defer`. Print the

current count each time a new client connects. Confirm with `proxyBench.zig --conns 20` that the counter reaches 20 before any session closes.

- Modify `fanOut.zig` so that the number of parallel tasks is read from the command line instead of being hardcoded. Each task should still sleep for `300 + id * 100` milliseconds. Run the program with one, five and ten tasks and confirm that the wall-clock time stays close to the slowest individual task.
- Extend `proxyBench.zig` with a `--rounds N` flag that repeats the full benchmark `N` times and prints the minimum, maximum and average wall-clock times across all rounds. Use this to quantify run-to-run variance between `tcpProxy.zig` and `proxyAsync.zig`.
- Run `proxyBench.zig` against `proxyAsync.zig` with `--conns 50` and `--bytes` set to `512`, `4096`, `16384` and `65536` in turn. Plot throughput in MB/s against payload size. Explain why throughput rises with larger payloads in terms of per-connection setup cost relative to data transferred.
- Rewrite the main loop of `tcpProxy.zig` so that it becomes concurrent without changing `handleSession()` at all. The only permitted modification is in `main()`: replace the direct `handleSession()` call with a mechanism from `std.Io` that fire-and-forgets the session. Verify with `proxyBench.zig` that wall-clock time no longer scales linearly with `--conns`. Discuss what you changed and why `handleSession()` itself required no modification.
- The `tcpProxy.zig` program resolves the remote host using `Io.net.IpAddress.resolve(io, remote_host, remote_port)`. As shown in `ch06/echoClientResolve.zig`, Zig provides `std.Io.net.HostName.init` combined with `hn.connect()` as an alternative way to resolve a hostname and open a connection in a single step. Refactor `handleSession()` in `tcpProxy.zig` to remove the `remote_addr` parameter entirely. Instead, accept the raw `remote_host` string and `remote_port` number, construct an `Io.net.HostName` from the host string and call `hn.connect()` directly to obtain the remote stream. Update main accordingly so that it no longer resolves the address upfront and passes the host and port through to `handleSession()` instead. Verify that the proxy still forwards traffic correctly after the refactor.

Additional resources

- Zig 0.16.0 Released: `https://ziglang.org/news/0.16.0-released/`

10

Building a High-Performance In-Memory Cache Server

The design of a high-performance in-memory cache server represents a quintessential challenge in systems programming, requiring a balance between raw throughput, predictable latency, and memory efficiency. In modern distributed architectures, the cache often serves as the primary defense against database bottlenecks, making its internal implementation a critical factor in overall system reliability. By the end of this chapter, you will have built `zcache` — a non-trivial cache server that demonstrates the core techniques: a custom binary protocol, a Least Recently Used (LRU) eviction policy, TTL-based expiry and a thread-per-connection networking layer, tested by three purpose-built clients that verify correctness, exercise the command interface, and measure throughput. Production cache servers such as Redis, memcached and KeyDB build on these same foundations but add sharded locking, graceful shutdown, Transport Layer Security (TLS), authentication, persistence and replication on top. The closing section of this chapter maps out exactly those gaps, giving you a clear picture of what separates a solid teaching implementation from a system you would deploy under real load.

This chapter covers:

- Developing `zcache`
- Doubly Linked List and Hash Map
- Implementing a state machine to parse streaming TCP data
- Developing three clients: test client, CLI, and benchmark

The required theory

At the hardware level, the performance of an in-memory system is often limited not by CPU cycles but by the efficiency of CPU cache utilization. Accessing main memory is orders of magnitude slower than accessing L1 or L2 caches; therefore, the data structures chosen must be designed to be cache-friendly. `std.StringHashMap`, which powers the `zcache` storage engine, uses open addressing internally — a layout where all entries live in a single contiguous array rather than scattered heap nodes — so a lookup that misses the map's first probe is still likely to find its target within the same or an adjacent cache line. Furthermore, the theory of cache eviction is paramount. Since memory is a finite resource, a cache must intelligently decide which items to discard when it reaches capacity. The **Least Recently Used algorithm** is the industry standard for this: the intuition is that data accessed recently is more likely to be accessed again than data that has not been touched for a long time. Its implementation requires an intrusive doubly linked list embedded directly inside each data record, so that when the CPU fetches a node to read its value, the metadata needed to update its position in the access order arrives in the same cache line at no extra cost. Concurrency theory further complicates the implementation, as a server must handle simultaneous requests without becoming mired in lock contention. The `zcache` implementation wraps the entire cache in a single `std.Io.Mutex`, which is the correct starting point for a thread-per-connection server, since each connection thread only acquires the mutex briefly while processing a single request. In a production system serving requests across many CPU cores, a single global lock would become a bottleneck — threads would spend more time waiting than processing data. The standard upgrade path is sharding, where the key space is partitioned into N independent cache segments, each with its own lock, so that requests hashing to different segments proceed in parallel — this is left as an exercise for the reader. Understanding this progression — from a single mutex to sharded locks to lock-free structures built on atomics and careful memory ordering — is essential context for reasoning about where the current implementation sits on the performance spectrum and what the cost of each upgrade step would be.

With these theoretical foundations established — the importance of cache-friendly data layouts, the LRU eviction strategy, and the trade-offs between simplicity and concurrency — we can now turn to the concrete implementation. Zcache is designed to make each of these trade-offs explicit and visible in the code so that the gap between theory and practice is as narrow as possible.

Developing zcache

Zcache is a high-performance in-memory cache server written in Zig, designed around three cleanly separated layers. At its core sits the storage engine, which implements an LRU cache by combining a hash map and a doubly linked list — the hash map provides *O(1)* key lookup while the linked list maintains access order, keeping every get, set, and eviction *O(1)* regardless of cache size. **Time-to-live (TTL)** expiry is handled lazily: rather than running a background sweep thread, entries are checked and evicted on the first access after their lifetime elapses, keeping the hot path simple and latency predictable. On top of the storage engine sits ZEMP (**Zcache Exchange Message Protocol**), a custom binary wire protocol where every message begins with a fixed 8-byte prefix containing a magic byte, version, command type, and payload length. That fixed-width prefix is the key design decision: the parser always knows exactly how many bytes to read next without scanning for delimiters, which makes the networking layer straightforward to implement correctly. The outermost layer is a thread-per-connection server where the main thread accepts incoming connections in a blocking loop and hands each one off to a dedicated OS thread via `std.Thread.spawn()`. Each connection thread runs its own synchronous I/O loop, reading the fixed 8-byte frame prefix first and then the payload, so partial reads are handled naturally by blocking until the required bytes arrive rather than by a state machine returning to an event loop. Because each thread owns its connection exclusively, a slow or misbehaving client blocks only that thread and has no effect on any other connection. The entire system shares a single allocator passed from `main()` down through every layer, making the memory ownership model explicit and the allocator itself easy to swap out — replacing `init.gpa` with a pool allocator tuned to a specific workload requires changing exactly one line.

Before writing a single line of implementation code, the most consequential decision must be made: *how will the server handle multiple simultaneous clients?* The answer to that question determines the shape of every component that follows — the connection state, the read buffer strategy, and the way the protocol parser is structured. We examine the two dominant models and explain why one is the right fit for `zcache`.

Architecture: Event-driven vs. Thread-per-connection

The choice between an event-driven architecture and a thread-per-connection model defines the fundamental scaling characteristics of a high-performance server. In the **thread-per-connection** approach, the OS assigns a dedicated kernel thread to every incoming client. While this model is conceptually simple and allows for straightforward synchronous code, it suffers from significant overhead as the number of concurrent connections grows. Each thread requires its own stack memory — often several megabytes by default — and the cost of context switching between thousands of threads can lead to a "thrashing" effect where the CPU spends more time managing task metadata than executing application logic. This model is generally preferred only when the total connection count is low and the workload is compute-intensive rather than I/O-bound.

In contrast, an **event-driven architecture** utilizes a single-threaded or small-pool execution model centered around a non-blocking I/O loop. By leveraging system calls like `epoll(2)` on Linux or `kqueue(2)` on BSD and macOS, the server can monitor thousands of file descriptors simultaneously without the memory footprint of multiple stacks. When a socket becomes ready for reading or writing, the kernel notifies the application, which then dispatches a callback or resumes a task to process the data. This approach maximizes throughput by keeping the CPU pipeline full of useful work and minimizing the overhead of the operating system scheduler. In Zig, this pattern is particularly powerful because its explicit nature allows for precise control over the event loop, memory allocation, and the state machines required to track asynchronous requests.

The decision to implement one over the other in a cache server depends largely on the expected latency profile and hardware concurrency. For a system designed to handle the ten thousand concurrent connections problem, the event-driven model is the industry standard. However, to fully utilize modern multi-core processors, a *hybrid* "multi-threaded event loop" is often employed, where a small number of threads each run an independent event loop. This prevents a single slow request from blocking the entire server while avoiding the memory exhaustion associated with the legacy thread-per-connection style. By aligning the number of event loops with the number of physical CPU cores, we achieve mechanical sympathy, ensuring that the cache server operates at the theoretical limits of the underlying hardware.

The server uses a **thread-per-connection architecture**. The main thread binds and listens via `std.Io.net.IpAddress.listen()`, then loops on `listener.accept(io)`. Each accepted connection is wrapped in a heap-allocated `ConnCtx` struct — holding the `std.Io`, the stream, the cache pointer, the allocator, and the configured buffer size — and handed off to a detached OS thread via `std.Thread.spawn()`. Heap allocation is necessary because the spawned thread outlives the stack frame that created it; the thread owns the context and frees it on exit. Each connection thread runs `serveClient()`, which allocates two per-connection byte slices (one for reading, one for writing) and wraps the stream in a buffered reader and a buffered writer from `std.Io.net.Stream`. It then enters a synchronous loop: read exactly 8 bytes into a prefix buffer with `readSliceAll()`, parse the frame header to extract the payload length, read exactly that many bytes, parse the command, dispatch to `handleRequest()`, and repeat. `readSliceAll()` blocks until the buffer is exactly full or raises `error.EndOfStream` on a clean or mid-frame disconnect — both are treated as a normal close by the caller. Because the I/O is blocking, there is no `WouldBlock` bookkeeping, no event loop, and no `poll(2)`, `fcntl(2)`, or `O_NONBLOCK` anywhere in the codebase. `handleRequest()` receives the already-parsed `proto.Request` value and the buffered writer. It switches exhaustively over the tagged union — the Zig compiler rejects the code if any command variant is unhandled — calls the appropriate cache method, writes a response with `proto.writeResponse()`, and flushes the writer so the client never waits on buffered data. The GET branch allocates a temporary encoding buffer via `encodeGetPayload()` and frees it with `defer` immediately after writing; by the time the deferred free runs, the bytes have already been copied into the write buffer. The only shared state is the Cache, which carries its own Mutex. Everything else — buffers, frame staging, the buffered reader, and writer — is private to the connection thread.

Thread-per-connection is the right choice for this implementation given the workload characteristics. Each cache operation — a hash map lookup, an LRU list update, a mutex acquire and release — completes in microseconds. At that speed, the per-operation cost dominates the per-connection overhead, and the simplicity of blocking I/O with no event loop, no `poll(2)`, and no `O_NONBLOCK` bookkeeping makes the code straightforward to read, test, and debug. The model does not scale to thousands of simultaneous connections — each thread carries its own stack, typically 8 MiB on Linux, so a thousand connections consume roughly 8 GB of virtual address space before a single byte of cache data is stored. Scaling beyond a few hundred connections would require combining sharded locking with an async front end of the kind built in the previous chapter, replacing the per-connection thread with a lightweight task and keeping the fast synchronous cache operations on worker threads. That combination is left as an exercise — the groundwork is already in place from the previous chapters, and zcache is a natural starting point for applying it.

With the architecture chosen, the next question is what the server and its clients will say to each other. A server is only as robust as its protocol parser — if the protocol requires scanning for delimiters or makes ambiguous frame boundaries possible, the state machine becomes fragile and error-prone. We therefore design the wire protocol first, before writing any networking code, so that the parser has a solid specification to implement against.

Wire protocol: designing a binary protocol (ZEMP)

The **Zcache Exchange Message Protocol** (ZEMP) is designed to eliminate the overhead of text-based parsing by using a fixed-width binary header that allows the parser to determine the exact byte length of an incoming message without scanning for delimiters. This approach makes the protocol robust against payloads containing arbitrary bytes, such as newlines or null characters, which often break simpler text protocols. By using big-endian u32 integers for length fields and u16 for key lengths, ZEMP ensures a consistent machine-readable format that maps efficiently to Zig's memory-backed structures.

A protocol specification is only useful if it translates into an unambiguous byte layout. We now define that layout precisely, because every subsequent component — the state machine, the request parser, and the response encoder — derives its correctness from the guarantees the frame structure provides.

Defining the binary frame structure (header, length, payload)

The binary frame structure begins with an 8-byte prefix consisting of a 4-byte `FrameHeader` and a 4-byte payload length. The header is declared as a `packed struct(u32)`, which guarantees a 4-byte footprint with no padding, mapping the four fields directly onto the wire layout: a magic byte (`0x5A`) that catches misaligned reads, a version byte, a type byte that carries either a command identifier in a request or a status code in a response, and a reserved flags byte that must be `0x00`. The packed struct(u32) declaration is the correct Zig idiom here — it makes the on-wire layout and the in-memory layout identical, so the compiler can reason about the struct size and field offsets without any hidden padding. Following the header, the remaining four bytes of the prefix carry the payload length as a big-endian `u32`, giving the parser the exact byte count it needs before reading the variable-length body.

The frame structure tells us what a complete message looks like. The state machine tells us how to recognize one when bytes arrive in arbitrary fragments over a TCP stream. These two concerns are deliberately separated: the frame structure is a static specification, while the state machine is the dynamic process of assembling bytes into frames over time.

Implementing a state machine to parse streaming TCP data

To interpret this stream, the server implements a state machine that tracks the parser position within each frame. The connection starts in the Reading Prefix state, where `readSliceAll()` blocks the thread until exactly 8 bytes have arrived. Once the header is parsed and the expected payload length is known, the machine transitions to the Reading Payload state. This separation of concerns ensures that the protocol logic remains deterministic regardless of how TCP fragments the incoming data across multiple reads.

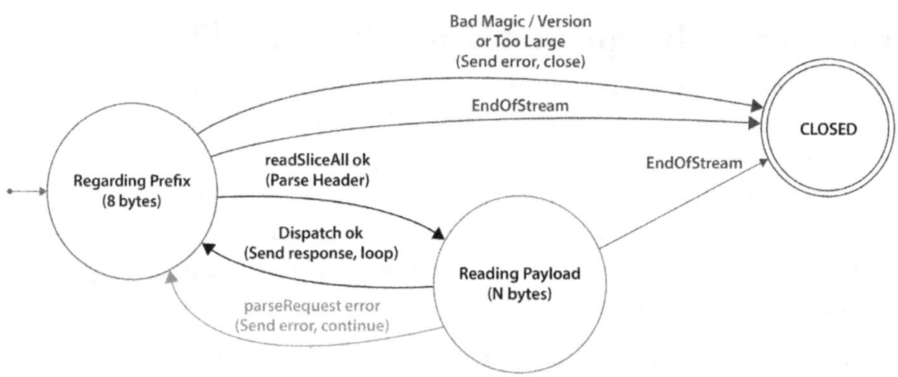

Figure 10.1 – The State Machine

The logic behind this graph reflects the synchronous, blocking nature of the thread-per-connection model. From Reading Prefix, a successful `readSliceAll()` and header parse transitions the machine to Reading Payload. Once the payload is fully read and dispatched, a successful response transitions the machine back to Reading Prefix, ready to process the next frame on the same connection. A `parseRequest` error also returns to Reading Prefix after sending an error response, allowing the connection to continue. The `CLOSED` terminal state is reached from either state on `EndOfStream` — a clean or mid-frame disconnect — and from Reading Prefix when prefix parsing detects a bad magic byte, unsupported version, or a payload length exceeding the 64 MiB `MAX_PAYLOAD_LEN` limit, all of which cause the server to send an error and close the connection immediately.

> **Note**
>
> The frame parser does not use an explicit state machine — no `State` enum, no state field on the connection struct, no transition table. The thread call stack and program counter serve that role instead. When `readSliceAll()` blocks waiting for bytes that have not yet arrived, the thread is paused at exactly the point in the call stack where it needs more data. When the bytes arrive, execution resumes from the same point. The two-phase read — first the fixed 8-byte prefix, then the variable-length payload — is simply two sequential blocking calls. Blocking I/O makes this natural: the call stack encodes the parser position for free, without any bookkeeping. An event-driven implementation cannot rely on this property, which is precisely why the async proxy in the previous chapter requires explicit state to track where each connection is in its read sequence.

The state machine defines the transitions between parser states but says nothing about what happens when the bytes needed for a transition have not yet arrived. That is the problem of partial reads and buffer fragmentation — the practical reality of working with TCP — and it is where the state machine design pays off most clearly.

Handling partial reads and buffer fragmentation

Handling partial reads and buffer fragmentation is a core requirement of this architecture, as TCP does not guarantee that data arrives in the same chunks it was sent. If a read call provides only a fraction of a frame, the blocking `readSliceAll()` call simply waits on the thread until the remaining bytes arrive, then continues from exactly where it left off — no state needs to be saved between calls because the thread itself preserves the execution context. Conversely, if a single connection delivers multiple frames back to back, the connection thread processes every complete frame in sequence before the next `readSliceAll()` call is issued, ensuring that no data is lost or skipped between iterations.

With the networking layer fully specified, we turn inward to the component that gives `zcache` its purpose: the storage engine. Before writing any code, it is worth understanding precisely why the LRU cache requires two data structures rather than one, because that reasoning directly determines the shape of every struct and every function in `cache.zig`.

Why do we need both a hash map and a linked list

The efficiency of a high-performance cache is primarily determined by its ability to perform two disparate operations in constant time: *data retrieval* and *metadata maintenance*. A hash map is the natural choice for the former, providing *O(1)* average-case complexity for looking up a value by its key. Without the hash map, the server would be forced to perform linear searches through memory, a process that becomes catastrophically slow as the dataset grows. However, while a hash map excels at addressing data, it is inherently unordered. It possesses no internal mechanism to track the "age" or "relevance" of an entry, which is a critical requirement for implementing an eviction policy like **Least Recently Used** (LRU). To solve the problem of knowing which item to discard when the cache is full, a second data structure must be overlaid onto the first. *Integrating a doubly linked list alongside the hash map provides the necessary ordering to track access patterns without sacrificing lookup speed.* In this hybrid strategy, each entry in the hash map contains pointers to its neighbors in the linked list. When an item is accessed or inserted, it is moved to the "front" of the list, marking it as the most recently used. Conversely, the item at the "tail" of the list is identified as the least recently used and becomes the first candidate for eviction. By maintaining these pointers, we can reorder the elements in *O(1)* time. This dual-structure approach ensures that the "hot" data remains easily accessible while the "cold" data naturally migrates toward the exit, allowing the cache to self-manage its memory footprint with minimal computational overhead. The logic behind this redundancy is a trade-off between memory consumption and temporal complexity. While storing two sets of pointers for every entry increases the memory overhead per item, it eliminates the need for periodic "scans" or sorting operations that would introduce latency spikes. In a systems language like Zig, we can optimize this further by using "intrusive" linked lists. Instead of allocating a separate node for the list that points to our data, we embed the `next` and `prev` pointers directly within the data record itself. This layout improves spatial locality and reduces the number of calls to the allocator, ensuring that when the CPU fetches a cache entry to check its value, it also pulls the metadata required to update its position in the

The argument for combining a hash map with a doubly linked list is now clear. What remains is to turn that argument into working Zig code — implementing the Node, the list primitives, and the public API in a way that keeps the invariants visible and the memory ownership unambiguous.

Storage engine: implementing the LRU cache

The storage engine implements an LRU cache by combining a hash map for O(1) lookups with a doubly linked list for *O(1)* eviction and promotion. Each entry is stored as a `Node` that embeds its key, value, expiry timestamp, and two pointers to its neighbors in the list, allowing the cache to track access order efficiently. When a key is accessed via `get()`, the corresponding node is promoted by detaching it from its current position and reattaching it at the head of the list — making it the most recently used entry. When the cache reaches its capacity, `set()` immediately evicts the node at the tail of the list before allocating the new entry, ensuring memory usage never exceeds the configured bound. TTL expiry is handled separately and lazily: rather than running a background sweep thread, each `get()` checks whether the entry's timestamp has elapsed and evicts it on the spot if so, returning null to the caller as if the key were absent. This distinction matters — capacity eviction is eager and happens on every insert when the cache is full, while TTL expiry is deferred until the next access, keeping the implementation simple and the hot path free of timer machinery.

The implementation of the LRU cache begins at the bottom of the data structure stack, with the building block that makes *O(1)* eviction and promotion possible. Before the hash map can be introduced, the linked list must exist because every pointer the map stores points to a node in the list. We start by defining that node and the two primitive operations — detach and attachHead — that all higher-level cache operations are composed from.

The doubly linked list

The **doubly linked list** is the ordering backbone of the LRU cache. Every entry is represented by a `Node` struct that embeds its key, value, expiry timestamp, and two pointers — `prev` toward the most-recently-used head and `next` toward the least-recently-used tail. Embedding the pointers directly inside the data record rather than in a separate wrapper node is the "intrusive" list pattern: when the CPU fetches a node to read its value, the `prev` and `next` pointers arrive in the same cache line at no extra cost. All mutations to the list are confined to two private functions. `detach` splices a node out of its current position by bridging its neighbors together, leaving the node floating with both pointers set to null. `attachHead` prepends a floating node at the **Most Recently Used** (MRU) end by wiring it in front of the current head. Every higher-level operation — `get`, `set`, and `eviction` — is composed entirely from these two primitives, which makes the list invariants easy to audit: `head.prev` is always null, `tail.next` is always null, and for every node `N` in the list, `N.prev.next == N` and `N.next.prev == N`.

The following are the only functions allowed to mutate `head`, `tail`, `prev` and `next`:

```
fn detach(self: *Cache, node: *Node) void {
    if (node.prev) |p| p.next = node.next
    else self.head = node.next;

    if (node.next) |n| n.prev = node.prev
    else self.tail = node.prev;
    node.prev = null;
    node.next = null;
}
```

`detach()` removes a node from wherever it sits in the doubly linked list without freeing it. It closes the gap left by the removal by rewiring the neighboring nodes: if the node has a predecessor, that predecessor's next pointer is updated to skip over the removed node; if it does not, the node was the head of the list, and its successor becomes the new head. The same logic applies on the right side — if the node has a successor, that successor's prev pointer is updated; if it does not, the node was the tail and its predecessor becomes the new tail. Finally, the node's own prev and next pointers are set to null, leaving it floating and ready to be repositioned or freed. The function is the single place in the cache that touches head, tail, prev, and next for removal — nothing else in the implementation unlinks a node directly.

attachHead() takes a floating node and prepends it at the head of the list, making it the most recently used entry. It sets the node's next pointer to the current head and clears its prev pointer, then updates the current head's prev to point back at the new node before installing the new node as head. The final guard handles the empty list case: if tail is null, the list was empty before this insertion, and the new node is both head and tail.

```
fn attachHead(self: *Cache, node: *Node) void {
    node.next = self.head;
    node.prev = null;
    if (self.head) |h| h.prev = node;
    self.head = node;
    if (self.tail == null) self.tail = node;
}
```

Together, detach() and attachHead() are the only two functions that mutate the list structure — every cache operation that needs to reorder entries, whether a get() promoting a hit or a set() inserting a new entry, composes these two primitives.

The linked list provides ordered access to every entry in the cache, but it cannot answer the question "does key X exist?" in better than O(n) time. That is the role of the hash map: to give the server a direct pointer to any node in constant time, turning what would be a list traversal into a single lookup.

The Hash Map wrapper

The **Hash Map** is a std.StringHashMap(*Node) that maps a key string to a pointer to its corresponding Node in the linked list. It provides the *O(1)* lookup that makes promotion and deletion fast: given a key, the map returns a direct pointer to the node, which can then be detached and reattached in the list without any traversal. The critical memory detail is that the key stored in the map is not the caller's slice — it is a slice pointing into node.key, the heap-allocated copy owned by the node itself. This means the map key remains valid for the entire lifetime of the node and is never left dangling when the caller's original slice goes out of scope.

The map is pre-allocated at initialization time via ensureTotalCapacity to avoid rehashing on early inserts, which would otherwise cause unpredictable latency spikes during the warm-up phase of a live cache.

With both data structures in place, the cache is functionally complete. What remains is to account for every byte it allocates. In a long-running server, a single missed free is not a bug that surfaces in testing — it is a slow leak that accumulates over days until the process is killed by the OS. We close the storage engine discussion by auditing every allocation site and its paired deallocation.

Memory management

The cache owns all memory associated with every entry. On insertion, three allocations are made: one allocator.create(Node) for the node struct itself, one allocator.dupe(u8, key) for an owned copy of the key, and one allocator.dupe(u8, value) for an owned copy of the value. All three are paired with corresponding frees inside freeNode, which is the single deallocation site called by every eviction path — LRU eviction, explicit delete, TTL expiry, and deinit. The use of errdefer immediately after each allocation ensures that a failure partway through an insert — for example, an out-of-memory error when duplicating the value — correctly frees the key and node that were already allocated, leaving the cache in a consistent state with no leak. On set updates to an existing key, only the value is reallocated; the key is unchanged, and its owned slice is reused, halving the allocator pressure for write-heavy workloads. The entire cache is driven by a single std.mem.Allocator interface passed in at init time. In the current server, main() provides an init.gpa which detects leaks and double-frees in debug builds. Swapping it for a fixed-buffer or pool allocator tuned to a known entry-size distribution requires no changes to the cache itself — the allocator interface is the only contract between the storage engine and its memory source.

Here is the removeNode() implementation:

```
fn removeNode(self: *Cache, node: *Node) void {
    _ = self.map.remove(node.key);
    self.detach(node);
    self.freeNode(node);
    self.len -= 1;
}
```

removeNode() is the single entry point for fully deleting a cache entry. It performs three operations in sequence: it removes the key from the hash map via self.map.remove(), unlinks the node from the doubly linked list via detach(), and frees all memory associated with the node via freeNode(). It then decrements the cache length counter. The ordering is important — the node must be unlinked from both the map and the list before its memory is freed; otherwise, the map or list could hold a dangling pointer to deallocated memory.

And here is the freeNode() implementation:

```
fn freeNode(self: *Cache, node: *Node) void {
    self.allocator.free(node.key);
    self.allocator.free(node.value);
    self.allocator.destroy(node);
}
```

freeNode() handles the memory side of deletion. A node owns three heap allocations: the key slice, the value slice, and the node struct itself. freeNode() frees all three in order — key first, then value, then the node — using the same allocator that created them. The doc comment makes the contract explicit: the caller is responsible for removing the node from the list and map before calling freeNode(). Calling it on a node that is still reachable from the list or map would leave dangling pointers behind. In practice, freeNode() is only ever called from removeNode(), which enforces that contract, and from the cache's deinit() method, which tears down the entire structure at once.

To bridge the gap between architectural theory and a running binary, we must examine how these disparate components are wired together by presenting actual code.

Learning about server implementation details

Moving from the abstract design of an architectural model to a working implementation requires translating high-level goals into concrete Zig structures that manage the lifecycle of the cache. In this section, we examine the internal mechanics of zcache. All files that follow are orchestrated by build.zig, which defines five build targets (run, client, cli, bench, test). Among them, the benchmark is compiled with ReleaseFast while everything else uses the default Debug mode. Last, zig build test runs the unit tests across cache.zig and protocol.zig.

main.zig is the entry point of zcache. It is deliberately thin as its only job is to parse command line flags, wire the three layers together, and call server.run(). It uses a single init.gpa and passes it down to both Cache.init() and Server.init(), forming the single - allocator ownership model that the rest of the codebase depends on. The four supported flags — --host, --port, --capacity, and --max-clients (this is left as an exercise for the reader) — map directly onto ServerConfig and CacheConfig structs with sensible defaults, so the server can be started with no arguments at all. A fatal() helper handles argument errors by logging and calling `std.process.exit(1)`, avoiding the runtime stack trace that `return error.X` from `main()` would produce. The banner printed on startup summarizes the active configuration so that the operator can confirm settings at a glance without reading a config file.

The `cache.zig` file implements the entire storage engine and has no knowledge of networking. It is organized into six numbered sections. The `Node` struct in section one is the building block of the doubly linked list: it embeds the key slice, value slice, an optional expiry timestamp, and `prev`, `next` pointers directly inside the record — the intrusive list pattern that ensures metadata and data arrive in the same cache line. Section two defines `CacheConfig`, a small struct holding the capacity limit and a hash map pre-allocation hint. Section three defines the `Cache` struct itself, which combines a `std.StringHashMap(*Node)` for *O(1)* key lookup with the linked list for *O(1)* access-order maintenance and wraps both in a `std.Io.Mutex`. The public API — `get()`, `set()`, `delete()`, and `count()` — all acquire the mutex on entry and release it via `defer`. `get()` performs a lazy TTL check on every hit, evicts, and returns null if the entry has expired. The `set()` function handles three distinct paths: an in-place update when the key already exists, an eager eviction of the tail node when the cache is at capacity, and a fresh allocation for new keys, using `errdefer` at each allocation site to guarantee no leak on partial failure. Section four contains the two list primitives, `detach()` and `attachHead()`, which are the only functions permitted to mutate `head`, `tail`, `prev`, and `next`; all higher-level operations compose from these two. Section five documents the memory ownership model in comments, and section six contains six unit tests covering basic operations, LRU eviction order, in-place updates, deletion idempotency, TTL expiry, and hit/miss statistics. Let us see some of its parts in more detail, starting with `Node`:

```
pub const Node = struct {
    key: []const u8,
    value: []const u8,
    expires_at_ms: ?i64,
    prev: ?*Node,
    next: ?*Node,
};
```

The `Node` structure defines the fundamental unit of storage in the storage engine, serving as the connective tissue between the hash map and the access-ordered list. As memory ownership is a primary concern in this design, the `key` and `value` fields are constant byte slices that refer to heap-allocated copies managed entirely by the cache. This isolation protects the storage engine from external mutations or premature freeing of memory by the caller. The `prev` and `next` fields are optional pointers that form the doubly linked list. These links allow for *O(1)* reordering: when an entry is touched, the server can detach it from its current position and prepend it to the head of the list by updating exactly four pointers. This mechanism allows the storage engine to maintain a strict gradient from **Most Recently Used** (MRU) at the head to **Least Recently Used** (LRU) at the tail, ensuring that the eviction candidate is always known without requiring a linear scan of the dataset.

Let us continue with the `get()` public function implementation:

```
pub fn get(
    self: *Cache,
    io: std.Io,
    gpa: std.mem.Allocator,
    key: []const u8,
) !?[]const u8 {
    try self.mutex.lock(io);
    defer self.mutex.unlock(io);

    const node = self.map.get(key) orelse {
        self.stats.misses += 1;
        return null;
    };

    // Lazy TTL check: evict on first access after expiry.
    if (isExpired(node)) {
        self.stats.expirations += 1;
        self.stats.misses += 1;
        self.removeNode(node);
        return null;
    }

    // Promote to MRU – the heart of LRU semantics.
    self.detach(node);
    self.attachHead(node);
    self.stats.hits += 1;

    // Copy the value while still holding the lock (see doc comment).
    return try gpa.dupe(u8, node.value);
}
```

The `get()` method is the primary entry point for data retrieval, and its implementation reveals the interplay between concurrency control, temporal safety, and the Least Recently Used (LRU) eviction policy. We begin by acquiring the cache internal mutex to ensure that the hash map lookup and the subsequent modification of the linked list pointers occur as a single atomic operation. By using the `defer` keyword to unlock the mutex, we guarantee that the lock is released regardless of whether the function results in a hit, a miss, or a lazy expiration, maintaining system stability without manual cleanup boilerplate. The lookup itself utilizes the hash map to provide the average-case *O(1)* performance necessary for high-performance caching. If the key is not present, we record the miss in our runtime statistics and return `null`. However, finding a node in the map is only the first step; we must then perform a lazy expiration check. Instead of employing a background worker to scan for stale data, we evaluate the time-to-live (TTL) at the moment of access, which keeps the system execution profile deterministic and simplifies the design. If the absolute expiration timestamp has passed, the `removeNode()` helper is called to purge the entry from both the map and the list. For a successful hit, the final responsibility of the method is to maintain the temporal integrity of the LRU queue. We call `detach()` to splice the node out of its current neighbors in the doubly linked list and `attachHead()` to place it at the "most recently used" end. The method does not return a pointer into the node's memory. While still holding the lock, it duplicates the value into a fresh, caller-owned allocation. This copy is what makes `get()` safe under concurrency: the moment the mutex is released, another thread may `set()` or `delete()` this same key and free the underlying bytes — so any slice that aliased the node's storage would dangle. By copying before unlocking, we ensure the value the caller receives outlives the next mutation. *This decision prioritizes performance by avoiding a memory copy but requires the caller to understand that the returned slice aliases* the cache memory and is only valid until the next mutation of the storage engine.

Next, we present the `delete()` function, which removes a key from the cache and reports whether the key was present:

```
pub fn delete(self: *Cache, io: std.Io, key: []const u8) !bool {
    try self.mutex.lock(io);
    defer self.mutex.unlock(io);
    const node = self.map.get(key) orelse return false;
    self.removeNode(node);
    return true;
}
```

The function begins by acquiring the mutex, with `defer self.mutex.unlock(io)` guaranteeing the lock is released regardless of which path the function takes — a pattern used consistently across the entire public API. The single line of logic that follows combines the lookup and the absent-key check in one expression: `self.map.get(key)orelse return false` attempts to find the key in the hash map and returns `false` immediately if it is not present, without touching the linked list at all. This is what makes `delete()` idempotent — calling it on a key that does not exist is not an error, it is a defined and safe outcome. If the key is found, `removeNode()` handles all three cleanup operations atomically: removing the entry from the hash map, splicing the node out of the doubly linked list via `detach()`, and freeing the node's key slice, value slice, and struct memory via `freeNode()`. The function then returns `true` to inform the caller that a deletion took place. The `bool` return type is an intentional design choice worth noting. Rather than returning an error for a missing key — which would force every call site to handle a `try` — the function treats *key not found* as a normal, expected outcome and communicates it through the return value. The command line client and the test client both rely on this: the `NOT_FOUND` response sent back to a `DEL` command for an absent key comes directly from this `false` return value being checked in `handleRequest()` (from `src/server.zig`), which is presented next:

```
fn handleRequest(
    io: std.Io,
    request: proto.Request,
    cache: *Cache,
    allocator: std.mem.Allocator,
    w: anytype,
) !void {
    switch (request) {
        .ping => {
            try proto.writeResponse(w, .ok, "PONG");
        },
        .get => |req| {

            if (try cache.get(io, allocator, req.key)) |value| {
                defer allocator.free(value);
                const encoded = try proto.encodeGetPayload(
                    allocator,
                    value,
                );
                defer allocator.free(encoded);
                try proto.writeResponse(w, .ok, encoded);
            } else {
                try proto.writeResponse(w, .not_found, "");
            }
        },
        .set => |req| {
            try cache.set(io, req.key, req.value, req.ttl_ms);
            try proto.writeResponse(w, .ok, "");
        },
```

```
            .del => |req| {
                const deleted = try cache.delete(io, req.key);
                const status: proto.Status =
                    if (deleted) .ok else .not_found;
                try proto.writeResponse(w, status, "");
            },
        }
        // Flush after every response so the client never waits in a buffer.
        try w.flush();
    }
```

`handleRequest()` is where the protocol layer and the storage engine meet. It receives an already-parsed `proto.Request` value and a writer rather than a raw payload slice and a connection. The `switch` on the tagged union remains exhaustive: the Zig compiler will reject the code if any command variant is unhandled, making it impossible to silently ignore a new command added to the protocol. Each branch calls the appropriate cache method (now with an `io` parameter for async-aware I/O) and writes a response directly via `proto.writeResponse()`. The `GET` branch still allocates a temporary buffer via `encodeGetPayload()` and frees it with `defer` immediately after writing — the response bytes have been copied into the writer by that point, so the temporary allocation is no longer needed. After every branch, the writer is explicitly flushed so the client never waits on buffered data.

Last, we present the implementation of `set()`, which is the entry point for both inserting new data and updating existing entries while enforcing the cache capacity limits.

```
pub fn set(
    self: *Cache,
    io: std.Io,
    key: []const u8,
    value: []const u8,
    ttl_ms: u64,
) !void {
    try self.mutex.lock(io);
    defer self.mutex.unlock(io);
    const expiry = toExpiry(ttl_ms);

    if (self.map.get(key)) |node| {
        // Replace value in-place – no need to reallocate the key.
        self.allocator.free(node.value);
        node.value = try self.allocator.dupe(u8, value);
```

```
        node.expires_at_ms = expiry;
        self.detach(node);
        self.attachHead(node); // update counts as a "use"
        return;
    }

    if (self.len >= self.capacity) {
        if (self.tail) |lru| {
            self.stats.evictions += 1;
            self.removeNode(lru);
        }
    }

    const node = try self.allocator.create(Node);
    errdefer self.allocator.destroy(node);
    const owned_key = try self.allocator.dupe(u8, key);
    errdefer self.allocator.free(owned_key);
    const owned_value = try self.allocator.dupe(u8, value);
    errdefer self.allocator.free(owned_value);
    node.* = .{
        .key = owned_key,
        .value = owned_value,
        .expires_at_ms = expiry,
        .prev = null,
        .next = null,
    };

    try self.map.put(node.key, node);
    self.attachHead(node);
    self.len += 1;
}
```

Once again, the code acquires a mutex lock to ensure thread safety, followed immediately by calculating an absolute expiry timestamp using the provided time-to-live duration.

The method prioritizes updates to existing keys by checking the hash map first. If a match is found, the engine performs an in-place update by freeing the old value and duplicating the new one, thereby avoiding the cost of reallocating the key or the node structure itself. This update also triggers an LRU promotion, detaching the node from its current position and reattaching it at the head to reflect its fresh status. When handling a new key, the engine must first ensure that memory is available. If the cache is at capacity, it performs a preemptive eviction by identifying the tail of the linked list — the least recently used item — and removing it from both the map and the list. Following the eviction, the engine proceeds to allocate the new node and its components. The use of `errdefer` here is a crucial Zig idiom, as it ensures that if any subsequent allocation (like duplicating the value) fails, previously allocated memory for the node or the key is automatically cleaned up. Finally, the new node's key slice is used as the key for the hash map entry, ensuring that the map refers to memory owned by the cache rather than the caller's transient stack. Once the map is updated and the node is attached to the head, the total count is incremented to reflect the new state.

The unit tests in `cache.zig` verify that the implementation matches the theory described in the preceding sections. The most instructive of the six tests is the LRU eviction order test, which confirms that the doubly linked list and hash map cooperate correctly to evict the right entry when the cache reaches capacity:

```
test "LRU eviction: least-recently-used entry is removed first" {
    // Insert A, B, C  → access order (MRU→LRU):  C · B · A
    // GET "A"            → promote A  → order:      A · C · B
    // SET "D"  (full) → evict tail B → order:    D · A · C
    var t: std.Io.Threaded = .init_single_threaded;
    const io = t.io();
    var cache = try Cache.init(
        std.testing.allocator,
        .{ .capacity = 3 },
    );
    defer cache.deinit();

    const a = std.testing.allocator;
    // ttl_ms = 0 means "no expiry";
    // these entries leave only via LRU eviction.
    try cache.set(io, "A", "1", 0);
    try cache.set(io, "B", "2", 0);
    try cache.set(io, "C", "3", 0);

    if (try cache.get(io, a, "A")) |v| a.free(v);
    try cache.set(io, "D", "4", 0);



    try std.testing.expect(try cache.get(io, a, "B") == null);
    inline for (.{ "A", "C", "D" }) |k| {
        const v = (try cache.get(io, a, k)).?;
```

```
            a.free(v);
        }
        try std.testing.expectEqual(
            @as(u64, 1),
            cache.stats.evictions,
        );
}
```

The test inserts three entries into a capacity-3 cache in order `A`, `B`, and `C`. At that point, the access order from MRU to LRU is `C → B → A`, because each insertion lands at the head. A `get("A")` then promotes `A` to the head, shifting the order to `A → C → B`, making `B` the least recently used entry at the tail. When `D` is inserted, and the cache is full, `set()` evicts the tail (`B`) before allocating the new node. The assertions confirm that `B` is gone, that `A`, `C`, and `D` are all present, and that exactly one eviction was recorded in the statistics. Running `zig build test` should report all tests passing across both `cache.zig` and `protocol.zig`.

The `protocol.zig` source code file defines ZEMP and contains no networking code; it only serializes and deserializes bytes. The file header documents the complete wire format: every frame begins with an 8-byte prefix consisting of a magic byte `0x5A`, a version byte, a type byte carrying either a command or a status code, a reserved flags byte, and a big-endian `u32` payload length. The payload layout varies by command — `PING` carries nothing, `GET` and `DEL` carry a `u16`-prefixed key, and `SET` carries a key, a `u32`-prefixed value, and a `u64` TTL. The `parsePrefix()` function validates the magic byte and version, rejects payloads exceeding the 64 MiB `MAX_PAYLOAD_LEN` limit, and returns both the parsed `FrameHeader` and the declared payload length — the two error transitions in the state machine diagram both originate here. The `Request` type is a tagged union over the `Command` enum, allowing the compiler to enforce exhaustive handling of every command type in `handleRequest`. The `parseRequest()` function is zero-copy: all key and value slices in the returned `Request` point directly into the caller's payload buffer. Response emission is split across three functions: `writeResponse()` builds the 8-byte prefix on the stack and writes it with the payload in two calls, while `encodeGetPayload()` and `encodeErrorPayload()` heap-allocate the specific payload shapes needed for `GET` hits and error responses. Eight unit tests cover prefix validation, bad magic detection, payload size rejection, and round-trip encoding for every command type.

> **Note**
>
> `MAX_PAYLOAD_LEN` and the per-connection `read_buf_size` both count payload bytes, but they are independent settings that answer different questions, and it is worth keeping them straight. `MAX_PAYLOAD_LEN` (64 MiB) is a protocol-level policy: the largest

> value a client is permitted to store in a single request. `read_buf_size` (a few kilobytes by default) is an I/O-level mechanism: the size of the staging buffer the connection reader uses to pull bytes off the socket. There is no requirement that they match, and good reason that they do not. When a legitimate client sends a value near the 64 MiB ceiling, the server allocates one payload buffer of the exact declared size and then calls `readSliceAll()` to fill it; because the socket delivers data in whatever chunks the network hands over and the reader's own buffer is only kilobytes wide, that single logical read becomes many small physical reads, looping until the full payload has been assembled. This is correct and intended. Sizing every connection's standing buffer to the largest payload the protocol allows would waste megabytes per idle connection to optimize a request shape that is rare; instead, the small fixed buffer handles the common case cheaply, and the one allocation that scales with the request — the exact-sized payload buffer — exists only for the lifetime of that request before `deferallocator.free(payload)` reclaims it. The apparent mismatch between a 64 MiB protocol limit and a kilobyte-scale buffer is therefore not an inconsistency to reconcile but an intentional separation of concerns: the limit bounds what the client is allowed to send, while the buffer governs how much data is resident in memory at once while that request is read.

The `parsePrefix()` function acts as the primary gatekeeper for the messaging protocol, responsible for validating and decomposing the first eight bytes of any incoming frame:

```
pub fn parsePrefix(buf: *const [FRAME_PREFIX_LEN]u8) !struct {
    header: FrameHeader,
    payload_len: u32,
} {
    const magic = buf[0];
    if (magic != MAGIC) return error.BadMagic;
    const version = buf[1];
    if (version != VERSION) return error.UnsupportedVersion;

    const header = FrameHeader{
        .magic = magic,
        .version = version,
        .type_byte = buf[2],
        .flags = buf[3],
    };
```

```
    const payload_len = std.mem.readInt(u32, buf[4..8], .big);
    if (payload_len > MAX_PAYLOAD_LEN) return error.PayloadTooLarge;
    return .{ .header = header, .payload_len = payload_len };
}
```

The logic begins with a strict verification of the "magic" byte, which serves as a coarse-grained filter for stream alignment; if the first byte does not match our defined constant, the server immediately rejects the connection to prevent interpreting garbage data as a valid command. Similarly, verifying the protocol version ensures that both the client and server are operating on the same structural assumptions, preventing the subtle bugs that arise from mismatched feature sets or shifted header offsets. Once the metadata is verified, the function reconstructs the `FrameHeader` by mapping the first four bytes into a packed structure. This is followed by the extraction of the payload length from the remaining four bytes. A design decision here is the use of big-endian byte ordering via `std.mem.readInt()`, which standardizes the protocol across different hardware architectures, ensuring that a little-endian machine and a big-endian machine interpret the length field identically without requiring manual bit-shifting. The final step in the logic is a vital security check: validating that the declared `payload_len` does not exceed our maximum allowed threshold of 64 megabytes. Without this check, the server would be vulnerable to memory exhaustion attacks where a malicious client sends a small header claiming a multi-gigabyte payload, causing the server to crash during buffer allocation. By returning an error if the length is suspect, the function ensures that the subsequent parsing stages always operate within safe, pre-allocated memory boundaries.

Here is the `writeResponse()` implementation:

```
pub fn writeResponse(
    writer: anytype,
    status: Status,
    payload: []const u8,
) !void {
    // Build the 8-byte prefix on the stack — no heap allocation needed.
    var prefix: [FRAME_PREFIX_LEN]u8 = undefined;
    prefix[0] = MAGIC;
    prefix[1] = VERSION;
    prefix[2] = @intFromEnum(status);
    prefix[3] = 0x00; // flags — reserved
    std.mem.writeInt(
        u32,
        prefix[4..8],
```

```
        @intCast(payload.len),
        .big,
    );

    try writer.writeAll(&prefix);
    try writer.writeAll(payload);
}
```

`writeResponse()` serializes a ZEMP response frame into the caller-supplied writer without allocating any heap memory. It builds the 8-byte frame prefix entirely on the stack: byte 0 is the magic constant that identifies a ZEMP frame, byte 1 is the protocol version, byte 2 is the status code cast from the `Status` enum to its underlying integer representation, and byte 3 is the flags field, currently reserved and always zero. Bytes 4 through 7 carry the payload length as a big-endian `u32`, written using `std.mem.writeInt()` which handles the byte-order conversion and writes directly into the prefix slice. Once the prefix is assembled, two sequential `writeAll()` calls send it to the writer, followed by the payload bytes. The function takes an `anytype` writer rather than a concrete type, which means it works with any writer the caller provides — a buffered stream writer, a test buffer, or a direct socket writer — without requiring a separate implementation for each. The caller is responsible for flushing the writer after the response is written if the underlying implementation buffers output.

Last, we have the `encodeGetPayload()` function implementation:

```
pub fn encodeGetPayload(
    allocator: std.mem.Allocator,
    value: []const u8,
) ![]u8 {
    const buf = try allocator.alloc(u8, 4 + value.len);
    std.mem.writeInt(u32, buf[0..4], @intCast(value.len), .big);
    @memcpy(buf[4..], value);
    return buf;
}
```

`encodeGetPayload()` constructs the payload portion of a GET response frame. It allocates a buffer large enough to hold a 4-byte big-endian length prefix followed by the value bytes, then writes the value length into the first four bytes using `std.mem.writeInt()` and copies the value into the remainder using `@memcpy()`. The resulting buffer is returned to the caller, who owns it, and is responsible for freeing it after use. The length prefix is necessary because ZEMP GET responses carry the value as a length-prefixed byte string rather than relying on the outer frame's payload length alone — the receiver needs to know where the value ends in order to parse it correctly. The allocation is intentional: the value slice passed in may reference internal cache memory that cannot be held across a lock release, so `encodeGetPayload()` produces an independent copy that the caller can write to the network and then free safely. In `handleRequest()`, a `defer allocator.free(payload)` statement immediately follows the `encodeGetPayload()` call, ensuring the buffer is released as soon as the write completes.

The `server.zig` source code file is the largest and most structurally significant file, implementing the thread-per-connection server. It is divided into four sections. Section one defines `ServerConfig` with defaults for host, port, maximum concurrent connections, and the per-connection read buffer size. Section two defines the `Server` struct, whose `run()` method contains the main accept loop: it calls `std.Io.net.IpAddress.parseIp4()` to resolve the configured address, binds, and listens via `addr.listen(io, .{})` and then blocks on `listener.accept(io)` waiting for incoming connections. Section three defines `ConnCtx`, a heap-allocated struct holding the `std.Io` handle, the stream, the cache pointer, the allocator, and the configured buffer size and `connThread()`, the entry point for each spawned OS thread: it allocates the per-connection read and write buffers, calls `serveClient()`, and frees the context on exit. Section four contains `serveClient()`, `handleRequest()`, and `sendError()`. `serveClient()` enters a `while (true)` loop that reads exactly 8 bytes for the frame prefix via `readSliceAll()`, parses the header to extract the payload length, reads exactly that many bytes for the payload, dispatches the command to `handleRequest()` and repeats — blocking at each `readSliceAll()` call until the required bytes arrive rather than breaking out and yielding to an event loop.

The `run()` function serves as the orchestrator of the server lifecycle, transitioning the system from a static configuration to an active network service:

```
pub fn run(self: *Server, io: std.Io) !void {
    const addr = try std.Io.net.IpAddress.parseIp4(
        self.config.host,
        self.config.port,
    );
    var listener = try addr.listen(io, .{});
    defer listener.deinit(io);
    std.log.info(
        "zcache listening on {s}:{d}",
        .{ self.config.host, self.config.port },
    );
    while (true) {
        const stream = listener.accept(io) catch |err| {
            std.log.warn("accept error: {s}", .{@errorName(err)});
```

```
                continue;
            };

            const ctx = self.allocator.create(ConnCtx) catch |err| {
                std.log.warn(
                    "connection context allocation failed: {s}",
                    .{@errorName(err)},
                );
                stream.close(io);
                continue;
            };
            ctx.* = .{
                .io = io,
                .allocator = self.allocator,
                .stream = stream,
                .cache = self.cache,
                .buf_size = self.config.read_buf_size,
            };
            const thread = std.Thread.spawn(
                .{},
                connThread,
                .{ctx},
            ) catch |err|
                {
                    std.log.warn(
                        "thread spawn failed: {s}",
                        .{@errorName(err)},
                    );
                    stream.close(io);
                    self.allocator.destroy(ctx);
                    continue;
                };
            thread.detach();
        }
    }
```

The code begins by resolving the configured host and port into a binary address using `std.Io.net.IpAddress.parseIp4()` and calling `addr.listen(io, .{})` to bind and begin accepting connections. The `defer listener.deinit(io)` ensures the socket is released cleanly on exit. The function then enters an infinite loop, blocking on `listener.accept(io)` until a client connects. Accept errors are logged and skipped with `continue` rather than crashing the server, so a transient failure does not bring down all existing connections. For each successful connection, a `ConnCtx` struct is heap-allocated and populated with the `io` handle, allocator, stream, cache pointer, and buffer size. Heap allocation is necessary because the spawned thread outlives the current stack frame — the thread takes ownership of the context and is responsible for freeing it on exit. If the allocation fails, the stream is closed immediately to avoid a file descriptor leak. `std.Thread.spawn()` then launches `connThread()` with the context pointer and `thread.detach()` tells the runtime that the main loop will not join the thread later, allowing each connection to run its full lifecycle independently. If spawning fails, both the stream and the context are freed before the loop continues. The decision to use a thread-per-connection model keeps the concurrency logic straightforward: each connection gets its own blocking I/O loop with no `WouldBlock` bookkeeping, trading the per-thread memory overhead for a significant reduction in implementation complexity.

> **Note**
>
> A production deployment would set `TCP_NODELAY` on each accepted stream — disabling Nagle's algorithm — to avoid the tens-of-millisecond stalls that can occur when small cache responses interact with the receiver's delayed-ACK timer. Memcached, Redis, and HAProxy all set `TCP_NODELAY` on every accepted connection for exactly this reason.

A sharp-eyed reader will notice that `run()` is an unconditional `while (true)` loop with no way out: there is no signal handler, no shutdown flag, and no connection drain. Press Ctrl+C and the process is gone instantly — whatever request was mid-parse is abandoned, and the listening socket is left to expire through the kernel `TIME_WAIT` state rather than being closed deliberately. This is a real limitation, and in a service you intend to operate, you would close it. The standard remedy is small and well understood: a process-global `g_running: std.atomic.Value(bool)`, a `SIGTERM` handler whose only job is to flip that flag to false, and an accept loop that consults it each iteration — or that waits on the socket with a timeout via `Io.Select` — so the loop can fall through, run its `defer` cleanup, and let `main()` return in an orderly fashion. We have deliberately left this out of the chapter's server, and the omission is worth defending rather than hiding. The honest reason is pedagogical economy: a correct, graceful shutdown is not the four lines the flag suggests. A flag flipped from a signal handler does nothing to wake a thread already blocked inside `accept()`, so you must additionally arrange for that syscall to be interrupted, closed, or timed out; and because every connection is served on a detached thread, the server holds no handle to the work in flight and so cannot actually drain it — a true shutdown would mean abandoning detached threads for joinable ones tracked in a shared registry. Each of those concerns is a worthwhile topic, but each pulls attention away from the chapter's actual subject, which is the cache: its hash-map-plus-linked-list structure, its TTL semantics, and its concurrency control. Rather than bolt on a shutdown path that looks complete but quietly drops in-flight connections — arguably worse than an obvious `while (true)`, because it dresses an unsolved problem in the costume of a solved one — we keep the loop honestly minimal and name the gap explicitly here. Treat closing it as the natural next exercise: install the handler, make `accept()` interruptible, switch to joinable connection threads, and you will have converted a teaching server into a deployable one.

With the server implementation fully examined and verified against the theory that motivated it, attention turns to the tools needed to interact with it.

Developing a client

A cache server is only as useful as the tools available to interact with it. Rather than building a single monolithic client and trying to make it serve every purpose, we develop three focused clients, each designed for a specific role in the development workflow. The first is a test client (`zemp_client.zig`) that connects to the server and executes a fixed sequence of commands, verifying that every protocol operation — PING, SET, GET, DEL, TTL expiry, large values — produces the correct response. The second is a command-line tool (`zcache_cli.zig`) that follows the Unix philosophy: one invocation, one command, one result, making it practical for manual inspection and shell scripting. The third is a benchmark client (`bench.zig`) that floods the server with a configurable number of operations and reports throughput and latency statistics, turning the architectural claims made earlier in the chapter into measurable numbers. Separating these concerns into three tools keeps each file small, single-purpose, and easy to reason about.

Have in mind that after executing `zig build` (inside `ch10/zcache`), you are going to have four binaries in `./zig-out/bin/`: one for the server and three binaries for the clients. While testing each one of the clients, make sure that you have already executed the `zcache` server as `./zig-out/bin/zcache` – expect to get the following kind of output:

```
$ ./zig-out/bin/zcache
info:

      Zcache - in-memory cache

  host      : 127.0.0.1
  port      : 7777
  capacity  : 10000 entries
  max conn  : 512
  protocol  : ZEMP v1 (binary)
```

```
info: zcache listening on 127.0.0.1:7777
```

We begin by describing the test client as found in `zemp_client.zig`.

Explaining zemp_client.zig

This file is a test client that exercises every command against a running server in a fixed sequence. It implements the full client side of ZEMP: a `Client` struct wrapping a `std.Io.net.Stream`, with `ping()`, `get()`, `set()`, and `del()` methods that each call `sendFrame()` and return a heap-allocated `Response`; `get()`, `set()`, and `del()` build their payloads using `ArrayListUnmanaged` before sending. The `readResponse()` function creates a buffered reader from the stream and uses `readSliceAll()` to read the 8-byte prefix and then the payload — the same blocking read pattern as the server, so partial reads are handled transparently by the I/O layer. The `runTests()` function connects to the server and executes a fixed test sequence covering basic commands, lazy TTL expiry with a 150 ms sleep, in-place updates, deletion, and a 65,000-byte large value. The results are printed using `std.debug.print()` with status labels and decoded values. This file is primarily a verification and demonstration tool rather than production code.

The test client connects to the server and works through four groups of operations, each verifying a different aspect of the implementation:

```
$ ./zig-out/bin/zemp_client

Connecting to zcache at 127.0.0.1:7777 …

── Basic commands ──────────────────────────────────────
  PING                  → OK            value=PONG
  SET name=zcache       → OK
  SET version=1         → OK
  GET name              → OK            value=zcache
  GET version           → OK            value=1
  GET missing_key       → NOT_FOUND

── TTL expiry ──────────────────────────────────────────
  SET ttl_key (100ms)   → OK
  GET ttl_key (now)     → OK            value=bye soon
  GET ttl_key (150ms)   → NOT_FOUND

── Update & Delete ─────────────────────────────────────
  SET name=updated      → OK
```

```
  GET name (updated)      → OK            value=zcache-updated
  DEL name                → OK
  GET name (deleted)      → NOT_FOUND
  DEL name (gone)         → NOT_FOUND

— Large value ─────────────────────────────────────────────
  SET big (65 000 B)      → OK
  GET big                 → OK            value length=65000 bytes

All tests completed.
```

The basic commands group confirms that the fundamental protocol round-trip is working correctly. A PING returns PONG, proving the connection is live and the server is processing frames. Two SET operations store the keys `name` and `version`, both returning OK. The subsequent GET operations retrieve the correct values, and a GET for a key that was never inserted returns `NOT_FOUND` rather than an error — confirming that a cache miss is handled as a normal response, not a failure condition. The TTL expiry group verifies the lazy expiry mechanism. A key is stored with a 100 millisecond time-to-live and retrieved immediately, returning its value correctly. The client then sleeps for 150 milliseconds — long enough for the TTL to elapse — and issues the same GET again. This time the server returns NOT_FOUND, confirming that `isExpired()` fired during the second `get()` call and the node was evicted on the spot. No background thread was involved; the expiry happened at the moment of access. The update and delete group exercises the remaining write operations. Setting `name` a second time with a different value returns OK, and the subsequent GET returns the new value, confirming that the update path in `set()` replaced the value in place without inserting a duplicate entry. The DEL command removes the key and returns OK, the following GET returns NOT_FOUND, confirming the deletion, and a second DEL on the same key also returns NOT_FOUND — confirming that `delete()` is idempotent and handles an absent key gracefully rather than returning an error. The large value group sends a 65,000-byte value in a single SET and retrieves all 65,000 bytes back intact. This confirms that the `u32` payload length field in the frame prefix correctly handles values well beyond what would fit in a single network packet, and that the state machine's partial-read handling reassembled the fragmented payload correctly on both the send and receive paths.

Next, we are turning to the command-line client.

Explaining zcache_cli.zig

This file implements a subcommand-style command line client where each invocation opens one TCP connection, sends exactly one command, prints the response, and exits — the Unix tool philosophy applied to cache access. Argument parsing collects `--host` and `--port` flags and a positional subcommand (`ping`, `get`, `set`, `del`) with its arguments into a `Frame` struct — a locally defined type holding a type byte and a heap-allocated payload — using labeled block expressions to satisfy the requirement that every `const` be assigned at its declaration site. All user-facing errors call `std.process.exit(1)` rather than returning an error, so that a mistyped command prints a usage message and exits cleanly without a stack trace or a build-system failure. The `printResponse()` function decodes the response payload according to its status byte, printing the value string for GET hits, `(nil)` for misses, and an `(error)` prefix for server-side errors.

Each invocation of `zcache_cli` is a complete, self-contained operation: the binary connects to the server, sends exactly one ZEMP frame, prints the response, and exits. There is no persistent connection between invocations — each command is independent:

```
$ ./zig-out/bin/zcache_cli ping
PONG
$ ./zig-out/bin/zcache_cli set name Mihalis 5000
OK
$ ./zig-out/bin/zcache_cli get name
Mihalis
$ ./zig-out/bin/zcache_cli del name
OK
$ ./zig-out/bin/zcache_cli get name
(nil)
```

The first command sends a `PING` frame with an empty payload and receives `PONG`, confirming the server is reachable and the binary protocol is functioning correctly. The second command stores the key `name` with the value `Mihalis` and a TTL of `5000` milliseconds — five seconds — receiving OK to confirm the entry was written to the cache. The third command retrieves the value by key and prints `Mihalis` directly, with no surrounding quotes or metadata, because `printResponse()` extracts the raw bytes from the `[value_len: u32][value]` payload layout and prints only the value string. The fourth command deletes the key and receives OK, confirming the entry was found and removed. The fifth command attempts to retrieve the same key again and receives `(nil)` — the client-side representation of a NOT_FOUND response — confirming that the deletion took effect and the key no longer exists in the cache. This interaction also illustrates the TTL in action implicitly: if the `get` after the `del` had been issued more than five seconds after the `set`, the result would have been `(nil)` even without the explicit deletion, because the lazy expiry check inside `cache.get()` would have evicted the entry on that access. The explicit delete simply made it happen immediately and unconditionally.

Last, let us explain the benchmarking utility.

Explaining bench.zig

This file is a performance measurement tool that connects to a running server and hammers it with a configurable number of operations, reporting throughput, and latency statistics. It is built with `optimize = .ReleaseFast` in `build.zig` so its own overhead does not contaminate the measurements. The `fmtKey()` function formats integer keys into a stack-allocated `[32]u8` buffer inside the hot loop, keeping heap allocations out of the measurement path. The `Histogram` struct records per-operation nanosecond timestamps in a heap-allocated slice and computes mean, minimum, maximum, and p99 latency by sorting the samples after the run. The `runPhase()` function is generic over a `comptime phase` enum with four variants — `set`, `get`, `del`, and `mix` — allowing the compiler to eliminate the branch inside the hot loop entirely for each variant. The mix mode simulates a realistic workload of 60% SET, 30% GET, and 10% DEL operations. Throughput is computed by dividing the operation count by the elapsed nanoseconds and scaling to operations per second, and all results are printed in a fixed-width table format for easy comparison across runs.

The following benchmark runs 100,000 operations for each of the three command types in sequence, using 64-byte values and 1,000 distinct keys, and measures the complete round-trip time for each operation — from the moment the frame is sent until the response is fully received:

```
$ ./zig-out/bin/bench --ops 100000

  zcache benchmark
  host=127.0.0.1  port=7777  ops=100000  value=64B  keys=1000  mix=false

  SET
  ─────────────────────────────────────
  ops           : 100000
  total time    : 3853 ms
  throughput    : 25951 ops/sec
  latency mean  : 38 µs
  latency min   : 24 µs
  latency p99   : 65 µs
  latency max   : 162 µs

  GET
  ─────────────────────────────────────
  ops           : 100000
  total time    : 5391 ms
  throughput    : 18546 ops/sec
```

```
latency mean : 53 µs
latency min  : 32 µs
latency p99  : 85 µs
latency max  : 182 µs

DEL
────────────────────────────────────
ops          : 100000
total time   : 2802 ms
throughput   : 35686 ops/sec
latency mean : 27 µs
latency min  : 18 µs
latency p99  : 51 µs
latency max  : 116 µs
```

The SET phase completes 100,000 operations in just under four seconds, achieving roughly 26,000 operations per second with a mean latency of 38 microseconds. The minimum latency of 24 microseconds represents the best-case round-trip: a frame sent, immediately processed, and a response received with no queueing delay. The p99 latency of 65 microseconds means that 99 out of every 100 operations completed within 65 microseconds — only 1,000 operations in the entire run exceeded that threshold. The maximum of 162 microseconds is a single outlier, likely caused by an OS scheduling interruption or a TCP buffer flush delay rather than anything in the cache itself. The GET phase is noticeably slower than SET, taking 5.4 seconds and achieving only about 18,500 operations per second with a mean latency of 53 microseconds. This is somewhat counterintuitive — a GET should be simpler than a SET since it involves no allocation. The difference is explained by the response payload: a GET hit must encode the value into a `[value_len: u32][value]` response payload via `encodeGetPayload()`, allocate a temporary heap buffer, write it to the connection write buffer, and then free it — whereas a SET response is an empty OK frame with no payload at all. The allocator round-trip on the GET response path is the likely source of the additional latency. The DEL phase is the fastest of the three at roughly 36,000 operations per second and a mean latency of 27 microseconds. Like SET responses, DEL responses carry an empty payload, avoiding the allocation on the response path. But DEL is also simpler on the cache side than SET: it only needs to find the node, remove it from the map and list, and free it — there is no eviction check, no key duplication, and no value duplication, all of which SET must perform on the insert path.

One important caveat about these numbers: the benchmark uses a pool of only 1,000 distinct keys across 100,000 operations, which means every GET after the initial SET phase is a cache hit. The latency and throughput figures for GET therefore reflect the best-case scenario — a key that is always present and always near the head of the LRU list. A more representative benchmark would vary the key space to introduce cache misses. Using 200,000 distinct keys against a cache sized for 1,000 entries would produce a miss rate of roughly 50%, forcing the server to return not-found responses for half of all GET operations and showing how the miss path performs relative to the hit path. Readers sizing a real deployment should treat the numbers above as an upper bound on GET throughput rather than a typical figure. The second caveat is architectural. The benchmark sends one request and waits for one response before sending the next — a serial round-trip pattern that includes the full loopback TCP stack overhead on every operation. This measures per-operation latency accurately but understates the server's actual throughput ceiling, since the server spends most of its time waiting for the next request to arrive rather than processing work. A pipelined client — one that sends multiple frames before reading any responses — would saturate the server's processing capacity and reveal its true throughput limit. Exercise 5 takes a step in this direction by introducing a concurrent client; pipelining within a single connection is a further improvement worth exploring.

Two things are worth noting about these numbers in context. First, this benchmark uses a single synchronous connection — one request is fully sent and its response fully received before the next request is issued. A pipelined client that sends multiple frames before reading responses would achieve substantially higher throughput by keeping both the client and server busy simultaneously rather than waiting at each step. Second, the server and benchmark are running on the same machine, so the measured latency includes loopback network overhead rather than real network latency. On a production deployment with the server on a separate host, the numbers would be dominated by network round-trip time rather than the cache's own processing cost. And now with mixed workload, which is the most realistic run because it reflects how a cache server is used in production — predominantly writes and reads with occasional deletions, rather than a single operation type in isolation. The `60/30/10` split across SET, GET, and DEL is a reasonable approximation of a typical application access pattern, where new data is written frequently, existing data is read more selectively, and deletions are relatively rare:

```
$ ./zig-out/bin/bench --ops 100000 --mix
  zcache benchmark
  host=127.0.0.1  port=7777  ops=100000  value=64B  keys=1000  mix=true

  MIXED  (60% SET / 30% GET / 10% DEL)
  ────────────────────────────────────
  ops           : 100000
  total time    : 3455 ms
  throughput    : 28936 ops/sec
  latency mean  : 34 µs
  latency min   : 20 µs
```

```
latency p99   : 63 µs
latency max   : 146 µs
```

The mixed run achieves roughly 29,000 operations per second with a mean latency of 34 microseconds, which sits between the SET and GET figures from the sequential benchmark and is closer to the SET numbers. This makes sense given the weighting: 60% of operations are SETs with their empty response payloads, 10% are DELs, which are the cheapest of all, and only 30% are GETs with their allocated response payloads. The aggregate cost is pulled toward the cheaper operations by the distribution. The p99 latency of 63 microseconds is almost identical to the SET p99 of 65 microseconds from the sequential run, which suggests that the tail latency of the mixed workload is dominated by the SET path rather than the GET path. The maximum of 146 microseconds is the lowest of all four benchmark runs, which is a mild surprise — one would expect the mixed workload to occasionally produce a GET maximum that approaches the 182 microseconds GET maximum from the sequential run. The likely explanation is that the sequential GET run performed 100,000 consecutive allocations on the response path, increasing the chance of an occasional slow allocation, whereas in the mixed run, only 30,000 of the 100,000 operations trigger that path, reducing the exposure to allocator tail latency.

Every benchmark so far has driven the server through a single connection, which faithfully measures the cost of one cache operation but quietly sidesteps the chapter's central design claim. We chose a thread-per-connection model precisely so that many clients could be served at once; a one-connection benchmark can never tell us whether that promise holds under load. To put it to the test, we run the same workload at three levels of concurrency — one connection, fifty, and two hundred — each level spawning that many independent client connections, each one on its own thread with its own socket, all hammering the single shared cache in parallel. Holding the total operation count fixed across the three runs lets us read the result as a scaling curve rather than three unrelated numbers: if the design scales, throughput should climb as we add clients; if it does not, throughput will plateau while latency, especially the p99 tail, climbs in its place. As we will see, the curve bends the second way, and the reason is the one piece of shared state every operation must pass through — the cache's single mutex. These measurements are what turn the earlier hand-wave about sharded locking from a plausible idea into a quantified, justified next step: we will not merely assert that one lock becomes a bottleneck, we will watch it happen.

Here is the generated output:

```
$ ./zig-out/bin/bench --port 7777 --ops 200000 --concurrency 1

  zcache benchmark
  host=127.0.0.1  port=7777  ops=200000  value=64B  keys=1000  conc=1  mix=false

  SET   (concurrency=1)
```

```
  ─────────────────────────────────────
  ops          : 200000
  total time   : 21674 ms
  throughput   : 9227 ops/sec
  latency mean : 108 µs
  latency min  : 89 µs
  latency p99  : 134 µs
  latency max  : 893 µs

  GET   (concurrency=1)
  ─────────────────────────────────────
  ops          : 200000
  total time   : 34032 ms
  throughput   : 5876 ops/sec
  latency mean : 170 µs
  latency min  : 135 µs
  latency p99  : 201 µs
  latency max  : 402 µs

  DEL   (concurrency=1)
  ─────────────────────────────────────
  ops          : 200000
  total time   : 12131 ms
  throughput   : 16486 ops/sec
  latency mean : 60 µs
  latency min  : 43 µs
  latency p99  : 73 µs
  latency max  : 329 µs
$ ./zig-out/bin/bench --port 7777 --ops 200000 --concurrency 50

  zcache benchmark
  host=127.0.0.1  port=7777  ops=200000  value=64B  keys=1000  conc=50  mix=false

  SET   (concurrency=50)
  ─────────────────────────────────────
  ops          : 200000
  total time   : 23059 ms
  throughput   : 8673 ops/sec
  latency mean : 4645 µs
  latency min  : 104 µs
  latency p99  : 83190 µs
```

```
  latency max  : 275394 µs

  GET   (concurrency=50)
  ─────────────────────────────────────
  ops          : 200000
  total time   : 37648 ms
  throughput   : 5312 ops/sec
  latency mean : 8570 µs
  latency min  : 154 µs
  latency p99  : 78791 µs
  latency max  : 751237 µs

  DEL   (concurrency=50)
  ─────────────────────────────────────
  ops          : 200000
  total time   : 11691 ms
  throughput   : 17106 ops/sec
  latency mean : 1719 µs
  latency min  : 40 µs
  latency p99  : 1117 µs
  latency max  : 7518888 µs
$ ./zig-out/bin/bench --port 7777 --ops 200000 --concurrency 200

  zcache benchmark
  host=127.0.0.1  port=7777  ops=200000  value=64B  keys=1000  conc=200  mix=false

  SET   (concurrency=200)
  ─────────────────────────────────────
  ops          : 200000
  total time   : 23114 ms
  throughput   : 8652 ops/sec
  latency mean : 18171 µs
  latency min  : 108 µs
  latency p99  : 157321 µs
  latency max  : 334410 µs

  GET   (concurrency=200)
  ─────────────────────────────────────
  ops          : 200000
  total time   : 38131 ms
  throughput   : 5244 ops/sec
```

```
latency mean : 36021 µs
latency min  : 158 µs
latency p99  : 157644 µs
latency max  : 1083667 µs

DEL   (concurrency=200)
─────────────────────────────────────
ops          : 200000
total time   : 11813 ms
throughput   : 16929 ops/sec
latency mean : 5120 µs
latency min  : 41 µs
latency p99  : 162 µs
latency max  : 8059660 µs
```

At `--concurrency 1`, the server achieves roughly 9,200 SET ops/sec, 5,900 GET ops/sec, and 16,500 DEL ops/sec — a clean baseline that reflects per-operation round-trip cost with no contention. At `--concurrency 50`, the aggregate throughput is nearly unchanged — 8,700 SET ops/sec, 5,300 GET ops/sec, 17,100 DEL ops/sec — but the latency picture changes dramatically: mean SET latency jumps from 108 µs to 4,645 µs. The p99 reaches 83 ms, meaning 1% of operations are waiting tens of milliseconds for the mutex. At `--concurrency 200`, the throughput numbers barely move — 8,600 SET, 5,200 GET, 16,900 DEL — confirming that the server is not doing more useful work as connections increase; it is simply distributing the same throughput across more waiting threads. Mean SET latency climbs to 18 ms and the p99 to 157 ms. The ceiling is the single mutex: every connection thread serializes through it on every operation, so adding more threads adds contention without adding capacity. This is precisely the gap that **sharded locking** addresses.

The three clients together close the loop that the chapter opened. The test client confirms that the state machine, the frame parser, and the LRU cache all behave correctly under the conditions the theory predicted. The CLI demonstrates that the binary protocol is practical to work with from outside the Zig ecosystem. And the benchmark puts concrete numbers against the architectural claims — showing the throughput and latency that result from the thread-per-connection model, the fixed-width binary protocol, and the *O(1)* cache operations working together. The chapter progression mirrors the typical development workflow: you build the server, verify it with a test client, interact with it manually via the CLI, then measure its performance with a benchmark.

Summary

In this chapter, we evolved from a simple set of requirements into a functional server that manages memory and network resources. The emphasis of Zig on precise memory management and the lack of a hidden runtime are instrumental in ensuring that these operations remain deterministic and free from the latency spikes often introduced by background garbage collection. The design of this cache server serves as a template for systems where mechanical sympathy — the alignment of software logic with hardware reality — is the primary goal.

In the next chapter, we shift focus to another essential domain in systems and application development: working with structured data and databases. You will learn how to read and write JSON data, perform file I/O to persist structured content, and interface with an SQLite3 database. Whether you are building data pipelines, backend services, or configuration tools, managing structured data is crucial. Let us dive in and see how Zig helps you stay efficient and in control, even when working with higher-level abstractions.

Exercises

- Implement Sharded Locking: The current `zcache` implementation protects the entire cache with a single mutex. Under concurrent load, all threads contend for the same lock regardless of which keys they are accessing, which limits throughput as the number of connections grows. Redesign the cache to use `N` independent shards, each containing its own hash map, LRU list, and mutex. Use the hash of the key to select the shard — for example, `shard_index = hash(key) % N`. A thread operating on key A and a thread operating on key B will now only contend if both keys map to the same shard. Once the implementation is complete, benchmark it against the single-mutex version using the existing benchmark client with `--conns 50` and `--conns 200`. Observe where throughput plateaus in each implementation and measure how the sharded version responds as the connection count increases. A shard count of 16 or 64 is a reasonable starting point — experiment with different values and note the effect on both throughput and latency.
- Implement a `TOUCH` command that resets the TTL of an existing key without modifying its value. If the key does not exist or has already expired, `TOUCH` should return a not-found response. Add the corresponding opcode to the ZEMP protocol, implement the handler in `cache.zig`, and add a unit test that verifies the TTL is correctly extended.
- Implement an `INCR` command that atomically increments a numeric value stored under a key. If the key does not exist, treat its value as zero and set it to one. If the value cannot

be parsed as an integer, return an error response. This command must hold the mutex for the duration of the read-modify-write to prevent a race between two concurrent `INCR` calls on the same key.

- The `--max-clients` flag is parsed and stored but never enforced in `run()`. Add a connection counter protected by an atomic and reject new connections — by closing the accepted socket immediately — when the counter reaches the configured limit. Verify the behavior by running the benchmark client with more connections than the limit allows and confirming that excess connections are refused cleanly rather than queued indefinitely.
- Replace the single-client benchmark with a concurrent client: The current benchmark client sends requests serially. Rewrite it using `Io.Group` to dispatch multiple concurrent connections, each sending a configurable number of `SET`/`GET` pairs. Run the concurrent benchmark at `--conns 10`, `--conns 50`, and `--conns 200` and compare the throughput and latency figures against the serial baseline.
- Add graceful shutdown: Implement a `SIGTERM` handler that sets an atomic flag, stops the accept loop from accepting new connections, and waits for in-flight requests to complete before freeing the cache and exiting. Verify the behavior by sending SIGTERM while the benchmark client is running and confirming that no requests are lost and no memory is leaked.
- Implement a simple persistence mechanism: on shutdown, serialize the cache contents to a binary file on disk; on startup, reload the file if it exists and re-populate the cache before accepting connections. Use the ZEMP frame format as the on-disk representation so the serialization code can be shared with the network layer.
- Implement a `STATS` command that returns a structured response containing the current hit count, miss count, eviction count, entry count, and memory usage. Extend the `Stats` struct in `cache.zig` to track evictions and memory usage, and add a corresponding handler in the server. Verify the output using the CLI client.
- Replace the thread-per-connection model with an async front end: The current `zcache` server spawns one OS thread per connection, which limits scalability to a few hundred concurrent connections before thread stack memory becomes the bottleneck. Redesign the server networking layer to use `Io.Group` and `io.concurrent` from the previous chapter in place of `std.Thread.spawn`, so that each connection is handled by a lightweight concurrent task rather than a dedicated OS thread. Keep the cache layer — `cache.zig`, the mutex, and all cache operations — unchanged. Only the connection acceptance and dispatch logic is in `server.zig` needs to change. Once the async front

end is in place, combine it with the sharded locking implementation from Exercise 3 and benchmark the result at `--conns 50`, `--conns 200`, and `--conns 1000`. Compare throughput and latency against the original thread-per-connection baseline and observe how the two implementations diverge as the connection count grows.

- The current `zcache` server runs an unconditional `while (true)` accept loop with no shutdown path. Pressing Ctrl+C abandons any request mid-parse and leaves the listening socket to expire through the kernel's `TIME_WAIT` state rather than being closed deliberately. Implement a correct graceful shutdown in three steps. First, declare a process-global `g_running: std.atomic.Value(bool)` and install a `SIGTERM` handler that sets it to `false` using `.release` ordering. Second, make the accept loop consult the flag on each iteration — but note that a flag alone is insufficient, since a thread already blocked inside `accept()` will not wake up when the flag changes. You must also arrange for the blocking `accept()` call to be interrupted, either by setting a timeout via `Io.Select` or by closing the listening socket from the signal handler. Third, replace the detached connection threads with joinable ones tracked in a shared registry, so the server can call `join()` on each in-flight connection before `main()` returns. Without this step, the server cannot drain in-flight requests — it can only stop accepting new ones. Once all three steps are in place, verify the behavior by sending `SIGTERM` while the benchmark client is running and confirming that in-flight requests complete cleanly, no memory is leaked, and the listening socket is closed before the process exits.
- The current `zcache` server does not disable Nagle's algorithm on accepted connections. Nagle's algorithm batches small writes to reduce the number of packets sent, but combined with the receiver's delayed-ACK timer, it can stall a request-response protocol by tens of milliseconds per operation — a significant penalty for a cache server whose entire value proposition is low latency. Add a `setNoDelay()` helper function that takes a stream file descriptor and calls `setsockopt(2)` with `TCP_NODELAY` via `std.c.setsockopt()`. Call it immediately after each `listener.accept(io)` in `run()`. A failure to set the option should be logged, but should not abort the connection. Once the change is in place, measure its effect using the benchmark client. Run the benchmark against a loopback address first — where `TCP_NODELAY` has little effect since loopback bypasses the network stack — and then against a remote host or a virtual machine on the same network, where the Nagle plus delayed-ACK interaction is visible in the latency numbers. Compare the average per-connection latency before and after the change and note the difference.

Additional resources

- Mitchell Hashimoto on YouTube interview – *new way of writing code*: `https://www.youtube.com/watch?v=WjckELpzLOU`

11

Persisting Structured Data with SQLite3

In the modern software landscape, *data is everything*. Applications often need to load, store and manipulate structured information — whether it is configuration files, API responses or persistent storage. At its core, working with structured data is an act of imposing order on chaos — a deeply human impulse rooted in our need to understand, remember, and make decisions. Structured data represents the world not as it is but as we choose to interpret it: rows and columns become stand-ins for relationships, identities and meaning. This structure reduces cognitive load. It allows us to externalize memory, enabling software to recall details we would forget, to make connections we might miss, and to operate at a scale far beyond human capacity. So structured data and databases allow us to store facts, model the world, reason about it and ultimately to build systems that help us think more clearly.

In this chapter, we explore how Zig helps you work with structured data formats like JSON. You will learn how to read and write JSON files, parse their contents into usable data structures, and generate JSON from in-memory data. But we will not stop at files. You will also gain hands-on experience connecting to an SQLite3 database from Zig. If you are looking for a simple, fast, and reliable way to store structured data without the overhead of managing a complete database server, then SQLite3 is the tool for the job. In fact, it is one of the most widely deployed databases in the world, used everywhere from web browsers and smartphones to embedded devices and even spacecraft. And the best part? You do not need a DBA or server infrastructure because SQLite3 stores everything in a single file, making it perfect for local applications, testing, prototyping, and lightweight systems. Back to reality and being practical now. Although Zig does not yet have as many mature database libraries as more established languages, it can interface with C libraries, allowing us to integrate popular database systems like SQLite3, PostgreSQL or MySQL through C bindings. This approach enables Zig programs to leverage existing, battle-tested database engines while benefiting from the compile-time safety checks of Zig and performance optimizations.

This chapter covers:

- Working with JSON and Nested Structures
- Using SQLite3
- Building a note-taking service
- Building a client for the note-taking service

Working with JSON and nested structures

JSON is a very popular and widely used plain text file format. Developing Zig applications that work with JSON data involves writing code that can parse, manipulate, and generate JSON while maintaining control over performance and memory usage. In this section, we are going to learn how to read nested JSON records and put them into structures. After all, data is rarely linear. Handling nested data structures requires a clear mapping between the serialized format and the internal types. In this example, we define an `Address` struct and embed it within a `Person` struct, creating a hierarchy that mirrors the organization of a typical JSON object. `std.json.parseFromSlice()` is recursive as it traverses the JSON tree and populates the nested address field automatically because the relationship is defined in the type system. This approach replaces manual parsing logic with a declarative structure, where the organization of the data in the source file is handled by the composition of structs in the code. Here is the example code of `ch11/nestedJSON.zig`:

```
const std = @import("std");

const Address = struct {
    street: []const u8,
    city: []const u8,
    postal: []const u8,

    pub fn print(self: Address) void {
        std.debug.print("  Street: {s}\n", .{self.street});
        std.debug.print("  City:   {s}\n", .{self.city});
        std.debug.print("  Postal: {s}\n", .{self.postal});
    }
};

const Person = struct {
```

```
    id: u32,
    name: []const u8,
    address: Address,

    pub fn print(self: Person) void {
        std.debug.print("ID: {}\n", .{self.id});
        std.debug.print("Name: {s}\n", .{self.name});
        std.debug.print("Address:\n", .{});
        self.address.print();
        std.debug.print("\n", .{});
    }
};
```

The code defines two structures, `Address` and `Person`. This design choice treats an address as a first-class entity rather than a loose collection of strings, which is a sensible way to organize data that naturally belongs together. The use of `[]const u8` for the string fields is a characteristic Zig idiom; these are slices that point to constant memory, providing a lightweight way to handle text without the overhead of the allocations typically associated with high-level string objects. Logic is further organized by the inclusion of `print()` methods within each struct. The `Address.print()` method encapsulates the formatting of location data, making the output consistent regardless of where it is called.

Here is the `main()` implementation that acts as the supervisor for a pipeline that transforms raw bytes from a file into structured data in memory:

```
pub fn main(init: std.process.Init) !void {
    const io = init.io;
    const allocator = init.gpa;
    const args = try init.minimal.args.toSlice(init.arena.allocator());

    if (args.len < 2) {
        std.debug.print("Usage: {s} <jsonFile>\n", .{args[0]});
        return error.MissingFilename;
    }

    const fp = args[1];
    const file = std.Io.Dir.cwd().openFile(io, fp, .{}) catch |err| {
        switch (err) {
            error.FileNotFound => {
                std.debug.print("File not found: {s}\n", .{fp});
```

```
            },
            else => {
                std.debug.print(
                    "Failed to open file {s}: {}\n",
                    .{ fp, err },
                );
            },
        }
        return err;
    };
    defer file.close(io);

    const stat = try file.stat(io);
    const contents = try allocator.alloc(u8, stat.size);
    defer allocator.free(contents);

    _ = try file.readPositionalAll(io, contents, 0);
    var parsed = try std.json.parseFromSlice(
        []Person,
        allocator,
        contents,
        .{},
    );
    defer parsed.deinit();
    for (parsed.value) |person| {
        person.print();
    }
}
```

The code verifies the presence of a filename before proceeding, using the zeroth argument to provide a helpful usage message if the input is insufficient. This prevents index errors and ensures the user understands the tool's requirements before any significant work begins. The `catch` block provides specific feedback for a `FileNotFound` error, allowing the user to troubleshoot the path without hunting through generic system codes. Once a handle is obtained, the program calculates the file size to allocate a buffer of the exact required length. This approach avoids the overhead and fragmentation associated with dynamic resizing during a read operation. The `readPositionalAll()` function then populates this buffer, preparing the ground for the deserialization process. However, the heart of the transformation lies in `std.json.parseFromSlice()`, which takes the raw buffer and maps it onto a slice of `Person` structs. This operation is more than a simple copy; the parser interprets the JSON keys and populates the corresponding fields in the `Person` and `Address` types, verifying that the schema of the file matches the expectations of the code. The use of `parsed.deinit()` ensures that the memory associated with the string fields within the structs — which may have been allocated during the parse — is properly released once the processing is finished. Finally, a loop traverses the resulting slice, calling the `print()` method on each object to deliver the formatted data to the standard output. Executing `ch11/nestedJSON.zig` on a sample nested JSON file (`ch11/nested.json`) produces the following kind of output:

```
$ zig run ch11/nestedJSON.zig -- ch11/nested.json
ID: 1
Name: Alice
Address:
  Street: 123 Main St
  City:   Zigville
  Postal: 12345

ID: 2
Name: Bob
Address:
  Street: 456 Side Rd
  City:   Compiletown
  Postal: 67890
```

Now that we have successfully parsed and printed structured, nested JSON data, we can turn our attention to a common yet often overlooked aspect of JSON record manipulation: working with date and time values. In real-world applications, timestamps frequently appear in different formats depending on the system or service generating the data. To ensure consistency, readability, or compatibility with other tools, it is often necessary to convert these date and time values into a standardized format — such as ISO 8601. In the next section, we will explore how to locate, parse, and reformat date and time fields within JSON records using Zig, enabling our programs to communicate more clearly with the outside world.

Converting date and time formats in JSON records

In this section, we are going to do something practical. We are going to read JSON records that contain dates and times, and we are going to parse and change their format and write the results to a different plain text file. We are going to begin by reading the JSON data from an external file and identifying valid and invalid JSON records, because you cannot make any conversions in invalid JSON records. We will build a system that not only parses JSON but also flags errors gracefully without halting execution, ensuring reliability and resilience. The presented Zig program reads and validates a JSON file that contains an array of records, each with a timestamp. The goal is to identify how many records follow the expected timestamp format, providing a simple form of data quality assurance. The core logic is centered around structured parsing and format validation.

The example code can be found in `ch11/writeJSON.zig` – the program logic is centered around the `Record` structure:

```
const Record = struct {
    id: u32,
    event: []const u8,
    timestamp: []const u8,

    pub fn isValid(self: Record) bool {
        return isIso8601(self.timestamp);
    }

    pub fn reformat(self: Record, allocator: Allocator) !Record {
        const s = self.timestamp;
        if (s.len != 20) return error.InvalidTimestampFormat;
        const new_ts = try std.fmt.allocPrint(
            allocator,
            "{s}-{s}-{s} {s}:{s}:{s}",
            .{
                s[8..10], // day
                s[5..7], // month
                s[0..4], // year
                s[11..13], // hour
                s[14..16], // minute
                s[17..19], // second
            },
        );
        const new_event = try allocator.dupe(u8, self.event);
        return Record{
            .id = self.id,
            .event = new_event,
            .timestamp = new_ts,
        };
    }
};
```

The Record struct has three fields: id, event, and timestamp, all of which are mapped directly from JSON fields. The isValid() method calls a helper function, isIso8601().

The reformat() method produces a more readable date string. Before any allocation occurs, the logic performs a defensive check on the timestamp length, returning an error if the input does not match the expected twenty-character ISO format. This prevents out-of-bounds slicing later in the function. Once validated, the method uses std.fmt.allocPrint() to construct a new string by reordering slices of the original timestamp. Rather than modifying the original string in place, which is impossible for const slices, the code creates an entirely new representation in a format specifically tailored for human consumption.

Because the newly created Record contains an allocated timestamp, we duplicate the event field using allocator.dupe(). This decision is critical for memory safety and ownership consistency. If we simply copied the pointer to the old event, the new Record would have a fractured ownership model where one field is a transient reference and another is a heap-allocated buffer. By duplicating both, the method returns a *clean* instance where the caller knows exactly which parts of the record need to be freed later.

The isIso8601() function is making sure that we are working with the ISO 8601 format:

```
fn isIso8601(s: []const u8) bool {
fn isIso8601(s: []const u8) bool {
    if (s.len != 20) return false;
    if (s[4] != '-' or s[7] != '-' or s[10] != 'T' or
        s[13] != ':' or s[16] != ':' or s[19] != 'Z') return false;

    const digit_positions = [_]usize{ 0, 1, 2, 3, 5, 6, 8, 9, 11, 12, 14, 15, 17,
18 };
    for (digit_positions) |i| {
        if (!std.ascii.isDigit(s[i])) return false;
    }

    const month = (s[5] - '0') * 10 + (s[6] - '0');
    const day = (s[8] - '0') * 10 + (s[9] - '0');
    const hour = (s[11] - '0') * 10 + (s[12] - '0');
    const minute = (s[14] - '0') * 10 + (s[15] - '0');
    const second = (s[17] - '0') * 10 + (s[18] - '0');

    return month >= 1 and month <= 12 and
        day >= 1 and day <= 31 and
```

```
        hour <= 23 and minute <= 59 and second <= 59;
}
```

The function validates two independent properties: structure and content. The separator check confirms that the string has the right shape — dashes, `T`, colons, and `Z` in the expected positions. The digit check confirms that every non-separator position contains an ASCII digit, rejecting strings like `XXXX-XX-XXTXX:XX:XXZ` that pass the structural check but contain no valid date data. Without both checks, `reformat()` would silently produce garbage output when given a malformed timestamp, since it slices the string at fixed positions without further validation.

We also have the `handleJsonValue()` helper function:

```
fn handleJsonValue(
    val: std.json.Value,
    allocator: Allocator,
    reformatted: *std.ArrayListUnmanaged(Record),
    counts: *Counts,
) !void {
    if (std.json.parseFromValue(Record, allocator, val, .{})) |rec| {
        defer rec.deinit();
        if (rec.value.isValid()) {
            const new_rec_result = rec.value.reformat(allocator);
            if (new_rec_result) |new_rec| {
                try reformatted.append(allocator, new_rec);
                counts.valid += 1;
            } else |_| {
                counts.invalid += 1;
            }
        } else {
            counts.invalid += 1;
        }
    } else |_| {
        counts.invalid += 1;
    }
}
```

The `handleJsonValue()` function transforms a generic, dynamic JSON value into a validated and reformatted `Record` instance. The logic is structured around a series of nested `if/let` blocks that enforce strict data integrity before any information is committed to the final output list. First, the function attempts to map the raw JSON value onto the `Record` struct using std.json.parseFromValue(). If the mapping fails, indicating a structural mismatch in the input, the code increments the invalid count and exits the function. We choose this fail-fast approach to ensure that the rest of the pipeline only ever interacts with data that conforms to our expected internal schema.

Once a record is successfully parsed, the function enters a secondary validation phase where it checks the logical consistency of the data via isValid() and attempts to execute the reformat() method. These nested blocks serve as a filter; the program only updates the global state, the reformatted array list and the success counter, once both the structural parse and the domain-specific transformation have succeeded. The use of defer rec.deinit() ensures that the transient memory used by the JSON parser is released regardless of whether the subsequent reformatting succeeds or fails.

Last, we utilize the processNDJSON() function:

```
fn processNDJSON(
    io: std.Io,
    path: []const u8,
    allocator: Allocator,
    reformatted: *std.ArrayListUnmanaged(Record),
    counts: *Counts,
) !void {
    var file = try std.Io.Dir.cwd().openFile(io, path, .{});
    defer file.close(io);

    const stat = try file.stat(io);
    const content = try allocator.alloc(u8, stat.size);
    defer allocator.free(content);
    _ = try file.readPositionalAll(io, content, 0);

    var it = std.mem.splitScalar(u8, content, '\n');
    while (it.next()) |line| {
        if (line.len == 0) continue;
        var val = try std.json.parseFromSlice(
            std.json.Value,
            allocator,
            line,
            .{},
        );
        defer val.deinit();
        try handleJsonValue(
```

```
                val.value,
                allocator,
                reformatted,
                counts,
            );
        }
    }
```

The processNDJSON() function processes files formatted as **Newline Delimited JSON**; unlike a standard JSON file, which contains a single massive array or object, an NDJSON file consists of multiple independent JSON objects, each appearing on its own line and separated by a newline character. The code treats the input file as a single contiguous stream, which it first consumes entirely into memory. By allocating a buffer equal to the file size and performing a single readAll() operation, the code favors a linear and predictable I/O pattern. This design choice assumes the file fits within the available heap, but in return, it avoids the complexity of manual stream buffering and the overhead of frequent, smaller system calls. The logic is anchored by the use of defer statements, which provide a guaranteed cleanup of both the file handle and the allocated buffer, ensuring the system remains stable even if an error occurs during the read process. Once the file content is safely in memory, the function employs a scalar splitter to iterate over the data line by line. This iterator produces slices that point directly into the original buffer, avoiding the need to allocate new strings for every record. The logic within the loop is defensive; it skips empty lines to account for trailing whitespace or malformed entries often found in log files. Each valid line is then passed to std.json.parseFromSlice() to be transformed into a generic std.json.Value. This intermediate representation allows the parser to build a flexible tree structure that can be inspected or validated before the program attempts to map it to a specific record type.

The lifecycle of each parsed object is tightly managed to prevent memory exhaustion during large batch operations. By calling val.deinit() at the end of each iteration via a defer block, the program ensures that the temporary tree structures and metadata created by the JSON parser are released immediately after the data is passed to handleJsonValue(). This keeps the memory footprint low, regardless of the number of lines in the input file. This architectural separation, dividing the task into file ingestion, line iteration, and object parsing, makes the function easier to maintain and modify. It embodies a classic systems programming approach: do the heavy lifting of I/O once, then iterate through the data with minimal overhead.

Before we can build reliable tools for processing JSON data, we need data to work with, ideally realistic and varied sample records. Creating sample JSON helps test and demonstrate your utilities, uncover edge cases, and explore performance under different conditions. It is also a critical step when building test suites or debugging data transformation pipelines. This Zig program generates a given number of JSON records and writes them to standard output in either standard JSON or NDJSON format. For this purpose, I have created a sample utility named `ch11/sampleJSON.zig`, which functions as a synthetic data generator that produces a specified number of event logs in either structured JSON or newline-delimited JSON formats. The implementation leverages an arena allocator for simplified memory management and uses the standard library epoch utilities to transform calculated time offsets into ISO 8601 strings, injecting occasional malformed timestamps on purpose to test the resilience of downstream parsing logic. The full source of `sampleJSON.zig` is available in the book GitHub repository. The program accepts two arguments: the number of records to generate and an optional format name. The default format is `json`, which produces a standard JSON array enclosed in `[` and `]`. Pass `ndjson` as the second argument to produce newline-delimited JSON instead — one record per line with no enclosing array.

Before continuing, let us create some sample data using `ch11/sampleJSON.zig`:

```
$ zig run ch11/sampleJSON.zig -- 25 > /tmp/sample.json
$ wc /tmp/sample.json
     126     202    2066 /tmp/sample.json
```

The command `sampleJSON.zig -- 25 > /tmp/sample.json` produces a JSON array, which `writeJSON.zig` handles via the `parseFromSlice([]std.json.Value, ...)` path. To produce NDJSON and trigger the `processNDJSON()` path instead, run `sampleJSON.zig -- 25 ndjson > /tmp/sample.json`.

With all that in mind, let us try `ch11/writeJSON.zig` on some sample JSON data:

```
$ zig run ch11/writeJSON.zig -- /tmp/sample.json /tmp/Output.json
Done.
Valid: 16
Invalid: 9
Output file: /tmp/Output.json
```

In this case, the program found 16 valid records, entries that met all the required conditions. It also found 9 invalid records, which failed validation. Such output is valuable when importing or cleaning data, as it provides a quick assessment of data quality before further processing or storage.

Having established a strong foundation in parsing and manipulating structured data formats like JSON, we turn our attention to persistent storage and efficient data retrieval through databases. SQLite3 offers a seamless bridge between in-memory data handling and long-term storage, enabling applications to maintain complex datasets without sacrificing performance or simplicity. In the upcoming section, we delve into how to harness the capabilities of SQLite3 by learning how to connect, query, and modify data.

Using SQLite3

Working with databases is a foundational skill for any systems engineer aiming to manage, query, and persist structured data efficiently. Among the many database engines available, **SQLite3** stands out for its simplicity, portability, and lightweight design. Unlike client-server databases, SQLite3 operates as an embedded library within your application, eliminating the need for a separate database server and configuration. This makes it ideal for applications where ease of deployment and minimal dependencies are critical. In this section, we will explore how to integrate SQLite3 with your systems code, focusing on performing reliable transactions, executing queries, and handling data safely — all while leveraging the power and flexibility that SQLite3 brings to database management.

Connecting to SQLite3

Before you can execute any SQL or interact with a database, you need to establish a connection to SQLite3. In Zig, this is done by calling the C function `sqlite3_open()`, which opens a database file or creates a new one if it does not already exist and returns a pointer to a sqlite3 database object. This subsection explains how to safely open a database, handle potential errors, and ensure the database connection is properly closed when no longer needed. Proper connection handling is critical for maintaining data integrity and avoiding resource leaks in your application. This program (`ch11/connectSQLite3.zig`) is the epicenter of working with SQLite3 databases because, without connecting to one, you cannot interact with it – the foundation of this program lies in the ability of Zig to interoperate directly with the C ecosystem without the need for complex bindings:

```
const std = @import("std");
const sqlite3 = @cImport({
    @cInclude("sqlite3.h");
});

pub fn main(init: std.process.Init) !void {
    _ = init;
    var db: ?*sqlite3.sqlite3 = null;
    try checkError(sqlite3.sqlite3_open("/tmp/test.db",&db));
    defer {
        if (db) |db_ptr| _ = sqlite3.sqlite3_close(db_ptr);
    }
```

```
    std.debug.print("Database opened successfully\n", .{});
}
```

By using `@cImport()`, the compiler parses the `sqlite3.h` header. The database handle (`db`) is defined as an optional pointer to an opaque C struct, which correctly represents the possibility that a connection attempt may fail. When we call `sqlite3_open()`, we pass the address of this pointer so the C library can initialize it. By utilizing the optional capture `if (db) |db_ptr|`, the code executes the cleanup only if the handle was successfully initialized, which ensures that the program is closing the connection only when it actually exists and avoids the undefined behavior of passing a null pointer to the C API.

The `try` keyword, paired with `checkError()`, converts the integer return codes used by the C library into Zig native error unions:

```
fn checkError(result: c_int) !void {
    if (result != sqlite3.SQLITE_OK and
        result != sqlite3.SQLITE_DONE and
        result != sqlite3.SQLITE_ROW)
    {
        std.debug.print(
            "SQLite error ({d}): {s}\n",
            .{ result, sqlite3.sqlite3_errstr(result) },
        );
        return error.SqliteError;
    }
}
```

The function serves as a translation layer between C-style integer return codes and Zig idiomatic error unions. In the SQLite C API, success is not represented by a singular value; while `SQLITE_OK` signifies a perfectly completed operation, codes like `SQLITE_ROW` and `SQLITE_DONE` are equally valid indicators of a successful, albeit specific, state. By consolidating these "non-error" codes into a single conditional check, the function establishes a clear boundary: any other result is treated as a failure that requires immediate intervention.

Running `ch11/connectSQLite3.zig` is easy, but with a twist. Using `connectSQLite3.zig` on an Arch Linux machine requires executing the following command:

```
$ zig run ./ch11/connectSQLite3.zig -lc -lsqlite3
Database opened successfully
```

The key here is linking to the SQLite3 library using `-lsqlite3` so that the Zig compiler can build and execute the binary executable file successfully. However, using `connectSQLite3.zig` on a macOS machine with HomeBrew installed is a bit more complex because you must deal with the multiple versions of the SQLite3 binary installed: one by HomeBrew and another by Apple. I found out that the best way to tell Zig to use the HomeBrew version of SQLite3 is by executing the following command, which explicitly points to the right directories, so you should do the same if you are working on macOS:

```
$ zig run ch11/connectSQLite3.zig -I/opt/homebrew/include -L/opt/homebrew/lib -
lsqlite3
Database opened successfully
```

The moral of the story here is that when compiling a program that depends on external C libraries, the command line must provide the compiler with a map of the system headers. Once a connection to an SQLite3 database is established, the next step is to put information into the database to have something to work with.

Inserting data into SQLite3

In real-world applications, you often need more than just reading from a database — you also need to write data back. The `INSERT` statement is the most fundamental way to add new rows to an SQLite3 table. In this subsection, we will explore how to construct and execute `INSERT` queries from Zig, using both simple `sqlite3_exec()` calls for one-off commands and prepared statements with parameter binding (`sqlite3_prepare_v2()` and `sqlite3_bind_*`) for repeated or user-supplied data. Here is the example code of `ch11/insertSQLite3.zig`, which is presented in multiple snippets:

```
const std = @import("std");
const sqlite3 = @cImport({
    @cInclude("sqlite3.h");
});

pub fn main(init: std.process.Init) !void {
    const allocator = init.gpa;
    _ = allocator;
    const args = try init.minimal.args.toSlice(init.arena.allocator());
    if (args.len != 5) {
        std.debug.print(
            "Usage: {s} <db_path> <name> <email> <age>\n",
            .{args[0]},
```

```
        );
        return error.InvalidArgument;
    }

    const db_path = args[1];
    const name = args[2];
    const email = args[3];
    const age_str = args[4];
    const age = try std.fmt.parseInt(i32, age_str, 10);

    var db: ?*sqlite3.sqlite3 = null;
    try checkError(sqlite3.sqlite3_open(db_path,&db));
    defer {
        if (db) |db_ptr| _ = sqlite3.sqlite3_close(db_ptr);
    }
    std.debug.print("Opened DB: {s}\n", .{db_path});
```

The code validates the argument count, requiring exactly five entries – program, database path, and three fields of user data — to ensure the application has sufficient state to proceed safely. As a result, a significant portion of the code is about data validation and resource management. As before, the SQLite3 connection is established via the `sqlite3_open()` function from the imported C library.

Next, we have the preparation of the SQL statement to create a database table:

```
    const create_table_sql =
        \\CREATE TABLE IF NOT EXISTS users (
        \\  id INTEGER PRIMARY KEY,
        \\  name TEXT NOT NULL,
        \\  email TEXT NOT NULL,
        \\  age INTEGER
        \\);
    ;
    try execSql(db, create_table_sql);
```

The multi-line string syntax in Zig, denoted by the double backslash \\, provides a clean way to embed formatted text like SQL directly into the source code without the clutter of escape sequences or manual newline characters. The SQL statement itself employs the `IF NOT EXISTS` clause, a defensive programming idiom that ensures the operation is idempotent. This means the program can be executed multiple times, such as during a server restart or a local development build, without triggering an error if the table has already been initialized. The schema defines the users table with specific constraints, such as NOT NULL, to enforce data integrity at the storage layer. By defining these rules within the database itself, the developer creates a secondary layer of validation that protects the system even if the application-level logic contains a flaw.

The next code snippet illustrates the standard procedure for executing data manipulation commands through *prepared statements*:

```
    const insert_sql =
        "INSERT INTO users (name, email, age) VALUES (?, ?, ?)";
    var stmt: ?*sqlite3.sqlite3_stmt = null;
    try checkError(
        sqlite3.sqlite3_prepare_v2(db, insert_sql, -1, &stmt, null),
    );

    defer {
        if (stmt) |stmt_ptr| _ = sqlite3.sqlite3_finalize(stmt_ptr);
    }

    try checkError(sqlite3.sqlite3_bind_text(
        stmt,
        1,
        name.ptr,
        std.math.cast(c_int, name.len) orelse
            return error.LengthOverflow,
        null,
    ));

    try checkError(sqlite3.sqlite3_bind_text(
        stmt,
        2,
        email.ptr,
        std.math.cast(c_int, email.len) orelse
            return error.LengthOverflow,
        null,
    ));
    try checkError(sqlite3.sqlite3_bind_int(stmt, 3, age));
    try checkError(sqlite3.sqlite3_step(stmt));
    std.debug.print("User inserted: {s}, {s}, {d}\n", .{
        name, email, age,
    });
}
```

By using a *template string with question mark placeholders*, the logic prevents SQL injection attacks, ensuring that user-provided data is never interpreted as executable SQL commands. The call to `sqlite3_prepare_v2()` compiles this template into an internal bytecode format, which is more efficient for the database engine to process. To maintain a leak-free environment, a `defer` block ensures that the statement resources are released via `sqlite3_finalize()` once the operation is complete. This design separates the structural intent of the query from the specific data it carries, allowing the compiler and the database engine to validate the operation before any actual records are modified.

The transition from Zig memory-safe slices to the C-based SQLite API is handled through explicit parameter binding. Since `usize` might not always fit into the `c_int` expected by the C library, the code employs `std.math.cast()` to perform a safe conversion, returning a length overflow error if the input string is too large for the library to handle. The `sqlite3_bind_text()` and `sqlite3_bind_int()` methods populate the placeholders. We use the `.ptr` field of the slice to provide the raw pointer that the C function requires. Once all parameters are firmly bound, the `sqlite3_step()` function is invoked to perform the actual insertion.

The `execSql()` function serves as a specialized wrapper for the `sqlite3_exec()` routine:

```
fn execSql(db: ?*sqlite3.sqlite3, sql: []const u8) !void {
    var err_msg: [*c]u8 = null;
    defer {
        if (err_msg) |msg| sqlite3.sqlite3_free(msg);
    }
    try checkError(
        sqlite3.sqlite3_exec(db, sql.ptr, null, null, &err_msg),
    );
}
```

The C library we are using communicates errors by allocating a string on the heap and returning its address through a pointer-to-a-pointer. In Zig, we represent this message variable as a `[*c]u8`, which is a C-compatible pointer that may be `null`. The logic behind the `defer` block is to bridge the gap between Zig automatic scope management and C manual memory requirements; by calling `sqlite3_free()` within the `defer`, we guarantee that any error message allocated by the library is released back to the system, preventing a memory leak regardless of how the function exits. When calling the underlying C function, we pass the raw pointer from the Zig slice using `sql.ptr`. We provide null values for the callback parameters, as this specific helper is intended for *fire-and-forget* commands where the results of a query are not needed. The function wraps the entire call in `try checkError()`, which ensures that any internal SQLite failure is translated into a native Zig error and reported to the caller with appropriate diagnostic information. So, the C library handles the heavy lifting of SQL execution while our Zig wrapper manages the safety, memory lifecycle, and error propagation. It is an excellent demonstration of how to build a robust, type-safe interface over a raw C API, keeping the application code focused on intent rather than the boilerplate of the bridge.

Execute `ch11/insertSQLite3.zig` to put some data into the database:

```
$ zig run ch11/insertSQLite3.zig -I/opt/homebrew/include -L/opt/homebrew/lib -
lsqlite3 -- /tmp/newDB.db Mihalis some@email.com 1
Opened DB: /tmp/newDB.db
User inserted: Mihalis, some@email.com, 1
```

A database that only accepts input is of little use; the real value of any storage system lies in its ability to return information quickly and accurately. So, we now turn our attention to the more complex task of retrieval.

Querying data

In this subsection, we focus on how to prepare and execute SQL `SELECT` statements using the SQLite3 C API from Zig. You learn how to bind query parameters, step through result rows, and extract values safely and efficiently. Querying data is essential for reading and responding to stored information, making it a core part of any database-driven program.

Here is the example code for querying SQLite3 as found in `ch11/querySQLite3.zig`:

```
pub fn main(init: std.process.Init) !void {
    const args = try init.minimal.args.toSlice(init.arena.allocator());
    if (args.len < 2) {
        std.debug.print("Usage: {s} <db_path>\n", .{args[0]});
        return error.InvalidArgument;
    }
    const db_path = args[1];
```

We begin by implementing a defensive check to ensure a database path is provided, returning an error if the argument count is insufficient.

After that, we establish a connection and shift focus to the preparation of the SQL query:

```
    var db: ?*sqlite3.sqlite3 = null;
    try checkError(sqlite3.sqlite3_open(db_path,&db));
    defer {
        if (db) |db_ptr| _ = sqlite3.sqlite3_close(db_ptr);
```

```
    }
    std.debug.print("Database opened successfully: {s}\n", .{db_path});

    const query_sql = "SELECT id, name, email, age FROM users";
    var query_stmt: ?*sqlite3.sqlite3_stmt = null;
    try checkError(sqlite3.sqlite3_prepare_v2(
        db,
        query_sql,
        -1,
        &query_stmt,
        null,
    ));
    defer {
        if (query_stmt) |stmt_ptr|
            _ = sqlite3.sqlite3_finalize(stmt_ptr);
    }
```

As before, we use the `sqlite3_prepare_v2()` function to compile a SQL string into a private bytecode format. In this case, we have a `SELECT` statement used for getting data from the database – note that a `SELECT` statement can return multiple rows back.

The final phase of the query process involves traversing the result set and transforming raw database columns into a human-readable table:

```
    std.debug.print("\nUser Records:\n", .{});
    std.debug.print(
        "{s: >5} | {s: <10} | {s: <20} | {s: >3}\n",
        .{ "ID", "Name", "Email", "Age" },
    );
    std.debug.print(
        "{s:-<5} | {s:-<10} | {s:-<20} | {s:-<3}\n",
        .{ "", "", "", "" },
    );

    while (sqlite3.sqlite3_step(query_stmt) == sqlite3.SQLITE_ROW) {
        const id = @as(
            u32,
            @intCast(sqlite3.sqlite3_column_int(query_stmt, 0)),
        );
        const name = std.mem.span(
            sqlite3.sqlite3_column_text(query_stmt, 1),
```

```
        );
        const email = std.mem.span(
            sqlite3.sqlite3_column_text(query_stmt, 2),
        );
        const age = @as(
            u32,
            @intCast(sqlite3.sqlite3_column_int(query_stmt, 3)),
        );

        std.debug.print(
            "{d: >5} | {s: <10} | {s: <20} | {d: >3}\n",
            .{ id, name, email, age },
        );
    }
}
```

The code begins by printing a header and a separator line. By using specifiers like `{s: >5}` for right-alignment and `{s: <10}` for left-alignment, the code ensures that the data columns remain vertically aligned regardless of the length of the individual strings. The logic of the retrieval is driven by a `while` loop that calls `sqlite3_step()` repeatedly, *advancing the internal database cursor until no more rows remain.* Inside the loop, we use type-specific functions like `sqlite3_column_int()` and `sqlite3_column_text()` to extract values from the current row. A critical transition occurs when handling text: since the SQLite C API returns null-terminated pointers, we use `std.mem.span()` to calculate the length and create a native Zig slice. This is a fundamental bridge between the two languages as it allows the remainder of the Zig program to treat the data as a safe, length-aware object rather than a bare pointer. Each row is then formatted and printed to the standard debug stream. Compared to the simple open-and-close example, this program shows the full lifecycle of a prepared statement: Prepare, step, extract, and finalize.

Note that `std.mem.span()` expects a valid non-null pointer — passing a null pointer to it is undefined behavior. This is safe in the examples here because both the `users` and `notes` tables declare their `TEXT` columns as `NOT NULL`, guaranteeing that `sqlite3_column_text()` never returns a null pointer. If you apply this pattern to a nullable column, check `sqlite3_column_type(stmt, i) == SQLITE_NULL` before calling `std.mem.span()` — on a `NULL` column, treat the value as missing and handle it explicitly rather than attempting to materialize a slice.

Now, let us use `ch11/querySQLite3.zig` – on a table with 4 records:

```
$ zig run ch11/querySQLite3.zig -I/opt/homebrew/include -L/opt/homebrew/lib -
lsqlite3 -- /tmp/newDB.db
Database opened successfully: /tmp/newDB.db

User Records:
   ID | Name       | Email                    | Age
----- | ---------- | -------------------- | ---
    1 | Mihalis    | some1@email.com      |   1
    2 | Mihalis    | some2@email.com      |  20
    3 | Mihalis    | some3@email.com      |  25
    4 | Mihalis    | some4@email.com      |  30
```

It is time to explore how to remove data when it is no longer needed. Whether you are cleaning up test entries or deleting outdated information, performing deletions in SQLite3 is just as straightforward. In the next subsection, we will write a Zig program that demonstrates how to delete user records based on specific criteria, ensuring that changes are applied securely and efficiently.

Deleting data

Deleting data from a database is an essential part of maintaining clean and relevant records. In this section, you will learn how to use Zig to connect to an SQLite3 database and remove specific entries from a table. So, we will focus on constructing and executing parameterized `DELETE` queries to delete records.

Here is the example code as found in `ch11/deleteSQLite3.zig`:

```
pub fn main(init: std.process.Init) !void {
    const args = try init.minimal.args.toSlice(init.arena.allocator());

    if (args.len != 3) {
        std.debug.print(
            "Usage: {s} <db_path> <name>\n",
            .{args[0]},
        );
        return error.InvalidArgument;
    }

    const db_path = args[1];
    const name = args[2];
```

```
var db: ?*sqlite3.sqlite3 = null;
try checkError(sqlite3.sqlite3_open(db_path,&db));
defer {
    if (db) |db_ptr| _ = sqlite3.sqlite3_close(db_ptr);
}
std.debug.print("Opened DB: {s}\n", .{db_path});
```

The program deletes a single record or multiple records from a SQLite3 database table. It begins by reading command-line arguments and validating that exactly two arguments are provided: the database path and the name value of the record or records to delete. It then opens the SQLite3 database using `sqlite3_open()` and ensures it will be closed at the end with `defer`.

Note

Unlike column values, table and column names cannot be bound as parameters in SQL prepared statements — the ? placeholder works only for values. Any function that accepts a table or column name and constructs a query from it must validate or escape that identifier at the application layer before it touches the SQL string. Passing an unvalidated identifier directly into a format string is a SQL injection vulnerability even when every value in the same query is safely parameterized.

Next, it constructs a parameterized `DELETE` SQL statement:

```
// Table and column names cannot be parameterized in
// SQL - only values can. Interpolating an identifier via fmt
// opens an SQL injection vector; use a hardcoded or
// whitelist-validated name instead.
const delete_sql = "DELETE FROM users WHERE name = ?";

var stmt: ?*sqlite3.sqlite3_stmt = null;
try checkError(
    sqlite3.sqlite3_prepare_v2(
        db,
        delete_sql,
        -1,
        &stmt,
        null,
    ),
);
```

```
    defer {
        if (stmt) |stmt_ptr| _ = sqlite3.sqlite3_finalize(stmt_ptr);
    }
```

The SQL statement is prepared for execution with `sqlite3_prepare_v2()`, and the name is bound to the first placeholder (?) using `sqlite3_bind_text()`:

```
    try checkError(sqlite3.sqlite3_bind_text(
        stmt,
        1,
        name.ptr,
        std.math.cast(c_int, name.len) orelse
            return error.LengthOverflow,
        null,
    ));
    try checkError(sqlite3.sqlite3_step(stmt));

    const changes = sqlite3.sqlite3_changes(db);
    std.debug.print(
        "Deleted {d} record(s) with name '{s}' from table 'users'.\n",
        .{ changes, name },
    );
}
```

The `sqlite3_step()` function executes the deletion, and `sqlite3_changes()` retrieves the number of records removed. Finally, it prints how many records with the given name were deleted from the hardcoded table. Let us now try the program on macOS using a database that contains four records where name equals `Mihalis` on a table named `users`:

```
$ zig run ch11/deleteSQLite3.zig -I/opt/homebrew/include -L/opt/homebrew/lib -
lsqlite3 -- /tmp/newDB.db Mihalis
Opened DB: /tmp/newDB.db
Deleted 4 record(s) with name 'Mihalis' from table 'users'.
$ zig run ch11/deleteSQLite3.zig -I/opt/homebrew/include -L/opt/homebrew/lib -
lsqlite3 -- /tmp/newDB.db Mihalis
Opened DB: /tmp/newDB.db
Deleted 0 record(s) with name 'Mihalis' from table 'users'.
```

The first time `ch11/deleteSQLite3.zig` successfully deleted four matching records. However, the second time, it found no records to delete, hence the generated output.

Using JSON for data interchange is a powerful asset but it lacks the indexing and relational constraints required for long-term storage and complex analysis. Having mastered the extraction of data from raw JSON buffers and the fundamental mechanics of SQLite3, we arrive at the natural intersection of these two technologies. We will now examine how to bridge these two worlds, using prepared statements, and type-safe parsing to build a robust, persistent data pipeline.

Putting JSON data into a database

The transformation of semi-structured JSON into a relational database requires a bridge between dynamic input and static types. In systems programming, we prefer this bridge to be built at compile time to avoid the overhead of a heavy runtime or a complex reflection engine. The naive approach — parsing JSON into a generic tagged union and then manually extracting fields — produces brittle code where every column name appears in at least three places: the struct definition, the JSON extraction, and the SQL binding. A single schema change breaks all three sites independently. By shifting the work of field mapping from the execution phase to the compilation phase, we ensure that the resulting machine code is as direct as if we had written a specialized routine for every table in our schema, while the source code maintains a single point of truth. The `Event` struct is that single point of truth. It is the only declaration that needs to change when the schema changes, and the rest of the program adapts automatically at the next build.

Advanced comptime

Zig treats compilation not just as a translation process but as an execution environment. The `comptime` keyword marks values, expressions, and parameters that must be fully resolved before any machine code is emitted. Unlike the macro systems found in other languages, which often rely on text substitution or a separate sub-language, Zig `comptime` is just Zig: the same type system, the same control flow, the same standard library functions. We use it here to build SQL strings through ++ concatenation at compile time. The resulting string literals live in the binary's read-only data segment, meaning `ensureTableExists()` makes no heap allocation and pays no formatting cost at runtime. The `comptime` string for a two-field struct is identical in the binary to one you would have written by hand. The compiler also enforces correctness: if a field has a type that `sqlType` does not handle, `@compileError` halts the build with a clear message before the program ever links, let alone runs.

Reflection: using @typeInfo to inspect struct fields

Introspection in Zig is handled by **@typeInfo**. This built-in function returns a tagged union of type `std.builtin.Type` describing the internal structure of any type. For a struct, the `.@"struct"` variant carries a slice of `std.builtin.Type.StructField` values, each containing the field's name as a comptime `[]const u8`, its type as a `type`, and its default value if one exists. We use this in `ensureTableExists()` to iterate over the fields of `Event` and synthesize column definitions. The `pk` variable is annotated `comptime` explicitly because, even inside an `inline for` where loop variables are comptime-known, the compiler does not automatically promote the result of a conditional expression — `comptime if (...)` forces the evaluation to happen during compilation so that the ++ operator, which requires both operands to be comptime-known slices, can proceed. The final `sql` constant is a single null-terminated string built entirely at compile time and passed to `sqlite3_exec()` via `.ptr`, which extracts the raw `[*c]const u8` pointer that the C function expects.

Using anytype for generic database mapping

The **anytype keyword** provides compile-time polymorphism: a function parameter declared `anytype` causes the compiler to generate a distinct, fully specialized copy of the function body for each concrete type it is called with. In `insertRecord` and `bindValue`, this means the compiler sees the exact struct layout and field types of `Event` at the call site and generates a flat sequence of SQLite bind calls with no branching or indirection. This is duck typing enforced at compile time — if the type passed to `insertRecord()` does not have fields that `bindValue()` can handle, the build fails. The `bindValue()` function demonstrates a second comptime pattern: a `switch` on `@TypeOf(val)` where each branch calls a different C function. Because `T` is known at compile time, the compiler eliminates all branches except the one that matches, producing a single direct call in the emitted code.

Using comptime to map SQL rows to Zig structs

Mapping a struct's fields to SQL `?` placeholders and then binding each field value is the mechanical core of `insertRecord()`. The placeholder string is built with a comptime `inlinefor` over `info.fields`, accumulating `"?"` and `", ?"` tokens with ++. Because the loop is `inline`, it does not exist at runtime — the compiler unrolls it entirely into a fixed sequence of concatenations. The bind loop that follows uses `@field(record, field.name)` to read each field by name. `@field` is a built-in that takes a comptime string and resolves it to the actual struct member access, so it compiles down to the same instruction as writing `record.id` or `record.event` directly. The index `i` drives the SQLite3 column index, which is one-based by convention, hence `i + 1`. Together, these two loops — one building the SQL, one executing the binds — replace what would otherwise be a hand-written function for every table in the schema.

Implementing the utility

The program (`ch11/popSQL.zig`) takes exactly two command-line arguments: a path to an SQLite database file and a path to a JSON file containing an array of `Event` records. The `Event` struct is the single source of truth for the schema, declaring three fields — `id` as `i64`, `event`, and `timestamp` as `[]const u8` — from which every subsequent database operation is derived automatically at compile time. The startup sequence opens the database with `sqlite3_open()` and immediately calls `ensureTableExists()`, passing the `Event` type as a `comptime` parameter. Inside that function, `@typeInfo(T).@"struct"` returns the field metadata at compile time and an `inline for` iterates over those fields to build the `CREATE TABLE` statement through `++` concatenation. The `sqlType()` function maps each Zig type to its SQLite equivalent — `i64` becomes `INTEGER`, `[]const u8` becomes `TEXT NOT NULL` — and a `comptime if` detects the `id` field by name to append the `PRIMARY KEY` constraint. The entire SQL string is resolved before any machine code is emitted, lives in the binary read-only data segment, and is passed to `sqlite3_exec()` via `.ptr` to satisfy the C API `[*c]const u8` expectation. Once the table is guaranteed to exist, the program reads the JSON file into a heap-allocated buffer with `readEntireFile()` and passes it to `std.json.parseFromSlice()` with `[]Event` as the target type. The parser maps JSON keys directly to struct fields — no dynamic tagged union, no runtime field inspection — so the resulting slice contains fully typed `Event` values ready for immediate use. Each record is then checked against the database with `idExists()`, which prepares a `SELECT 1` statement, binds the `id` field with `sqlite3_bind_int64()`, and returns `true` if `sqlite3_step()` produces a row. This duplicate check prevents primary key constraint violations from aborting the entire import when a partially populated database is reused across multiple runs. Records that pass the duplicate check are handed to `insertRecord()`, which uses `@typeInfo()` a second time to build the placeholder string `(?, ?, ?)` at compile time and then executes a second `inline for` to bind each field value. The binding is dispatched by `bindValue()`, which switches on `@TypeOf(val)` — a `comptime` switch — to call either `sqlite3_bind_int64()`, `sqlite3_bind_double()`, or `sqlite3_bind_text()` depending on the field type. Because the switch is resolved at compile time, the emitted code for the `Event` struct is a flat sequence of three bind calls with no branching. Any field type not covered by `bindValue` or `sqlType` produces a `@compileError` at build time, ensuring that schema changes which introduce unsupported types are caught before the program runs, rather than failing silently at the first insert.

Here is the `sqlType()` implementation, which maps a Zig type to a SQLite column type at compile time:

```
fn sqlType(comptime T: type) []const u8 {
    return switch (T) {
        i64, i32, c_int => "INTEGER",
        f64, f32 => "REAL",
        []const u8 => "TEXT NOT NULL",
```

```
        else => @compileError(
            "unsupported field type: " ++ @typeName(T),
        ),
    };
}
```

The function takes a single `comptime` parameter `T` of type `type` — meaning the argument must be a type known at compile time rather than a runtime value — and returns a string literal that names the corresponding SQLite type. The mapping is expressed as a `comptime` switch over the type itself: integer types `i64`, `i32`, and `c_int` map to `INTEGER`, floating-point types `f64` and `f32` map to `REAL`, and `[]const u8` — Zig's string slice type — maps to `TEXT NOT NULL`. The `NOT NULL` constraint is included directly in the type string because the chapter's schema treats all text columns as non-nullable by design. The `else` branch calls `@compileError()`, which halts compilation with a descriptive message if an unsupported type appears in the struct. This means type errors in the schema are caught at compile time rather than producing a malformed SQL string at runtime.

Next is the `bindValue()` function implementation, which dispatches to the correct `sqlite3_bind_*` at compile time based on type:

```
fn bindValue(
    stmt: *sqlite3.sqlite3_stmt,
    col: c_int,
    val: anytype,
) !void {
    const T = @TypeOf(val);
    switch (T) {
        i64, i32 => try checkError(
            sqlite3.sqlite3_bind_int64(stmt, col, @intCast(val)),
        ),
        f64, f32 => try checkError(
            sqlite3.sqlite3_bind_double(stmt, col, @floatCast(val)),
        ),
        []const u8 => try checkError(sqlite3.sqlite3_bind_text(
            stmt,
            col,
            val.ptr,
            @intCast(val.len),
            null,
        )),
```

```
        else => @compileError(
            "unsupported bind type: " ++ @typeName(T),
        ),
    }
}
```

`bindValue()` is a generic binding function that maps a Zig value of any supported type to the correct SQLite parameter binding call. The `val` parameter is declared as `anytype`, which tells the Zig compiler to infer the concrete type at each call site and generate a specialized version of the function for each distinct type used. Inside the function, `@TypeOf(val)` retrieves the inferred type as a compile-time constant, which is then used as the switch discriminant. The switch dispatches to the appropriate SQLite C API call based on the type: integer values use `sqlite3_bind_int64()` with `@intCast()` to widen narrower integer types to `i64`; floating-point values use `sqlite3_bind_double()` with `@floatCast()` to convert between `f32` and `f64`; and string slices use `sqlite3_bind_text()`, passing the slice's `ptr` and `len` fields separately since the C API expects a pointer and a byte count rather than a Zig slice. The final `null` argument tells SQLite to copy the string data rather than taking ownership of it. As with `sqlType()`, the `else` branch calls `@compileError()`, so passing an unsupported type to `bindValue()` is a compile-time error rather than a runtime failure. The result is a single call site — `try bindValue(stmt, col, value)` — that works correctly for any supported type without requiring the caller to know which SQLite binding function to use.

Last, here is `ensureTableExists()` that uses `@typeInfo` to inspect `T`'s fields at compile time and generate the `CREATE TABLE` statement:

```
fn ensureTableExists(
    db: *sqlite3.sqlite3,
    comptime T: type,
) !void {
    const info = @typeInfo(T).@"struct";
    comptime var sql: []const u8 =
        "CREATE TABLE IF NOT EXISTS events (\n";
    inline for (info.fields, 0..) |field, i| {
        const col_type = comptime sqlType(field.type);
        const comma = if (i == 0) "" else ",\n";
        const is_id = comptime std.mem.eql(u8, field.name, "id");
        const pk: []const u8 = if (is_id) " PRIMARY KEY" else "";
        sql = sql ++ comma ++
            "  " ++ field.name ++ " " ++ col_type ++ pk;
```

```
    }
    sql = sql ++ "\n);";
    try checkError(
        sqlite3.sqlite3_exec(db, sql.ptr, null, null, null),
    );
}
```

`ensureTableExists()` is deriving the table schema directly from struct field definitions. It takes a `comptime T: type` parameter — the struct type whose fields will become the table's columns — and begins by extracting the struct's field metadata using `@typeInfo(T).@"struct"`, which returns a `std.builtin.Type.Struct` value containing a slice of field descriptors. The SQL string is built using `comptime var sql`, which is a compile-time mutable string that accumulates the column definitions. The `inline for` loop iterates over every field in the struct at compile time — `inline for` is required here because the loop body references `comptime` values and calls `comptime` functions, which the runtime loop cannot do. For each field, `sqlType(field.type)` maps the Zig type to its SQLite equivalent, a comma separator is prepended for every column after the first, and a special check using `std.mem.eql()` detects whether the field is named `id` — if so, `PRIMARY KEY` is appended to that column definition. Each column definition is concatenated onto `sql` using the ++ operator, which performs string concatenation at compile time. Once the loop completes, the closing `\n);` is appended, and the fully formed SQL string is passed to `sqlite3_exec()` for execution. The entire schema generation happens at compile time — by the time the program runs, `sql` is a string literal baked into the binary, with no runtime allocation and no string construction overhead. Adding a field to the struct automatically adds a column to the generated schema, and removing a field removes the column, keeping the code, and the database schema in sync without any manual SQL maintenance.

With the implementation complete, the relationship between the `Event` struct and the generated SQL is mechanical: the compiler has already resolved the table definition, the placeholder string, and the bind sequence before a single byte of the JSON file is read. What remains is to observe that contract in action — to run the program against real data and confirm that the `comptime` guarantees translate into correct runtime behavior.

Using the utility

Running `ch11/popSQL.zig` requires two things: a JSON file containing an array of `Event` records in the format the struct expects and either an existing SQLite database or a path where one should be created. The program is self-initializing — `ensureTableExists()` runs unconditionally on startup, so there is no separate migration step and no requirement that the database file exist in advance. This means the same command works identically on a fresh database and on one that has been populated by a previous run, with duplicate records silently counted as rejected rather than treated as fatal errors. The sample data generated by `ch11/sampleJSON.zig` serves as a convenient input source, since its output format matches the `Event` struct directly — the `id`, `event`, and `timestamp` fields are present in every record. Records with `id` values that already exist in the database will be rejected and counted in the rejected total. Let us try to insert 1000 records into a new database. First, generate the sample data:

```
$ zig run ch11/sampleJSON.zig -- 1000 > /tmp/1000.json
```

Then insert the records into a new database named `/tmp/ch11.db`:

```
$ zig run ch11/popSQL.zig -I/opt/homebrew/include -L/opt/homebrew/lib -lsqlite3
-- /tmp/ch11.db /tmp/1000.json
Done.
Valid inserts: 1000
Rejected records: 0
```

SQLite wraps every statement that is not explicitly inside a transaction in its own implicit transaction. For a single `INSERT` or `DELETE` operation this is convenient — the statement either succeeds or fails atomically with no extra work. For a bulk operation like the 1,000-record insert in `popSQL.zig`, however, it is a significant performance liability: each implicit transaction flushes the write-ahead log to disk before the next statement can begin, turning 1,000 inserts into 1,000 sequential fsyncs. On a typical SSD this can add between 0.1 and 1 millisecond per statement, meaning the unoptimized bulk insert takes far longer than the application logic alone would require. Wrapping the entire batch in an explicit `BEGIN`/`COMMIT` pair tells SQLite to batch all writes into a single WAL flush on `COMMIT`, reducing 1,000 fsyncs to one — a speedup of one to two orders of magnitude that is immediately measurable even on a loopback benchmark. Transactions also provide atomicity across the batch: without an explicit transaction, a failure midway through the import leaves the database partially populated with no clean way to distinguish a complete import from an interrupted one. With an explicit transaction, a failure before `COMMIT` can be resolved with a `ROLLBACK`, leaving the database exactly as it was before the import began. The rule of thumb for SQLite is simple: any operation that touches more than one row should be wrapped in an explicit transaction, using `ROLLBACK` on error and `COMMIT` on success.

Trying to insert the same 1000 JSON records into the same SQLite3 database produces the following output, demonstrating that the duplicate detection works correctly:

```
$ zig run ch11/popSQL.zig -I/opt/homebrew/include -L/opt/homebrew/lib -lsqlite3
-- /tmp/ch11.db /tmp/1000.json
```

```
ID 1 already exists. Skipping.
ID 2 already exists. Skipping.
. . .
ID 999 already exists. Skipping.
ID 1000 already exists. Skipping.
Done.
Valid inserts: 0
Rejected records: 1000
```

So, `ch11/popSQL.zig` works as expected and does not include duplicate entries.

The `comptime` approach demonstrated here is not free of tradeoffs. The `Event` struct must be fully known at compile time, which means the schema cannot be determined from a configuration file or a database introspection query at startup. Every supported field type must be explicitly handled in `sqlType` and `bindValue`, and any gap produces a build error rather than a graceful runtime fallback. The SQL generated by `ensureTableExists()` is also minimal — it handles primary keys but not foreign keys, indexes, or constraints, all of which would require additional `comptime` logic or a separate migration system. What the approach does buy is a guarantee: the JSON parser, the table definition, and the bind sequence are provably consistent with one another because they all derive from the same struct declaration. In a codebase where schemas evolve frequently, that guarantee is worth more than the flexibility of a fully dynamic approach, because schema drift between the application and the database is one of the most common sources of bugs that only surface in production. The compiler becomes the enforcer of that contract, and the cost is paid once, at build time, by the developer who adds a field — not repeatedly, at runtime, by every user who hits the code path.

With the data pipeline established — generating, transforming, and persisting structured records through a chain of `comptime`-driven components — we now turn to the layer that sits above it all: an HTTP service that exposes those operations to a client over TCP/IP.

Building a note-taking service

The **note-taking service** has a minimal design: a single-file Zig program with no framework, no middleware, and no abstraction layer between the HTTP connection and the SQLite3 database. Every request goes through one function, every query is a prepared statement, and every response is plain text. This directness makes the code easy to follow and the failure modes easy to reason about.

Specifying the functionality of the web service

The note-taking server is a lightweight Zig-based web service built on top of the `std.http.Server` API, designed to handle client requests efficiently while interacting with a persistent SQLite database. It listens for incoming HTTP connections, parses requests and routes them to the appropriate handlers for listing, retrieving, creating or deleting notes. Internally, the server establishes a connection to an SQLite database containing a `notes` table with `id`, `title` and `content` columns. Each request handler validates input parameters, executes parameterized SQL queries to prevent injection attacks and returns plain text responses. The note-taking application exposes a small but powerful set of HTTP endpoints for interacting with stored notes. It is important to understand the available endpoints and their expected parameters. The server responds to `/status` with a simple text message confirming that it is operational. The `/list` endpoint returns all stored notes. The `/search` endpoint accepts a q query parameter and responds with notes whose title or content matches the search term. The `/insert` endpoint expects title and content parameters and adds a new note to the database. Finally, the `/delete` endpoint takes an id parameter to remove the corresponding note. Any requests that do not match these patterns return a plain-text `404 Not Found` error.

With the endpoints defined, we can now look at the implementation. The server startup sequence handles three concerns in order: parsing and validating the command line flags that configure the host, port, and database path; opening the SQLite3 database and ensuring the notes table exists; and entering the accept loop that keeps the process running. The argument parsing loop is the first of these and the most defensive, since a misconfigured server that starts silently is harder to diagnose than one that refuses to start at all.

Implementing the web service

As usual, we begin by looking at the most important part of `main()`'s implementation:

```
while (iter.next()) |arg| {
    if (std.mem.eql(u8, arg, "--host")) {
        host = iter.next() orelse {
            std.debug.print("Error: --host requires a value\n", .{});
            return error.InvalidArguments;
        };
    } else if (std.mem.eql(u8, arg, "--port")) {
        const port_str = iter.next() orelse {
            std.debug.print("Error: --port requires a value\n", .{});
            return error.InvalidArguments;
        };
        port = std.fmt.parseInt(u16, port_str, 10) catch {
```

```
                std.debug.print(
                    "Error: Invalid port '{s}'\n",
                    .{port_str},
                );
                return error.InvalidPort;
            };
            if (port == 0) {
                std.debug.print(
                    "Error: Port must be between 1 and 65535\n",
                    .{},
                );
                return error.InvalidPort;
            }
        } else if (std.mem.eql(u8, arg, "--db")) {
            db_path = iter.next() orelse {
                std.debug.print("Error: --db requires a value\n", .{});
                return error.InvalidArguments;
            };
            if (db_path.len == 0) {
                std.debug.print(
                    "Error: Database path cannot be empty\n",
                    .{},
                );
                return error.InvalidDatabasePath;
            }
        } else {
            std.debug.print("Error: Unknown argument '{s}'\n", .{arg});
            return error.InvalidArguments;
        }
    }
```

The argument parsing loop consumes the iterator one token at a time. For each token it checks whether the value matches one of three known flag names using `std.mem.eql()`, which performs a byte-by-byte comparison rather than pointer equality. When a flag is recognized, the loop immediately calls `iter.next()` a second time to consume the following token as the flag value. This eager consumption is why the iterator is stateful — advancing it inside a branch moves the cursor forward so the outer `while` condition sees the token after the value on its next iteration, not the value itself. The `orelse` block on each inner `next()` call handles the case where a flag appears as the last argument with nothing following it, printing a diagnostic, and returning a typed error rather than silently using a null or a default. The `--port` flag requires two additional validation steps beyond the others. First, `std.fmt.parseInt(u16, port_str, 10)` attempts to parse the string as a base-10 unsigned 16-bit integer. The `u16` type constrains the range to 0–65535 at the type level, so any string representing a number outside that range or any non-numeric string causes `parseInt()` to return an error, which the `catch` block intercepts. Second, even a successfully parsed value of zero is rejected with a dedicated check, because port zero has special meaning to the OS — it requests an ephemeral port assignment rather than binding to a fixed address — and accepting it silently would produce a server listening on an unpredictable port. The `--db` flag applies a simpler check: an empty string passes the `orelse` guard because it is technically a value, so `db_path.len == 0` catches it explicitly, preventing `sqlite3_open()` from receiving an empty path, which SQLite3 would interpret as a request to open a temporary in-memory database rather than a file. The final `else` branch rejects any unrecognized flag immediately. This is a stricter policy than silently ignoring unknown arguments, and it is the right choice for a server: an unrecognized argument is most likely a typo in a flag name, and silently ignoring it would cause the server to start with a default value the operator did not intend, which is harder to diagnose than an immediate error message at startup.

This is the accept loop at the bottom of `main()`, which is also very important:

```
while (true) {
    const stream = listener.accept(io) catch |err| {
        std.log.warn("accept error: {s}", .{@errorName(err)});
        continue;
    };
    handleConnection(io, stream, allocator, db_ptr) catch |err| {
        std.log.debug("connection error: {s}", .{@errorName(err)});
    };
}
```

`listener.accept()` blocks until a client connects. Once it returns, `handleConnection()` runs to completion — parsing the request, querying SQLite, and writing the response — before the loop iterates and `accept()` is called again. This means the server is strictly single-threaded: while one client is being served, every other client is waiting in the operating system's accept queue. A slow query, a large result set, or even a client that reads the response slowly will stall every subsequent connection for the duration. This is a deliberate simplification that keeps the code readable and the ownership model trivial. There is no shared mutable state to protect with a mutex, no allocator to make thread-safe, and no risk of two requests racing to modify the same SQLite connection. SQLite itself is not safe to use from multiple threads on the same connection without additional locking, so a single-threaded server sidesteps that constraint entirely. The practical consequence is that this server is suitable for local tooling, personal utilities, and low-concurrency internal services — exactly the kind of note-taking service this chapter builds. It is not suitable for production workloads where multiple clients may connect simultaneously. If concurrency becomes a requirement, the natural next step is to spawn a new `std.Thread` for each accepted connection, passing ownership of the `conn` value into the thread function. Each thread would need its own SQLite connection rather than sharing `db_ptr`, because a connection cannot be safely shared across threads without serialization. Alternatively, a connection pool — a fixed array of SQLite3 connections protected by a mutex, with threads checking out a connection for the duration of a request and returning it afterward — allows a bounded number of concurrent database operations without the overhead of opening a new connection per request. Both approaches require the allocator passed to `handleConnection()` to be thread-safe; `std.heap.GeneralPurposeAllocator` satisfies that requirement by design. The single-threaded version presented here is therefore not a dead end but a foundation: the accept loop, the connection handling and the SQLite functions all remain unchanged when threading is introduced. Only the loop body and the connection management strategy need to evolve.

> **Note**
>
> To be absolutely fair, the SQLite thread safety depends on the threading mode the library was compiled and opened with. There are three modes: single-thread mode (`SQLITE_THREADSAFE=0`), which performs no internal locking and is unsafe to use from multiple threads at all; multi-thread mode (`SQLITE_OPEN_NOMUTEX`), which is safe as long as no single connection is shared across threads; and serialized mode (`SQLITE_OPEN_FULLMUTEX`), which allows connections to be shared across threads with SQLite handling the internal locking. Most Linux distributions and the official SQLite amalgamation ship in serialized mode by default, which means sharing a connection across threads is technically safe on most systems readers will encounter. However, the mode can be overridden per-connection at open time.

Next, we have the `handleConnection()` implementation:

```
fn handleConnection(
    io: std.Io,
    stream: std.Io.net.Stream,
    alloc: std.mem.Allocator,
    db: *sqlite3.sqlite3,
) !void {
    defer stream.close(io);
```

```
    var reader_buf: [4096]u8 = undefined;
    var writer_buf: [4096]u8 = undefined;
    var r_impl = stream.reader(io,&reader_buf);
    var w_impl = stream.writer(io,&writer_buf);
    var http = std.http.Server.init(
        &r_impl.interface,
        &w_impl.interface,
    );
    var req = try http.receiveHead();
    const method = req.head.method;
    const target = req.head.target;
    const raw = getRawQuery(target);

    const path = getPath(target);
    std.debug.print("Path {s}\n", .{path});

    if (std.mem.eql(u8, path, "/status")) {
        try respondText(&req, "Server is running OK");
        return;
    }
    if (std.mem.eql(u8, path, "/list")) {
        try listNotes(db,alloc,&req);
        return;
    }
    if (std.mem.startsWith(u8, path, "/search")) {
        const q = lookupParam(raw, "q") orelse "";
        try searchNotes(db,alloc,&req,q);
        return;
    }
    if (std.mem.eql(u8, path, "/insert") and method == .GET) {
        const title = lookupParam(raw, "title") orelse "";
        const content = lookupParam(raw, "content") orelse "";
        try insertNote(db,alloc,&req,title,content);
        return;
    }
    if (std.mem.eql(u8, path, "/delete") and method == . POST) {
        const id_str = lookupParam(raw, "id") orelse "0";
        const id = std.fmt.parseInt(i32, id_str, 10) catch 0;
        try deleteNote(db,&req,id);
        return;
    }
```

```
        try req.respond("Error: Not found\n", .{
            .status = .not_found,
            .extra_headers = &.{
                .{ .name = "Content-Type", .value = "text/plain" },
            },
        });
    }
```

The `handleConnection()` function is the central request handler for the note-taking server, responsible for processing incoming client HTTP connections and routing them to the appropriate functionality. It begins by printing the request path for diagnostic purposes. The TCP stream must be wrapped explicitly: `conn.stream.reader()` and `conn.stream.writer()` each receive a stack-allocated buffer and return typed reader and writer values, whose `.interface()` and `&.interface` accessors provide the `*std.Io.Reader` and `*std.Io.Writer` pointers that `std.http.Server.init()` expects. The HTTP request header is then read using `receiveHead()`, from which the request method and target URL are extracted. The query string portion is obtained using `getRawQuery()`, while `getPath()` isolates the clean path without query parameters. Route matching then dispatches each path to its handler, with unrecognized paths returning a `404 Not Found` response in plain text.

> **Note**
>
> The `/insert` endpoint uses `GET` so that examples in this chapter are testable directly with a browser or curl without additional flags — passing `--data` or `--json` to `curl` is not introduced until later. In a production service, `/insert` should use `POST` with a JSON or form-encoded request body, and the server should read the body via `req.reader()` rather than parsing query parameters. Treat the `GET` approach here as an instructional simplification. The `/delete` endpoint uses `POST` to avoid the most serious consequence of the `GET` violation — a browser prefetch or HTTP crawler silently deleting records without any user action.

After that, we have `lookupParam()`:

```
fn lookupParam(raw: []const u8, key: []const u8) ?[]const u8 {
    var start: usize = 0;
    while (start < raw.len) {
        const idxFunc = std.mem.findScalarPos;
```

```
        const eq_pos = idxFunc(u8, raw, start, '=') orelse break;
        const amp_pos = idxFunc(u8, raw, eq_pos, '&')orelseraw.len;

        const k = raw[start..eq_pos];
        const v = raw[eq_pos + 1 .. amp_pos];

        if (std.mem.eql(u8, k, key)) {
            return v;
        }

        start = amp_pos + 1;
    }
    return null;
}
```

The `lookupParam()` function searches for and retrieves the value of a specific query parameter from a raw query string. It takes two byte slices: raw, representing the `raw` query (such as `id=123&name=alice`), and `key`, the parameter name to find. It iterates over the query string starting at position start, looking for an equal sign (=) using `std.mem.findScalarPos()` to separate each parameter name from its value. It also looks for an ampersand (&) to determine the end of the current parameter. The substring before the equals sign is stored as `k`, and the substring after it up to the ampersand is stored as `v`. If k matches the requested key using `std.mem.eql()`, the function returns `v`. If no match is found, it advances past the current parameter and continues searching. If the key is not present in the query string, the function returns null.

Next, we present the `getRawQuery()` implementation:

```
fn getRawQuery(target: []const u8) []const u8 {
    if ( std.mem.findScalar(u8, target, '?')) |p| {
        return target[p + 1 ..];
    }
    return "";
}
```

The `getRawQuery()` function extracts the query string portion of an HTTP request target. It takes a byte slice (`target`), which typically represents the requested URL path along with any query parameters. The function searches for the first occurrence of the ? character using `std.mem.findScalar()`. If found, the position is stored in `p`, and the function returns the substring starting immediately after p, which isolates the raw query part without the leading question mark. If no question mark is present, meaning there are no query parameters, the function returns an empty string slice.

Last, we present searchNotes():

```
fn searchNotes(
    db: *sqlite3.sqlite3,
    alloc: std.mem.Allocator,
    req: *std.http.Server.Request,
    query: []const u8,
) !void {
    const sql = "SELECT id, title, content FROM notes " ++
        "WHERE title LIKE ? OR content LIKE ?";
    var stmt: ?*sqlite3.sqlite3_stmt = null;
    try check(
        sqlite3.sqlite3_prepare_v2(db, sql, -1, &stmt, null),
    );
    defer {
        if (stmt) |s| {
            _ = sqlite3.sqlite3_finalize(s);
        }
    }

    std.debug.print("Query: {s}\n", .{query});
    const pattern = try std.fmt.allocPrint(alloc, "%{s}%", .{query});
    defer alloc.free(pattern);

    try check(sqlite3.sqlite3_bind_text(
        stmt.?,
        1,
        pattern.ptr,
        @as(c_int, @intCast(pattern.len)),
        null,
    ));
    try check(sqlite3.sqlite3_bind_text(
        stmt.?,
        2,
        pattern.ptr,
        @as(c_int, @intCast(pattern.len)),
        null,
```

```
    ));

    var aw: std.Io.Writer.Allocating = .init(alloc);
    defer aw.deinit();

    try aw.writer.writeAll("Search results for: ");
    try aw.writer.writeAll(query);
    try aw.writer.writeAll("\n\n");

    var count: i32 = 0;
    while (sqlite3.sqlite3_step(stmt.?) == sqlite3.SQLITE_ROW) {
        count += 1;
        const id = sqlite3.sqlite3_column_int(stmt.?, 0);
        const title = std.mem.span(
            sqlite3.sqlite3_column_text(stmt.?, 1),
        );
        const content = std.mem.span(
            sqlite3.sqlite3_column_text(stmt.?, 2),
        );

        try aw.writer.print("Note #{d}\n", .{id});
        try aw.writer.print("Title: {s}\n", .{title});
        try aw.writer.print("Content: {s}\n", .{content});
        try aw.writer.writeAll("---\n");
    }

    if (count == 0) {
        try aw.writer.writeAll("No matching notes found.");
    } else {
        try aw.writer.print(
            "Found {d} matching note(s).",
            .{count},
        );
    }

    try respondText(req, aw.writer.buffer[0..aw.writer.end]);
}
```

The `searchNotes()` function adds a search capability to the note-taking web service, allowing clients to query the SQLite3 database for notes whose title or content match a given substring. It constructs an SQL query with `LIKE` clauses to perform pattern matching, prepares the statement with `sqlite3_prepare_v2()`, and ensures proper cleanup with `sqlite3_finalize()` in a `defer` block. The search term is embedded into a pattern of the form `%query%`, which enables partial matches, and this pattern is bound to both the title and content parameters in the SQL query using `sqlite3_bind_text()`. Results are iterated over using `sqlite3_step()`, and for each matching note, the function retrieves the `id`, `title` and `content` fields, formatting them into a response buffer. The function also keeps a count of matches, appending either a `"No matching notes found."` message or a summary line with the total number of results. Finally, it sends the constructed output to the HTTP client via `respondText()`.

The server also registers a handler for the SIGINT signal — the signal the operating system delivers when the user presses Ctrl-C — so that the process exits cleanly rather than being torn down mid-request. This requires a second `@cImport` block alongside the SQLite3 one, this time pulling in the POSIX signal API from `signal.h`. Having two separate `@cImport` blocks is perfectly valid in Zig; each block is an independent translation unit that the compiler processes in isolation, so the SQLite3 and signal namespaces remain distinct and there is no risk of name collisions between the two C headers. The handler itself is a top-level function named `handle_sigint()`, and three of its details are worth examining closely. First, the `export` keyword gives it C-linkage visibility, making it addressable by name from outside the Zig object file; without it, the linker would not produce a symbol that the C `signal()` function can store as a function pointer. Second, `callconv(.c)` specifies the C calling convention explicitly. Signal handlers are called directly by the operating system, which follows the platform C ABI rather than Zig's own internal conventions, and mismatching calling conventions produces subtle stack corruption that only surfaces at runtime under the right conditions. Third, `_ = sig` is the standard Zig idiom for acknowledging a parameter that the function deliberately does not use. The signal number is passed by the OS but the handler has only one job — described below — so discarding it is correct, and the `_ =` assignment suppresses the unused-variable compiler error without introducing a dummy computation.

The body of `handle_sigint()` is a single atomic store: `g_running.store(false, .release)`. This is important. The POSIX standard defines a small list of async-signal-safe functions that may be called from a signal handler; almost everything else — including `printf`, `malloc` and `exit` as well as `std.debug.print` and `std.process.exit` — is explicitly excluded, because those functions may hold internal locks or be in the middle of flushing buffered I/O at the moment the signal arrives, and calling them again from the handler can deadlock or corrupt state. An atomic store on a value of type `std.atomic.Value(bool)` involves no locks and no I/O, so it is safe. The accept loop checks the flag on each iteration via `g_running.load(.acquire)`, and also checks it immediately after a failed `accept()` call so that a signal arriving while the server is blocked in `accept()` exits cleanly rather than logging a spurious error. The shutdown message is printed after the loop exits, in normal program context where it is safe to do so. Registration happens via `c.signal(c.SIGINT, handle_sigint)` at the very start of `main()`, before any networking or database state is established. The return value of `signal()` is the previous handler for `SIGINT`, which this server discards. Calling `signal()` early ensures the handler is in place before the process enters the blocking `listener.accept()` loop, so no Ctrl-C delivered at any point during the server's lifetime goes unhandled. For production use, `std.posix.sigaction()` is the preferred alternative to `c.signal()`: unlike `signal()`, whose behavior after handler delivery is implementation-defined on some platforms — some reset the disposition to `SIG_DFL`, meaning a second Ctrl-C kills the process immediately — `sigaction()` with `SA_RESTART` gives fully specified, portable behavior. *Chapter 7, Managing Threads, Processes, and Signals*, introduced `std.posix.sigaction()` in the context of `zcron`; the pattern here is kept simpler to focus on the atomic-flag technique, but a reader building a production service should prefer `sigaction()`.

With the server compiled and running, the next step is to verify that each route behaves correctly before writing any client code. The most direct tool for this is `curl(1)`. Because the note-taking service communicates entirely over plain HTTP/1.1 and returns plain text responses, `curl(1)` is sufficient to exercise every route — `status`, `list`, `search`, `insert`, and `delete` — and to observe exactly what the server sends back at the byte level. This matters in systems programming: before trusting a higher-level client, it is worth confirming that the wire behavior is correct, that query parameters are parsed as expected, that the SQLite operations commit and roll back cleanly, and that error paths return meaningful messages rather than silent failures.

Testing the web service with curl(1)

With `curl(1)`, you can simulate client behavior, inspect server responses, and catch errors in routing, input parsing, or output formatting. While not a substitute for full automated testing, `curl(1)` is invaluable for interactive debugging and validating individual API features one step at a time. Run the server before executing the `curl(1)` commands — in my case, I used `zig run ch11/noteServer.zig -I/opt/homebrew/include -L/opt/homebrew/lib -lsqlite3` on my macOS machine. Next, run the following:

```
$ curl http://127.0.0.1:8080/status
Server is running OK
$ curl http://127.0.0.1:8080/list
No notes found.
$ curl -G --data-urlencode "title=Shopping" --data-urlencode "content=Milk eggs
bread" http://127.0.0.1:8080/insert
Note successfully created with ID: 2
$ curl http://127.0.0.1:8080/list
```

```
Note #2
Title: Shopping
Content: Milk+eggs+bread
---
Total notes: 1
$ curl -G --data-urlencode "title=Idea" --data-urlencode "content=Learn Zig"
http://127.0.0.1:8080/insert
Note successfully created with ID: 3
$ curl "http://127.0.0.1:8080/search?q=Zig"
Search results for: Zig

Note #3
Title: Idea
Content: Learn+Zig
---
Found 1 matching note(s).
$ curl -X POST "http://127.0.0.1:8080/delete?id=2"
Note successfully deleted
$ curl http://127.0.0.1:8080/list
Note #3
Title: Idea
Content: Learn+Zig
---
Total notes: 1
$ curl "http://127.0.0.1:8080/insert?title=NoContent"
Error: title and content must not be empty
%
$ curl http://127.0.0.1:8080/list
Note #3
Title: Idea
Content: Learn+Zig
---
Total notes: 1
```

The session above walks through every route in order and reveals several behaviors worth understanding before writing production code against this server. The first two commands confirm the server is running and that the database starts empty. The `/status` route always returns the same string regardless of database state, making it a useful liveness check. The `/list` route returns `No notes found.` rather than an empty response or an error when the table has no rows, which is a deliberate usability choice in `listNotes()`. The first insert uses

`--data-urlencode` to send a content value containing spaces. The server assigns ID 2 rather than 1, which reveals that a previous session had already written to this database file — the `AUTOINCREMENT` counter is persistent across connections and never resets even if all rows are deleted. This is important to understand when writing tests that assert specific ID values: the IDs are not guaranteed to start at 1. When the list is retrieved after the insert, the content appears as `Milk+eggs+bread` rather than `Milk eggs bread`. This is because `--data-urlencode` encodes spaces as + rather than `%20` when constructing the query string, and the `lookupParam()` function returns the raw URL value without decoding it. The server has no URL decoding layer, so whatever encoding the client uses is stored verbatim in SQLite and returned verbatim in responses. The Zig client avoids this discrepancy by using `%20` encoding via `urlEncode()` but `curl(1)` with `--data-urlencode` uses + encoding, which is technically valid in a query string but produces visibly different stored content. The search command demonstrates the `LIKE` pattern matching. Sending `q=Zig` causes the server to execute `WHERE title LIKE '%Zig%'OR content LIKE '%Zig%'`, which matches note 3 because its content contains the substring `Zig`. The delete command removes note 2 by ID and the subsequent list confirms it is gone while note 3 remains, demonstrating that delete operates precisely on the specified row and does not affect others. Sending `/insert?title=NoContent` with no `content` parameter does not succeed.

With our web service up and running, accepting and responding to HTTP requests, it is time to shift our focus to building a more user-friendly way to interact with it. While tools like `curl(1)` are great for testing and exploration, they are not ideal for everyday use. In the next section, we will develop a dedicated command-line client in Zig. This client will allow users to add, search, and manage notes with simple commands, streamlining access to the web service without needing to craft raw HTTP requests by hand.

Building a client for the note-taking service

In this section, we develop a command-line client in Zig that communicates with our note-taking web service over HTTP. The goal is to create a lightweight tool that allows users to perform common operations — such as inserting, listing, searching, and deleting notes — directly from the terminal. This client will serve as both a practical utility and a concrete example of how to interact with web APIs programmatically in Zig. Along the way, you learn how to construct requests, handle responses, and manage user input effectively.

The client is a thin command-line wrapper around `std.http.Client` that translates subcommands and their arguments into HTTP GET requests against the note-taking server. Its design mirrors the server route table exactly: every path handled by the server has a corresponding subcommand in the client, and the client job is purely to construct the correct URL and print whatever the server sends back. The argument parsing strategy differs from the server.

Where the server expects only named flags with values, the client treats the first non-flag token as a command name and accumulates all subsequent tokens into a dynamic list using `ArrayListUnmanaged`. This two-phase approach — flags first, then positional arguments — allows the user to place `--host` and `--port` anywhere before the command without ambiguity. The `command_args` list is not interpreted until `buildUri()` is called, at which point each command has its own arity rules enforced: `status` and `list` reject any arguments, `search` requires at least one, `insert` requires at least two and `delete` requires exactly one. The URL construction in `buildUri()` is worth examining in detail. It writes into a fixed stack-allocated buffer of 4096 bytes using `std.fmt.bufPrint()`, which returns an error if the formatted string would overflow the buffer rather than silently truncating it. This is a deliberate safety choice: a sufficiently long title or content value could overflow a naive fixed buffer, and returning an error is preferable to writing past the end of the array. The ` search` and ` insert` commands require URL encoding because the query string values they carry — a search term, a title, a content body — may contain characters that have special meaning in a URL. The `urlEncode()` function handles this by iterating over each byte and either passing it through if `isUrlSafe()` returns `true` or replacing it with a `%XX` hex escape. The set of safe characters — alphanumeric plus `-`, `_`, `.` and `~` — follows the RFC 3986 definition of unreserved characters, which are the only bytes that can appear in a query string without being misinterpreted by an HTTP parser. The HTTP request itself is made with `std.http.Client.fetch()`, which handles connection establishment, request serialization, and response reading in a single call. The response body is captured using `std.Io.Writer.Allocating`: it accumulates bytes into a heap allocation that grows as needed and the final content is read from the writer's internal buffer once the fetch completes. The client checks only the HTTP status code to determine success; any non-200 response is treated as an error and its phrase and numeric code are printed. The server never returns structured error bodies, so there is nothing to parse. The `joinArgs()` helper deserves a brief mention because its behavior has a visible effect on the user experience. For the `insert` command, the title is taken from `args[0..1]` while the content is joined from `args[1..]`. This means a user can write multi-word content without quoting it: `insert Shopping milk eggs bread` produces a title of `Shopping` and a content of `milk eggs bread`. As a result, the title is always a single shell token – a multi-word title must be quoted at the shell level.

Let us now try `ch11/noteClient.zig`:

```
$ zig run ch11/noteClient.zig -- list
Note #3
Title: Idea
Content: Learn+Zig
---
```

```
Note #4
Title: NoContent
Content: 12345
---
Total notes: 2
$ zig run ch11/noteClient.zig -- insert Reading "Animal Farm"
Note successfully created with ID: 5
$ zig run ch11/noteClient.zig -- insert Idea "Learn Zig programming"
Note successfully created with ID: 6
$ zig run ch11/noteClient.zig -- list
Note #3
Title: Idea
Content: Learn+Zig
---
Note #4
Title: NoContent
Content: 12345
---
Note #5
Title: Reading
Content: Animal%20Farm
---
Note #6
Title: Idea
Content: Learn%20Zig%20programming
---
Total notes: 4
$ zig run ch11/noteClient.zig -- search Zig
Search results for: Zig

Note #3
Title: Idea
Content: Learn+Zig
---
Note #6
Title: Idea
Content: Learn%20Zig%20programming
---
Found 2 matching note(s).
$ zig run ch11/noteClient.zig -- search Learn Zig
Search results for: Learn%20Zig
```

```
Note #6
Title: Idea
Content: Learn%20Zig%20programming
---
Found 1 matching note(s).
$ zig run ch11/noteClient.zig -- delete 4
Note successfully deleted
$ zig run ch11/noteClient.zig -- delete 5
Note successfully deleted
$ zig run ch11/noteClient.zig -- list
Note #3
Title: Idea
Content: Learn+Zig
---
Note #6
Title: Idea
Content: Learn%20Zig%20programming
---
Total notes: 2
```

As we are using `zig run` instead of a compiled binary, the `--` separator is required here on every command invocation. The first `list` command shows the current database state. The two `insert` commands add notes 5 and 6. The IDs continue from where the previous session left off. When the list is retrieved afterward, the contrast between note 3 and note 6 is visible and instructive: note 3 content shows `Learn+Zig` because it was inserted by `curl(1)`, while note 6 content shows `Learn%20Zig%20programming` because it was inserted by the Zig client, which uses `%20` encoding. Both records contain the word `Zig` as a substring regardless of encoding, which is why the single-word search `search Zig` returns both. The two-word search `search Learn Zig` demonstrates `joinArgs()` in action. The client joins the two tokens into `Learn Zig`, encodes the space to produce `Learn%20Zig` and sends `q=Learn%20Zig` to the server. The server then constructs the pattern `%Learn%20Zig%` and executes `LIKE '%Learn%20Zig%'` against the stored content. This query matches note 6 because its content is `Learn%20Zig%20programming` but does not match note 3 because its content is `Learn+Zig`, which contains a `+` where the pattern expects `%20`. This is a subtle but important point: the search operates on the stored encoding, not on the decoded meaning. A server with a proper URL decoding layer would decode both values to `Learn Zig` before storing them, and both would then match either search form. The two `delete` commands remove notes 4 and 5, and the final `list` confirms the result: only notes 3 and 6 remain.

Summary

This chapter covered the full arc from raw structured data to a running networked service. You began by parsing nested JSON into typed Zig structs, learning how `std.json.parseFromSlice()` traverses a JSON tree and maps its fields onto struct hierarchies without manual extraction code. From there, you built a validation and reformatting pipeline that distinguished structurally valid records from invalid ones, converting ISO 8601 timestamps into human-readable form while maintaining clean ownership semantics through explicit allocation and duplication. The SQLite3 sections established the mechanics of working with a C library from Zig: opening connections safely with optional pointers, translating C integer return codes into Zig error unions via `checkError`, and using prepared statements with parameter binding to prevent SQL injection. The most technically demanding section used `@typeInfo`, `anytype`, `inline for` and `@field` to build a `comptime` driven JSON-to-database import pipeline where a schema change is a single-line edit to the Event struct and any unsupported field type becomes a build error rather than a runtime failure. The note-taking service brought all these pieces together into a working HTTP server built on `std.http.Server`, demonstrating the `std.Io` interface, query string parsing, parameterized SQL from HTTP parameters, and the tradeoffs of a single-threaded accept loop. The `curl(1)` session exposed a subtle but important consequence of the server having no URL decoding layer: the encoding used at insert time is preserved verbatim in the database, affecting search results in ways that only become visible when clients with different encoding strategies share the same database. The Zig command line client illustrated how `std.http.Client`, `std.Io.Writer.Allocating`, and a custom URL encoder combine into a tool that speaks the same protocol as ` curl ` but produces consistently encoded data.

The next chapter is about exploring something ambitious: writing a simple programming language. This journey will take us beneath the surface of the tools we have been using so far and into the world of *parsers, lexers,* and *interpreters*. By building a small language from scratch, we will see how programming languages translate human-readable instructions into the logic that computers can execute — and in doing so, we will deepen our understanding of how all code, including Zig itself, truly works.

Exercises

- To deepen your understanding, try modifying `ch11/connectSQLite3.zig` to accept the database path as a command-line parameter.
- Write a command-line utility that reads a JSON or NDJSON file and filters records based on a specific field and value (e.g., `"event": "login"`). Output should retain the same format as input.

- Add JSON support to the note-taking server and client. On the server, add a `respondJson()` helper that sets `Content-Type: application/json` and update `listNotes()` and `searchNotes()` to check the `Accept` request header — when it contains `application/json`, serialize the results with `std.json.fmt()` instead of building a plain-text buffer. On the client, add a `--json` flag that sends `Accept: application/json` via the `extra_headers` field of `FetchOptions`. The `insert()` and `delete()` commands return single-line status messages and do not need changes.
- The current `isIso8601()` function in `ch11/writeJSON.zig` verifies that the timestamp string has the correct length, separator positions, and digit content, but it does not check whether the numeric values are in valid ranges. A string like `9999-99-99T99:99:99Z` passes all current checks despite being an impossible date. Extend `isIso8601()` to validate the numeric ranges of each field. Parse the month from positions 5–6 and verify it falls between 01 and 12. Parse the day from positions 8–9 and verify it falls between 01 and 31. Parse the hour from positions 11–12 and verify it falls between 00 and 23. Parse the minutes from positions 14–15 and the seconds from positions 17–18 and verify both fall between 00 and 59. Use `std.fmt.parseInt()` to parse each field and return `false` if parsing fails or the value is out of range. Once the extended validation is in place, add unit tests covering both valid timestamps and each category of invalid input — wrong month, wrong day, wrong hour, wrong minute, and wrong second — and verify that `isIso8601()` correctly rejects all of them. As a further extension, implement day-of-month validation that accounts for the actual number of days in each month, including leap year handling for February.
- The examples in this chapter use shell flags to link against SQLite3. A real project would handle this in `build.zig` instead, making the build portable and reproducible without requiring the developer to remember the correct flags for their platform. So, add a `build.zig` for the note-taking service that links against SQLite3 using `b.linkSystemLibrary("sqlite3")` and `b.linkLibC()`. Define separate executables for `noteServer`, `noteClient`, and the benchmark client, each with the correct source file and SQLite linkage. Verify that `zig build run` works on both macOS and Linux without any manually specified include or library paths. As a further step, add a `zig build test` target that runs the unit tests for the SQL generation functions, so the build system covers both compilation and correctness in a single command.
- The note-taking service currently uses `GET` for `/insert`, passing note fields as query parameters. This violates the HTTP specification's requirement that `GET` requests are safe and have no side effects. Change the `/insert` endpoint to accept `POST` requests with

a JSON body containing the note's fields. Update the server to read the request body using `req.reader()`, parse the JSON payload, and extract the note data from it rather than reading query parameters. Similarly, update `noteClient.zig` to send a `POST` request with a properly formatted JSON body instead of appending fields to the URL. Confirm that a plain `curl http://localhost:8080/insert` without a method flag — which defaults to `GET` — returns a `405 Method Not Allowed` response rather than inserting a record.

- The current `lookupParam()` function in `ch11/noteServer.zig` returns raw URL-encoded values without decoding them, which means a search for `'Learn Zig'` behaves differently depending on whether the client encodes the space as `+` or `%20`. Fix this by implementing URL decoding in `lookupParam()` before the value is returned. The decoding requires two passes: first replace every `+` character with a space, since `application/x-www-form-urlencoded` uses `+` for spaces; after that, decode `%XX` percent-encoded sequences with `std.Uri.percentDecodeBackwards`. Once decoding is in place, verify that both `curl --data-urlencode` and `curl` with a manually percent-encoded query string produce identical search results for the same query.

Additional resources

- SQLite3: `https://sqlite.org/index.html`
- SQLite3 C Bindings: `https://sqlite.org/c3ref/intro.html`
- The `zig-sqlite` package: `https://github.com/vrischmann/zig-sqlite`
- DHH discusses SQLite: `https://www.youtube.com/watch?v=0rlATWBNvMw`

Get this book's PDF version and more

Scan the QR code (or go to `packtpub.com/unlock`). Search for this book by name, confirm the edition, and then follow the steps on the page.

UNLOCK NOW

Note: Keep your invoice handy. Purchases made directly from Packt don't require an invoice.

12

Developing a Domain-Specific Language

There is no better way to understand core programming concepts like syntax trees, scope, and evaluation strategies than by building a programming language from scratch. An interpreter is also a fitting capstone for a systems programming book because it draws on every discipline the previous chapters introduced: the lexer processes raw bytes into tokens using the same stream processing and buffer management covered in *Chapter 4, Processing Streams, Buffers, and Data Encoding*; the parser builds a tree from those tokens using recursive descent, allocating nodes with the same explicit memory ownership model established in *Chapter 3, Direct Memory Access and Binary Formats*; the evaluator walks that tree, managing scope and values in a way that mirrors the data structure design from *Chapter 8, Orchestrating Concurrency and Synchronization*; and the REPL ties everything together into an interactive tool, applying the same input handling and error propagation patterns used throughout the networking chapters. Building an interpreter from scratch is not a departure from systems programming — it is systems programming, applied to the problem of making a machine understand a new language. Zig's simplicity, strong Standard Library and excellent tooling make it an ideal choice for the task. In this chapter, we will construct the three pillars of an interpreter: a Lexer to transform raw text into tokens, a Parser to structure those tokens into a tree, and an Evaluator to execute the code, as well as an interactive shell, the Read-Eval-Print Loop, or REPL.

This chapter covers:

- The `zcalc` Language and the EBNF grammar of `zcalc`
- Lexing: Breaking strings into Tokens
- Parsing: Abstract Syntax Trees (AST) and Recursion

- Evaluation: Tree-Walking Execution
- REPL: Building an interactive shell

The zcalc language

In this section, we are going to describe the **zcalc language** before we implement it. We begin by formally defining the language using EBNF.

The EBNF grammar of zcalc

To translate a sequence of raw tokens into a meaningful abstract syntax tree, we rely on a formal specification written in **Extended Backus-Naur Form** (EBNF). This notation serves as the exact blueprint for our recursive descent parser, defining the legal syntactic structure of `zcalc` from the highest level of a complete program down to the smallest atomic characters. Reading the grammar is essentially reading the execution flow of the parser itself. Every rule defined on the left side of an equals sign maps directly to a discrete parsing function in our Zig implementation. The sequences on the right side dictate the specific tokens that the function must expect and consume, as well as the subsequent parsing functions it must invoke to satisfy the rule. This direct translation from a formal grammar to executable code ensures that the interpreter strictly adheres to the language design without ambiguity. Here is the EBNF grammar:

```
Program             = { Statement } ;
Statement           = LetStatement
                    | AssignmentStatement
                    | ReturnStatement
                    | ExpressionStatement
                    | IfStatement ;

LetStatement        = "let" Identifier "=" Expression [ ";" ] ;
AssignmentStatement = Identifier "=" Expression ";" ;
ReturnStatement     = "return" Expression [ ";" ] ;
ExpressionStatement = Expression [ ";" ] ;
IfStatement         = "if" Expression Block [ "else" Block ] ;

Block               = "{" { Statement } "}" ;

Expression          = Equality ;
Equality            = Relational { ("==" | "!=") Relational } ;
Relational          = Addition { ("<" | ">" | "<=" | ">=") Addition } ;
Addition            = Multiplication { ("+" | "-") Multiplication } ;
Multiplication      = Primary { ("*" | "/") Primary } ;
```

```
Primary              = Number
                     | String
                     | Identifier
                     | "(" Expression ")" ;

Identifier           = Letter { Letter | Digit | "_" } ;
Number               = Digit { Digit } ;
String               = "\"" { Character | Escape } "\"" ;
Letter               = "a"…"z" | "A"…"Z" ;
Digit                = "0"…"9" ;
Escape               = "\\\"" ;
```

Note

If you have not encountered the EBNF format before, the notation is straightforward. Each rule has a name on the left of the = sign and a definition on the right. A | separates alternatives — `'true' | 'false'` means either the literal `true` or the literal `false`. Parentheses group alternatives together. A ? means the preceding element is optional — it appears zero or one times. A * means zero or more repetitions, and a + means one or more. Terminal symbols — the literal characters and keywords that appear directly in source code — are enclosed in single quotes. Everything else is a rule name that refers to another definition elsewhere in the grammar. Reading a grammar rule from left to right tells you exactly what sequence of tokens is valid at that point in the language.

The **zcalc language** is designed as a compact, imperative programming environment focused on straightforward sequential execution and state management. At its core, a program in this language is constructed from a sequence of statements, executing from top to bottom. The language provides fundamental memory management through variable declarations initiated by the `let` keyword, alongside direct assignment statements used to mutate existing bindings. The logic behind strictly separating variable declaration from assignment ensures that the underlying environment can explicitly distinguish between the introduction of new identifiers into the current scope and the modification of existing state, which is a crucial distinction for catching runtime errors like undefined variables. Furthermore, the language supports conditional control flow through standard `if` and optional `else` constructs. By mandating that conditional branches be enclosed in explicit blocks surrounded by braces, the grammar deliberately avoids the notorious dangling-else ambiguity, ensuring that scoping boundaries remain rigidly clear to both the parser and the programmer.

> **Note**
>
> The string implementation in `zcalc` supports only one escape sequence: `\"`, which allows a double-quote character to appear inside a string literal without terminating it. Other escape sequences that you might expect (especially if you are coming from C, Go, or Python), like `\n` for newline, `\t` for tab, `\\` for a literal backslash, `\r` for carriage return, are not supported. The characters `\n` in a `zcalc` string are stored as the two literal bytes `\` and `n`, not as a newline character. Extending the lexer to support the standard escape sequences is left as an exercise for the reader — the `readString()` function is the only place that needs to change, and adding a `switch` over the character following each `\` is the natural implementation.

Evaluation in `zcalc` is driven by a carefully stratified expression grammar that natively enforces standard mathematical operator precedence. The recursive descent hierarchy encodes the rules of arithmetic directly into the syntax, ensuring that multiplication and division operations tightly bind to their operands before any addition or subtraction is evaluated. Relational operators for magnitude comparisons and equality checks logically occupy the lowest precedence levels; this design allows complex arithmetic expressions on either side of a comparison to be fully resolved before the Boolean evaluation occurs. Grouping via parentheses is supported at the primary level, granting the programmer the ability to manually override these built-in precedence rules. This layered approach to parsing simplifies the evaluator's internal implementation because the abstract syntax tree inherently reflects the correct order of operations without requiring additional sorting passes. In terms of data capabilities, `zcalc` operates on basic primitive types. The foundational components of any expression ultimately resolve down to numeric literals, which are defined purely as continuous digits representing integers, and string literals that support character escapes for basic text manipulation. Identifiers are formed using a traditional alphanumeric structure starting with a letter, providing a familiar nomenclature for variable naming. While the grammar as defined lacks complex compound data structures or explicit function definitions, the inclusion of a `return` statement indicates an architecture designed to support exiting a specific context or block with a computed value. Ultimately, `zcalc` presents a tightly focused foundation that provides the essential building blocks — sequence, conditional selection, and state manipulation — necessary for evaluating procedural logic and arithmetic.

The most critical architectural decision within this grammar is the strict, deliberate separation between *statements* and *expressions*. **Statements** form the structural backbone of the control flow; constructs like variable declarations, assignments, and conditional branches execute actions and modify the environment state, but they do not resolve to a distinct value. **Expressions** act as the computational engine, fundamentally designed to be evaluated down to a single primitive result. Within the expression subset, the grammar's most powerful feature is its stratified hierarchy, which natively enforces operator precedence. By forcing the parser to descend from broad equality checks down through relational operators, addition, and finally multiplication, the grammar inherently guarantees that mathematical operations bind more tightly than logical comparisons. This nested structure allows the abstract syntax tree to represent the correct order of operations purely by its physical shape, entirely bypassing the need for complex, secondary precedence-sorting algorithms.

To understand how `zcalc` operates from the moment code is written to the moment a result is produced, it is instructive to trace a complete program through the interpreter internal pipeline. Consider a simple script that calculates the area of a triangle and categorizes its size. The program defines a base and a height, computes the area, and uses a conditional branch to return a string describing whether the resulting area is large or small:

```
let base = 10;
let height = 5;
let area = (base * height) / 2;
if (area > 20) {
    return "Large";
} else {
    return "Small";
}
```

The lifecycle of this script begins with the *lexer*. As the interpreter reads the raw character stream, the lexer discards meaningless whitespace and categorizes the text into a sequence of discrete tokens. For the first line, it recognizes the characters `l-e-t` as a language keyword, emitting a distinct `Let` token. It then reads `b-a-s-e` and categorizes it as an `Identifier`, followed by an `Assign` token for the equals sign, an `Int` token containing the numeric value `10`, and a `SemiColon` to terminate the sequence. This converts a string of characters into a structured, predictable vocabulary that the next phase can easily digest. Once the token stream is generated, it is fed into the *parser*, which constructs the *Abstract Syntax Tree*. The parser imposes the language's grammar upon the flat sequence of tokens. When it encounters the `Let` token, it immediately knows it is building a `LetStatement` and expects an identifier followed by an assignment operator and an expression. The third line provides a clear example of how the parser handles precedence. It encounters the parentheses and recursively parses the internal multiplication as an isolated expression. This multiplication node is then attached as the left child of a division node, ensuring that the tree structurally represents the mathematical rule that the base and height must be multiplied together before the division occurs. The conditional structure is parsed into a node containing three distinct branches: a condition expression checking if the area exceeds 20, a consequence block containing the first return statement, and an alternative block containing the second. Execution begins when the evaluator traverses this fully constructed **Abstract Syntax Tree**. The evaluator maintains an environment, which is fundamentally a hash map acting as the program's memory. Walking the tree from the top down, it evaluates the first declaration by reducing the integer 10 to a runtime value and storing it in the environment under the key "base". The same process occurs for the height. When evaluating the area statement, the evaluator looks up the values for the two variables in the environment, performs the multiplication to get 50, divides by 2 to yield 25, and stores this result. Reaching the conditional, the evaluator compares the stored value of the area against 20. Finding the condition to be true, it ignores the alternative branch and steps directly into the consequence block. Finally, it evaluates the `return` statement, which wraps the string `Large` in a special control-flow object. This object signals the evaluator to immediately halt any further execution in the current block and bubble the final result back to the host program.

Before diving into the implementation, it is worth understanding how the source files are organized. The `lexer.zig` source code file is a standalone, self-contained program that implements only the lexer and includes a `main()` function for running it directly against an input file. The `parser.zig` source code file is also self-contained: it embeds a compact copy of the lexer alongside the full parser and its own `main()` function, so it can be compiled and run independently to inspect the AST of any source file. The `evaluator.zig` source code file follows the same pattern, embedding copies of both the lexer and the parser next to the evaluator logic. This deliberate redundancy means that each stage can be studied, compiled, and debugged in complete isolation, without managing build dependencies between files. The `repl.zig` source code file is the final, integrated artifact. It consolidates all three stages into a single compilation unit and adds the interactive shell on top. When working through the chapter, the progression from `lexer.zig` through to `repl.zig` mirrors the conceptual progression of the interpreter itself.

Let us now see the three stages in more detail, starting with lexing.

Lexing: breaking strings into tokens

A computer program begins its life as nothing more than a sequence of characters, an undifferentiated stream of bytes. Before we can make sense of the programmer's intent, we must group these raw characters into meaningful words, or tokens. This process is called **lexing**. The logic behind separating lexing from the rest of the interpreter is one of simplicity and isolation. By handling the messy details of ignoring spaces, skipping comments, and recognizing numbers and keywords early, we present a clean, structured sequence to the next phase. The **lexer** acts as a specialized filter, transforming a chaotic string into a manageable, predictable vocabulary.

Every token in `zcalc` belongs to one of the variants defined in the `TokenType` enum. The enum separates single-character punctuation from multi-character operators and from the reserved keywords of the language. The design principle here is *clarity*: by giving each distinct lexical category a named variant, every subsequent stage of the interpreter can switch on a clean, typed value rather than comparing raw strings. The `Token` struct that pairs a `TokenType` with a string literal slice is intentionally minimal. It holds a view into the original input buffer rather than copying bytes, which keeps allocation entirely out of the lexer's responsibility:

```
pub const TokenType = enum {
    Illegal, Eof, Ident, Int, String,
    Assign, Plus, Minus, Asterisk, Slash, Bang,
    Lt, Gt, LtEq, GtEq, Eq, NotEq,
    Comma, SemiColon, LParen, RParen, LBrace, RBrace,
    Let, Return, If, Else,
};

pub const Token = struct {
    type: TokenType,
    literal: []const u8,
};
```

The Lexer struct maintains three pieces of state: the full input slice, a `position` cursor pointing at the character currently under examination, and a `read_position` cursor pointing one character ahead. This two-pointer design is the heart of the lexer. It allows the lexer to consume the current character while simultaneously looking at the next one, which is necessary for distinguishing single-character tokens like `=` from two-character tokens like `==`. The field `ch` caches the current character so that every switch arm can inspect it without indexing the slice repeatedly:

```
pub const Lexer = struct {
    input: []const u8,
    allocator: std.mem.Allocator,
    position: usize = 0,
    read_position: usize = 0,
    ch: u8 = 0,


    pub fn init(
        allocator: std.mem.Allocator,
        input: []const u8,
    ) Lexer {
```

```
        var l = Lexer{ .input = input, .allocator = allocator };
        l.readChar();
        return l;
    }

    fn readChar(self: *Lexer) void {
        if (self.read_position >= self.input.len) {
            self.ch = 0;
        } else {
            self.ch = self.input[self.read_position];
        }
        self.position = self.read_position;
        self.read_position += 1;
    }

    fn peekChar(self: *Lexer) u8 {
        if (self.read_position >= self.input.len) return 0;
        return self.input[self.read_position];
    }
```

The sentinel value of zero for `ch` is a design choice. It represents end-of-input and maps cleanly to the `Eof` token without requiring any special-case branching in `readChar()`. When `init()` calls `readChar()` immediately, it primes the lexer so that the first call to `nextToken` finds the very first character already loaded into `ch`.

Three helper methods handle the reading of multi-character lexemes. `skipWhitespace()` simply advances past spaces, tabs, and newlines using the standard library predicate `std.ascii.isWhitespace()`. `readIdentifier()` and `readNumber()` each record a start position and then advance the position and `read_position` cursors forward until the character class changes, returning the slice of the input between the start and the new position. No heap allocation occurs; the returned slice is a window directly into the original input buffer.

```
fn skipWhitespace(self: *Lexer) void {
    while (std.ascii.isWhitespace(self.ch)) {
        self.readChar();
    }
}

fn readIdentifier(self: *Lexer) []const u8 {
    const start = self.position;
```

```
    while (std.ascii.isAlphabetic(self.ch) or
        self.ch == '_' or
        std.ascii.isDigit(self.ch))
    {
        self.readChar();
    }
    return self.input[start..self.position];
}

fn readNumber(self: *Lexer) []const u8 {
    const start = self.position;
    while (std.ascii.isDigit(self.ch)) {
        self.readChar();
    }
    return self.input[start..self.position];
}
```

String reading works slightly differently. Because the opening double-quote is the current character when `readString()` is invoked, the method first advances past it, then scans character by character until it reaches a closing quote or end of input. Rather than returning a slice of the source, it builds the decoded contents in an allocator-backed buffer: on encountering a backslash, it consumes the next byte and translates the escape (`\n`, `\t`, `\r`, `\0`, `\"` and `\\` taken literally). Because the byte after a backslash is always consumed as part of the escape, an escaped backslash correctly protects a following quote instead of confusing the terminator search. The caller owns the returned slice.

```
// readString consumes a double-quoted string and returns its decoded
// contents. Backslash escapes are translated explicitly: the byte after
// a backslash is taken literally (with the usual \n, \t, \r, \0
// mappings), so an escaped backslash (\\) correctly protects the
// following quote instead of confusing the terminator search. The
// caller owns the returned slice.
fn readString(self: *Lexer) ![]const u8 {
    var buf: std.ArrayListUnmanaged(u8) = .empty;
    errdefer buf.deinit(self.allocator);
    self.readChar(); // consume the opening quote
    while (self.ch != '"' and self.ch != 0) {
        if (self.ch == '\\') {
            self.readChar();
            if (self.ch == 0) break; // trailing backslash at EOF
```

```
            const decoded: u8 = switch (self.ch) {
                'n' => '\n',
                't' => '\t',
                'r' => '\r',
                '0' => 0,
                // \" \\ and any other escape are literal
                else => self.ch,
            };
            try buf.append(self.allocator, decoded);
        } else {
            try buf.append(self.allocator, self.ch);
        }
        self.readChar();
    }
    // The loop stops on a closing quote or on end of input.
    // Reaching EOF first means the literal was never closed,
    // e.g. `"hello;` - report it rather than silently returning
    // everything up to EOF as a string.
    if (self.ch != '"') return error.UnterminatedString;
    return buf.toOwnedSlice(self.allocator);
}
```

Keyword detection is factored into its own pure function, `lookupIdent()`. After `readIdentifier()` returns a slice, that slice is passed to `lookupIdent()`, which performs four equality checks against the reserved words of `zcalc`. If none match, it returns `.Ident`, meaning the text is a user-defined identifier. This separation means that the main token-dispatch method never needs to reason about keywords directly.

```
fn lookupIdent(ident: []const u8) TokenType {
    if (std.mem.eql(u8, ident, "let")) return .Let;
    if (std.mem.eql(u8, ident, "return")) return .Return;
    if (std.mem.eql(u8, ident, "if")) return .If;
    if (std.mem.eql(u8, ident, "else")) return .Else;
    return .Ident;
}
```

The public method `nextToken()` ties everything together:

```
pub fn nextToken(self: *Lexer) !Token {
        self.skipWhitespace();
```

```
        var tok: Token = undefined;

        switch (self.ch) {
            '=' => {
                if (self.peekChar() == '=') {
                    self.readChar();
                    tok = .{ .type = .Eq, .literal = "==" };
                } else {
                    tok = .{ .type = .Assign, .literal = "=" };
                }
            },
            // ... remaining single-character cases ...
            '"' => {
                tok.type = .String;
                tok.literal = try self.readString();
            },
            0 => tok = .{ .type = .Eof, .literal = "" },
            else => {
                if (std.ascii.isAlphabetic(self.ch)) {
                    const literal = self.readIdentifier();
                    tok.type = lookupIdent(literal);
                    tok.literal = literal;
                    return tok;
                } else if (std.ascii.isDigit(self.ch)) {
                    tok.type = .Int;
                    tok.literal = self.readNumber();
                    return tok;
                } else {
                    tok = .{ .type = .Illegal, .literal = "" };
                }
            },
        }
        self.readChar();
        return tok;
    }
```

The code first calls `skipWhitespace()` to discard any irrelevant characters, then switches on the current character `ch`. Single-character punctuation maps directly to a token literal. For operators that could be either one or two characters, `peekChar()` is called before consuming the second character: if a `=` is followed by another `=`, the lexer advances and emits `.Eq`; otherwise, it emits `.Assign`. Notice that `readIdentifier()` and `readNumber()` return early from `nextToken()` without calling the trailing `readChar()`. This is because those helpers already leave the cursor positioned at the first character that does not belong to the current lexeme. All other paths fall through to the `readChar()` call at the bottom of the method, which advances past the single character that was just tokenized.

The standalone `main()` function in `lexer.zig` exists purely for verification. It accepts a filename as a command line argument, reads the file into an arena-backed buffer, and drives the lexer in a loop until it encounters `.Eof`, printing each token type and literal to the debug output. Running `zig run lexer.zig --math.small` against one of the sample programs shows exactly what the parser will receive as input, making it a valuable diagnostic tool when extending the language with new syntax.

```
$ cat ch12/math.small
let a = 10;
let b = 5;
let c = a * 2 + b * 4;
return c;
$ zig run ch12/lexer.zig -- ch12/math.small
Lexing file: ch12/math.small
----------------
Type: .Let Literal: let
Type: .Ident Literal: a
Type: .Assign Literal: =
Type: .Int Literal: 10
Type: .SemiColon Literal: ;
Type: .Let Literal: let
Type: .Ident Literal: b
Type: .Assign Literal: =
Type: .Int Literal: 5
Type: .SemiColon Literal: ;
Type: .Let Literal: let
Type: .Ident Literal: c
Type: .Assign Literal: =
Type: .Ident Literal: a
Type: .Asterisk Literal: *
Type: .Int Literal: 2
Type: .Plus Literal: +
Type: .Ident Literal: b
Type: .Asterisk Literal: *
```

```
Type: .Int Literal: 4
Type: .SemiColon Literal: ;
Type: .Return Literal: return
Type: .Ident Literal: c
Type: .SemiColon Literal: ;
Type: .Eof Literal:
```

With the lexer in hand, the raw source text of a `zcalc` program has been reduced to exactly the kind of structured, predictable sequence shown above. Every keyword, operator, identifier, and literal has been given a name and a value. Whitespace has been discarded. The messy reality of character-by-character reading is entirely behind us. What remains is a flat, linear stream of tokens — and that word, flat, is precisely the problem. A sequence has no hierarchy. It cannot express the fact that the multiplication on line three must be resolved before the addition, or that the body of an if block belongs to the condition that precedes it and not to whatever statement comes after. To capture those relationships, we need to move from a sequence to a tree.

Parsing: abstract syntax trees (ASTs) and recursion

Once the lexer has reduced the source text to a sequence of tokens, the next task is to discover the grammatical structure of the program. Tokens alone lack hierarchy; a plus sign and a number mean little without knowing what they connect to. **Parsing** is the act of imposing the language grammar onto this flat sequence, building a hierarchical representation known as an **Abstract Syntax Tree**. We construct a tree because programming languages are inherently nested: expressions contain sub-expressions, and control structures contain blocks of statements. To navigate and build this nested reality, we rely heavily on recursion. A recursive descent parser translates our grammar rules directly into function calls, providing a straightforward, elegant mapping between the language specification and the code that implements it.

The **parser** operates on two distinct levels: the statement level and the expression level. This separation is encoded directly into the two tagged unions, `Stmt` and `Expr`. A `Stmt` can be one of five variants — `Let`, `Assign`, `Return`, `Expression`, or `If` — and it represents an action that modifies the program's state or controls its flow. An `Expr` resolves to a value and can be either a literal integer, a literal string, an identifier lookup, or a Binary node connecting two child expressions through an operator:

```
const BinaryOp = enum { Add, Sub, Mul, Div, Eq, NotEq, Lt, Gt, LtEq, GtEq };

const Expr = union(enum) {
    Integer:    i64,
    String:     []const u8,
    Identifier: []const u8,
```

```
    Binary: struct { left: *Expr, op: BinaryOp, right: *Expr },
};

const Stmt = union(enum) {
    Let:        struct { name: []const u8, value: Expr },
    Assign:     struct { name: []const u8, value: Expr },
    Return:     Expr,
    Expression: Expr,
    If: struct { condition: Expr, consequence: []Stmt, alternative: ?[]Stmt },
};
```

The `Binary` node requires heap-allocated pointers for its children because a tagged union in Zig cannot directly embed a recursive type — the compiler cannot determine the size of `Expr` if `Expr` can contain another `Expr` inline. The allocator passed to the parser at initialization is what makes this possible. Each time a `Binary` node is constructed, the parser calls `allocator.create(Expr)` twice — once for the left child and once for the right — which reserves space for each `Expr` on the heap and returns a pointer to it. The child expression is then written into that reserved space with `ptr.* = value`, and the resulting two pointers are stored inside the `Binary` node. The node itself knows its children only as `*Expr`, never as inline values, which breaks the recursive size dependency and allows the compiler to determine the size of `Expr` without ambiguity.

> **Note**
>
> All AST allocations come from a single allocator passed to the parser. In every program in this chapter — the standalone lexer/parser/evaluator tools and the REPL — that allocator is the process arena, obtained from the runtime via `init.arena.allocator()`, so all AST memory is freed in one operation when the process exits. This is why no `deinit` methods are defined. Note that the REPL uses this single arena for the entire session and does not reset it between input lines, so memory grows for as long as the REPL runs — acceptable for learning purposes but not what you would want in a long-lived interpreter. To reclaim memory mid-session, you would reset (or swap) the arena per evaluation or add explicit `deinit` methods that walk the tree and free each node.

The `Parser` struct holds the lexer, two token slots (`cur` and `peek`), and the allocator. The two-token look-ahead mirrors the same two-pointer design used in the lexer. When `init()` calls nextToken() twice, it primes cur_token with the first token and peek_token with the second, so that every parsing function can inspect the upcoming token without consuming it.

```
const Parser = struct {
    l: Lexer,
    cur_token: Token,
    peek_token: Token,
    allocator: Allocator,

    fn init(allocator: Allocator, l: Lexer) Parser {
        var p = Parser{
            .l = l,
            .allocator = allocator,
            .cur_token = undefined,
            .peek_token = undefined,
        };
        p.nextToken();
        p.nextToken();
        return p;
    }

    fn nextToken(self: *Parser) void {
        self.cur_token = self.peek_token;
        self.peek_token = self.l.nextToken();
    }
};
```

parseProgram() is the top-level entry point. It loops until it sees .Eof, parsing one statement per iteration and appending it to an ArrayList. The call to toOwnedSlice() at the end transfers ownership of the backing memory to the caller and returns a plain Zig slice, which is the canonical form the evaluator expects.

```
fn parseProgram(self: *Parser) anyerror![]Stmt {
    var statements = std.ArrayList(Stmt).empty;
    while (self.cur_token.type != .Eof) {
        const stmt = try self.parseStatement();
        try statements.append(self.allocator, stmt);
        self.nextToken();
    }
```

```
    return statements.toOwnedSlice(self.allocator);
}
```

Statement dispatch in parseStatement() uses a switch on cur_token.type. The interesting case is the .Ident branch, which uses a one-token look-ahead: if peek is .Assign, the identifier begins an assignment statement; otherwise, it is the start of an expression statement. This lookahead is the minimum context required to resolve the ambiguity without backtracking:

```
fn parseStatement(self: *Parser) anyerror!Stmt {
    switch (self.cur_token.type) {
        .Let => return self.parseLetStatement(),
        .Return => return self.parseReturnStatement(),
        .If => return self.parseIfStatement(),
        .Ident => {
            if (self.peek_token.type == .Assign) {
                return self.parseAssignStatement();
            }
            return self.parseExpressionStatement();
        },
        else => return self.parseExpressionStatement(),
    }
}
```

parseLetStatement() advances three times: first to move cur_token to the identifier, then twice more to skip over the identifier and the = sign so that cur_token lands on the first token of the value expression:

```
fn parseLetStatement(self: *Parser) anyerror!Stmt {
    try self.expectPeek(.Ident);
    const name = self.cur_token.literal;
    try self.expectPeek(.Assign);
    self.nextToken();
    const value = try self.parseExpression();
    if (self.peek_token.type == .SemiColon) self.nextToken();
    return Stmt{ .Let = .{ .name = name, .value = value } };
}

fn parseAssignStatement(self: *Parser) anyerror!Stmt {
    const name = self.cur_token.literal;
    self.nextToken(); // move to =
```

```
    self.nextToken(); // move past =
    const value = try self.parseExpression();
    if (self.peek_token.type == .SemiColon) self.nextToken();
    return Stmt{ .Assign = .{ .name = name, .value = value } };
}
```

parseAssignStatement() follows the same logic but begins with the identifier already in cur_token, needing only two advances. Both functions consume the optional trailing semicolon using a conditional peek rather than requiring it unconditionally, which makes the parser more forgiving of omissions.

The if-statement parser illustrates how blocks are handled. After parsing the condition expression, parseIfStatement() looks ahead to the { delimiter, then delegates to parseBlock. The alternative branch is parsed only if peek holds .Else after the consequence block is complete:

```
fn parseIfStatement(self: *Parser) anyerror!Stmt {
    self.nextToken();
    const condition = try self.parseExpression();
    try self.expectPeek(.LBrace);
    const consequence = try self.parseBlock();
    var alternative: ?[]Stmt = null;
    if (self.peek_token.type == .Else) {
        self.nextToken();
        try self.expectPeek(.LBrace);
        alternative = try self.parseBlock();
    }
    return Stmt{ .If = .{
        .condition = condition,
        .consequence = consequence,
        .alternative = alternative,
    } };
}
```

parseBlock() is structurally identical to parseProgram(), differing only in its termination condition: it stops when it sees .RBrace rather than .Eof. This makes the block parser naturally composable with the if-statement parser and keeps the overall structure flat and easy to follow.

The expression parsing functions form the most mechanically important part of the parser. Each function handles one precedence level and calls the function one level below it. This descent from parseEquality() down to parsePrimary() means that lower-precedence operators are always recognized last, and by the time the tree is built, higher-precedence operations sit deeper in the tree and will therefore be evaluated first by the evaluator. The while-loop structure at each level correctly handles left-associativity: the left operand accumulates successive right-hand sides before any of them are returned. `parseAddition()` illustrates the pattern shared by all four expression-level functions:

```
fn parseAddition(self: *Parser) anyerror!Expr {
    var left = try self.parseMultiplication();
    while (self.peek_token.type == .Plus or
            self.peek_token.type == .Minus)
        {
        self.nextToken();
        const op: BinaryOp = if (self.cur_token.type == .Plus)
            .Add
        else
            .Sub;
        self.nextToken(); // Advance past operator
        const right = try self.parseMultiplication();
        const left_ptr = try self.allocator.create(Expr);
        left_ptr.* = left;
        const right_ptr = try self.allocator.create(Expr);
        right_ptr.* = right;
        left = Expr{
            .Binary = .{.left = left_ptr, .op = op, .right = right_ptr},
        };
    }
    return left;
}
```

The method handles integer literals by parsing them immediately with `std.fmt.parseInt()`, string literals by capturing the slice already stored in the token, identifiers by recording the name, and grouped expressions by recursing back up to `parseExpression()` after consuming the `(`. The pattern is uniform: every primary produces a value and leaves cur at the last token it consumed.

Let us now try `ch12/parser.zig` with `ch12/math.small`:

```
$ zig run ch12/parser.zig -- ch12/math.small
Parsing file: ch12/math.small
----------------
Successfully parsed 4 statements.
Stmt 0: .{ .Let = .{ .name = a, .value = .{ .Integer = 10 } } }
Stmt 1: .{ .Let = .{ .name = b, .value = .{ .Integer = 5 } } }
```

```
Stmt 2: .{ .Let = .{ .name = c, .value = .{ .Binary = .{ ... } } } }
Stmt 3: .{ .Return = .{ .Identifier = c } }
```

The parser output shown above makes the tree structure concrete. What was a flat sequence of tokens is now a hierarchy of nested nodes, each one encoding both a value and its relationship to the values around it. The `Binary` node for the third statement does not merely record that `a`, `*`, `2`, `+`, `b`, `*`, and `4` appeared in the source; it records that `a*2` and `b*4` are independent multiplications whose results are the two operands of the addition. That structural fact, baked into the shape of the tree by the precedence hierarchy of the parser, is exactly what the evaluator needs. It never has to reason about operator precedence or parse order. It simply walks the tree from the top down, and the correct order of operations emerges naturally from the depth at which each node sits.

Evaluation: tree-walking execution

With a fully formed syntax tree in memory, the evaluator's task is to traverse it and reduce every node to a runtime value. The runtime type system of `zcalc` is encoded in the `RuntimeVal()` union, which can hold a 64-bit integer, a string slice, a Boolean, or a special `ReturnWrapper()` variant. The `ReturnWrapper` is not a user-visible type but a control-flow signal. When the evaluator encounters a return statement, it boxes the resulting value inside a `ReturnWrapper()` and propagates it up through every recursive call until the outermost loop detects it and unwraps the final result:

```
const RuntimeVal = union(enum) {
    Integer:       i64,
    String:        []const u8,
    Boolean:       bool,
    Void,
    ReturnWrapper: *RuntimeVal,
};
```

The program's memory is an `Environment` struct wrapping a `StringHashMap`. `get()` and `set()` are thin methods over the map's own get and put. The allocator is stored inside the environment so that the `ReturnWrapper` heap allocation and string concatenation can both draw from the same arena without needing to pass an allocator to every evaluation function individually.

```
const Environment = struct {
    store: std.StringHashMap(RuntimeVal),
    allocator: Allocator,
```

```
    fn init(allocator: Allocator) Environment {
        return Environment{
            .store = std.StringHashMap(RuntimeVal).init(allocator),
            .allocator = allocator,
        };
    }
    fn get(self: *Environment, name: []const u8) ?RuntimeVal {
        return self.store.get(name);
    }
    fn set(self:*Environment, name:[]const u8, val:RuntimeVal) !void {
        try self.store.put(name, val);
    }
};
```

The top-level `eval()` function dispatches on the statement variant. `Let` and `Assign` both reduce their value expression and store it in the environment; the only difference between them at the evaluation stage is the name used as the map key, which was already validated at parse time. The `Return` case evaluates its expression, allocates a `RuntimeVal()` on the heap, and wraps it before returning. The `If` case calls `isTruthy()` on the condition and then delegates either to the consequence slice or the optional alternative.

```
fn eval(node: Stmt, env: *Environment) anyerror!RuntimeVal {
    switch (node) {
        .Expression => |expr| return evalExpr(expr, env),
        .Return => |expr| {
            const val = try evalExpr(expr, env);
            const ptr = try env.allocator.create(RuntimeVal);
            ptr.* = val;
            return RuntimeVal{ .ReturnWrapper = ptr };
        },
        .Let => |let_stmt| {
            const val = try evalExpr(let_stmt.value, env);
            try env.set(let_stmt.name, val);
            return .Void;
        },
        .Assign => |assign_stmt| {
            const val = try evalExpr(assign_stmt.value, env);
            try env.set(assign_stmt.name, val);
            return .Void;
        },
```

```
            .If => |if_stmt| {
                const cond = try evalExpr(if_stmt.condition, env);
                if (isTruthy(cond)) {
                    return evalBlock(if_stmt.consequence, env);
                } else if (if_stmt.alternative) |alt| {
                    return evalBlock(alt, env);
                }
                return .Void;
            },
        }
    }
```

`evalBlock()` iterates over a slice of statements and short-circuits the moment it encounters a `ReturnWrapper`:

```
fn evalBlock(stmts: []Stmt, env: *Environment) anyerror!RuntimeVal {
    var result: RuntimeVal = .Void;
    for (stmts) |stmt| {
        result = try eval(stmt, env);
        if (result == .ReturnWrapper) return result;
    }
    return result;
}
```

This function implements the mechanism that makes return exit not just the current statement but the entire enclosing block. Next, `isTruthy()` formalizes the truth rules of the language:

```
fn isTruthy(val: RuntimeVal) bool {
    switch (val) {
        .Boolean => |b| return b,
        .Integer => |i| return i != 0,
        else => return true,
    }
}
```

A `Boolean` is checked directly. An integer is truthy if it is not zero. Every other value — including strings and Void — is truthy by default. This is a simple convention that keeps conditional evaluation predictable. `evalExpr()` handles the four expression variants:

```
fn evalExpr(expr: Expr, env: *Environment) anyerror!RuntimeVal {
    switch (expr) {
        .Integer => |i| return RuntimeVal{ .Integer = i },
        .String => |s| return RuntimeVal{ .String = s },
        .Identifier => |name| {
            if (env.get(name)) |val| return val;
            // std.debug.print is safe
            std.debug.print("Runtime Error: Identifier not found '{s}'\n", .
{name});
            return error.IdentifierNotFound;
        },
        .Binary => |bin| {
            const left = try evalExpr(bin.left.*, env);
            const right = try evalExpr(bin.right.*, env);

            if (left == .Integer and right == .Integer) {
                const l = left.Integer;
                const r = right.Integer;
                return switch (bin.op) {
                    .Add => RuntimeVal{ .Integer = l + r },
                    .Sub => RuntimeVal{ .Integer = l - r },
                    .Mul => RuntimeVal{ .Integer = l * r },
                    .Div => RuntimeVal{ .Integer = @divTrunc(l, r) },
                    .Eq => RuntimeVal{ .Boolean = l == r },
                    .NotEq => RuntimeVal{ .Boolean = l != r },
                    .Lt => RuntimeVal{ .Boolean = l < r },
                    .Gt => RuntimeVal{ .Boolean = l > r },
                    .LtEq => RuntimeVal{ .Boolean = l <= r },
                    .GtEq => RuntimeVal{ .Boolean = l >= r },
                };
            }
            if (left==.String and right==.String and bin.op == .Add) {
                const s = try std.fmt.allocPrint(
                    env.allocator,
                    "{s}{s}",
                    .{ left.String, right.String },
                );
```

```
                return RuntimeVal{ .String = s };
            }

            return error.TypeMismatch;
        },
    }
}
```

`Integer` and `String` literals are wrapped and returned immediately. An `identifier` lookup queries the environment map and returns an error if the name is not found, which surfaces as a runtime error. The `Binary` case recursively evaluates both operands, checks that they are both integers, and then dispatches the arithmetic or comparison. The one exception is string addition: if both operands are strings and the operator is `.Add`, the evaluator concatenates them by formatting into a newly allocated buffer, returning a fresh string slice owned by the arena.

Now, let us discuss some of the limitations of the language as they appear in the evaluator. The binary operator support is narrow, and it is worth knowing exactly where the boundaries are before you start writing programs against it. When both operands are integers, every operator is available: `+`, `-`, `*` and `/` produce a new integer, while `==`, `!=`, `<`, `>`, `<=` and `>=` produce a boolean. Strings are far more limited — the only operator they accept is `+`, which concatenates them into a new string. Every other combination falls through to a single `error.TypeMismatch`: a string compared with `==` or ordered with `<`, an integer added to a string, or any expression with a boolean operand on either side. That last point produces the most surprising gap. Comparisons create boolean values, but no branch of the evaluator ever accepts a boolean as an operand, so an expression like `true == false` — or even `(1 < 2) == (3 < 4)` — is a type error rather than the `true` you might expect. The asymmetry between strings is just as easy to stumble over: because `+` is for concatenation but `==` is not, `"foo" + "bar"` succeeds and yields `"foobar"`, yet `"foo" == "foo"` raises a `TypeMismatch`. One outcome sits outside the type system entirely. Integer division is truncating and is not checked against a zero divisor, so `10 / 0` does not become a `TypeMismatch` — it reaches `@divTrunc` and panics. When reasoning about what a given operator-and-operand combination will do, then, there are really three possible results to keep in mind: a computed value, a `TypeMismatch` for an unsupported combination, and a hard crash for division by zero.

> **Note**
>
> Please have in mind that the evaluator in this chapter uses **tree-walking evaluation** — it recursively visits AST nodes and uses the call stack as its implicit evaluation stack. This is the simplest and most readable approach to evaluation and the right choice for a first interpreter. A production language implementation would typically take a second step:

> compiling the AST to bytecode and running it on a virtual machine with an explicit value stack. The bytecode approach separates the compilation phase from the execution phase, enables optimizations that are difficult or impossible in a tree-walker, and produces significantly better performance for compute-intensive programs.

Consider running the `math.small` sample program through this pipeline:

```
$ zig run ch12/evaluator.zig -- ch12/math.small
Running ch12/math.small...
----------------
Parsed AST:
Stmt 0: .{ .Let = .{ .name = a, .value = .{ .Integer = 10 } } }
Stmt 1: .{ .Let = .{ .name = b, .value = .{ .Integer = 5 } } }
Stmt 2: .{ .Let = .{ .name = c, .value = .{ .Binary = .{ ... } } } }
Stmt 3: .{ .Return = .{ .Identifier = c } }
----------------
----------------
Evaluator Result: 40
```

The evaluator stores `10` under `a` and `5` under `b`. When it reaches the third statement, it walks the binary tree rooted at `+`. The left subtree is a `*` node whose children are the identifier `a` and the integer `2`; looking up `a` yields `10`, and multiplying gives `20`. The right subtree is another `*` node whose children are `b` and `4`; the lookup yields `5`, and the product is `20`. The root `+` node adds those two results to produce `40`, which is stored as `c`. The return statement wraps `40` in a `ReturnWrapper`, and the main loop prints `40`.

At this point, all three stages of the interpreter exist as independent, verifiable programs. The lexer can be run against any source file to inspect the token stream. The parser can be run to confirm that the resulting AST has the expected shape. The evaluator can be run to produce a result from a script on disk. Each stage is a useful diagnostic tool, and that isolation is precisely what made them straightforward to build and reason about. What is missing is the glue that binds them into a single, ergonomic tool — one that a programmer can sit down with, type an expression, and get an answer without writing a file, invoking a build step, or reading raw debug output. That is what `ch12/repl.zig` provides.

REPL: building an interactive shell

The `ch12/repl.zig` file is the complete, self-contained interpreter. It merges the lexer, parser, and evaluator into a single compilation unit and provides two distinct execution modes controlled by whether a command-line argument is present. This design means the tool is equally useful as a batch script runner and as an interactive playground, selectable at launch without any configuration flags.

Output is handled by the `printVal()` function, which formats each `RuntimeVal()` variant into a human-readable line and writes it to standard output using `writeStreamingAll()`:

```
fn printVal(allocator: Allocator, io: std.Io, val: RuntimeVal) anyerror!void {
    const stdout = std.Io.File.stdout();
    switch (val) {
        .Integer => |i| {
            const msg = try std.fmt.allocPrint(
                allocator,
                "{d}\n",
                .{i},
            );
            defer allocator.free(msg);
            try stdout.writeStreamingAll(io, msg);
        },
        .String => |s| {
            const msg = try std.fmt.allocPrint(
                allocator,
                "\"{s}\"\n",
                .{s},
            );
            defer allocator.free(msg);
            try stdout.writeStreamingAll(io, msg);
        },
        .Boolean => |b| {
            const msg = try std.fmt.allocPrint(allocator, "{}\n", .{b});
            defer allocator.free(msg);
            try stdout.writeStreamingAll(io, msg);
        },
        .Void => {},
        .ReturnWrapper => |r| try printVal(allocator, io, r.*),
    }
}
```

The `ReturnWrapper` case recurses on the inner value, ensuring that the printed result reflects the unwrapped content regardless of how deeply nested the return is.

`readLine()` is for interactive input. The function allocates an `ArrayList` on each call and appends bytes one at a time from standard input until it encounters a newline or end-of-file:

```
fn readLine(allocator: Allocator, io: std.Io) !?[]u8 {
    const stdin = std.Io.File.stdin();
    var rbuf: [256]u8 = undefined;
    var reader_impl = stdin.reader(io,&rbuf);
    constreader=&reader_impl.interface;

    var list = std.ArrayList(u8).empty;

    while (true) {
        var byte: [1]u8 = undefined;
        const amt = try reader.readSliceShort(&byte);
        if (amt == 0) {
            if (list.items.len == 0) return null;
            break;
        }
        if (byte[0] == '\n') break;
        try list.append(allocator, byte[0]);
    }

    return try list.toOwnedSlice(allocator);
}
```

If read returns zero bytes on a completely empty input, the function returns `null` to signal the end of the interactive session. The caller owns the returned slice and must free it. Because the REPL loop uses an arena allocator, that cleanup happens automatically when the arena is released at program exit.

The `main()` function opens with a single arena allocator and a single `Environment`. The environment persisting across the entire session is what gives the REPL its interactive quality: variables declared in one line remain in scope for every subsequent line. When a filename argument is present, the file is read into the arena, parsed, and evaluated in one pass. The loop checks each statement result for `.ReturnWrapper` and, if found, prints the unwrapped value and exits immediately, matching the semantics of the batch evaluator:

```
// FILE MODE
if (args.len >= 2) {
    const filename = args[1];
    const file = try std.Io.Dir.cwd().openFile(io, filename, .{});
```

```
        defer file.close(io);
        const stat = try file.stat(io);
        const input = try allocator.alloc(u8, stat.size);
        _ = try file.readPositionalAll(io, input, 0);
        const l = Lexer.init(input);
        var p = Parser.init(allocator, l);
        const program = p.parseProgram() catch {
            try stdout.writeStreamingAll(io, "Parsing Error\n");
            return;
        };
        for (program) |stmt| {
            const result = try eval(stmt,&env);
            if (result == .ReturnWrapper) {
                try printVal(allocator, io, result.ReturnWrapper.*);
                break;
            }
        }
        return;
    }
```

In REPL mode, the loop prints a prompt, reads a line, and trims it to check for the exit command:

```
// REPL MODE
try stdout.writeStreamingAll(
    io,
    "Zig REPL (v0.1)\nType 'exit' to quit.\n",
);
while (true) {
    try stdout.writeStreamingAll(io, ">> ");
    const line = try readLine(allocator, io);
    if (line == null) break;
    const input = line.?;
    if (std.mem.eql(u8, std.mem.trim(u8, input, "\r\t "), "exit"))
        break;
    const l = Lexer.init(input);
    var p = Parser.init(allocator, l);
    const program = p.parseProgram() catch {
        try stdout.writeStreamingAll(io, "Syntax Error\n");
        continue;
    };
    for (program) |stmt| {
```

```
        const result = eval(stmt, &env) catch {
            try stdout.writeStreamingAll(io, "Runtime Error\n");
            break;
        };
        try printVal(allocator, io, result);
    }
}
```

> **Note**
>
> This REPL is minimal: it reads raw bytes a line at a time, with no history, no in-line editing, and no tab completion. Adding readline-style input is a natural next step and a good exercise — you could bind a C library such as `linenoise` or write a small terminal-mode handler that interprets the arrow-key and backspace escape sequences yourself.

Each line is then treated as a complete program: a fresh lexer and parser are constructed from the single input string, and the resulting statements are evaluated against the persistent environment. Any parsing failure emits a Syntax Error message and continues to the next iteration rather than terminating the session. Any runtime error emits Runtime Error and breaks out of the inner statement loop, leaving the REPL alive for the next prompt.

To run a script from the command line, pass the filename as the sole argument:

```
$ zig run ch12/repl.zig -- ch12/math.small
40
```

To enter the interactive shell, run `ch12/repl.zig` with no arguments:

```
$ zig run ch12/repl.zig
Zig REPL (v0.1)
Type 'exit' to quit.
>> let x = 7;
>> let y = x * 6
>> return y;
42
>> exit
```

The two sample programs demonstrate the range of the language cleanly. `math.small` exercises, variable declaration, multiplication, addition, and a return statement. `logic.small` adds an assignment mutation inside a conditional branch, confirming that let, and Assign are handled independently and that environment state survives across the `if`-statement boundary. Both programs serve as minimal but meaningful integration tests for the full interpreter pipeline.

> **Note**
>
> `zcalc` uses a single global environment for all variable bindings — there are no nested scopes. A variable declared with `let` inside an `if` block remains visible after the block exits, which means `let` in `zcalc` behaves more like a global assignment than a scoped declaration in the C or Go sense.

Running `logic.small` through the same pipeline confirms that the conditional branch and the assignment mutation both evaluate correctly:

```
$ cat ch12/logic.small
let x = 10;
let y = 20;
if (x < y) {
  x = x * 2;
} else {
  x = 0;
}
return x;
$ zig run ch12/repl.zig -- ch12/logic.small
20
```

The program sets x to 10 and y to 20. The condition x < y is true, so the consequence block executes, multiplying x by 2 and storing 20 back into the environment. The `return` statement then surfaces that value through the `ReturnWrapper()` mechanism and the main loop prints 20.

The domain-specific language developed here serves primarily as a practical illustration of the capabilities of Zig. This implementation may fit your immediate needs, or it may not; like any non-trivial software, it may contain latent bugs. The point of this exercise is not to hand you a flawless, production-ready interpreter. Instead, your goal should be to internalize the logic, the design of the data structures, and the idioms of Zig. Do not merely copy the code; understand the decisions behind it so that you are equipped to detect and correct errors and to adapt the architecture to your own specific problems. The mastery of systems programming demands the iterative practice of writing code. Keep programming. Zig is a rigorous but rewarding tool for this work, teaching you to respect memory and explicit control flow. *Learn by doing*; build your own tools, make mistakes, study good code, and rewrite your programs until they achieve simplicity and clarity.

Before closing, it is worth noting what `zcalc` does not handle. Division by zero causes a runtime panic rather than a friendly error message. Arithmetic is integer-only, so `7 / 2` returns `3` rather than `3.5`. The language has no function definitions or closures, no loop constructs such as `while` or `for`, and no variable shadowing — a `let` inside a block uses the same global environment as the outer scope, so inner declarations overwrite outer ones rather than creating a new binding. String escape handling supports only `\"` and has an edge case with consecutive backslashes that can prevent a closing quote from being recognized. Integer overflow is another unhandled case: any arithmetic result that exceeds the range of `i64` panics in debug builds and is undefined behavior in `ReleaseFast`. A script like let `x = 9223372036854775807; let y = x + 1;` crashes the interpreter rather than producing an error message.

Most importantly, build tools and software that you want to use and let others try them. The most enduring programs in our field — from the earliest UNIX utilities to modern compilers — almost always began as simple solutions to the immediate problems of their developers. When you write code to serve your own needs, you inherently prioritize utility, clarity, and performance over abstract architectural purity. When you release that code to the world, you subject your design to the unpredictable realities and edge cases of other users. This iterative cycle of scratching your own itch and then embracing public refinement is the true engine of software engineering. *Find a problem that annoys you, open your editor, and start typing.*

Summary

We have come a long way in this chapter. Designing and implementing a programming language from the ground up is not an easy task. By building a lexer to dissect raw text, a parser to impose grammatical structure, and an evaluator to execute the resulting abstract syntax tree, we have demystified exactly how software understands code. The inherent difficulty of this process demands strict logical precision, but the reward is a profound, structural understanding of the tools you use every day, forever changing how you read and write software. Congratulations!

This is the final chapter of the book that you are reading. Reaching the final pages of this book is not the conclusion of your journey but rather the equipping of your workshop. The mastery of systems programming cannot be acquired solely by reading; it demands the relentless, iterative practice of writing code. Zig is a remarkable language for this endeavor. By stripping away hidden control flow and opaque abstractions, it forces you to confront the realities of memory and machine logic directly. Treat the compiler not as an enemy but as a mentor guiding you toward building robust and efficient software. The only true way to internalize these concepts is by doing, building small tools, making mistakes, reading the code of others, and continually rewriting your own solutions until they achieve clarity and elegance. Keep programming, keep experimenting, and let the discipline and absolute control that Zig provides become the foundation of your craft.

Exercises

- Negative number literals. The current lexer has no concept of a leading minus sign; the expression let `x = -5;` will fail to parse. Extend the grammar with a unary negation rule at the `Primary` level. In the parser, detect a `.Minus` token in `parsePri` and, if found, parse the following primary and wrap it in a `Binary` node that subtracts from zero. Verify that expressions like `let x = -5; return x + 3;` evaluate to `-2`.
- A `print` statement. Add a `Print` variant to `TokenType` and teach `lookupIdent()` to recognize the keyword `print`. Add a corresponding `Print` variant to `Stmt` and parse it in `parseStmt()` by consuming the keyword and then delegating to `parseExpr()`. In `eval()`, handle the `.Print` case by evaluating the expression and writing its value to standard output without wrapping it in a `ReturnWrapper()`. This exercise forces you to touch all three stages of the pipeline for a single feature.
- A `while` loop. Extend the EBNF grammar with the rule `WhileStatement = "while" Expression Block ;` and implement it following the same pattern as `parseIf`. In the evaluator, the `while` case must repeatedly evaluate the condition and, if truthy, call `evalBlock()` on the body. The loop must also propagate a `ReturnWrapper()` immediately if one surfaces from inside the block, so that a `return` statement inside a `while` loop terminates the enclosing program correctly.
- Division-by-zero detection. The current evaluator calls `@divTrunc(l, r)` without checking whether `r` is zero. In Zig, integer division by zero causes a runtime panic rather than returning a defined value, which abruptly terminates the interpreter. Add a guard before the `.Div` branch that returns `error.DivisionByZero` when the right operand is zero. Then update the REPL's inner evaluation loop to catch that specific error and print a descriptive message rather than crashing.
- The `evalExpr()` function performs arithmetic directly on `i64` values using `+`, `-`, `*` and `@divTrunc()`. Therefore, any operation that exceeds the range of `i64` causes an overflow. Fix this by replacing the arithmetic operators in `evalExpr()` with overflow-checked alternatives. Use `@addWithOverflow`, `@subWithOverflow`, and `@mulWithOverflow` for addition, subtraction, and multiplication, respectively. Each returns a tuple containing the result and a boolean overflow flag — check the flag and return `error.IntegerOverflow` if it is set. Handle `error.IntegerOverflow` in the REPL's error path and print a friendly message such as `'error: integer overflow'` rather than

crashing the interpreter. Once the fix is in place, verify that `let x = 9223372036854775807; let y = x + 1;` produces a clean error message.

Additional resources

- Thorsten Ball, *Writing An Interpreter In Go*, Thorsten Ball (2016). The closest practical companion to this chapter. It builds a similar tree-walking interpreter from scratch in Go, covering a superset of the features implemented here, including functions and closures. The approach to lexing and parsing is conceptually identical to zcalc.
- Robert Nystrom, *Crafting Interpreters* (2021). The most comprehensive treatment of interpreter construction available. The first half builds a tree-walking interpreter in Java; the second builds a bytecode virtual machine in C, which represents the natural next step beyond the architecture described in this chapter. The complete text is freely available at `https://craftinginterpreters.com/`.
- The formal definition of Extended Backus-Naur Form is specified in ISO/IEC 14977. A concise and readable treatment is available in the Zig language reference itself, which uses EBNF to specify the entire Zig grammar at `https://ziglang.org/documentation/master/`.

13

Unlock Your Exclusive Benefits

Your copy of this book includes the following exclusive benefits:

Follow the guide below to unlock them. The process takes only a few minutes and needs to be completed once.

Unlock this Book's Free Benefits in 3 Easy Steps

Step 1

Keep your purchase invoice ready for *Step 3*. If you have a physical copy, scan it using your phone and save it as a PDF, JPG, or PNG.

For more help on finding your invoice, visit `https://www.packtpub.com/en-us/unlock?step=1`.

> **Note**
>
> If you bought this book directly from Packt, no invoice is required. After *Step 2*, you can access your exclusive content right away.

Step 2

Scan the QR code or go to `packtpub.com/unlock`.

On the page that opens (similar to *Figure 13.1* on desktop), search for this book by name and select the correct edition.

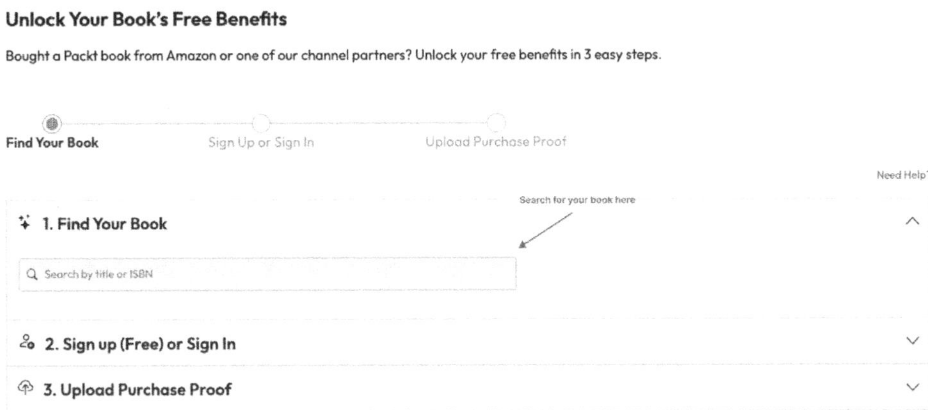

Figure 13.1 – Packt unlock landing page on desktop

Step 3

After selecting your book, sign in to your Packt account or create one for free. Then upload your invoice (PDF, PNG, or JPG, up to 10 MB). Follow the on-screen instructions to finish the process.

Need Help

If you get stuck and need help, visit `https://www.packtpub.com/unlock-benefits/help` for a detailed FAQ on how to find your invoices and more. This QR code will take you to the help page.

> **Note**
>
> If you are still facing issues, reach out to `customercare@packt.com`.

Other Books You May Enjoy

If you enjoyed this book, you may be interested in these other books by Packt:

Learning Zig

Alex Rios

ISBN: 9781835085127

- Find out how to maintain low-level control over system resources
- Set up a Zig development environment across different operating systems
- Organize maintainable projects with proper structure and build systems
- Implement error handling using Zig's unique approach to managing failures
- Leverage Zig's standard library effectively for everyday programming tasks
- Build applications that use files, external libraries, and C code
- Cross-compile and package Zig applications for multiple platforms

Practical Systems Programming in Go

Mihalis Tsoukalos

ISBN: 9781806112197

- Create command-line utilities using Go
- Work with files, directories, and UNIX signals
- Build TCP/IP clients and servers in Go
- Write concurrent programs using goroutines and channels
- Develop web services and networked applications
- Implement interpreters for custom programming languages
- Process and analyze time series data
- Understand Go internals and system-level performance

Packt is searching for authors like you

If you're interested in becoming an author for Packt, please visit `authors.packt.com` and apply today. We have worked with thousands of developers and tech professionals, just like you, to help them share their insight with the global tech community. You can make a general application, apply for a specific hot topic that we are recruiting an author for, or submit your own idea.

Share your thoughts

Now you've finished *Systems Programming with Zig*, we'd love to hear your thoughts! Scan the QR code below to go straight to the Amazon review page for this book and share your feedback or leave a review on the site that you purchased it from.

https://packt.link/r/1807426432

Your review is important to us and the tech community and will help us make sure we're delivering excellent quality content.

Subscribe to Deep Engineering

Index

Symbols

#NAME? 55

@typeInfo 438

A

Arena Allocator 49

abstract syntax trees (ASTs) 472, 479

acquire ordering 304

active operating system
- finding 190, 191

anytype keyword 439

async 343
- TCP proxy, refactoring 357 – 360
- using 344 – 348
- using, for write operations 348, 349

asynchronous TCP proxy 351 - 356

asynchrony 341, 342

atomic operations 302
- variable, modifying 305, 306

atomics 303, 304
- Producer-Consumer pattern, implementing 319 – 322

await 343
- TCP proxy, refactoring 357 – 360
- using 344 – 348
- using, for write operations 348, 349

B

BFQ (Budget Fair Queuing) 162

Base64 146

Breadth-First Search (BFS) 332

backing allocator 97

bench.zig 403 - 406, 409

binary frame structure 377

bitwise manipulation operations 146

branch prediction 144

breaking changes 5

buffer fragmentation 379

buffer size
- effect, on writing speed 157, 158
- reading speed, benchmarking for 154 – 157

build system as infrastructure as code 61

build.zig 62 - 64

build.zig.zon
- dependencies, managing 61, 62

C

C code
- calling, from Zig 31 – 33

Central Directory 98

Concurrent File Indexer 331

Counts struct 136

canonicalization 169

characters
- counting 136 – 139

chmod logic
- implementing 198 – 200

chown logic
- implementing 200 – 203

client
- building, for note-taking service 458 – 461
- developing 399

comptime 438
- implementing 439 – 443
- protocol correctness, enforcing 250 – 254
- using 439, 443, 444
- wire format correctness, enforcing 106 – 113

concurrency 341

concurrent TCP client
writing 274 – 277

concurrent TCP server
writing 271 – 273

condition variable
Producer-Consumer, implementing 322 – 324

config.zig 278

containers 223

coroutines 342

coverage analysis 78

curl(1)
note-taking service, testing 456 – 458

custom memory allocator
programming 90 – 98

D

Debug Allocator 48

Docker 223

Docker images
creating 223 – 226

data corruption, in shared writing
preventing 308 – 310
with atomic operations 310, 311
without atomic operations 308

date and time formats
converting, in JSON records 419 – 425

dependencies
managing, with build.zig.zon 61, 62

directory
deleting 180 – 182
recursively walking 183, 186, 187

directory entries
listing 172, 173

documentation
generating 55 – 60

doubly linked list 381, 382

E

Echo server
testing 208
writing, with TCP 206 – 208

End of Central Directory (EOCD) 98

Endianness
working with 113, 114

Extended Backus-Naur Form (EBNF) 468

encoder logic
implementing 147 – 150

environment variables
reading 27

event loop 192 - 198, 343

event-driven architecture 375

expressions 470

external libraries
fetching 60
using 60

F

Fixed Buffer Allocator (FBA) 49

file
deleting 179, 180
kind of file, finding 174, 175
moving 182, 183
opening 13 – 18
reading 13 – 18

file events 191

file metadata
finding 175 – 177

file permissions 168

file seeking
benchmarking, with sequential reading 159 – 163

filtering tests 78

fire and forget pattern 273

G

General Purpose Allocator (GPA) 48

GitHub
Zig library, hosting 70, 71

gather phase 333

H

HTTP clients

developing 232 – 239

HTTP protocol
minimal web server, developing 226 – 228
web service, creating to generate random numbers 229 – 232
working with 226

hard link **169**

hash map **379, 382**

heap **88, 89**

high-performance text counting
with SIMD 140 – 143

I

I/O loop **23, 24**

information
logging, concurrently 330, 331

inode **168**

inotify **191**

inter-process communication (IPC) mechanisms **262**

interactive shell
building 490 – 496

io_uring **343, 364**

J

JSON **416**

JSON data
putting, into database 438

JSON records
date and time formats, converting 419 – 425

JSON serialization **246**

K

kqueue **191, 343, 364**

L

LRU cache
implementing 380

Least Recently Used (LRU) **374, 380, 386**

Little-Endian integers
reading, from raw bytes 115 – 117

latency **341**

lexer **471, 472**

lexing **472 - 479**

library
compiling, to create executable binary 64 – 66

library, from zuuid code
making 70, 71
tests, writing 72, 73

lines
counting 136 – 139

linked list **380**

low-level I/O multiplexing **364 - 369**

low-level hostname resolution
performing 211 – 213

M

Most Recently Used (MRU) **381, 386**

main.zig **278**

memory
sharing 294 – 296

memory allocators **45 - 50**
benchmarking 120 – 126
using, for each thread 313 – 316

memory info server
improving 312, 313

memory information
reading 240 – 244

memory leaks
detecting, automatically during tests 54, 55

memory management **383, 384**

mq-deadline **161**

mutex **294 - 296**

N

Newline Delimited JSON **424**

nested structures **417, 418**

nonblocking code
writing 343

none scheduler **161**

noop **161**

note-taking service **445**

client, building for 458 – 461
functionality 446
implementing 446 – 452, 455, 456
testing, with curl(1) 456 – 458

null-terminated C strings
composing 86 – 88

O

OS primitives
using 191

OS threads **342**

Optional Pointer **85**

offset addressing **84**

P

PATH environment variable
splitting 28

Producer-Consumer pattern **318, 319**
implementing, with atomics 319 – 322
implementing, with condition variable 322 – 324

parser **479 - 485**

parsing **267, 479**

partial reads **379**

pointer arithmetic **83 - 85**

pointers **82**

port numbers **205**

print on screen
ways 7, 8

process **262**

process forking **263, 264**

proxies
performance, comparing 361 – 364

R

RwLock
using 296 – 299

race conditions
avoiding 294, 299 – 302

random values
generating 33 – 35

raw byte slices
casting, to structured data types 117 – 120

raw bytes
Little-Endian integers, generating from 115 – 117

reading speed
benchmarking, for buffer sizes 154 – 157

relative path
resolving, to absolute path 169 – 172

release ordering **304**

repl.zig **278**

ring buffer pattern
data structure 325 – 329

S

SIGCHLD **285**

SIGTERM **285**

SIMD (Single Instruction, Multiple Data) **139**
high-performance text counting 139 – 143

SQLite3
connecting to 426 – 428
data, deleting 435 – 437
data, inserting into 428 – 432
data, querying 432 – 434
using 426

Scatter-Gather pattern **333**
implementation details 333 – 337

scatter phase **333**

schedule.zig **278**

self-pipe trick **279**

sequential consistency memory ordering **311**

sequential reading
file seeking, benchmarking 159 – 163

service client **246 - 250**

service process **245, 246**

sharded locking addresses **409**

shell commands
executing 268 – 271

signals **257**

signals.zig **278**

sliding pointer **83**

spawning **267**

stack **88 - 90**

standard error **4**

standard input **4**

standard output **4**

state machine
- implementing, to parse streaming TCP data 378, 379

statements **470**

std.ArrayList **9 - 11**

std.fmt
- strings, formatting 42 – 45

std.testing
- unit tests, writing 50

storage engine **380**

stream processing **129**

streams
- decoding 150 – 153

strings
- formatting, with std.fmt 42 – 45

symbolic links **169**
- creating 178, 179

synchronizing **267**

system monitor service
- creating 240

T

TCP Echo client
- improving 214 – 216
- writing 208 – 211

TCP proxy
- refactoring, with async and await 357 – 360

Transmission Control Protocol (TCP)
- Echo server, writing 206 – 208

Transmission Control Protocol/Internet Protocol (TCP/IP) **205**

tee(1) command **4**

tests
- writing, for zwhich 50 – 54

thread pools **316, 317**

thread-per-connection architecture **375 - 377**

threads **262, 263**
- CPU, working with 265, 266
- variable number of threads, running 266, 267

time-to-live (TTL) **374**

tree-walking evaluation **489**

tree-walking execution **485 - 489**

U

UDP Echo client
- writing 220 – 223

UDP Echo server
- writing 216 – 219

UNIX fork-and-exec pattern **283**

UNIX signals
- handling 258, 259
- using intentionally 259 – 261

Universally Unique Identifier (UUID) **66**

User Datagram Protocol (UDP) **216**

unit tests
- writing, with std.testing 50

unpredictable passwords
- generating 36, 37

user input
- reading 11 – 13

V

Virtual File System (VFS) **168**

variable
- modifying, with atomic operations 305, 306

variable number of threads
- running 266 – 268

vnode **168**

W

Writergate (Zig 0.15.1) **5**

wc
- versus zwc 145, 146

words
- counting 136 – 139

wrapper allocator **97**

X

XDG (Cross-Desktop Group) **289**

Z

ZEMP (Zig Exchange Memory Protocol) **251**

ZWC implementations
- comparing 144

Zcache Exchange Message Protocol (ZEMP) **374, 377**

Zig **3**
- C code, calling 31 – 33
- features 37

Zig 0.16
- breaking changes 5, 6

Zig Object Notation (ZON) **62**

Zig programs
- practical guidance 163

Zunzip **98 - 106**

z64
- developing 146

zcache **374, 375**
- server implementation details 384 – 398

zcache_cli.zig **401, 402**

zcalc language **468**
- EBNF grammar 468 – 472

zcat
- developing 130 – 132
- system calls 132 – 135

zcat.zig **132**

zcron **278**
- characteristics 279
- creating 278
- design decisions 278 – 280
- fork and exec, using to run periodic tasks 282 – 284
- implementation details 285 – 290
- SIGCHLD, handling 285
- SIGTERM, handling 285
- terminal, detaching 280 – 282

zemp_client.zig **400, 401**

zlocate **331, 332**
- using 338 – 340

zpass
- unpredictable passwords, generating 36, 37

ztee **4**
- implementing 19 – 23
- testing 25, 26

ztree
- developing 187 – 189
- implementing 183

zuuid
- benchmarking, against uuidgen 77
- developing 66 – 70
- using 73 – 76

zwatch
- implementing 190

zwc
- developing 135
- versus wc 145, 146

zwhich **27**
- implementing 29 – 31
- tests, writing for 50 – 53

Made in the USA
Monee, IL
16 September 2026

63035033R00299